Pro Exchange 2019 and 2016 Administration

For Exchange On-Premises and Office 365

Second Edition

Michel de Rooij
Jaap Wesselius

Apress®

Pro Exchange 2019 and 2016 Administration: For Exchange On-Premises and Office 365

Michel de Rooij
VLEUTEN, Utrecht, The Netherlands

Jaap Wesselius
MARKNESSE, Flevoland, The Netherlands

ISBN-13 (pbk): 978-1-4842-7330-2
ISBN-13 (electronic): 978-1-4842-7331-9
https://doi.org/10.1007/978-1-4842-7331-9

Managing Director, Apress Media LLC: Welmoed Spahr
Acquisitions Editor: Smriti Srivastava
Development Editor: Laura Berendson
Coordinating Editor: Shrikant Vishwakarma

Cover designed by eStudioCalamar

Cover image designed by Pexels

Distributed to the book trade worldwide by Springer Science+Business Media LLC, 1 New York Plaza, Suite 4600, New York, NY 10004. Phone 1-800-SPRINGER, fax (201) 348-4505, e-mail orders-ny@springer-sbm.com, or visit www.springeronline.com. Apress Media, LLC is a California LLC and the sole member (owner) is Springer Science + Business Media Finance Inc (SSBM Finance Inc). SSBM Finance Inc is a **Delaware** corporation.

For information on translations, please e-mail booktranslations@springernature.com; for reprint, paperback, or audio rights, please e-mail bookpermissions@springernature.com, or visit http://www.apress.com/rights-permissions.

Apress titles may be purchased in bulk for academic, corporate, or promotional use. eBook versions and licenses are also available for most titles. For more information, reference our Print and eBook Bulk Sales web page at http://www.apress.com/bulk-sales.

Any source code or other supplementary material referenced by the author in this book is available to readers on GitHub via the book's product page, located at www.apress.com/978-1-4842-7330-2. For more detailed information, please visit http://www.apress.com/source-code.

Printed on acid-free paper

Table of Contents

About the Authors

Michel de Rooij is a consultant and Microsoft MVP since 2013. He lives in the Netherlands and has been working in the IT industry for over 20 years. Michel helps customers with their journeys related to Microsoft 365, with a focus on Exchange and Identity, but also related technologies such as Microsoft Teams or email in general. Michel has a developer background, but after some long-term dedicated Exchange-related work for a large multinational, he switched to Exchange and never looked back. He is also a big fan of automating processes and procedures related to infrastructure, being either supporting projects or automating administrator tasks. Michel is also active in online communities, such as the Microsoft Tech Community, and on social media such as Twitter (@mderooij). He runs an Exchange-related blog at eightwone.com, guest authors for several other sites, and speaks at international events.

Jaap Wesselius is an independent consultant based in the Netherlands. As a consultant, Jaap has been working with Exchange server since Exchange 5.0 in 1997. After working for Microsoft, he became an independent consultant in 2006. For his work in the (Exchange) community, Jaap has received a Microsoft MVP award in 2007, an award he still holds in 2021. The first MVP category was Exchange server, but over the years that has changed to Office Apps and Services. Besides working with Exchange, Jaap also works with Office 365, identity management, privacy, and security. He is 54 years old, married, has three (almost) grown-up sons, and likes to ride his motorcycle, when possible.

About the Technical Reviewers

Kay Sellenrode works as a freelance consultant/architect, focusing on unified messaging solution, that is, Exchange server and Exchange Online/Office 365. He has been actively working with Exchange since 5.5 and is a Microsoft Certified Master (MCM) and Architect (MCA) on Exchange Server.

In all those years, he has seen environments from small businesses to large and from simple setups to complex multiforest mergers or splits of Exchange.

As a speaker, he has spoken at several events like TechEd US and local events in the Netherlands and is always willing to share his knowledge.

Vikas Sukhija has over a decade of IT infrastructure experience with expertise in messaging, collaboration, and IT automations. He is a blogger, architect, Microsoft MVP, and is known as TechWizard. As an experienced professional, he assists small to large enterprises in architecting and implementing Office 365 and Azure.

Community Contributions from him can be found at:

@Blog `http://TechWizard.cloud`

@Page `www.facebook.com/TechWizard.cloud`

@Twitter `https://twitter.com/techwizardcloud`

@Coderepo`https://github.com/VikasSukhija`

Acknowledgments

Another book! When Jaap asked me if I wanted to join him in writing the successor to our previous book that we both co-authored in 2014, I immediately got enthusiastic again. And now, after a few months, the fruit of our labor has once more seen the light. It always is an interesting and rewarding experience. The amount of depth and widening is intense, especially in the cloud era where the rate of change is insane. Then, when you finish writing, you feel you achieved something. Something useful for people that are on their own learning path, be it Exchange or Microsoft 365, something to help them understand and grow.

Again, a word of thanks to Jaap Wesselius for getting me on board this project. Finally, I am grateful to my wife Juliana, two kids, and family who had to share me in the evenings with this project as well. This, while already working from home during the pandemic. Also to the community, and especially the MVPs, intelligent people that are never hesitant to help out or exchange ideas. To you and everybody else I forgot, I say thank you.

—Michel

Introduction

I have been working with Exchange since 1997 when Microsoft introduced Exchange server 5.0. Over the years, a lot has changed in Exchange, or as they say in marketing terms, "it has been built from the ground up," and with the move writing Exchange in managed code (i.e., .NET), that's completely true.

But there's this other beast called Exchange Online, part of Office 365. It is not a big secret that Microsoft wants everybody to move to Office 365, and for a lot of customers, that is the best solution. All Microsoft developments and new features are in the cloud, and Exchange server on-premises is in a status quo. There are not a lot of new developments, and all updates are about stability and security.

But why a book about Exchange server? There still is a demand for Exchange server on-premises. Sometimes, organizations are running Exchange server for the wrong reason ("the cloud is too expensive," for example), but there are organizations that do not want to be the first, or they cannot move to the cloud for legal reasons. Do not forget there are still millions of mailboxes on-premises, and this book is targeted for administrators that are completely moving to the cloud anytime soon and still have Exchange servers on-premises. This can be a full on-premises environment and I still have these types of customers, but also in a hybrid environment where Exchange server on-premises is configured with Exchange Online.

This book is divided into four parts:

1. **Exchange Infrastructure**—In this part, we cover an introduction and how to install and configure Exchange server. We will also cover the Client Access and the mailbox services, which were dedicated server roles in previous Exchange versions. Managing Mailboxes and mail transport are also included in this part.

2. **Upgrading Exchange Server**—In this part, we discuss the upgrade path from Exchange 2010 to Exchange 2016 and from Exchange 2013 to Exchange 2019. Why an Exchange 2010 upgrade path? In our experience, a lot of customers are still running

Exchange 2010, and they must move to Exchange 2016 anytime soon since Exchange 2010 is not supported at all anymore. From a security perspective, this is an unacceptable situation.

3. **Integration with Office 365**—Although this is a book about Exchange server on-premises, customers are running an Exchange hybrid environment, and we should not close our eyes to this. And running Exchange hybrid can be the best of both worlds. This part covers identities, directory synchronization, Exchange federations, Autodiscover in a hybrid environment, and Exchange Online Protection.

4. **Security and Compliance**—This is perhaps one of the most important aspects of running any environment. In this part, we cover authentication methods, including Hybrid Modern Authentication, Multi-Factor Authentication, and Role-Based Access Control (RBAC). Chapter 11 focuses more on safeguarding the information with features like journaling, in-place hold and eDiscovery, messaging records management, data loss prevention, and auditing.

There still is demand for Exchange server on-premises, and there still is demand for an up-to-date book about Exchange server on-premises. This book is about Exchange 2019 and also covers Exchange 2016 and Exchange 2013 where appropriate. Exchange server is not dead, since Microsoft already announced a new version of Exchange on-premises, at the time of writing, referred to as "Exchange vNext." From the information publicly available, I do not expect too much changes in Exchange vNext.

But until then, enjoy Exchange 2019 and never stop learning.

PART 1

Exchange Infrastructure

CHAPTER 1

Introduction to Exchange 2019

In April 1996, Microsoft released the first version of Exchange server which was Exchange server 4.0. At the time of writing, we are 25 years later, and Exchange is still around. The current version is Exchange server 2019, released by the end of 2018, but a new version has already been announced by Microsoft with the codename Exchange vNext. Although the Microsoft cloud shows a tremendous growth month over month, there is still a demand for an on-premises version of Exchange server.

Looking back over the years, three real major changes can be identified in Exchange server:

- **Use of Active Directory**—The first versions of Exchange server had their own X.500 directory which was used in combination with the NT4 directory. User accounts were created in the NT4 domain, and mailboxes were created in the Exchange directory. Exchange 2000 was the first version of Exchange that was using Active Directory, and it still is until today.
- **64-bit architecture**—Exchange server 2007 was the first version that was built on the X64 platform, although a 32-bit version for testing purposes was still available. Exchange server was growing tremendously, and it hit the boundaries of the 32-bit architecture of Exchange server 2003 which resulted in major performance issues. By moving to a 64-bit architecture, Microsoft was able to work on the performance issues, and performance has been improved with each new version.

M. de Rooij and J. Wesselius, *Pro Exchange 2019 and 2016 Administration*,
https://doi.org/10.1007/978-1-4842-7331-9_1

- **Managed code**—Exchange server 2013 was the first version that was 100% built on top of the .NET Framework, and as such it was really built from the ground up. I do not want to sound like a marketing guy, but this really was a big change. Another big change with the introduction of Exchange server 2013 was that Exchange server 2013 and Exchange Online shared the same codebase which means that all releases and Cumulative Updates (CUs) of Exchange server 2013 are a spin-off of Exchange Online. This was continued with Exchange server 2016 but stopped with Exchange 2019 which now is a separate product compared to Exchange Online. From Exchange 2019 on, it is a separate product compared to Exchange Online. This was clearly visible when the HAFNIUM vulnerability hit—Exchange servers on-premises were vulnerable, but Exchange Online was not.

Starting with Exchange server 2013, Microsoft introduced a new servicing model based on Cumulative Updates or CUs. Microsoft is releasing a CU on a quarterly basis which contains fixes and new features when available. Microsoft stepped away from the concept of service packs; all features are now included in CUs. Because of the cumulative nature of the CUs, a CU contains all features and fixes of earlier CUs. Therefore, you can "jump" over several CUs, for example, from Exchange server 2019 CU7 to Exchange server 2019 CU10. There is no need to install CUs that are between those versions.

CUs are only released when the product is in mainstream support. When critical security issues are found and a product is in extended support, a Security Update (SU) is released. This happened in March 2021, when Microsoft released Security Updates for all Exchange servers in mainstream and in extended support for the HAFNIUM vulnerability. SUs are also cumulative, so the March 2021 security updates contain all security updates included in previous SUs for the same CU. SUs are also CU specific, so a SU for Exchange Server 2019 CU9 is different from a SU for Exchange Server 2019 CU8. Microsoft typically releases SUs only for the current CU and the previous CU. For the HAFNIUM vulnerability, an exception was made. Because of the critical and dangerous nature of the HAFNIUM vulnerability, SUs were released for older CUs and even out-of-support Exchange builds as well, but this should really be considered an exception.

Exchange Servers 2013, 2016, and 2019 are very similar and to some extent compatible. Over the years, there have not been major changes to the product, but lots of improvements.

The first area of improvement is security with support for Windows Server Core, TLS 1.2, and blockage of the Exchange Control Panel and Exchange Management Shell externally.

Another area of improvement is performance and reliability. Performance improvement in Exchange server 2019 is achieved by modern hardware support (Exchange server 2019 now supports up to 256 GB memory!), a new search engine (which also improves failover times), and the MetaCache database, a combination of large JBOD disks and SSDs.

There are also several client improvements, such as the "do not forward" option in meeting invites, improved out-of-office support, and the option to remove calendar events (using PowerShell), possibly the most requested feature.

Of course, there are differences between Exchange servers 2013, 2016, and 2019, especially when it comes to features. But these versions also work together quite well. For example, it is possible to create a load-balanced array for Exchange servers with all three versions in this array. It does not matter on which Exchange server a client connection is terminated; the request is automatically proxied to the correct mailbox server. This is extremely useful when upgrading your Exchange environment to Exchange server 2019.

There is one major difference between Exchange server 2013 and Exchange servers 2016 and 2019. Exchange server 2013 does have two server roles, the Client Access server role and the Mailbox server role. In Exchange server 2016 and up, these two roles are combined, and only the Mailbox server role is available. The different components are still there, but only available in one server role. The Edge Transport server role is still available in Exchange servers 2016 and 2019.

Exchange server 2019 is targeted toward large enterprise customers; as such Exchange server 2019 is only available via the volume license center (VLC). Smaller customers can still use Exchange server 2016 or move to Exchange Online, not surprisingly the Microsoft recommended approach. Exchange Online contains the latest and greatest features; Exchange server 2019 is the rock-solid solution for enterprise customers that need a solid mail environment.

This book is about Exchange server 2019, but where needed a sidestep to Exchange server 2016 is made. The reason to add Exchange server 2016 is because of the upgrade path from Exchange server 2010, a version still in use by a lot of customers.

Exchange 2016 or Exchange 2019?

In the beginning of 2021, two versions of Exchange server were available:

- **Exchange Server 2016**—Mainstream support for Exchange server 2016 ended in October 2020, but Exchange Server 2016 is in extended support until October 2025.
- **Exchange Server 2019**—Mainstream support for Exchange server 2019 will end in January 2024, but Exchange Server 2019 is in extended support only until October 2025.

This is shown in Figure 1-1.

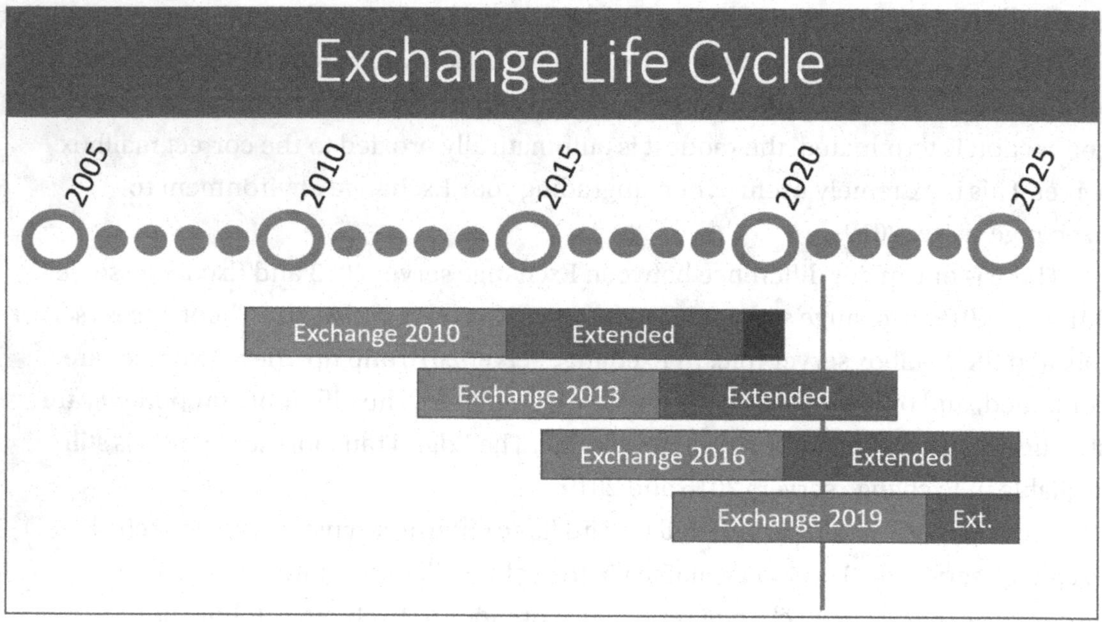

Figure 1-1. *Support life cycle of various Exchange server versions*

It is expected that Microsoft will release a new version of Exchange server by the end of 2021, at the time of writing, with the codename "Exchange vNext."

This raises the question which version one must use. There are several answers to this question, and "it depends":

- If you do not have a volume license agreement with Microsoft, you do not have access to Exchange server 2019, so Exchange server 2016 is your only option for an on-premises deployment.
- When building a brand-new Exchange environment, a so-called greenfield deployment, Exchange server 2019 is the way to go.
- If you are currently running Exchange server 2010 and are going to upgrade, then move to Exchange server 2016. You can then decide to move to Exchange server 2019.
- If you are in Exchange server 2010, 2013, or 2016 hybrid and have moved all mailboxes to Exchange Online, keep one Exchange server 2016 server for management purposes. You can use a free "hybrid license" for this. A free hybrid license is not available for Exchange server 2019.
- If you are on Exchange server 2013 or 2016, you can move to Exchange server 2019.

When possible, move to Exchange server 2019 because of Exchange vNext. Although nothing has been released yet, Microsoft announced that the integration of Exchange vNext into an Exchange server 2019 environment will be very easy. It is compatible on the protocol level, so you can add an Exchange vNext server into a load-balanced array of previous Exchange servers. But what is more interesting, the Mailbox databases are also compatible, so you can add Exchange vNext Mailbox servers into an Exchange server 2019 Database Availability Group. This will make upgrading from Exchange server 2019 to Exchange vNext "a piece of cake."

Getting Started

To begin, let's take a general look at Exchange 2019. First, we will consider the two Exchange 2019 editions and review their features. Then, we will look at their features compared to previous versions of Exchange.

Exchange Server 2019 Editions

Exchange 2019 is available in two editions:

- **Exchange 2019, Standard Edition**—This is a "normal" Exchange 2019 but limited to five mailbox databases per Mailbox server.
- **Exchange 2019, Enterprise Edition**—This version can host up to 100 mailbox databases per Mailbox server.

Except for the number of mailbox databases per Exchange server, there are no differences between the two versions; the binaries are the same.

Entering the Exchange 2019 license key changes the limit of maximum mailbox databases for that server. Besides the Exchange 2019 server license, there is also a Client Access License (CAL), which is required for each user or device accessing the server software.

There are two types of CALs available:

- **Standard CAL**—This CAL offers standard email functionality from any platform. The license is for typical Exchange and Outlook usage.
- **Enterprise CAL**—This more advanced CAL offers functionality such as integrated archiving, compliance features, and information protection capabilities. The CAL is an add-on to the Standard CAL, so both licenses need to be purchased!

This is not a complete list of all available features for the different CALs. For a complete overview, visit the Microsoft licensing page at `http://bit.ly/X2019Licensing`.

Note An Exchange server 2019 server license is always needed. But an Exchange Online P1 or P2 of Office 365 E1 or E3 license can also be used for a CAL. When an Exchange server 2016 server is used in a hybrid environment, and all mailboxes are in Exchange Online, customers might be eligible for a free "hybrid server license" from Microsoft.

What's New in Exchange Server 2019?

So, what are the new features and improvements in Exchange server 2019? There are a lot of new features, valuable both from an administrator's point of view and from that of an end user. Let us discuss the most important changes here, compared to previous versions of Exchange server 2019:

- **Support for Windows Server 2019 server core**—Exchange server 2019 is supported on Windows server 2019, both the Desktop Experience and Server Core. Windows server 2019 server core is the recommended operating system for Exchange server 2019 because of the lower footprint and improved security. Windows Server 2019 is also the only supported operating system for Exchange server 2019. Please note that Exchange server 2016 is only supported on Windows server 2016 (Desktop Experience only, no server core support) and Windows Server 2012 R2.
- **TLS 1.2**—To improve the client to server connections, the default protocol for encrypting traffic between clients and the Exchange server 2019 server. Older versions are still available but are disabled by default. Please note that a client in this respect can also be another (Exchange) server that is communicating with the Exchange server 2019 server.
- **Block external access of ECP and EMS**—In Exchange server 2019, it is possible to block external access to the Exchange Control Panel (ECP) and Exchange Management Shell (EMS) using Client Access Rules. Based on conditions, exceptions, and actions, Client Access Rules help you to control access to ECP and EMS in a very granular manner.
- **Improved search infrastructure**—The search infrastructure in Exchange server 2019 is improved and is now based on the Bing search technology. Its codename is "Big Funnel," something you can still see in Exchange server 2019 under the hood. Search indexes are no longer stored in a separate directory on the disk containing the Mailbox database, but they are stored in the user's mailbox. Because of this, search data replication is always up to date, and Mailbox database failovers are much faster, therefore improving performance of the Exchange server 2019 server.
- **Modern hardware support**—Exchange server 2019 supports more modern hardware, up to 256 GB memory and up to 48 CPU cores. The minimum recommended amount of memory for Exchange server 2019 is also 128 GB (it can run with less memory though), and

performance greatly benefits from this large amount of memory. Large memory and multiple processor cores also enable switching from Workstation Garbage Collection (GC) to Server GC. This setting in .NET Framework can handle more requests per second, thus improving performance.

- **MetaCache database**—Exchange server 2019 has a new feature called metacache database (MCDB). This feature uses SSD disks to store frequently accessed data from Mailbox databases. Mailbox databases are still stored on slow JBOD disks, but frequently accessed data can now be cached on SSD disks. For every four (slow) JBOD disks, one SSD disk is used to cache information. This greatly improves performance and latencies, which is very beneficial for Remote Desktop or Citrix environments where Outlook clients are running in online mode.
- **Dynamic database cache**—Mailbox database information is kept in memory. While this is useful for active Mailbox databases, it does not make much sense for passive Mailbox databases in a Database Availability Group. Previous versions of Exchange did not differentiate between these two, therefore "wasting" valuable memory on passive Mailbox databases. Exchange server 2019 has a dynamic database cache, which means that passive Mailbox databases use less memory than active Mailbox databases. In other words, active Mailbox databases in Exchange server 2019 can use memory than they could in Exchange server 2016. This also improves overall Exchange server 2019 performance.
- **A different look and feel for client interfaces**—The Outlook Web App (OWA) or Outlook on the Web as it is called these days did not change much since Exchange server 2013. The overall themes have changed a bit or the location of buttons, but that is basically it. But when moving from Exchange server 2010 to Exchange server 2016, users will see a completely new user interface with a different look and feel. It also comes with several new features in OWA, like Bing Maps integration as shown in Figure 1-2, support for server-side

apps, or offline use in a browser. Exchange server 2016 and Exchange server 2019 also support Microsoft Teams integration, making it possible to use the on-premises calendar in Microsoft Teams. This only works in a hybrid environment with Exchange Online.

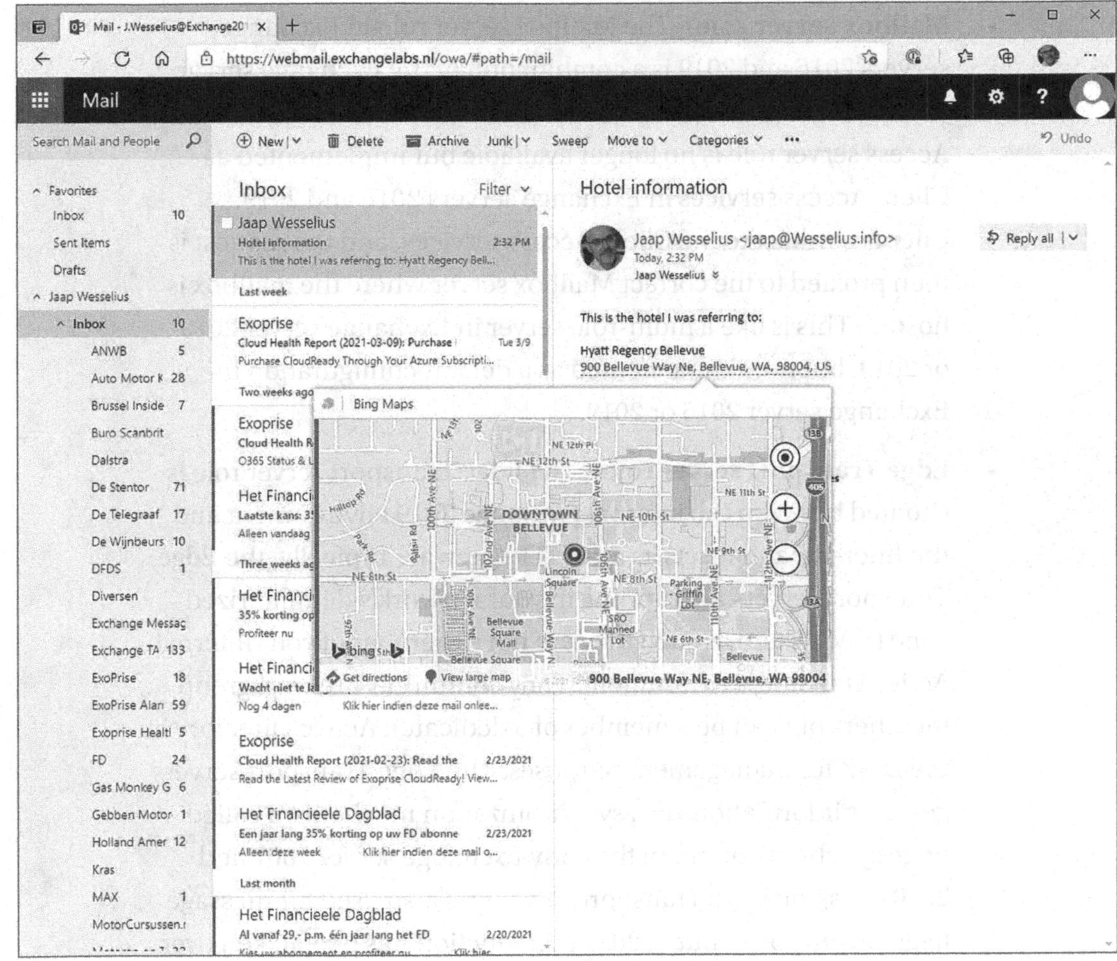

***Figure 1-2.** Outlook Web App (OWA) in Exchange server 2019 with Bing Maps integration*

- **Exchange 2019** architecture—Previous versions of Exchange server had multiple server roles, ranging from five server roles in Exchange server 2007 and Exchange server 2010 to three server roles in Exchange server 2013. Exchange servers 2016 and 2019 only have two server roles:
    - **Mailbox server role**—The Mailbox server role in Exchange servers 2016 and 2019 is a combination of the Exchange server 2013 Mailbox server and Client Access server role. The Client Access server role is no longer available but implemented as Client Access services in Exchange servers 2016 and 2019. Clients connect to the Client Access services, and the request is then proxied to the correct Mailbox server where the mailbox is hosted. This is like a multi-role server in Exchange server 2010 or 2013, but now implemented as a default configuration in Exchange server 2016 or 2019.
    - **Edge Transport server role**—The Edge Transport server role is situated between the internal Exchange 2019 environment and the Internet, and it acts as an SMTP gateway. Typically, the Edge Transport servers are running in your network's demilitarized zone (DMZ), and as such they are not a member of your internal Active Directory environment. They commonly are workgroup members but can be a member of a dedicated Active Directory in the DMZ for management purposes. The Edge Transport servers get their information via a synchronization mechanism called Edge synchronization. In the early Exchange server 2007 and 2010 days, the Edge Transport server was also used for message hygiene purposes, but in 2021 that function has been taken over by various cloud services like Exchange Online Protection (or any other message hygiene vendor).
- **Managed Availability**—Not new in Exchange server 2019 but introduced in Exchange server 2013 and carried forward is the Managed Availability feature. It looks like some sort of "self-healing" feature, and it is responsible for monitoring all critical services in Exchange server 2019. When needed, it takes appropriate action.

Managed Availability consists of probes, monitors, and actions. Probes are constantly checking for certain services, and they feed the results into the monitors. The monitors evaluate the results from the probes. When needed, Managed Availability can perform certain actions. For example, it can check if OWA is up and running; if it is not, it can start or recycle the application pool where OWA is running or reset the Internet Information Services (IISRESET). Similarly, Managed Availability has probes for mailbox databases; if a mailbox database is found to be corrupted, Managed Availability can take action to automatically fail over that mailbox database to another Mailbox server in the Database Availability Group (DAG) and perform an automatic reseed of the corrupted mailbox database. This way, problems can be resolved even before end users notice the failures, thereby reducing the number of calls to the help desk.

Of course, there are more new features in Exchange 2019, but these are the most important and interesting ones.

What Has Been Removed from Exchange Server

Every new version of Exchange Server introduces new features, but at the same time, other features are discontinued, deprecated, or available only in some other form or scenario. The most important changes or discontinued features in Exchange 2019 are

- **Unified Messaging server role**—The Unified Messaging (UM) server role has been removed from Exchange server 2019 but is still available in Exchange server 2016. Since the UM role is no longer available in Exchange server 2019, it is out of scope for this book. The UM role in Exchange server 2016 has not changed since Exchange server 2013, so when information is needed about the UM role, you are kindly referred to our Exchange server 2013 SP1 book.
- **Client Access server role**—The Client Access server role is no longer available in Exchange 2016 and 2019 and is replaced by Client Access services running on the Mailbox server role.

- **MAPI/CDO library**—When moving from Exchange server 2013 to Exchange server 2019, you will see that the MAPI/CDO library is no longer available. The functionality of the MAPI/CDO library has been replaced by Exchange Web Services (EWS), Exchange ActiveSync (EAS), or REST APIs.
- **RPC/HTTP**—RPC/HTTP (also known as Outlook Anywhere) is deprecated in Exchange server 2019 and is replaced by MAPI/HTTP. Although being deprecated, this is still a requirement for installing Exchange 2019 for compatibility purposes.
- **Cluster administrative access points for DAGs**—Database Availability Groups in Exchange 2019 no longer support failover-cluster administrative access points.

When moving from Exchange server 2010 to Exchange server 2016, the following features are discontinued:

- **Support for Outlook 2003 and older**—Outlook 2003 is not supported in Exchange 2016. Not only is it unsupported, but it is also not working. Outlook 2003 depends on system folders, free/busy, and offline address book distribution folders in public folders, and these system folders have been discontinued. This might look silly in a book about Exchange servers 2016 and 2019, but it still happens when moving from Exchange server 2010 to Exchange server 2016. Users start complaining that Outlook no longer runs, and at closer inspection, it turns out they are still running Outlook 2003!
- **RPC/TCP access for Outlook clients**—The traditional RPC/TCP access for Outlook clients is no longer supported in Exchange 2013 and higher. All Outlook clients will only connect using MAPI/HTTP or Outlook Anywhere, although the latter is being deprecated as well. But, when moving mailboxes from Exchange server 2010 to Exchange server 2016, the clients will reconnect and switch from RPC/TCP to MAPI/HTTP or Outlook Anywhere. This is a change you must be aware of when moving from Exchange server 2010.

- **Exchange Management Console and Exchange Control Panel—** In Exchange server 2010, the Exchange Management Console (EMC) was the primary graphical UI for managing the Exchange environment. In Exchange server 2013 and higher, this is replaced by the Exchange Admin Center (EAC) and Exchange Management Shell (EMS). Exchange server 2010 administrators need to get used to the new management tools. The preferred way of managing Exchange 2013 and higher is the EMS. EMS contains all configurable options. EAC can be used for configuring Exchange 2013 and higher but is missing nitty-gritty details.

Integration with Active Directory

Active Directory is the foundation for Exchange server 2019, as it has been for Exchange Server since Exchange 2000 was released 14 years ago. Earlier versions of Exchange Server—that is, Exchange 5.5 and earlier—relied on their own directory, which was separate from the (NT4) user directory. Active Directory stores most of Exchange's configuration information, both for server/organization configuration and for mail-enabled objects.

A Microsoft Windows Active Directory Directory Service (ADDS) is best described as a forest; this is the highest level in the Directory Service and is the actual security boundary. The forest contains one or more Active Directory domains; a domain is a logical grouping of resources, such as users, groups, and computers. An Exchange 2019 organization is bound to one forest, so even if you have an environment with one Active Directory forest and over 100 Active Directory domains, there can be only one Exchange organization.

Active Directory sites also play an important role in Exchange deployment. An Active Directory site can be seen as a location, well connected with high bandwidth and low latency—for example, a data center or an office. Active Directory sites can contain multiple Active Directory domains, but an Active Directory domain can also span multiple Active Directory sites.

Exchange 2019 depends heavily on ADDS, and these need to be healthy. The minimum levels in ADDS need to be Windows 2012 R2 Forest Functional Level (FFL) and Windows 2012 R2 Domain Functional Level (DFL). The Domain Controllers need to be at a minimum level of Windows Server 2012 R2.

Active Directory Partitions

A Microsoft Windows ADDS consists of three system-provided partitions:

- **Schema partition**—The schema partition is the blueprint for all objects and properties that are available in Active Directory. For example, if a new user is created, a user object is instantiated from the schema, the required properties are populated, and the user account is stored in the Active Directory database. All objects and properties are in the schema partition, and therefore it depends which version is used. Windows 2019 Active Directory has much newer objects and newer (and more) properties than, for example, Windows 2012 R2 Active Directory. The same is true, of course, for applications like Exchange Server. Exchange 2019 adds a lot of new objects and attributes to Active Directory that make it possible to increase functionality. Therefore, every new version of Exchange Server, or even the cumulative updates or service packs, needs to make schema changes.

  There is only one schema partition in the entire Active Directory forest. Even if you have an Active Directory forest with 100 domains and 250 sites worldwide, there is only one schema partition. This partition is replicated among all Domain Controllers in the entire Active Directory forest. The most important copy of the schema partition is running on the schema master, which is typically the first Domain Controller installed in the forest. This copy is the only read-write copy in the entire Active Directory forest.

- **Configuration partition**—The configuration partition is where all non-schema information is stored that needs to be available throughout the Active Directory forest. Information that can be found in the configuration partition is, for example, about Active Directory sites, about public key infrastructure, about the various partitions that are available in Active Directory, and of course about Exchange Server. Just like the schema partition, there is only one configuration partition. It replicates among all Domain Controllers in the entire Active Directory environment so that all the Exchange servers have access to the same, consistent set of information. All information regarding the Exchange server configuration, like the Exchange servers themselves, the routing infrastructure, or the number of domains that Exchange Server is responsible for, is stored in the configuration partition.

- **Domain partition**—The domain partition is where all domain-specific information is stored.

  There is one partition per domain, so if you have 100 domains in your Active Directory forest, you have 100 separate domain partitions. User objects, contacts, and security and distribution groups are stored in the domain partition.

The best tool for viewing the three Active Directory partitions is the ADSI Edit MMC (Microsoft Management Console) snap-in, which is shown in Figure 1-3.

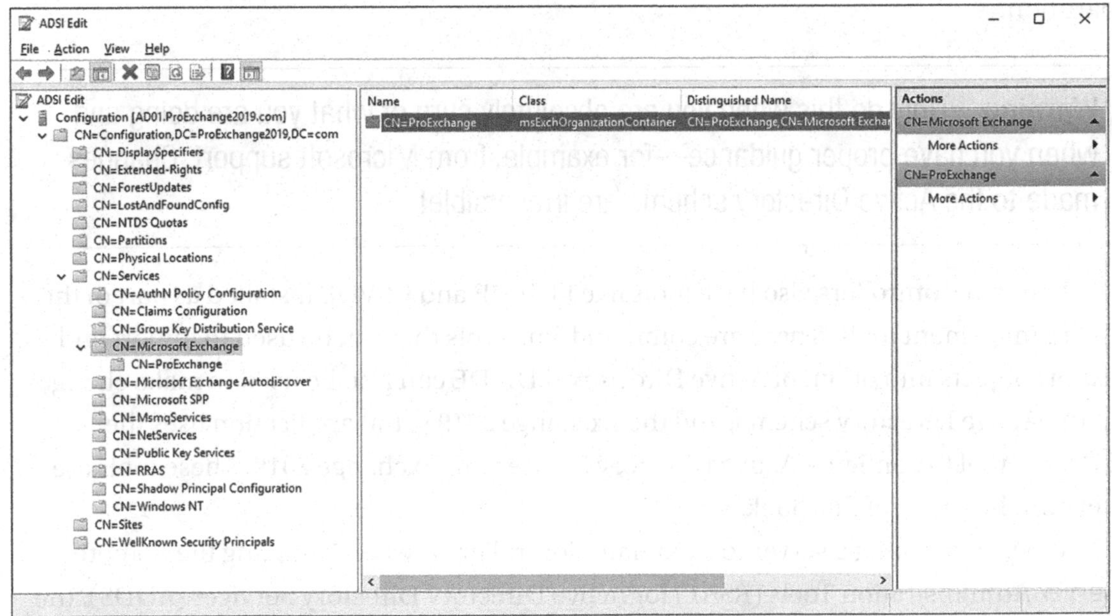

***Figure 1-3.** The Exchange information is stored in the configuration partition*

Warning There is very little safeguarding in this tool, so it is easy to destroy critical parts in Active Directory when you are just clicking around!

In Windows Server 2019, the Active Directory Administrative Center (ADAC) is the preferred tool to manage the Active Directory environment, but Active Directory Users and Computer (ADUC) can also be used. Using either tool is relatively safe since the tool prevents messing around with objects in a way that Active Directory does not like. The advantage of the Administrative Center is (in my opinion) that it can show deleted objects when the Active Directory Recycle Bin is enabled. This has saved me from mess-ups in the past.

The Active Directory Sites and Services (ADSS) MMC snap-in reads and writes information from the configuration partition. All changes made here are visible to all domains in the forest; the same is true for the Active Directory Domains and Trusts MMC snap-in.

A very powerful tool regarding Active Directory is the Schema MMC snap-in, which is usually run on the Domain Controller that holds the schema master role. Using the Schema MMC snap-in, it is possible to make changes to the Active Directory schema partition.

Warning Only do this when you are absolutely sure of what you are doing and when you have proper guidance—for example, from Microsoft support. Changes made to the Active Directory schema are irreversible!

Domain Controllers also have tools like LDIFDE and CSVDE installed as part of the AD management tools. These are command-line tools that can be used to import and export objects into or out of Active Directory. LDIFDE can also be used to make changes to the Active Directory schema, and the Exchange 2019 setup application uses the LDIFDE tool to configure Active Directory for use with Exchange 2019. These tools are beyond the scope of this book.

When promoting a server to a Domain Controller, or when installing the Remote Server Administration Tools (RSAT) for Active Directory Directory Services (ADDS), the PowerShell Active Directory module is installed as well. This module enables Active Directory functionality in PowerShell, making it possible to manage Active Directory using PowerShell cmdlets.

Active Directory Permissions

There are three partitions in Active Directory. Each of these partitions has separate permissions requirements, and not everybody has (full) access to these partitions. The following are the default administrator accounts or security groups that have access to each partition.

- **Schema Admins security group**—The Schema Admins have full access to the schema partition. The first administrator account is the top-level domain, which is the first domain created. To make the necessary changes to the schema partition for installing Exchange Server, the account that is used needs to be a member of this security group. Any other domain administrator in the forest is, by default, not a member of this group.
- **Enterprise Admins security group**—The Enterprise Admins have full access to the configuration partition. Again, the first administrator account in the top-level domain is a member of this group and as such can make changes to the configuration partition. Since all Exchange Server configuration information is stored in the configuration partition, the account used for installing Exchange Server needs to be a member of this group. Please note that the Enterprise Admins security group does not have permission to make changes to the schema partition.
- **Domain Admins security group**—The Domain Admins have full access to the domain partition of the corresponding domain. If there are 60 domains in an Active Directory environment, there are 60 domain partitions and thus 60 different Domain Admins security groups. The first administrator account in the top-level domain is a member of the Domain Admins security group in this top-level domain.

Why is this important to know? In the early days of Active Directory, Microsoft recommended using multiple domains in an Active Directory forest, preferably with an empty root domain. This empty root domain is a domain without any resources, and its primary purpose was for Active Directory management. All resources like servers, computers, users, and groups were located in child domains. Needless to say, this has some implications for the use of various administrator accounts. It is a delegated model, where the administrator accounts in the top-level domain have control over all Active Directory domains, whereas the administrators in the other domains have administrative rights only in their respective Active Directory domains. These other administrators do not have administrative privileges in other domains, let alone permission to modify the configuration partition or the schema partition.

But things have changed, and although an empty root Active Directory domain environment can still be used, it is no longer actively recommended. Mostly recommended these days is a “single forest, single domain” environment unless there are strict legal requirements that dictate using another Active Directory model.

Chapter 10 will explain about security in great detail and will explore the various options available for delegated administration and split permissions. But in short, the default administrator account that is created in the top-level Active Directory domain has enough permissions for installing Exchange 2019.

Active Directory Sites

Active Directory sites play an important role in any Exchange server deployments. As stated earlier, an Active Directory site can be seen as a (physical) location with good internal network connectivity, high bandwidth, and low latency—that is, a local LAN. An office or data center is typically a good candidate for an Active Directory site.

An organization can have multiple locations or multiple data centers, resulting in multiple Active Directory sites. Sites are typically interconnected, with lower bandwidth, higher latency connections. An Active Directory site can also have multiple domains, but at the same time, an Active Directory domain can span multiple sites.

An Active Directory site also is a replication boundary. Domain Controllers in an Active Directory site replicate their information almost immediately among Domain Controllers in the same site. If a new object is created, or if an object is changed, the other Domain Controllers in that same site are notified immediately, and the information is replicated within seconds. All Domain Controllers in an Active Directory site must contain the same information.

Information exchanged between Domain Controllers in different Active Directory sites is replicated on a timed schedule, defined by the administrator. A typical time frame can be 15 minutes, but depending on the type of connection or the bandwidth used to a particular location (you do not want your replication traffic to interfere with normal production bandwidth), it can take up to several hours. This means that when changes are made to Active Directory—for example, when installing Exchange 2019—it can take a serious amount of time before all the information is replicated across all the Domain Controllers and the new changes are visible to the entire organization.

Active Directory sites are created using the Active Directory Sites and Services MMC snap-in. The first step is to define the network subnets in the various locations in the snap-in, and then tie the actual Active Directory site to the network subnet. For example, a data center in the Amsterdam site has IP subnet 10.38.96.0/24, while the data center in the London site has IP subnet 10.83.4.0/24. This is shown in Figure 1-4.

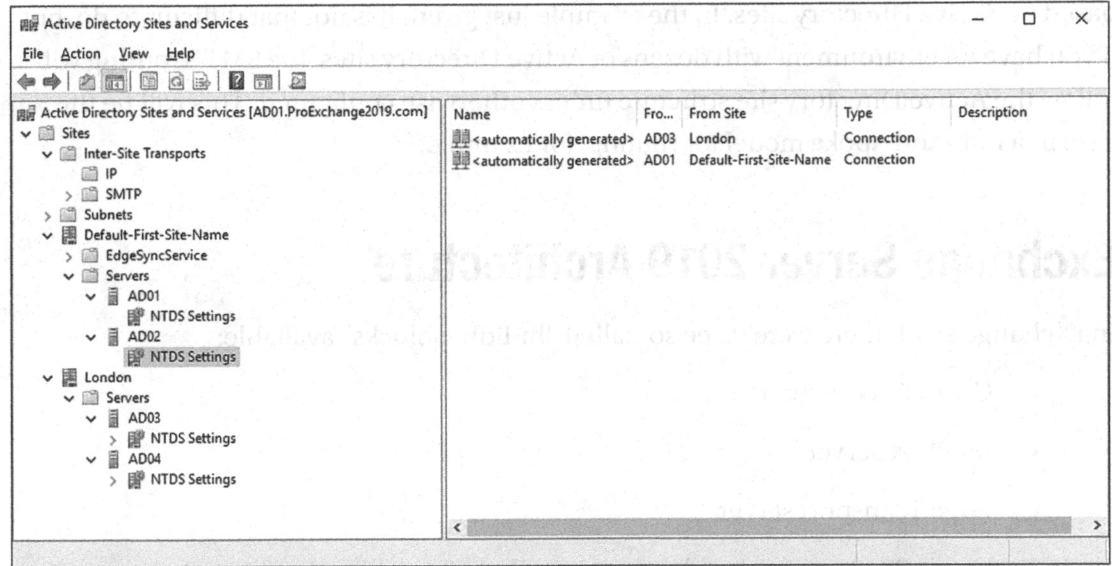

***Figure 1-4.** Two different subnets and sites, as shown in Active Directory Sites and Services*

A location like a data center in London or in Amsterdam (which corresponds with the Active Directory sites) can be "Internet facing" or "non-Internet facing," a descriptor that indicates whether the location has Internet connectivity or not. This is important for Exchange 2019, since it determines how namespaces are configured and thus how external clients are connected to their mailboxes in the different locations.

For example, the environment in Figure 1-4 has two Active Directory sites. If the data center in Amsterdam has an Internet connection and the data center in London does not, all clients from the Internet are connected initially to the Exchange 2019 servers in Amsterdam. If a user's mailbox is in London, the client request is proxied to the Exchange 2019 servers in London.

But, if the data center in London also has an Internet connection and the Exchange servers are configured accordingly, the London-based clients can access the Exchange 2019 servers from the Internet in Amsterdam, though the request will be redirected to the Exchange 2019 servers in London and thus connect directly to the servers in London.

Also, the routing of SMTP messages through the Exchange organization is partly based on Active Directory sites. In the example just given, it is not that difficult to do, but if you have an environment with dozens of Active Directory sites, the SMTP routing will follow the Active Directory site structure unless otherwise configured. This will be the case in a hub-and-spoke model for routing, for example.

Exchange Server 2019 Architecture

In Exchange 2013, there were three so-called "building blocks" available:

- Client Access server
- Mailbox server
- Edge Transport server

In Exchange 2013, it was already recommended to combine the Client Access and Mailbox servers into a multi-role server. In Exchange 2016, a multi-role server is enforced, and this is continued in Exchange server 2019. In Exchange 2019, two building blocks are available:

- **Mailbox server**—As just explained, the Exchange 2019 Mailbox server contains previous Client Access and Mailbox server roles, but now there are services:
    - **Client Access service**—The Client Access service (CAS) is the server where all clients connect. The CAS consists of two parts: Client Access Front End (CAFE) and the Front-End Transport service (FETS). The CAS performs authentication of a client request, it locates the location of the client's mailbox, and it

proxies or redirects the client request to the appropriate Mailbox server, where the actual client mailbox is located. The CAS in Exchange 2019 is sometimes also referred to as the "front end."

- **Mailbox service**—The Mailbox service is the component where the actual mailbox data is stored. Clients do not access the Mailbox service directly; all requests are routed through the CAS. The Mailbox service in Exchange 2019 is sometimes also referred to as the "back end." Rendering for clients like OWA, transport transcoding for SMTP always takes place on the back end.

- **Edge Transport server**—The Edge Transport server acts as an SMTP gateway between your internal Exchange environment and the Internet, typically situated in the perimeter network. When an Edge Transport server is used, all messages are routed through this server. Using an Edge Transport server is not mandatory; there are lots of customers who have decided not to use an Edge Transport server and use a third-party solution instead or route SMTP messages directly from a cloud message hygiene solution into the Mailbox servers.

Exchange 2019 Client Access Services

The Client Access service (CAS) performs only authentication of a client request; after authentication, the client request is proxied to the Mailbox server where the destination mailbox is located. The CAS in itself does not perform any processing with respect to mail data. According to Microsoft, its connections are stateless, but the connections are not really stateless because the SSL connection is terminated at the CAS and then processed. If a CAS goes offline, all connections are terminated and must be set up again on another CAS (which would not be the case in a true stateless setup). The reason that Microsoft calls it "stateless" is that there is no persistent storage on Exchange 2019 CAS.

Client connections are proxied from the CAS to the Mailbox server hosting the user's mailbox. This can be the same server, but it can also be another Exchange server 2019 server in the same organization. The protocol used to communicate with the Mailbox server is the same as the client connection, so when a client uses HTTP to connect to the CAS, the HTTP request is proxied to the correct Mailbox server. The only difference is the port that is used. The client uses port 443 to connect to the CAS; the CAS uses port 444 to connect to the Mailbox server. This is also true for other protocols like POP3, IMAP4, and SMTP. Figure 1-5 shows two Exchange 2019 servers (EXCH01 and EXCH02) with the Exchange services.

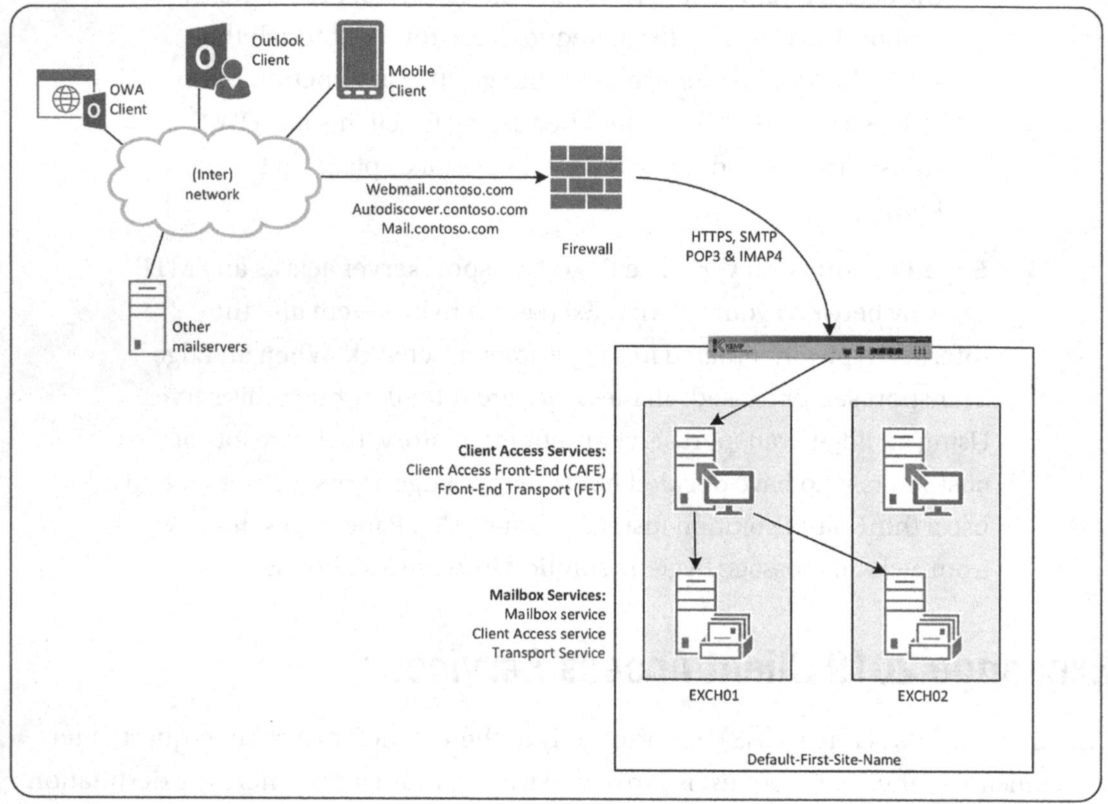

Figure 1-5. *CAS and Mailbox services in an Exchange 2019 Mailbox server*

As stated before, the CAS is a "thin" service and does not store any information from the sessions, except for the various protocol logs like Autodiscover, Outlook Anywhere, or IIS logging. This is true for both regular client requests and SMTP requests.

The Front-End Transport service that is responsible for handling SMTP messages on the CAS does not store messages on the server itself but passes the SMTP messages directly to the appropriate Mailbox server where the intended recipient's mailbox is located, or to a down-level Hub Transport server if the recipient is located on a down-level Mailbox server. The Front-End Transport service does not inspect message content.

Exchange 2019 Mailbox Services

The Mailbox service is where all the processing regarding messages takes place. Clients connect to the CAS, but the requests are proxied or redirected to the appropriate Mailbox service. All message rendering takes place on the Mailbox server.

SMTP Transport is also located on the Mailbox server and consists of three separate services:

- The Transport service
- The Mailbox Transport Delivery service
- The Mailbox Transport Submission service

The Transport service handles all SMTP message flow within the organization, such as routing, queuing, bifurcation, message categorization, and content inspection. Important to note is that the Transport service never communicates directly with the mailbox databases.

Communication between the Transport service and the mailbox database is performed by the Mailbox Transport Delivery service and the Mailbox Transport Submission service. These services connect directly to the mailbox database to deliver or retrieve messages from the mailbox database. As with the Front-End Transport service, the Mailbox Transport Delivery and Mailbox Transport Submission services do not queue any messages on the Mailbox server; the Transport service does queue information on the Mailbox server. (The transport mechanism is covered in detail in Chapter 6).

The most important part of this, of course, is the mailbox components that run on the Mailbox server. The Information Store, or store process, is responsible for handling all mailbox transactions and for storing these transactions in a mailbox database. The database is not a relational database like SQL server; it is running on its own engine, the Extensible Storage Engine or ESE. The ESE database engine has been fully optimized for the past 25 years for use with Exchange Server, so it performs very well and is very reliable. The ESE database is a transactional database using a database, log files, and a checkpoint file. Mailbox database internals are discussed in depth in Chapter 4.

The Exchange Replication service is another important service running on the Mailbox server. This service is responsible for replicating mailbox data from one mailbox database on one Mailbox server to a mailbox database running on another Mailbox server. The collection of Mailbox servers replicating data between each other is called the Database Availability Group, or DAG. A DAG can take up to 16 Exchange 2019

Mailbox servers. Each mailbox database has 1 active mailbox database copy and may have up to 16 mailbox database copies. There is always 1 active mailbox database copy and up to 15 passive mailbox database copies.

Note An Exchange server 2019 DAG can only contain Exchange server 2019 mailbox servers. Adding a previous version of Exchange is not supported and will not work. As mentioned earlier, Exchange 2019 will only support Exchange server vNext in hosting copies of the same database on different product versions.

The database in Exchange 2019 has been greatly improved compared to earlier versions, for instance:

- Exchange 2010 generates 0.1 I/O per second (IOPS) per mailbox.
- Exchange 2013 generates 0.07 IOPS per mailbox.
- Exchange 2016 and 2019 generate 0.044 IOPS per mailbox.

So, Exchange server 2019 generates less than 50% of the IOPS compared to Exchange 2010, making it now possible to store multiple databases, including their log files, on one physical disk.

Note Storing the Mailbox database and their log files on one disk can only be done in a high availability environment.

The decrease in IOPS is shown in Figure 1-6.

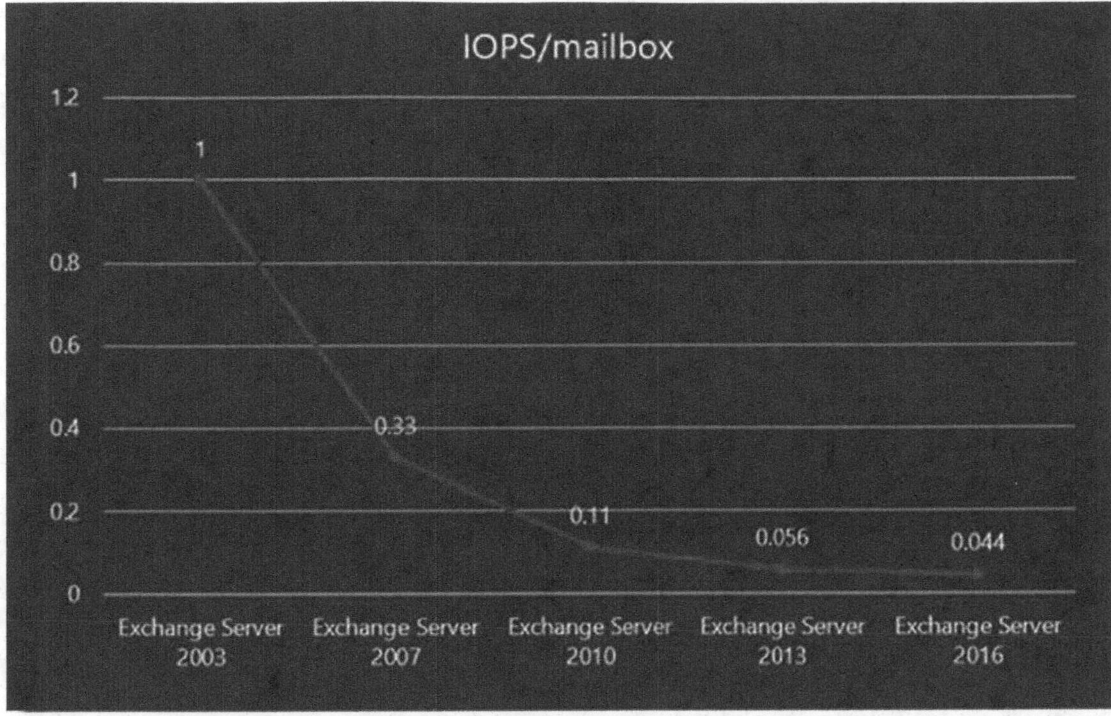

Figure 1-6. *Decrease in IOPS from Exchange server 2003 until Exchange 2016*

Exchange Server 2019 Management

There are two options for managing your Exchange 2019 environment:

- **Exchange Admin Center**—The HTML-based GUI that offers the most basic options for managing your Exchange 2019 environment
- **Exchange Management Shell**—The command-line interface running on top of Windows PowerShell and offering all nitty-gritty options when managing your Exchange 2019 environment

I will discuss these in more detail, as follows.

Exchange Admin Center

The Exchange Admin Center (EAC) is the web-based administration portal for managing your Exchange 2019 environment. The EAC can be managed from the internal network as well as from the external network. From a safety perspective, it is recommended to disable external access to the EAC. The EAC is accessible via a URL like `https://exch01/ecp` internally or `https://webmail.contoso.com/ecp` externally.

When the EAC is opened, a window like the one shown in Figure 1-7 appears.

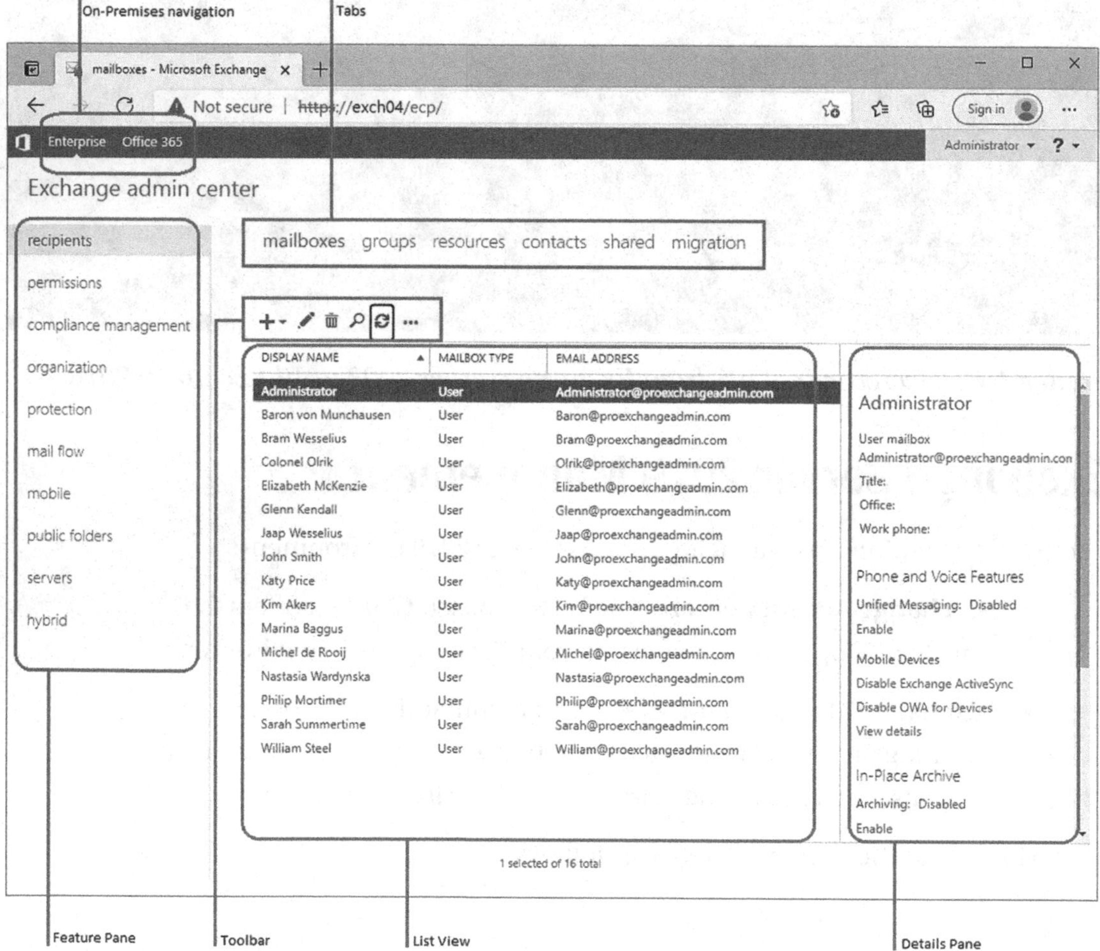

***Figure 1-7.** The Exchange Admin Center in Exchange server 2019*

In the left-hand menu, there are various components of Exchange server 2019 that can be managed in the EAC. The left-hand menu is also called the "Feature pane" and consists of the following features:

- **Recipients**—All recipients, like mailboxes, groups, contacts, shared mailboxes, and resource mailboxes, are managed from the Recipients option.
- **Permissions**—In the Permissions option, you can manage administrator roles, user roles, and Outlook Web App policies. The first two roles are explained in more detail in the RBAC section later in this chapter.
- **Compliance Management**—In the Compliance Management option, you can manage In-Place eDiscovery and Hold, auditing, data loss prevention (DLP), retention policies including retention tags, and journal rules.
- **Organization**—The Organization option is the highest level of configuration, and this is the place where you will manage your Exchange organization, including federated sharing, Outlook apps, and address lists.
- **Protection**—In the Protection option, you can manage anti-malware protection for the Exchange 2019 organization.
- **Mail Flow**—The Mail Flow option contains all choices regarding the flow of messages, including transport rules, delivery reports, accepted domains, email address policies, and send and receive connectors.
- **Mobile**—All settings regarding mobile devices are managed from the Mobile option. You can manage mobile device access and mobile device mailbox policies.
- **Public Folders**—From the Public Folders option, you can manage Exchange 2019 public folders.
- **Servers**—The Exchange 2019 servers can be managed from the Servers option. This also includes databases, database availability groups (DAGs), virtual directories, and certificates.

- **Hybrid**—In this section, you can connect to Office 365, download the Hybrid Configuration Wizard, and create a hybrid environment.

Note Functions available in the EAC are limited by the permissions enforced by Role-Based Access Control.

When working with the EAC, all actions are translated to PowerShell commands and then executed. The EAC has a command logging option so you can see what commands are executed. This is great for learning PowerShell and understanding what is happening under the hood.

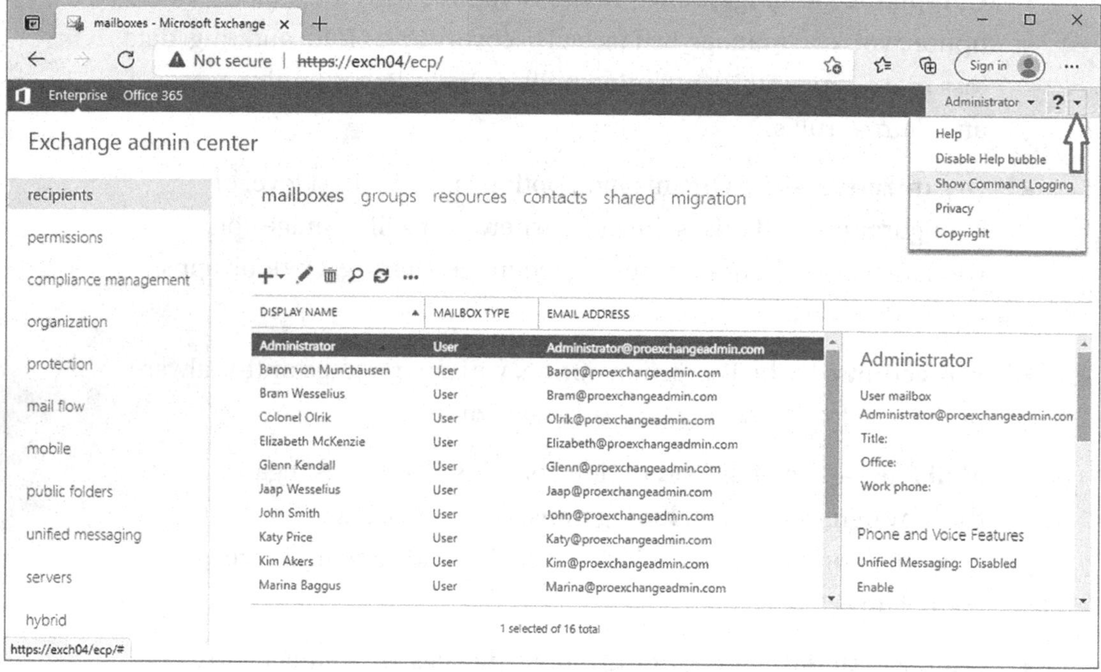

Figure 1-8. *The command log is available in the upper-right menu in EAC*

The tabs in the top-level menu are context sensitive. In other words, they change when a different feature in the Feature pane is selected.

All actions are associated with an icon. Table 1-1 describes each of the icons.

Table 1-1. *Available Options (Icons) in the EAC Toolbar*

Icon	Name	Description
+▾	Add, New	Use this for adding a new object. Sometimes, a down arrow is shown like here; this means multiple options are available for creating a new object.
✎	Edit	Use this for editing a selected object.
🗑	Delete	Use this for deleting a selected object.
⌕	Search	Use this for searching for a particular object.
⟳	Refresh	Use this for refreshing the objects listed in the list view.
•••	More options	This is shown when more action options are available. For example, in **Recipients** and **Mailboxes** the following additional options are available: Add/Remove columns, Export data to a CSV file, Connect a mailbox, and Advanced search.
↑↓	Up/Down	Use this option when changing the priority of an object in the list view. You will find this, for example, in **mail flow** and **email address policies**.
⧉	Copy	Use this to copy an object to a new object and start editing this new object. The original object will be kept and not changed.
+ −	Add/ Remove	Use to add or remove an item from a list. For example, the remove option is available in the Public Folders permissions dialog box to remove users from the allowed users list.

The EAC is capable of listing up to only 500 objects in one page at the same time, and if you want to view objects that aren't listed in the Details pane, you need to use Search and Filter options to find those specific objects. In Exchange 2019, the viewable limit from within the EAC list view is approximately 20,000 objects. In addition, paging is included so you can page to the results. In the Recipients list view, you can also configure the page size and export the data to a CSV file.

When you select an object from the list view, information about that object is displayed in the Details pane. In some cases (e.g., with mailboxes), the Details pane includes quick management tasks. For example, if you navigate to Recipients and then Mailboxes and select a mailbox from the list view, the Details pane displays an option to enable or disable the archive for that mailbox. The Details pane can also be used to bulk-edit several objects.

Simply press the CTRL key, select the objects you want to bulk-edit, and use the options in the Details pane. For example, selecting multiple mailboxes allows you to bulk-update users' contact and organization information, custom attributes, mailbox quotas, Outlook Web App settings, and more.

Note Supported browsers for the EAC are Microsoft Edge, the latest version of Mozilla Firefox or Google Chrome, and Apple Safari 6 or later.

Exchange Management Shell

The Exchange Management Shell (EMS) is the core of Exchange Server management. This is the place where you can configure everything—every little, tiny tidbit of Exchange Server. The EMS is not new; its first version appeared with Exchange Server 2007, and EMS has become more and more important over the years. There remain features which are only manageable from using EMS, and not from the EAC, such as the Client Access Rules.

EMS is running on top of the Windows PowerShell, and as such it can use all functionality that is available in PowerShell, like pipelining, formatting output, saving to local disk, ordering the output, or using filtering techniques.

We will discuss the most important basics here but also at various points throughout this book.

PowerShell

Lots of Microsoft server applications have their own management shell, and all are running on top of Windows PowerShell; and whether you like it or not, PowerShell is an industry standard for Windows management and for applications that run on top of Windows. And it is not only Microsoft that is using PowerShell for managing their applications; third-party vendors are also writing PowerShell add-ons for their products. Examples of these are HP, for their EVA storage management solutions; VMware, for their virtualization platform; and KEMP, for their load balancing solutions.

The first version of PowerShell was a downloadable add-on for Windows 2003, but Windows Server 2008 was the first operating system that came with PowerShell built into the product.

PowerShell is a command-line shell and scripting environment, and it uses the power of the .NET Framework. But PowerShell is not text based, it is object based, and as such it supports nice features such as pipelining, formatting, or redirecting the output. All objects have properties or methods that can be accessed and used in PowerShell.

The last feature we are going to discuss is additional modules, such as the Server Manager, Active Directory, and the Exchange module.

How do you identify the differences between the various PowerShell modules? It depends if you are running Windows 2019 Server Core or Windows 2019 Desktop Edition. In Windows 2019 Server Core, the various modules are identified as follows:

- The Windows command prompt has a black background and is identified with C:\>. This is the command prompt that is shown directly after logging on.
- Windows PowerShell typically has a black background, and the command prompt is identified with PS C:\>.
- Exchange Management Shell typically has a blue background, and the command prompt can be identified with the square brackets around the PS letters: [PS] C:\>.

In Windows 2019 Desktop Edition, the various modules are identified as follows:

- The Windows command prompt has a black background, and the command prompt is identified with C:\>.
- Windows PowerShell has a blue background, and the command prompt is identified with PS C:\>.
- Exchange Management Shell has a black background, and the command prompt is identified with [PS] C:\>.

Object Model

Although a command-line interface, PowerShell uses an object-oriented model stemming from the .NET Framework on which top it is build. This means you are working with objects and not with normal text, as in a regular command prompt or Unix-like shell environment.

Since an object is returned, it can be manipulated using methods related to the object, or you can check certain attributes or properties. For example, you can request information regarding an Exchange server with the following command:

```
[PS] C:\> Get-ExchangeServer -Identity EXCH01
```

Although it is returned as text on the console, it is an object being returned, and you can treat it this way, for example:

```
[PS] C:\> (Get-ExchangeServer -Identity EXCH01).AdminDisplayVersion
```

This will return the AdminDisplayVersion property of the Exchange server. Or, when moving mailboxes and you want to check the number of mailboxes that are in the queue waiting to be processed, you can use the following command:

```
[PS] C:\> (Get-MoveRequest -MoveStatus Queued).count
```

So, the output of a command is an object, and you can continue working with this object. This way, you can use the output (object) of one command as actual input for another command, a technique which is called pipelining. This technique is very often used in managing Exchange environments.

Pipeline

You can see a pipeline as a series of connected segments of pipe where all items or objects pass through each segment. Each segment has its own functionality or purpose and can alter the objects. To create a new pipeline, the pipe operator "|" is used with the various commands. The simplest form of a pipeline is to use a Get command in conjunction with a Set command, for example:

```
[PS] C:\> Get-Mailbox | Set-Mailbox
```

In this command, a pipeline is created between the Get-Mailbox and the Set-Mailbox commands. The Get-Mailbox command retrieves one or more mailbox objects, and these objects are sent through the pipeline to the Set-Mailbox command, which can make certain changes to the mailbox objects.

Personally, I use this pipelining a lot when administering Exchange server. You can use the various Get commands to retrieve objects from Exchange, and you can actually see if you have the right objects. Then you can pipe them into the corresponding Set command and you are done. Very valuable!

Objects and Members

Each object in PowerShell has members, and members can be properties or methods. A property is something that has a value—for example, the name of a mailbox. A method is something that can be executed against an object—for example, to configure mailbox properties.

To see all members of a particular mailbox, you can use the following command:

```
[PS] C:\>Get-Mailbox Administrator | Get-Member

   TypeName: Microsoft.Exchange.Data.Directory.Management.Mailbox

Name                  MemberType              Definition
----                  ----------              ----------
Clone                 Method                  System.Object Clone(),
                                              System.Object
                                              ICloneable.Clone()
CopyChangesFrom       Method                  void IConfigurable.
                                              CopyChangesFrom
                                              (Microsoft.
                                              Exchange.D...
Equals                Method                  bool Equals(System.
                                              Object obj)
GetHashCode           Method                  int GetHashCode()
GetProperties         Method                  System.Object[]
                                              GetProperties(System.
                                              Collections.Generi...
GetProxyInfo          Method                  System.Object GetProxy
                                              Info(), System.Object
                                              ICmdletProx...
GetType               Method                  type GetType()
PSComputerName        NoteProperty            string PSComputerName=
                                              exch01.proex
                                              changeadmin.com
PSShowComputerName    NoteProperty            bool PSShowComputer
                                              Name=False
RunspaceId            NoteProperty            guid RunspaceId=
                                              a19837e5-7683-455b-
                                              affe-c745d90e2ad8
Item                  ParameterizedProperty   System.Object
                                              Item(Microsoft.
                                              Exchange.Data.
                                              PropertyDefi...
```

```
AcceptMessagesOnlyFrom              Property            Microsoft.Exchange.
                                                        Data.MultiValuedProper
                                                        ty[Microsoft.E...
AcceptMessagesOnlyFromDLMembers     Property            Microsoft.Exchange.
                                                        Data.MultiValuedProper
                                                        ty[Microsoft.E...
ArchiveGuid                         Property            guid ArchiveGuid {get;}
CustomAttribute1                    Property            string
                                                        CustomAttribute1
                                                        {get;set;}
DisplayName                         Property            string DisplayName
                                                        {get;set;}
IsValid                             Property            bool IsValid {get;}
OrganizationalUnit                  Property            string
                                                        OrganizationalUnit
                                                        {get;}
SCLDeleteEnabled                    Property            System.Nullable[bool]
                                                        SCLDeleteEnabled
                                                        {get;set;}
WhenChanged                         Property            System.Nullable
                                                        [datetime] WhenChanged
                                                        {get;}
WhenChangedUTC                      Property            System.Nullable
                                                        [datetime]
                                                        WhenChangedUTC {get;}
WhenCreated                         Property            System.
                                                        Nullable[datetime]
                                                        WhenCreated {get;}
WhenCreatedUTC                      Property            System.
                                                        Nullable[datetime]
                                                        WhenCreatedUTC {get;}
WhenMailboxCreated                  Property            System.Nullable
                                                        [datetime] WhenMailbox
                                                        Created {get;}

[PS] C:\>
```

When you use PowerShell to retrieve an object, only a limited set of members is shown. This is purely practical; your console would be overwhelmed with data if all members were shown.

Formatting

It is possible to format the output as shown on the console using cmdlets that start with the Format verb. The following are used throughout this book:

- **Format-List**—This is abbreviated to FL and is used to show all properties of a certain object. To retrieve all properties of the Administrator mailbox, you would use Get-Mailbox -Identity | FL.
- **Format-Table**—This is abbreviated to FT and can be used to retrieve certain properties of an object. The Get-Mailbox command, for example, returns only the Name, Alias, ServerName, and ProhibitSendQuota properties. To retrieve the Name, Alias, Database, and ArchiveState, a command similar to Get-Mailbox -Identity Administrator | FT -Property Name, Alias, Database, ArchiveState can be used.
- **Format-Wide**—This command is abbreviated to FW and shows only one property of an object. Typically, it shows only the default property of an object; for a mailbox, this would be its name, but you can select another property using the -Property option.

In addition to these Format verbs, you can use the -Wrap and -AutoSize parameters in PowerShell to format the output of the Format-Table command, as shown on the console. The -Wrap option does not truncate output in a column, but it wraps all output in its column, thereby showing the entire property. The -AutoSize option varies the width of the column, depending on the data that is shown in the column.

Important to note is that PowerShell expects the first column to be the most important, decreasing the importance with subsequent columns. As such, later columns can even be removed from the output when there is too much information to be shown. If this happens, you can change the order of information shown on the console by reordering the properties using the -Property option.

Normally, the output of commands is shown on the console. It is possible to redirect the output elsewhere using the Out verb in PowerShell. The following options are available in PowerShell:

- **Out-Host**—The Out-Host option redirects the output to the console, which is the default option. You can use the -Paging option to show only a limited amount of information at one time. You can use the <SPACE> to view another page with information on the console.
- **Out-Null**—The Out-Null option immediately discards any information without showing it on the console. However, any error message or, more specifically, output from the error stream will be shown on the console.
- **Out-Printer**—The Out-Printer option redirects any output directly to the printer. The default printer is used if no printer name is provided; otherwise, a command similar to Out-Printer -Name "HP LaserJet 1200 Series PCL 5" can be used.
- **Out-File**—The Out-File command is often used because it redirects any output to a (Unicode) file on the local hard disk. If a pure ASCII-coded file is needed, the -Encode ASCII option can be used—for example, Out-File -FilePath C:\Logging\Mailboxes.txt -Encode ASCII.
- **Out-GridView**—The Out-GridView option will output objects to a graphically presented grid where users can perform limited additional searching and sorting. Note that GridView allows for selections, which are passed through the pipeline for further processing.

These methods and concepts are widely referenced throughout this book.

Grouping

Another useful parameter to organize output is the GroupBy control. Long output listings that are hard to view offer the option to group the output based on a property. For example, it is possible to retrieve all users from Active Directory and group the output by the value of their company attribute, like this:

```
[PS] C:\> Get-User | Format-Table -Property Name,SamAccountName,Company
-Sort Company -GroupBy Company
```

Filtering

It is also possible to filter the output of the Get-User command with the -Filter parameter. For example, to mailbox-enable all users whose company attribute is set to "Fourth Coffee," enter the following command:

```
[PS] C:\> Get-User -Filter {Company -eq "Fourth Coffee"}
```

Note Whenever possible, you should use the –Filter option. This will only send the objects to the console that pass the filter conditions on the server side, resulting in much more efficient processing.

If you want to be even more specific—for example, to mailbox-enable all users whose company attribute is set to "Fourth Coffee" and whose department attribute is set to "Marketing," enter the following command:

```
[PS] C:\> Get-User -Filter {(Company -eq "Fourth Coffee") -AND
(Department -eq "Marketing")}
```

In short, the following operations are available for the -Filter option:

- -and
- -or
- -not
- -eq (equals)
- -ne (does not equal)
- -lt (less than)
- -gt (greater than)
- -like (compare strings by using wildcard rules)
- -notlike (compare strings by using wildcard rules)

Conversion

It is possible to convert objects to a certain format—for example, HTML or CSV. This can be useful if you want to just collect data or you want to process it using applications like Excel. For instance, to collect a simple list of mailboxes and export that information to a CSV file that you can import in Excel, enter the following cmdlet:

```
[PS] C:\> Get-Mailbox | Select DisplayName, PrimarySmtpAddress | Export-CSV
-Path C:\Install\Mailboxes.csv -NoTypeInformation
```

When exporting output into a CSV file, PowerShell writes the type of object onto the first line of the CSV file—something like #TYPE Selected.Microsoft.Exchange.Data.Directory.Management.Mailbox, as shown in Figure 1-9.

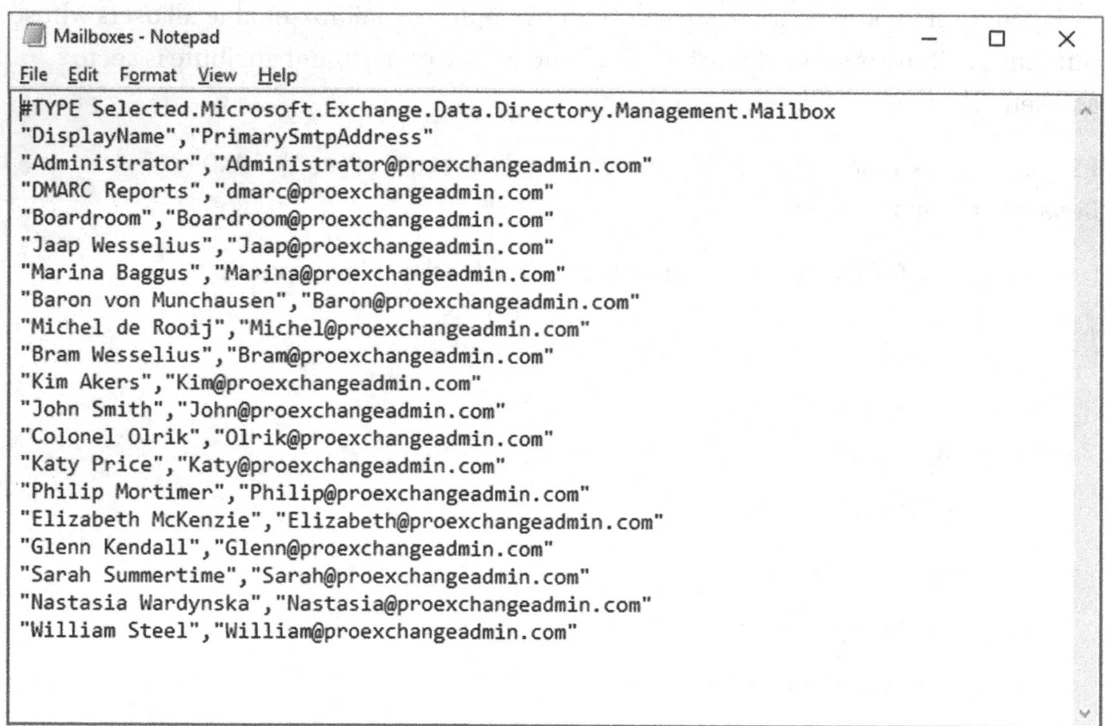

Figure 1-9. *The Export-CSV creates an additional #Type entry in the CSV file*

The -NoTypeInformation option prevents this line in the output file.

Conversion cmdlets also have an import counterpart—that is, Import-CSV—which allows you to import information that is stored in a certain format.

Variables

Using variables is not really specific for PowerShell, but every command-line interface or scripting engine can use variables, and that is no different in PowerShell.

As explained earlier, PowerShell is using objects, and you can store objects in variables so you can use them later on. This can be used in a PowerShell script, but also on the command line. An object is kept alive as long as the PowerShell window is open or until it is destroyed.

Variables are identified with a $ character, followed by any name you want. Of course, it is good practice to use an easy-to-identify name.

To create a variable called $AdminMailbox and store the Administrator mailbox object in it, you can use the following command:

```
[PS] C:\> $AdminMailbox = Get-Mailbox -Identity Administrator
```

The mailbox object is now stored in the variable $AdminMailbox and ready for use directly, or for later use. To view the contents of the variable, you can type in its name in the PowerShell window:

```
[PS] C:\Windows\system32>$AdminMailbox
Name          Alias               ServerName          ProhibitSendQuota
----          ----- ----------  ----------          -----------------
Administrator   Administrator   ams-exch01           Unlimited

[PS] C:\Windows\system32>
```

You can see that the output is identical to a normal Get-Mailbox command. To view all members of the object stored in this variable, you can request them, just like a normal object:

```
[PS] C:\> $AdminMailbox | Get-Member
```

All members of this variable will now be shown on the console.

It is also possible to store multiple objects in a variable. To store all mailboxes running on server EXCH01 in a variable called $Mailboxes, you can use the following command:

```
[PS] C:\> $Mailboxes = Get-Mailbox -Server EXCH01
```

To do "something" with all these mailboxes, you can create a conditional loop in PowerShell, along the lines of

```
[PS] C:\> $Mailboxes = Get-Mailbox -Server AMS-EXCH01
[PS] C:\> ForEach ($Mailbox in $Mailboxes){Do Something with each $Mailbox}
```

It is also possible to use system environment variables like the name of the server you are working on. To use a variable called $ServerName and populate it with the name of the server, you can use the following:

```
[PS] C:\> $ServerName = $env:COMPUTERNAME
```

To retrieve the name of the Active Directory domain you are logged on to and to create the FQDN you will use to configure the OWA virtual directory, you can use the following commands:

```
[PS] C:\> $Domain = $env:UserDnsDomain
[PS] C:\> $FQDN = "webmail." + $Domain
```

As with many programming environments, there are often more ways to accomplish things. For example, the preceding last cmdlet could also be replaced with

```
[PS] C:\> $FQDN = "webmail.$Domain"
```

Double quotes allow for embedding variables which will be replaced by its value at runtime. Another alternative is

```
[PS] C:\> $FQDN = 'webmail.' + $Domain
```

Single quotes are similar to double quotes, except single quotes take everything inside literally, not substituting variables at runtime.

Note This example is based on the assumption that your Active Directory domain name is identical to your external domain name.

If this is not the case in your environment, you can also use the Read-Host command to request user input on the PowerShell console and combine this with the "webmail" string to create the FQDN:

```
[PS] C:\> $Domain = Read-Host "Please enter your external domain name"
[PS] C:\> $FQDN = "webmail." + $Domain
```

By using these variables, it is possible to set the OWA virtual directory like this:

```
[PS] C:\> Get-OWAVirtualDirectory -Server $ServerName | Set-
OWAVirtualDirectory
-ExternalURL "https://$FQDN/owa" -InternalURL "https://$FQDN/owa"
```

In this example, you see the pipelining technology combined with the use of variables. In this book, you will learn how to use several kinds of these scripts to manage your Exchange 2019 environment.

Additional Modules

PowerShell is interesting to use, but it gets more interesting when you are using additional modules. The Server Manager module is used, for example, to use Server Manager features using PowerShell. When installing Exchange 2019, you need to install the prerequisite Server Roles and Features. You can do this using the Server Manager, but you can also load the Server Manager module in PowerShell, followed by the Server Role or Server Feature you want to install. For example, if you want to install the Remote Server Administration Tools, you can use the following commands:

```
[PS] C:\> Import-Module ServerManager
[PS] C:\> Install-WindowsFeature RSAT-ADDS
```

To install the IIS web server, you can use commands similar to the following:

```
[PS] C:\> Import-Module ServerManager
[PS] C:\> Install-WindowsFeature Web-Server
```

Note In Windows Servers 2016 and 2019, the Server Manager module is automatically loaded. It is referenced here for clarity.

Another interesting module when administering your Exchange 2019 environment is the Active Directory module, which can be loaded using the following command:

```
[PS] C:\> Import-Module ActiveDirectory
```

When the Active Directory module is loaded, the following options will be available in PowerShell:

- Account management
- Group management
- Organizational unit management
- Search and modify objects in Active Directory
- Forest and domain management
- Domain Controller management
- Operations Master management

To create a new user in Active Directory called "Sarah Summertime" in the OU=Users in the Accounts Organization Unit, a command similar to the following can be used:

```
[PS] C:\> Import-Module ActiveDirectory
[PS] C:\> New-ADUser -SamAccountName Sarah -Name "Sarah Summertime"
-GivenName Sarah -SurName Summertime -AccountPassword (ConvertTo-
SecureString -AsPlainText "Pass1word" -Force) -Enabled $TRUE -Path "OU=Users,
OU=Account,DC=Proexchangeadmin,DC=COM"
```

Note The ConvertTo-SecureString is used because the AccountPassword parameter does not accept any clear text as input for a password. In addition, AsPlainText and Force are required to convert plain text to a secure string.

For a complete overview of all PowerShell administration in Active Directory, you can check the Microsoft TechNet pages "Active Directory Administration" with PowerShell on `http://bit.ly/ADPowershell`.

Another module that is often used in Exchange management using PowerShell is the Web Administration module. Using this module, you can manage websites and their properties on your Exchange 2019 server. For example, to load the Web Administration module and clear the SSL offloading flag on the OWA virtual directory, you can use the following commands:

```
[PS] C:\> Import-Module WebAdministration
[PS] C:\> Set-WebConfigurationProperty -Filter //security/access -name
sslflags
-Value "None" -PSPath IIS:\ -Location "Default Web Site/OWA"
```

The last module I want to discuss is the Exchange module. The Exchange Management Shell (EMS) is best started using the EMS icon on the Start menu. This will make sure the binaries are loaded correctly. What basically happens is that PowerShell is started, a special Exchange management script is loaded, and the session is connected to an Exchange 2019 server. This can be the local Exchange server you are logged on to, but it can also be another server, as long as it is in the same Active Directory site. This is called Remote PowerShell, even when it is connected locally.

Remote PowerShell

When you open the EMS on the Exchange server, it is running on the local server, and you need access to the console of the server. But it is possible to use a remote PowerShell as well, thereby making connection a local Windows PowerShell instance to an Exchange server at a remote location. The workstation does not have to be in the same domain; if the proper credentials and authentication method are used, it will work. With this kind of function, it is now as easy to manage your Exchange 2019 servers in other parts of the building as those servers in data centers in other parts of the country. Needless to say, if you are using a non-domain-joined client for remote PowerShell, you cannot use Kerberos. You must change authentication on the PowerShell virtual directory to Basic Authentication for this to happen.

When the Exchange Management Shell is opened, it will automatically try to connect to the PowerShell virtual directory on the Exchange 2019 server you are logged on to. However, this is only true if you are logged on to an Exchange server (Console or RDP) at the time. If you are on a management workstation with the Exchange management tools installed, it will choose any Exchange server within your Active Directory site. Alternatively, by using the remote option, it is possible to connect to a remote Exchange server at this stage.

To use the remote PowerShell with Exchange 2019, make sure that the workstation (or server) supports remote signed scripts. Owing to security constraints, this is disabled by default. You can enable the support for remote signed scripts by opening a PowerShell command prompt with elevated privileges and enter the following command:

```
[PS] C:\> Set-ExecutionPolicy RemoteSigned
```

The next step is to create a session that will connect to the remote Exchange server. When the session is created, it can be imported into PowerShell:

```
[PS] C:\> $Session = New-PSSession -ConfigurationName Microsoft.Exchange
-ConnectionUri "https://Exch04.proexchangeadmin.com/PowerShell"
-Authentication Kerberos
[PS] C:\> Import-PSSession $Session
```

Note When using Kerberos authentication, it is only possible to use the FQDN to connect to a specific Exchange server. Also, using HTTPS to connect to a specific Exchange server requires a valid SSL certificate. Using a more general FQDN like webmail.proexchangeadmin.com is not possible with Kerberos authentication, unless the Service Principal Name (SPN) is registered to that system. If not, basic authentication must be used.

The PowerShell on the workstation will now connect to the remote Exchange server using a default SSL connection, and, RBAC permitting, all Exchange cmdlets will be available. It is incredibly easy, as can be seen in Figure 1-10.

Administrator: Windows PowerShell

```
PS C:\> $Session = New-PSSession -ConfigurationName Microsoft.Exchange -ConnectionUri "http://Exch04.proexchangeadmin.co
m/PowerShell" -Authentication Kerberos
PS C:\> Import-PSSession $Session
WARNING: The names of some imported commands from the module 'tmp_4225ykpg.13i' include unapproved verbs that might
make them less discoverable. To find the commands with unapproved verbs, run the Import-Module command again with the
Verbose parameter. For a list of approved verbs, type Get-Verb.

ModuleType Version    Name                                ExportedCommands
---------- -------    ----                                ----------------
Script     1.0        tmp_4225ykpg.13i                    {Add-ADPermission, Add-AvailabilityAddressSpace, Add-Conte...

PS C:\> Get-Mailbox

Name                      Alias                ServerName       ProhibitSendQuota
----                      -----                ----------       -----------------
Administrator             Administrator        exch04           Unlimited
DiscoverySearchMailbox... DiscoverySearchMa... exch04           50 GB (53,687,091,200 bytes)
DMARC Reports             dmarc                exch04           Unlimited
Boardroom                 Boardroom            exch04           Unlimited
Jaap Wesselius            Jaap                 exch04           Unlimited
Marina Baggus             Marina               exch03           Unlimited
Baron von Munchausen      Baron                exch03           Unlimited
Michel de Rooij           Michel               exch03           Unlimited
Bram Wesselius            Bram                 exch03           Unlimited
Kim Akers                 Kim                  exch03           Unlimited
John Smith                John                 exch03           Unlimited
Colonel Olrik             Olrik                exch03           Unlimited
Katy Price                Katy                 exch03           Unlimited
Philip Mortimer           Philip               exch03           Unlimited
Elizabeth McKenzie        Elizabeth            exch03           Unlimited
Glenn Kendall             Glenn                exch03           Unlimited
Sarah Summertime          Sarah                exch03           Unlimited
Nastasia Wardynska        Nastasia             exch03           Unlimited
William Steel             William              exch03           Unlimited

PS C:\> _
```

***Figure 1-10.** Using remote PowerShell on a local workstation to manage Exchange 2019*

To end the remote PowerShell session, just enter the command:

```
[PS] C:\> Remove-PSSession $session
```

Note It is also possible to set up an Exchange session using the Add-PSSnapin Microsoft.Exchange.Management.PowerShell.E2010 command. While the result looks similar, it is not. This does connect, but it bypasses the RBAC configuration, and it is not supported. More on RBAC in Chapter 10.

The example in Figure 1-10 is from a Windows 10 workstation that is also a member of the same Active Directory domain. To connect to a remote Exchange 2019 from a non-domain-joined workstation, Kerberos authentication cannot be used. Instead, basic authentication must be used.

The first step is to create a variable $Credential in the PowerShell session that contains the username and password for the remote session. When using the Get-Credential command, a pop-up box will appear, requesting a username and password for the remote Exchange environment. Once you have filled in the credentials, the following command will create a new session that will set up a connection to the Exchange environment. The $Credential variable is used to pass the credentials to the Exchange environment, and then the session is imported into PowerShell. See Figure 1-11.

```
[PS] C:\> $Credential = Get-Credential
[PS] C:\> $Session = New-PSSession -ConfigurationName Microsoft.Exchange
-ConnectionUri "https://webmail.proexchangeadmin.com/PowerShell"
-Authentication Basic
-Credential $Credential
[PS] C:\> Import-PSSession $Session
```

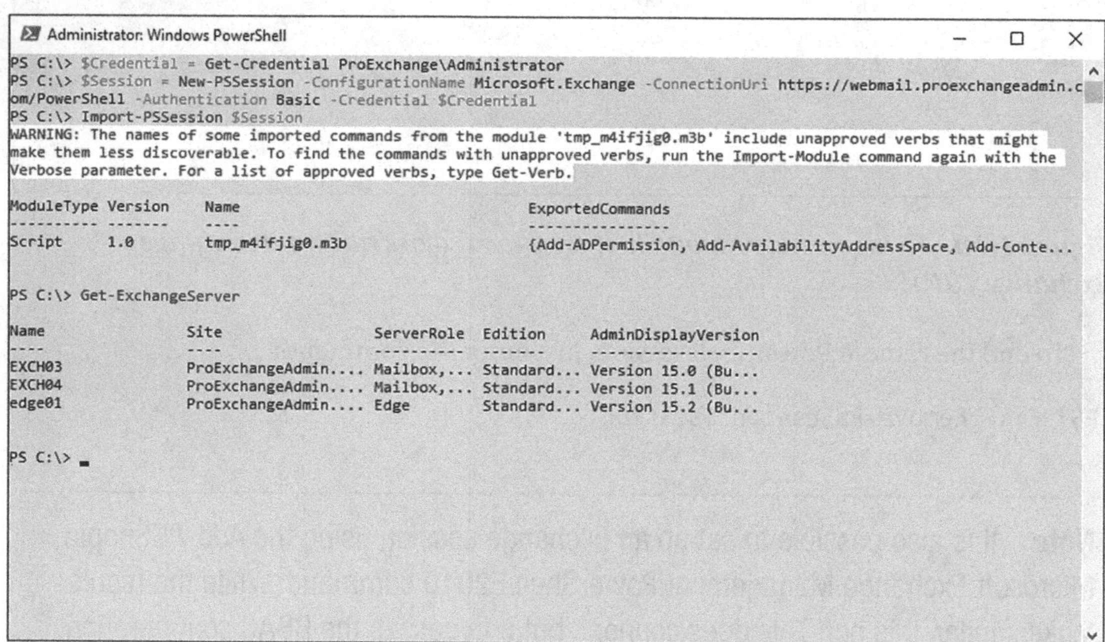

Figure 1-11. *Using remote PowerShell on a remote workstation to manage Exchange 2016*

Note If you want to use basic authentication with Remote PowerShell, do not forget to enable basic authentication on the PowerShell virtual directory. Using Remote PowerShell via the Internet is possible, but not recommended from a security perspective.

These examples were for the Active Directory domain administrator, who automatically has the Remote Management option enabled. To enable another account for remote management, you can use the following command:

```
[PS] C:\> Set-User <username> -RemotePowerShellEnabled $True
```

Tip You can use the Prefix parameter with Import-PSSession to prefix imported cmdlets. This may come in handy when working against multiple Exchange environments or Exchange on-premises and Exchange Online. For example, when using -Prefix Contoso, all imported Exchange cmdlets for that session are prefixed with ProExchange, for example, Get-ProExchangeMailbox. Do note that while convenient, it also means things like scripts need to be adjusted accordingly.

PowerShell ISE

When you want to create PowerShell scripts, you can use a basic tool like Notepad or Notepad++ (downloadable via `http://bit.ly/np-plus-plus`), but you can also use the PowerShell Integrated Scripting Environment, or ISE. Using ISE, you can run single commands, but you can also write, test, and debug PowerShell scripts. ISE supports multiline editing, tab completion, syntax coloring, and context-sensitive help. When debugging, you can set a breakpoint in a script to stop execution at that point. Windows PowerShell ISE can be found at the Administrative Tools menu, but when selecting a PowerShell script in Windows Explorer, you can also edit the script using ISE.

It is fully supported to use the remote PowerShell functionality and import Exchange sessions as explained in the previous section in ISE, making it possible to use all Exchange 2019–related cmdlets in ISE and to create your own Exchange 2019 scripts. This is shown in Figure 1-12.

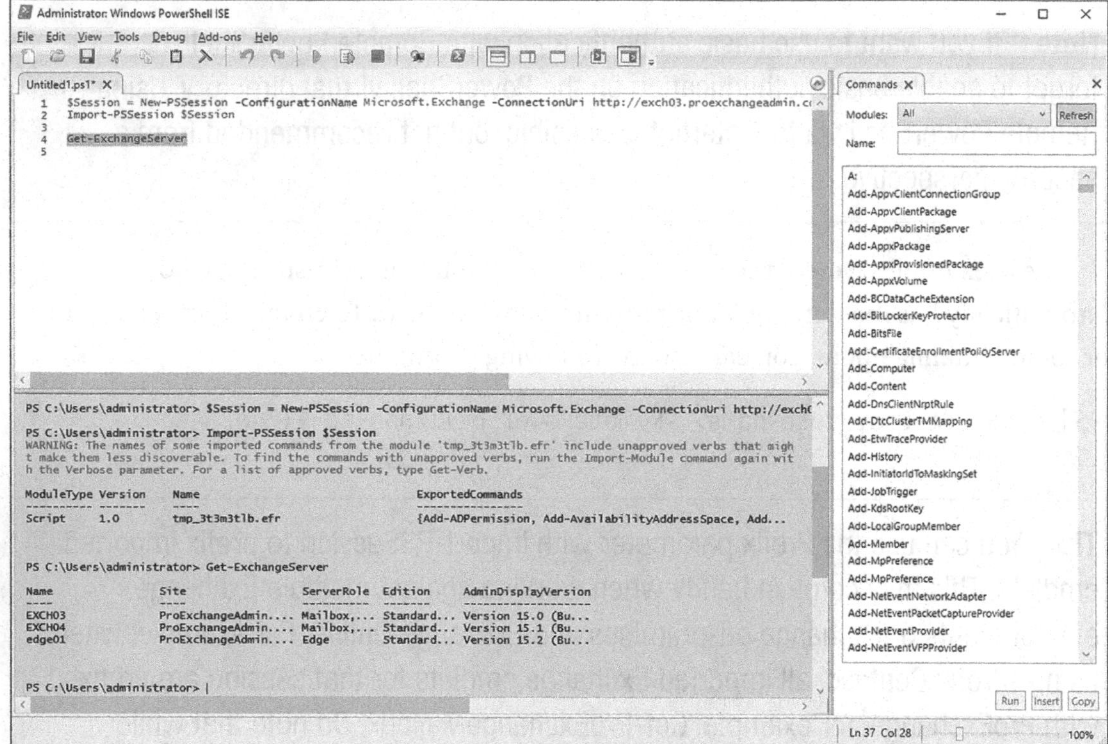

***Figure 1-12.** Using remote PowerShell in ISE to get access to the Exchange 2019 modules*

While ISE is convenient as it is available out of the box on Windows servers, other tools for writing and maintaining PowerShell code are available as well. Another popular one is Visual Studio Code or VSCode, which is freely available from Microsoft at `https://code.visualstudio.com`. This environment also has add-in support for things such as GitHub or PSAnalyzer for quickly analyzing your scripts and supports other languages and file types as well (e.g., C, XML, JSON).

If you want to read a lot more about Windows PowerShell in general, you can visit the Windows PowerShell User's Guide at `http://bit.ly/WinPowershellGuide`.

Virtualization

When looking at the minimum recommended hardware, you might think that virtualizing Exchange 2019 is no longer supported. But that is not the case, a virtualized Exchange server 2019 server is fully supported!

When virtualizing Exchange server 2019, there are some specific requirements for the hypervisor platform, but these are more general requirements or recommendations. There are also more specific requirements for storage, memory, and high availability solutions. We will discuss these in more detail.

Requirements for Hardware Virtualization

Exchange server 2019 is fully supported on one of the following virtualization solutions:

- Any version of Windows Server with Hyper-V or Microsoft Hyper-V Server.
- Any third-party hypervisor solution that is validated under the Microsoft Server Virtualization Validation Program (SVVP). More information regarding SVVP can be found at `http://bit.ly/ExSVVP`.

When it comes to Exchange server 2019, this must be installed on Windows Server 2019, but that is not different than deploying Exchange server 2019 on bare metal.

The most tested virtualization platform for Exchange Server is, of course, Hyper-V. Every day the Microsoft Exchange team is testing thousands of Exchange servers, all running on Hyper-V in Microsoft Azure, Office 365, and on-premises. Since it is the same company, there is a close ongoing cross-group engineering relationship, and there is a direct feedback loop between the Exchange team, the Windows team, and the Hyper-V team. A lot of the recommendations are directly targeted to Hyper-V, but they apply to other virtualization solutions as well.

Note Exchange server 2019 can also be installed on Microsoft Azure. This is supported if all storage volumes used for Exchange databases and their transaction log files are configured for Azure Premium storage.

When it comes to the virtualization platform, there are a couple of things you must be aware of. Let's discuss these.

The Virtualization Host

The hosts running Hyper-V are designed to run Hyper-V and nothing else. Although it might be tempting to install other software on the Hyper-V host, especially when it is running a normal version of Windows as the host or parent partition, it is absolutely not supported and not recommended. It works and I have seen customers do it, but from a performance point of view, it is not a good idea. The applications installed on the Hyper-V host consume valuable resources, especially memory, that are no longer available for virtual machines running on that host.

The only software that is supported and can be installed on the Hyper-V host is management software like a System Center Configuration Manager (SCCM) client, a System Center Operations Manager (SCOM) client and a Virtual Machine Manager (SVMM) agent, a backup client, or a Microsoft Endpoint Protection (anti-virus) client. No other software should be installed on the virtualization host. Also, the Hyper-V host itself should never be configured as a Domain Controller!

Virtual Processors

When using server virtualization, there are a given number of processors and processor cores available on the virtualization host and virtually unlimited number of virtual processors. However, you cannot give away an unlimited amount of processor cycles, so you must be aware of the number of virtual processors—that is, the processors that are assigned to virtual machines—and the number of logical processors or actual processors on the virtualization host.

The Microsoft Exchange product team supports a virtual to logical processor ratio of 2:1. In other words, when your virtualization host has eight processor cores installed, you should not use more than 16 virtual processor cores to virtual machines on that host. The ratio of 2:1 is officially supported by the Exchange product team, but their recommendation for the ratio is actually 1:1.

When it comes to processors on your virtualization host, there is also something called hyperthreading. This is Intel's implementation of Simultaneous Multithreading (SMT), used to improve parallel processing of instructions within the processor. Although the number of cores doubles when hyperthreading is enabled, the performance is not doubled at the same time. It is true, however, that performance increases when hyperthreading is enabled, though not more than by approximately 20%.

Hyperthreading improves performance, but there are two scenarios you must be aware of:

- Enabling hyperthreading when running Exchange server 2019 on Windows Server 2019 bare metal (without virtualization) adds a layer of complexity to the processors and the way Windows handles them. This can increase the amount of memory that is utilized by the Exchange server 2019 server by approximately 2 GB per core. Given the fact that hyperthreading only increases performance by 20%, it can result in a performance loss.
- Enabling hyperthreading when running Exchange server 2019 does increase performance since the processor complexity is "hidden" for the guest operating system. Be aware though that enabling hyperthreading only increases performance by 20%. When designing, count the number of processor cores without hyperthreading enabled.

More information can be found on `http://bit.ly/HyperThreadingStory`.

It looks tempting to enable hyperthreading to improve performance, but there is also a downside. Hyperthreading poses a security risk that includes speculative execution side-channel vulnerabilities. To protect against this risk, customers may want to disable hyperthreading. More information can be found on the Microsoft support site at `http://bit.ly/HyperthreadingVulnerabilities`.

Storage Requirements for Virtual Machines

When it comes to storage, there are two ways of looking at it. There is the storage used on the virtualization host itself, which is where the virtualization host's operating system is installed, and there are the storage solutions used by the virtual machines. The latter are the virtual hard disks. I will discuss both.

Virtualization Host Storage

There are multiple types of storage solutions used on a virtualization host. First, there are the disks used by the operating system running the virtualization software. Typically, there are two disks for this operating system, configured in a RAID-1 setup so the disks are mirrored. These disks should be the fastest disks you can get—preferably solid-state disks (SSD). At all times, you must make sure this operating system is located on disks different from where the virtual machines are located.

Data disks are disks where the virtual machines are stored; these disks can be

- **Direct-attached storage (DAS)**—When using DAS, the data disks are local to the virtualization host. These should also be fast disks, preferably in a RAID-10 configuration offering the best performance and redundancy.
- **iSCSI storage**—When iSCSI is used, the disks (LUNs) are presented to the virtualization software, which can access them just as local disks. Interesting to note is that iSCSI disks can also be accessed from within the virtual machine via a network connection.
- **SAN storage**—When a SAN is used, the virtualization host typically uses a Fibre Channel (FC) solution to access the disks (LUNs). This is a fast and redundant solution, but at the same time costly.

Caution I have seen several virtualized Exchange deployments using SAN storage where performance was inadequate. Exchange was suffering from disk issues, but the SAN storage was running fine. Most of the time, it turned out that the fiber switches between the virtualization hosts and the SAN storage were a bottleneck.

All three solutions are fully supported when running the virtualized Exchange 2019 server. These storage solutions are block-level storage solutions. The host "owns" the file system on the storage solution and therefore controls the storage solution.

I have also seen numerous implementations of VMware where the virtual disks (.vmdk) are stored on an NFS volume, mostly NetApp solutions. This is a file-level storage solution. The operating system—that is, VMware—does not own and thus does not control the underlying file system where the virtual disks are stored. While this works fine in most scenarios, it can yield unpredictable results due to performance issues, especially when using other solutions that also access the NFS storage. Therefore, this is not a supported scenario.

Note In this section, I am discussing the storage requirements, recommendations, and supported scenarios from a hypervisor point of view when it comes to running a virtualized Exchange. In the next chapter, I will discuss designing Exchange 2019 and the storage requirements from an Exchange server point of view.

So, storing your virtual disks on a NAS solution is not supported. Storing the virtual disks on an SMB 3.0 share is supported, but only when the SMB 3.0 share is backed by a block-level storage solution. So, block-level storage is key when it comes to virtual Exchange servers!

Here is one last remark regarding the separation of disk spindles. In a normal physical environment, it is best practice to store the Windows operating system on one disk and the mailbox database files on another disk or set of disks. Of course, this is not different when virtualizing the Exchange servers. But you must be careful to store the actual virtual hard disks that contain the Windows operating system and the mailbox database files on separate hard disks on the virtualization host. This gives the best performance within your virtualized Exchange servers; but in case of a disk failure, you will lose only one, either the operating system or the mailbox database. If you lose one, it is always recoverable provided there is a backup available. It is most likely quite a bit of work.

Virtual Hard Disks

Virtual machines are using virtual hard disks. In Hyper-V, these are the VHDX files; in VMware, they are the VMDK files. These are large, single files holding the operating system or the data from the virtual machines and are stored on one of the three storage solutions mentioned before. Also note these files should be located outside of the disks holding the virtualization host operating system.

In Hyper-V, there are four types of virtual hard disks available:

- Fixed size
- Dynamically expanding

- Differencing disk
- Pass-through disk

I will discuss these in more detail.

Fixed Disks

A fixed-size virtual disk is a pre-created and fully allocated virtual disk. If you create a fixed-size virtual disk of 100 GB, a VHDX file is created of 100 GB in size on the virtualization host's storage solution. Yes, it takes time to create the VHDX file and fill it up with nothing but zeroes, but it saves you from experiencing performance issues later on. Also, since the disk is pre-created before creating the actual virtual machine, you will not run into "disk full" situations when using other types of VHDX files, as explained in the next sections.

The fixed-size virtual hard disk is the only virtual hard disk supported in virtualized Exchange 2019 solutions.

Dynamically Expanding Disks

A dynamically expanding virtual disk is also pre-created, but it does not contain any data at the time of creation and therefore has only a couple of megabytes after the initial creation.

When data is stored on this type of virtual disk—that is, when an operating system is installed or when a mailbox database located on this disk is expanding—it is automatically expanding. Although small, there is a performance penalty when the disk is expanding, however. More importantly, there is a serious risk of overcommitting the underlying disk when you are using this type of virtual disk. You won't be the first, and certainly not the last, person to use a dynamically expanding disk to discover that it is completely filled and the virtual machines have stopped working.

Therefore, dynamically expanding disks are not supported for running Exchange 2019 in a production environment, but for a lab environment, it is a great solution, as it will save you a lot of disk space.

Differencing Disks

A differencing disk is an interesting solution, as it consists of two virtual hard disks linked together in a parent-child relationship. The first disk is known as the "parent" disk, and this is typically the most important one. This disk is used as read-only, which means that data is read from this disk and never written to this disk. Thus, it will never change, and typically it is stored where the actual virtual hard disk is stored. In a differencing disk scenario, you cannot afford to lose this disk.

The second disk is known as the "child" disk, and this is a read-write disk. Data is read from the child disk, but data can also be stored on the disk. It is possible to create multiple differencing disks, based on the same parent disk.

This is shown in Figure 1-13, with the Diff 1, 2, and 3 VHDX.

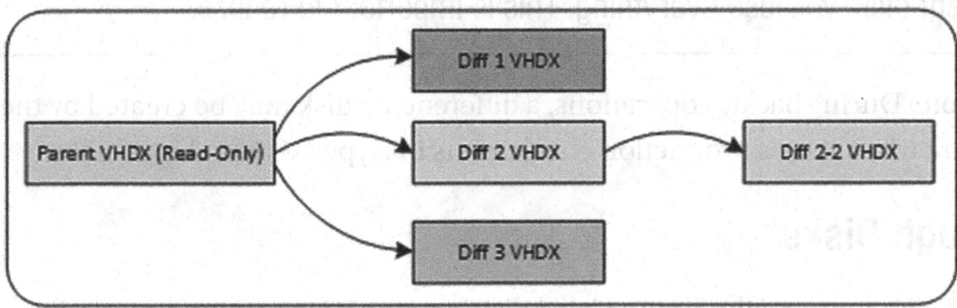

***Figure 1-13.** Multiple differencing disks with one parent disk*

Why use a differencing disk? Imagine you create a virtual machine with Windows server 2019 installed, and it is fully configured and operational. You shut down the virtual machine, and based on this VHDX, you create a new differencing disk. Your next step is to create a new virtual machine, based on this differencing disk. When the new VM is started, the configuration is read from the parent disk, but all changes are written to the child disk, leaving the parent disk untouched. This way, it is possible to return to the point where you originally shut down the first virtual machine. You have created a point-in-time mechanism.

Even better, before you create the differencing disk, you can use the sysprep utility to prepare the virtual machine for a fresh "mini setup." When you create a new differencing disk based on the sysprepped VHDX, you can create a new virtual machine based on the mini setup of sysprep. Since you can create multiple differencing disks based on the same sysprepped parent partition, you can create multiple new virtual machines in a matter of minutes. If you store the parent VHDX file on one hard disk and the child VHDX file on another, you get acceptable performance as well.

The downside of this is that differencing disks are not supported in Exchange Server scenarios by Microsoft. The main reason for this is that Exchange Server is unaware of what's going on in the background. When a differencing disk is removed, you can get back to a previous state, but Exchange Server is not aware of that.

Nevertheless, differencing disks are a great solution for lab and test environments because they allow you to quickly create multiple virtual machines for testing purposes.

Note As you might now understand, if you lose the child disk, you lose data, but since you still have the parent disk, there is a situation you can return to. If you lose the parent disk, you lose everything. This is important to realize.

Another note. During backup operations, a differencing disk may be created by the backup software when it uses production checkpoints in Hyper-V virtual machines.

Pass-Through Disks

A pass-through disk is not really a virtual hard disk because it is not stored as a VHDX or VMDK file, as with the previous types of virtual disks, but a pass-through disk can be used by a virtual machine.

A pass-through disk can be a physical disk or a LUN on a SAN presented directly to the SCSI adapter of the virtual machine. Sometimes, a pass-through disk is also referred to as a "raw disk."

Checkpoints

A checkpoint, previously known as "snapshot," is a point-in-time recovery method for virtual machines. A checkpoint captures the moment of creation when the current state of the virtual machine memory and hard disk is stored on the Hyper-V host. Since everything is stored on disk at that moment, it is possible to return to this exact point in time and thus to this exact state. Over the years, there has been a huge development and improvement in Hyper-V checkpoint technology. Hyper-V in Windows Server 2016 and Windows Server 2019 contains two kinds of checkpoints:

- **Standard snapshots**—This will create a consistent checkpoint that captures the state of the virtual machine and its applications.
- **Production snapshots**—This will create a consistent snapshot and use backup technology in the guest operating system to create data-consistent snapshots. Under the hood, the Virtual Shadow Copy Service (VSS) is used to achieve this.

When a checkpoint is created, the following occurs:

- The current virtual hard disk is frozen, a new differencing disk is created, and the current virtual hard disk will act as a new parent disk. Of course, the new differencing disk is linked to this parent disk.
- The volatile state of the virtual machine is frozen at the same time and stored on the virtualization host. VSS is used at this point to create an application-aware state of any running applications. In our scenario, that is Exchange of course.

Several files are used to create a checkpoint and store information:

- **Configuration file (.VMCX)**—This contains the configuration file of the virtual machine. In older versions of Hyper-V, this was a .XML file. The XML file was replaced because too many administrators were editing the XML file, causing issues.
- **Runtime state file (.VMRS)**—This contains the running state (which is volatile data) of the virtual machine. When creating checkpoints of running virtual machines, these files can be very large in size.
- **Virtual hard disk (.VHDX) and automatic virtual hard disk (.AVHDX)**—This is the "original" virtual hard disk and the automatically created differencing disk, also known as automatic virtual hard disk.
- **Checkpoint files (.VMCX and .VMRS)**—Created when the configuration of a virtual machine is changed *after* a checkpoint was made. This makes it possible to revert to a previous configuration file.

Note The configuration, runtime, and checkpoint files are stored in the Hyper-V virtual machine folder. By default, this is C:\ProgramData\Microsoft\Windows\Hyper-V. Make sure you change this location to prevent the system disk to fill up quickly with additional Hyper-V files. This can be configured in Hyper-V Settings of Hyper-V Manager or in System Center Virtual Machine Manager host configuration.

When done, the virtual machine continues running normally, but all data will now be stored in the newly created differencing disk. It is possible to create multiple, consecutive checkpoints, making it conceivable to return to multiple points in time. This is shown in Figure 1-14, where a checkpoint is created at point T=1 and later another checkpoint is created at T=2.

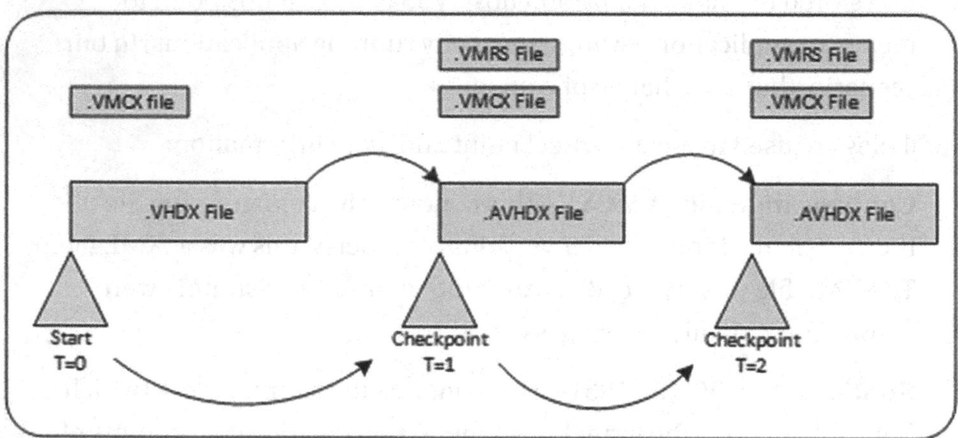

***Figure 1-14.** Two checkpoints at different points in time*

Although VSS is used when a checkpoint is created, a backup is not created. VSS is only used to bring the mailbox database in a consistent state. It does not purge any logfiles, and as such it differs from a regular VSS backup.

When creating a checkpoint of a running Exchange server, the following warning message is returned on the console of the Hyper-V server:

"Backup technology in the guest operating system was used to create a production checkpoint. The running application state wasn't included in the checkpoint operation. You can configure checkpoint options under the virtual machine settings."

This is shown in Figure 1-15.

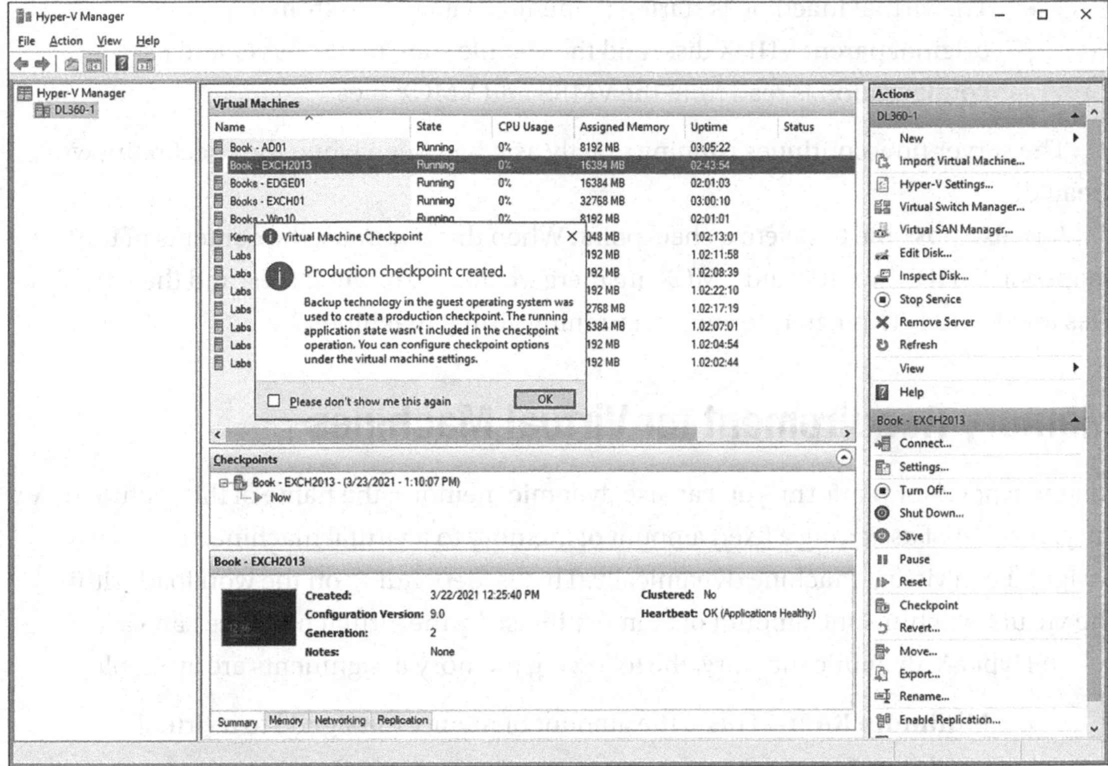

***Figure 1-15.** Warning message when creating a production snapshot of an Exchange server*

Note Checkpoints in Hyper-V are not supported as a backup solution, despite the use of VSS inside the virtual machine to create an application-aware checkpoint. VSS backups are fully supported, but this is an entirely different mechanism. Backup, restore, and disaster recovery are discussed in detail in Chapter 4. However, checkpoints are automatically created by backup software. Once the backup is safely stored, the checkpoint is also automatically deleted.

When reverting a checkpoint, the following occur:

- The virtual machine is stopped. Since the situation at that moment will be destroyed, the virtual machine is powered off.
- The differencing disk is deleted, and a new differencing disk is created.

- The virtual machine is started manually, data is read from the original parent VHDX disk, and the volatile state of the server and its configuration is read from the VMRS and VMCX files.

The server now continues running exactly as it had been when the checkpoint was created.

It is also possible to delete a checkpoint. When this happens, the contents of the snapshot AVHDX, VMRS, and VMCX are merged into the original files, and the snapshot files are deleted. This can be done on a running virtual machine.

Memory Requirement for Virtual Machines

In any hypervisor platform, you can use dynamic memory; the name of this feature may vary. Instead of assigning a fixed amount of memory to a virtual machine, memory is assigned to a virtual machine dynamically. That is, depending on the workload within the virtual machine, the amount of memory in use by the virtual machine can vary.

In Hyper-V dynamic memory, the following memory assignments are available:

- **Minimum RAM**—This is the amount of memory assigned to a virtual machine at boot time.
- **Maximum RAM**—This is the maximum amount of memory that can be assigned to a virtual machine when running. You can set this to an extremely high value, but it will never grow beyond the amount of physical memory in the Hyper-V host.
- **Memory buffer**—A small but configurable amount of memory that is reserved for the virtual machine, useful for memory bursts.

A fourth setting is about the memory weight. This determines the importance of the virtual machine when it comes to reassigning memory. A higher weight means more important and thus a better assignment of memory.

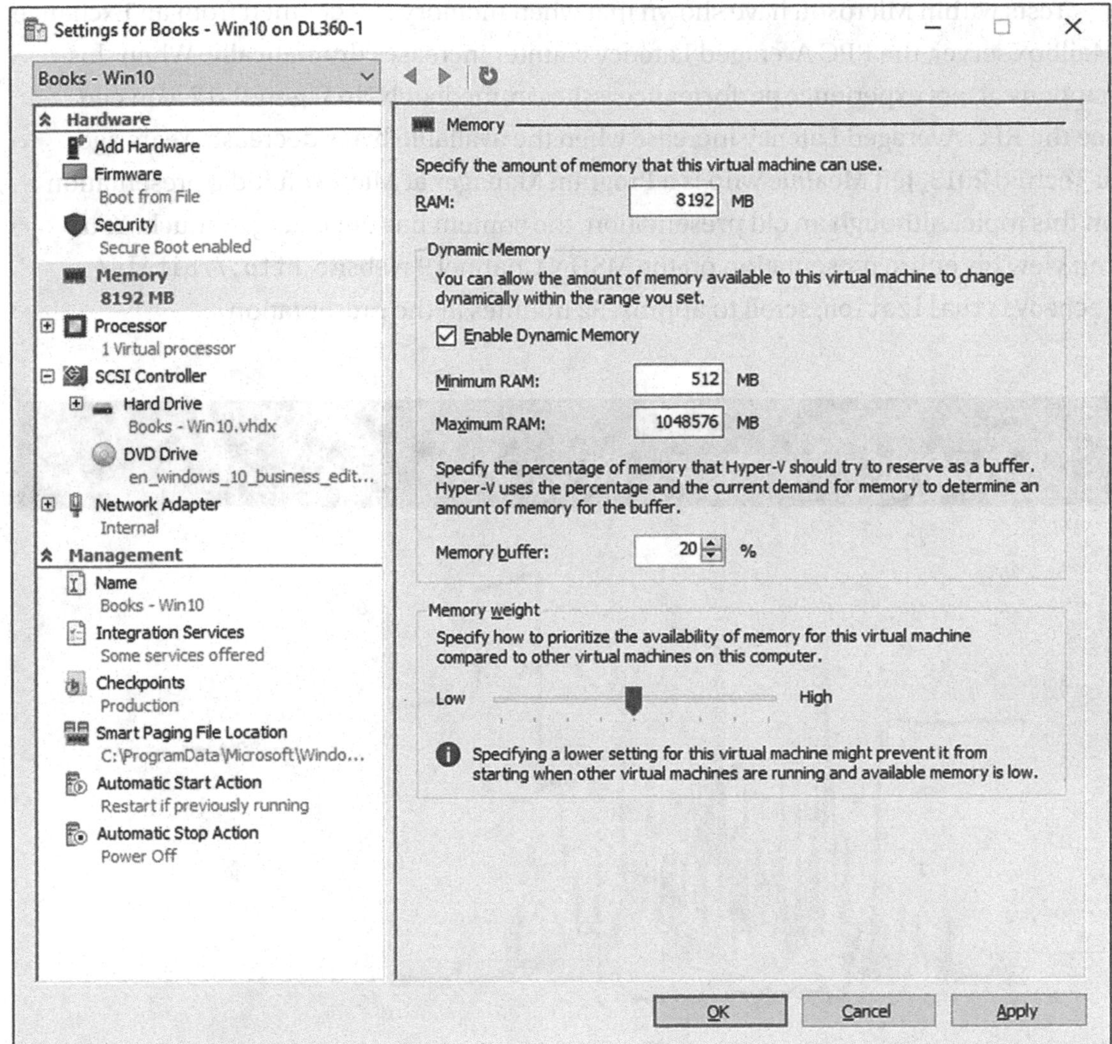

Figure 1-16. *Dynamic memory assignments*

When a virtual machine is started, it gets the minimum amount of RAM assigned, but as soon as it is needed, more RAM is assigned to the virtual machine; over time, you will see the amount of memory stabilizing. But when other virtual machines need more memory, the hypervisor needs to reclaim memory from some virtual machines.

When the hypervisor reclaims memory, a process called ballooning takes place inside the virtual machine to reclaim any non-used memory pages inside the virtual machine. But when there aren't any pages available, the kernel inside the virtual machine starts paging to disk to reclaim memory. As you might know, paging typically has a dramatic effect on server performance.

Tests within Microsoft have shown that when memory is reclaimed from an Exchange Mailbox server, the RPC Averaged Latency counter increases dramatically. When this happens, users experience performance issues immediately. In Figure 1-17, you can see the RPC Averaged Latency increase when the available bytes decrease. Years ago, at TechEd 2013, Jeff Mealiffe who is a Program Manager at Microsoft did a presentation on this topic. Although an old presentation, the content has not changed much. You can view his entire presentation on the MSDN Channel 9 website, `http://bit.ly/TechedVirtualization`, scroll to approx. 52 minutes in the presentation.

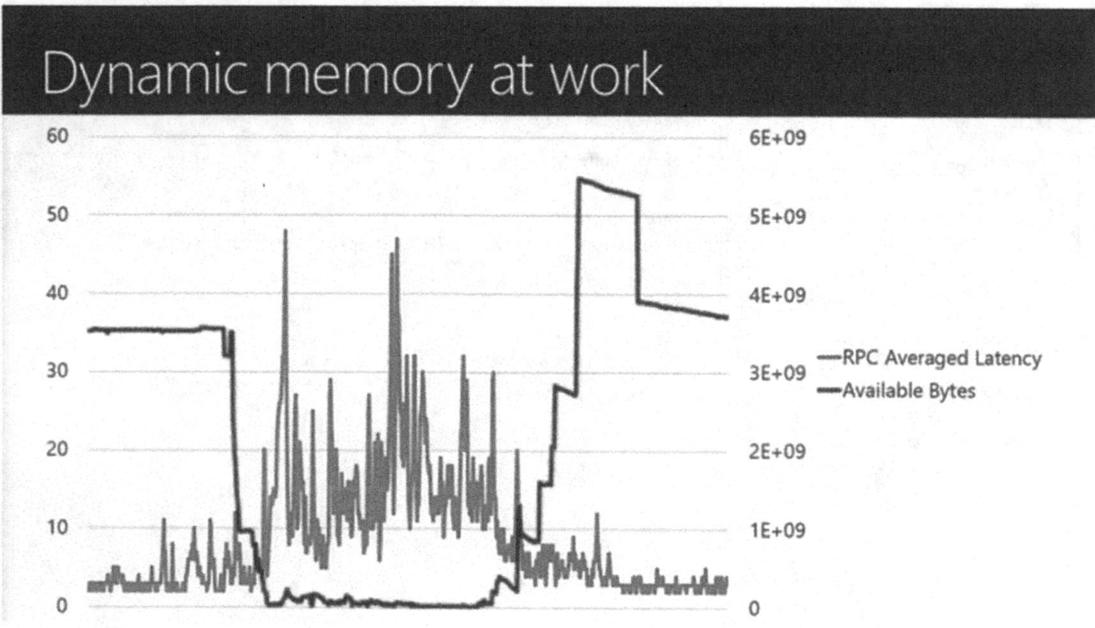

Figure 1-17. *The RPC Averaged Latency increases dramatically when dynamic memory kicks in*

Dynamic memory is useful for applications that need a memory boost on a temporary basis, like a web server or a file server. Exchange does not need a memory boost; it needs all its memory all the time. Therefore, the use of dynamic memory on any Exchange server version is not supported in a production environment. The same is true for any solution that manipulates the memory inside virtual machines when running Exchange server, such as oversubscription of memory.

High Availability Solutions

When it comes to high availability solutions in a virtualized Exchange 2019 environment, there are basically two solutions:

- **Host clustering**—This is a solution whereby the virtualization hosts form a cluster where the virtual machines are created as a cluster resource. When a host fails, the virtual machine is moved to another host in the cluster. Please note that when a host fails, the virtual machine will crash as well and perform a cold boot on the other cluster node. When a planned migration occurs, the virtual machine is gradually moved from one cluster node to another, preferably without any downtime.
- **Guest clustering**—This is a solution where several virtual Exchange server 2019 servers are running in a database availability group (DAG). When a virtualization host fails, the DAG member on that host will fail, and another virtual machine that is part of the DAG will take over the Exchange service, most likely without any downtime for the users. Guest clustering—that is, the database availability group—will be discussed in detail in Chapter 4.

When using host clustering, Microsoft fully supports Live Migration and similar third-party technologies like VMware's VMotion. All Exchange server versions are fully supported with these technologies. Please note that all third-party vendors should have their solutions validated through the SVVP program, as stated earlier. Microsoft can support Exchange Server, but cannot support these third-party solutions, so you must make sure that running Exchange Server on these solutions is fully supported by these third-party vendors.

What Microsoft does not support is any other migration solution that uses a point-in-time or saved state technology, including the Hyper-V quick migration solution.

Note A "saved state" is a state in which the virtual machine is "brought to sleep." The virtual machine is turned off, and its memory contents are stored in a separate file on disk. When the machine is returned to service, the memory contents are read from the file, and the virtual machine returns to the state it was in before the move. When it comes to Exchange (any version), this is not supported.

It is important to realize that when you are running an Exchange server on a host-based clustering solution, you still have one copy of an Exchange server. That is, there is redundancy on a host level, but not on the Exchange level. If the Exchange server fails inside the virtual machine, you end up with a high availability virtual machine and an unwilling Exchange server. If redundancy in Exchange Server is important, it is recommended you use guest clustering—that is, a database availability group in a host-based clustering solution. This way, you can survive failures on a hypervisor level as well as on an Exchange level.

Related to this, I have received several questions regarding the Hyper-V replica, and if this is a useful solution for Exchange Server. Unfortunately, it is not. The first thing to know is that Hyper-V replica is a disaster recovery solution and not a high availability solution. Hyper-V replica uses a special Hyper-V replication technology whereby special log files (not Exchange log files) are shipped asynchronously to a remote Hyper-V server. And with asynchronous replication technology, this introduces the most horrible situations with Exchange Server. Therefore, Hyper-V replica is not supported by Exchange Server. The same is true for Azure Site Recovery and Exchange server.

There is a lot of information on Microsoft TechNet—for example, server virtualization on `http://bit.ly/VirtualX2019`.

Sizing Virtual Exchange Servers

Virtualization is a pretty cool solution and very interesting for a lot of customers to use, but CPU resources don't appear out of thin air. What I mean is that there is overhead in the virtualization layer. For Hyper-V, for example, you must calculate an additional 10% CPU overhead. For third-party solutions, you must follow the vendor's guidance for processor overhead in their virtualization solutions.

The best recommendation when you are virtualizing is to use the Exchange 2019 Server Role Requirements Calculator. You will find two options in this requirements calculator for virtualization: the Server Role Virtualization option and the Hypervisor CPU Adjustment factor. These are explained in the next chapter.

Other important factors to consider are the memory recommendations made earlier in this section; also, note that storage is as important as before. Storage should be optimized for IO latency and high availability, for both host clustering and guest clustering.

Virtualization has major advantages when it comes to networks. You can use the hypervisor networking flexibility to provide availability and performance. The general recommendation is to design a physical Exchange 2019 environment and apply it to a virtual Exchange 2019 environment. However, I have seen too many customers create virtual Exchange servers without enough memory, too many virtual machines using the same network interface, or too many virtual hard disks on the same set of physical disks. These combinations are recipes for disaster!

Summary

At the time of writing, Exchange has been around for almost 25 years. The current version is Exchange server 2019, but a successor with the codename Exchange vNext is already announced. If you want the latest and greatest of Exchange features, you should move to Exchange Online. If you want a rock-solid messaging platform without too many bells and whistles, you can implement Exchange server 2019.

Exchange server 2019 is only available via the Volume License Portal. This means that smaller customers do not have access to Exchange server 2019. These customers can stay on Exchange server 2016 (still supported until 2025) or move to Exchange Online.

Exchange server 2019 has been a continuous development and improvement from Exchange server 2013. Differences with Exchange server 2016 are minor when it comes to user features, but there are improvements when it comes to security and performance. Examples of this are default support for TLS 1.2, support for Windows 2019 Server Core, modern hardware support, and the metacache database.

The next chapter is about designing your Exchange 2019 infrastructure and installing Exchange 2019.

CHAPTER 2

Installing Exchange Server 2019

In the previous chapter, we have discussed some of the basics of Exchange server 2019 with some sidesteps to Exchange server 2016. This chapter will cover the installation of Exchange server 2019. Primarily, we will cover Exchange server 2019 on Windows server 2019 Server Core since this is the recommended installation, but additionally we will also cover the Desktop Experience version of Windows server 2019. Where needed, we will also discuss the differences in installing Exchange Server 2016 on Windows Server 2016.

The first section of this chapter is about designing your Exchange 2019 environment. The Exchange server 2019 Role Requirements Calculator will be used to design an environment for our 2000-user fictitious company called ProExchangeAdmin.

The second section of this chapter is about installing Exchange server 2019 on Windows Server 2019. Where needed, we will do a small sidestep to Exchange server 2016 on Windows Server 2016.

Installing Exchange Server 2019 can be done in a clean and fresh Active Directory by in what is called a "greenfield" deployment. While this is certainly useful, chances are you already have an existing, earlier version of Exchange Server running. In this case, you must upgrade the environment, which is covered in Chapters 7 and 8.

In the third section of this chapter, we will install an Exchange server 2019 Edge Transport server as an SMTP gateway between the Exchange server 2019 Mailbox server and the Internet.

The last section covers the update and patching process of your Exchange Server 2019 environment with cumulative updates and security updates.

M. de Rooij and J. Wesselius, *Pro Exchange 2019 and 2016 Administration*,
https://doi.org/10.1007/978-1-4842-7331-9_2

Designing Your Exchange Server 2019 Environment

When you want to deploy Exchange 2019 for any number of users, you must make a proper design of your Exchange Server environment. You must do an inventory of all business and legal requirements and write these down in a design document. Together with the user requirements, such as the number of users (i.e., mailboxes), the mailbox sizing, and so on, you create a design of your Exchange 2019 environment based on the proper design decisions. If you fail to do so, most likely you will run into capacity issues when you run your Exchange 2019 environment.

Business, legal, and user requirements include answers to the following questions:

- What is the average mailbox size?
- What is your backup strategy?
- If you have backups, how long do you need to keep these backups, and do you need to store the backups at an off-site location?
- What is the average message size used by your users, and how many messages are sent and received on average?
- What are the normal business hours?
- What does your service-level agreement (SLA) look like? In your SLA, you will define your answers to such questions as follows:
    - Is there a need for 24x7, or will 5x12 do as well?
    - How long does it take to create a backup, and, more importantly, how long does it take to restore data, and what type of data can be restored (e.g., mailbox or item level)?
    - In case of an emergency, what amount of data are you allowed to lose, or is it allowed to resume with initial empty mailboxes where data will be restored to over time (dial-tone recovery)?
    - How long does it take to restore a mailbox, a mailbox database, or an entire Exchange 2019 server?
    - Are there guaranteed delivery times for messages?
- What is the user concurrency? That is, how many users are online at the same time?

These are some of the questions you need to answer when designing a proper Exchange 2019 environment. They are a different kind of question from the ones you, as an Exchange administrator, are accustomed to answering, such as "How much memory do I need in my server?" or "How about the disk configuration of my Exchange 2019 server?"

In our fictitious ProExchangeAdmin.com company, we have 2000 users, we anticipate a 5 GB mailbox for each user, and for high availability purposes, we will use two Exchange 2019 servers in a Database Availability Group.

Exchange 2019 Server Role Requirements Calculator

One of the best tools to determine the sizing of your Exchange 2019 server is the Exchange 2019 Server Role Requirements Calculator. This is basically a spreadsheet created by the Microsoft Exchange Product Group that will perform the sizing calculations for an Exchange 2019 deployment based on the requirements, which you must provide as input. Initially, the Exchange server 2019 Requirements Calculator was only made available via the Exchange server 2019 ISO image. However, in September 2020, the calculator for Exchange 2019 is also available as a separate download via `https://aka.ms/excalc`.

When you open the calculator, you will see an Excel spreadsheet with nine tabs. The first tab is where you enter the requirements that will be used as input for the actual design.

Important requirements you must enter here are, for example:

- **If you are virtualizing your Exchange servers**—As explained in Chapter 1, virtualizing your Exchange 2019 servers is not a problem if the virtualization solution is validated in the SVVP program, and the virtualization vendor supports running Exchange 2019 in its solution.
- **How many Mailbox servers you will use**—This is a tricky matter; the number you choose depends on the number of mailboxes you will be hosting on your Mailbox server. You must start somewhere, and as a rule of thumb, I always start with approximately 2500 mailboxes on one Mailbox server, so for 10,000 mailboxes I start with four Mailbox servers. Depending on the sizing that comes out of the Requirements Calculator, I can always adjust the number of Mailbox servers.

- **How many mailboxes in your environment**—This is a hard number to ascertain for setting your requirements, but when you are designing your Exchange 2019 environment, keep future growth in mind. You can define a percentage growth in the calculator for this.
- **How many messages sent and received per mailbox each day**—This number is also known as the usage profile, and it might be quite difficult to ascertain. One way to find good numbers for this is to analyze message tracking in your existing environment and calculate average values for this.
- **How large the mailbox size**—In our contoso.com environment, we set this to 5 GB. Quite a lot of people still have doubts about large mailboxes, but Exchange 2019 does not have trouble with 50 GB mailboxes, especially not if the MetaCache Database is used (more about this in Chapter 4).
- **The backup architecture**—A traditional backup is VSS based, whether it is a hardware VSS solution or a software VSS one. There is a backup server running in your network and backup clients on your Exchange servers. Microsoft System Center DPM is an example of this, but there are a lot more from Symantec, IBM, HP, and others. The Exchange Native Data Protection is another way of safeguarding your information, sometimes also referred to as a “backupless” environment.

In our ProExchangeAdmin environment, the requirements are based on an HP DL380 Gen10 server with a dual Intel Xeon Gold 6242, running at 2.8 GHz. This data is fed into the Requirements Calculator as listed in Table 2-1.

Table 2-1. *Requirements Used As Input for the ProExchangeAdmin Exchange Server Configuration*

Requirement	Value
Server role virtualization	Yes
High availability deployment	Yes
Use metacache database	No
Number of non-lagged database copies	2
Number of mailboxes	2000
Total send/receive messages per mailbox per day	100
Number of days per workweek	5
Average message size	75 KB
Initial mailbox size	2.5 GB
Mailbox size limit	5 GB
Maximum database size	1 TB
Backup methodology	Software VSS backup/restore
System and boot disk	600 GB, 15 krpm SAS
Database disk	4 TB, 7200 rpm, 3½ SAS disk
Log disk	4 TB, 7200 rpm, 3½ SAS disk
Restore volume	4 TB, 7200 rpm, 3½ SAS disk
Server SPECint2017 rate value[1]	203
Process cores/server	

These are the most important settings for the first page of the Requirements Calculator; all other requirements can be left at their default settings at this point.

When you have entered all data into the Requirements Calculator, you can navigate to the second tab for viewing the Role Requirements. On this sheet, you will find the sizing of the Exchange 2019 servers, based on the input you have just entered.

[1] The SPECint2017 value for a given server can be retrieved from `www.spec.org`

You will find the number of mailboxes, the number of mailbox databases, the IOPS generated, and the amount of memory needed in the Exchange server, just to name a few. In our example, the most important results are listed in Table 2-2.

Table 2-2. *Calculated Requirements of Our ProExchangeAdmin Exchange 2019 Environment*

Requirement	Value
Number of mailboxes	2000
Number of mailboxes per database	144
Transaction logs generated per mailbox per day	20
IOPS profile per mailbox	0.08
Number of mailbox databases	14
Available database cache per mailbox	16.25
Recommended RAM configuration	128 GB
Server CPU Megacycles requirements	16,549
Number of processor cores utilized	5
Primary data center server CPU utilization	7%
Database space required (per database)	988 GB
Log space required (per database)	261 GB
Database space required (per server)	13,825 GB
Log space required (per server)	3644 GB
Total database required IOPS (per server)	185
Total log required IOPS (per server)	89

As you can see, Exchange 2019 needs quite some resources according to the Requirements Calculator; on the other hand, it could be said that this calculation is a worst-case scenario in which all resources are stressed to the max. In real life, the resources used by Exchange 2019 are probably much less, but when your design is according to the Requirements Calculator, you know it is fully supported. When you assign fewer resources to your Exchange 2019 server, especially memory, there is a serious risk of experiencing performance issues.

So, 14 mailbox databases are used by these Exchange 2019 servers. The "Volume Requirements" tab in the Requirements Calculator shows the number of mailbox databases and the volumes used where the mailbox databases are stored. Since Exchange 2019 supports multiple mailbox databases on one volume, only seven volumes are used, and the mailbox databases are spread across these seven volumes.

The Storage Design tab in the Requirements Calculator tells you how many disks are used for each volume. For the mailbox database, six disks are used; six disks are in a RAID-5 configuration. The transaction log files of all mailbox databases are stored on a separate volume, consisting of two disks in a RAID-10 configuration.

A special volume is used for restoring purposes. If you want to restore one or more mailbox databases from a backup, a special volume is used for this. In our example, three disks in a RAID-5 configuration are used to create this restore volume.

So, in total, this Exchange 2019 server is using 11 physical disks of 4 TB each for storing 2000 mailboxes of max 5 GB in size. The server itself is using two disks in a RAID-1 configuration for the operating system and the Exchange 2019 server software. A graphic representation of this distribution is shown in Figure 2-1.

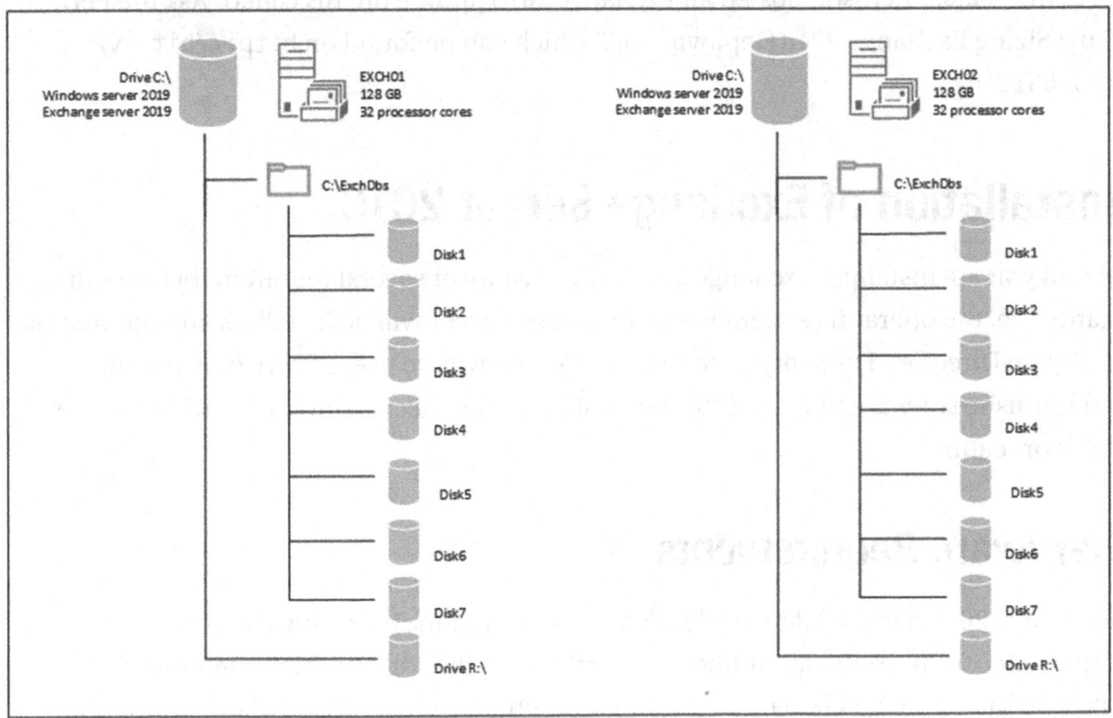

Figure 2-1. *The Exchange 2019 server design for a 2000-mailbox ProExchangeAdmin environment*

For smaller Exchange servers, drive letters can be used for the disks holding the mailbox databases. For larger environments, it is recommended to use mount points. When using mount points, a structure like this is used:

- C:\ExchDbs\Disk1
- C:\ExchDbs\Disk2
- C:\ExchDbs\Disk2
- C:\ExchDbs\Disk3
- Etc.

When using mount points, it is also possible to use features like AutoReseed and the metacache database. AutoReseed is discussed in Chapter 4 as part of the high availability section.

Microsoft has an excellent white paper on sizing Exchange 2013, called "Ask the Perf Guy: Sizing Exchange 2013 Deployments," and it can be found at `http://bit.ly/X2013Sizing`. I know it is an old white paper, but the overall technology has not changed over the years. Microsoft posted an Exchange 2016 update on this called "Ask the Perf Guy: Sizing Exchange 2016 Deployments," which can be found on `http://bit.ly/X2016Sizing`.

Installation of Exchange Server 2019

When you are installing Exchange 2019, you must meet several requirements regarding hardware, the operating system where Exchange Server will be installed, and the version of Active Directory Directory Services (ADDS) that will be used. There is also some prerequisite software that needs to be installed in advance, including Windows Server roles or features.

Hardware Requirements

Exchange 2019 has the following hardware requirements, based on Microsoft's experience from Exchange Online. One could think that these requirements seem to have been established by a marketing department. As we have seen in the previous section, the normal hardware requirements are a bit different, depending on the expected usage. The following are the bare minimum requirements for a supported Exchange Server 2019 deployment:

- X64 architecture from Intel or AMD.
- 128 GB of RAM for the Mailbox server.
- 64 GB of RAM for the Edge Transport server.
- At least 30 GB of free space where Exchange 2019 will be installed. (Add 500 MB for every UM language pack. All disks must be formatted with the NTFS or ReFS file system.)
- An additional hard disk of 500 MB where the Transport Queue database is stored.

For a full and up-to-date overview of all Exchange 2019 requirements, visit the Exchange Server system requirements on Microsoft docs at `http://bit.ly/Ex2019Requirements`.

Note The requirements look substantial at first sight, especially when comparing to previous versions of Exchange. Please bear in mind that these numbers are based on Exchange Online experiences, where the previous numbers were dictated by the marketing department. These numbers are a recommendation; your mileage may vary though. Also, keep in mind Exchange is now designed with the end-user experience in mind, which translates to low latencies made possible by plenty of resources and substantial caching of data.

Software Requirements

Exchange server 2019 can be installed on the following Windows operating systems:

- Windows Server 2019 Datacenter Edition, both Desktop Experience and Server Core
- Windows Server 2019 Standard Edition, both Desktop Experience and Server Core

Note Exchange Server 2019 is only supported on Windows Server 2019. It will not work on Windows Server 2016. At the same time, Exchange server 2016 is not supported on Windows Server 2019. Exchange server 2016 is only supported on Windows server 2016 and Windows server 2012 R2. Also, Exchange server 2016 is not supported on Windows server 2016 Server Core.

The Exchange 2019 Management Tools can be installed on the following Windows operating systems:

- Windows Server 2019 Datacenter Edition
- Windows Server 2019 Standard Edition
- Windows 10, 64-bit edition

When it comes to Active Directory, the following requirements can be identified:

- Domain Controllers must be Windows 2012 R2 or higher.
- The Active Directory functional level must be Windows 2012 R2 or higher.
- The Active Directory site where Exchange server 2019 is installed should have at least one writeable Domain Controller that also holds the Global Catalog server.

Several DNS namespace scenarios are supported in Exchange 2019, although these requirements have not changed in years. The following namespaces can be used with Exchange 2019:

- **Contiguous namespace**—This is a normal namespace where all domain names in the environment are contiguous. For example, a root domain would be proexchangeadmin.com, and the child domains would be emea.proexchangeadmin.com, na.proexchangeadmin.com, or asia.proexchangeadmin.com. Go one level deeper, and it would be prod.emea.proexchangeadmin.com and rnd.na.proexchangeadmin.com.

- **Noncontiguous namespace**—This is a namespace where the different trees in an Active Directory forest do not have similar names. For example, one tree in the Active Directory forest can be proexchangeadmin.com, while another tree in the same Active Directory forest can be Exchange2019.nl, and a third tree can be Exchangelabs.nl. They form separate domain trees in one forest.

  A special example of a noncontiguous namespace is where one tree would be proexchangeadmin.com and another tree would be proexchangeadmin.net. In this scenario, you would run into problems with the NetBIOS name of these domains. By default, the NetBIOS name of the domains would be proexchangeadmin, but since you cannot have two identical NetBIOS names in one network, you have to create another NetBIOS name for the second proexchangeadmin domain.

- **Single-label domain**—A single-label domain is a domain name that does not contain a DNS suffix, for example, no .com, .net, .org, or .corp. A normal domain name would be proexchangeadmin.com, but a single-label domain would be proexchangeadmin. A single-label domain is supported by Exchange 2019, but the use of single-label domains is not recommended by Microsoft.
- **Disjoint namespace**—A disjoint namespace is a namespace where the primary DNS suffix of a server does not match the DNS name of the Active Directory domain. For example, you can have an Exchange server called AMS-EXCH01 with a primary DNS suffix research. proexchangeadmin.com in the Active Directory domain emea. proexchangeadmin.com.

For a complete overview of supported DNS namespaces and additional resources, you can check the support for DNS namespace planning in the Microsoft server products article at `http://bit.ly/ExNamespace`.

Note The installation of Exchange 2019 on domain controllers is supported but not recommended. The recommended way of installing Exchange 2019 is on a member server in an Active Directory domain.

Installing the Exchange Server

One of the requirements of Exchange 2019 is that it can only be installed on Windows Server 2019. This can be the GUI version ("Desktop Experience") or Server Core; both are supported. Although more difficult to manage for the more traditional Windows GUI administrator, I always recommend using Server Core because of the lower footprint and attack surfaces. The prerequisites for Windows 2019 Server Core and Desktop Experience are similar, but where needed information for the Desktop Experience is added.

Note Take special care when deciding whether to use Server Core or Desktop Experience. In Windows 2019, it is not possible to change between the two after installation.

Installing Windows 2019

Exchange uses multiple disks for its operation. Of course, there is the system and boot disk (drive C:\), but there are also disks for storing the SMTP Queue databases and the mailbox databases. For small deployments, you can use regular drive letters for the mailbox database disk, but for larger deployments, mount points are recommended to avoid running out of drive letters. Also, when using mount points, you can take advantage of interesting features like AutoReseed (Exchange 2013 and higher) and MetaCache database (Exchange 2019). Throughout this book, we will be using drive D:\ as the disk holding the SMTP Transport database and SMTP logfiles, and drive Z:\ will be assigned to the DVD drive. Mailbox databases will be stored on disk configured as mount points, located in C:\ExchDbs\Disk1, C:\ExchDbs\Disk2, C:\ExchDbs\Disk3, etc. The focus will be on Windows 2019 server core since it is more complex to configure than Windows 2019 Desktop Experience. The commands in the following sections are PowerShell commands for Windows 2019 Server Core but can be used on Windows 2019 and Windows 2016 Desktop Experience as well of course.

Disk Configuration

To assign drive letter Z: to the DVD drive, use the following PowerShell command:

```
PS C:\> Get-WmiObject -Class Win32_volume -Filter "DriveType=5" | Select
-First 1 | Set-WmiInstance -Arguments @{DriveLetter="Z:"}
```

To get an overview of the disks that are available on the Windows 2019 server, you can use the Get-Disk command in PowerShell. For an Exchange server with a disk configuration as mentioned earlier, it will look like shown in Figure 2-2.

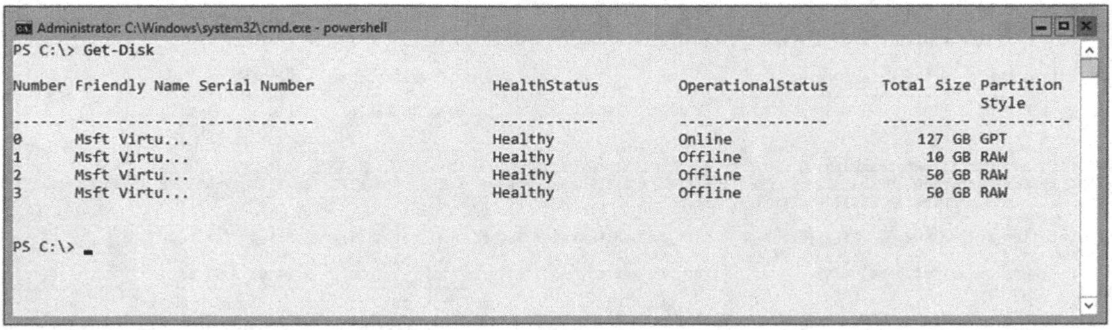

```
PS C:\> Get-Disk

Number Friendly Name Serial Number                    HealthStatus         OperationalStatus      Total Size Partition
                                                                                                              Style
------ ------------- -------------                    ------------         -----------------      ---------- ---------
0      Msft Virtu...                                  Healthy              Online                     127 GB GPT
1      Msft Virtu...                                  Healthy              Offline                     10 GB RAW
2      Msft Virtu...                                  Healthy              Offline                     50 GB RAW
3      Msft Virtu...                                  Healthy              Offline                     50 GB RAW


PS C:\>
```

Figure 2-2. *Disk configuration shown in PowerShell*

Disk number 0 is the boot and system disk; disk number 1 will be used for storing the SMTP Queue databases which will be drive D:\.

To bring this disk online and initialize it, use the following PowerShell command:

```
PS C:\> Get-Disk -DiskNumber 1 | Initialize-Disk -PartititionStyle GPT
PS C:\> New-Partition -DiskNumber 1 -UseMaximumSize
PS C:\> Add-PartitionAccessPath -DiskNumber 1 -PartitionNumber 2
-AccessPath D:
PS C:\> Get-Partition -DiskNumber 1 -PartitionNumber 2 | Format-Volume
-FileSystem NTFS -NewFileSystemLabel "Queue Database" -AllocationUnitSize
65536 -Confirm:$false
```

This is shown in Figure 2-3.

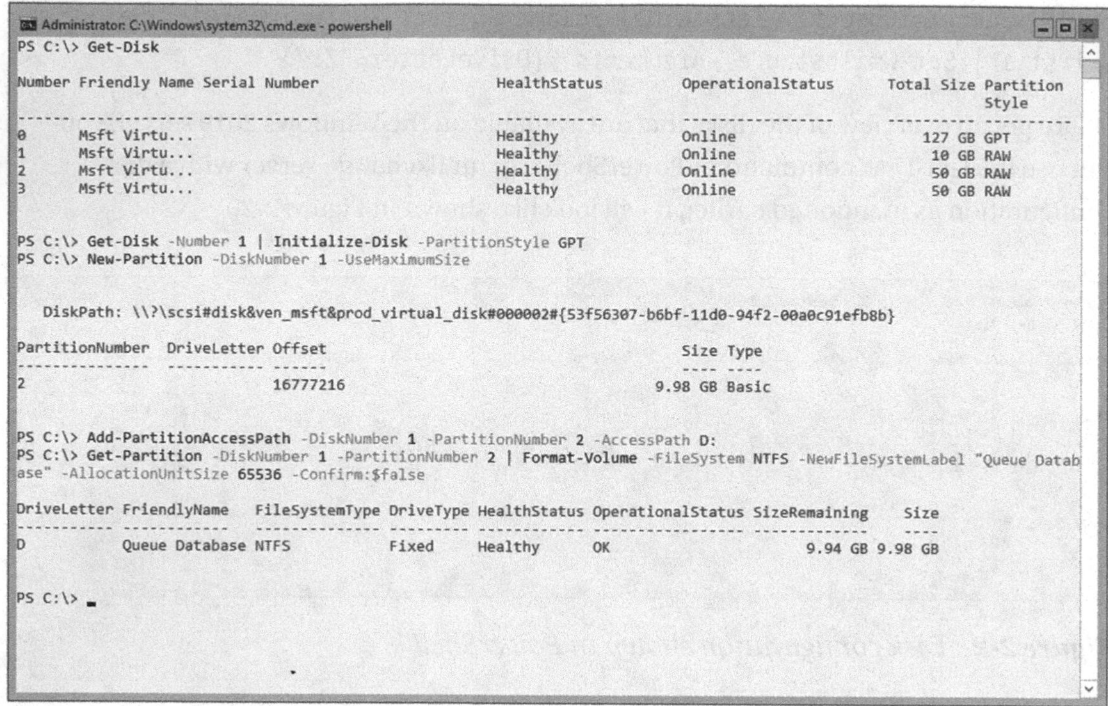

Figure 2-3. Initializing and formatting drive D: using PowerShell

For formatting the disks that will hold the mailbox databases in mount points, the process is similar. When using the Add-PartitionAccessPath command in PowerShell, the -AccessPath option will have the value "C:\ExchDbs\Disk1" instead of a drive letter.

The set of PowerShell commands to run is

```
PS C:\> MD C:\ExchDbs\Disk1
PS C:\> Get-Disk -Number 2 | Initialize-Disk -PartititionStyle GPT
PS C:\> New-Partition -DiskNumber 2 -UseMaximumSize
PS C:\> Add-PartitionAccessPath -DiskNumber 2 -PartitionNumber 2
-AccessPath "C:\ExchDbs\Disk1"
PS C:\> Get-Partition -Disknumber 2 -PartitionNumber 2 | Format-Volume
-FileSystem NTFS -NewFileSystemLabel "Disk1" -AllocationUnitSize 65536
-Confirm:$false
```

The output of these commands is very similar to the output shown in Figure 2-3.

Note For the PowerShell purists, instead of the MD command it is also possible to use the `New-Item C:\ExchDbs\Disk1 -ItemType Directory` command.

Installing Prerequisite Software

When installing the Exchange 2019 Mailbox server on Windows 2019, the following prerequisite Windows features as well as additional runtimes are required:

- Windows Server Roles and Features and the Active Directory Remote Server Administration Tools (RSAT-ADDS)
- .NET Framework 4.8 (Exchange 2019 CU4 and higher, earlier versions of Exchange server 2019 were running on .NET Framework 4.7.2)
- Visual C++ Redistributable Package for Visual Studio 2012
- Visual C++ Redistributable Package for Visual Studio 2013
- Microsoft Unified Communications Managed API 4.0 Core Runtime

Note When installing Exchange server 2016 on Windows server 2016, the same prerequisite software must be installed. Windows server should be fully patched before starting any installation.

The easiest way to install any prerequisite software is using PowerShell. Log on to the Windows 2019 server with an administrative account and execute the following commands in a PowerShell command window with elevated privileges:

To download the .NET Framework 4.8

```
PS C:\> New-Item C:\Install -ItemType Directory
PS C:\> Start-BitsTransfer -Source "https://download.visualstudio.
microsoft.com/download/pr/7afca223-55d2-470a-8edc-6a1739ae3252/
abd170b4b0ec15ad0222a809b761a036/ndp48-x86-x64-allos-enu.exe" -Destination
C:\Install
```

To download the Visual C++ Redistributable Package for Visual Studio 2012

```
PS C:\> New-Item C:\Install\VS2012 -ItemType Directory
```

```
PS C:\> Start-BitsTransfer -Source "https://download.microsoft.com/
download/1/6/B/16B06F60-3B20-4FF2-B699-5E9B7962F9AE/VSU_4/vcredist_x64.exe"
-Destination C:\Install\2012
```

To download the Visual C++ Redistributable Package for Visual Studio 2013

```
PS C:\> New-Item C:\Install\VS2013 -ItemType Directory
PS C:\> Start-BitsTransfer -Source "https://download.microsoft.com/
download/2/E/6/2E61CFA4-993B-4DD4-91DA-3737CD5CD6E3/vcredist_x64.exe"
-Destination C:\Install\2013
```

Finally, to download the Microsoft Unified Communications Managed API 4.0, Core Runtime 64-bit.

```
PS C:\> Start-BitsTransfer -Source "http://download.microsoft.com/
download/2/C/4/2C47A5C1-A1F3-4843-B9FE-84C0032C61EC/UcmaRuntimeSetup.exe"
-Destination C:\Install
```

Note All PowerShell commands in this book are available via the Apress GitHub.

The Microsoft Unified Communications Managed API 4.0, Core Runtime 64-bit, needs to be downloaded for the Desktop Experience version of Windows 2019 only. For Windows 2019 Server Core, there is a special Server Core version of the Microsoft Unified Communications Managed API 4.0 available on the Exchange 2019 installation media in the \UCMARedist folder.

Make sure that the directories where the installation files are downloaded exist. Both Visual C++ Redistributable Packages have identical names, so they need to be stored in separate directories or renamed after downloading.

To install the prerequisite software, use the following PowerShell commands:

```
PS C:\> Start-Process -FilePath "C:\Install\ndp48-x86-x64-allos-enu.exe"
-ArgumentList "/q" -Wait
PS C:\> Start-Process -FilePath "C:\Install\2012\vcredist_x64.exe"
-ArgumentList "/q" -Wait
PS C:\> Start-Process -FilePath "C:\Install\2013\vcredist_x64.exe"
-ArgumentList "/q" -Wait
```

For Windows Server 2019 Desktop Experience

```
PS C:\> Start-Process -FilePath "C:\Install\UcmaRuntimeSetup.exe"
-ArgumentList "/q" -Wait
```

For Windows Server 2019 Server Core

```
PS C:\> Start-Process -FilePath "Z:\UcmaRedist\setup.exe" -ArgumentList
"/q" -Wait
```

Note Installing .NET Framework 4.8 unattended will automatically restart the server.

When the prerequisite software is installed, the prerequisite Windows Server Roles and Features can be installed. This must be installed using PowerShell.

To install the Windows Server Roles and Features on Windows 2019 Server Core, use the following command:

```
PS C:\> Install-WindowsFeature Server-Media-Foundation, NET-Framework-
45-Features, RPC-over-HTTP-proxy, RSAT-Clustering, RSAT-Clustering-
CmdInterface, RSAT-Clustering-PowerShell, WAS-Process-Model, Web-Asp-Net45,
Web-Basic-Auth, Web-Client-Auth, Web-Digest-Auth, Web-Dir-Browsing, Web-Dyn-
Compression, Web-Http-Errors, Web-Http-Logging, Web-Http-Redirect, Web-Http-
Tracing, Web-ISAPI-Ext, Web-ISAPI-Filter, Web-Metabase, Web-Mgmt-Service,
Web-Net-Ext45, Web-Request-Monitor, Web-Server, Web-Stat-Compression, Web-
Static-Content, Web-Windows-Auth, Web-WMI, RSAT-ADDS, Telnet-Client
```

To install the Windows Server Roles and Features on Windows 2019 Desktop Experience, use the following command:

```
PS C:\> Install-WindowsFeature Server-Media-Foundation, NET-Framework-
45-Features, RPC-over-HTTP-proxy, RSAT-Clustering, RSAT-Clustering-
CmdInterface, RSAT-Clustering-Mgmt, RSAT-Clustering-PowerShell,
WAS-Process-Model, Web-Asp-Net45, Web-Basic-Auth, Web-Client-Auth, Web-
Digest-Auth, Web-Dir-Browsing, Web-Dyn-Compression, Web-Http-Errors,
Web-Http-Logging, Web-Http-Redirect, Web-Http-Tracing, Web-ISAPI-Ext,
Web-ISAPI-Filter, Web-Lgcy-Mgmt-Console, Web-Metabase, Web-Mgmt-Console,
```

```
Web-Mgmt-Service, Web-Net-Ext45, Web-Request-Monitor, Web-Server, Web-
Stat-Compression, Web-Static-Content, Web-Windows-Auth, Web-WMI, Windows-
Identity-Foundation, RSAT-ADDS, Telnet-Client
```

Installing the prerequisite Server Roles and Features on Windows 2019 Desktop Experience is shown in Figure 2-4.

Note The Telnet-Client is not a prerequisite for any version of Exchange, but it is a very useful tool for basic troubleshooting Exchange, so I install it on any Exchange server.

When the Exchange server is configured to be a member of a Database Availability Group, the Failover-Clustering feature should be included in both commands as well.

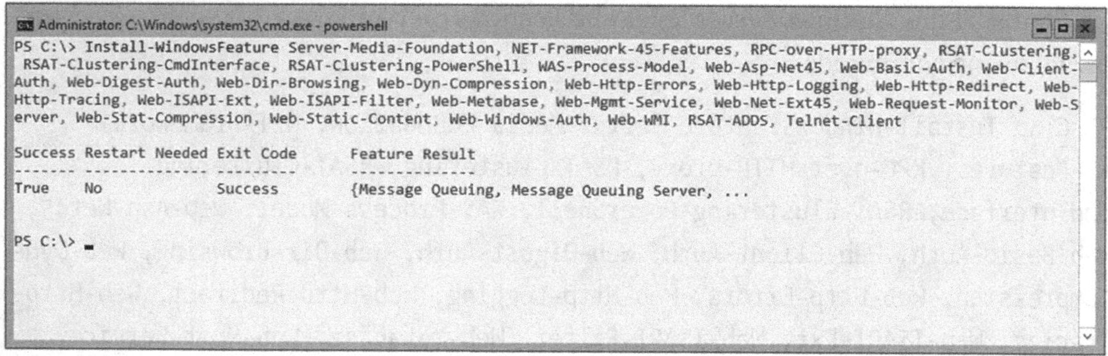

Figure 2-4. *Installing prerequisite Server Roles and Features on Windows 2019 Server core*

When installing Exchange server 2016 on Windows server 2016, the following Windows Server Roles and Features need to be installed:

```
[PS] C:\> Install-WindowsFeature NET-Framework-45-Features, Server-
Media-Foundation, RPC-over-HTTP-proxy, RSAT-Clustering, RSAT-Clustering-
CmdInterface, RSAT-Clustering-Mgmt, RSAT-Clustering-PowerShell,
WAS-Process-Model, Web-Asp-Net45, Web-Basic-Auth, Web-Client-Auth, Web-
Digest-Auth, Web-Dir-Browsing, Web-Dyn-Compression, Web-Http-Errors,
Web-Http-Logging, Web-Http-Redirect, Web-Http-Tracing, Web-ISAPI-Ext,
Web-ISAPI-Filter, Web-Lgcy-Mgmt-Console, Web-Metabase, Web-Mgmt-Console,
```

```
Web-Mgmt-Service, Web-Net-Ext45, Web-Request-Monitor, Web-Server, Web-
Stat-Compression, Web-Static-Content, Web-Windows-Auth, Web-WMI, Windows-
Identity-Foundation, RSAT-ADDS, Telnet-Client
```

Installing the Exchange 2019 Mailbox Server

When the prerequisite software and Server Roles and Features are installed and the Windows server is fully patched, the Exchange 2019 Mailbox server can be installed.

As discussed in Chapter 1, the Exchange server depends heavily on Active Directory, and before Exchange can be installed, Active Directory needs to be prepared. This consists of three different consecutive steps:

- Prepare the Schema partition.
- Prepare the Configuration partition.
- Prepare the Domain partition.

This will be discussed in the following sections.

Note that Exchange GUI as well as unattended setup can also take care of this, but for clarity in the process and since many organizations have different teams and thus change processes for Active Directory and Exchange, we will describe the manual process here.

Prepare the Schema Partition

To prepare the schema for Exchange 2019, log in using an account which is part of the Schema Admin security group. Then, open a command prompt with elevated privileges and enter the following command:

```
Z:\Setup.exe /PrepareSchema /IAcceptExchangeServerLicenseTerms
```

The read-write copy of the Active Directory Schema partition is hosted on the Domain Controller that hosts the Schema Master FSMO role. Therefore, this command must be run on the Domain Controller holding the Schema Master FSMO role, any other Domain Controller in the same Active Directory site as where the Schema Master is installed or the new Exchange servers as long as it is in the same Active Directory site and Active Directory domain. In a multi-domain environment, this must be run in the root domain.

If you try to prepare the Schema partition from a server in a different Active Directory site, the error message is returned on the console:

```
Setup encountered a problem while validating the state of Active Directory:
Exchange organization-level objects have not been created, and setup cannot
create them because the local computer is not in the same domain and site
as the schema master. Run setup with the /PrepareAD parameter on a computer
in the domain <contoso> and site Default-First-Site-Name, and wait for
replication to complete. See the Exchange setup log for more information on
this error.
```

Preparing the Active Directory Schema partition for the installation of Exchange 2019 CU8 is shown in Figure 2-5.

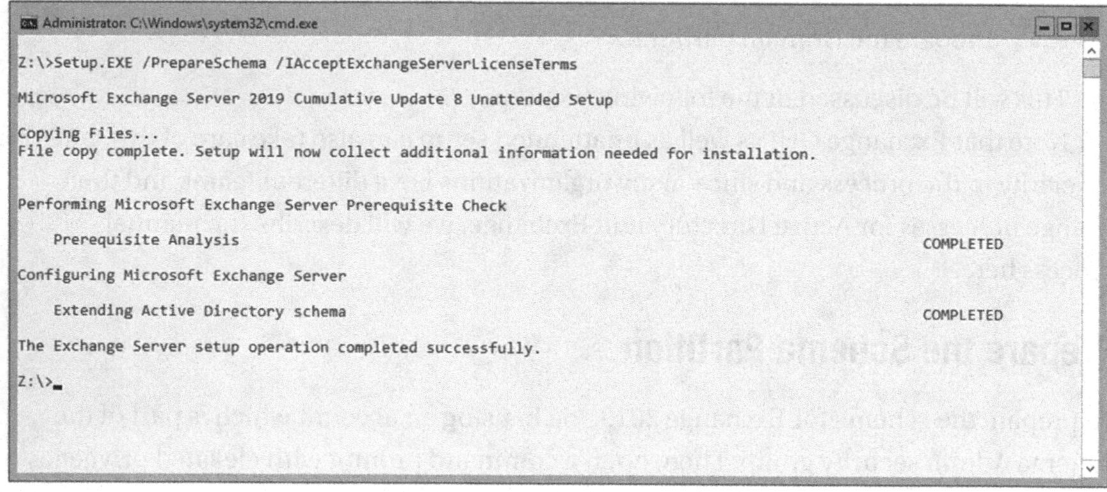
Administrator: C:\Windows\system32\cmd.exe
Z:\>Setup.EXE /PrepareSchema /IAcceptExchangeServerLicenseTerms
Microsoft Exchange Server 2019 Cumulative Update 8 Unattended Setup
Copying Files...
File copy complete. Setup will now collect additional information needed for installation.
Performing Microsoft Exchange Server Prerequisite Check
Prerequisite Analysis
COMPLETED
Configuring Microsoft Exchange Server
Extending Active Directory schema
COMPLETED
The Exchange Server setup operation completed successfully.
Z:\>

Figure 2-5. *Preparing the Active Directory Schema*

How do you know this worked? First, if you do not see any error messages on the console, you can be sure that it worked correctly.

You can also check the Exchange version in the Active Directory Schema, which is also important when upgrading your Exchange deployment. Open ADSI Edit and navigate to the ms-Exch-Schema-Version-PT. Open its properties and check the rangeUpper property. For Exchange 2019 CU2 and higher, it should have a value of 17001; for Exchange 2019 CU8 and CU9, this should have a value of 17002 as shown in Figure 2-6.

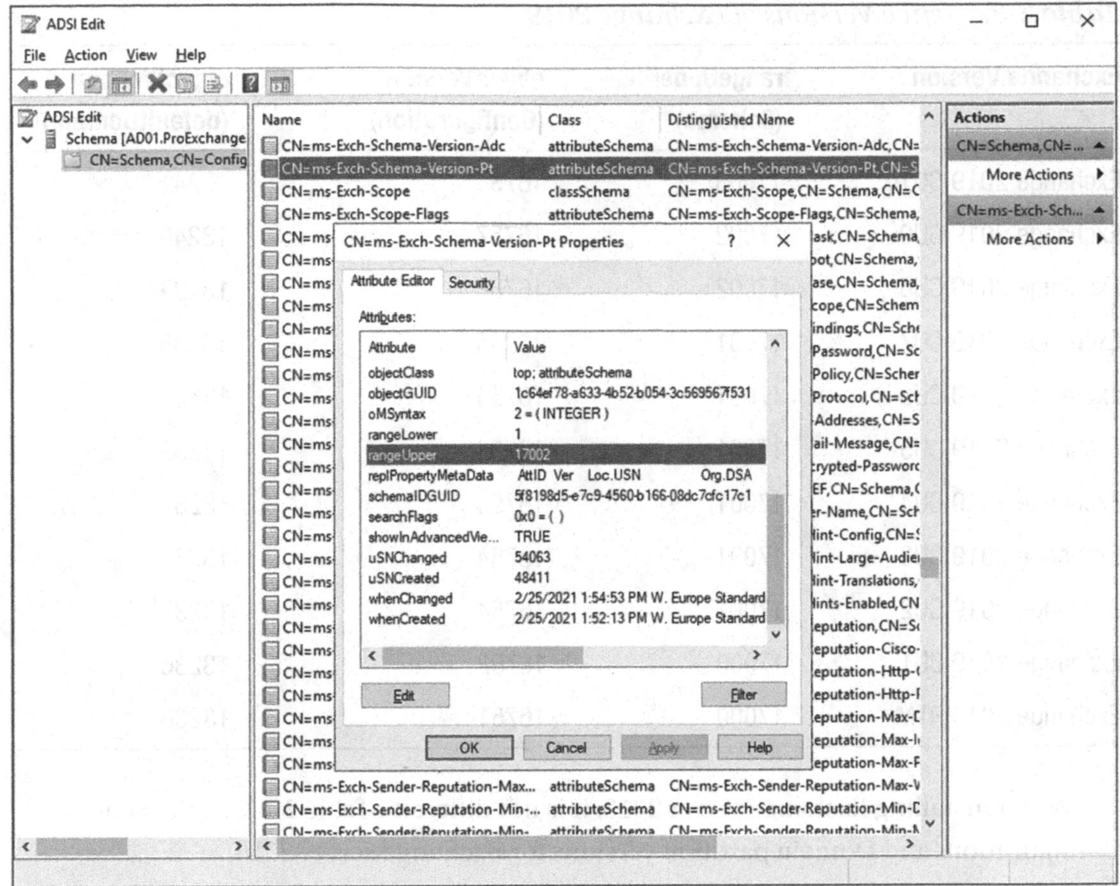

Figure 2-6. *Checking the Schema version after preparing for Exchange 2019 CU8*

It is also possible to check the Schema version using PowerShell by using the following commands:

```
PS C:\> $Root = [ADSI]"LDAP://RootDSE"
PS C:\> ([ADSI]("LDAP://CN=ms-Exch-Schema-Version-Pt," + $Root.
schemaNamingContext)).rangeUpper
```

This will return the value of the rangeUpper property.

Table 2-3 lists the Schema, Configuration, and Domain partition versions of Active Directory for all Exchange 2019 versions.

Table 2-3. *Active Versions of Exchange 2019*

Exchange Version	rangeUpper (Schema)	objectVersion (Configuration)	objectVersion (defaultDomain)
Exchange 2019 CU10	17003	16758	13241
Exchange 2019 CU9	17002	16757	13240
Exchange 2019 CU8	17002	16756	13239
Exchange 2019 CU7	17001	16755	13238
Exchange 2019 CU6	17001	16754	13237
Exchange 2019 CU5	17001	16754	13237
Exchange 2019 CU4	17001	16754	13237
Exchange 2019 CU3	17001	16754	13237
Exchange 2019 CU2	17001	16754	13237
Exchange 2019 CU1	17000	16752	13236
Exchange 2019 RTM	17000	16751	13236

When installing Exchange server 2016, it is not different. Table 2-4 lists the Schema, Configuration, and Domain partition versions for Exchange server 2016.

Table 2-4. *Active Directory Versions of Exchange 2016*

Exchange Version	rangeUpper (Schema)	objectVersion (Configuration)	objectVersion (defaultDomain)
Exchange 2016 CU21	15334	16221	13241
Exchange 2016 CU20	15333	16220	13240
Exchange 2016 CU19	15333	16219	13239
Exchange 2016 CU18	15332	16218	13238
Exchange 2016 CU17	15332	16217	13238
Exchange 2016 CU16	15332	16217	13237

(continued)

Table 2-4. (*continued*)

Exchange Version	rangeUpper (Schema)	objectVersion (Configuration)	objectVersion (defaultDomain)
Exchange 2016 CU15	15332	16217	13237
Exchange 2016 CU14	15332	16217	13237
Exchange 2016 CU13	15332	16217	13237
Exchange 2016 CU12	15332	16215	13236
Exchange 2016 CU11	15332	16214	13236
Exchange 2016 CU10	15332	16213	13236
Exchange 2016 CU9	15332	16213	13236
Exchange 2016 CU8	15332	16213	13236
Exchange 2016 CU7	15332	16213	13236
Exchange 2016 CU6	15330	16213	13236
Exchange 2016 CU5	15326	16213	13236
Exchange 2016 CU4	15326	16213	13236
Exchange 2016 CU3	15326	16212	13236
Exchange 2016 CU2	15325	16212	13236
Exchange 2016 CU1	15323	16211	13236
Exchange 2016 RTM	15317	16210	13236

For an up-to-date list of all versions, you can check the Active Directory version information on Microsoft docs at `http://bit.ly/ExADVersions`.

Prepare the Configuration Partition

When the Active Directory Schema partition is prepared for Exchange and all changes have been replicated throughout the forest, you can continue with preparing the Active Directory Configuration partition. This partition holds information about the entire Exchange configuration.

The Configuration partition can be prepared using the following command, started in an elevated command prompt, and using an account which is a member of the Enterprise Admins security group:

```
Z:\> Setup.exe /PrepareAD /OrganizationName:<Name> /
IAcceptExchangeServerLicenseTerms
```

If you do not have any Exchange version in your organization, you must run this command including the /OrganizationName option. This will create the Exchange organization in the Active Directory configuration partition, and it will hold all information regarding the Exchange deployment.

When running this for the first time, a warning message is displayed on the console about no previous Exchange server available in your organization. Running the Exchange 2019 setup with the /PrepareAD and /OrganizationName in a new Active Directory will return the following warning:

```
Setup will prepare the organization for Exchange Server 2019 by using
'Setup /PrepareAD'. No Exchange Server 2016 roles have been detected in
this topology. After this operation, you will not be able to install any
Exchange Server 2016 roles.
For more information, visit: https://docs.microsoft.com/Exchange/plan-and-
deploy/deployment-ref/readiness-checks?view=exchserver-2019
```

This warning makes sense since this is the initial deployment, but care must be taken. If there are any applications or services that require Exchange 2016 in your organization, then you must run the Exchange 2016 setup with the /PrepareAD and / OrganizationName first. This will prepare the Active Directory Configuration partition for Exchange 2016 and thus makes it possible to install an Exchange 2016 server when needed. When the Exchange 2016 setup with /PrepareAD and /OrganizationName has been executed, the process continues with running the Exchange 2019 setup with the / PrepareAD switch. In this case, the /OrganizationName is not needed anymore.

When preparing the Active Directory Configuration partition, if an Exchange organization already exists, you can omit the /OrganizationName option and only use the following command:

```
Z:\> Setup.exe /PrepareAD /IAcceptExchangeServerLicenseTerms
```

This is shown in Figure 2-7.

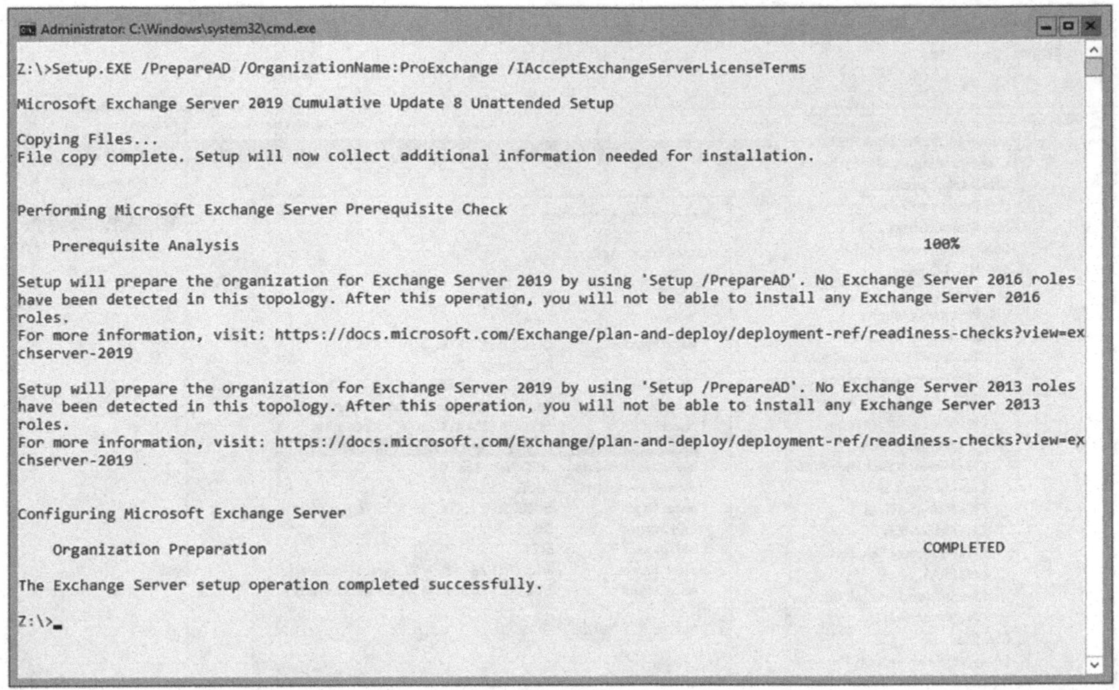
Administrator: C:\Windows\system32\cmd.exe
Z:\>Setup.EXE /PrepareAD /OrganizationName:ProExchange /IAcceptExchangeServerLicenseTerms
Microsoft Exchange Server 2019 Cumulative Update 8 Unattended Setup
Copying Files...
File copy complete. Setup will now collect additional information needed for installation.
Performing Microsoft Exchange Server Prerequisite Check
Prerequisite Analysis 100%
Setup will prepare the organization for Exchange Server 2019 by using 'Setup /PrepareAD'. No Exchange Server 2016 roles have been detected in this topology. After this operation, you will not be able to install any Exchange Server 2016 roles.
For more information, visit: https://docs.microsoft.com/Exchange/plan-and-deploy/deployment-ref/readiness-checks?view=exchserver-2019
Setup will prepare the organization for Exchange Server 2019 by using 'Setup /PrepareAD'. No Exchange Server 2013 roles have been detected in this topology. After this operation, you will not be able to install any Exchange Server 2013 roles.
For more information, visit: https://docs.microsoft.com/Exchange/plan-and-deploy/deployment-ref/readiness-checks?view=exchserver-2019
Configuring Microsoft Exchange Server
Organization Preparation COMPLETED
The Exchange Server setup operation completed successfully.
Z:\>

***Figure 2-7.** Preparing the Active Directory Configuration partition for Exchange 2019 CU8*

Again, when no error message is returned on the console, you can be sure that no errors occurred while preparing the Active Directory Configuration partition.

You can check the version of the Configuration partition using ADSI Edit. In ADSI Edit, open the configuration partition and navigate to CN=Microsoft Exchange, CN=Services, CN=Configuration, DC=Domain, DC=Com object, and check the value of the objectVersion property. This is shown in Figure 2-8.

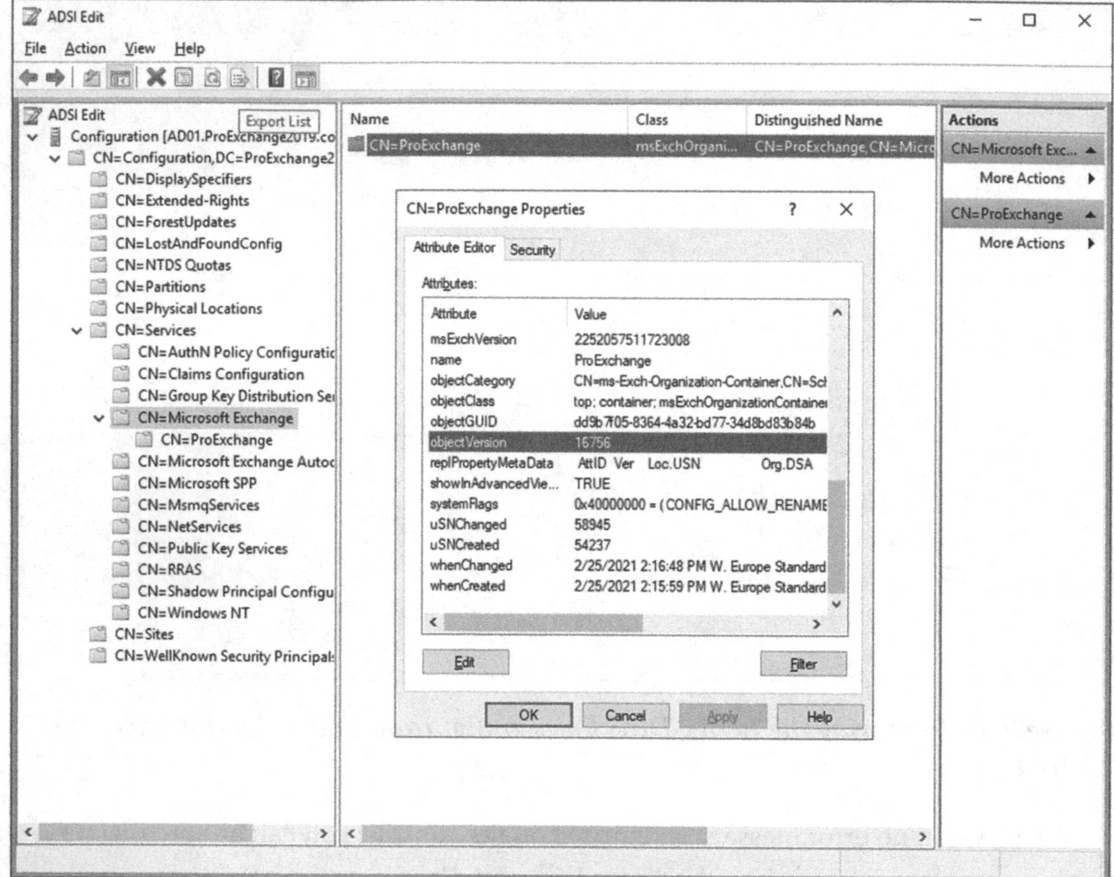

***Figure 2-8.** Checking the version of the Active Directory Configuration partition*

Possible values for the objectVersion property are listed in Table 2-3 earlier in this chapter.

You can also use PowerShell to retrieve the objectVersion property of this object by executing the following commands:

```
PS C:\> $Root = [ADSI]"LDAP://RootDSE"
PS C:\> ([ADSI]("LDAP://CN=<OrganizationName>,CN=Microsoft
Exchange,CN=Services," + $Root.configurationNamingContext)).objectVersion
```

This will return the value of the objectVersion property of the object.

This step also creates a hidden container called CN=Microsoft Exchange System Objects in the Active Directory root domain. At this stage, it only contains a security group called **Exchange Install Domain servers** and another container called

Monitoring Mailboxes which is still empty. This container is only visible when **View Advanced Features** is selected in Active Directory Users and Computers.

In the CN=Users container in the Active Directory domain, there are nine accounts created that will be used as System Mailboxes when the first Exchange server is installed.

When the configuration partition is prepared for Exchange, an Exchange container named CN=Microsoft Exchange is created under CN=Services,CN=Configuration, DC=<your domain>,DC=Com. This container is created in a greenfield scenario where no Exchange information is available in Active Directory. When it is already available from a previous version of Exchange, it is updated with the latest information.

The CN=Microsoft Exchange container contains multiple other Exchange-specific containers and objects:

- CN=Address Lists Container
- CN=AddressBook Mailbox Policies
- CN=Addressing
- CN=Administrative Groups
- CN=Approval Applications
- CN=Auth Configuration
- CN=Availability Configuration
- CN=Client Access
- CN=Connections
- CN=ELC Folders Container
- CN=ELC Mailbox Policies
- CN=ExchangeAssistance
- CN=Federation
- CN=Federation Trusts
- CN=Global Settings
- CN=Hybrid Configuration
- CN=Mobile Mailbox Policies
- CN=Mobile Mailbox Settings

- CN=Monitoring Settings
- CN=OWA Mailbox Policies
- CN=Provisioning Policy Container
- CN=Push Notification Settings
- CN=RBAC
- CN=Recipient Policies
- CN=Remote Accounts Policies Container
- CN=Retention Policies Container
- CN=Retention Policy Tag Container
- CN=ServiceEndpoints
- CN=System Policies
- CN=Team Mailbox Provisioning Policies
- CN=Transport Settings
- CN=Workload Management Settings
- CN=UM AutoAttendant Container
- CN=UM DialPlan Container
- CN=UM IPGateway Container
- CN=UM Mailbox Policies

These containers can be viewed using ADSI Edit as shown in Figure 2-9. The last four UM containers are only for Exchange 2013 and Exchange 2016 and are not created when preparing Active Directory for Exchange 2019.

The CN=Transport Settings container contains information regarding Exchange Transport that must be available throughout the entire forest:

- CN=Accepted Domains
- CN=ControlPoint Config
- CN=DNS Customization
- CN=Interceptor Rules

- CN=Malware Filter
- CN=Message Classifications
- CN=Message Hygiene
- CN=Rules
- CN=MicrosoftExchange329e71ec88ae4615bbc36ab6ce41109e

When the containers are added, the appropriate permissions are set. The setup application does this by importing and processing the information found in the rights.ldf file from the installation media.

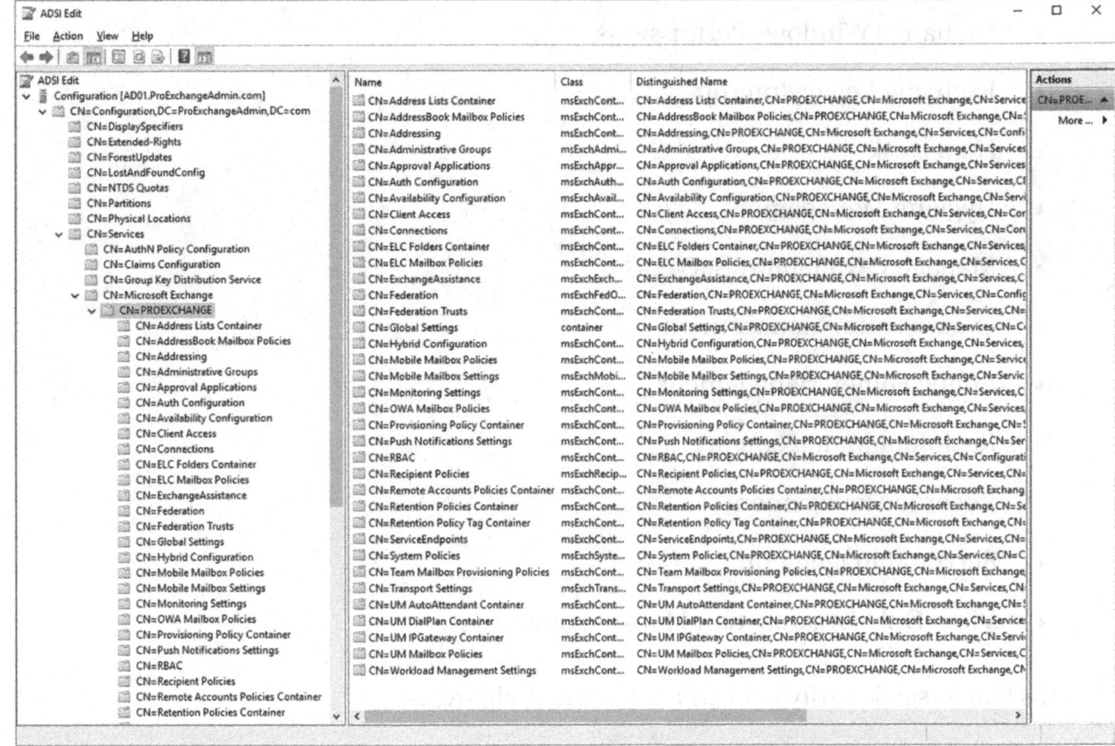

***Figure 2-9.** The CN=Microsoft Exchange container in the configuration partition of Active Directory*

When preparing the configuration partition, an Organizational Unit named OU=Microsoft Exchange Security Groups is created (if it does not exist) in the root domain of the Active Directory forest, and the following Universal Security Groups are created:

- Compliance Management
- Delegated Setup
- Discovery Management
- Exchange Servers
- Exchange Trusted Subsystem
- Exchange Windows Permissions
- ExchangeLegacyInterop
- Help Desk
- Hygiene Management
- Managed Availability Servers
- Organization Management
- Public Folder Management
- Recipient Management
- Records Management
- Server Management
- View-Only Organization Management

This Universal Security Groups are shown in Figure 2-10.

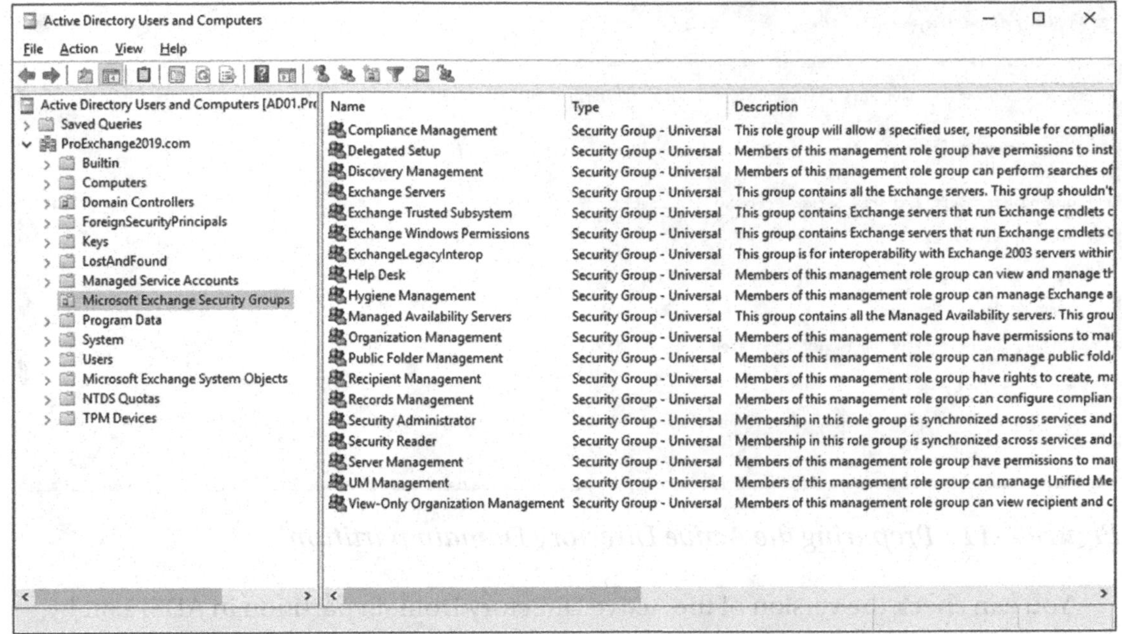

Figure 2-10. The Exchange-specific Univeral Security Groups in the root domain of the Active Directory forest

Prepare the Domain Partition

The last step in preparation before installing Exchange 2019 is preparing the Active Directory Domain partition, or partitions if you have multiple Domain partitions that contain mail-enabled objects.

To prepare the Active Directory Domain partition, execute the following command in an elevated command prompt:

```
Z:\> Setup.exe /PrepareDomain /IAcceptExchangeServerLicenseTerms
```

This command should be run in every domain in Active Directory that contains mail-enabled recipients. The setup application has an option to prepare all domains in just one command by using the /PrepareAllDomains switch. The command to prepare one Active Directory domain is shown in Figure 2-11.

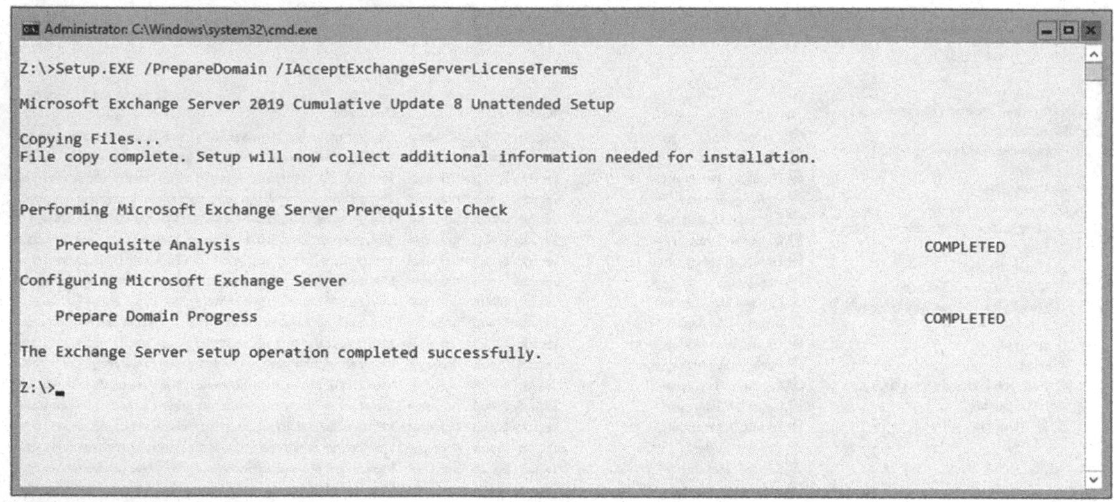
Administrator: C:\Windows\system32\cmd.exe
Z:\>Setup.EXE /PrepareDomain /IAcceptExchangeServerLicenseTerms
Microsoft Exchange Server 2019 Cumulative Update 8 Unattended Setup
Copying Files...
File copy complete. Setup will now collect additional information needed for installation.
Performing Microsoft Exchange Server Prerequisite Check
Prerequisite Analysis COMPLETED
Configuring Microsoft Exchange Server
Prepare Domain Progress COMPLETED
The Exchange Server setup operation completed successfully.
Z:\>

Figure 2-11. *Preparing the Active Directory Domain partition*

You can check the version of the Active Directory Domain partition in ADSI Edit by navigating to the CN=Microsoft Exchange System Objects container in Active Directory and retrieve its properties. The objectVersion property should have a value listed in Table 2-3. Checking the objectVersion property is shown in Figure 2-12.

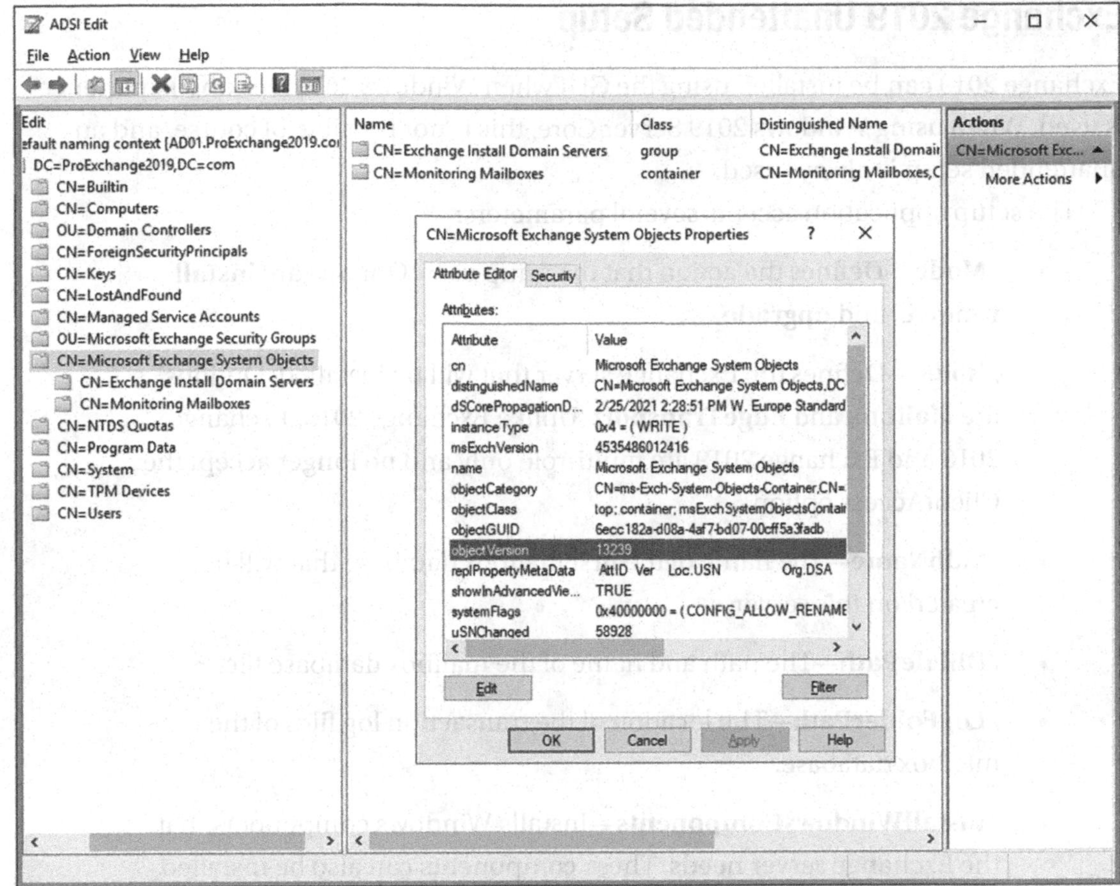

***Figure 2-12.** Checking the Domain version after preparing for Exchange 2019 CU8*

As always, checking the objectVersion of the Microsoft Exchange System Objects container in PowerShell is much easier and faster. Execute the following commands:

```
PS C:\> $RootDSE= ([ADSI]"").distinguishedName
PS C:\> ([ADSI]("LDAP://CN=Microsoft Exchange System Objects,$RootDSE")).
objectVersion
```

This will show the value of the objectVersion property.

When Active Directory is fully prepared, the Exchange servers themselves can be installed. This can be done using the setup application in graphical mode (GUI setup) or from the command line (unattended setup). This will be discussed in the following sections.

Exchange 2019 Unattended Setup

Exchange 2019 can be installed using the GUI when Windows 2019 Desktop Experience is used. When using Windows 2019 Server Core, this is not possible of course, and an unattended setup is always used.

The setup application accepts several parameters:

- **/Mode**—Defines the action that the setup uses. Options are **install**, **remove**, and **upgrade**.
- **/Roles**—Defines the Exchange server that will be installed. Options are **Mailbox** and **EdgeTransport**. Unlike Exchange 2013, Exchange 2016 and Exchange 2019 are multi-role only and no longer accept the ClientAccess option.
- **/MdbName**—The name of the first mailbox database that will be created on this server.
- **/DbFilePath**—The path and name of the mailbox database file.
- **/LogFolderPath**—The location of the transaction log files of the mailbox database.
- **/InstallWindowsComponents**—Installs Windows components that the Exchange server needs. These components can also be installed as part of the prerequisite software installation.
- **/IAcceptExchangeServerLicenseTerms**—Indicates you agree to the Microsoft license terms.

To install an Exchange 2019 mailbox server unattended, run the following command from the command line:

```
Setup.exe /Mode:Install /Roles:Mailbox /MdbName:"MDB01" /DbFilePath:"C:\
ExchDbs\Disk1\MDB01.edb" /LogFolderPath:"C:\ExchDbs\Disk1\LogFiles" /
InstallWindowsComponents /IAcceptExchangeServerLicenseTerms
```

This is shown in Figure 2-13.

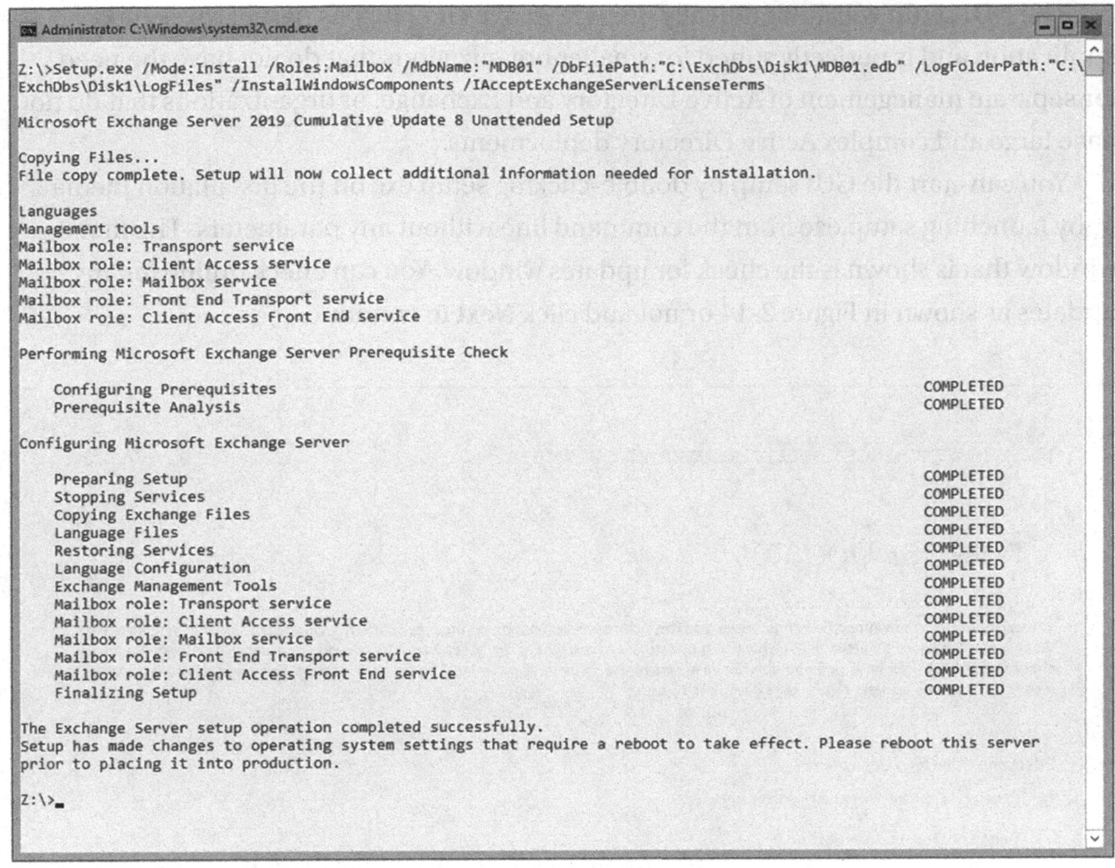

Administrator: C:\Windows\system32\cmd.exe
Z:\>Setup.exe /Mode:Install /Roles:Mailbox /MdbName:"MDB01" /DbFilePath:"C:\ExchDbs\Disk1\MDB01.edb" /LogFolderPath:"C:\ExchDbs\Disk1\LogFiles" /InstallWindowsComponents /IAcceptExchangeServerLicenseTerms
Microsoft Exchange Server 2019 Cumulative Update 8 Unattended Setup
Copying Files...
File copy complete. Setup will now collect additional information needed for installation.
Languages
Management tools
Mailbox role: Transport service
Mailbox role: Client Access service
Mailbox role: Mailbox service
Mailbox role: Front End Transport service
Mailbox role: Client Access Front End service
Performing Microsoft Exchange Server Prerequisite Check
Configuring Prerequisites COMPLETED
Prerequisite Analysis COMPLETED
Configuring Microsoft Exchange Server
Preparing Setup COMPLETED
Stopping Services COMPLETED
Copying Exchange Files COMPLETED
Language Files COMPLETED
Restoring Services COMPLETED
Language Configuration COMPLETED
Exchange Management Tools COMPLETED
Mailbox role: Transport service COMPLETED
Mailbox role: Client Access service COMPLETED
Mailbox role: Mailbox service COMPLETED
Mailbox role: Front End Transport service COMPLETED
Mailbox role: Client Access Front End service COMPLETED
Finalizing Setup COMPLETED
The Exchange Server setup operation completed successfully.
Setup has made changes to operating system settings that require a reboot to take effect. Please reboot this server prior to placing it into production.
Z:\>

Figure 2-13. *Unattended setup of Exchange 2019 CU8*

When the server is rebooted, the Exchange server 2019 server can be configured.

Exchange 2019 Graphical Setup

Instead of using the command line for an unattended setup, it is also possible to use the GUI version of the Exchange setup. The GUI setup is a very basic wizard that asks some questions regarding the installation and installs Exchange on your server. It is straightforward, not much room for error, and requires additional configuration after the initial install. The additional configuration is a bit more than when using the unattended setup.

In the previous sections, the preparation of Active Directory for Exchange was explained. Preparing Active Directory in advance is recommended for large deployments of Active Directory and Exchange or for organizations that have different departments for managing Active Directory and for Exchange server.

The GUI setup will automatically prepare Active Directory as part of the setup application and is perfectly suited for smaller organizations that do not have the need for separate management of Active Directory and Exchange, or organizations that do not have large and complex Active Directory deployments.

You can start the GUI setup by double-clicking setup.exe on the installation media or by launching setup.exe from the command line without any parameters. The first window that is shown is the check for updates window. You can check online for any updates as shown in Figure 2-14 or not and click **Next** to continue.

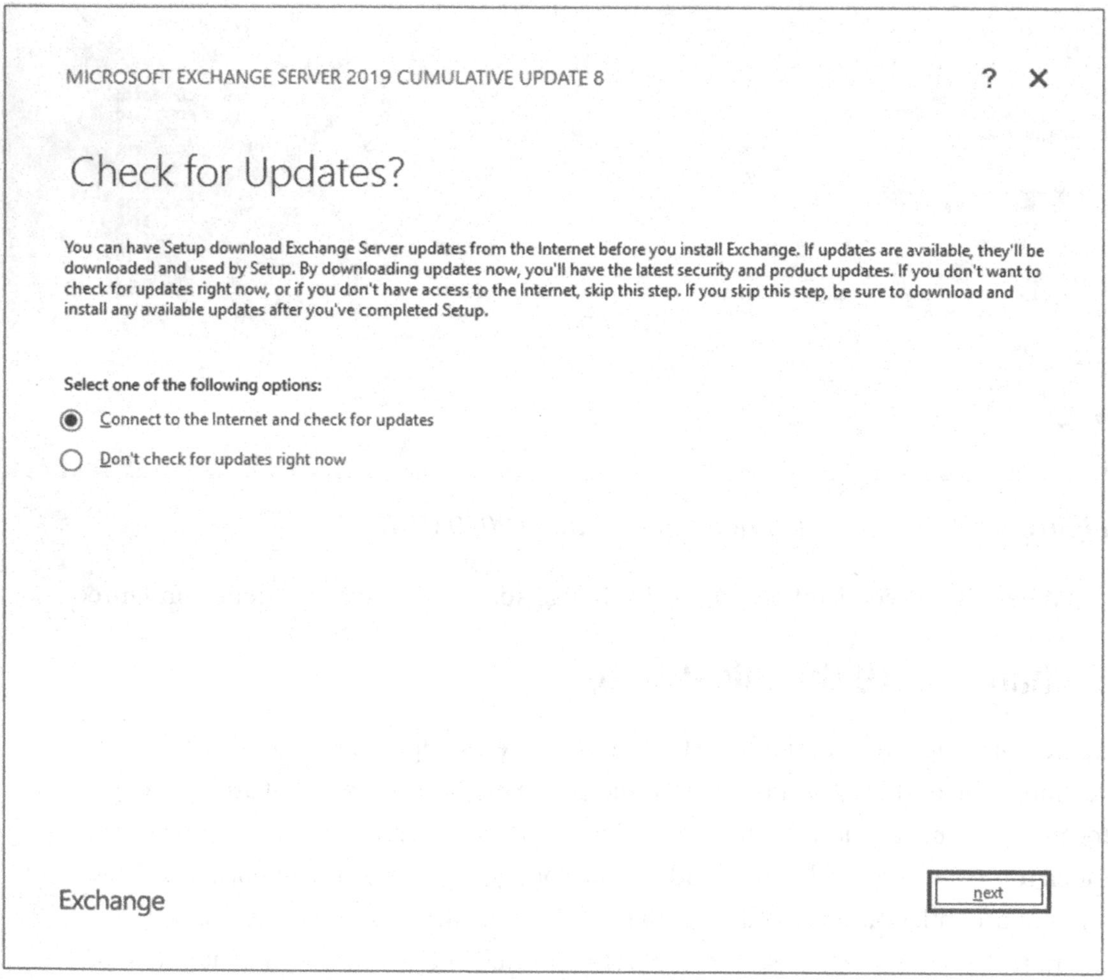

MICROSOFT EXCHANGE SERVER 2019 CUMULATIVE UPDATE 8 ? ✕

Check for Updates?

You can have Setup download Exchange Server updates from the Internet before you install Exchange. If updates are available, they'll be downloaded and used by Setup. By downloading updates now, you'll have the latest security and product updates. If you don't want to check for updates right now, or if you don't have access to the Internet, skip this step. If you skip this step, be sure to download and install any available updates after you've completed Setup.

Select one of the following options:

◉ Connect to the Internet and check for updates

○ Don't check for updates right now

Exchange next

Figure 2-14. *Check for updates when installing Exchange*

Follow the wizard, accept the license agreement, select **recommended settings** for usage reporting, and when you reach the **Server Role Selection** window as shown in Figure 2-15, select the server role that must be installed.

Server roles are mutually exclusive. When the mailbox server is selected, the Edge Transport role is automatically grayed out. Also, when the mailbox role is selected, the management tools are automatically included. Check the **Automatically install Windows server roles and features** checkbox when prerequisite server roles and features are not installed in advance. I always check this box, even when the server roles and features are installed, just in case a server role or feature was accidentally not installed.

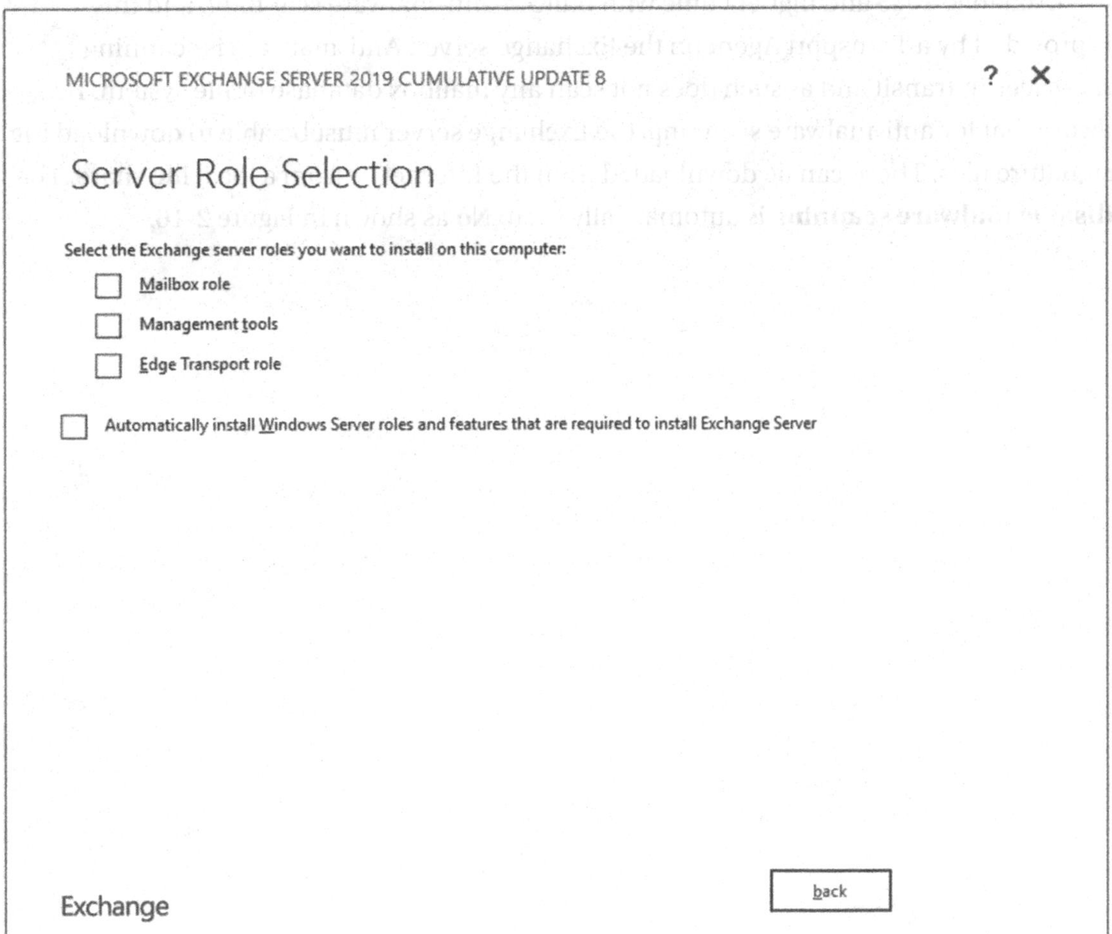

Figure 2-15. *Server role selection*

The default location for installing Exchange is C:\Program Files\Microsoft\Exchange Server\V15, but any other location can be used. The advantage of using another disk for installing Exchange is that the system disk is not filled up with Exchange information, causing the server to stop unexpectedly.

Note Exchange 2019 still uses the V15 folder, same as Exchange 2016 and Exchange 2013 before. The reason is that the Exchange 2019 major version number still is 15 (15.2.x to be exact), where Exchange 2016 was 15.1.x and Exchange 2013 15.0.x.

Exchange 2013 and higher come with built-in anti-malware scanning, and this is provided by a Transport Agent on the Exchange server. Anti-malware is scanning messages in transit and as such does not scan any mailbox database or file system. Be aware that for anti-malware scanning, the Exchange server must be able to download the signature files. These can be downloaded from the Internet or from a local file share. The **disable malware scanning** is automatically set to **No** as shown in Figure 2-16.

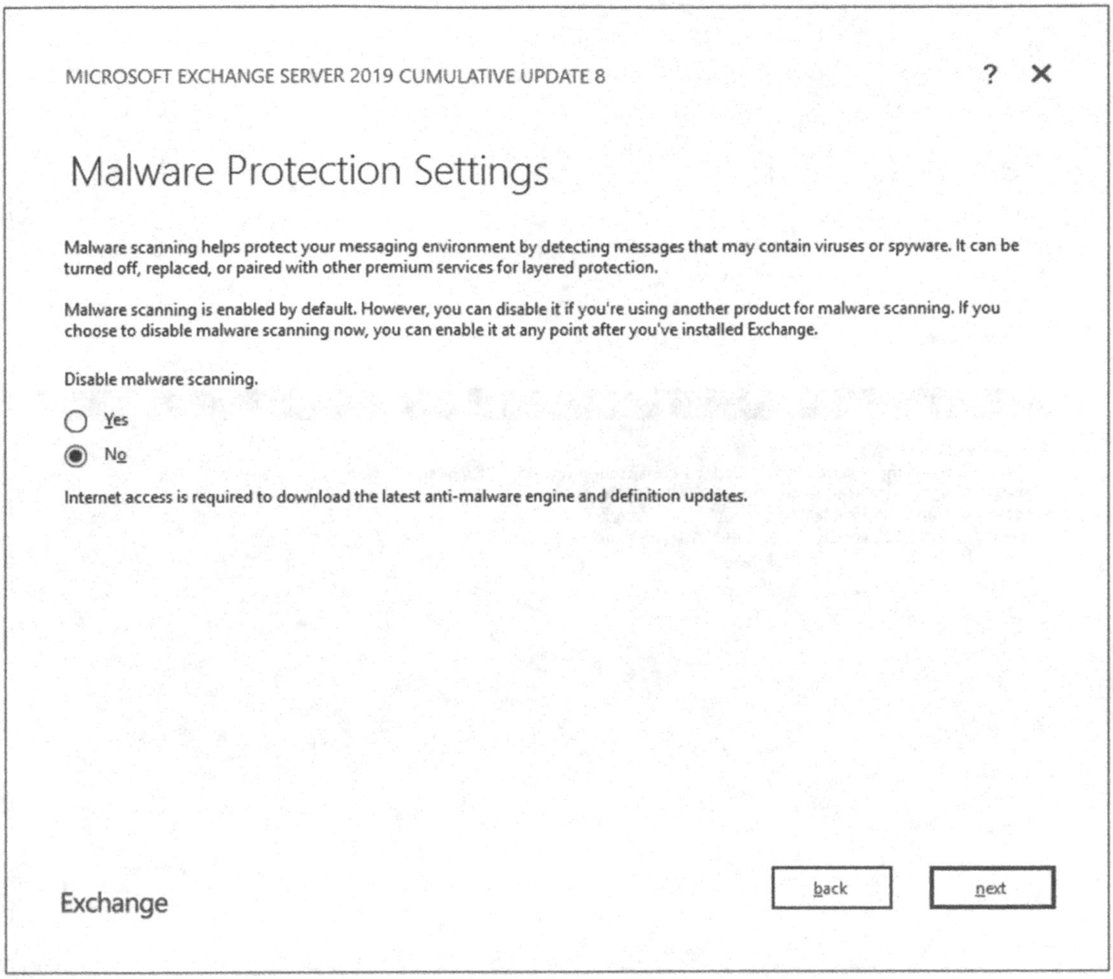

MICROSOFT EXCHANGE SERVER 2019 CUMULATIVE UPDATE 8 ? ✕

Malware Protection Settings

Malware scanning helps protect your messaging environment by detecting messages that may contain viruses or spyware. It can be turned off, replaced, or paired with other premium services for layered protection.

Malware scanning is enabled by default. However, you can disable it if you're using another product for malware scanning. If you choose to disable malware scanning now, you can enable it at any point after you've installed Exchange.

Disable malware scanning.

○ Yes

◉ No

Internet access is required to download the latest anti-malware engine and definition updates.

Exchange back next

Figure 2-16. *Disabling malware scanning is not a good idea*

Malware scanning in Exchange is explained in detail in Chapter 6.

At the end of the wizard, the setup will perform a prerequisite check to see if all prerequisites for installing Exchange 2019 are met. Sometimes, the prerequisite check will generate a warning message. For example, when upgrading from Exchange 2013 to Exchange 2016 or Exchange 2019, a warning message will be shown that the Exchange organization does not have MAPI over HTTP enabled, as shown in Figure 2-17.

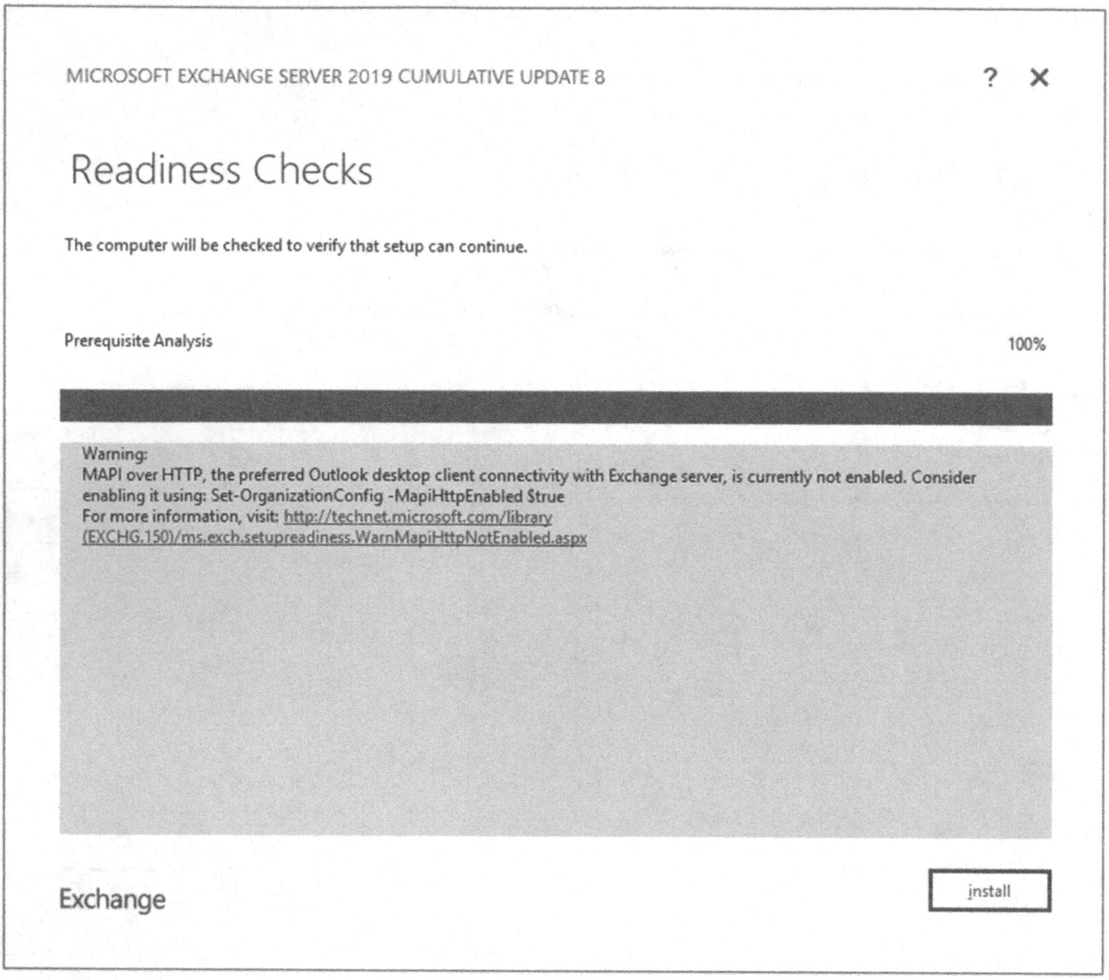

Figure 2-17. *Warning message about MAPI over HTTP not being enabled when Active Directory is on the Exchange 2013 level*

Warning messages can be ignored, but error messages must be fixed before installation can continue. If no errors are generated, click **install** to start the installation of Exchange. The installation of Exchange consists of 14 different steps, starting at preparing Active Directory as shown in Figure 2-18.

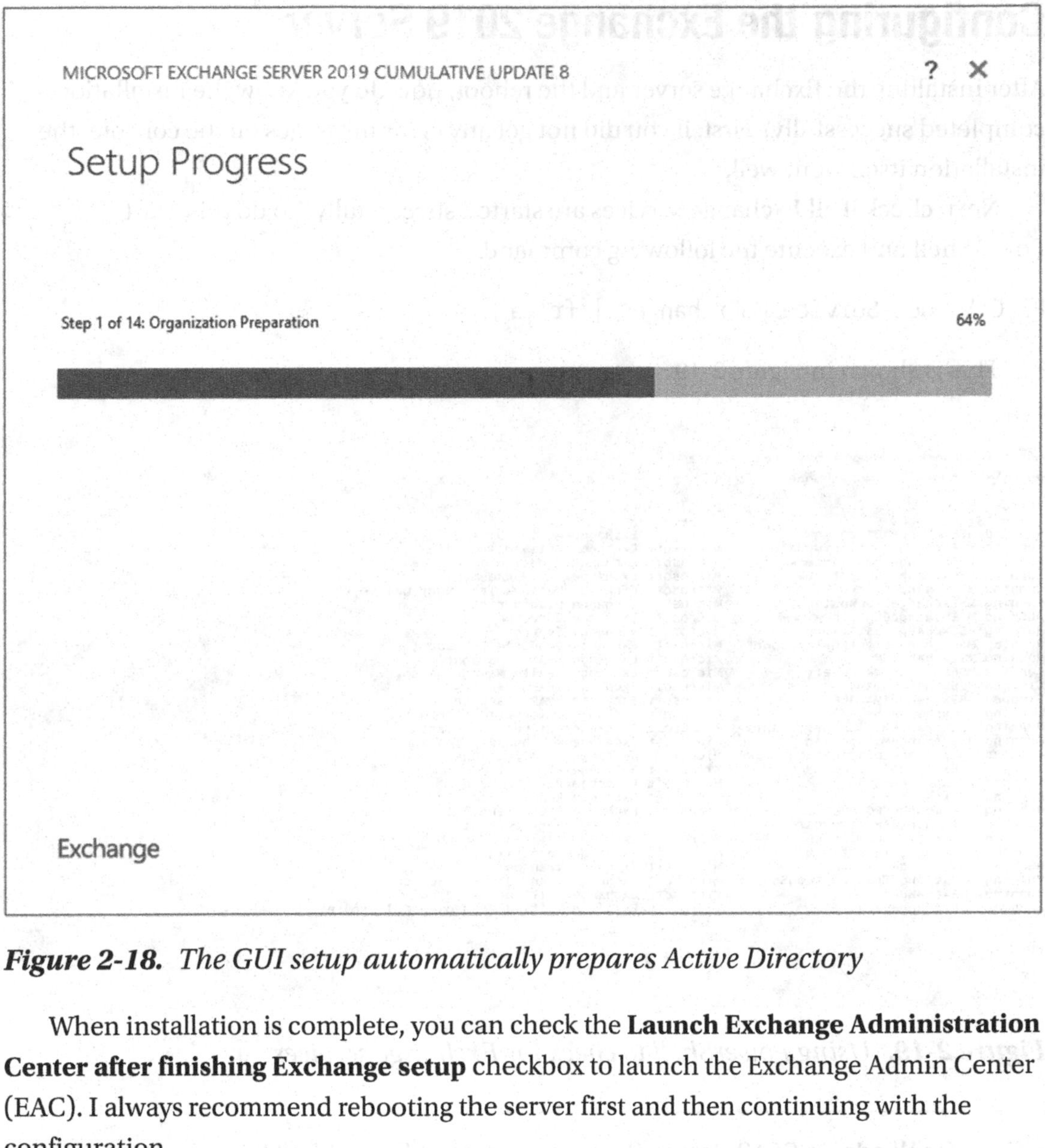

MICROSOFT EXCHANGE SERVER 2019 CUMULATIVE UPDATE 8

Setup Progress

Step 1 of 14: Organization Preparation 64%

Exchange

Figure 2-18. *The GUI setup automatically prepares Active Directory*

When installation is complete, you can check the **Launch Exchange Administration Center after finishing Exchange setup** checkbox to launch the Exchange Admin Center (EAC). I always recommend rebooting the server first and then continuing with the configuration.

When the server is rebooted, the Exchange server 2019 server can be configured.

Configuring the Exchange 2019 Server

After installing the Exchange server and the reboot, how do you know the installation completed successfully? First, if you did not get any error messages on the console, the installation itself went well.

Next, check if all Exchange services are started successfully. To do this, start PowerShell and execute the following command:

```
PS C:\> Get-Service MSExchange* | ft -a
```

This is shown in Figure 2-19.

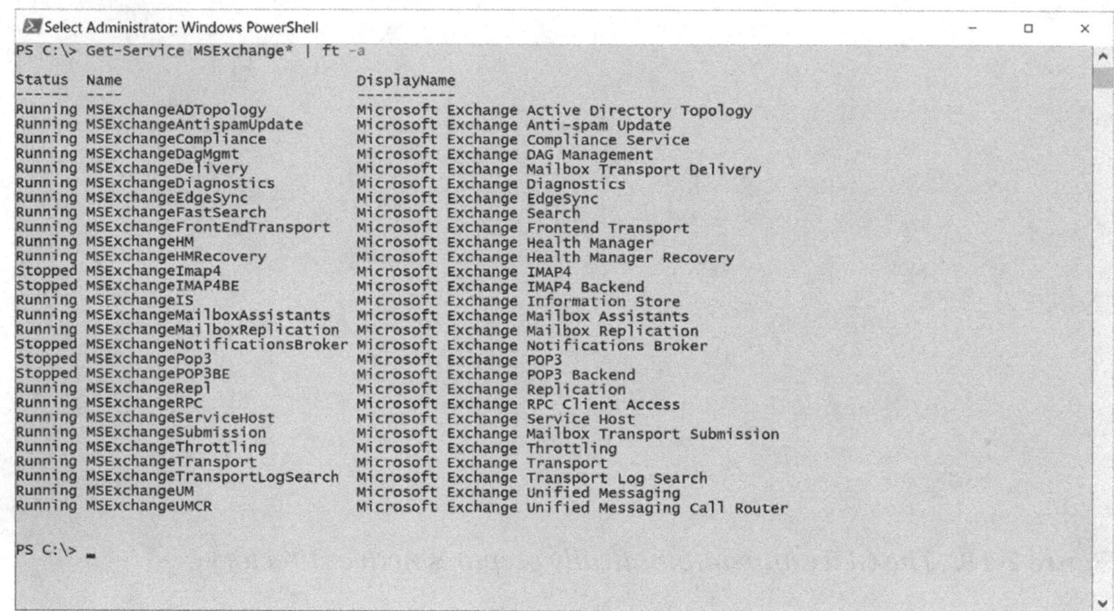

Figure 2-19. *Using PowerShell to check for Exchange services*

Tip On Windows 2019 Server Core, you can start PowerShell by executing the command "PowerShell" on the command prompt. To launch the Exchange Management Shell (EMS), execute the command "LaunchEMS".

When you are using Exchange 2019 on Windows 2019 Desktop Experience, you can also use the Services MMC snap-in; the Exchange services should be running as shown in Figure 2-20.

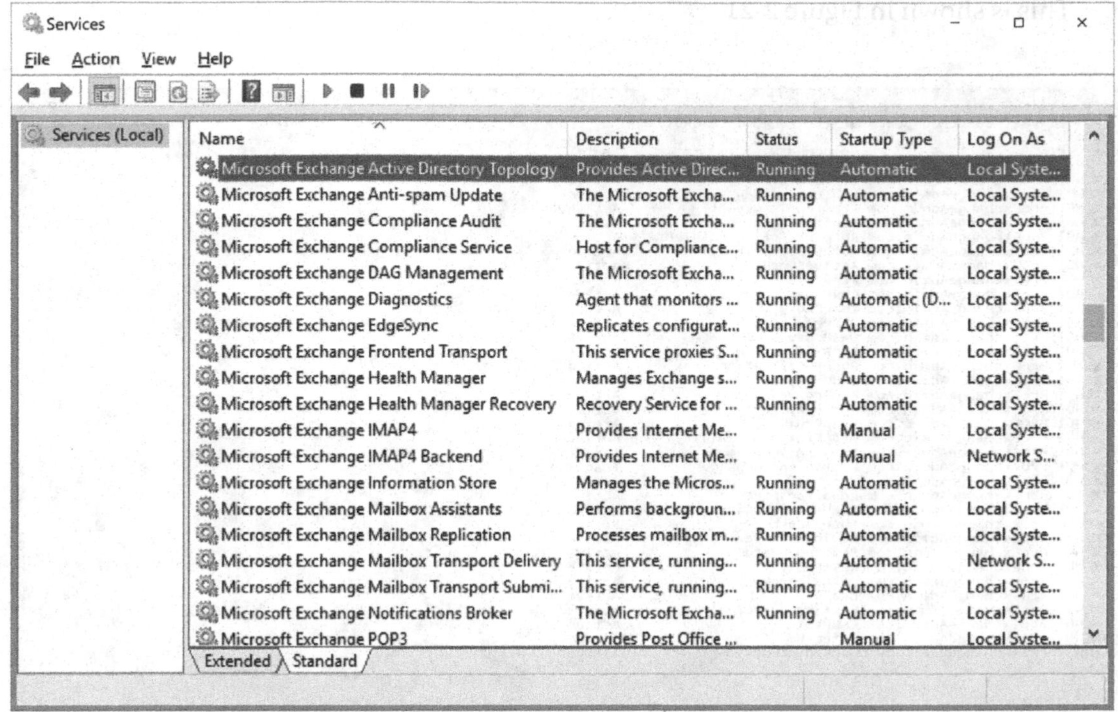

***Figure 2-20.** Most services must be running and have Automatic for Startup Type*

For both versions, Server Core and Desktop Experience, all services should be running and have set the Startup Type to Automatic, except

- Microsoft Exchange IMAP4
- Microsoft Exchange IMAP4 Backend
- Microsoft Exchange POP3
- Microsoft Exchange POP3 Backend
- Microsoft Exchange Server Extension for Windows Server Backup

These services have set their Startup Type to Manual right after installation and thus should not be running.

Another server-side test is to use the EMS command `Get-ServerComponent` state which is a part of the Microsoft Managed Availability. Health Manager is a part of Managed Availability and is checking the state of all Exchange components. To check this, execute the following command in EMS:

```
[PS] C:\> Get-ServerComponentState -Identity EXCH01
```

This is shown in Figure 2-21.

```
Machine: EXCH01.ProExchangeAdmin.com
[PS] C:\>Get-ServerComponentState -Identity EXCH01

Server                      Component                     State
------                      ---------                     -----
EXCH01.ProExchangeAdmin.com ServerWideOffline             Active
EXCH01.ProExchangeAdmin.com HubTransport                  Active
EXCH01.ProExchangeAdmin.com FrontendTransport             Active
EXCH01.ProExchangeAdmin.com Monitoring                    Active
EXCH01.ProExchangeAdmin.com RecoveryActionsEnabled        Active
EXCH01.ProExchangeAdmin.com AutoDiscoverProxy             Active
EXCH01.ProExchangeAdmin.com ActiveSyncProxy               Active
EXCH01.ProExchangeAdmin.com EcpProxy                      Active
EXCH01.ProExchangeAdmin.com EwsProxy                      Active
EXCH01.ProExchangeAdmin.com ImapProxy                     Active
EXCH01.ProExchangeAdmin.com OabProxy                      Active
EXCH01.ProExchangeAdmin.com OwaProxy                      Active
EXCH01.ProExchangeAdmin.com PopProxy                      Active
EXCH01.ProExchangeAdmin.com PushNotificationsProxy        Active
EXCH01.ProExchangeAdmin.com RpsProxy                      Active
EXCH01.ProExchangeAdmin.com RwsProxy                      Active
EXCH01.ProExchangeAdmin.com RpcProxy                      Active
EXCH01.ProExchangeAdmin.com XropProxy                     Active
EXCH01.ProExchangeAdmin.com HttpProxyAvailabilityGroup    Active
EXCH01.ProExchangeAdmin.com ForwardSyncDaemon             Inactive
EXCH01.ProExchangeAdmin.com ProvisioningRps               Inactive
EXCH01.ProExchangeAdmin.com MapiProxy                     Active
EXCH01.ProExchangeAdmin.com EdgeTransport                 Active
EXCH01.ProExchangeAdmin.com HighAvailability              Active
EXCH01.ProExchangeAdmin.com SharedCache                   Active
EXCH01.ProExchangeAdmin.com MailboxDeliveryProxy          Active
EXCH01.ProExchangeAdmin.com RoutingUpdates                Active
EXCH01.ProExchangeAdmin.com RestProxy                     Active
EXCH01.ProExchangeAdmin.com DefaultProxy                  Active
EXCH01.ProExchangeAdmin.com Lsass                         Active
EXCH01.ProExchangeAdmin.com RoutingService                Active
EXCH01.ProExchangeAdmin.com E4EProxy                      Active
EXCH01.ProExchangeAdmin.com CafeLAMv2                     Active
EXCH01.ProExchangeAdmin.com LogExportProvider             Active

[PS] C:\>_
```

***Figure 2-21.** Check the state of the Exchange components*

Note All components should return Active for their state, except the ForwardSyncDaemon and ProvisioningRps components. These are not actively used in Exchange 2019.

Another check is to see if you can open OWA in the browser using https://exch01/owa and log on as the account you used to install the Exchange server. You can ignore the SSL certificate warning; this is caused by using a self-signed SSL certificate on the Exchange server. After logging on and selecting the region and language, you should see OWA as shown in Figure 2-22.

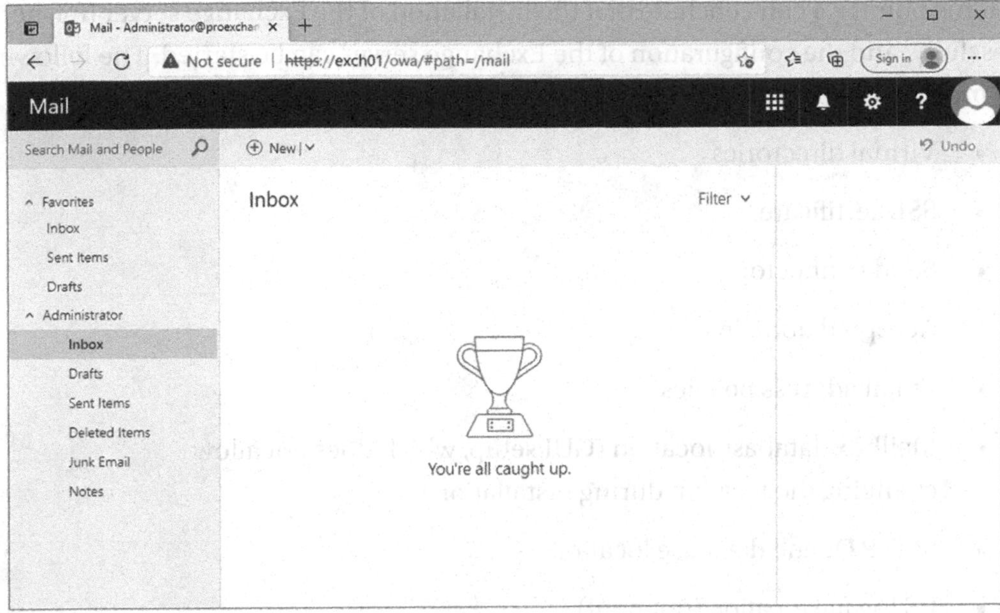

***Figure 2-22.** Outlook for the Web directly after installation*

When the URL is changed to https://exch01/ecp as shown in Figure 2-23, the Exchange Admin Center is shown. This is used for the configuration of the Exchange server.

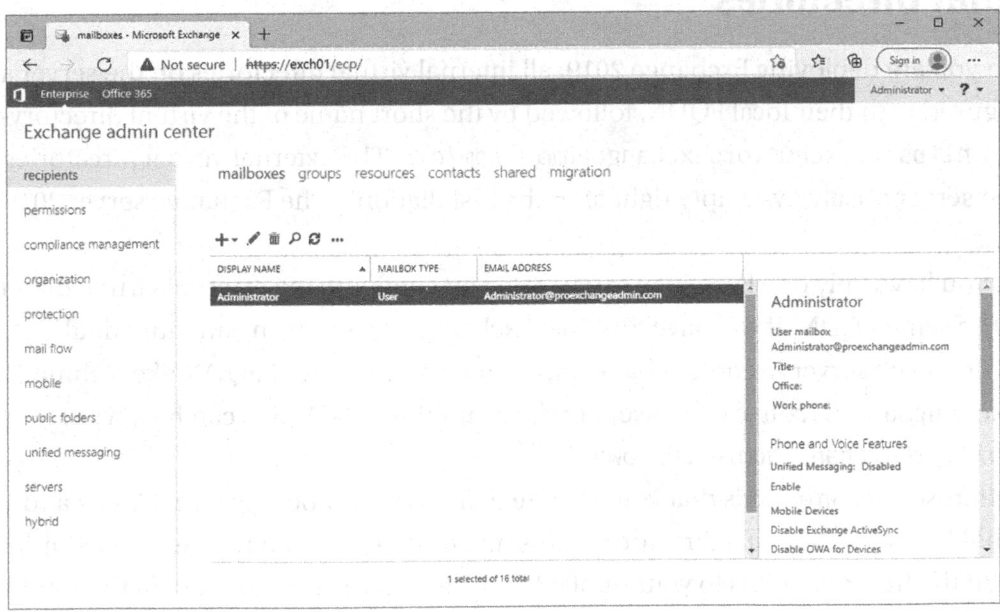

***Figure 2-23.** Exchange Admin Center right after installation*

At this point, we can conclude that the installation of the Exchange server finished successfully, and the configuration of the Exchange server can be started. The following items must be configured to get to a fully operational Exchange server:

- Virtual directories
- SSL certificate
- Send connector
- Accepted domains
- Email address policies
- Mailbox database location (GUI setup, which does not allow changing the location during installation)
- SMTP Queue database location
- IIS log file location (optional)
- Exchange server 2019 product key

Configuring these items will be discussed in the following sections.

Virtual Directories

When you are deploying Exchange 2019, all internal virtual directories on the server are configured with their local FQDN, followed by the short name of the virtual directory—that is, `https://exch01.proexchangeadmin.com/owa`. The external virtual directories on the server are always empty right after the installation of the Exchange server 2019 server.

If you have only one Exchange server, you can configure the external virtual directory with the same FQDN. If you have multiple Exchange servers, using an individual FQDN on each server becomes challenging, and a more general FQDN like webmail.proexchangeadmin.com can be used. In the example of OWA, this can be `https://webmail.proexchangeadmin.com/owa`.

Microsoft recommends that you use one namespace for both external URLs and internal URLs for all virtual directories. This means that webmail.proexchangeadmin.com on the Internet points to your public IP address on the Internet; but at the same time, webmail.proexchangeadmin.com points to the private IP address on the internal network. This is called a "split DNS" configuration.

In Exchange 2019, the following directories need to be configured:

- OWA virtual directory
- ECP virtual directory
- EWS (web services) virtual directory
- ActiveSync virtual directory
- OAB (offline address book) virtual directory
- PowerShell virtual directory
- MapiHttp virtual directory

Table 2-5 lists the values for the InternalURL and ExternalURL properties for all virtual directories in Exchange 2019. For our proexchangeadmin installation, the same URL is used for the internalURL and externalURL properties. The reason for this and background information will be discussed in more detail in Chapter 3.

Table 2-5. *Virtual Directory Settings*

Virtual Directory	InternalURL and ExternalURL
OWA Virtual Directory	`https://webmail.proexchangeadmin.com/owa`
ECP Virtual Directory	`https://webmail.proexchangeadmin.com/ecp`
ActiveSync Virtual Directory	`https://webmail.proexchangeadmin.com/microsoft-Server-ActiveSync`
EWS Virtual Directory	`https://webmail.proexchangeadmin.com/ews/exchange.asmx`
OAB Virtual Directory	`https://webmail.proexchangeadmin.com/oab`
PowerShell Virtual Directory	`https://webmail.proexchangeadmin.com/powershell`
MapiHttp Virtual Directory	`https://webmail.proexchangeadmin.com/mapi`

When you look closely at Table 2-5, you will notice that the Autodiscover virtual directory is not mentioned. This is correct because there is no need to set the internal URL and external URL properties of this virtual directory.

Note Autodiscover functionality is discussed in more detail in Chapter 3.

You can change these virtual directory settings using PowerShell commands like Set-OWAVirtualDirectory, Set-ECPVirtualDirectory, or Set-MAPIVirtualDirectory. I find it easier to combine the Set- commands with the corresponding Get- command.

To configure all virtual directories on an Exchange 2019 server, you can use the following commands:

```
[PS] C:\> Get-OWAVirtualDirectory -Server EXCH01 | Set-OWAVirtualDirectory
-InternalURL https://webmail.proexchangeadmin.com/owa -ExternalURL https://
webmail.proexchangeadmin.com/owa
[PS] C:\> Set-ECPVirtualDirectory -Identity "EXCH01\Ecp (Default Web Site)"
-InternalURL https://webmail.proexchangeadmin.com/ecp -ExternalURL https://
webmail.proexchangeadmin.com/ecp
[PS] C:\> Set-WebServicesVirtualDirectory -Identity "EXCH01\EWS (Default
Web Site)" -InternalURL https://webmail.proexchangeadmin.com/ews/Exchange.
asmx -ExternalURL https://webmail.proexchangeadmin.com/ews/Exchange.asmx
[PS] C:\> Set-ActiveSyncVirtualDirectory -Identity "EXCH01\Microsoft-
Server-ActiveSync (Default Web Site)" -InternalURL https://webmail.
proexchangeadmin.com/Microsoft-Server-ActiveSync -ExternalURL https://
webmail.proexchangeadmin.com/Microsoft-Server-ActiveSync
[PS] C:\> Set-OABVirtualDirectory -Identity "EXCH01\OAB (Default Web Site)"
-InternalURL https://webmail.proexchangeadmin.com/OAB -ExternalURL https://
webmail.proexchangeadmin.com/OAB
[PS] C:\> Set-MapiVirtualDirectory -Identity "EXCH01\Mapi (Default Web
Site)" -InternalURL https://webmail.proexchangeadmin.com/mapi -ExternalURL
https://webmail.proexchangeadmin.com/mapi -IISAuthenticationMethods Ntlm,
OAuth, Negotiate
[PS] C:\> Set-PowerShellVirtualDirectory -Identity "EXCH01\PowerShell
(Default Web Site)" -InternalURL https://webmail.proexchangeadmin.com/
PowerShell -ExternalURL https://webmail.proexchangeadmin.com/PowerShell
```

This is shown in Figure 2-24.

```
Machine: EXCH01.ProExchangeAdmin.com
[PS] C:\>Get-OWAVirtualDirectory -Server EXCH01 | Set-OWAVirtualDirectory -InternalURL https://webmail.proexchangeadmin.
com/owa -ExternalURL https://webmail.proexchangeadmin.com/owa
WARNING: You've changed the InternalURL or ExternalURL for the OWA virtual directory. Please make the same change for
the ECP virtual directory in the same website.
[PS] C:\>Set-OWAVirtualDirectory -Identity "EXCH01\Ecp (Default Web Site)" -InternalURL https://webmail.proexchangeadmin
.com/ecp -ExternalURL https://webmail.proexchangeadmin.com/ecp
[PS] C:\>Set-WebServicesVirtualDirectory -Identity "EXCH01\EWS (Default Web Site)" -InternalURL https://webmail.proexcha
ngeadmin.com/ews/Exchange.asmx -ExternalURL https://webmail.proexchangeadmin.com/ews/Exchange.asmx
[PS] C:\>Set-ActiveSyncVirtualDirectory -Identity "EXCH01\Microsoft-Server-ActiveSync (Default Web Site)" -InternalURL h
ttps://webmail.proexchangeadmin.com/Microsoft-Server-ActiveSync -ExternalURL https://webmail.proexchangeadmin.com/Micros
oft-Server-ActiveSync
[PS] C:\>Set-OABVirtualDirectory -Identity "EXCH01\OAB (Default Web Site)" -InternalURL https://webmail.proexchangeadmin
.com/OAB -ExternalURL https://webmail.proexchangeadmin.com/OAB
[PS] C:\>Set-MapiVirtualDirectory -Identity "EXCH01\Mapi (Default Web Site)" -InternalURL https://webmail.proexchangeadm
in.com/mapi -ExternalURL https://webmail.proexchangeadmin.com/mapi -IISAuthenticationMethods Ntlm, OAuth, Negotiate
[PS] C:\>Set-PowerShellVirtualDirectory -Identity "EXCH01\PowerShell (Default Web Site)" -InternalURL https://webmail.pr
oexchangeadmin.com/PowerShell -ExternalURL https://webmail.proexchangeadmin.com/PowerShell
[PS] C:\>_
```

Figure 2-24. *Setting the Exchange 2019 virtual directories*

You can play around a bit with variables in the commands mentioned earlier. For example, the FQDN of the server is always identical in this example, so it makes sense to use a variable called $FQDN. The server name in this example is also always EXCH01, so you can use a variable called $Server for this as well.

Combined with the other commands, we will get something like

```
[PS] C:\> $FQDN = "webmail.proexchangeadmin.com"
[PS] C:\> $Server = $ENV:ComputerName
[PS] C:\> Get-OWAVirtualDirectory -Server $Server | Set-OWAVirtualDirectory
-InternalURL "https://$FQDN/owa" -ExternalURL "https://$FQDN/owa"
```

Note Instead of executing the individual commands, you can also use a PowerShell script to configure all virtual directories. On the Apress GitHub, you can find such a script called change_vdir_settings.ps1.

MapiHttp is a protocol for Outlook clients that was introduced in Exchange 2013 SP1. For Outlook, you need to use a fully patched Outlook 2010 or higher client. MapiHttp is enabled on an organizational level, so it is turned on or off for the entire environment. To enable MapiHttp for Exchange server 2019, execute the following PowerShell command:

```
[PS] C:\> Set-OrganizationConfig -MapiHttpEnabled $true
```

If you are still running outdated and unsupported clients like Outlook 2007, you must enable Outlook Anywhere by entering the following command in EMS:

```
[PS] C:\> Set-OutlookAnywhere -Identity "EXCH01\Rpc (Default Web Site)"
-ExternalHostname "webmail.proexchangeadmin.com" -ExternalClientsRequireSsl
:$true -ExternalClientAuthenticationMethod:NTLM -InternalHostname "webmail.
proexchangeadmin.com" -InternalClientsRequireSsl:$true -InternalClientAuthe
nticationMethod:NTLM
```

If you do not use Outlook Anywhere, this configuration step can be omitted. When omitted, there is no need to configure Outlook Anywhere in the load balancer that is in front of the Exchange server.

Although not really a virtual directory, the service connection point (SCP) for Autodiscover purposes must be configured at this point as well. The SCP can only be configured using PowerShell; there is no GUI available for this. To configure the SCP, execute the following command in EMS:

```
[PS] C:\> Set-ClientAccessService -identity EXCH01
-AutoDiscoverServiceInternalUri https://autodiscover.proexchangeadmin.com/
autodiscover/autodiscover.xml
```

The configuration of the SCP is shown in Figure 2-25.

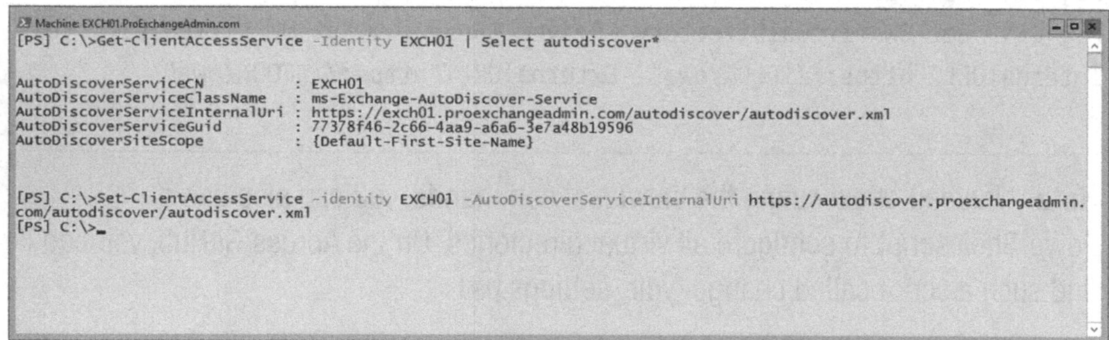

***Figure 2-25.** Configuring the service connection point*

It is also possible to configure the virtual directories in EAC. In EAC, navigate to **Servers ➤ Virtual Directories** and select the server you want to configure in the Select Server drop-down box. Select a virtual directory in the details pane as shown in Figure 2-26 and use the wrench icon to configure it.

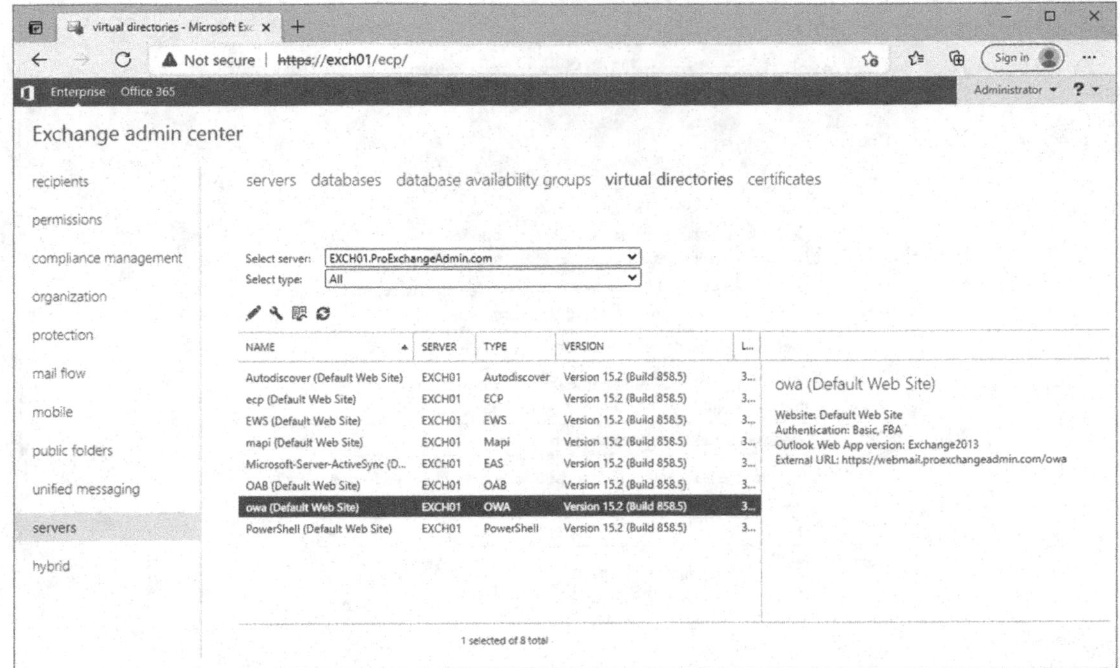

***Figure 2-26.** Virtual directory settings in the Exchange Admin Center*

To configure Outlook Anywhere in EAC, navigate to **Servers ➤ Servers** and select the Exchange server you want to configure Outlook Anywhere for. In the toolbar, click the pencil icon to edit the server's profile. In this navigation pane, select Outlook Anywhere and fill in the details over the internal and external hostname and the authentication method. Click save to store the configuration and close the window. This is shown in Figure 2-27.

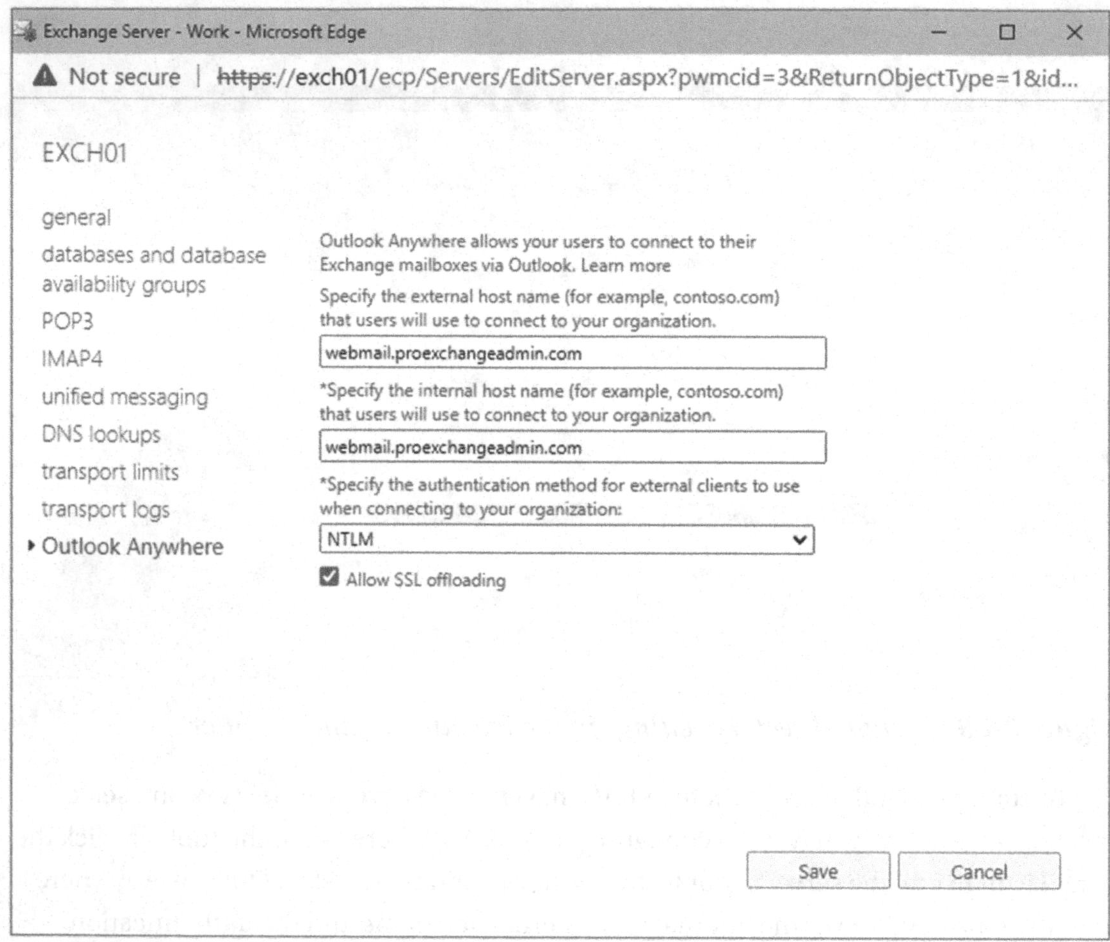

Figure 2-27. Configure Outlook Anywhere in the EAC

Configure an SSL Certificate

By default, a self-signed certificate is installed on each Exchange server during installation, regardless of its version. This self-signed certificate has the NetBIOS name of the server as its common name and the fully qualified domain name (FQDN) of the server configured in the Subject Alternative Name field of the certificate (see Figure 2-28).

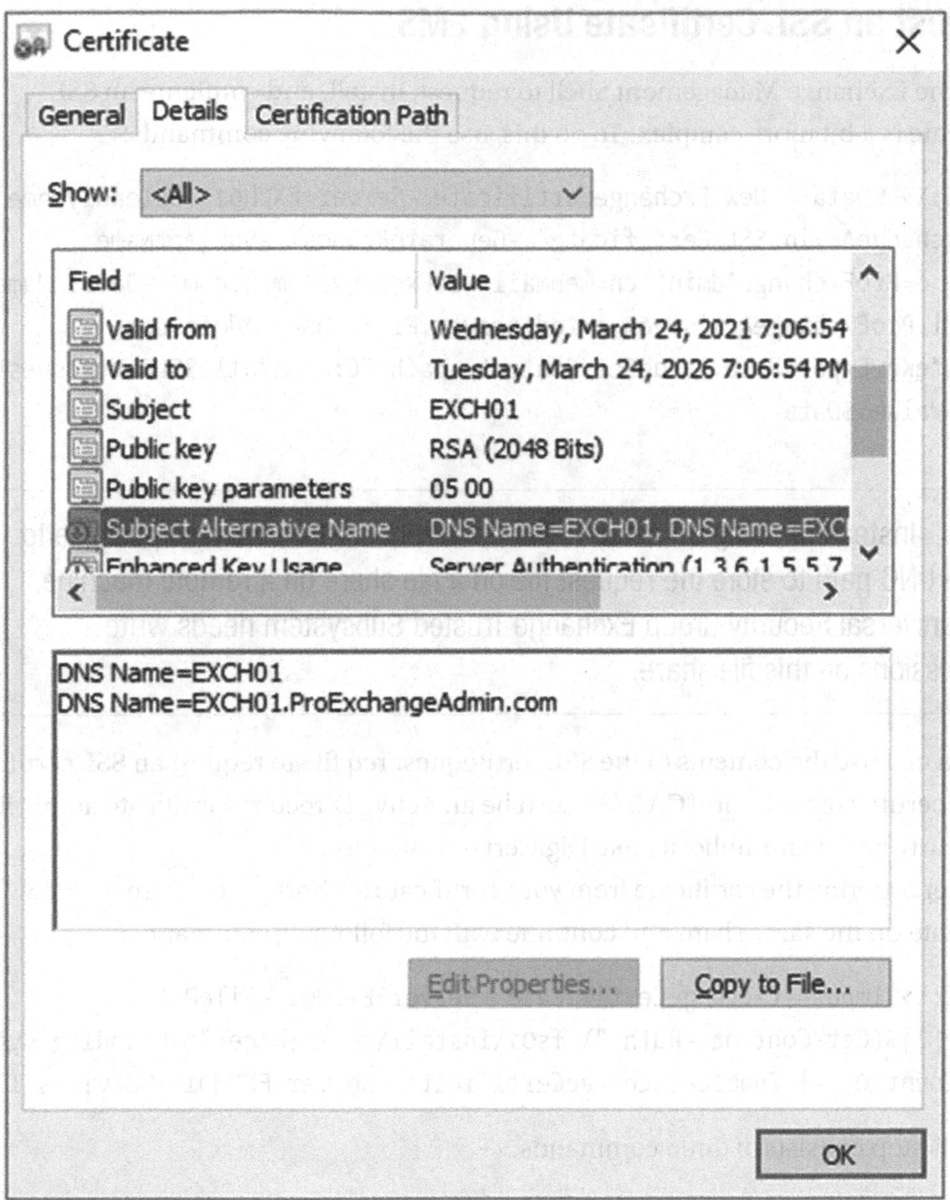

***Figure 2-28.** The hostname and root domain will be included by default as well in the certificate request*

The self-signed certificate works fine for testing OWA and EAC, but should never be used for production purposes. Requesting a valid SSL certificate is the only option.

Request an SSL Certificate Using EMS

Using the Exchange Management Shell to request, install, and configure an SSL certificate is a bit more complex. To do this, use the following commands:

```
[PS] C:\> $Data = New-ExchangeCertificate -Server EXCH01 -FriendlyName
"ProExchangeAdmin SSL Certificate" -GenerateRequest -SubjectName
"c=US, o=ProExchangeAdmin, cn=webmail.ProExchangeAdmin.com" -DomainName
webmail.ProExchangeAdmin.com,autodiscover.ProExchangeAdmin.com
-PrivateKeyExportable $trueSet-Content -path "C:\Install\SSLCertRequest.
req" -Value $Data
```

Note Instead of using C:\Install to store the request file, it is also possible to use a UNC path to store the request file on a file share on a remote machine. The Universal Security Group Exchange Trusted Subsystem needs write permissions on this file share.

You can use the contents of the SSLCertRequest.req file to request an SSL certificate from a certificate authority (CA). This can be an Active Directory certificate authority or a third-party certificate authority like DigiCert or Comodo.

After ordering the certificate from your certificate authority, you store the new certificate on the same share and continue with the following commands:

```
[PS] C:\> Import-ExchangeCertificate -Server EXCH01 -FileData
([Byte[]]$(Get-Content -Path "\\fs01\install\certnew.cer" -Encoding byte
-ReadCount 0)) | Enable-ExchangeCertificate -Server EXCH01 -Services IIS
```

This step consists of three commands:

1. The Import-ExchangeCertificate, which imports the SSL certificate (the .cer file) that was returned from the CA into the local certificate store of the Exchange 2019 server.

2. The Get-Content cmdlet, which reads the certificate file from disk and sends it as byte data to the Import-ExchangeCertificate cmdlet.

3. The Enable-ExchangeCertificate cmdlet, which receives its input from the Import-ExchangeCertificate cmdlet. This cmdlet enables the newly imported SSL certificate to be used with the Internet Information Service.

In this example, only two domain names are used:

- Webmail.proexchangeadmin.com
- Autodiscover.proexchangeadmin.com

For a typical environment, this is sufficient.

Exporting an Existing SSL Certificate

When a new SSL certificate is created and installed on an Exchange server, it is recommended to export the certificate. This export can be stored somewhere safe, but it can also be used to import the certificate on other Exchange servers or on a load balancer, for example.

To export the SSL certificate on the Exchange server, you can use the following command:

```
[PS] C:\> Export-ExchangeCertificate -Thumbprint
3FE6DBADB4336D796E6F27A9D723569BD37F331E -FileName "\\FS01\Install\webmail_
proexchangeadmin_com.pfx" -BinaryEncoded -Password (ConvertTo-SecureString
-String "P@ssw0rd01" -AsPlainText -Force)
```

The thumbprint value can be retrieved using the Get-ExchangeCertificate command. The password that is used for the exported certificate cannot be a plain text password, hence the ConvertTo-SecureString function.

The file webmail_proexchangeadmin_com.pfx in the c:\install directory can be copied to other Exchange servers for import or stored on a safe place for disaster recovery purposes.

Importing an Existing SSL Certificate

When you already have a valid SSL certificate, you can import that on an Exchange server as well. For example, if we want to install the SSL certificate from the Exchange server 2019 server EXCH01 to another Exchange server 2019 server called EXCH02, we can use the following command:

```
[PS] C:\> Import-ExchangeCertificate -Server EXCH02 -FileData
([Byte[]]$(Get-Content -Path "\\FS01\install\webmail_proexchangeadmin_com.
pfx" -Encoding byte -ReadCount 0)) -Password:(Get-Credential).password |
Enable-ExchangeCertificate -Server EXCH01 -Services IIS
```

The -Password:(Get-Credential).password parameter shows a Windows pop-up in which you enter the password while importing the certificate. The output of the Import-ExchangeCertificate command is piped directly to the Enable-ExchangeCertificate command.

Request an SSL Certificate Using EAC

Personally, I prefer to request new SSL certificates using PowerShell, but it is also possible to create this using the EAC although it is a bit more work. Certificate vendors might also provide methods to specify certificate properties.

1. In the EAC, navigate to Servers ➤ Certificates and click the + Icon to start the **new Exchange certificate** wizard.
2. Select the **Create a request for a certificate from a certification authority** radio button and click **Next** to continue.
3. Type a **friendly name** for the certificate, this can be something like **Microsoft Admin Exchange**, and click Next to continue. If a wildcard certificate is needed, check the **Request a wildcard certificate** checkbox; click **Next** to continue.
4. The request should be generated and stored on an Exchange server; use the browse button to select an Exchange server. If this is the first server to be configured, you can only select the server you are logged on to now. Click **Next** to continue.
5. Select the domains you want to be included in the certificate. In a typical environment, this will be something like webmail.contoso.com and Autodiscover.contoso.com. Sometimes, the name of the Exchange server is included as well, but this is not a hard requirement, and it is even a bad practice as it might expose internal server names and FQDNs to the outside world. When the domain names are selected, click **Next** to continue.

6. In the next window, it is possible to configure domain names for all virtual directories. By default, the values of the -InternalURL and -ExternalURL properties of the virtual directories are selected. You can leave this default, or you can change them to anything you want by clicking the pencil icon. Click **Next** to continue.

7. In the wizard, it will now show the domain names that it wants to include, based on the names that were selected in the previous step. It will include the hostname of the Exchange server as shown in Figure 2-29, but this is not supported by any third-party vendor, so this can be removed using the – icon. In a typical environment, the root domain is not needed, so this can be removed as well.

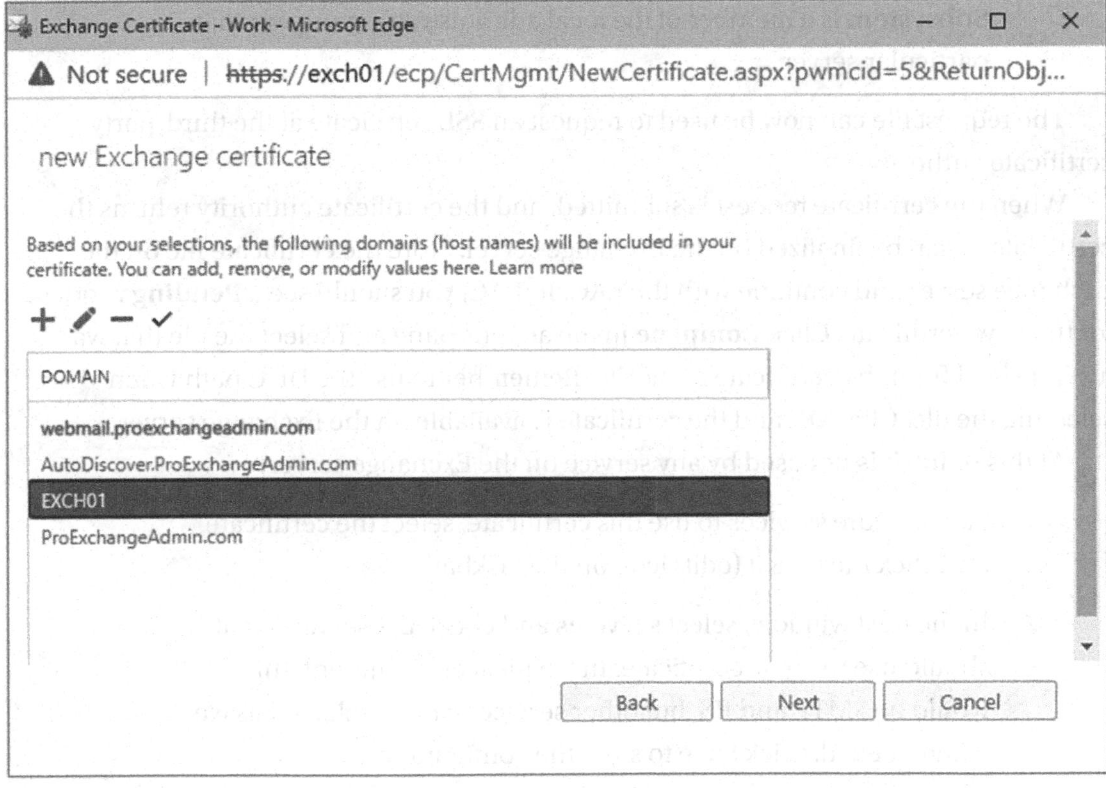

***Figure 2-29.** The hostname and root domain will be included by default as well in the certificate request*

1. When the localhost name and root domain are removed, click **Next** to continue. In the next window, specify the organization details like the organization name, department name, and country. Correct information must be added here since the certificate authority will check the WHOIS information database for this database. If it does not match, the certificate authority will come back with additional questions and an additional proof of ownership.

2. The last step is to store the request file on a server. A UNC name must be used; a name like C:\Install\SSL.req is not accepted, and a name like \\FS01\Install\SSL.req is accepted. It can be any server, as long as the Universal Security Group **Exchange Trusted Subsystem** is a member of the local administrator group on that particular server.

The request file can now be used to request an SSL certificate at the third-party certificate authority.

When the certificate request is submitted, and the certificate authority returns the certificate, it can be finalized on the Exchange server. Store the certificate file on the Exchange server and continue with the EAC. In EAC, you should see a **Pending request** for the new certificate. Click **Complete** in the actions pane and select the file that was just received from the certificate authority. Remember to use the UNC path when selecting the file. Click **OK** and the certificate is available on the Exchange server.

At this point, it is not used by any service on the Exchange server:

1. To configure services to use this certificate, select the certificate and click the pencil (edit) icon on the taskbar.

2. In the next window, select **services** and check the services that should use the new certificate. In a typical environment, this would be SMTP and IIS, but other services can be selected as well when needed. Click **Save** to store the configuration.

3. When a warning pops up regarding the overwrite of the existing default SMTP certificate, click **No**.

Chapter 6 will discuss certificates for SMTP purposes in detail.

Create a Send Connector

Out of the box, Exchange server can receive messages on its Receive Connectors, but it cannot send messages to the external world because no default Send Connectors are created (unless you are deploying in an existing environment, of course).

When creating a new Send Connector, it needs a name, an address space, and a source transport server, that is, which server can use this connector to send email to the outside world. You can use the following PowerShell command to create a new Send Connector:

[PS] C:\> New-SendConnector -Internet -Name "Internet Send Connector" -AddressSpaces "*" -SourceTransportServers "RTD-EXCH01.msexchangebooks.com"

It is also possible to use EAC to create a new Send Connector. To do this, open the EAC and navigate to **mail flow ➤ send connectors**. Click the + icon and follow the wizard to create a new Send Connector:

- Give the Send Connector a name, select the **Internet** radio button, and click **Next.**
- Select the **MX record associated with the recipient domain** radio button and click **Next.**
- Under **address space**, click the + icon and enter * in the **Fully Qualified Domain Name** textbox and click **Save** and then click **Next.**
- The **Source Server** is the server that is participating in the Send Connector; use the + icon to add the newly created Exchange server and click **Finish.**

A new Send Connector that sends mail to the Internet using public MX records is now created.

Receive Connectors

Besides send connectors, Exchange server 2019 also has receive connectors. There are default receive connectors for receiving messages from other SMTP hosts, and there are client receive connectors used so that authenticated clients can send SMTP messages. The latter may sound strange, but the Exchange server 2019 server is receiving messages from the client and, when needed, routes those messages to the Internet.

A default Exchange server 2019 server named EXCH01 has the following receive connectors:

- **Client Frontend EXCH01**—Listening on port 587, this receive connector is used by clients like Mozilla Thunderbird that want to use authenticated SMTP to send email. This port needs users to authenticate to use the service.
- **Client Proxy EXCH01**—Listening on port 465, this connector receives the client's messages from the Client Access services on the Exchange server 2019 server or any other Exchange server 2019 server in the same Active Directory site.
- **Default EXCH01**—Listening on port 2525, this is the SMTP service accepting messages from the Default Frontend Receive Connector on the Exchange server 2019 server or any other Exchange server 2019 server in the same Active Directory site. This connector is not scoped for regular clients to be used.
- **Default Frontend EXCH01**—Listening on port 25, this is the receive connector for regular inbound SMTP messages. Servers that connect to this port can be other SMTP servers, Exchange 2010 Hub Transport services, other Exchange 2013/2016/2019 servers in the organization, or applications or devices that need to submit messages to mailboxes.
- **Outbound Proxy Frontend EXCH01**—This connector accepts messages from the Transport service on the Exchange server and relays the messages to external hosts. This only takes place on Send Connectors that have the front-end proxy option enabled.

These connectors are shown in Figure 2-30.

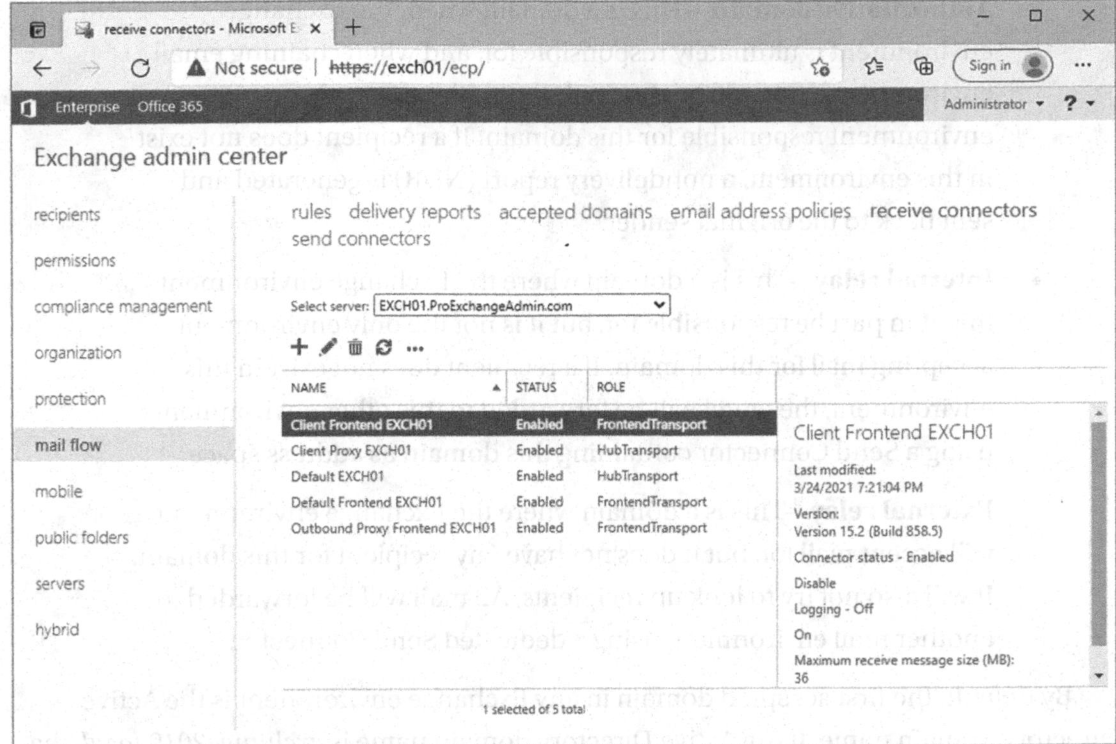

***Figure 2-30.** Default Receive Connectors in Exchange server 2019*

Note At first sight, five different Receive Connectors on one Exchange server 2019 server look strange. In Chapter 6, this is discussed in detail.

When installing Exchange server 2019 out of the box, there is no need to configure anything on the receive connector; it just works. You configure the firewall to forward SMTP to TCP/25 on the Exchange server 2019 server, and you are ready to go.

Accepted Domains

An accepted domain in Exchange server is a domain used for email services which this specific Exchange environment will accept messages for. There are three types of accepted domains:

- **Authoritative domain**—This is a domain where the Exchange environment is ultimately responsible for, and when chaining email environments, this will be the final destination. There is no other mail environment responsible for this domain. If a recipient does not exist in this environment, a nondelivery report (NDR) is generated and sent back to the original sender.
- **Internal relay**—This is a domain where the Exchange environment might in part be responsible for, but it is not the only environment accepting mail for this domain. If a recipient does not exist in this environment, the email will be forwarded to this other environment using a Send Connector containing this domain as address space.
- **External relay**—This is a domain where the Exchange environment will accept mail for, but it does not have any recipient for this domain. It will also not try to look up recipients. All mail will be forwarded to another mail environment using a dedicated Send Connector.

By default, the first accepted domain in any Exchange environment is the Active Directory domain name. If the Active Directory domain name is *exchange2019.local*, the first accepted domain is also *exchange2019.local*. In this book, the Active Directory name is *proexchangeadmin.com* which is automatically the first authoritative accepted domain in the Exchange environment. The Exchange server will accept all mail for this domain, and if a recipient in the @proexchangeadmin.com address space is not found, an NDR is generated.

To create a new authoritative domain in Exchange with address space @proexchange2019.com, execute the following command in PowerShell:

```
[PS] C:\> New-AcceptedDomain -Name "Pro Exchange 2019" -DomainName
ProExchange2019.com -DomainType Authoritative
```

This is shown in Figure 2-31.

```
Machine: EXCH01.ProExchangeAdmin.com
[PS] C:\>New-AcceptedDomain -Name "Pro Exchange 2019" -DomainName ProExchange2019.com -DomainType Authoritative

Name                  DomainName              DomainType          Default
----                  ----------              ----------          -------
Pro Exchange 2019     ProExchange2019.com     Authoritative       False

[PS] C:\>_
```

Figure 2-31. *Create a new Accepted Domain in Exchange server 2019*

Note that for subdomains, you have the option to explicitly specify the subdomain as an accepted domain, or you can set the MatchSubdomains property of the Accepted Domain to $true. The MatchSubDomains option is not available in the `New-AcceptedDomain` command, but must be set using the `Set-AcceptedDomain` command. This is useful in environments where Exchange is responsible for accepting inbound email to hand off to other systems responsible for subdomains, for example, list servers or Unix/Linux systems which might be sending email using their hostname.

You will not be surprised, but it is also possible to create a new Accepted Domain using EAC. This can be achieved by opening the EAC and navigating to **mail flow ➤ accepted domains** and clicking the + icon. Give the new accepted domain a name, enter the domain name, and select one of the radio buttons for the type of accepted domain. Click **Save** to store the information. This is shown in Figure 2-32.

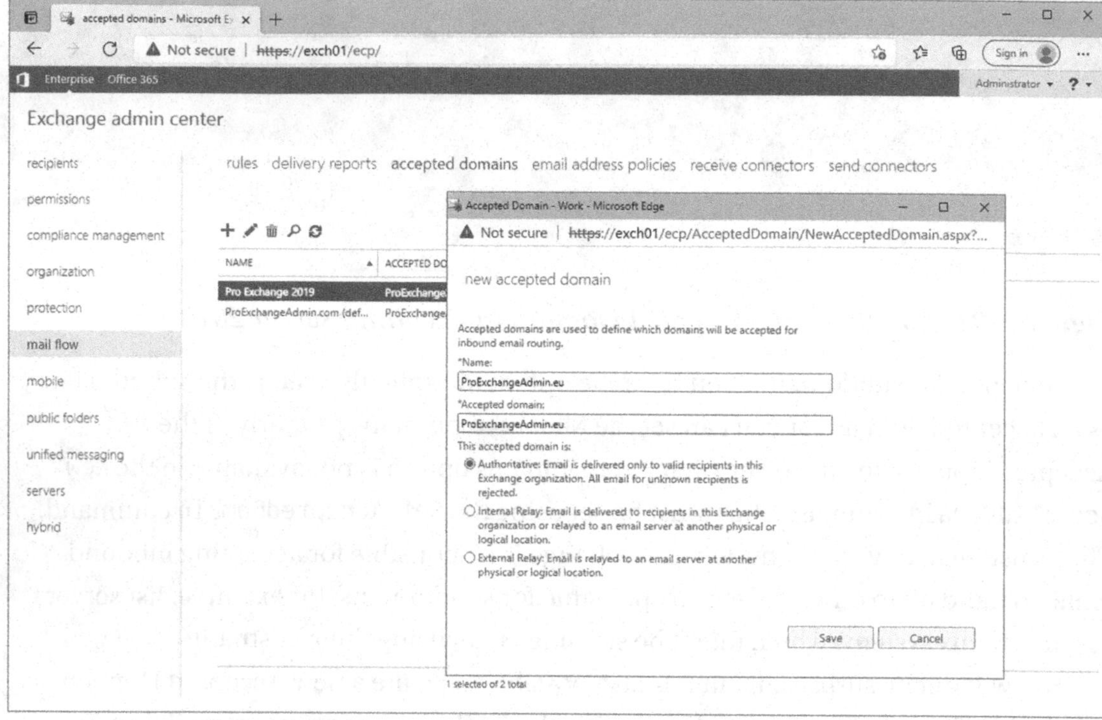

Figure 2-32. *Create a new Accepted Domain in EAC*

Create an Email Address Policy

When an Accepted Domain is created, you can add email addresses manually to recipients. It is much more efficient to assign email addresses automatically. This is what an Email Address Policy does. Email addresses are automatically applied to recipients based on certain criteria, such as the recipient type, a recipient container in Active Directory, or a certain attribute of the recipient. Also, the format of the email address is defined in an Email Address Policy. An email address policy is applied on a recipient when the recipient is created, but an email address policy can also be generally applied. In this case, all recipients that match a filter in the email address policy will have that policy applied.

An email address policy has

- A name.
- An email address format.

- A type of recipient.
- A rule that defines how or where to find the recipients in Active Directory.

In Exchange, there is always a default Email Address Policy which is applied to all recipients in the Exchange organization; this email address policy uses the default accepted domain. An email address policy can only be created with an accepted domain in that Exchange organization.

Multiple Email Address Policies can be created.

To create a new additional Email Address Policy that assigns an email address <alias>@ProExchange2019.com to all recipients that exist in the OU=Users,OU=Accounts in Active Directory, execute the following PowerShell command:

```
[PS] C:\> New-EmailAddressPolicy -Name ProExchange2019 -IncludedRecipients
AllRecipients -RecipientContainer "proexchangeadmin.com/accounts/users"
-EnabledEmailAddressTemplates "SMTP:%m@ProExchange2019.com"
```

This policy stamps an SMTP email address on each user that is within the reach of this policy with a format of %m@ProExchange2019.com, where %m means the user's alias in Exchange. To apply this newly created email address policy, you can use the following command:

```
[PS] C:\> Update-EmailAddressPolicy -Identity ProExchange2019
```

Figure 2-33 shows the process completed successfully.

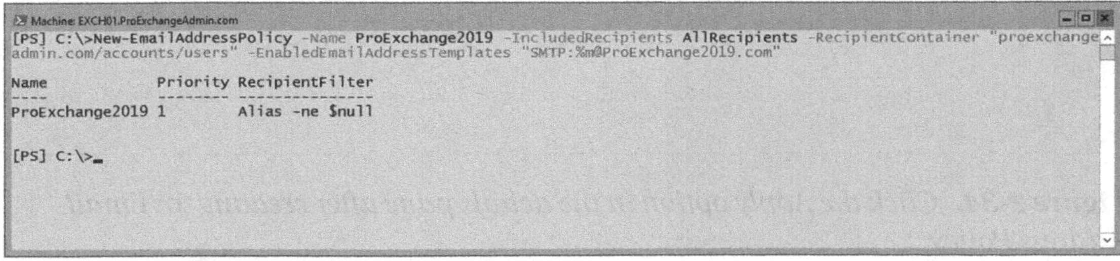

***Figure 2-33.** Creating an email address policy using the Exchange Management Shell*

To create a new email address policy in EAC, navigate to **mail flow ➤ email address policies** and click the + icon to start the new email address policy wizard.

Give the policy a unique and preferably an identifiable name and click the + icon to change the email address format. Here, you can select the accepted domain that needs to be used, and you can select the format of the email address. Click **Save** to store this information and go back to the previous window. Scroll down and select the recipient type that must have this policy applied. Click the **Add a rule** button to create a rule to specify which recipients must have this policy applied.

When you click **Save**, the policy is stored, but it has not been applied yet. In the details pane, click the **Apply** option. This is shown in Figure 2-34.

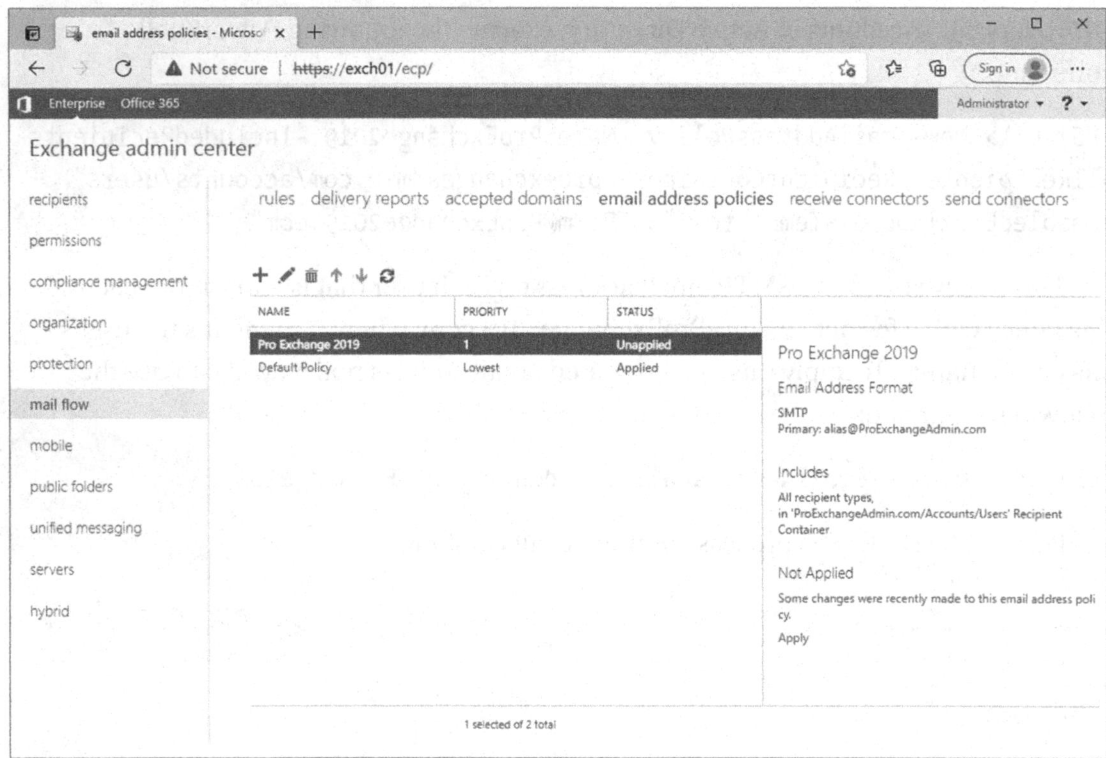

***Figure 2-34.** Click the Apply option in the details pane after creating an Email Address Policy*

By default, there is one email address policy that filters all recipients and assigns the default accepted domain to all these new recipients. To create a new email address policy using the fabrikam.com SMTP domain, for users in the Fabrikam OU under the Accounts organizational unit, you open the Exchange Management Shell and enter the following command:

```
[PS] C:\> New-EmailAddressPolicy -Name Fabrikam -IncludedRecipients
AllRecipients -RecipientContainer "contoso.com/accounts/fabrikam"
-EnabledEmailAddressTemplates "SMTP:%1@fabrikam.com"
```

Relocate the Initial Mailbox Database (GUI Setup Only)

When performing an unattended installation of Exchange server 2019, the initial Mailbox database is defined as an option of the setup application. This includes the name of the Mailbox database, but also the name and location of the Mailbox database file and the transaction log files.

When performing an Exchange server 2019 GUI setup, you cannot configure this during setup. Instead, a new Mailbox database with a random name located in C:\Program Files\Microsoft\Exchange Server\V15\Mailbox\Mailbox Database <number> is created. The name of this initial Mailbox database is "Mailbox Database" followed by a random ten-digit number. This initial Mailbox database is shown in Figure 2-35.

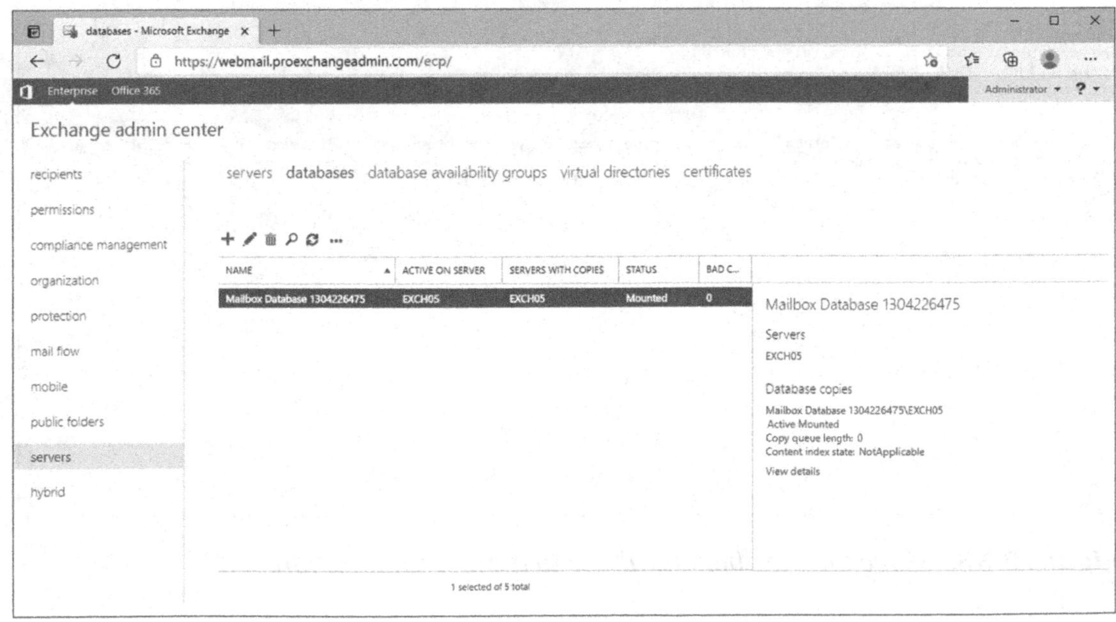

Figure 2-35. *The Mailbox database that was created by the GUI setup*

It is possible to change the name of the default Mailbox database by clicking the pencil icon. Change the name of the Mailbox database, for example, to MDB05 and click Save to store the new name in Active Directory. Besides the name of the Mailbox database, no other properties including the location of the Mailbox database can be changed in EAC. To change the location of the Mailbox database file and change the name of the actual Mailbox database file (the .edb file), you must use the Move-DatabasePath command in PowerShell.

To rename the Mailbox database file and move the files to a different location, execute the following PowerShell command:

```
[PS] C:\> Move-DatabasePath -Identity MDB05 -EdbFilePath C:\ExchDbs\Disk1\
MDB05.edb -LogFolderPath C:\ExchDbs\Disk1\LogFiles
```

When a Mailbox database is renamed or moved to another location, it will automatically be dismounted. When dismounted, users are disconnected, so this must be done outside of business hours. Of course, this is not an issue when an empty (new) Mailbox database is relocated. When executing this command, a warning message is shown on the console about the Mailbox database dismount. This is shown in Figure 2-36.

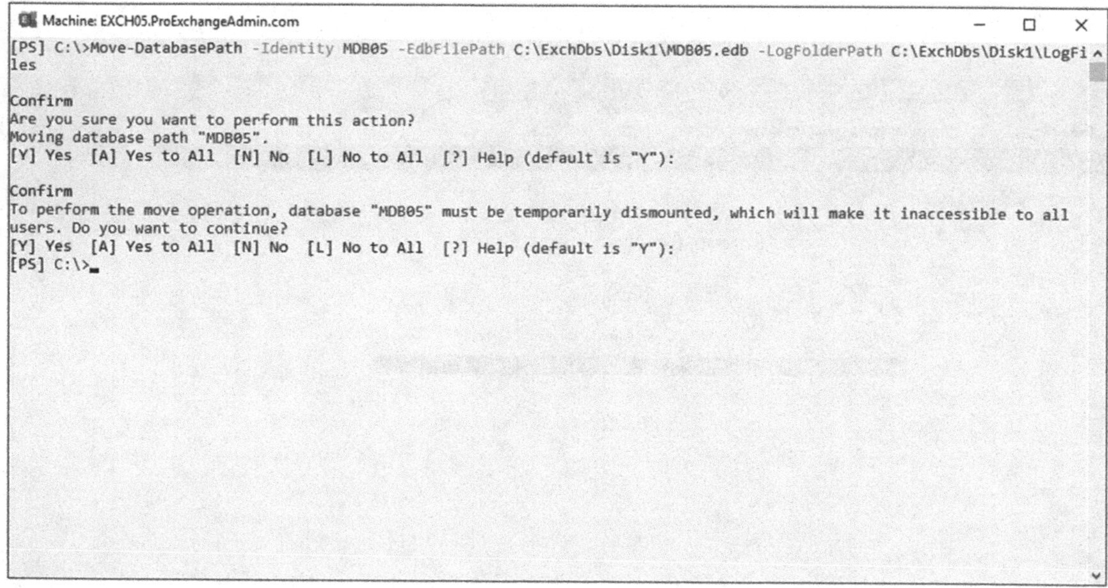

Figure 2-36. *Move the mailbox database to a different location*

Note Exchange Management Shell on Windows 2019 Desktop Experience has a black background instead of a blue background.

Relocate the SMTP Queue Database

SMTP messages that are sent and received by an Exchange server are always queued and stored in a queue database. By default, this queue database is stored on the same disk as where the Exchange server software is installed. Typically, this is the C:\Program Files\Microsoft\Exchange Server\V15\TransportRoles\data\Queue directory.

The queue database is used to temporarily store every message that is stored or received, and it can grow rapidly. You would not be the first administrator that faces an Exchange server that goes offline because of the C:\ drive completely filled up.

The recommendation is to relocate the queue database to another disk, preferably a dedicated disk with sufficient storage. This is not included in the Role Requirements Calculator!

The configuration of the transport service is stored in a configuration file called EdgeTransport.exe.config which is located in the C:\Program Files\Microsoft\Exchange Server\V15\Bin directory of the Exchange server. It is possible to change the settings for the file locations manually, but there is also a PowerShell script available on the Exchange server that takes care of this. The Exchange server scripts directory has an alias $ExScripts. The following example uses a variable called $LogPath to make it a bit more easier to read and use:

```
[PS] C:\> CD $ExScripts
[PS] C:\> $LogPath = "D:\Program Files\Microsoft\Exchange Server\V15\
TransportRoles\data"
[PS] C:\> .\Move-TransportDatabase.ps1 -queueDatabasePath "$LogPath\
Queue" -queueDatabaseLoggingPath "$LogPath\Queue" -iPFilterDatabasePath
"$LogPath\IpFilter" -iPFilterDatabaseLoggingPath "$LogPath\IpFilter"
-temporaryStoragePath "$LogPath\Temp"
```

The script will stop the MSExchangeTransport service, copy the Queue database and accompanying files to the new location, and start the MSExchangeTransport service again. Because of the copy of the Queue database, no messages will be lost during the move.

Note This configuration is not stored in Active Directory. When a new Cumulative Update is installed and a new configuration file is needed, the previous configuration file is overwritten. All changes are lost and need to be reapplied.

Relocate IIS Logfiles

Another component on an Exchange server that is notorious for using lots of disk space is Internet Information Server (IIS), the web server hosting the Exchange client access front-end components. IIS logging takes place on

- **C:\inetpub\logs\LogFiles\W3SVC1**—Here are the client access front-end component logfiles located.
- **C:\inetpub\logs\LogFiles\W3SVC2**—Here are the client access back-end component logfiles located.

All HTTPS client requests of all clients, direct or proxied, are logged. Log files are clear text and take up a tremendous amount of disk space, with 10 GB per logfiles, and multiple log files per day for a heavily loaded Exchange server.

Just with the SMTP Queue database, IIS logging can fill up the default disk, and the Exchange server will come to a halt. I always recommend relocating the IIS log files to another disk. To achieve this, use the following PowerShell commands to locate IIS log files to the D:\ drive:

```
PS C:\> Import-Module WebAdministration
PS C:\> $LogPath = "D:\Inetpub\Logs\LogFiles"
PS C:\> New-Item $LogPath -type directory
PS C:\> ForEach($site in (Dir iis:\sites\*)){Set-ItemProperty IIS:\
Sites\$($site.Name) -name logFile.directory -value "$LogPath"}
```

Restart IIS for these changes to take effect.

Enter a Product Key

When the Exchange server is fully configured, a product key can be installed on the server. Without the product key, the Exchange server is running as an unlicensed server and is limited to only five mounted Mailbox databases. More can be configured, but they cannot be mounted.

```
[PS] C:\> Set-ExchangeServer -Identity EXCH01 -ProductKey xxx-xxx-xxx-xxx-xxx
```

After registering the product key, the Information Store needs to be restarted, but I always reboot the server before bringing the server into production.

At this point, we have a fully configured and operational Exchange 2019 server that can be used by clients to send and receive email, use calendaring, etc.

The next section is about the Exchange server 2019 Edge Transport server.

Install Exchange Server 2019 Edge Transport Server

Most customers do not install their Exchange server directly behind the firewall or do not allow a direct connection from the Internet to their Exchange servers. Instead, they use an SMTP gateway in their (perimeter) network. Email messages are delivered from the Internet (or Microsoft Exchange Online Protection) to the SMTP gateway and then to the Exchange server 2019 servers. This SMTP gateway can be any mail server, but from a Microsoft perspective, this should be an Edge Transport server. Edge Transport servers are also the only supported option to transport email from an Exchange on-premises environment to Exchange Online in Hybrid deployments.

The Edge Transport server was introduced in Exchange server 2007 and still exists in Exchange server 2019. The Edge Transport server does have some anti-spam functionality, but personally I would not rely on this functionality in a production environment but use an anti-spam solution in front of the Edge Transport server, such as Exchange Online Protection.

The next sections are about installing and configuring the Exchange server 2019 Edge Transport server on Windows server 2019. Just like the Exchange server 2019 Mailbox server, Windows server 2019 server core is the recommended operating system. There are minor differences with the Exchange server 2016 Edge Transport server, except that this server is running on Windows Server 2016 (Desktop Experience). The following sections are valid both for Exchange Server 2019 and 2016.

Installing Windows Server 2019

Installing an Exchange 2019 Edge Transport server involves four main steps:

- Prepare the server.
- Install the Edge Transport server role.
- Create an Edge subscription.
- Start Edge synchronization.

These steps are discussed in the following sections.

Prepare the Edge Transport Server

The Exchange server 2019 Edge Transport server can only be installed on Windows Server 2019, and the recommendation is to use Windows server 2019 Server Core, but the Desktop Experience version can be used as well. Please note that the Edge Transport server itself can only be managed using PowerShell; there is no EAC to manage the Edge Transport server.

The Edge Transport server is not a member of the internal Active Directory forest as it is typically installed in the perimeter network. It can be a member of a perimeter network Active Directory for management purposes.

The Edge Transport server needs an FQDN, and this FQDN must be configured before installing the Edge Transport server role. If the FQDN is changed after installing the Edge Transport role, the Exchange server will break beyond repair and needs to be rebuild.

When using Windows Server 2019 Server Core, the server can be configured using the SCONFIG tool, including the server name. The DNS suffix however cannot be configured using SCONFIG and needs to be set in the registry of the server. Execute the following PowerShell command to set the correct DNS suffix of the Edge Transport server:

```
PS C:\> Set-ItemProperty -Path HKLM:\SYSTEM\CurrentControlSet\Services\
Tcpip\Parameters -Name 'NV Domain' -Value "proexchangeadmin.com"
```

Reboot the server for the change to take effect.

Note Do not forget to add an additional disk for the SMTP Queue database.

When it comes to server features, only the Active Directory Lightweight Directory Server (ADLDS) needs to be installed. ADLDS is an LDAP server and is used to store specific information that the Edge Transport server needs for sending and receiving messages.

To install ADLDS, execute the following PowerShell command:

```
PS C:\> Install-WindowsFeature ADLDS, Telnet-Client
```

This is shown in Figure 2-37.

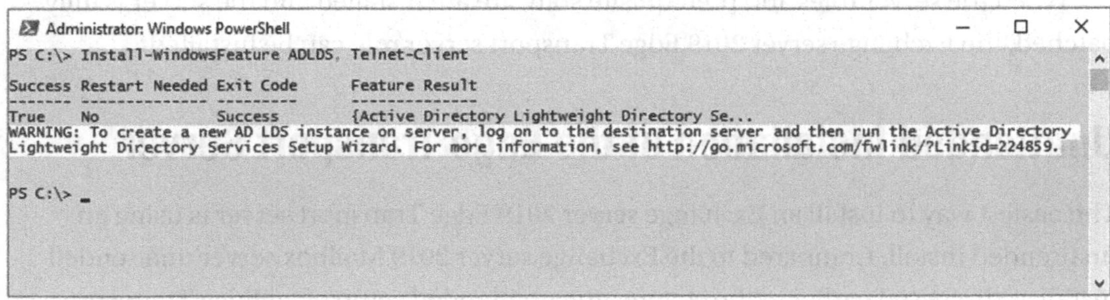

***Figure 2-37.** Installing the Windows server features*

The following prerequisite software needs to be installed on the Edge Transport server role as well:

- .NET Framework 4.8
- Visual C++ Redistributable Package for Visual Studio 2012

Use the following PowerShell commands to download the software:

```
PS C:\> New-Item C:\Install -ItemType Directory
# .NET Framework 4.8
PS C:\> Start-BitsTransfer -Source "https://download.visualstudio.
microsoft.com/download/pr/7afca223-55d2-470a-8edc-6a1739ae3252/
abd170b4b0ec15ad0222a809b761a036/ndp48-x86-x64-allos-enu.exe" -Destination
C:\Install
```

```
# Visual C++ Redistributable package for Visual Studio 2012
PS C:\> Start-BitsTransfer -Source "https://download.microsoft.com/
download/1/6/B/16B06F60-3B20-4FF2-B699-5E9B7962F9AE/VSU_4/vcredist_x64.exe"
-Destination C:\Install
```

And use the following PowerShell commands to install the prerequisite software unattended:

```
PS C:\> Start-Process -FilePath "C:\Install\ndp48-x86-x64-allos-enu.exe"
-ArgumentList "/q" -Wait
PS C:\> Start-Process -FilePath "C:\Install\vcredist_x64.exe" -ArgumentList
"/q" -Wait
```

When the server roles and prerequisite software are installed and the server is fully patched, the Exchange server 2019 Edge Transport server role can be installed.

Unattended Installation of the Edge Transport Server

The easiest way to install an Exchange server 2019 Edge Transport server is using an unattended install. Compared to the Exchange server 2019 Mailbox server unattended install as discussed earlier in the chapter, the unattended setup of an Edge Transport server only accepts one option, the /Mode option which can take the value “install,” “remove,” or “upgrade.”

To install an Exchange server 2019 Edge Transport server in unattended mode, start a command prompt with elevated privileges, navigate to the installation media, and execute the following command:

```
Z:\> Setup.exe /mode:install /Roles:EdgeTransport /
IAcceptExchangeServerLicenseTerms
```

This is shown in Figure 2-38.

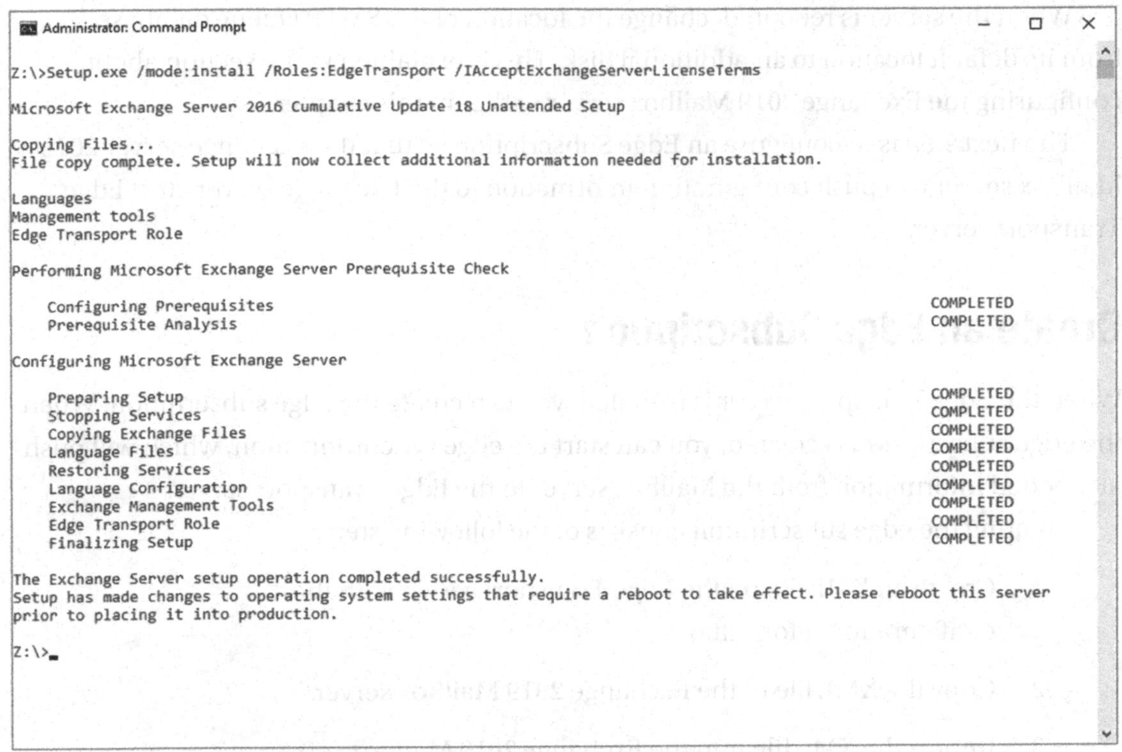
Administrator: Command Prompt
Z:\>Setup.exe /mode:install /Roles:EdgeTransport /IAcceptExchangeServerLicenseTerms
Microsoft Exchange Server 2016 Cumulative Update 18 Unattended Setup
Copying Files...
File copy complete. Setup will now collect additional information needed for installation.
Languages
Management tools
Edge Transport Role
Performing Microsoft Exchange Server Prerequisite Check
Configuring Prerequisites COMPLETED
Prerequisite Analysis COMPLETED
Configuring Microsoft Exchange Server
Preparing Setup COMPLETED
Stopping Services COMPLETED
Copying Exchange Files COMPLETED
Language Files COMPLETED
Restoring Services COMPLETED
Language Configuration COMPLETED
Exchange Management Tools COMPLETED
Edge Transport Role COMPLETED
Finalizing Setup COMPLETED
The Exchange Server setup operation completed successfully.
Setup has made changes to operating system settings that require a reboot to take effect. Please reboot this server prior to placing it into production.
Z:\>_

***Figure 2-38.** An unattended install of the Edge Transport server role*

Tip You can add the /DoNotStartTransport switch when installing the Edge Transport server. This will prevent the server from accepting messages from outside and allow configuration first. Another option is to disable the Transport Service directly after setup. This will always prevent the service from starting, regarding any other setting.

When the installation has finished, reboot the server.

Note Make sure that the Edge Transport server can resolve the Exchange server 2019 Mailbox servers on the internal network. This can be achieved by using DNS on the internal network (depending on your preferred server configuration, of course) or by using a HOSTS file where the FQDN and the IP addresses of the internal Exchange 2019 Mailbox servers are entered.

When the server is rebooted, change the location of the SMTP Queue database from its default location to an additional disk. This is explained in the section about configuring the Exchange 2019 Mailbox server earlier in this chapter.

The next step is to configure an Edge Subscription so that the Exchange server 2019 Mailbox server can push configuration information to the Exchange server 2019 Edge Transport server.

Create an Edge Subscription

When the Edge Transport server is installed, you can create the edge subscription. When the edge subscription is created, you can start the edge synchronization, which will push all needed information from the Mailbox server to the Edge Transport server.

Creating the edge subscription consists of the following steps:

1. Create an XML file on the Edge Transport server with the configuration information.
2. Copy the XML file to the Exchange 2019 Mailbox server.
3. Import the XML file into the Exchange 2019 Mailbox server.
4. Start the edge synchronization.

To create the configuration XML file on the Exchange server 2019 Edge Transport server, execute the following PowerShell command on the Edge Transport server:

```
[PS] C:\> New-EdgeSubscription -FileName C:\Install\Edge01.xml
```

This will create an XML file with all information from the Edge Transport server that is needed by the Exchange server 2019 Mailbox server. Copy the XML file to the Exchange 2019 Mailbox server, and on the Mailbox server, you execute the following PowerShell command:

```
[PS] C:\> [byte[]]$FileData = Get-Content -Path C:\Install\edge01.xml
-Encoding Byte -ReadCount 0
[PS] C:\> New-EdgeSubscription -FileData $FileData -Encoding Byte
-Site Default-First-Site-Name -CreateInternetSendConnector $true
-CreateInboundSendConnector $true
```

This will begin the Edge Subscription. Please note the –Site parameter that defines which Active Directory site the Edge Transport server will be bound to.

In my experience, it can take up to ten minutes before the Edge Subscription is fully active on the internal Exchange organization.

So, after ten minutes or so, execute the following PowerShell command on the Exchange server 2019 Mailbox server:

```
[PS] C:\> Start-EdgeSynchronization
```

As mentioned before, for synchronization to work properly you must make sure that the Exchange server 2019 Mailbox server can resolve the Exchange server 2019 Edge Transport server using DNS; this typically involves adding the Edge Transport server to the DNS on your internal network.

Another pitfall is a firewall between the Exchange server 2019 Mailbox server and the Exchange server 2019 Edge Transport server. The Edge Synchronization (EdgeSync) is using port 50636 (outbound) by default to push information to the Edge Transport server, so you must make sure that this port is open on the firewall to the perimeter network. This EdgeSync process runs on every Exchange server in the Active Directory site associated with the Edge Transport server. Needless to say, in addition to port 50636, port 25 should also be open between all Edge Transport servers and all the Hub Transport servers in the Active Directory site those Edge Transport servers are subscribed to. Of course, port 25 should be open inbound and outbound.

Note If for some reason you need to alter the default port used for EdgeSync, you can use the ConfigureAdam.ps1 script provided with Exchange. Modify the port on the Edge Transport server before you create the Edge Subscription.

When the name resolution and the firewall are properly configured, the edge synchronization should start immediately, as shown in Figure 2-39.

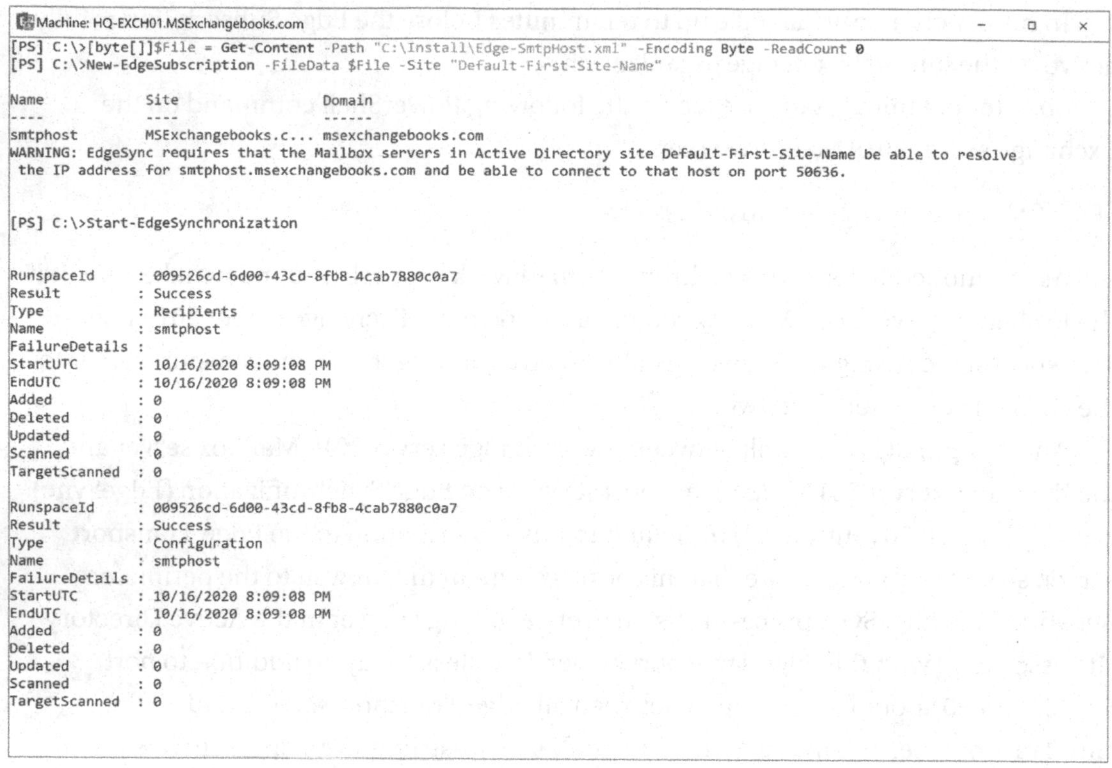

Machine: HQ-EXCH01.MSExchangebooks.com
[PS] C:\>[byte[]]$File = Get-Content -Path "C:\Install\Edge-SmtpHost.xml" -Encoding Byte -ReadCount 0
[PS] C:\>New-EdgeSubscription -FileData $File -Site "Default-First-Site-Name"
Name Site Domain
---- ---- ------
smtphost MSExchangebooks.c... msexchangebooks.com
WARNING: EdgeSync requires that the Mailbox servers in Active Directory site Default-First-Site-Name be able to resolve the IP address for smtphost.msexchangebooks.com and be able to connect to that host on port 50636.
[PS] C:\>Start-EdgeSynchronization
RunspaceId : 009526cd-6d00-43cd-8fb8-4cab7880c0a7
Result : Success
Type : Recipients
Name : smtphost
FailureDetails :
StartUTC : 10/16/2020 8:09:08 PM
EndUTC : 10/16/2020 8:09:08 PM
Added : 0
Deleted : 0
Updated : 0
Scanned : 0
TargetScanned : 0
RunspaceId : 009526cd-6d00-43cd-8fb8-4cab7880c0a7
Result : Success
Type : Configuration
Name : smtphost
FailureDetails :
StartUTC : 10/16/2020 8:09:08 PM
EndUTC : 10/16/2020 8:09:08 PM
Added : 0
Deleted : 0
Updated : 0
Scanned : 0
TargetScanned : 0

Figure 2-39. *Starting the Edge Synchronization successfully*

That is all it takes to install the Exchange 2019 Edge Transport server, create an Edge Subscription, and start the Edge Synchronization. All relevant settings configured on the internal Exchange server 2019 organization for proper functioning of the mail flow are synchronized at this point, including the accepted domains, connector information, and recipient information.

If you want to make changes to certain settings on the Edge Transport server, you must make these on the Exchange server 2019 Mailbox server. For example, if you want to enable logging on to the send connector of the Exchange server 2019 Edge Transport server, you must issue the command on the Exchange 2019 Mailbox server. To enable protocol logging, for example, you open the Exchange Management Shell on the Exchange server 2019 Mailbox server and enter the following command:

```
[PS] C:\> Get-SendConnector <outbound connector> | Set-SendConnector -
ProtocolLoggingLevel Verbose
```

To change the FQDN of the Edge Transport server when an EHLO command is sent from another host to another FQDN, you can execute the following command, again on the Exchange 2019 Mailbox server:

```
[PS] C:\> Get-ReceiveConnector <Name> | Set-ReceiveConnector -Fqdn
smtphost.contoso.nl
```

When it comes to making changes to the Exchange server 2019 Edge Transport server, you always must be conscious of where you are making those changes. Changes related to message flow have to be made on the Exchange server 2019 Mailbox server, but server-specific settings can be made on the Exchange server 2019 Edge Transport server itself.

Note Like the Exchange server 2019 Mailbox server, the Exchange server 2019 Edge Transport server is also configured with a self-signed certificate. This certificate is used for setting up an encrypted connection with other mail servers using TLS 1.2. This works fine for regular SMTP traffic, but there are situations where a regular third-party SSL certificate must be used. Be careful though, this self-signed certificate is also used for authentication in the Edge Subscription. This is discussed in Chapter 6.

Exchange Server 2019 Patch Management

Every administrator knows they must patch their servers, and this is of course not different for an Exchange server 2019 server. Windows server 2019 is patched using Windows Update, WSUS, or maybe even SCCM. For the Exchange server, it is a bit different. Updates are released on a regular basis and called Cumulative Updates (CUs). CUs are not released through Windows Update but are only available as a separate download.

Sometimes, an interim update is released for Exchange with security fixes, but only in case of a critical vulnerability. These updates are called Security Updates (SUs) and are released on an ad hoc basis. In contrast to CUs, SUs are released through Windows Update (and thus WSUS) but are also available as a manual download.

CUs and SUs are discussed in the following sections.

Cumulative Updates

Microsoft releases Cumulative Updates for Exchange server versions that are in standard support every three months. When a version of Exchange server is in extended support, Cumulative Updates are no longer released, but only Security Updates when updates are marked as critical.

Note Exchange server 2016 went into extended support in October 2020, so CUs were planned to stop by then. Microsoft made the decision to release two additional CUs for Exchange server 2016. CU20 was released in March 2021, and before the summer of 2021, CU21 will be released as well. This will only contain fixes for issues that were raised in 2020 but not yet released.

As the name implies, Cumulative Updates contain the current updates, but also all previously released updates. As such, every Cumulative Update is a full version of Exchange server and can be used for a new or recovery installation of Exchange server as well.

A Cumulative Update supports an in-place upgrade of Exchange server, but only for that version of Exchange. It is not possible to perform an in-place upgrade of Exchange server 2016 to Exchange server 2019.

Note Microsoft announced during Ignite in 2020 that the next version of Exchange server (vNext) is going to support in-place upgrades from Exchange 2019, for a period of approximately two years following release of vNext.

Exchange server 2019 is a .NET application, and there are different .NET dependencies, based on the version of the Cumulative Update. If you are running on the latest CU of Exchange server, you are safe and you will not encounter difficulties when upgrading to a new Cumulative Update. If you are running a Cumulative Update that's years behind, for example, when running Exchange 2016 CU11, you will run into .NET difficulties when upgrading to CU18. Exchange 2016 CU11 is running on .NET Framework 4.7.2 which is not supported on Exchange 2018 CU18, which runs on .NET Framework 4.8.

At the same time, .NET Framework 4.8 is not supported on Exchange 2016 CU11, so you must upgrade to Exchange 2016 CU14 first, then upgrade to .NET Framework 4.8 followed by an upgrade to Exchange 2016 CU18.

Fellow MVP Michel de Rooij wrote an interesting blogpost about Exchange server CU upgrades and .NET dependencies. You can find this blogpost on `https://eightwone.com/2017/12/21/upgrade-paths-for-cus-net/`.

As explained earlier in this chapter, you must prepare Active Directory before installing an Exchange server. Some Cumulative Updates for Exchange server come with Schema changes and configuration changes. It does not happen that often anymore, but especially when upgrading from a very old Cumulative Update, there is a chance the Schema or Configuration partition must be upgraded. Details on version numbers can be found in Tables 2-3 and 2-4 earlier in this chapter.

When needed, you can prepare the Active Directory using the following commands:

```
Z:\> Setup.exe /PrepareSchema /IAcceptExchangeServerLicenseTerms
Z:\> Setup.exe /PrepareAD /IAcceptExchangeServerLicenseTerms
Z:\> Setup.exe /PrepareDomain /IAcceptExchangeServerLicenseTerms
```

In earlier versions of Exchange server, it was important to install Exchange server and updates in the following order:

- Internet-facing sites first
- Followed by non-Internet-facing sites
- Edge Transport server last

Although Exchange server versions are getting more and more compatible with each other, the preceding list is still the recommended approach.

Installing the Cumulative Update on an Exchange server is straightforward. Use the setup application with the /Mode:Upgrade switch:

```
Z:\> Setup.exe /Mode:Upgrade /IAcceptExchangeServerLicenseTerms
```

This is shown in Figure 2-40.

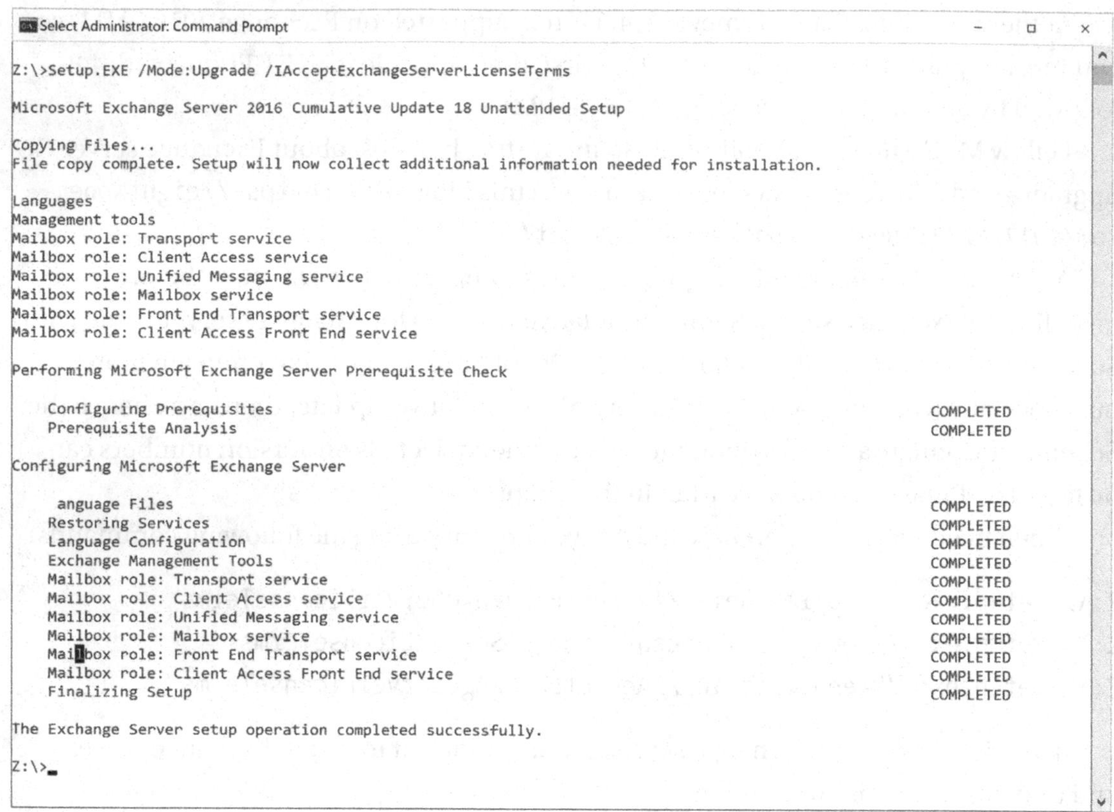
Select Administrator: Command Prompt
Z:\>Setup.EXE /Mode:Upgrade /IAcceptExchangeServerLicenseTerms
Microsoft Exchange Server 2016 Cumulative Update 18 Unattended Setup
Copying Files...
File copy complete. Setup will now collect additional information needed for installation.
Languages
Management tools
Mailbox role: Transport service
Mailbox role: Client Access service
Mailbox role: Unified Messaging service
Mailbox role: Mailbox service
Mailbox role: Front End Transport service
Mailbox role: Client Access Front End service
Performing Microsoft Exchange Server Prerequisite Check
Configuring Prerequisites COMPLETED
Prerequisite Analysis COMPLETED
Configuring Microsoft Exchange Server
anguage Files COMPLETED
Restoring Services COMPLETED
Language Configuration COMPLETED
Exchange Management Tools COMPLETED
Mailbox role: Transport service COMPLETED
Mailbox role: Client Access service COMPLETED
Mailbox role: Unified Messaging service COMPLETED
Mailbox role: Mailbox service COMPLETED
Mailbox role: Front End Transport service COMPLETED
Mailbox role: Client Access Front End service COMPLETED
Finalizing Setup COMPLETED
The Exchange Server setup operation completed successfully.
Z:\>

Figure 2-40. *Upgrading Exchange 2016 to a newer Cumulative Update*

Upgrading a single Exchange server with the latest Cumulative Update is straightforward; installing a Cumulative Update on a member of a Database Availability Group (DAG) involves a bit more work. In a DAG, the workload is distributed dynamically, and you do not want any changes in workload during an upgrade to a newer Cumulative Update. To prevent this, members in a DAG need to be in maintenance mode during the installation of a Cumulative Update so a failover to an updated DAG member will not occur. Also, SMTP processing is suspended when in maintenance mode, so no activity will take place.

To place an Exchange server 2019 Mailbox server in a DAG, the following Exchange PowerShell commands can be used:

```
[PS] C:\> $Computer = $ENV:ComputerName
[PS] C:\> Set-ServerComponentState $Computer -Component HubTransport -State
Draining -Requester Maintenance
[PS] C:\> Redirect-Message -Server $Computer -Target <other Exchange
Server> -Confirm:$False
 # Prevent DAG member becoming PAM
[PS] C:\> Suspend-ClusterNode $Computer
 # Move all Mailbox Databases and prevent hosting copies on current server
[PS] C:\> Set-MailboxServer $Computer
-DatabaseCopyActivationDisabledAndMoveNow $True
[PS] C:\> Set-MailboxServer $Computer -DatabaseCopyAutoActivationPolicy
Blocked

# Put the Exchange server in Maintenance Mode:
[PS] C:\> Set-ServerComponentState $Computer -Component ServerWideOffline
-State Inactive -Requester Maintenance
```

To check if a server is in suspended mode the following Exchange PowerShell command can be used:

```
[PS] C:\> Get-ServerComponentState $Computer | ft Component,State -Autosize
```

This is shown in Figure 2-41.

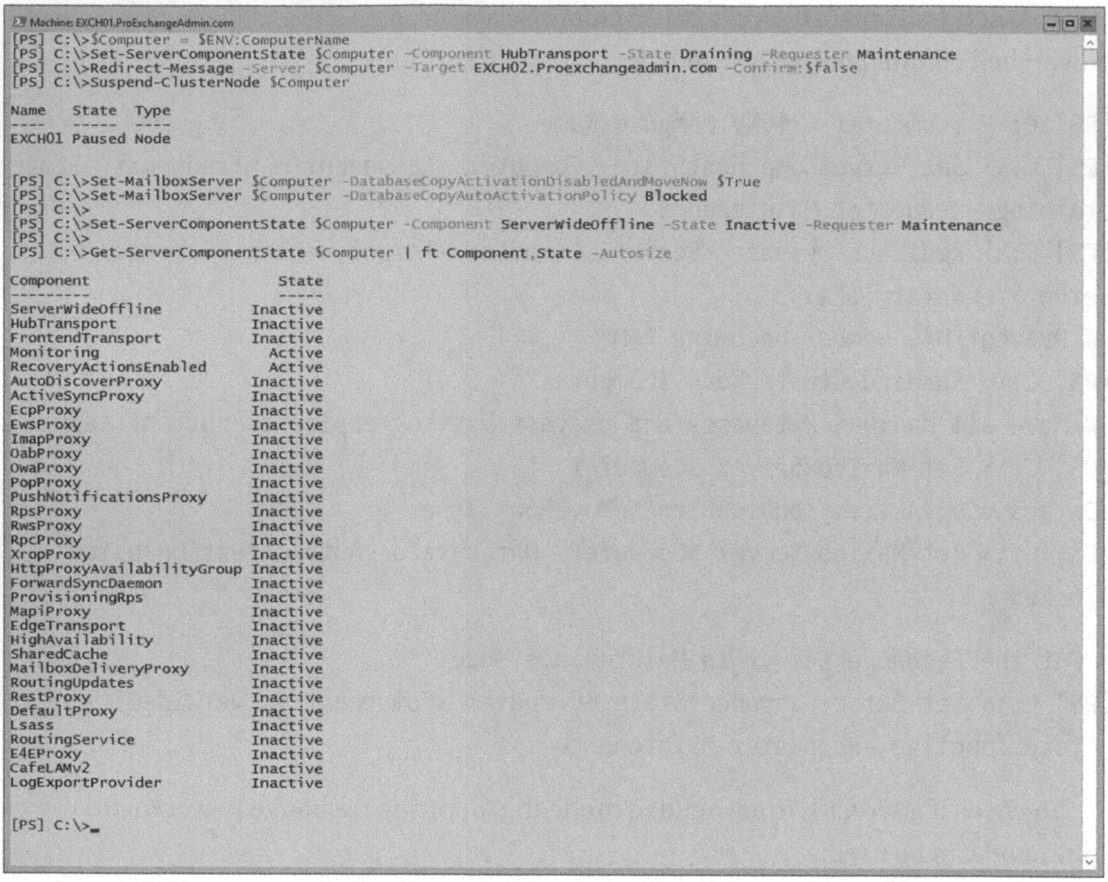

```
Machine: EXCH01.ProExchangeAdmin.com
[PS] C:\>$Computer = $ENV:ComputerName
[PS] C:\>Set-ServerComponentState $Computer -Component HubTransport -State Draining -Requester Maintenance
[PS] C:\>Redirect-Message -Server $Computer -Target EXCH02.Proexchangeadmin.com -Confirm:$false
[PS] C:\>Suspend-ClusterNode $Computer

Name   State  Type
----   -----  ----
EXCH01 Paused Node


[PS] C:\>Set-MailboxServer $Computer -DatabaseCopyActivationDisabledAndMoveNow $True
[PS] C:\>Set-MailboxServer $Computer -DatabaseCopyAutoActivationPolicy Blocked
[PS] C:\>
[PS] C:\>Set-ServerComponentState $Computer -Component ServerWideOffline -State Inactive -Requester Maintenance
[PS] C:\>
[PS] C:\>Get-ServerComponentState $Computer | ft Component,State -Autosize

Component                         State
---------                         -----
ServerWideOffline              Inactive
HubTransport                   Inactive
FrontendTransport              Inactive
Monitoring                       Active
RecoveryActionsEnabled           Active
AutoDiscoverProxy              Inactive
ActiveSyncProxy                Inactive
EcpProxy                       Inactive
EwsProxy                       Inactive
ImapProxy                      Inactive
OabProxy                       Inactive
OwaProxy                       Inactive
PopProxy                       Inactive
PushNotificationsProxy         Inactive
RpsProxy                       Inactive
RwsProxy                       Inactive
RpcProxy                       Inactive
XropProxy                      Inactive
HttpProxyAvailabilityGroup     Inactive
ForwardSyncDaemon              Inactive
ProvisioningRps                Inactive
MapiProxy                      Inactive
EdgeTransport                  Inactive
HighAvailability               Inactive
SharedCache                    Inactive
MailboxDeliveryProxy           Inactive
RoutingUpdates                 Inactive
RestProxy                      Inactive
DefaultProxy                   Inactive
Lsass                          Inactive
RoutingService                 Inactive
E4EProxy                       Inactive
CafeLAMv2                      Inactive
LogExportProvider              Inactive


[PS] C:\>_
```

***Figure 2-41.** Checking a DAG member for maintenance mode*

When the DAG members are in maintenance mode, the Cumulative Update can be installed. This is for a DAG member not different than for a single Exchange server.

After installation and reboot, the DAG members can be resumed using the following Exchange PowerShell commands:

```
[PS] C:\> $Computer = $ENV:ComputerName
[PS] C:\> Set-ServerComponentState $Computer -Component ServerWideOffline
-State Active -Requester Maintenance
[PS] C:\> Resume-ClusterNode $Computer
[PS] C:\> Set-MailboxServer $Computer
-DatabaseCopyActivationDisabledAndMoveNow $False
[PS] C:\> Set-MailboxServer $Computer -DatabaseCopyAutoActivationPolicy
Unrestricted
```

```
[PS] C:\> Set-ServerComponentState $Computer -Component HubTransport -State
Active -Requester Maintenance
[PS] C:\> Restart-Service MSExchangeTransport
[PS] C:\> Restart-Service MSExchangeFrontEndTransport
```

To verify if all Exchange components are available again, the following Exchange PowerShell command can be used:

```
[PS] C:\> Get-ServerComponentState $Computer | ft Component,State -Autosize
```

This is shown in Figure 2-42.

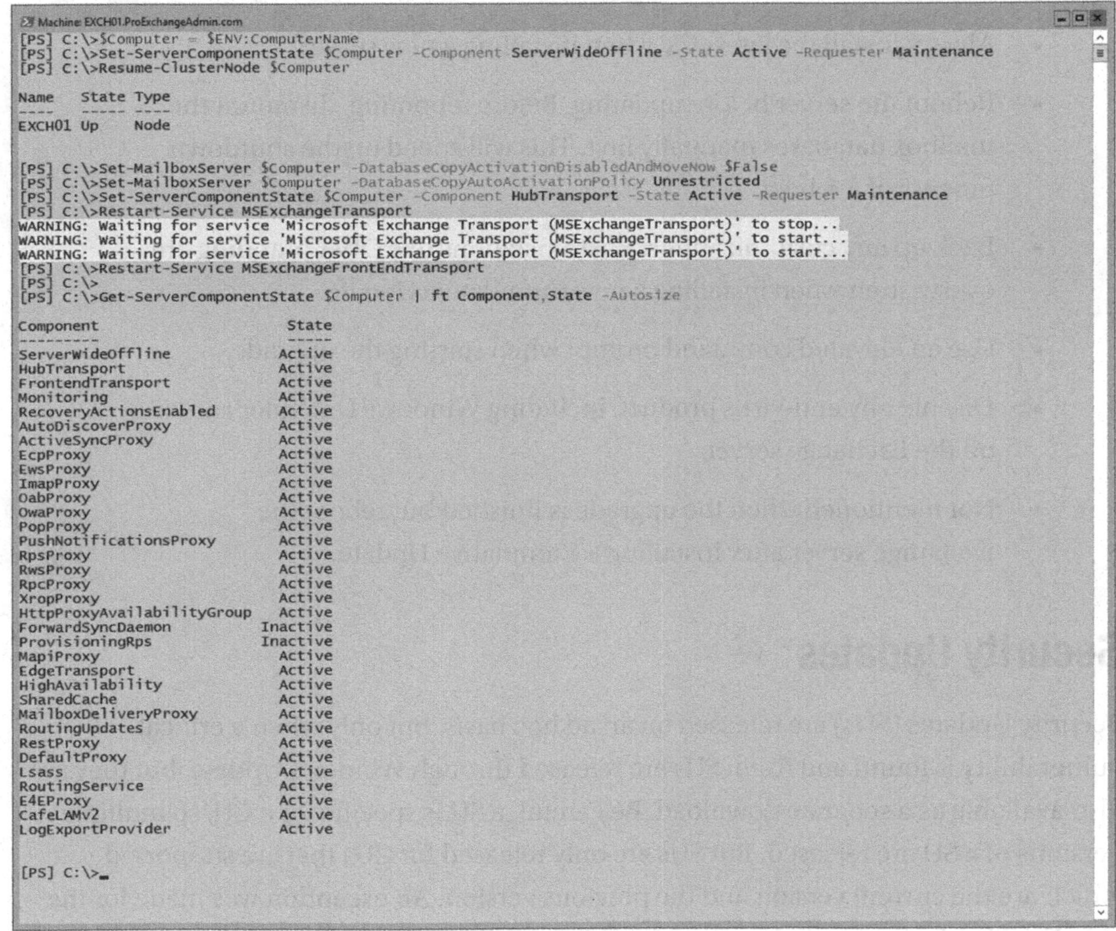

***Figure 2-42.** Checking if all components are available again*

When installing Exchange Cumulative Updates, the following tips or best practices can be used:

- Test a new CU before bringing in production. This sounds logical, but there are a lot of customers still installing a new CU in their production environment without testing. Especially when using third-party solutions like backup and anti-virus, it is recommended to deploy in test first.
- Keep the Exchange servers up to date. Running the last or one last Cumulative Update is not a problem, but try to avoid running a Cumulative Version that is eight versions old.
- Always install the latest CU when installing a new server.
- Reboot the server before updating. Before rebooting, dismount the mailbox databases manually first. This will speed up the shutdown process of a reboot.
- Back up any customizations! Customizations like OWA branding are overwritten when installing a new Cumulative Update.
- Use an elevated command prompt when starting the upgrade.
- Disable any anti-virus product, including Windows Defender running on the Exchange server.
- Not mentioned when the upgrade is finished but reboot the Exchange server after installing a Cumulative Update.

Security Updates

Security Updates (SUs) are released on an ad hoc basis, but only when a critical vulnerability is found and fixed. SUs are released through Windows Update, but they are also available as a separate download. Be careful, a SU is specific for a CU, so multiple versions of a SU are released. But SUs are only released for CUs that are supported which are the current version and the previous version. An exception was made for the HAFNIUM vulnerability in March 2021. This was such a critical issuc that Microsoft released this SU for older CUs of both Exchange server 2019 and Exchange server 2016, and even unsupported Exchange versions 2013 and 2010 received security updates.

When installing a SU, make sure it is started with elevated privileges ("Run As Administrator"). The only way to achieve this is to start a command prompt with elevated privileges, and from there start the SU. This is shown in Figure 2-43.

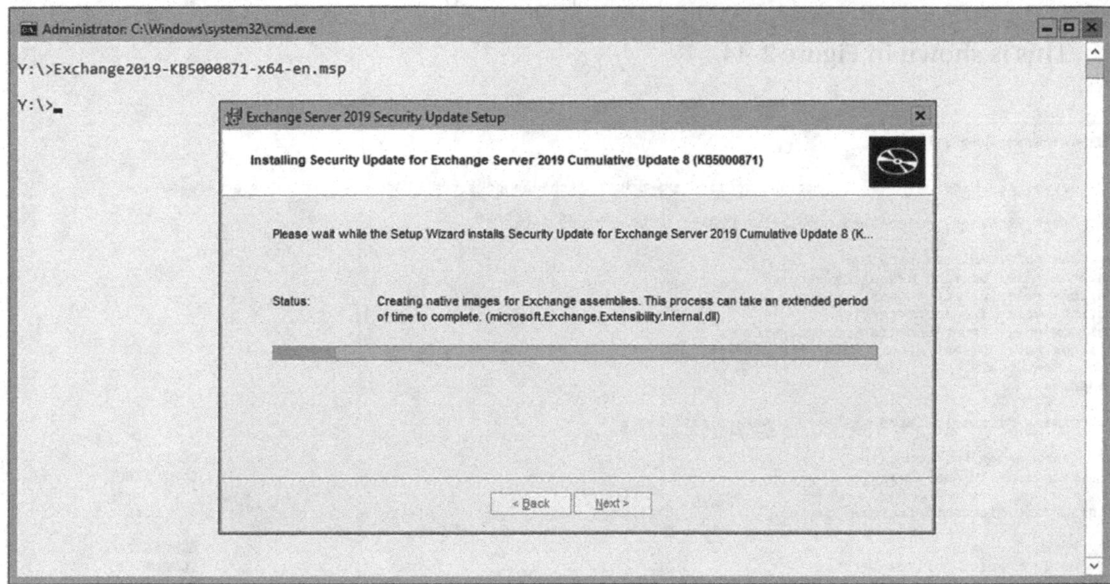

Figure 2-43. *Installing a security update on Exchange Server 2019 CU8*

Note When installing a Security Update via Windows Update or WSUS, the installation of the update is automatically started with elevated privileges.

Uninstalling Exchange Server 2019

Sometimes, it is necessary to remove an Exchange server from the network. Just removing a virtual machine is never a good idea. Since the Exchange server is registered in Active Directory, other Exchange servers still "see" the removed Exchange server and try to access it.

Before an Exchange server can be uninstalled, all resources need to be removed from that server. So, remove it from the DAG (when configured in a DAG), move any mailboxes to other Exchange servers, remove mailbox databases, and remove the Exchange server from any Send Connectors that are configured in the Exchange organization.

The proper way to remove an Exchange server is to uninstall it the official way. Again, the easiest way to remove an Exchange server is to use the unattended setup with the /Mode:Uninstall option, like this:

```
Z:\> Setup.exe /Mode:Uninstall /IAcceptExchangeServerLicenseTerms
```

This is shown in Figure 2-44.

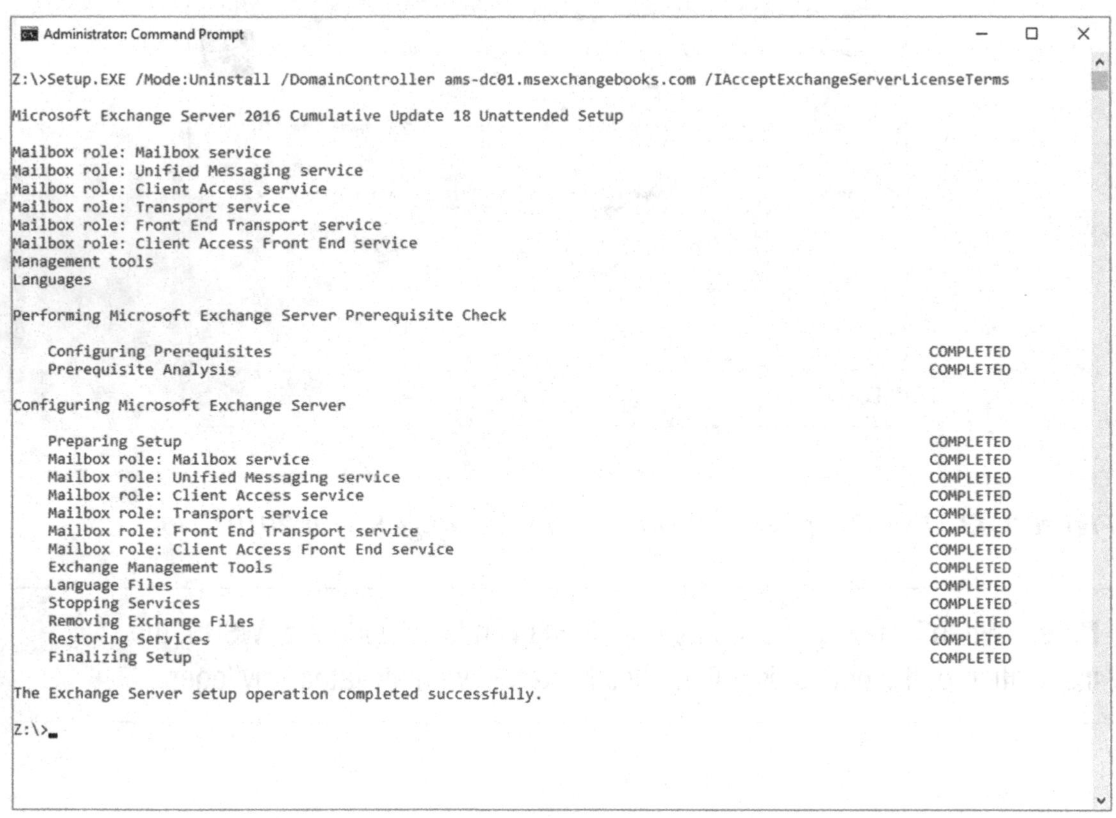
Administrator: Command Prompt
Z:\>Setup.EXE /Mode:Uninstall /DomainController ams-dc01.msexchangebooks.com /IAcceptExchangeServerLicenseTerms
Microsoft Exchange Server 2016 Cumulative Update 18 Unattended Setup
Mailbox role: Mailbox service
Mailbox role: Unified Messaging service
Mailbox role: Client Access service
Mailbox role: Transport service
Mailbox role: Front End Transport service
Mailbox role: Client Access Front End service
Management tools
Languages
Performing Microsoft Exchange Server Prerequisite Check
Configuring Prerequisites COMPLETED
Prerequisite Analysis COMPLETED
Configuring Microsoft Exchange Server
Preparing Setup COMPLETED
Mailbox role: Mailbox service COMPLETED
Mailbox role: Unified Messaging service COMPLETED
Mailbox role: Client Access service COMPLETED
Mailbox role: Transport service COMPLETED
Mailbox role: Front End Transport service COMPLETED
Mailbox role: Client Access Front End service COMPLETED
Exchange Management Tools COMPLETED
Language Files COMPLETED
Stopping Services COMPLETED
Removing Exchange Files COMPLETED
Restoring Services COMPLETED
Finalizing Setup COMPLETED
The Exchange Server setup operation completed successfully.
Z:\>

Figure 2-44. *Removing an Exchange server*

This will remove the Exchange 2019 software from the server, and it will remove all Exchange information regarding this server from Active Directory. This is the only supported way to remove an Exchange server.

Summary

Installing Exchange 2019 is not that difficult, and the process does not differ much from previous versions of Exchange Server. Install Windows, configure the storage, install the prerequisite software and server roles and features, and install Exchange server 2019.

My personal preference is to use an unattended setup. This way, there is no interaction via the console, and you get a consistent deployment when installing multiple Exchange servers. Other than that, it is a great method for using installation scripts.

Before installing Exchange server 2019, you need to make a proper design. To do this, you can use the Exchange 2019 Server Role Requirements Calculator, which can be found on the Exchange server 2019 ISO image. For Exchange server 2016, it can be downloaded from the Microsoft website.

Based on the input requirements, the calculator determines the best configuration for your Exchange servers. This configuration might look like serious overkill, but when you assign fewer resources to your Exchange 2019 server, especially memory, you risk serious performance issues.

After installing and configuring an Exchange server 2019 Mailbox server, you can continue with installing an Exchange server 2019 Edge Transport server which is optional or start working on your message hygiene (Chapter 6) and start migrating resources (Chapters 7 and 8).

Cumulative Updates for Exchange server that are in standard support are released on a quarterly basis. At the time of writing, that was only true for Exchange server 2016. For Exchange server 2013 and 2016 no Cumulative Updates are released anymore. Ad hoc updates for critical vulnerabilities are called Security Updates, and these are specific for a Cumulative Update. Only the current and the previous CU are supported, so typically only Security Updates are released for these versions. At all times, Security Updates need to be installed with elevated privileges. If not, installation will fail.

The next two chapters will discuss the Exchange server 2019 Mailbox server. Chapter 3 will focus on clients accessing the Mailbox server, and Chapter 4 will focus on the mailbox databases, mailboxes, and recipients.

Summary

CHAPTER 3

Exchange Client Access Services

Starting in Exchange server 2016, the Client Access Server role and Mailbox Server role were no longer individual server roles but were combined into one role, the Exchange server 2016 Mailbox server. This is the same in Exchange server 2019; there is only the Exchange server 2019 Mailbox server role.

In Exchange server 2013, the Microsoft recommendation was to combine the Client Access and Mailbox server roles into a multi-role server. This is exactly what the Exchange server 2016 and 2019 Mailbox server is. As such, the Exchange server Mailbox server role consists of client access services and mailbox services. Notice the difference between "server" and "services" in this naming. It can also be seen as "front-end" and "back-end" services, something that is also visible in the names of various services. In this chapter, I will talk about Exchange server 2019 client access services; in the next chapter, I will talk about the Exchange server 2019 Mailbox services. Although one server role, these topics are divided into two chapters to prevent one massive chapter. All topics that are discussed apply to Exchange server 2019, unless otherwise noted.

Note There is also the Exchange server 2016 and 2019 Edge Transport server role, but these are discussed in Chapter 6.

In this chapter, I will cover the following client access topics:

- Client Access services
- Virtual directories
- Namespaces

M. de Rooij and J. Wesselius, *Pro Exchange 2019 and 2016 Administration*,
https://doi.org/10.1007/978-1-4842-7331-9_3

- SSL certificates
- Clients
- Autodiscover
- Client access high availability

Maybe you are expecting a section like clients earlier in this chapter. I have chosen to discuss sections like namespaces, virtual directories, and SSL certificates first because they all are a major component of all clients.

Client Access Services

The Client Access services on an Exchange server 2019 server consist of the following roles or services:

- Client Access Front End (CAFE), which is used to authenticate client requests and proxy connections to the correct Mailbox service.
- Front-End Transport Service (FETS), which is used to accept inbound SMTP messages from other SMTP hosts. FETS can also be used to route outbound messages to other SMTP hosts, but this is optional.

Exchange server 2016 has a third front-end component, the Unified Messaging Call Router (UMCR). This is used by the SIP protocol to redirect inbound voice messages to the correct Exchange server 2016 mailbox service.

A client connects via a load balancer to a load-balanced array of Exchange servers. From the load balancer, the client connects to the Client Access Front-End service, and after authentication the client request is proxied to the mailbox service hosting the user's mailbox. This can be the same server, but it can also be another mailbox server hosting the user's mailbox. This is shown in Figure 3-1, where a client connects to CAFE on server EXCH01, but the Mailbox is on server EXCH02.

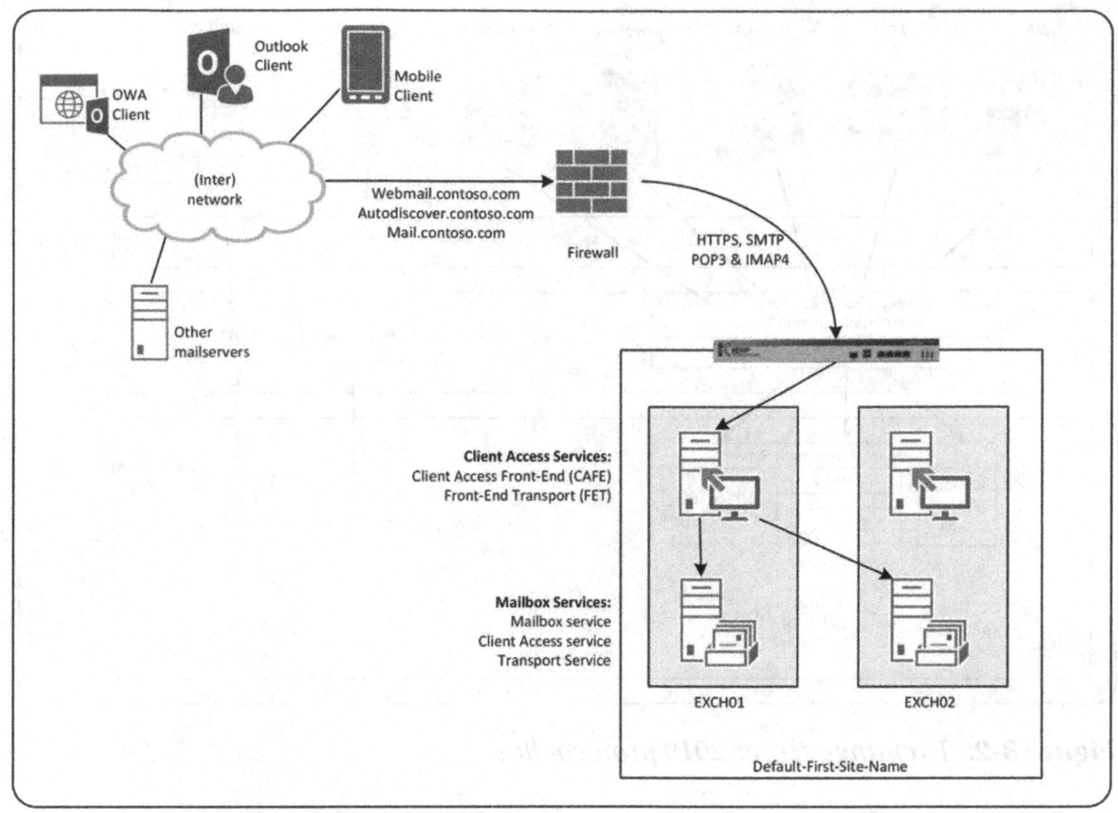

***Figure 3-1.** Exchange server 2019 services*

When looking a bit closer, the client connects to CAFE which in turn uses Internet Information Server. After authentication, the request is proxied to the Client Access service in the back end where the user's mailbox is hosted, which is also running on Internet Information Server. This can be the same Exchange server, but it can also be another Exchange server.

POP3 and IMAP4 have their own services running on both CAFE and the Mailbox server. Again, after authentication the POP3 or IMAP4 service determines where the user's mailbox is hosted and proxies the request to this Mailbox server.

SMTP works similar. When an email is sent to the Exchange server, the Front-End Transport service (FETS) accepts the connection. It determines which server hosts the Mailbox and proxies the SMTP connection to the transport services running on this server for delivery to the mailbox. The protocol flow is shown in Figure 3-2.

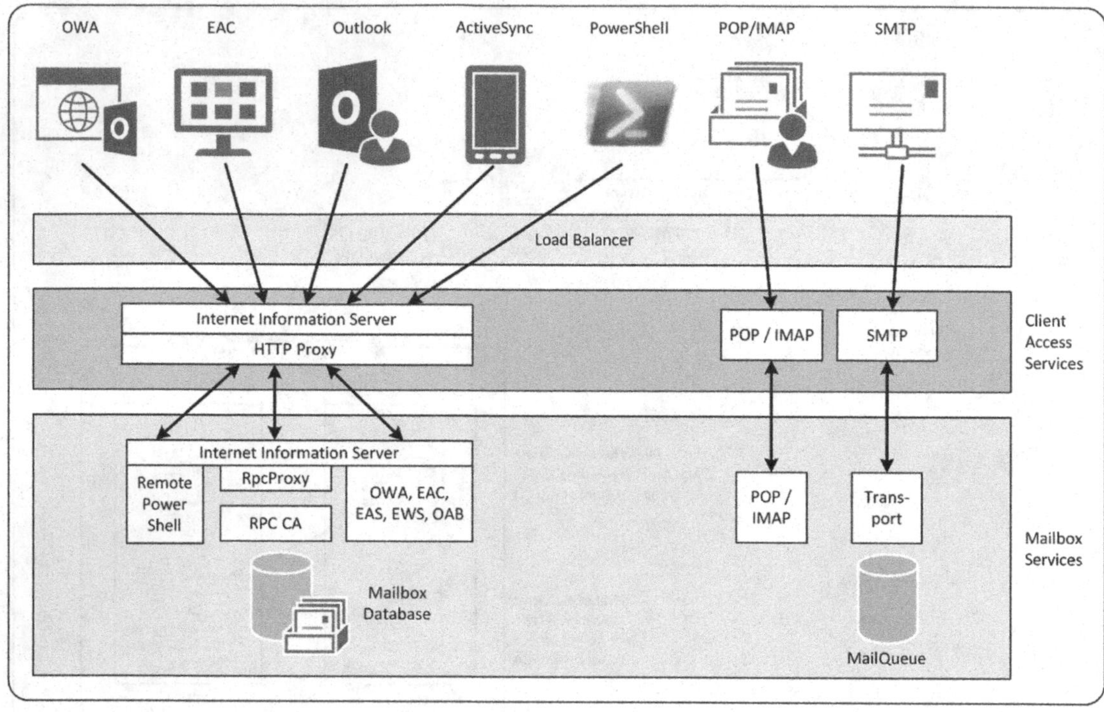

***Figure 3-2.** Exchange server 2019 protocol flow*

To prevent conflicts on an Exchange server, CAFE and the Client Access service have their own application in Internet Information Server, each using their own port. CAFE is using the default port 443, but the Client Access service is using port 444.

POP3 clients connect using port 110 (unencrypted) or port 995 (encrypted) to the CAFE. After authentication, the request is proxied to the Mailbox server hosting the mailbox. The POP3 service here is using port 1995. For IMAP4, ports 143 (unencrypted) and 995 (encrypted) are used at CAFE; the mailbox server is using port 1995 for IMAP4.

For SMTP, multiple ports are used. The default front-end connector as part of FETS is listening on port 25. This is the port where all SMTP hosts connect to, and this is anonymous access. This is regular SMTP traffic from the Internet or internal SMTP hosts that need to deliver SMTP messages to mailboxes. For simplicity, I skip the message hygiene part here as this is covered in Chapter 6. FETS determines the mailbox server hosting the user's mailbox and forwards the message to the Transport Service running on the Mailbox server. This Transport service is using port 2525 for connections from FETS or from an Exchange Transport server when used.

Authenticated SMTP is using port 587; this is used by mail clients like Mozilla Thunderbird or applications that do not or cannot submit SMTP messages anonymously. After authentication, the submitted SMTP message follows the regular path for either mailbox delivery or to the Internet.

A "strange" port used by SMTP is port 717 by the FETS. This port is used for outbound SMTP traffic from a Send Connector that is configured to use an outbound front-end proxy which is delivered by FETS.

Table 3-1 lists all ports used by the Client Access Front-End services and the Mailbox services. This table is valid for Exchange server 2019, Exchange server 2016, but also for Exchange server 2013.

Table 3-1. *Used Ports by the Client Access Front-End and Mailbox Services*

Protocol	Client Access Front End	Client Access Back End
IIS	443	444
POP3	110/995	1995
IMAP4	143/993	1993
SMTP	25	2525
Authenticated SMTP	587	465
Outbound SMTP proxy	717	n/a

Note An Exchange server is a domain-joined server in the corporate forest, and because of this, it is automatically located on the internal network. An Exchange server located in the perimeter network as a port of the internal organization is not supported. For an Exchange administrator, this may look strange, but I see this question frequently after a penetration test (pentest) is performed by a security department. One of their recommendations is often to place a server in the perimeter network.

Virtual Directories

So, all services on an Exchange server have front-end and back-end components. For IIS, this is clearly visible when opening IIS Manager on an Exchange server as shown in Figure 3-3.

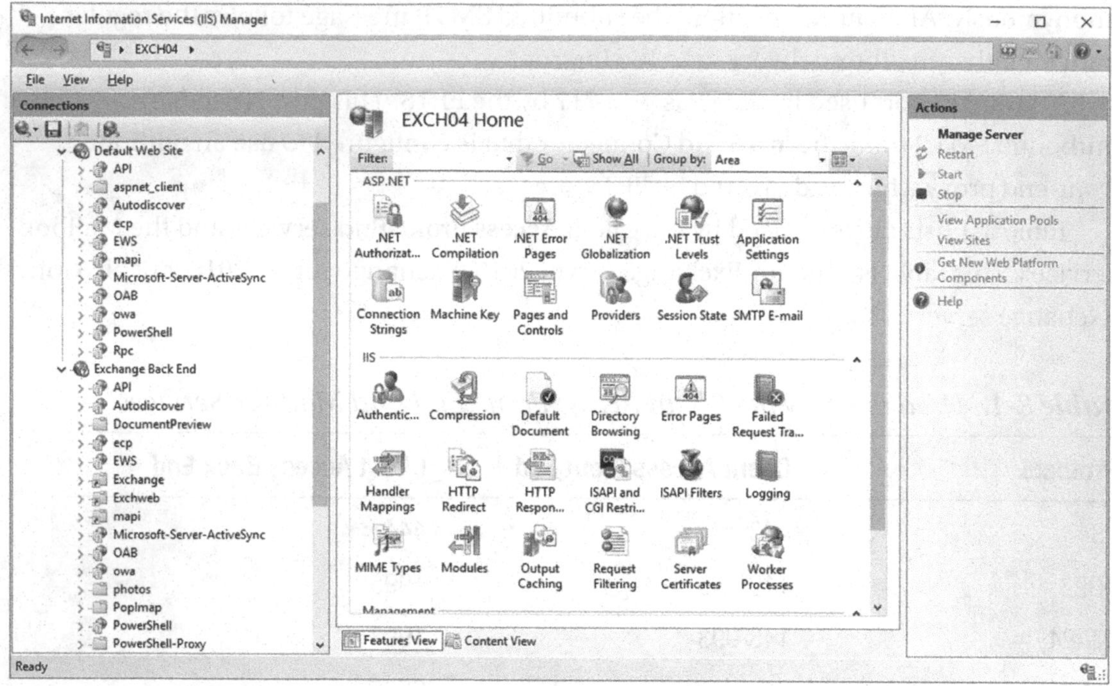

***Figure 3-3.** Front-end and back-end IIS components on an Exchange server*

Exchange server can use multiple authentication methods. The defaults that are used when installing Exchange are sufficient for normal use. For large and complex organization, or when working with previous versions of Exchange like an Exchange 2010/2016 coexistence scenario, authentication methods become more important. Also, after being authenticated by the CAFE and when proxied to another server, the credential is passed to the server where the connection is proxied to.

The following authentication methods are available in a typical Exchange server deployment:

- **Form-based authentication (FBA)**—This is the authentication method used when logging on to Outlook on the Web or the Exchange Admin Center. The user enters the credentials which are encrypted and sent to the Exchange server.
- **Basic Authentication**—Typically identified by a small pop-up window requesting the credentials. The credentials are sent across the wire unencrypted, so basic authentication must always be used in combination with SSL.

- **Kerberos authentication**—This is the native Windows client-server authentication method. Originally developed by the Massachusetts Institute of Technology (MIT) and later incorporated in Active Directory in Windows 2000. Kerberos allows secure network authentication, but a connection to the Key Distribution Center (KDC) running on a Domain Controller needs to be always available. This works fine on the internal network, but not for clients on the Internet, non-domain-joined clients, or non-Windows clients like MacBooks or Linux clients. Once a client has a valid Kerberos token, it can use this token to access other resources on the internal network.
- **NTLM**—This stands for New Technology LAN Manager. Despite the name, it is an older Microsoft technology. It uses a challenge/response sequence and sends the credentials encrypted across the wire. However, it can easily be compromised using modern brute-force techniques.
- **Integrated Windows Authentication (IWA)**—This is the native client-server authentication method used by IIS, and it can use both NTLM and Kerberos authentication when enabled.

All client protocols are treated independently by an Exchange server, and it does this by means of a virtual directory. The following virtual directories are available on an Exchange server:

- **OWA virtual directory**—Used for Outlook on the Web.
- **ECP virtual directory**—Used for the Exchange Admin Center. The name ECP comes from earlier versions of Exchange where the name Exchange Control Panel was used for this.
- **ActiveSync virtual directory**—Used for mobile clients.
- **OAB virtual directory**—Used by Outlook clients to download the Offline Address Book.

- **EWS virtual directory**—EWS is the Exchange Web Services virtual directory and used by clients for requesting free/busy services, mail tips, or out-of-office replies, but also used by the Mailbox Replication Service (MRS) to move mailboxes between Exchange servers. Exchange Web Services are also used in a hybrid scenario with Exchange Online.
- **PowerShell virtual directory**—Used for PowerShell and Exchange Management Shell remote access.
- **MAPI virtual directory**—Used by Outlook clients to connect to an Exchange server.
- **RPC virtual directory**—Used by Outlook clients using Outlook Anywhere to connect to an Exchange server.
- **Autodiscover virtual directory**—Used by Outlook clients to request the Exchange configuration where a mailbox is located.

Each virtual directory has two URLs, one for internal use (the -InternalURL property) and one for external use (the -ExternalURL property). Clients use these properties to determine how to connect to the virtual directory. It is therefore important that both URLs are resolvable and that clients can connect to either one URL. For example, Outlook will use the Autodiscover mechanism to determine how to connect to an Exchange server. It receives the -InternalURL and -ExternalURL properties and will try to connect. It is up to Outlook to determine based on the network settings which URL is used to connect. First, it will try to connect using the -InternalURL, and if that fails, it will try to connect using the -ExternalURL property. If that fails as well, Outlook decides it cannot connect to the Exchange server, and it will stay in a disconnected state.

When an Exchange server is installed, the -InternalURL property of all virtual directories is set with the FQDN of the server, while the -ExternalURL property is empty. When requesting the properties of the MAPI virtual directories, for example, it returns the following output:

```
[PS] C:\>Get-MapiVirtualDirectory -Server EXCH01 | select *ternal* | fl
InternalUrl                    : https://exch01.proexchange2019.com/mapi
InternalAuthenticationMethods : {Ntlm, OAuth, Negotiate}
ExternalUrl                    :
```

```
ExternalAuthenticationMethods : {Ntlm, OAuth, Negotiate}
[PS] C:\>
```

And when requesting the properties of Outlook Anywhere, it returns the following output:

```
[PS] C:\>Get-OutlookAnywhere -Server EXCH01 | select *ternal*
ExternalHostname                  :
InternalHostname                  : exch01.proexchange2019.com
ExternalClientAuthenticationMethod : Negotiate
InternalClientAuthenticationMethod : Ntlm
ExternalClientsRequireSsl         : False
InternalClientsRequireSsl         : False
[PS] C:\>
```

As shown in the previous outputs, each virtual directory also has its own authentication method, which is configured independently of other virtual directories. Therefore, it is possible to configure OWA, for example, with basic authentication and configure Outlook Anywhere with NTLM authentication.

There is also a difference in authentication between internal and external clients. Unless you are in a coexistence environment, for example, Exchange 2010/2016, and the migration guidance explicitly tells you to change settings, it is best to leave these settings as default.

For regular maintenance of Exchange and the virtual directories, the IIS Manager is not used at all; all Exchange server maintenance is done using EMS or EAC. When using EMS, you can configure every little detail of the Exchange virtual directories, but in EAC only the most important parts of the virtual directories can be configured, so EMS is the preferred management interface.

As explained before, each virtual directory has an -internalURL and -externalURL property, used by clients to connect to the Exchange server. For OWA and EAC, it is not a big deal. You can use any URL to access OWA as long as the name is resolved to the IP address of the Exchange server. You will see a certificate warning when the name in the request does not match the name on the certificate, but other than that, you can access the service.

For Outlook clients and mobile clients, it is different because these clients get their Exchange configuration via Autodiscover. And if something is configured incorrectly, the wrong data is returned to the client, and the client in turn cannot connect to the various services.

The question is how to configure the virtual directories and what URL is needed. When only one Exchange server is used, the default setting of the local FQDN of the Exchange server can be used if it is configured with a valid SSL certificate. With one server, the same FQDN can be used for the externalURL as well if it is publicly resolvable.

When multiple Exchange servers are used, things become a bit more complicated when a load balancer is used in front of the Exchange server. Typically, a general server name like webmail is used, and the FQDN will be something like webmail.proexchangeadmin.com. This FQDN should resolve to the virtual service on the load balancer, and the request will be forwarded from the load balancer to one of the Exchange servers.

The Microsoft recommendation is to use split DNS, so webmail.proexchangeadmin.com will resolve to the external address when on the Internet and resolve to the internal address when on the internal network. This way, both the internalURL and externalURL are configured with the same value like webmail.proexchangeadmin.com.

The virtual directories can be configured using EMS. Each virtual directory has its own set of PowerShell commands, like Get-OWAVirtualDirectory and Set-OWAVirtualDirectory or Get-WebServicesVirtualDirectory and Set-WebServicesVirtualDirectory.

Note: To get a list of all PowerShell commands available in EMS, execute the Get-Command *VirtualDirectory in EMS.

To change all virtual directories of Exchange server EXCH01 to webmail.proexchangeadmin.com for both the internalURL and externalURL, execute the following commands in EMS:

```
[PS] C:\> Set-OWAVirtualDirectory -Identity "EXCH01\OWA (Default Web Site)"
-ExternalURL https://webmail.proexchangeadmin.com/owa -InternalURL https://
webmail.proexchangeadmin.com/owa

[PS] C:\> Set-ECPVirtualDirectory -Identity "EXCH01\ECP (default web
site)"-ExternalURL https://webmail.proexchangeadmin.com/ecp -InternalURL
https://webmail.proexchangeadmin.com/ecp
```

```
[PS] C:\> Set-ActiveSyncVirtualDirectory -Identity "EXCH01\Microsoft-
Server-ActiveSync (Default Web Site)" -ExternalURL https://webmail.
proexchangeadmin.com/Microsoft-Server-ActiveSync -InternalURL https://
webmail.proexchangeadmin.com/Microsoft-Server-ActiveSync

[PS] C:\> Set-WebServicesVirtualDirectory -Identity "EXCH01\EWS (Default
Web Site)" -ExternalURL https://webmail.proexchangeadmin.com/ews/Exchange.
asmx -InternalURL https://webmail.proexchangeadmin.com/ews/Exchange.asmx

[PS] C:\> Set-OABVirtualDirectory -Identity "EXCH01\OAB (Default Web Site)"
-ExternalURL https://webmail.proexchangeadmin.com/OAB -InternalURL https://
webmail.proexchangeadmin.com/OAB

[PS] C:\> Set-PowershellVirtualDirectory -Identity "EXCH01\PowerShell
(Default Web Site)" -ExternalURL https://webmail.proexchangeadmin.com/
Powershell -InternalURL https://webmail.proexchangeadmin.com/Powershell

[PS] C:\> Set-MAPIVirtualDirectory -Identity "EXCH01\Mapi (Default Web
Site)" -ExternalURL https://webmail.proexchangeadmin.com/mapi -InternalURL
https://webmail.proexchangeadmin.com/mapi
```

The RPC virtual directory is not configured this way. There are no *-RpcVirtualDirectory commands available. The RPC virtual directory is part of Outlook Anywhere and configured using the Set-OutlookAnywhere command in EMS.

Note: The Autodiscover virtual directory also has the internalURL and externalURL properties, but they are not used. Therefore, there is no need to configure them.

If there are multiple Exchange servers, be very careful when configuring the various options in the virtual directories; this is even more critical when using multiple Exchange servers in a load-balanced array. If one of the Exchange servers in the array is misconfigured, you will see erratic results. This will not be consistent, though, because the remaining servers might be configured correctly. You will see problems arise every now and then, and these problems are the toughest to troubleshoot. I have seen this happening in a large environment with 32 Exchange servers in a load balancer where two (newly added) Exchange servers were configured incorrectly. This resulted in more than 1000 Outlook clients (out of 40,000) with corrupt Outlook profiles.

Since all communication is going via virtual directories (in IIS) on the Exchange server, a lot of logging takes place on an IIS level. The default location of IIS log files is the directory C:\inetpub\logs\LogFiles\W3SVC1, and for typical Exchange server, it is not uncommon that hundreds of megabytes of data are stored daily. This amount of data can quickly fill up the system and boot disk of your Client Access server, so you need to act accordingly.

Former Exchange Server MVP Paul Cunningham has written a script that will compress the log files into monthly archives and store the archive files in a central archive location. You can find more information regarding this script and a download option on his ExchangeServerPro.com website at `https://practical365.com/powershell-script-iis-logs-cleanup/`.

Another option is to relocate the IIS logfiles to another disk as explained in Chapter 2.

Namespaces

Namespaces play an increasingly important role in Exchange Server; this started with the introduction of Autodiscover and its namespace back in the days of Exchange server 2007.

A namespace is a domain name used by clients to access the Exchange environment. An example of a namespace can be webmail.proexchangeadmin.com. Browsers can use webmail.proexchangeadmin.com/owa to access a mailbox, mobile devices can use webmail.proexchangeadmin.com/Microsoft-Server-ActiveSync to retrieve content from the mailbox, and Outlook Anywhere can use webmail.proexchangeadmin.com as the RPC proxy server to access the mailbox.

An additional namespace being used in an Exchange server environment is autodiscover.proexchangeadmin.com. This is used by Outlook clients to send the Autodiscover requests to the Exchange server to retrieve information on where to find and how to access a mailbox.

The minimum number of namespaces in an Exchange environment is two: the protocol namespace and the Autodiscover namespace, as mentioned earlier. It is possible to add more protocol-specific namespaces. I have seen customers use smtp.proexchangeadmin.com for SMTP purposes. Another well-known namespace is pop.proexchangeadmin.com for POP3 and imap.proexchangeadmin.com for IMAP4 clients.

Note In Exchange 2010, there was another namespace used by the RPC Client Access service, something like outlook.proexchangeadmin.com. This namespace was implemented for the RPC Client Access Array (also referred to as CAS array) and used by internal Outlook clients as the RPC endpoint. Since RPC/TCP is no longer used in Exchange, the RPC CAS array is no longer used.

Namespaces are important to consider, especially when using multiple data centers. Another important factor is SSL certificate usage. More namespaces automatically mean more domain names on your SSL certificate. In a typical environment, the webmail.proexchangeadmin.com and autodiscover.proexchangeadmin.com namespaces are used, and therefore these are the only names that need to be configured on the SSL certificate.

From a load balancing perspective as well, namespaces are an important factor to consider. A layer 4 load balancer cannot do any content inspection and therefore cannot determine which protocol is used in a particular namespace. For example, a load balancer on layer 4 cannot determine whether a request is for Exchange Web Services, the MAPI virtual directory, or ActiveSync; it only knows the IP address of the Exchange server. As a result, the load balancer cannot check the health of the individual services.

It is possible to work around this by terminating the SSL connection at the load balancer, do the content inspection of the incoming traffic, and reencrypt the traffic. Reencrypting the traffic is optional. Some customers have a requirement for this, but Exchange fully supports SSL offloading, so unencrypted traffic from the load balancer to the Exchange server is possible too. However, I do not recommend this. Both SSL offloading and load balancing are discussed later in this chapter.

Split DNS

In the previous section, namespaces were briefly discussed, but these were external namespaces—that is, namespaces used by clients that do not reside on the internal network. Internal clients need to connect to the Exchange environment as well, so namespaces are also used on the internal network.

When an Exchange server is installed, it is typically accessed using its fully qualified domain name (FQDN), which can be something like

- Exch01.proexchangeadmin.com

- Exch02.proexchangeadmin.com
- Exch03.proexchangeadmin.com

While these are all valid names and can be safely used, it makes life much easier if the same namespace is used on the internal as on the external network—that is, webmail.proexchangeadmin.com. Using one namespace is not only clearer, there is also no need to use additional names on an SSL certificate.

When webmail.proexchangeadmin.com is used from the Internet, the external IP address of the load-balanced array of Exchange server is resolved—for example, 178.251.192.3. When webmail.proexchangeadmin.com is used on the internal network, the IP address of the internal load-balanced array of the Client Access server is resolved, as in 10.38.96.233.

This configuration is called a split DNS configuration and is the recommended approach for namespace planning.

Single Common Namespace

One of the advantages of the loosely coupled architecture of Exchange server is its unified namespace. It is now possible to use only one or two namespaces for the entire Exchange organization. It is even possible to use only one namespace like webmail.proexchangeadmin.com for all Exchange servers, even if there is worldwide deployment.

For example, a user called John logs on to webmail.proexchangeadmin.com when he is in Amsterdam. This is where his mailbox is located. He is authenticated by the local Exchange server, and his request is proxied to the appropriate Mailbox server, also in Amsterdam.

When John is traveling to New York, he still accesses webmail.proexchangeadmin.com. The Geo-DNS solution resolves to a local Exchange server in New York where his request is authenticated. The Exchange server detects that John's mailbox is in Amsterdam and proxies the request, over the internal network, to the Mailbox server in Amsterdam (see Figure 3-4).

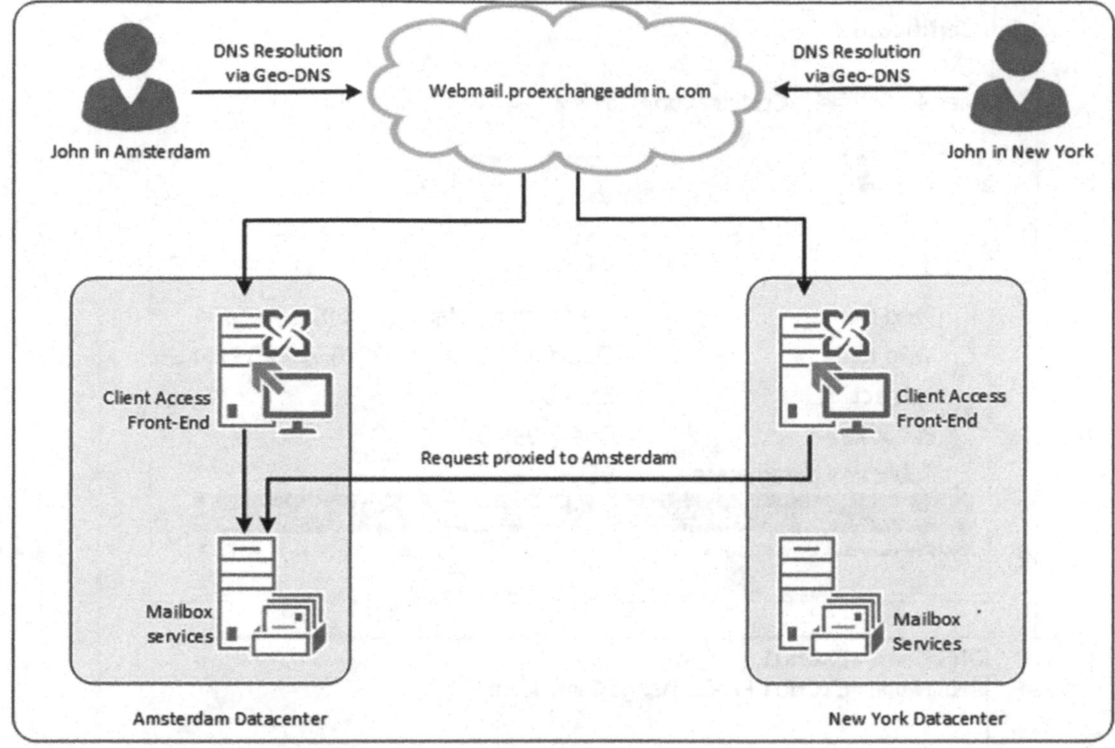

Figure 3-4. *A single, common namespace using a Geo-DNS solution*

SSL Certificates

Because Exchange server extensively uses HTTP to communicate between the client and the Exchange Client Access Front-End services, the SSL certificates are very important. When an Exchange server is installed, a self-signed SSL certificate is created (see Figure 3-5). This self-signed certificate contains only the NetBIOS name of the server as its common name and the FQDN of the server in the "subject alternative name" field. Such a certificate can be used for encryption, but it cannot be used for server authentication, since its issuer (the Exchange server itself) is not trusted by any other machine.

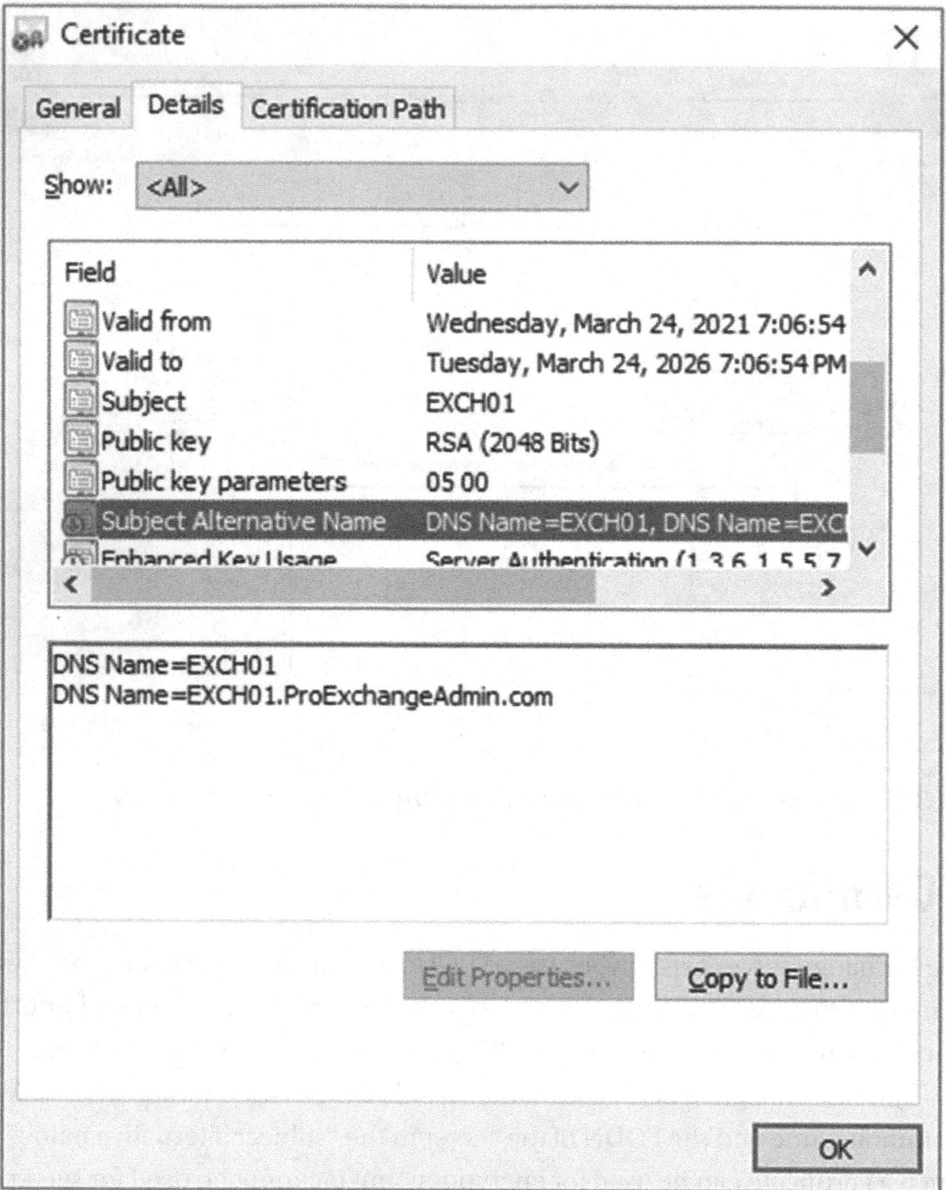

***Figure 3-5.** The self-signed certificate on a Client Access server*

An exception to this is the "Default SMTP Certificate" in an Edge Subscription. When the Edge Subscription is created, the thumbprint of the certificate is copied from the Edge Transport to the Exchange 2019 server. This in turn is used for server authentication. This is discussed in detail in Chapter 5.

For the Exchange server, this self-signed certificate can be used for testing purposes to see if OWA and EAC are working correctly and to configure the server, but it is not meant for production purposes.

A normal SSL certificate has only one name on it; this is the certificate's common name (CN), and it will work perfectly when the server that is configured with this certificate is accessed by a URL that is equal to the common name.

For example, an Exchange server can be accessed using a URL like `https://exch01.proexchangeadmin.com/owa`, and its certificate would have a common name of CN=exch01.proexchangeadmin.com. If this Exchange is now accessed with a URL like `https://mail.proexchangeadmin.com/owa` (assuming DNS would resolve this address to the Exchange server EXCH01), it will result in a certificate error as shown in Figure 3-6, saying "Your connection isn't private" and "This server couldn't prove that it is mail.proexchangeadmin.com; its security certificate is from webmail.proexchangeadmin.com. This may be caused by a misconfiguration or an attacker intercepting your connection."

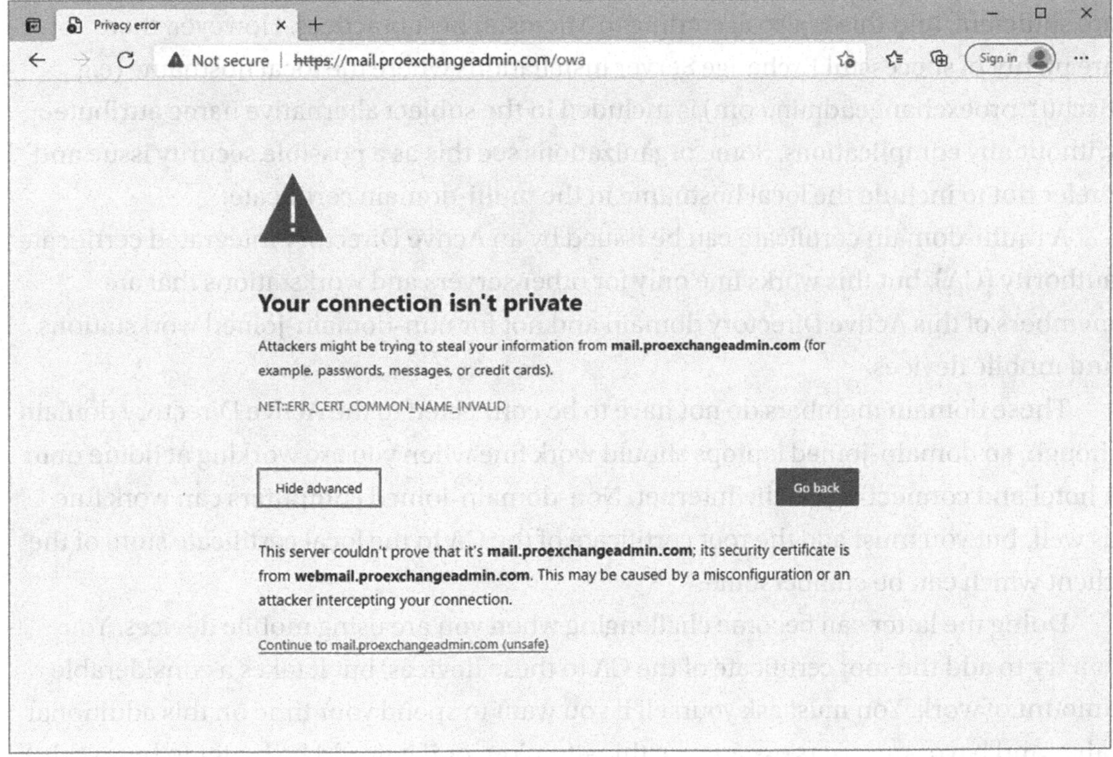

***Figure 3-6.** Certificate warning when the URL does not match the certificate's common name*

If you select "Continue to mail.proexchangeadmin.com (unsafe)," you can proceed with access, but you will see a "Not secure" certificate warning in the browser's navigation bar.

The "problem" with an Exchange server and its clients is that this server can be accessed using a normal URL like webmail.proexchangeadmin.com, but external Outlook clients (that do not have access to Active Directory) automatically try to access the Exchange server using the FQDN autodiscover.proexchangeadmin.com. If you have a normal SSL certificate, this attempt will fail because the autodiscover.proexchangeadmin.com server name does not match the CN=webmail.proexchangeadmin.com name.

To work around this problem, you can use a multi-domain certificate. This multi-domain certificate can hold multiple server names next to its normal common name. These additional server names are stored in an attribute called "subject alternative name." A typical multi-domain certificate for proexchangeadmin.com would have a CN=webmail.proexchangeadmin.com and autodiscover.proexchangeadmin.com entries. If a split DNS configuration is used in your environment, these server names are sufficient, and this is also according to Microsoft best practices. However, there are plenty of successful Exchange Server installations where the local hostname (e.g., Exch01.proexchangeadmin.com) is included in the subject alternative name attribute without any complications. Some organizations see this as a possible security issue and prefer not to include the local hostname in the multi-domain certificate.

A multi-domain certificate can be issued by an Active Directory integrated certificate authority (CA), but this works fine only for other servers and workstations that are members of this Active Directory domain and not for non-domain-joined workstations and mobile devices.

These domain members do not have to be connected to the Active Directory domain though, so domain-joined laptops should work fine when you are working at home or in a hotel and connecting via the Internet. Non-domain-joined computers can work fine as well, but you must add the root certificate of the CA to the local certificate store of the client which can be cumbersome.

Doing the latter can become challenging when you are using mobile devices. You can try to add the root certificate of the CA to these devices, but it takes a considerable amount of work. You must ask yourself if you want to spend your time on this additional labor and have your users experience this situation, or if it would be better to buy a third-party certificate. This is not a matter of cost anymore these days; you can buy a decent certificate for less than US$ 100.

The preferred way is to use a third-party certificate from a trusted third-party CA. Both well-known and Microsoft-supported CAs include, for example, Verisign (now owned by Symantec), Entrust, Comodo, and DigiCert.

Request a New SSL Certificate

To request a new SSL certificate, log on to the Exchange server (or multi-role server, for that matter) as an Exchange administrator and enter a command in EMS like the following:

```
[PS] C:\> $Data = New-ExchangeCertificate -Server EXCH01 -FriendlyName
"Exchange Certificate" -GenerateRequest -SubjectName "c=US,o=Contoso,
cn=webmail.contoso.com" -DomainName webmail.contoso.com, autodiscover.
contoso.com -PrivateKeyExportable $true
[PS] C:\> Set-Content -path "\\FS01\Install\SSLCertRequest.req" -Value
$Data
```

Note A management server with the Exchange Management Tools installed can also be used to request a new SSL certificate.

It is possible to use a UNC path for this, but a direct path like C:\Install is also possible. You can use the contents of this file to request an SSL certificate from the Active Directory integrated CA or from your third-party CA, whichever you prefer. When the SSL certificate is returned from the CA, it is important that you finish the SSL certificate creation from the server (in our example, this is Exchange server EXCH01) you used for generating the initial request. In EMS, use a command like the following to finalize the SSL certificate creation:

```
[PS] C:\> Import-ExchangeCertificate -Server EXCH01 -FileData
([Byte[]]$(Get-Content -Path "\\FS01\Install\certnew.p7b" -Encoding byte
-ReadCount 0)) | Enable-ExchangeCertificate -Server EXCH01 -Services IIS
```

In this example, the certificate is only bound to IIS for all HTTPS-based communication. If you want to use this certificate also for POP3 and IMAP4, you can use `-Services IIS,IMAP,POP`.

You can also use this certificate for SMTP; this is explained in detail in Chapter 6.

Export an SSL Certificate

When the SSL certificate is installed and configured correctly, you can use the Export-ExchangeCertificate command to create a backup file of the Exchange certificate. This backup file can be stored in a safe location, but it can also be used to import on additional Exchange 2013 Client Access servers.

To create an export file of the SSL certificate, you first must find out the thumbprint of the SSL certificate. This thumbprint is a unique identifier of the SSL certificate within the Exchange environment. The thumbprint of the SSL certificates is shown when executing a Get-ExchangeCertificate command in EMS:

```
[PS] C:\> Get-ExchangeCertificate -Server EXCH01
Thumbprint                                Services   Subject
----------                                --------   -------
D4FA1A0243A929AEEBF4D77DE93D50B691DB0A79  IP.WS..    CN=EXCH01
EB3A32C2079C31B281736FDB065310516E69C17A  .......    CN=WMSvc-SHA2-EXCH01
C7DDAE9409B27CD08C9E5863A4906B1D75B3A617  ....S..    CN=Microsoft Exchange
Server Auth Certificate
54C1DF64138E27A56CBB4E8ABE1C2AE0EB430BF7  ...W...    CN=webmail.
proexchangeadmin.com
To request the properties of the webmail.proexchangeadmin.com certificate,
execute the following command in EMS:
[PS] C:\> Get-ExchangeCertificate -Server EXCH01 -Thumbprint
54C1DF64138E27A56CBB4E8ABE1C2AE0EB430BF7 | FL
AccessRules          : {System.Security.AccessControl.CryptoKeyAccessRule,
                       System.Security.AccessControl.CryptoKeyAccessRule}
CertificateDomains : {webmail.proexchangeadmin.com, autodiscover.
                       proexchangeadmin.com}
HasPrivateKey        : True
IsSelfSigned         : False
Issuer               : CN=GeoTrust TLS DV RSA Mixed SHA256 2020 CA-1,
                       O=DigiCert Inc, C=US
NotAfter             : 3/8/2022 12:59:59 AM
NotBefore            : 3/7/2021 1:00:00 AM
```

```
PublicKeySize        : 2048
RootCAType           : ThirdParty
SerialNumber         : 0608314C846CD0C43BF8777A5B930A48
Services             : IIS
Status               : Valid
Subject              : CN=webmail.proexchangeadmin.com
Thumbprint           : 54C1DF64138E27A56CBB4E8ABE1C2AE0EB430BF7
```

To export the certificate into a .PFX file, you first must create a variable containing an export file of the SSL certificate and then write the contents of the variable to disk. To do this, execute the following commands in EMS:

```
$ExportFile = Export-ExchangeCertificate -Server EXCH01 -Thumbprint
54C1DF64138E27A56CBB4E8ABE1C2AE0EB430BF7 -binaryencoded:$true -password
(Get-Credential).password
Set-Content -Path \\FS01\management\webmail_proexchangeadmin_com.pfx -Value
$ExportFile.FileData -Encoding Byte
```

Note The Get-Credential command in the previous example shows a dialog box where credentials can be entered. For the Export-ExchangeCertificate command, only the password is used.

Instead of using the Get-Credential command for the password, it is also possible to use a string for the password and use the ConvertTo-SecureString command. The previous command would then be

```
$ExportFile = Export-ExchangeCertificate -Server EXCH01 -Thumbprint
54C1DF64138E27A56CBB4E8ABE1C2AE0EB430BF7 -binaryencoded:$true -password
(ConvertTo-SecureString -String 'P@ssw0rd1' -AsPlainText -Force)
Set-Content -Path \\FS01\management\webmail_proexchangeadmin_com.pfx -Value
$ExportFile.FileData -Encoding Byte
```

Again, instead of the UNC path, a direct path can be used here as well.

Import an SSL Certificate

When you have an export file of an SSL certificate, you can use PowerShell to import this SSL certificate on additional Exchange servers. To do this, you can use commands like the following in EMS:

```
[PS] C:\> Import-ExchangeCertificate -Server EXCH02 -FileData
([Byte[]]$(Get-Content -Path \\fs01\install\webmail_proexchangeadmin_com.
pfx -Encoding byte -ReadCount 0)) -Password:(Get-Credential).password |
Enable-ExchangeCertificate -Server EXCH02 -Services IIS
```

Note If you have a load-balanced array of Exchange servers, it is important that the SSL certificates used on these servers be identical.

Clients

When using Exchange server, multiple email clients are available:

- Outlook
- Web-based clients
- Autodiscover
- Mobile clients
- Exchange Web Services

I will discuss these clients in the following sections.

Outlook

One of the most important changes in Exchange Server 2013 and higher is that Outlook no longer uses direct MAPI (RPC over TCP); Exchange servers are only accessible using Outlook Anywhere (RPC/HTTPS) or MapiHttp.

Outlook clients rely heavily on HTTP (and thus IIS), not only for MapiHttp but also for Exchange Web Services (EWS), Offline Address Book, and Autodiscover. Using EWS, Outlook clients can request availability information (free/busy) or set an out-of-office message. The Offline Address Book is downloaded by Outlook clients running in cached mode. Outlook for Mac also runs 100% on HTTPS communication; this Outlook client fully utilizes the Exchange Web Services for all communications.

Finally, Autodiscover is used by Outlook clients to find their initial configuration when configuring their Outlook profile. But that is not all; Outlook uses Autodiscover every hour to check for any configuration changes.

Note With all these HTTP dependencies, it is not hard to imagine that namespaces and SSL certificates play an important role in every Exchange and Outlook deployment. A small configuration error will always result in connection errors, pop-up boxes for authentication, or SSL certificate warnings.

Outlook clients can run in cached mode or in online mode where cached mode is the default (and preferred) mode. When run in cached mode, Outlook works with a copy of the mailbox on the local machine, and all changes are made to this "cached" copy. Outlook automatically synchronizes this copy in the background with the mailbox on the Exchange Server. All processing takes place on the Outlook client's workstation, not on the Exchange Server, thereby reducing processor cycles and (expensive) disk I/O on the Exchange Server.

When run in online mode, Outlook works directly against the Exchange Server, and there is no copy of the mailbox on the local workstation. It is obvious that this will increase the load on the Exchange Server, plus the Outlook client will always need to be online. Offline working—for example, while traveling—is not possible in this scenario. Outlook running in online mode can be seen when used in a terminal server environment, but when using a tool like FSLogix, it is possible to run Outlook in cached mode in a terminal server environment as well. As a side note, FSLogix is also often seen in terminal server environments with Office 365.

MAPI/HTTP

MAPI/HTTP was introduced in Exchange server 2013 SP1 as the successor of RPC/HTTPS, also known as Outlook Anywhere. RPC is an ancient protocol, developed in the 1960s for servers running on a normal and stable network (like in your office) but not on flaky networks like WiFi or the Internet. Even though Outlook Anywhere in itself is stable, when you have an intermittent network connection, your HTTPS connection can deal with that, but RPC within the HTTPS packets cannot.

Microsoft Exchange can work perfectly with HTTPS connections. Look at ActiveSync, for example, or OWA; they can work fine on a flaky network like the Internet. If you lose the Internet connection for a small period because you are connecting to another wireless network, OWA continues to work. The same is true for ActiveSync. You can travel throughout the country without noticing that your mobile device is switching networks all the time.

Another issue with Outlook Anywhere is that it relies on the RPC Proxy service on the Windows Server. As such, the RPC Proxy service is not a responsibility of the Exchange Product Group at Microsoft but is of the Windows Product Group at Microsoft. Now you may think this is not a big deal but consider this. When a bug is discovered in Outlook Anywhere and it turns out to be an issue with the RPC Proxy service, the Exchange Product Group needs to submit an incident to the Windows Product Group and hopes the latter will fix the problem. This is a less than desirable situation.

To overcome this problem, Microsoft has developed MapiHttp, which is basically native HTTPS traffic. The Outlook client is no longer using RPC for its MAPI communication but instead is using HTTPS directly. The difference is shown in Figure 3-7.

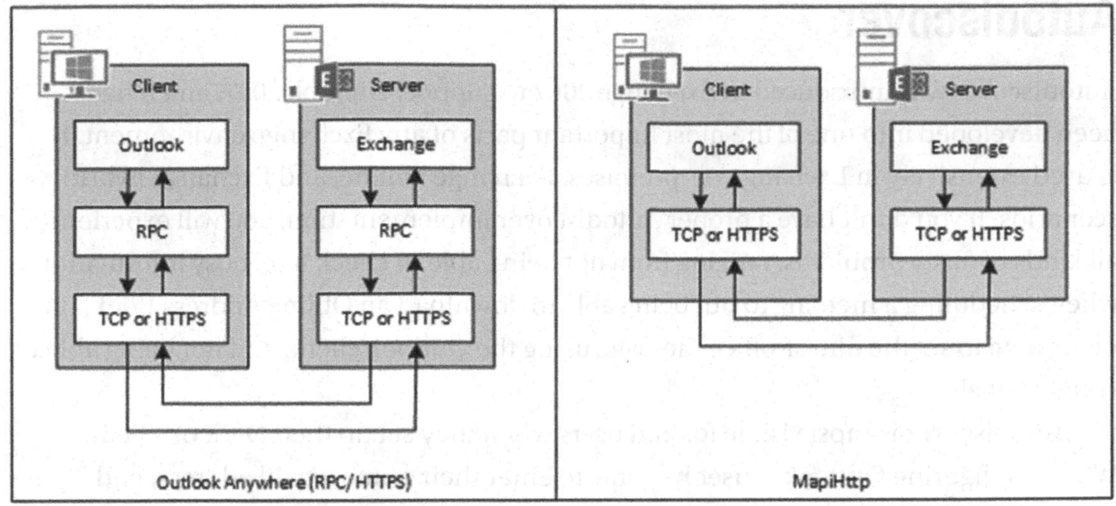

Figure 3-7. *The difference between RPC/HTTPS and MapiHttp*

MapiHttp is enabled on a global level; you enable it in the entire organization at one moment. To enable MapiHttp, open the Exchange Management Shell and enter the following command:

```
[PS] C:\> Set-OrganizationConfig -MapiHttpEnabled $TRUE
```

Please note that it can take some time for this change to take effect.

Note When moving from Exchange server 2010 to Exchange server 2016, you will notice a difference in clients connecting to the Exchange server. Older Outlook clients were using RPC/TCP (the traditional MAPI) to connect to the mailbox databases. As an RPC endpoint, the RPC CAS array was used. Microsoft has moved away from RPC/TCP; the only two protocols are Outlook Anywhere (but this is deprecated) and MAPI/HTTP. This is the default protocol in Exchange server 2019, but also in Exchange Online. So, when moving from Exchange server 2010 to Exchange server 2016, you will see that clients reconnect using a different protocol when moving mailboxes. Also, when moving from Exchange 2013 or Exchange 2016 to Exchange 2019, MAPI/HTTP is not automatically enabled. This is something to be aware of.

Autodiscover

Autodiscover was introduced in Exchange 2007 to support Outlook 2007, and it has been developed into one of the most important parts of any Exchange environment. It is used extensively in Exchange on-premises, Exchange Online, and Exchange hybrid scenarios. If you don't have a proper Autodiscover implementation, you will experience all kinds of nasty problems, ranging from not being able to check free/busy information when scheduling a meeting to not being able to download an Offline Address Book, not being able to set the out-of-office message using the Outlook client, and not being able to connect at all.

Autodiscover is most visible for end users when they set up their Outlook client. When configuring Outlook, a user has only to enter their name, email address, and Active Directory password, and the Outlook client will configure itself automatically. It discovers all the information regarding the Exchange Server implementation and uses this information to configure the Outlook profile. But not only does it do this on the initial setup, but it also performs this action on a regular basis to check for any changes in the Exchange environment.

Autodiscover works by sending an XML request to the Exchange server. The Exchange server checks Active Directory for the location of the user's mailbox and, when needed, proxies the request to the Exchange server hosting the mailbox. The Autodiscover process on this Exchange server processes the request, gathers all information, and returns this to the client. The client in turn configures the Outlook profile. This is shown in Figure 3-8.

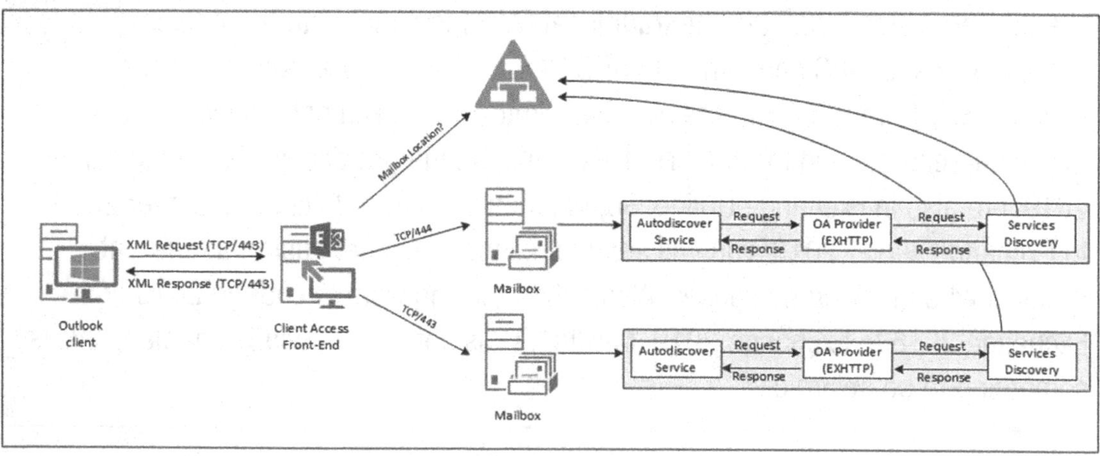

Figure 3-8. *Autodiscover information flow*

How does the Outlook client discover which Exchange server to send its request to? The answer is twofold:

- Domain-joined Outlook clients who are logged on to the Active Directory domain retrieve this information directly from Active Directory.
- Non-domain-joined Outlook clients, or domain-joined Outlook clients who cannot access Active Directory (when working at home, for example), build the Autodiscover URL based on the user's SMTP address.

Both scenarios are covered in the next two sections.

Domain-Joined Clients

When an Exchange server is installed, a computer object is created in the configuration partition of Active Directory. Besides this computer object, a service connection point (SCP) is also created in Active Directory. For every Exchange server that is installed, a corresponding SCP is created. So, if you have six Exchange servers, you also have six SCPs.

An SCP has a well-known GUID (Global Unique Identifier) that's unique for the type of application that's using the SCP. In the case of Exchange Server, this application is Outlook. All service connection points created by installing Exchange servers have the same well-known GUID, and Outlook clients query Active Directory for this GUID. This GUID is stored in the keywords attribute together with the Active Directory site name where the Exchange server is installed, as shown in Figure 3-9.

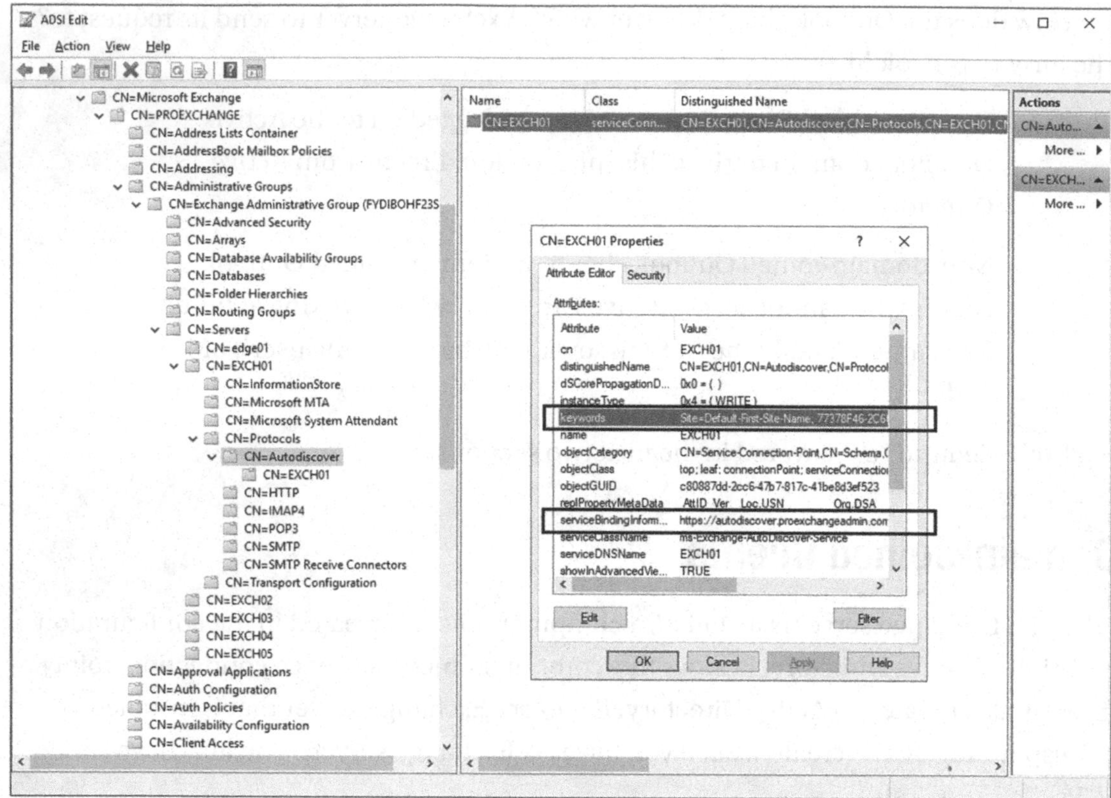

***Figure 3-9.** The service connection point in Active Directory, with keywords and serviceBindingInformation properties*

Once found, the serviceBindingInformation attribute is retrieved, and, by default, this value contains the FQDN of the Exchange server—for example, Exch01.proexchangeadmin.com. If there are multiple Exchange servers in the Active Directory site of the Exchange environment, a virtual IP (VIP) on the load balancer should be created. This VIP should be the IP address of a load-balanced FQDN (e.g., autodiscover.proexchangeadmin.com), and it should contain all Exchange servers. Clients connect to this VIP instead of to an individual Exchange server, and all client requests are distributed across all Exchange servers.

The Outlook client retrieves the Autodiscover FQDN from Active Directory and sends an HTTP post command to this URL. The Exchange server then accepts the request and proxies it to the Exchange server hosting the user's mailbox. This Mailbox server gathers all the required information and returns this as an XML package to the Outlook client. The Outlook client then can use the XML package to configure its profile (when it is a new setup) or reconfigure its profile (when changes are detected in the Exchange environment).

This process happens always, not only during the initial setup of the Outlook client; the request is sent once an hour to determine if there are any changes in the Exchange configuration. Since it is an HTTP request that must be secured, the SSL certificates come into play. The autodiscover.proexchangeadmin.com FQDN needs to be in the certificate as well, next to the webmail.proexchangeadmin.com name.

The Autodiscover URL is configurable only by using the Exchange Management Shell. To configure this, open EMS and execute the following command:

```
[PS] C:\> Set-ClientAccessService -Server EXCH01
-AutoDiscoverServiceInternalUri https://autodiscover.proexchangeadmin.com/
autodiscover/autodiscover.xml
```

If all the Client Access servers need to be configured with this URL, the following command can be used:

```
[PS] C:\> Get-ClientAccessService | Set-ClientAccessService
-AutoDiscoverServiceInternalUri https://autodiscover.proexchangeadmin.com/
autodiscover/autodiscover.xml
```

Note Change the SCP record using the Set-ClientAccessService command directly after installing an Exchange server to prevent Outlook clients accidentally retrieving wrong information from the newly installed Exchange server.

Autodiscover will retrieve all information from the Exchange environment, including information regarding virtual directories, Offline Address Book downloads, and Exchange Web Services. These Exchange Web Services are used for retrieving free/busy information or for setting the out-of-office information.

Therefore, if you have any issues with free/busy information or setting out-of-office messages in Outlook, I always recommend checking the same functionality in OWA first, followed by checking the Autodiscover configuration.

In 99% of cases, any complications with Autodiscover are caused by SSL certificate errors. When using a browser to connect to an Exchange server and a certificate error arises, it is possible to continue despite the error message. That is a great advantage of OWA, but Outlook is much more sensitive.

It is possible to verify the Autodiscover functionality from within Outlook. When Outlook is running, check the system tray for the Outlook icon. Press CTRL while right-clicking the Outlook icon and select "Test Email AutoConfiguration"; this is shown in Figure 3-10.

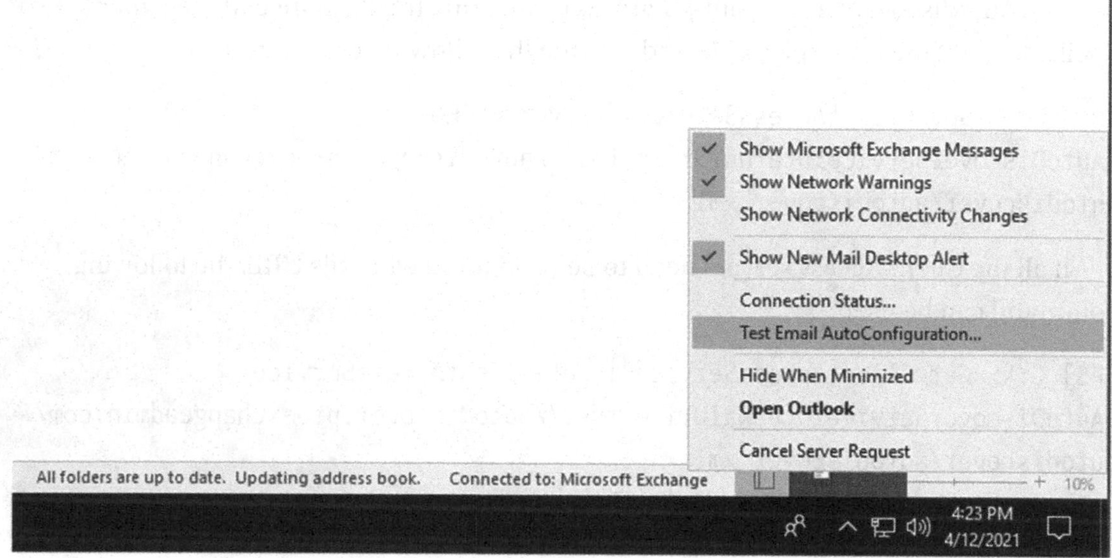

***Figure 3-10.** Testing Autodiscover from within the Outlook client*

You then enter the email address and password, clear both the "Use Guessmart" and the "Secure Guessmart Authentication" checkboxes, and click the Test button. The Outlook client will perform an Autodiscover check against the Exchange Server and display the information as shown in Figure 3-11.

There are three tabs visible:

- **Results**—The returned information is shown in a readable format.
- **Log**—The various options are shown for how the Outlook client tried to retrieve the information.
- **XML**—The raw XML data that is returned from the Exchange server is shown.

This utility is extremely useful when troubleshooting the Exchange environment.

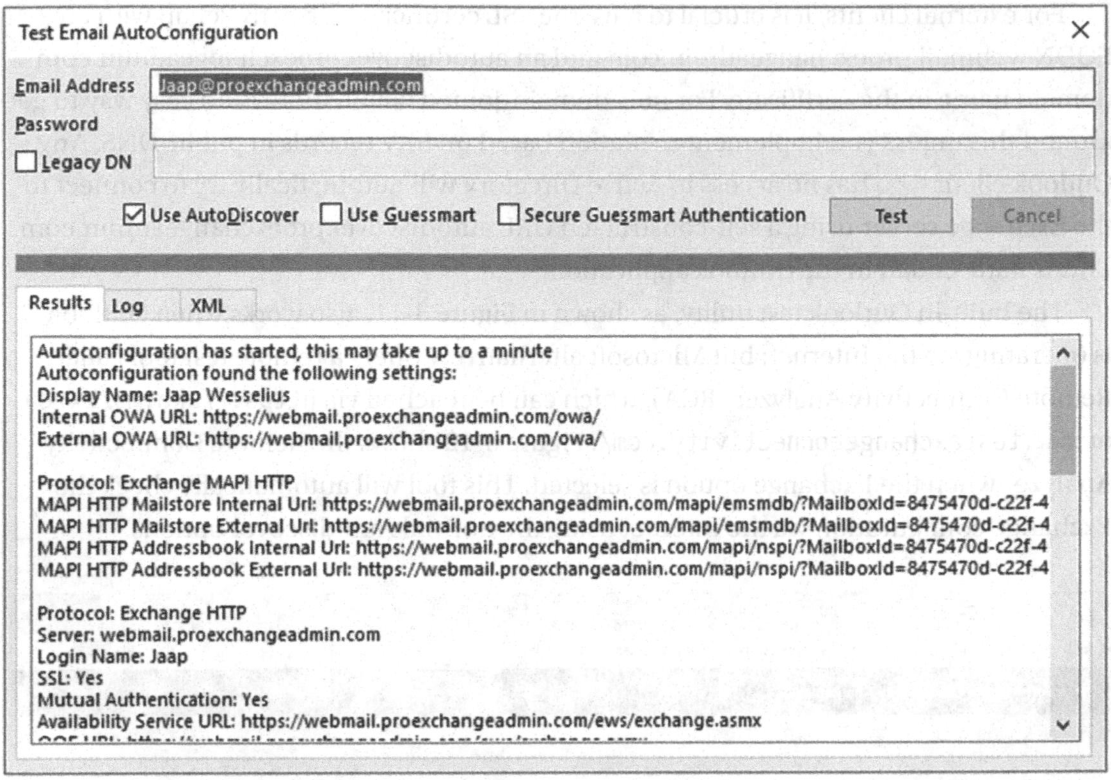

Test Email AutoConfiguration

Email Address Jaap@proexchangeadmin.com
Password
Legacy DN
Use AutoDiscover Use Guessmart Secure Guessmart Authentication Test Cancel

Results Log XML

Autoconfiguration has started, this may take up to a minute
Autoconfiguration found the following settings:
Display Name: Jaap Wesselius
Internal OWA URL: https://webmail.proexchangeadmin.com/owa/
External OWA URL: https://webmail.proexchangeadmin.com/owa/

Protocol: Exchange MAPI HTTP
MAPI HTTP Mailstore Internal Url: https://webmail.proexchangeadmin.com/mapi/emsmdb/?MailboxId=8475470d-c22f-4
MAPI HTTP Mailstore External Url: https://webmail.proexchangeadmin.com/mapi/emsmdb/?MailboxId=8475470d-c22f-4
MAPI HTTP Addressbook Internal Url: https://webmail.proexchangeadmin.com/mapi/nspi/?MailboxId=8475470d-c22f-4
MAPI HTTP Addressbook External Url: https://webmail.proexchangeadmin.com/mapi/nspi/?MailboxId=8475470d-c22f-4

Protocol: Exchange HTTP
Server: webmail.proexchangeadmin.com
Login Name: Jaap
SSL: Yes
Mutual Authentication: Yes
Availability Service URL: https://webmail.proexchangeadmin.com/ews/exchange.asmx

Figure 3-11. *Autodiscover information returned from the Autodiscover check*

Non-domain-Joined Clients

Non-domain-joined clients, or domain-joined clients who do not have access to Active Directory, use a different approach for getting Autodiscover information.

Initially, Outlook will construct an FQDN based on the right-hand part of the email address. So, if the user's email address is john@proexchangeadmin.com, Outlook will start looking at `https://proexchangeadmin.com/autodiscover/autodiscover.xml` to try to get to an Exchange server.

Often, this is causing issues, since the root domain "proexchangeadmin.com" is used for a company website and not for Autodiscover purposes. In this scenario, it helps to deny the /Autodiscover requests on the company firewall to speed up the Autodiscover process.

Once the URL is constructed, Outlook will automatically send an HTTP XML post request to the Autodiscover URL and will get all the necessary information as it does for an internal Outlook client. If that does not work, Outlook will fall back to the same URL, but with an Autodiscover prefix, like `https://autodiscover.proexchangeadmin.com/autodiscover/autodiscover.xml`. In most cases, this will work.

For external clients, it is crucial to have the SSL certificate correctly set up with an FQDN webmail.proexchangeadmin.com and an autodiscover.proexchangeadmin.com domain name in the certificate. For non-domain-joined client, there is no easy way to get around this unless you implement a solution based on SRV records in public DNS. Any Outlook client who has no access to Active Directory will automatically try to connect to the Exchange server using a self-constructed URL autodiscover.proexchangeadmin.com. This is hard-coded in the Outlook application!

The built-in Outlook test utility, as shown in Figure 3-11, also works when Outlook is operating via the Internet; but Microsoft alternatively offers a remote test tool called Remote Connectivity Analyzer (RCA), which can be reached via `https://aka.ms/exrca` or `www.testexchangeconnectivity.com/`. Figure 3-12 shows the Remote Connectivity Analyzer when the Exchange option is selected. This tool will automatically check the Exchange configuration via the Internet using the normal Autodiscover options.

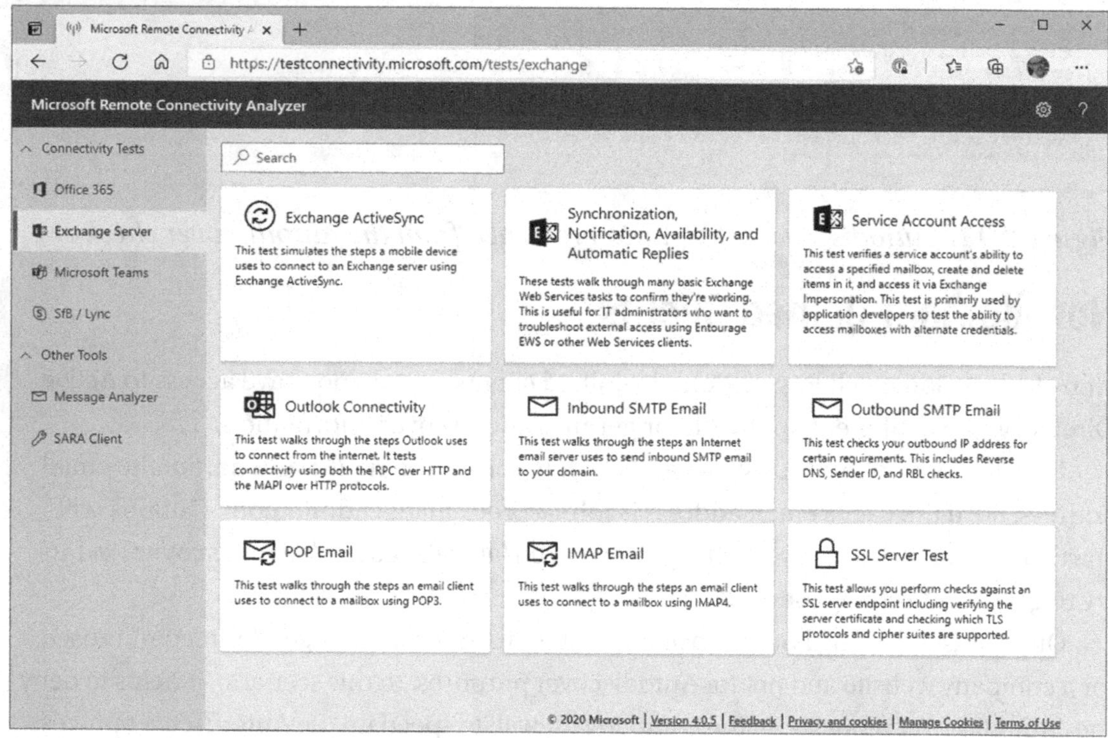

***Figure 3-12.** The Remote Connectivity Analyzer*

To use this tool, select Outlook Connectivity, and enter the email address, username (can be UPN or Domain\Username), and password of the user account. Check the "I understand that I must use the credentials of a working account..." checkbox and enter the characters in the verification box. You can click the verify button or proceed to the Perform Test button directly as this will start the verification automatically.

There are multiple methods for retrieving Autodiscover information, and these are shown as a red circle with a white cross in it, a green circle with a white checkbox in it, or an orange triangle with an exclamation mark. When one method fails, Outlook (and RCA) will automatically continue with the next available option. There is no need to panic when you see the red circle; only when you only see red circles and no green ones is it time to start worrying. Figure 3-13 shows the output of RCA. The MAPI/HTTP tests are all successful, but the Outlook Anywhere tests show a warning. In this test, it was just a warning about RPC encryption, so no need to worry.

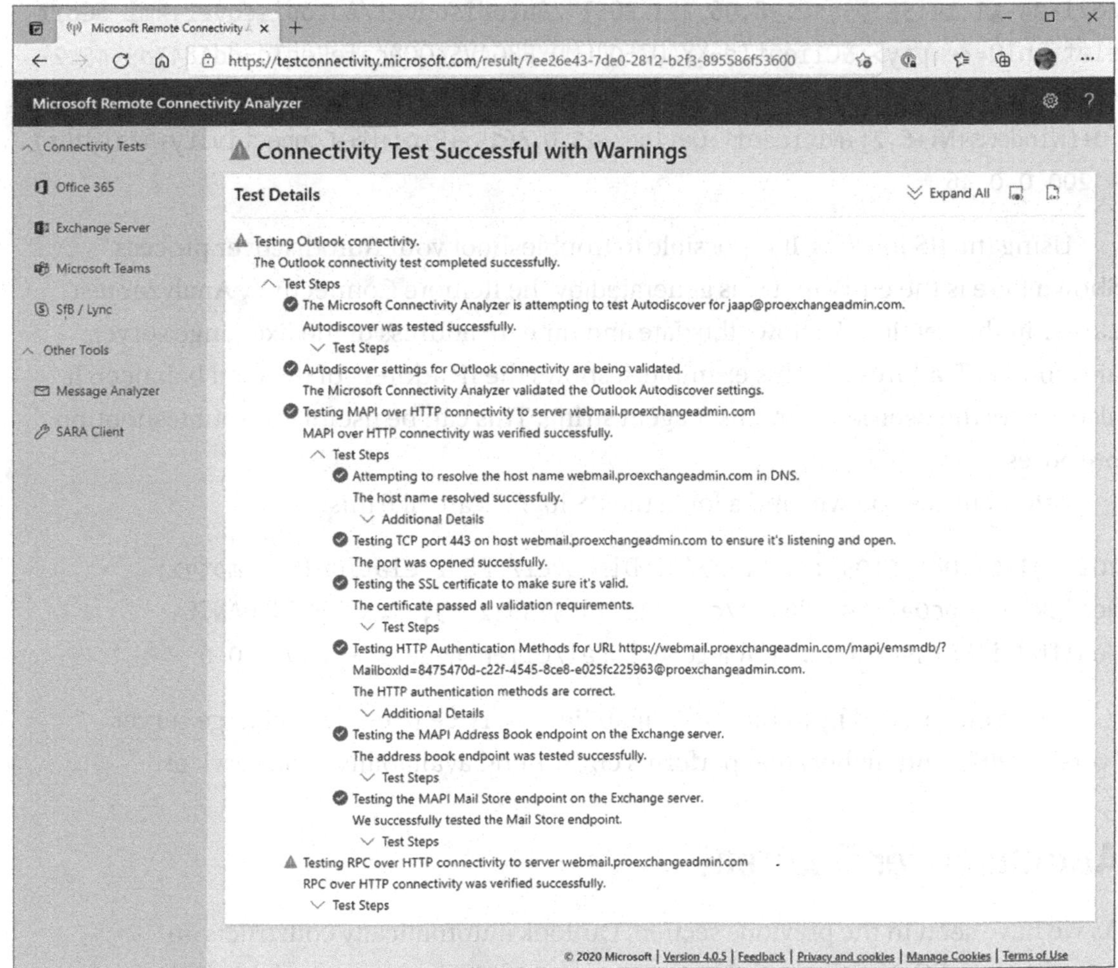

Figure 3-13. *The RCA results*

Note The Remote Connectivity Analyzer is a publicly available tool to test your Exchange environment. Since it must access your Exchange environment from the Internet, your Exchange server needs to be accessible from the Internet. One pitfall I enter occasionally is that the Exchange server is behind either a VPN solution or an MFA solution. In both cases, the RCA does not work.

It also needs a valid and trusted third-party SSL certificate on the Exchange server. Important: It does not work with the default self-signed certificate.

If you check the IIS log files, which can be found by default on %SystemDrive%\inetpub\logs\LogFiles\W3SVC1, you will see numerous entries like

```
2021-04-11 19:58:05 10.38.96.223 POST /Autodiscover/Autodiscover.xml &Corr
elationID=<empty>;&ClientId=XYAOZEOJEMDYFBGAVSKQQ&cafeReqId=dd1847b5-45e2-
4e01-9fe1-43a9ac7f7494; 443 proexchange\jaap 10.38.96.9 Microsoft+Office/15
.0+(Windows+NT+6.2;+Microsoft+Outlook+15.0.4615;+Pro;+MS+Connectivity+Analyzer)
- 200 0 0 46
```

Using the IIS log files, it is possible to troubleshoot your Autodiscover process. Shown here is the entry that was generated by the Remote Connectivity Analyzer test earlier in this section. It shows the date and time, IP address of the Exchange server, and source IP address. In this example, it shows the IP address of the load balancer. It also shows the username and user agent string. This can be useful for troubleshooting purposes.

Other entries you will find a lot in the IIS logfiles are like this:

```
2021-04-13 08:41:03 ::1 GET /AutoDiscover/ &CorrelationID=<empty>;
&cafeReqId=8c0af66b-3865-47c7-b221-7a4525d32a49; 443 PROEXCHANGE\
HealthMailbox39af3e9 ::1 AMProbe/Local/ClientAccess - 200 0 0 6
```

These are created by Managed Availability, a service in every Exchange server (version 2013 and higher) that performs end-to-end availability of all services.

Autodiscover Redirect

As we have seen in the previous section, Outlook automatically constructs an Autodiscover FQDN based on the user's primary SMTP address, and this FQDN needs to be on the Exchange 2013 Client Access server's SSL certificate. While this works fine if you have only one or two primary SMTP domains in your Exchange organization, things become challenging when you have a lot of SMTP domains.

One of my clients is a worldwide publisher, and over the years, it has acquired several hundred small publishing companies all over the globe, each with its own identity. It is not hard to imagine that an SSL certificate with so many domains is difficult to work with. Most third-party SSL certificate vendors support up to 20 or 25 domain names on an SSL certificate. This is a practical limitation set by these vendors. When you have a lot of domain names in your SSL certificate, it takes a lot of time to validate all those domain names—plus, the cost of such an SSL certificate skyrockets.

Suppose in the proexchangeadmin.com Exchange environment there is another SMTP domain hosted name inframan.nl, but the SSL certificate on the Exchange server only has the webmail.proexchangeadmin.com and Autodiscover.proexchangeadmin.com domain names.

For this scenario, Microsoft has developed the Autodiscover Redirect option. What happens is that the Exchange server has an additional website (listening on port 80) with an FQDN called autodiscoverredirect.proexchangeadmin.com. Internally, in IIS, requests for this site are automatically redirected to autodiscover.proexchangeadmin.com. The additional domain inframan.nl has an Autodiscover record in public DNS, but it is not an A record but a CNAME record. This CNAME record for Autodiscover.inframan.nl refers to autodiscoverredirect.proexchangeadmin.com, which in turn is located on the Exchange server.

When an external user with a primary SMTP address M.Jones@inframan.nl opens his Outlook, Outlook wants to connect automatically to autodiscover.inframan.nl. This attempt will fail because the Exchange server responds with an SSL warning message.

Outlook's next try is to check for an HTTP redirect option. Outlook will access the Exchange server and check for an HTTP/302 redirect. If this is detected, Outlook will continue with the Autodiscover process using the website found in the redirect string.

From here, the process is the same; Outlook will send an HTTP POST command to the Exchange server, and the Autodiscover service running on the Exchange server will gather all information and send it as an XML file back to the Outlook client.

This can be seen in Figure 3-14, where Outlook will receive an HTTP/302 redirect from the Exchange server and continue with the Autodiscover process.

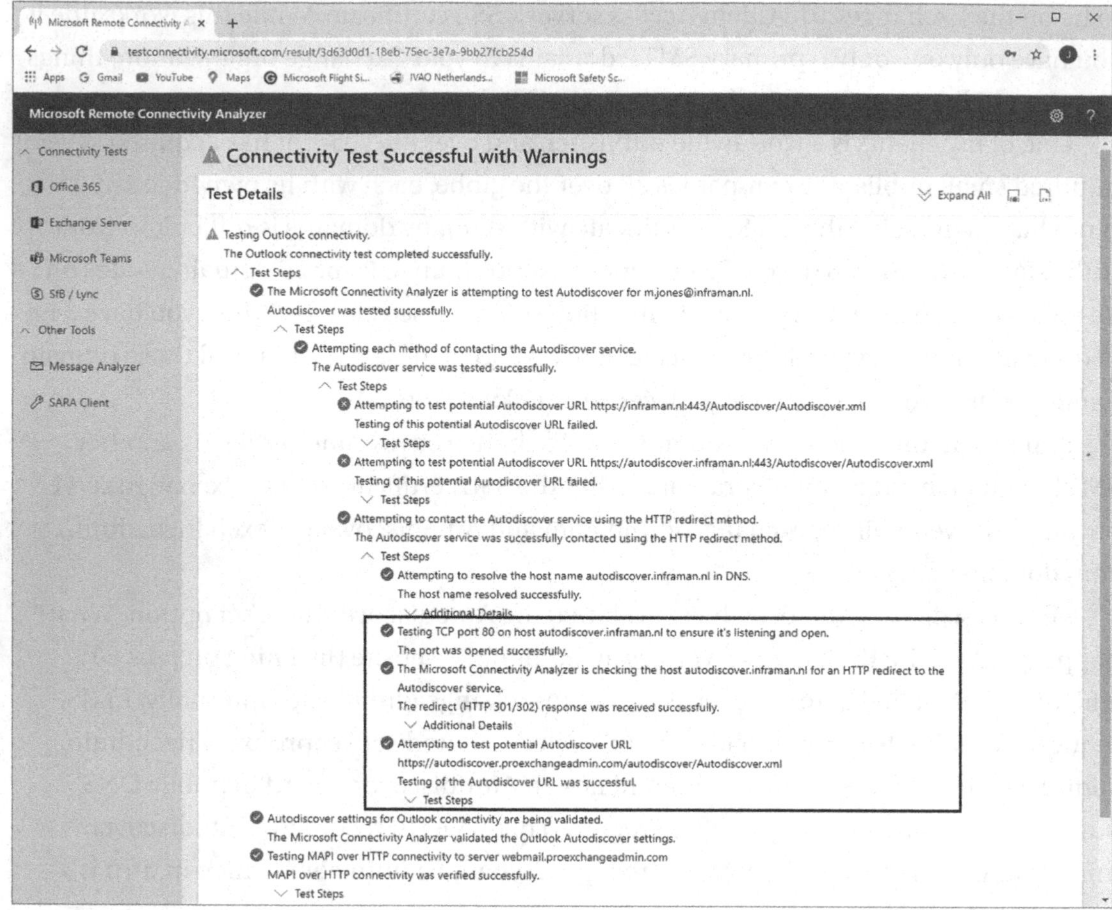

Figure 3-14. *The autodiscoverredirect option in the RCA*

Clearly visible in Figure 3-14 is that the tests for `https://inframan.nl/Autodiscover/Autodiscover.xml` and `https://autodiscover.inframan.nl/Autodiscover/Autodiscover.xml` fail but succeed on the HTTP redirect method. Just as in the earlier examples, there is no need to panic because of the red circles with the white crosses; if there is one green circle, you are fine.

To implement the Autodiscover redirect method on Exchange server, you must

1. Add an additional IP address to the Exchange server.
2. Create an additional website on the Exchange server.
3. Set the bindings and the IP addresses correctly.
4. Set the redirection on the additional website to the original (Autodiscover) site.

The following commands can be used in the Exchange Management Shell to configure Autodiscover redirect:

```
# Add an additional IP address to the Exchange server
[PS] C:\> New-NetIPAddress -InterfaceAlias "Ethernet" -IPAddress
"10.38.96.241" -PrefixLength 24
# Remote the default bindings (all IP addresses on port 443) from the
default website
[PS] C:\> Import-Module WebAdministration
[PS] C:\> Remove-WebBinding -Name 'default web site' -BindingInformation
"*:443:"

# Bind the server IP address to the default website
[PS] C:\> New-WebBinding -Name "Default Web Site" -IPAddress "10.38.96.241"
-Port 443 -Protocol https

# Create new directories on disk for AutodiscoverRedirect
[PS] C:\> New-Item -ItemType Directory -Path $env:systemdrive\Inetpub\
AutodiscoverRedirect
[PS] C:\> New-Item -ItemType Directory -Path $env:systemdrive\Inetpub\
AutodiscoverRedirect\Autodiscover

# Create a new Website and Virtual Directory for AutodiscoverRedirect
[PS] C:\> New-WebSite -Name AutodiscoverRedirect -Port 80 -PhysicalPath
"$env:systemdrive\inetpub\AutodiscoverRedirect" -IPAddress "10.38.96.241"
[PS] C:\> New-WebVirtualDirectory -Name Autodiscover -Site
AutodiscoverRedirect -PhysicalPath "$env:systemdrive\inetpub\
AutodiscoverRedirect\Autodiscover"

# Point the virtual directory to the default website for Autodiscover.
[PS] C:\> Set-WebConfiguration system.webServer/httpRedirect "IIS:\sites\
autodiscoverredirect\autodiscover" -Value @{enabled="true";destination="htt
ps://autodiscover.proexchangeadmin.com/autodiscover/autodiscover.xml";exact
Destination="false";httpResponseStatus="Found"}
```

Note These commands can also be downloaded from the Apress GitHub.

Multiple websites on one server need unique combinations of IP addresses and port number. Therefore, you see the Default Web Site listing on port 443 and the Exchange Back End website on port 443. This way, both can use the same IP address. Instead of using an additional IP address on the Exchange server, it is also possible to use a different port number. I have been testing with the Autodiscoverredirect website on the same IP address, but listing on port 81. Then create a virtual service on the load balancer for the Autodiscoverredirect website and connect to the Exchange server on port 82. This will save you the hassle and potential challenges of additional IP addresses.

I can imagine you want to use the GUI when making this kind of infrastructural change to your Exchange environment. Since there is no IIS Manager on the Exchange server 2019 server when running on Windows server 2019 server core, you can start IIS Manager from another server and connect to the Exchange server. You can use the following steps to implement the Autodiscover redirect method:

1. Configure an additional IP address on the Exchange server.
2. In IIS Manager, bind the default website to the original IP address of the Exchange server for port 443, as shown in Figure 3-15. Before you continue, make sure the Exchange server still works correctly with this new binding.

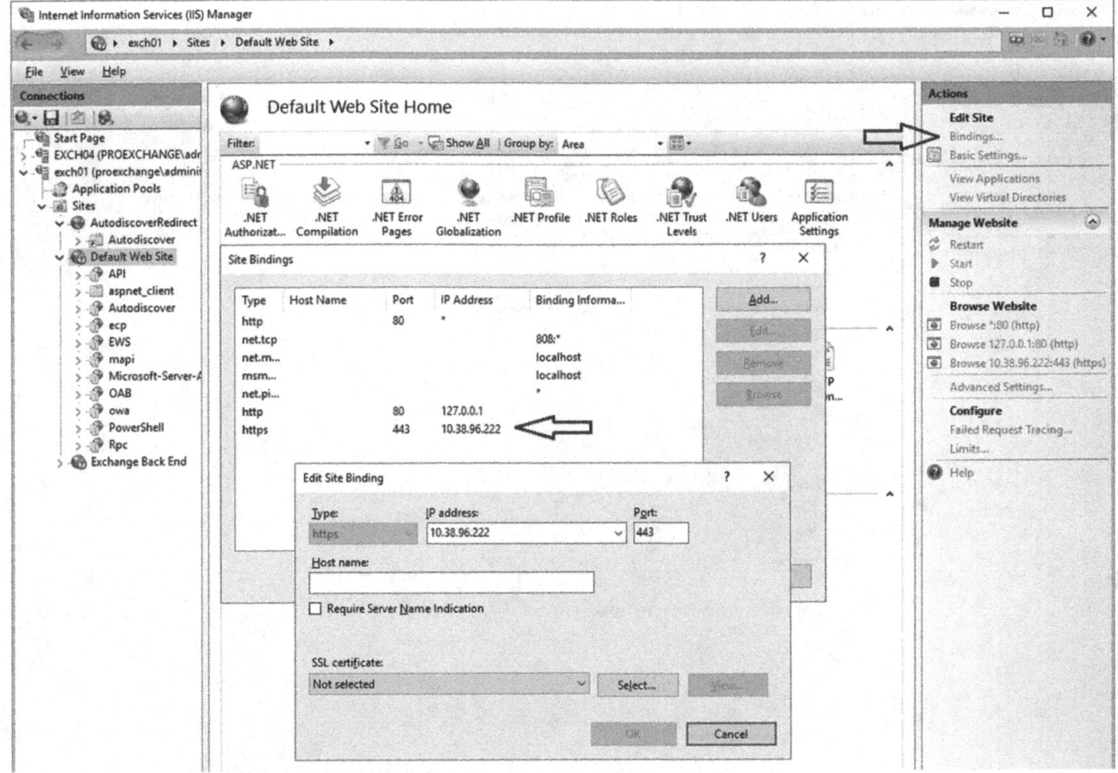

***Figure 3-15.** Configure one IP address to the default website*

3. On the Exchange server, create two additional directories: C:\Inetpub\AutodiscoverRedirect and C:\Inetpub\AutodiscoverRedirect\Autodiscover.

4. In IIS Manager, create a new website, name it AutodiscoverRedirect, and use the C:\Inetpub\Autodiscover as its physical path. Make sure the binding of this website is set to the additional IP address we configured earlier, as shown in Figure 3-16.

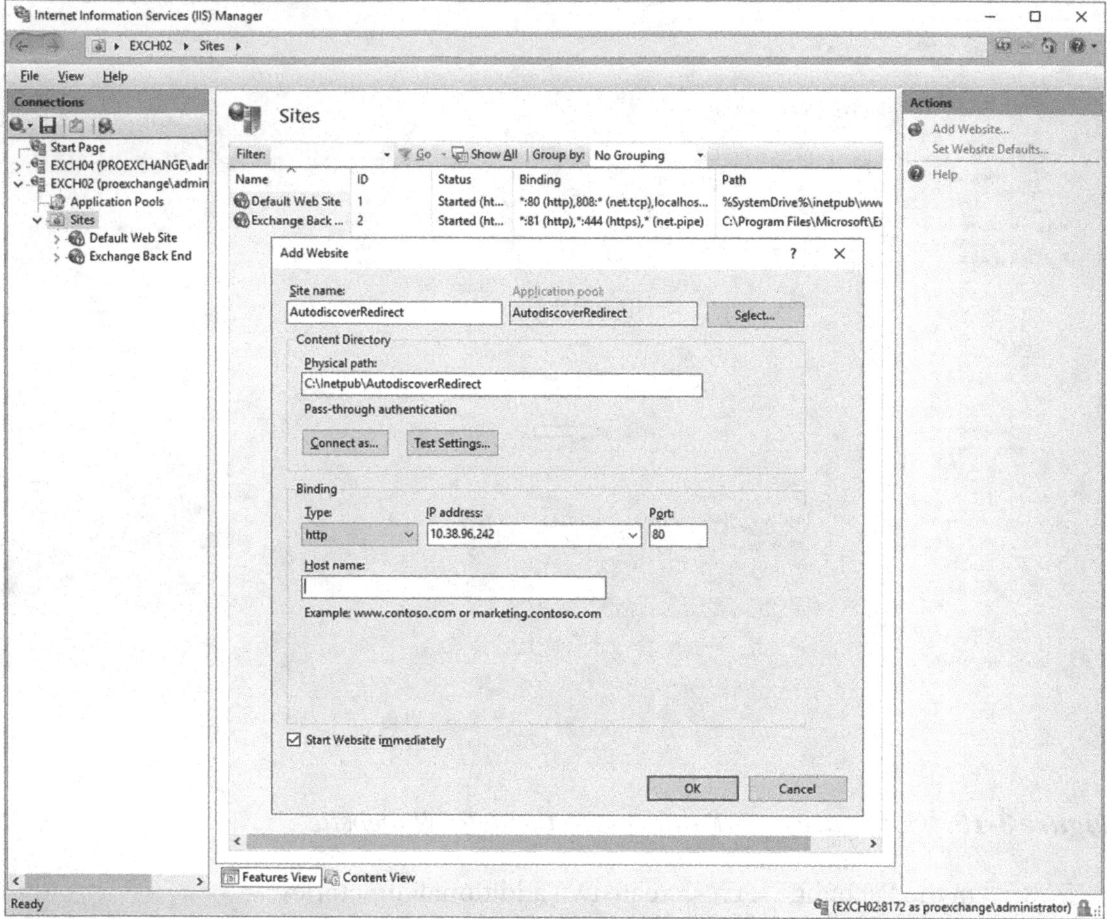

Figure 3-16. *Add a new website to the Exchange server and assign an IP address and port number.*

5. In the AutodiscoverRedirect website in IIS Manager, you will see an Autodiscover virtual directory show up. Select this Autodiscover virtual directory, and in the details pane, double-click "HTTP Redirect."

6. In the HTTP Redirect window, check the "Redirect" request to this destination and enter the normal Autodiscover URL, like `https://autodiscover.proexchangeadmin.com/autodiscover`, as shown in Figure 3-17.

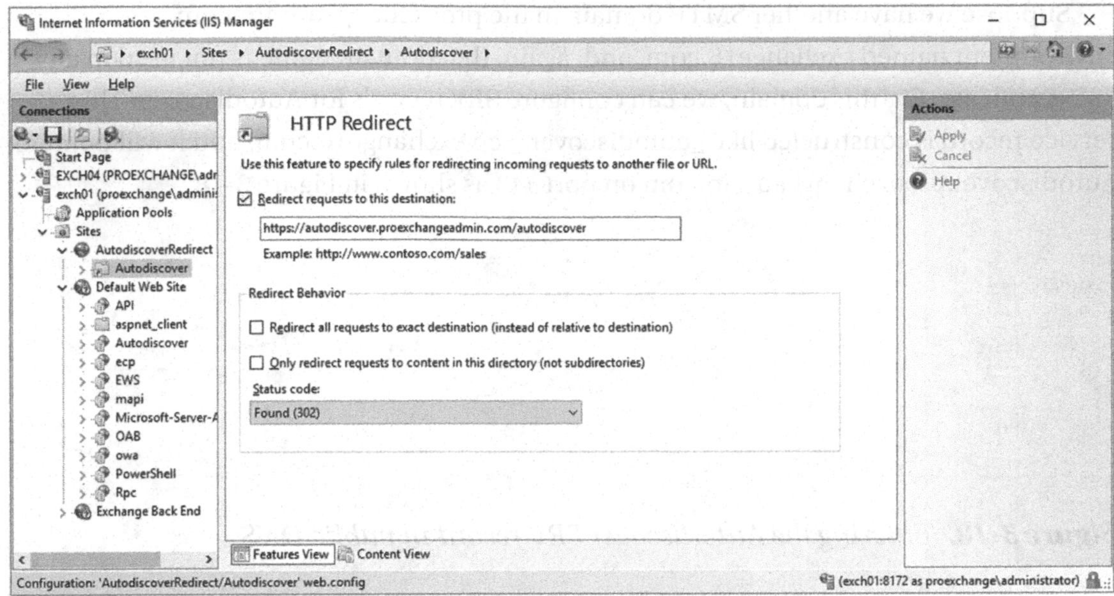

***Figure 3-17.** Configure the redirect option to use the original Autodiscover website*

When the Autodiscoverredirect website is up and running, configure a virtual IP address on the load balancer to make it externally accessible. The last step is to create a public DNS record for autodiscoverredirect.proexchangeadmin.com, which should point to the additional IP address. The autodiscover.inframan.nl DNS record should be a CNAME record and point to autodiscoverredirect.proexchangeadmin.com.

Now, when you test this configuration using the RCA, you should see similar results to those as shown in Figure 3-14 earlier in this chapter.

Note Why is this interesting, or important, to know? Microsoft is using the HTTP redirect option for Autodiscover in Exchange Online extensively.

Autodiscover SRV Records

If you do not want to configure the additional website on your Exchange server—for example, because you don't have enough public IP addresses—there is another way for Autodiscover to access your Exchange server, and that's the use of Service Records (SRV) in public DNS. Be aware that not all clients support SRV records for Autodiscover purposes. Mobile clients, for example, often do not support this.

Suppose we have another SMTP domain in the proexchangeadmin.com environment named exchange16.com, and, again, that domain name is not used in any SSL certificate. For this domain, we can configure SRV records for Autodiscover. This service record is constructed like _autodiscover._tcp.exchange16.com, and it will point to Autodiscover.proexchangeadmin.com on port 443 as shown in Figure 3-18.

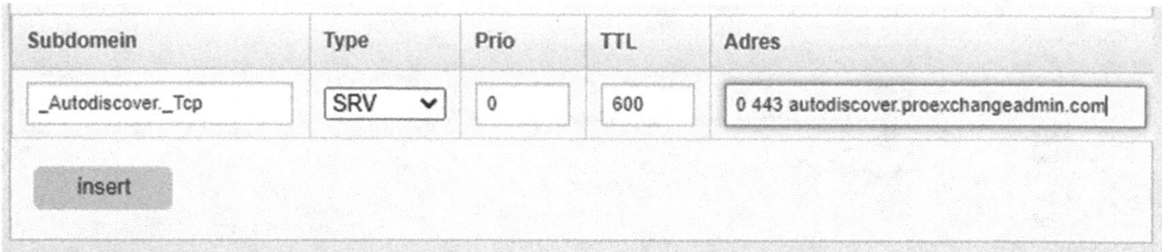

Figure 3-18. *Entering the Autodiscover SRV record in public DNS*

When using a tool like MXToolbox.com (or any other tool of course) to check the SRV entry, you will see something similar to that shown in Figure 3-19.

srv:_autodiscover._tcp.exchange16.com Find Problems srv

Type	Service	Protocol Name	TTL	Priority	Weight	Port	Target
SRV	autodiscover	tcp	10 min	0	0	443	autodiscover.proexchangeadmin.com

	Test	Result
✔	DNS Record Published	DNS Record found

dns lookup smtp diag blacklist http test

Reported by **ns2.argewebhosting.com** on 4/13/2021 at **6:54:37 AM (UTC -5)**, just for you. Transcript

Figure 3-19. *Resolving the Autodiscover SRV record in DNS using MXToolbox.com*

Now, when checking with the RCA, you will see that the Autodiscover redirect options fail, but that the SRV option succeeds, as shown in Figure 3-20.

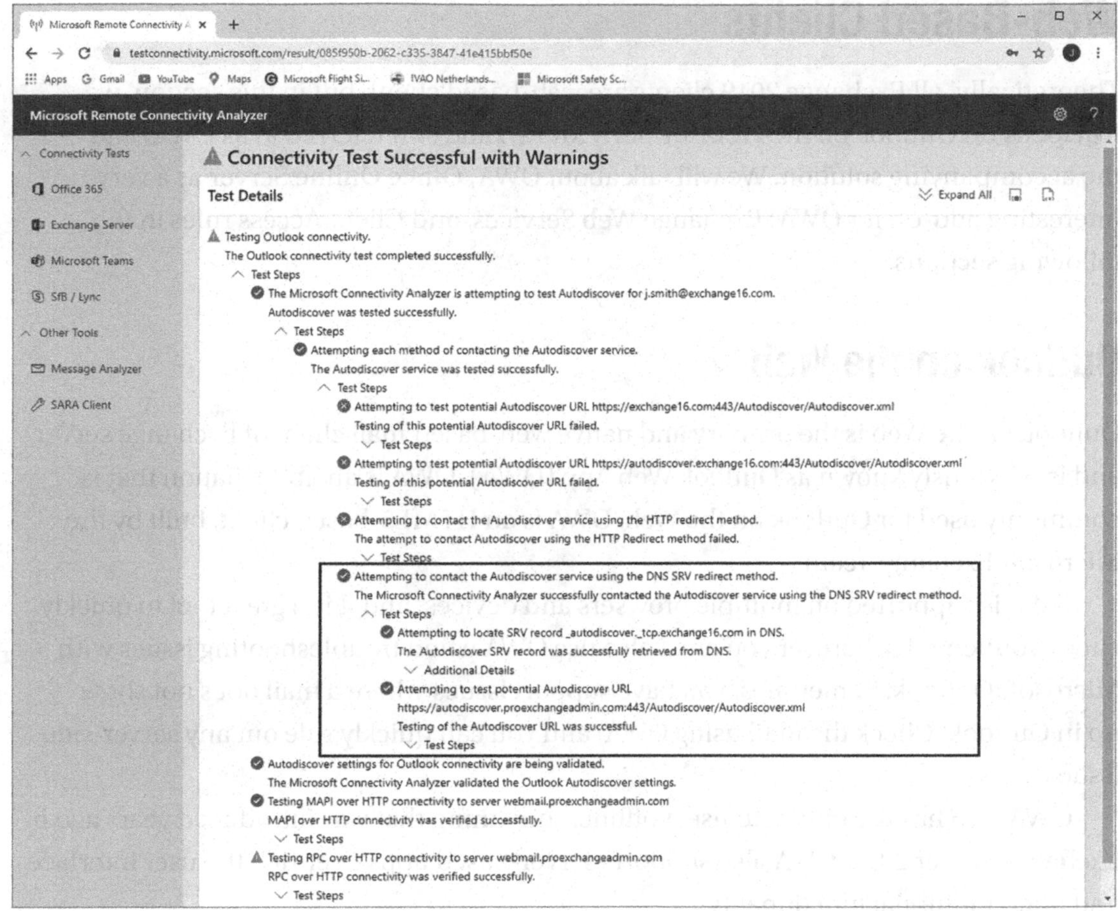

Figure 3-20. The Autodiscover SRV records test in the RCA

Note When using SRV records for Autodiscover, you can use any FQDN you like. This way, you can configure your Exchange server with only webmail.proexchange.com and use an SRV record for Autodiscover and point it to webmail.proexchange.com. In the early days of Exchange, this was sometimes used to save some money on SSL certificates, but nowadays that is no longer a valid business justification with the low pricing of SSL certificates. But it is still possible.

Web-Based Clients

Theoretically, all Exchange 2019 clients are web-based client, but in this section, we will focus on Outlook on the Web, formerly known and still referred to as OWA, and the accompanying solution. We will talk about OWA, Office Online Server as a very interesting add-on for OWA, Exchange Web Services, and Client Access rules in the following sections.

Outlook on the Web

Outlook on the Web is the primary and native web-based mail client of Exchange server and is previously known as Outlook Web App (OWA). OWA is an abbreviation that is commonly used for Outlook on the Web. OWA is an HTML5-based client, built by the Microsoft Exchange team.

OWA is supported on multiple browsers and devices, and it is a great tool to quickly check your email, wherever you are. I also use OWA when troubleshooting issues with Microsoft Outlook. Sometimes, you have support issues where a mail does not show up in Outlook. Check the mail using OWA, and you can quickly rule out any server-side issues.

OWA also has the option to use it offline, something that was introduced years ago in Exchange server 2013. OWA also supports server-based apps to enrich the user interface and offer additional functionality.

Official Microsoft browser support is quite simple. The latest versions of Microsoft Edge, Firefox, Safari, and Chrome are supported.

OWA Offline

Most browsers support the offline use of OWA, and it is easy to enable. Click the settings icon and select Offline settings as shown in Figure 3-21.

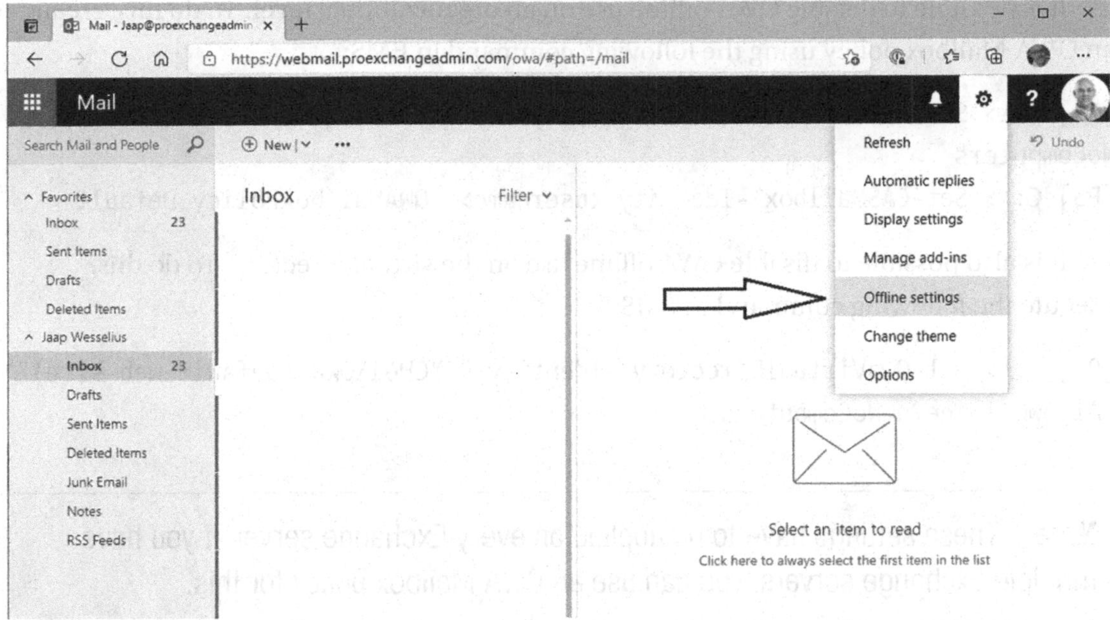

***Figure 3-21.** Enable Offline use in OWA*

Check the turn on offline access checkbox and follow the wizard to enable offline use.

A couple of remarks:

- Mail data is stored on the local computer. This can pose a security risk when other people are using the computer as well. Data is stored in a web database located in the user profile (C:\Users\<username>\AppData\Local\Microsoft\Edge\User Data\Default\databases).
- OWA uses a predetermined amount of storage on the computer. It can happen more storage is needed, and a pop-up box appears asking for more storage.
- When offline, a bookmark is the best way to access OWA offline.
- By default, only the Inbox and Drafts folders are synchronized for offline use. Five other folders that are recently used are synced as well, but other folders can be selected.

It is possible to disable OWA offline use on an organizational level. To do this, create an OWA Mailbox policy using the following command in EMS:

```
[PS] C:\> Set-OwaMailboxPolicy -Identity Default -AllowOfflineOn
NoComputers
[PS] C:\> Set-CASMailbox -Identity <username> -OWAMailboxPolicy Default
```

It is also possible to disable OWA offline use on the virtual directory. To do this, execute the following command in EMS:

```
[PS] C:\> Set-OwaVirtualDirectory -Identity "EXCH01\Owa (default web site)"
-AllowOfflineOn NoComputers
```

Note These settings have to be applied on every Exchange server. If you have multiple Exchange servers, you can use an OWA Mailbox policy for this.

Outlook Apps

Outlook apps were introduced in Exchange server 2013 and still exist in Exchange 2019. With Outlook apps, you can customize the functionality of OWA and Outlook. One nice example that's available by default in Exchange is "Bing Maps." When there is a street address in an email, Exchange will automatically detect it, contact Bing Maps, and provide additional information as shown in Figure 3-22.

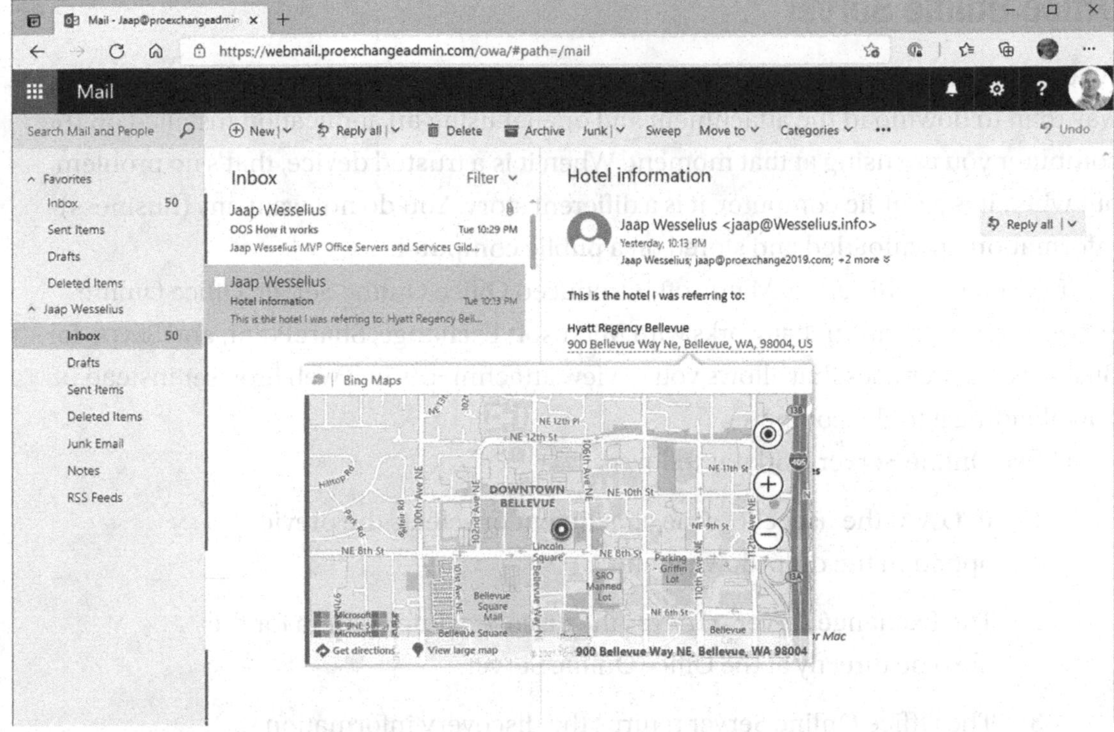

Figure 3-22. *Bing Maps in OWA*

By default, there are five apps available in Exchange:

- Action Items
- Bing Maps
- My Templates
- Suggested Meetings
- Unsubscribe

To add additional Outlook apps, open EAC and navigate to **Organization ➤ Add-ins**. Here, you will see the five default Outlook apps, but when you click the + icon and select **Add from the Office store**, you will be redirected to the Microsoft store. Filter on **Exchange** and you will see all available apps for Exchange which can be used in OWA (shown as web app) and Outlook.

Office Online Server

When you are using OWA and receive an email with an attachment, there is no other way than to download the attachment and open it using an application installed on the computer you are using at that moment. When it is a trusted device, that's no problem, but when it is a public computer, it is a different story. You do not want any (business) information downloaded and stored on a public computer.

To overcome this issue, Microsoft introduced Office Online Server. Office Online Server is an application that works with Microsoft Exchange, SharePoint, and Skype for Business on-premises that allows you to view attachments in a web browser instead of downloading it to the computer.

Office Online Server works as follows:

1. In OWA, the user clicks the attachment or selects the preview option in the drop-down menu.
2. The Exchange server retrieves the discovery information for the file type directly at the Office Online Server.
3. The Office Online Server returns the discovery information directly to the Exchange server with a unique URL.
4. Exchange creates in <iFrame> for the attachment and uses the unique URL that was retrieved in the previous step. This information is sent to the OWA client.
5. The OWA client uses the unique URL with a token to access the Office Online Server directly within the <iFrame>.
6. Exchange transfers the attachment to the Office Online Server.
7. Office Online Server renders the contents from the attachments and returns this directly to the OWA client.

This is shown in Figure 3-23.

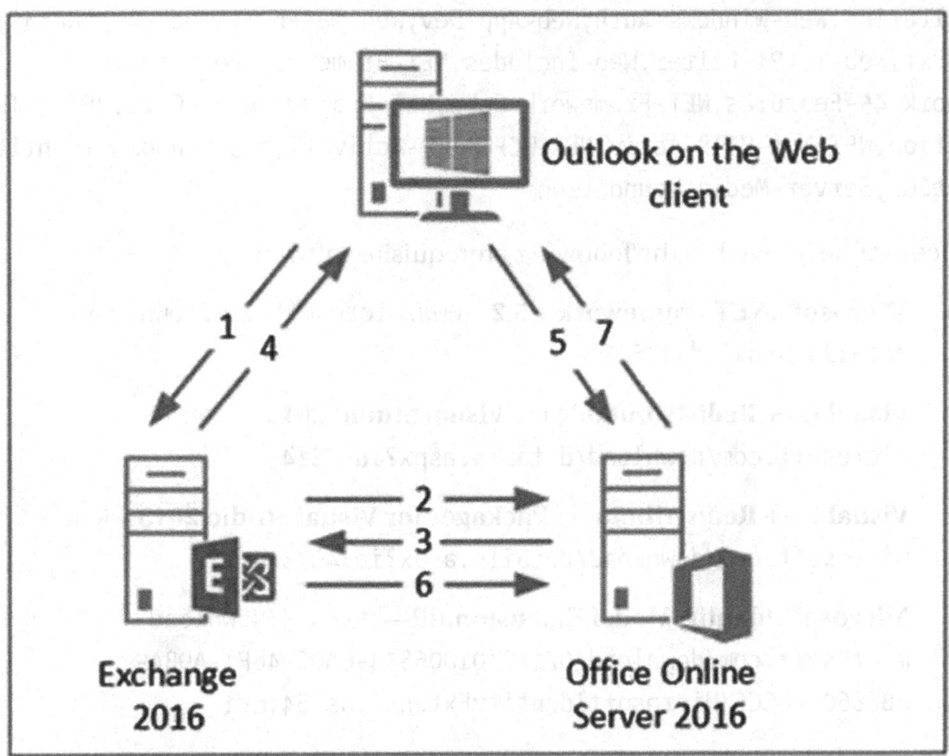

***Figure 3-23.** Data flow between Exchange, Office Online Server, and the OWA client*

When the user has read the information from the attachment and closes the <iFrame>, all data is deleted, and nothing remains on the (public) computer.

Note Office Online Server is not part of Exchange server; it is available as part of a Volume Licensing Agreement and as such a separate download. Also, Office Online Server only runs on Windows 2016 and not on Windows 2019. This is not supported.

Installing the Office Online Server is straightforward. Install Windows 2016 server and add the following prerequisite Server Roles and Features:

```
PS C:\> Add-WindowsFeature Web-Server,Web-Mgmt-Tools,Web-Mgmt-Console,
Web-WebServer,Web-Common-Http,Web-Default-Doc,Web-Static-Content,Web-
Performance,Web-Stat-Compression,Web-Dyn-Compression,Web-Security,
```

```
Web-Filtering,Web-Windows-Auth,Web-App-Dev,Web-Net-Ext45,Web-Asp-Net45,Web-
ISAPI-Ext,Web-ISAPI-Filter,Web-Includes,NET-Framework-Features,NET-
Framework-45-Features,NET-Framework-Core,NET-Framework-45-Core,NET-HTTP-
Activation,NET-Non-HTTP-Activ,NET-WCF-HTTP-Activation45,Windows-Identity-
Foundation,Server-Media-Foundation
```

Office Online Server has the following prerequisite software:

- **Microsoft .NET Framework 4.5.2**—`www.microsoft.com/download/details.aspx?id=42643`
- **Visual C++ Redistributable for Visual Studio 2015**—`www.microsoft.com/download/details.aspx?id=48145`
- **Visual C++ Redistributable Packages for Visual Studio 2013**—`www.microsoft.com/download/details.aspx?id=40784`
- **Microsoft.IdentityModel.Extension.dll**—`https://download.microsoft.com/download/0/1/D/01D06854-CA0C-46F1-ADBA-EBF86010DCC6/MicrosoftIdentityExtensions-64.msi`

The Server Roles and Features need to be installed before the prerequisite software. The Microsoft Identity Extensions model depends on the Windows Identity Foundation v1.0 which is installed with the Server Roles and Features.

Note Windows Server 2016 comes with .NET Framework 4.6.2, so the first prerequisite software does not have to be downloaded and installed.

A valid third-party SSL certificate is also needed on the Office Online Server. In the proexchangeadmin environment, the FQDN of the Office Online Server is office.proexchangeadmin.com, and an SSL request is created for the FQDN. Unlike the Exchange server, no additional names are used on the certificate. Also, this FQDN is used externally and internally. Figure 3-24 shows the Internet Information Server Manager (IIS Manager) when creating the certificate request.

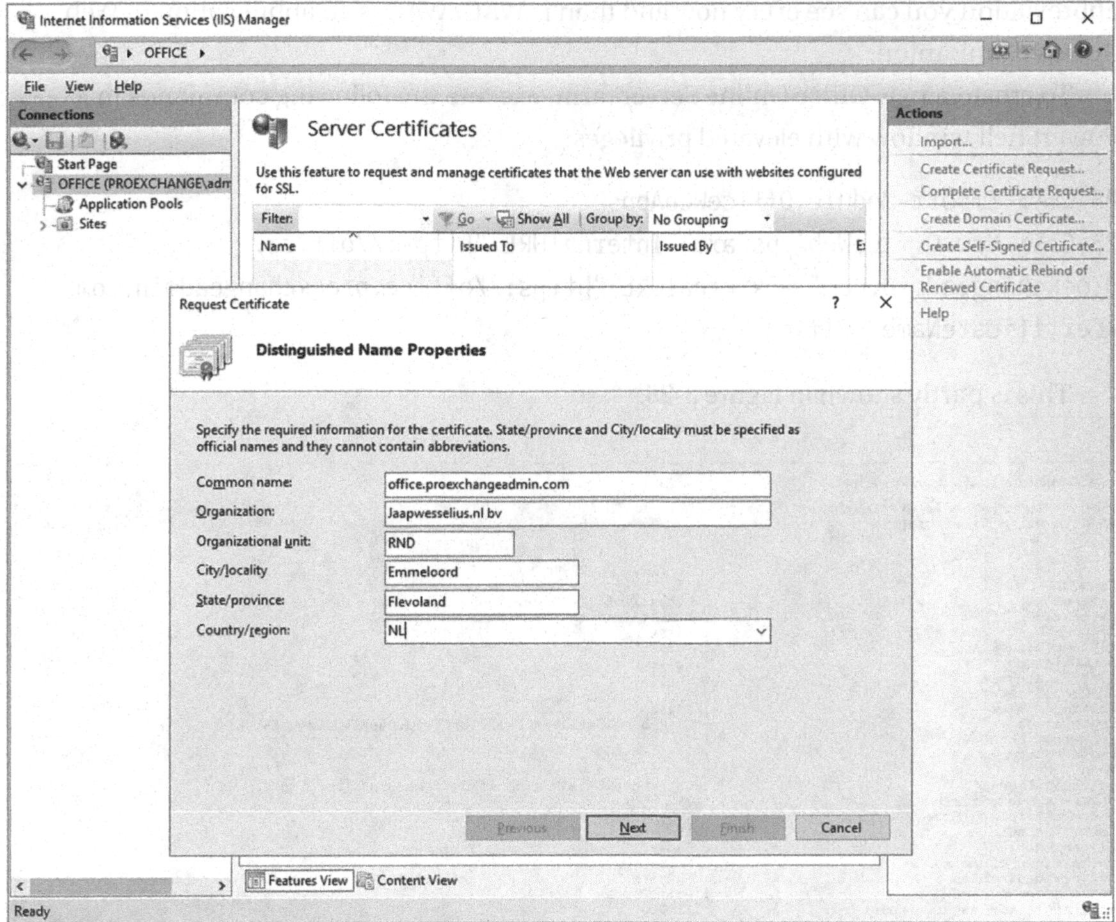

***Figure 3-24.** Create a certificate request in IIS Manager*

Tip Use an easy to identify friendly name for the certificate. This is used later in the process when creating an Office Online Server farm.

When the Windows 2016 server is installed and configured, the Office Online Server binaries can be installed. Open the setup application on the installation media and follow the wizard. The only configuration change that can be made during installation is the location of the software.

When the software is installed and ready, the server can be rebooted, and the Office Offline Server farm can be installed. Although the application is called "Office Online Server," under the hood it is still called "Office Web Apps." An even older name or abbreviation you can see every now and then is WAC. WAC is an abbreviation of Web Access Companion.

To create a new Office Online Server farm, execute the following commands in a PowerShell window with elevated privileges:

```
PS C:\> Import-Module OfficeWebApps
PS C:\> New-OfficeWebAppsFarm -InternalURL "https://office.
proexchangeadmin.com" -ExternalURL "https://office.proexchangeadmin.com"
-CertificateName "Office"
```

This is partly shown in Figure 3-25.

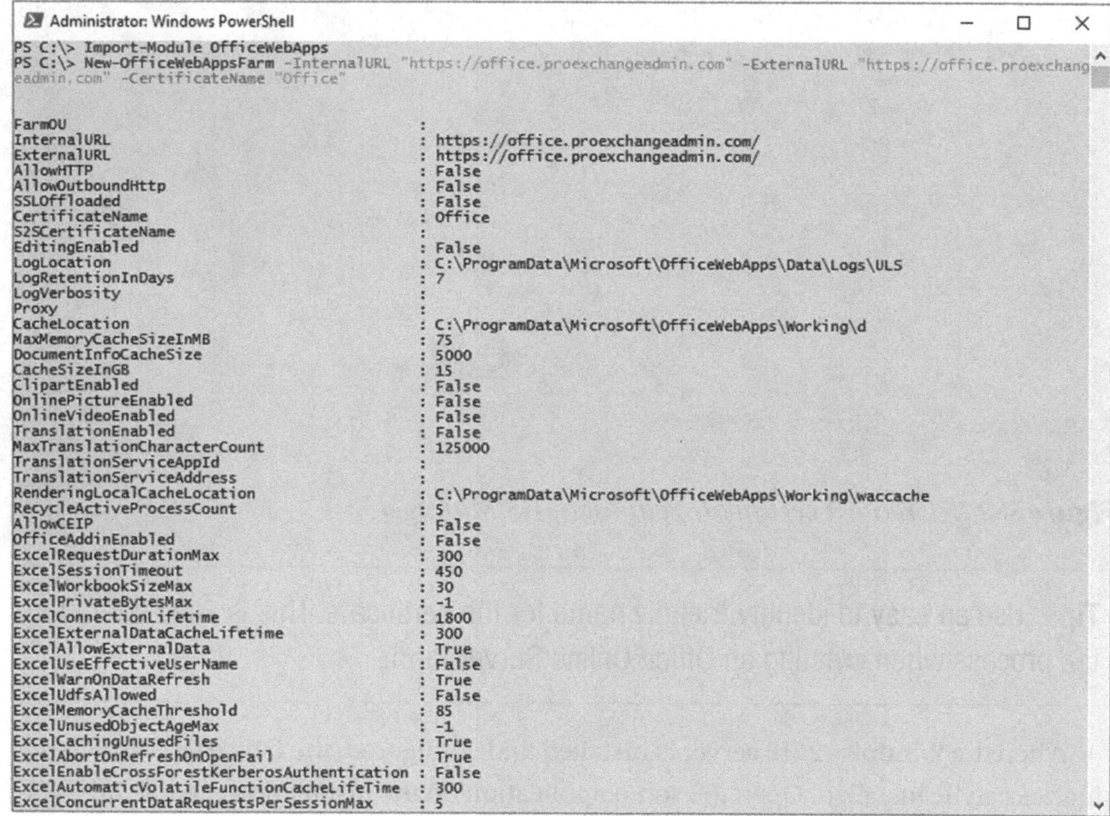

***Figure 3-25.** Creating a new Office Online Server farm*

Note The -certificatename option is the friendly name of the SSL certificate that was created earlier in this section.

When you access an email with an attachment, you can select the Preview option, and the attachment will be visible in the browser as shown in Figure 3-26. This example is a PowerPoint presentation; you can use the arrow buttons to scroll through the presentation.

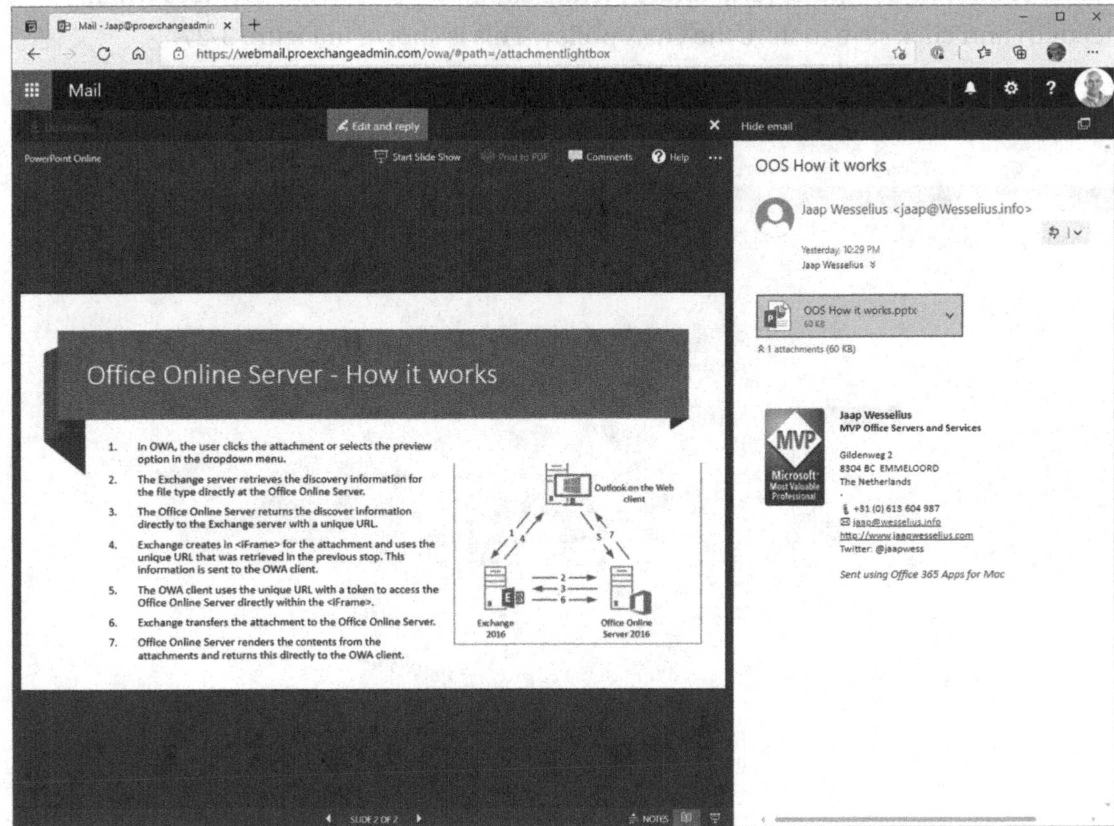

***Figure 3-26.** Opening an attachment with Office Online Server and OWA*

So, after installing Office Online Server, there is a new option "Preview" next to the download option in OWA. But on public computers, you want to disable the download option at all, so that only the preview option remains for attachments.

This can be achieved by the file access option in the OWA policies. To disable file access in OWA, execute the following commands in EMS:

```
[PS] C:\> Get-OwaMailboxPolicy | Set-OwaMailboxPolicy
-DirectFileAccessOnPublicComputersEnabled $false
-DirectFileAccessOnPrivateComputersEnabled $false
```

```
[PS] C:\> Set-CASMailbox -Identity jaap@proexchangeadmin.com
-OwaMailboxPolicy default
```

To change the OWA policy in EAC, navigate to **Permissions ➤ Outlook Web App policies** and open the Default policy. Uncheck the **Direct file access** options under Public or Shared Computer (and under Private computer or OWA for Devices when needed) and click save to store the OWA policy. This is shown in Figure 3-27.

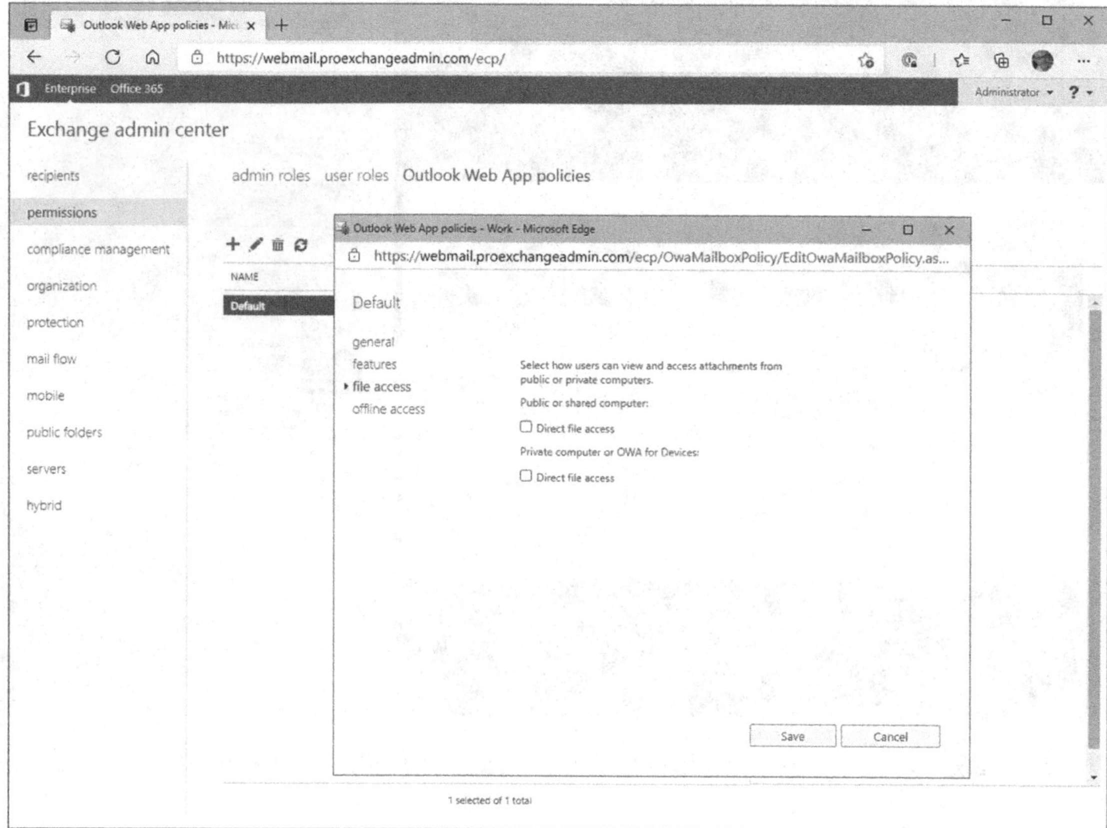

***Figure 3-27.** Change the OWA policies to block attachment downloads*

Note Office Online Server is difficult to patch. If you must patch this server, the farm must be removed, the server must be patched, and the farm recreated.

Exchange Admin Center

The Exchange Admin Center is the HTML5-based management interface for Exchange server. You can access the EAC using your browser by navigating to a URL like `https://webmail.proexchangeadmin.com/ecp`. The name of the EAC virtual directory is ECP, a leftover from the past when it was called Exchange Control Panel in Exchange 2010.

The EAC is accessible for everyone, both users and Exchange administrators. Depending on the permissions granted to the account, you can have a variety of functions available. Normal users have very limited permissions; they can only manage their own user and mailbox properties, but even that is limited. The Exchange administrators can manage most of the functions available in EAC. That is most, but not all, because there are features not available by default, even not for Exchange administrators like the Enterprise Search function or Export to PST functionality. Permissions are controlled via Role-Based Access Control (RBAC), which is discussed in Chapter 10.

It is possible to disable access to the EAC; to accomplish this, execute the following command in EMS:

```
[PS] C:\> Set-ECPVirtualDirectory -Identity "EXCH01\Ecp (default web site)"
-AdminEnabled $false
```

It will take approximately five minutes for this change to take effect. To expedite this change, you can always reset Internet Information Server using IISRESET.

Note: Only the administrative components of EAC will be disabled; the user components are still available. This is true for both external and internal access. So be careful with this setting, since it is not possible to make changes to the Exchange environment using EAC. For a more granular approach, I recommend using Client Access Rules to restrict access.

More information on how to manage your Exchange environment using EAC can be found in Chapter 1.

Exchange Web Services

The Exchange Web Services is not a client but an application programming interface (API) that is available via the network or when using Exchange Online via the Web.

EWS clients can access mailbox items on the Exchange server by sending a SOAP[1]-based XML message. Well-known EWS clients are Microsoft Outlook and Outlook for Mac, but there are also a lot of PowerShell scripts that use EWS to access mailboxes. Also, third-party applications can use EWS to interact with mailboxes. The use case for Outlook is availability information (free/busy), mail tips, and out-of-office settings.

The Exchange Web Services architecture is shown in Figure 3-28.

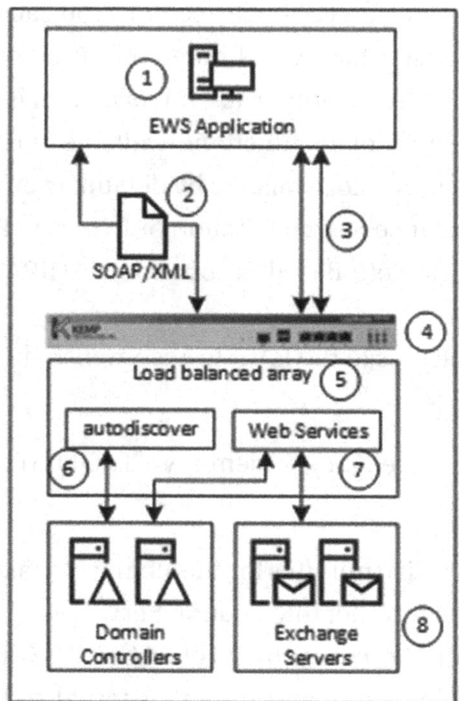

Figure 3-28. *Exchange Web Services architecture*

The following items are shown in the Exchange Web Services architecture:

1. **EWS application**—This can be any client like Microsoft Outlook or Outlook for Mac, custom application, PowerShell script, or third-party application. For custom application or PowerShell scripts, you must install the Microsoft Exchange Web Services managed API, which can be downloaded from `http://bit.ly/EWSAPIDownload`. More information, including code samples,

[1] SOAP stands for Simple Object Access Protocol, an HTTP-based communication protocol

can be found on the MSDN Office | Dev Center—in particular, the "Explore the EWS Managed API" page at `http://bit.ly/ExploreEWS`.

2. **SOAP/XML message**—An XML message is a SOAP envelope that is sent to the Exchange server. HTTPS is strongly recommended for communication between the client and the Exchange server.

3. **Authentication method**—EWS include Basic Authentication, Windows Integrated Authentication (NTLM), and OAuth. The latter is used for authentication for Microsoft Teams accessing a mailbox on the Exchange server.[2]

4. **Load balancer**—The load balancer distributes the client request among multiple Exchange servers.

5. **Array of Exchange servers**—An array of Exchange servers, but this can be only one for small environments. The Exchange server, or in more detail the Client Access Front-End service, performs an Autodiscover lookup to find the Exchange server hosting the user's mailbox, and the request is proxied to that Exchange server.

6. **Autodiscover service**—The Autodiscover performs service discovery by using Active Directory to find the Exchange server hosting the user's mailbox.

7. **Exchange Web Service**—The Exchange Web Service is described by three files:

   - **Services.wsdl**—Describes the contract between the client and the server
   - **Messages.xsd**—Defines the request and response SOAP messages
   - **Types.xsd**—Defines the elements used in the SOAP messages

8. **Database Availability Group**—Highly Available Exchange servers hosting mailbox databases. DAGs are described in more detail in Chapter 4.

[2] Teams integration with on-premises Exchange is supported from Exchange 2016 CU3 and higher

When an EWS application requests information from the Exchange store, an XML request message that complies with the SOAP standard is created and sent to the Exchange server. When the Exchange server receives the request, it verifies the credentials that are provided by the client and automatically parses the XML for the requested data. The server then builds a SOAP response that contains XML data that represents the requested information. The XML data is sent back to the application in an HTTP response and processed by the application.

Client Access Rules

Earlier in this chapter, I explained how to limit the functionality of the Exchange Admin Center, but even then, the EAC is still accessible. It is also possible to disable access to the EAC in the load balancer, but in that scenario, it is not accessible at all which is not always the right approach.

New in Exchange server 2019 are Client Access Rules which can help you limit access to both EAC and Remote PowerShell. Client Access Rules are much like Transport Rules in Exchange. Based on certain criteria, you can limit access to the EAC. These criteria are the IP address of the client (IPv4 and IPv6), authentication type, and user property values.

Examples of Client Access Rules are

- Disable client access to remote PowerShell (and thus Exchange Management Shell).
- Allow access to EAC only from certain IP addresses, like remote offices or even home IP addresses from Exchange administrators.

A Client Access Rule consists of the following components:

- **Condition**—Identify the client connection and when the connection matches a condition and apply an action. When a client connection matches a condition and an action is applied, rule evaluation stops.
- **Exception**—Identify client connections that the action should NOT be applied to.
- **Action**—Valid actions that can be applied are
    - AllowAccess
    - DenyAccess

- **Priority**—Higher priority rules (that have a lower number) are processed before lower priority rules. The highest priority for a rule has a value of "1".

Note Client Access Rules are applied to internal and external client connections, so you must consider how Client Access Rules impact your internal clients. As a best practice, you can create a Client Access Rule with the highest priority that allows connections from your internal network.

To create a new Client Access Rule that will restrict access to the EAC, but only allows clients from an internal subnet 10.38.96.0/4, execute the following command in EMS:

```
[PS] C:\> New-ClientAccessRule -Name "Restrict EAC" -Action DenyAccess
-AnyOfProtocols ExchangeAdminCenter -ExceptAnyOfClientIPAddressesOrRanges
10.38.96.0/24
```

This is shown in Figure 3-29.

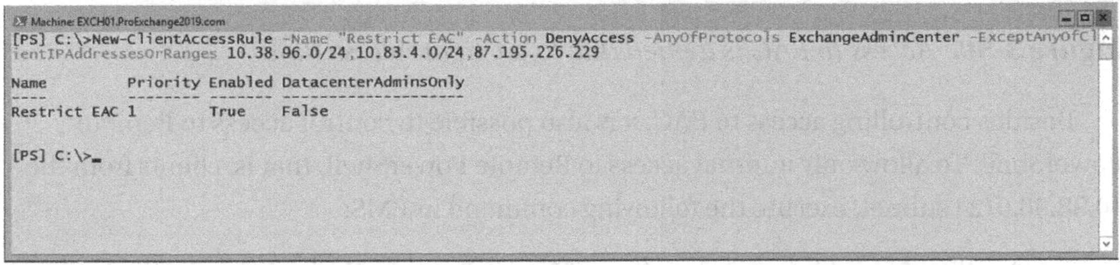

***Figure 3-29.** Creating a new Client Access Rule*

When the Client Access Rule is active and you navigate to the Exchange Admin Center, you can log in, but a warning is displayed as shown in Figure 3-30. You cannot access EAC, but you can redirect to OWA if you want, or you can opt to log out.

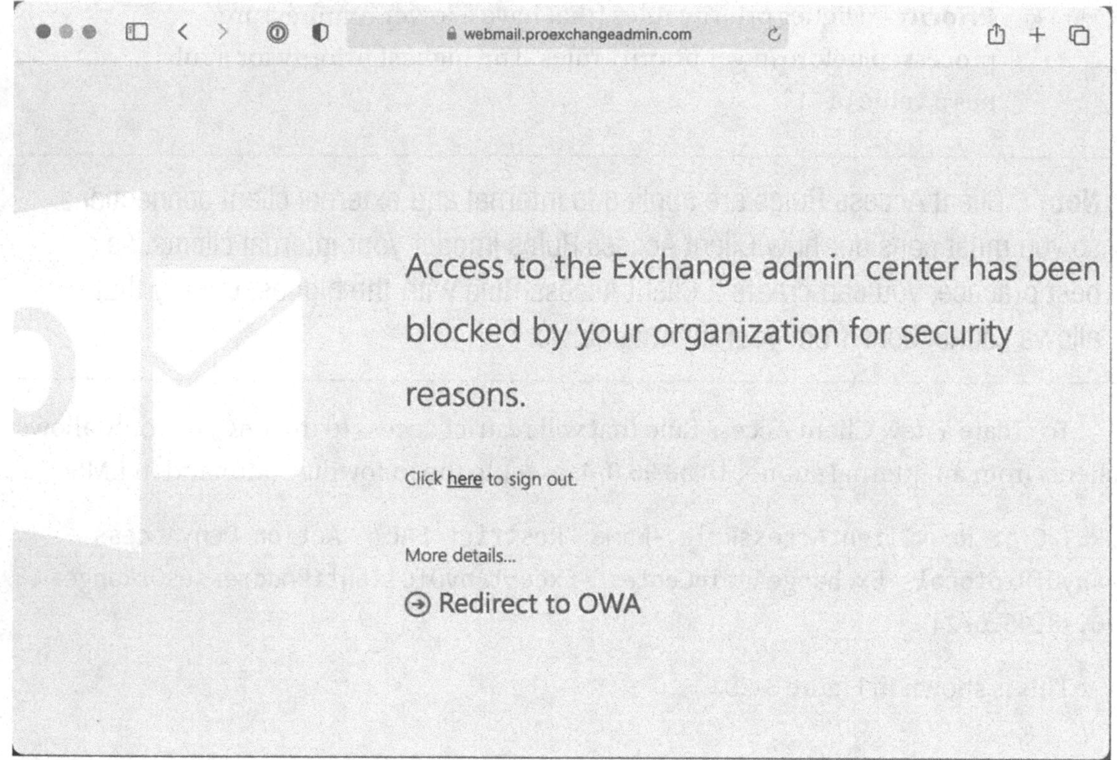

Figure 3-30. *Access to EAC is denied due to a Client Access Rule*

Besides controlling access to EAC, it is also possible to control access to Remote PowerShell. To allow only internal access to Remote PowerShell, that is, clients from the 10.38.96.0/24 subnet, execute the following command in EMS:

```
[PS] C:\> New-ClientAccessRule -Name "Block PowerShell" -Action DenyAccess
-AnyOfProtocols RemotePowerShell -ExceptAnyOfClientIPAddressesOrRanges
10.38.96.0/24
```

For performance reasons, Client Access Rules are cached. This automatically implies that changes do not take effect immediately. For the first rule that is created, it can take up to 24 hours before it becomes effective. Additional Client Access Rules are effective in approximately one hour.

Another pitfall is the load balancer in front of the Exchange servers. Client Access Rule results depend on how the load balancer is configured with transparency. When the virtual service on the load balancer is configured with transparency disabled, all requests on the Exchange server originate from the internal IP address of the load balancer. As a result, Client Access Rules will never show the desired behavior.

Note Transparency and load balancing will be discussed in the "Client Access High Availability" section later in this chapter.

Mobile Clients

Exchange ActiveSync (EAS) is the protocol used by mobile clients connecting to the Exchange environment over the Internet. Mobile clients are mostly smartphones and tablets running iOS or Android. The default mail client on Windows 10 also uses EAS to retrieve email from the Exchange server.

Microsoft is licensing the EAS protocol and its interfaces to third parties and independent software vendors. It is up to the vendor to write actual applications to use the EAS protocol. One of the problems with this is that Microsoft "forgot" to enforce standard implementations or quality control. Therefore, each vendor has its own interpretation of using the EAS protocol, resulting in some applications that run fine but others that are horrible to use from an Exchange perspective. Additionally, there are applications that have a major performance impact on the Exchange server.

Mobile clients are typically very sensitive when it comes to SSL certificates, and not all SSL certificates are accepted by mobile clients. To get EAS working properly, there needs to be a supported third-party SSL certificate.

Most mobile clients rely on the Autodiscover function of the Exchange server, as do Outlook clients, so again having a fully working Autodiscover environment is a prerequisite for running EAS successfully.

Earlier versions of Exchange were able to use OWA of iPad or OWA for iPhone clients, but these are discontinued in 2018. The successor of these clients is Outlook Mobile, sometimes referred to as Outlook for iOS and Outlook for Android. Outlook Mobile is a cloud-backed application. It is a local app on the mobile device, combined with a scalable service in the Microsoft cloud. As such, it uses a different approach when connecting to a mailbox in Exchange on-premises. Outlook Mobile is using an unmanaged mailbox in Exchange Online, and it communicates with this mailbox using a native Microsoft Sync technology. The unmanaged mailbox in turn is using EAS to communicate with the on-premises Exchange server as shown in Figure 3-31.

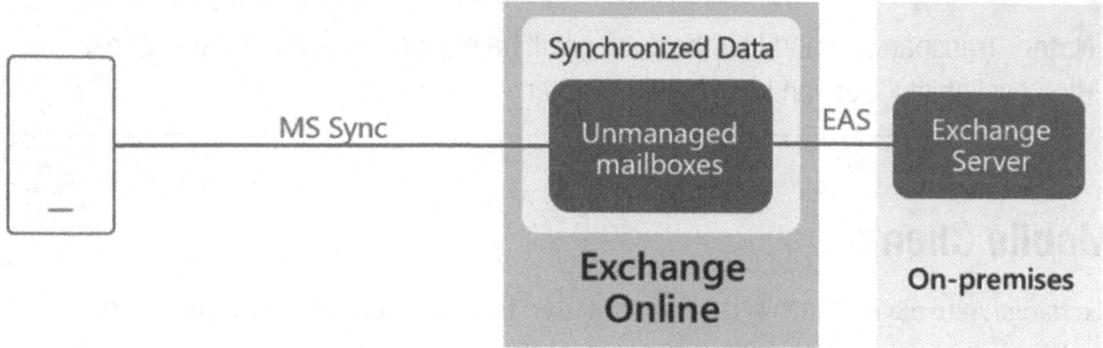

Figure 3-31. *Outlook Mobile is using unmanaged mailboxes in Exchange Online for communicating with an on-premises mailbox*

This is clearly visible in the IIS logs. When connecting with Outlook Mobile on an iPhone, the following is logged in the IIS logfile:

```
2021-05-04 09:45:54 10.38.96.222 POST /Microsoft-Server-ActiveSync/default.
eas Cmd=Ping&User=baron%40proexchangeadmin.com&DeviceId=db4f7bbcccf845a185
da5b9f2d9783ec&DeviceType=Outlook&CorrelationID=<empty>;&cafeReqId=634618
5e-3f3d-4eac-8e66-98acac9920d7; 80 baron@proexchangeadmin.com 52.98.169.237
Outlook-iOS-Android/1.0 - 200 0 0 180023
```

The IP address 10.38.96.222 is the internal IP address of the Exchange 2019 server; the IP address 52.98.169.237 is a Microsoft IP address from Dublin. The external IP address of the iPhone is 5.159.33.188; this IP address is not logged anywhere.

A similar test with Outlook Mobile on an Android phone reveals the same:

```
2021-05-04 10:08:35 10.38.96.222 OPTIONS /Microsoft-Server-ActiveSync/
default.eas Cmd=Options&User=proexchange%5Cphilip&DeviceId=OPCC2F2ECD5DFC67
882009735E484A84&DeviceType=Outlook&CorrelationID=<empty>;&cafeReqId=31e4ca
1e-1eeb-46ea-a929-3b182a0187a1; 80 proexchange\philip 52.97.216.13 Outlook-
iOS-Android/1.0 - 401 1 1326 91
```

The external IP address of the Android phone is 80.255.255.55; the IP address 52.97.216.13 is a Microsoft address from Paris.

The unmanaged mailbox in Exchange Online contains four weeks of email, all calendaring data, all contact data, and out-of-office status. The connection and synchronization between the unmanaged mailbox and the on-premises mailbox is ongoing and independent of user behavior. This will ensure the user always gets the best performance.

Using the services of the Microsoft will enable features like the focused inbox, customized experience for travel and calendar, and improved search speed. It also gives a consistent look and feel on the client, independent of the underlying Exchange servers.

POP3 and IMAP4

Although still widely used and still under active development, POP3 and IMAP4 are not commonly employed in a Microsoft environment. POP3 and IMAP4 are primarily used in (low-cost) hosting environments running some Unix flavor, but they can also be configured for use on Exchange Server. There are also business applications that can access a particular mailbox using the POP3 or IMAP4 protocol to retrieve messages.

POP3 and IMAP4 are installed on the Exchange server by default, but the relevant services are set to "manual start," so if they are needed, the POP3 or IMAP4 service has to be reset to "automatically start." Also, the authentication (encrypted login or plain text login) needs to be set. Exchange Server allows the basic POP3 and IMAP4 protocols, but also allows the encrypted version—that is, POP3S (POP3 over SSL) and IMAPS (IMAP4 over SSL).

Note The POP3 and IMAP4 protocols are only used for retrieving messages. The mail client should be configured for sending outbound mail via an SMTP mailhost. Of course, this can be the Exchange server running the Client Front-End connector.

If you want to use a third-party certificate with POP3 or IMAP4, you must configure the respective service to use it, very similar to the process with IIS. To enable an SSL certificate for POP3 and IMAP4, execute the following command in EMS:

```
[PS] C:\> Get-ExchangeCertificate -Server EXCH01 -Thumbprint <thumbprint> |
Enable-ExchangeCertificate -Server EXCH01 -Services POP,IMAP
```

Restart the POP3 and IMAP4 services, and you are good to go.

Client Access High Availability

If you are running multiple Exchange servers, most likely you want to use a load balancer for redundancy and performance reasons. For this, you can use a load balancer solution. Using a load balancer, you can distribute the load from clients among multiple Exchange servers. This will distribute the load across the Exchange servers, and if one server fails, client connections will be distributed among the remaining Exchange servers.

Load balancing solutions can be hardware load balancers, software load balancers (which are often like the hardware load balancers but running in a virtual machine on your own hardware), and Microsoft Network Load Balancing (NLB).

In the early days of Exchange Server, there was hardly any load balancing, and the Microsoft solution for load balancing was to use NLB. Although NLB works fine, it has some drawbacks:

- NLB is a service in Windows Server and thus is dependent on the server.
- The scalability of an NLB cluster is not that great and is limited to eight nodes.
- The only option for affinity is source IP.
- When you are adding or removing nodes to or from an NLB cluster, all clients are automatically disconnected and must reconnect.
- When NLB is used in unicast mode, it is possible that port or switch flooding occurs.
- There is no service awareness, thus causing a possible "black hole."
- NLB cannot be combined with a database availability group (DAG) on a multi-role server. A DAG is using failover clustering software that cannot be combined with NLB software.

That last bullet is an issue when using DAGs as well. Up to Exchange 2013, it was possible to separate the server roles, and you could install dedicated Client Access servers, so the DAG conflicts were not an issue. But to be honest, the last time I have seen NLB in any Exchange deployment is years ago. At the same time, it is a general recommendation to use a load balancer solution instead of NLB.

Layer 4 and Layer 7 Load Balancing

In Exchange, it is possible to use two ways of load balancing:

- Layer 4 (L4) load balancing, a relatively "dumb" load balancing solution where an inbound client connection is forwarded one on one to an Exchange Server.
- Layer 7 (L7) load balancing, where the inbound SSL client connection is terminated at the load balancer and then forwarded to an Exchange server.

Let us compare load balancing layers to the OSI model. A layer 7 load balancer is a solution whereby the load balancing takes place on the application layer. The SSL session is terminated at the load balancer, and the load balancer can do smart things to the connection, like modifying the HTTP headers or using cookie information in the HTTP stream. This information is then employed to identify the session and make sure the session is always connected to the same Exchange server.

With a layer 4 load balancer, the load balancing takes place on the network layer. An incoming connection is accepted and distributed across multiple Exchange servers "as is"—no processing takes place at all. The Exchange server, in turn, accepts the connection, and after authentication the connection is forwarded to the appropriate Mailbox server. Since the connections to the Exchange server are stateless, there is no need to worry about affinity. If an Exchange server fails the connection, it is rerouted to another Exchange server. There will be a minor performance penalty, owing to automatic reauthentication, but the connection on the Mailbox server is preserved.

The load balancer is configured with a virtual service, and this virtual service has an FQDN (like webmail.proexchangeadmin.com) and an IP address. The IP address is referred to as the "virtual IP," or VIP. A client connects to this VIP and thus connects to the load balancer. The load balancer keeps track of the source IP of the connection request and forwards the request to one of the Exchange servers.

Keep in mind that, in a layer 4 load balancer, the SSL connection is terminated at the Exchange server and not at the load balancer. Therefore, the load balancer cannot inspect any of the traffic between the client and the Exchange server.

To overcome this problem, there are two possible solutions:

- Use multiple VIPs for various services so that the individual VIPs can be checked for health (see Figure 3-32).

- Use a layer 7 load balancer so that the load balancer can inspect the traffic for the individual services. This can be combined with SSL offloading.

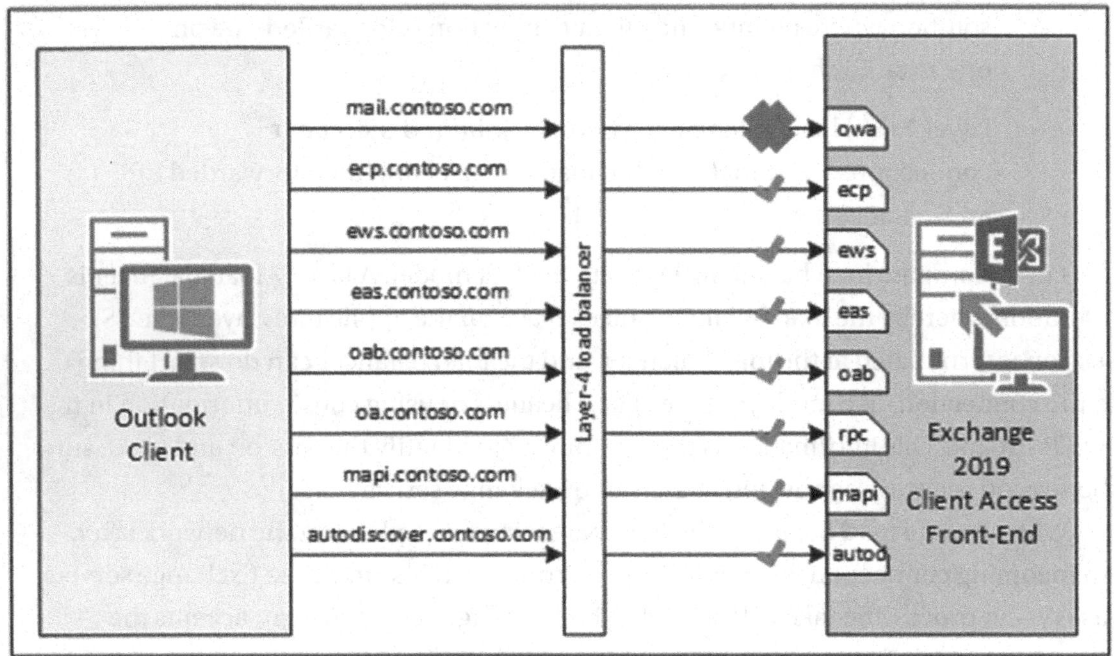

Figure 3-32. *Multiple VIPs on the load balancer for the Exchange server*

In Figure 3-32, there are eight separate VIPs—one VIP for each server—and they are independent of each other. When the OWA AppPool on the Exchange server fails, only the OWA traffic is redirected to another Exchange server, and other traffic continues to be serviced by this Exchange server.

With layer 7 load balancer, the connection from the client is terminated at the load balancer. After termination, the load balancer can do content inspection. It can detect whether an incoming connection is for OWA, EWS, or MAPI and redirect the connection to the respective virtual directory on the Exchange server. So, you can use one VIP for both webmail and Autodiscover, including all the virtual directories. When the connection is terminated at the load balancer, the load balancer determines which virtual directory to send the request to. When one service fails, the load balancer can initiate a failover for only that specific virtual directory to another Exchange server.

This is shown in Figure 3-33 where the OWA virtual directory fails. In this case, the load balancer will redirect to another Exchange server, but all other virtual directories on this specific server will remain active and support clients.

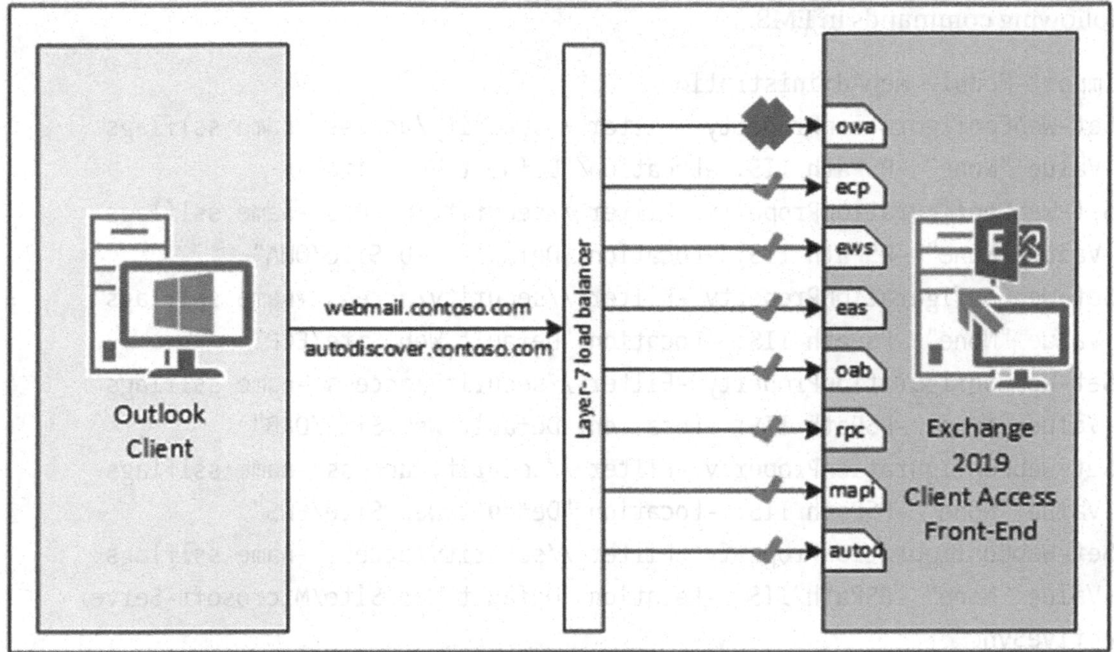

***Figure 3-33.** One VIP on the load balancer and multiple virtual directories on the Exchange server*

Note When using layer 7 load balancing, the connection is terminated at the load balancer. As such, the VIP on the load balancer is the endpoint for the client, and the load balancer must be configured with the proper SSL certificate.

SSL Offloading

When using SSL offloading, the SSL traffic is terminated at the load balancer; beyond the load balancer, the traffic can continue unencrypted. With SSL offloading, it is possible to perform content inspection and thus evaluate the individual client request and then proxy these individual client requests to individual virtual directories on the Client

Access server. SSL offloading is also needed for transparency purposes as described in the next section.

SSL offloading for the individual web services is not enabled by default, so it must be enabled on each virtual directory on the Exchange server. To achieve this, execute the following commands in EMS:

```
Import-Module WebAdministration
Set-WebConfigurationProperty -Filter //security/access -name sslflags
-Value "None" -PSPath IIS: -Location "Default Web Site"
Set-WebConfigurationProperty -Filter //security/access -name sslflags
-Value "None" -PSPath IIS: -Location "Default Web Site/OWA"
Set-WebConfigurationProperty -Filter //security/access -name sslflags
-Value "None" -PSPath IIS: -Location "Default Web Site/ECP"
Set-WebConfigurationProperty -Filter //security/access -name sslflags
-Value "None" -PSPath IIS: -Location "Default Web Site/OAB"
Set-WebConfigurationProperty -Filter //security/access -name sslflags
-Value "None" -PSPath IIS: -Location "Default Web Site/EWS"
Set-WebConfigurationProperty -Filter //security/access -name sslflags
-Value "None" -PSPath IIS: -Location "Default Web Site/Microsoft-Server-
ActiveSync"
Set-WebConfigurationProperty -Filter //security/access -name sslflags
-Value "None" -PSPath IIS: -Location "Default Web Site/Autodiscover"
Set-WebConfigurationProperty -Filter //security/access -name sslflags
-Value "None" -PSPath IIS: -Location "Default Web Site/MAPI"
```

Note These commands can be downloaded from the Apress website.

For Outlook Anywhere on an Exchange server, SSL offloading is enabled by default. If for some reason the SSL offloading for Outlook Anywhere is not enabled, you can use the following commands in EMS to enable SSL offloading:

```
[PS] C:\> Get-OutlookAnywhere -Server EXCH01 | Set-OutlookAnywhere -
SSLOffloading:$true -ExternalClientsRequireSsl:$true -ExternalHostName
webmail.contoso.com -ExternalClientAuthenticationMethod NTLM -Internal
```

```
ClientsRequireSSL:$true -InternalHostName webmail.proexchangeadmin.com
-InternalClientAuthenticationMethod NTLM
```

Customers often do not allow unencrypted traffic between the load balancer and the Exchange servers. To overcome this, you can enable the reencrypt option on the load balancer. This way, the SSL connection is terminated on the load balancer, the load balancer can perform its tasks, and the traffic to the Exchange server is still using an encrypted connection. The default self-signed certificate on the Exchange server can be used in this scenario. The self-signed certificate is only used for the encrypted connection, but not for server validation; hence, a third-party SSL certificate is not needed.

Load Balancer Transparency

To work effectively in a layer 7 configuration, two things need to happen:

1. Inbound traffic needs to flow through the load balancer.
2. Response traffic needs to flow through the load balancer on the way out.

To achieve this, the load balancer can be configured in L7 transparent mode or L7 nontransparent mode.

When traffic reaches the load balancer, its source IP address is that of the client to access the Exchange server, and the destination IP address is that of the virtual service on the load balancer:

- When configured in L7 **transparent mode**, the source IP address of the client is kept, but the destination IP is changed to the IP address of the Exchange server. Return traffic is sent to the original source address, but the return traffic must flow through the load balancer. The default gateway setting of the Exchange server MUST be the balancer; otherwise, the Exchange server will route the traffic via the regular network default gateway, causing the load balancer functionality to break. This is shown in Figure 3-34.
- When configured in L7 **nontransparent mode**, the load balancer will change the source IP address of the client traffic to the internal IP of the load balancer, and it will change the destination IP address to the

IP address of the Exchange server. The Exchange server will only see traffic coming from the internal IP address of the load balancer, and response traffic will always be routed via this internal IP address. In this scenario, no changes need to be made to the network settings of the Exchange server.

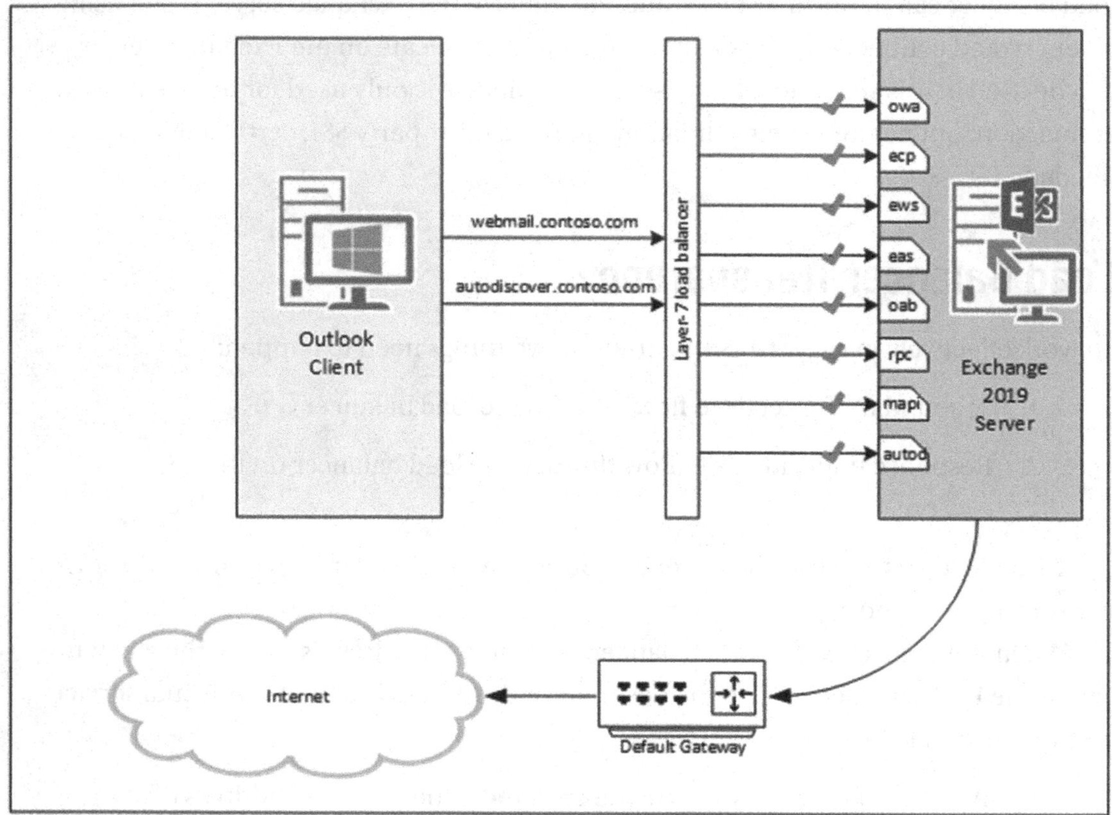

***Figure 3-34.** Regular traffic flows via the default gateway, but client traffic needs to go through the load balancer*

To enable transparency, the Exchange server needs to be configured first for SSL offloading as discussed in the previous section. You can check if SSL offloading works by using the healthcheck.htm page, which is part of Managed Availability and which the load balancer also uses for checking server availability. Open a browser and navigate to `http://exch01/owa/healthcheck.htm`, and you should see something like Figure 3-35.

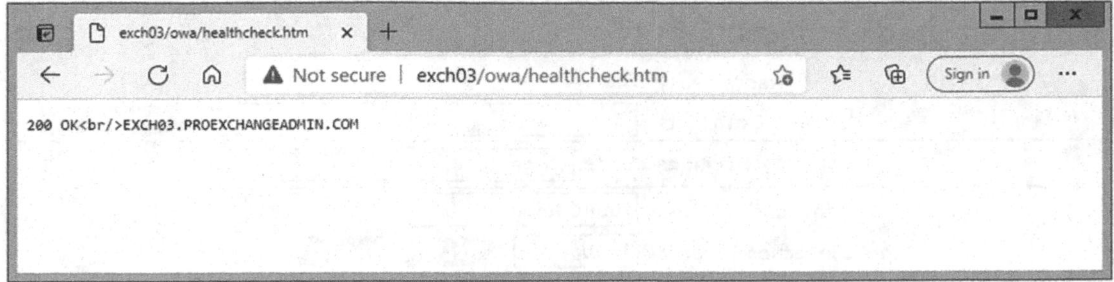

***Figure 3-35.** OWA is using an unencrypted connection via port 80*

The next step is to disable reencrypting traffic between the load balancer and the Exchange servers. It differs per vendor, but when using a Kemp LoadMaster, it is just a matter of unchecking the reencrypt checkbox as shown in Figure 3-36.

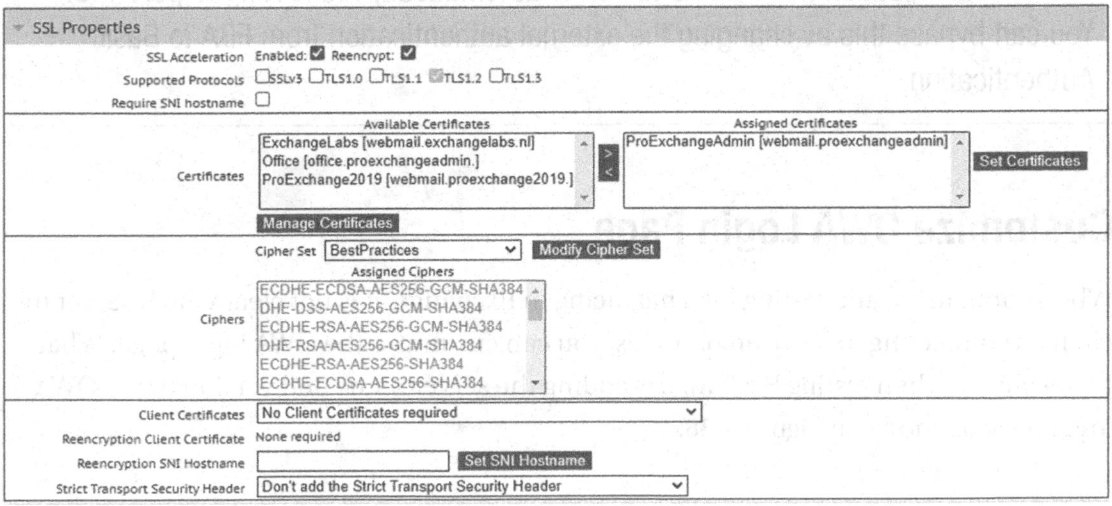

***Figure 3-36.** Uncheck the Reencrypt checkbox for IIS offloading*

The virtual service should remain "up," and the real servers (the Exchange servers) should remain healthy as well. Transparency should automatically switch to enabled when disabling reencrypting traffic from the load balancer to the Exchange server, as shown in Figure 3-37.

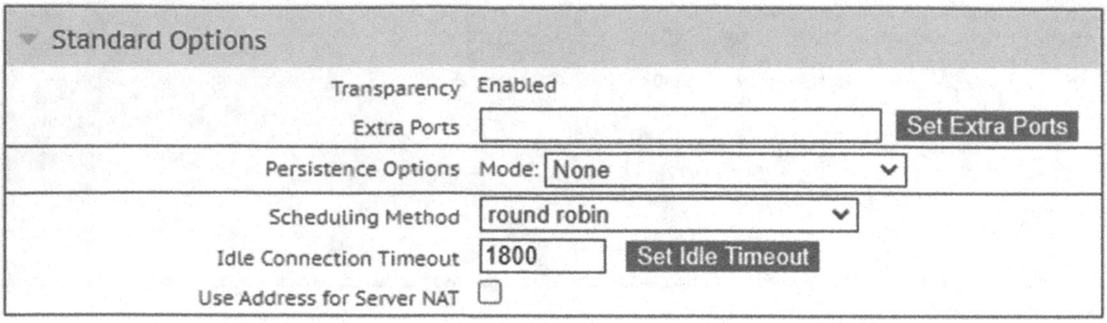

***Figure 3-37.** Transparency is automatically enabled when reencryption is disabled*

Tip When testing SSL offloading, be aware that OWA by default is using form-based authentication (FBA) and that FBA is automatically redirecting to port 443. You can bypass this by changing the external authentication from FBA to Basic Authentication.

Customize OWA Login Page

When configuring and testing load balancing in Exchange, it is not clear which server the client is connecting to. To overcome this, you can customize the OWA login page. What I typically do when testing Exchange is adding the server name and version to the OWA login page as shown in Figure 3-38.

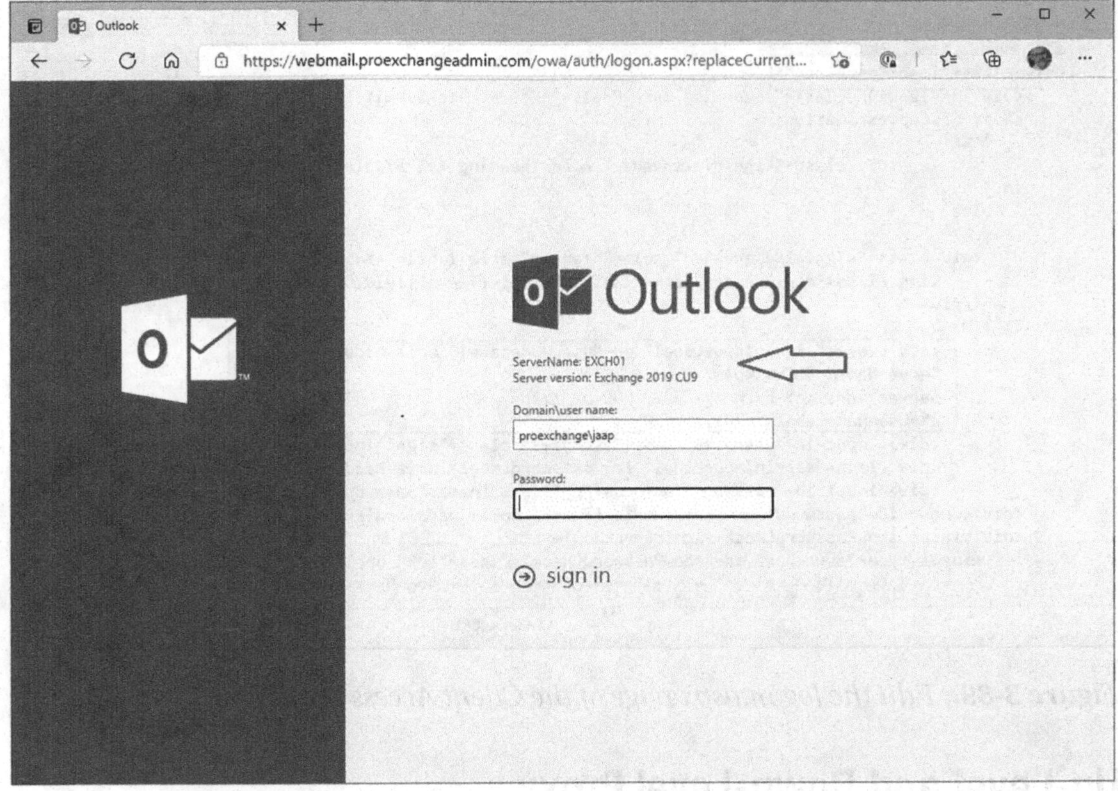

Figure 3-38. *The OWA login page shows the server name and version*

To do this, open the logon.aspx file that can be found in the C:\Program Files\Microsoft\Exchange Server\V15\FrontEnd\HttpProxy\owa\auth directory and scroll down to the *div class="logonContainer"* section and add the server name text just before the UserNameLabel variable, as shown in Figure 3-39.

```
<div class="logonContainer">
    <div id="lgnDiv" class="logonDiv" onKeyPress="return checkSubmit(event)">
    <% if (IsEcpDestination)
       { %>
               <div class="signInTextHeader" role="heading"><%=SignInHeader%></div>
    <% }
       else
       { %>
        <div class="signInImageHeader" role="heading" aria-label="<%=SignInHeader%>">
            <img class="mouseHeader" src="<%=InlineImage(ThemeFileId.OwaHeaderTextBlue)%>" alt="<%=
        </div>
    <% } %>
            <div class="signInInputLabel" id="userNameLabel" aria-hidden="true">
            ServerName: EXCH01<br />
            Server version: Exchange 2019 CU9<br /><br />
            <%=UserNameLabel%></div>
            <div><input id="username" name="username" class="signInInputText" role="textbox" aria-]
            <div class="signInInputLabel" id="passwordLabel" aria-hidden="true"><%=LocalizedString:
            <div><input id="password" onfocus="g_fFcs=0" name="password" value="" type="password" (
    <div><input id="passwordText" onfocus="g_fFcs=0" name="passwordText" value="" style="display: r
    <div class="showPasswordCheck signInCheckBoxText">
        <input type="checkbox" id="showPasswordCheck" class="chk" onclick="showPasswordClick()" />
```

Figure 3-39. *Edit the logon.aspx page of the Client Access Front End*

Up-Level and Down-Level Proxy

One of the nice features of Exchange 2013, 2016, and 2019 is that from a Client Access Front-End perspective, the servers are compatible with each other and that they can do both up-level and down-level proxy. What is up-level and down-level proxy?

- Down-level proxy means the mailbox is on Exchange 2016 and the client connects to the Exchange 2019 server; the client connection is proxied from Exchange 2019 to Exchange 2016.
- Up-level proxy means the mailbox is on Exchange 2016 and the client connects to the Exchange 2013 server; the client connection is proxied from Exchange 2013 to Exchange 2016.

This means you can create an array of load-balanced Exchange 2013, 2016, and 2019 servers without any issues. When testing, you can use the customize option as discussed in the previous section.

Note Up-level proxy works only from Exchange 2013 and higher. If you are in a coexistence mode with Exchange 2010 and Exchange 2016, you can only use down-level proxy. Up-level proxy does not work in this scenario. Compatibility is only true for the Client Access Front-End services. Mailbox databases are NOT compatible with each other, and as such, Exchange versions cannot be mixed in a Database Availability Group.

Summary

Although Exchange server 2019 and Exchange server 2016 have one server role, the Mailbox server role, under the hood there still are the Client Access services as we knew them in the Exchange 2013 Client Access Server.

The Client Access services consist of the Client Access Front-End and the Front-End Transport service. All clients connect to these services, so it is important to configure them well.

Exchange server 2013, Exchange server 2016, and Exchange server 2019 are compatible with each other from a Client Access perspective, so you can create an array of load-balanced servers with all three Exchange server versions. They will process all client requests, independent of the location of the mailbox.

It is important to configure the Exchange virtual directories and SSL certificates, according to your namespace design.

Another very important aspect is the Autodiscover functionality in every Exchange deployment. Autodiscover was first developed in Exchange server 2007, but even after 13 years, I see customers not fully understanding this functionality. Without a proper Autodiscover configuration, you will have difficulties in configuring Outlook clients, and Outlook clients will have issues with availability information, mail tips, and out-of-office settings.

After discussing the Client Access services in Exchange 2019, we will continue with the other components in Exchange, the mailbox server components. This will be the next chapter.

CHAPTER 4

Exchange 2019 Mailbox Services

In Exchange server 2019 and Exchange server 2016, the mailbox service is the back-end part of an Exchange server. Its primary role is to host mailboxes, but the Transport service and Client Access service (not to confuse with Client Access Front-End services) are also part of the Mailbox service. From an architectural point of view, it is very much comparable with the old Exchange server 2013 Mailbox server role. Clients connect to and are authenticated on the front-end services; all processing takes place in the back-end services.

As explained in the previous chapter, the Client Access services are a stateless protocol proxy, proxying user requests to the correct Mailbox service and Mailbox database. An important part of the Mailbox server is hosting the mailbox databases where all the mailboxes are located.

The database technology used in Exchange is the first part of this chapter, followed by the management tasks related to the mailbox databases. Then we will continue with High Availability on the Mailbox services using Database Availability Groups, followed by backup, restore, and disaster recovery on the Mailbox services. This also includes the "backupless environment" using compliance features offered by Exchange.

Mailbox Services

The Exchange 2019 Mailbox Service is like the Mailbox service in Exchange 2016 and the Mailbox server role in Exchange server 2013. It is responsible for processing all mail items, storing those items in the mailbox database, and showing them in the user's inbox.

M. de Rooij and J. Wesselius, *Pro Exchange 2019 and 2016 Administration*,
https://doi.org/10.1007/978-1-4842-7331-9_4

All mail items are stored in a mailbox, and all mailboxes are stored in a mailbox database. The first mailbox database is stored by default on the local hard disk of the Mailbox server, in the C:\Program Files\Microsoft\Exchange Server\V15\Mailbox\<<database name>> directory. The <<database name>> is a random number in a typical default Exchange installation.

As explained in Chapter 2, this location is only used by the GUI setup of Exchange. When using an unattended setup of Exchange, a different name and location can be used. In this chapter, the Exchange server EXCH01 has a Mailbox database called MDB01, which is in the directory C:\ExchDbs\Disk1, and the transaction log files are in the C:\ExchDbs\Disk1\LogFiles directory.

The following files are available for this configuration:

- The file Mailbox Database MDB01.edb is the actual mailbox database where all the individual mail items are stored.
- Tmp.edb is a temporary file used by Exchange Server. The Tmp.edb file is dynamically created and not always used.
- E00 and subsequent log files are log files used for the transactional processing of information.
- E00.chk is a checkpoint file that keeps track of the transactions still in the log files, as well as those that are already written to the mailbox database.
- E00res00001.jrs-E00res0000A.jrs are temporary log files reserved by Exchange Server in case of disk full problems.
- E00tmp.log is a temporary log file used by Exchange Server during creation of new transaction log files.

All these files belong together, and they make up one mailbox database. One Exchange server 2019 Enterprise server can mount up to 100 mailbox databases. Exchange 2019 also supports multiple databases on one physical disk if you have multiple copies of the mailbox databases in a Database Availability Group (DAG). The maximum number of mounted mailbox databases on an Exchange server 2019 Standard server however is limited to five. More Mailbox databases can be created, but only five can be mounted. These numbers are valid for Exchange server 2016 and Exchange server 2013 as well.

In the next sections, we will discuss all the mailbox database internals and how all fits together.

The Mailbox Database

The mailbox database is the primary repository of the Exchange Mailbox server information; it is where all the Exchange data is stored. In theory, the mailbox database can be 16 TB, which is the NTFS size limit of a file, but it is normally limited to a size you can handle within the constraints of your service-level agreement (SLA). The recommended maximum database size for a normal Exchange 2019 server is 2 TB when you have multiple copies of the mailbox database in a Database Availability Group. If this is not the case, the maximum recommended size is 200 GB—but in practice it is limited by your backup and restore solution and by the accompanying SLA.

The mailbox database in Exchange is an extensible storage engine (ESE) database. ESE is a low-level database technology, sometimes also referred to as a JET database. The ESE database has been used since Exchange Server 4.0. The Active Directory database, the WINS database, and the DHCP database also are ESE databases.

The ESE database processing follows the "ACID" principle:

- **Atomic**—A transaction is all or nothing; there is no "unknown state" for a transaction.
- **Consistent**—The transaction preserves the consistency of the data being processed.
- **Isolated**—A single transaction is the only transaction on this data, even when multiple transactions occur at the same time.
- **Durable**—The committed transactions are preserved in the database.

Transactions are part of everyday life. Suppose you go to the bank to transfer money from your savings account to your checking account. The money is withdrawn from your savings account and then added to your checking account, and both actions are recorded and maybe even printed on paper. Yet this can be seen as one transaction. You do not want the transaction to end with the first step, in which the money is withdrawn from your savings account, but it is not yet added to your checking account.

The same principle goes for Exchange Server. Suppose you move a message from your inbox to a folder named "Authoring." From a transaction point of view, it starts by adding the message to the Authoring folder, then it updates the message count for this folder, deletes the message from the inbox, and updates the message count for the inbox. All these actions can be seen as one transaction.

The data within a database is organized as a balanced tree, or B-tree. This binary arrangement can be easily envisioned as an upside-down tree where the leaves are at the bottom and the root at the top, as illustrated in Figure 4-1. The actual mail data is stored in the leaves. The mid-level pages contain the pointers. The upper level is the root. This B-tree design is an efficient way of storing data because it requires only two or three lookups to find a particular piece of data, and all the pointers can be kept in memory.

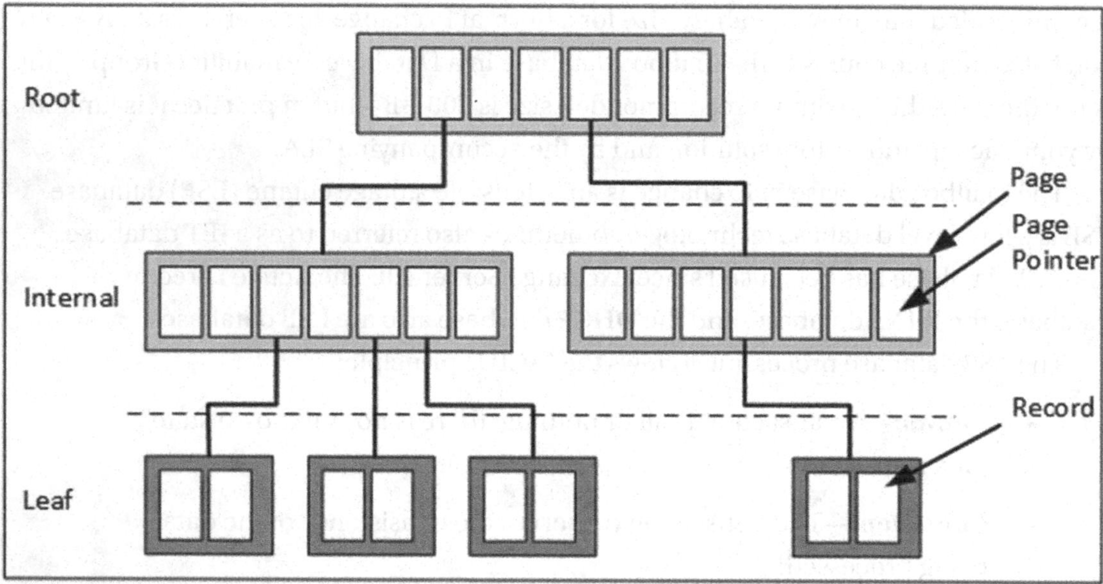

***Figure 4-1.** A balanced tree setup*

Exchange uses an enhanced version of a B-tree, called the B+ tree. This B+ tree contains pointers between the pages, so every page in a leaf has a pointer to the next page and to the previous page, making it even more efficient. This arrangement is also referred to as an indexed sequential access method (ISAM) database.

One of the functions of ESE is to balance the tree. It is not hard to imagine that when lots of data are added to the database, the tree becomes unbalanced. When this happens, ESE reorganizes the tree by splitting and merging the pointer pages.

Similarly, when a page becomes full, ESE splits the page into two adjacent pages. If this happens, an additional key is put into the secondary key's parent page.

The process continues until the parent page becomes full as well. Then, the parent page is split, and the new secondary page's parent page is updated with a new key.

It can happen that the root level becomes full, and then the root level needs to be split also. If this happens, an additional layer of pages is inserted into the tree, and the tree now has four layers instead of three. A balanced tree with four layers is shown in Figure 4-2. Obviously, a four-layer tree has many more leaves, containing more data.

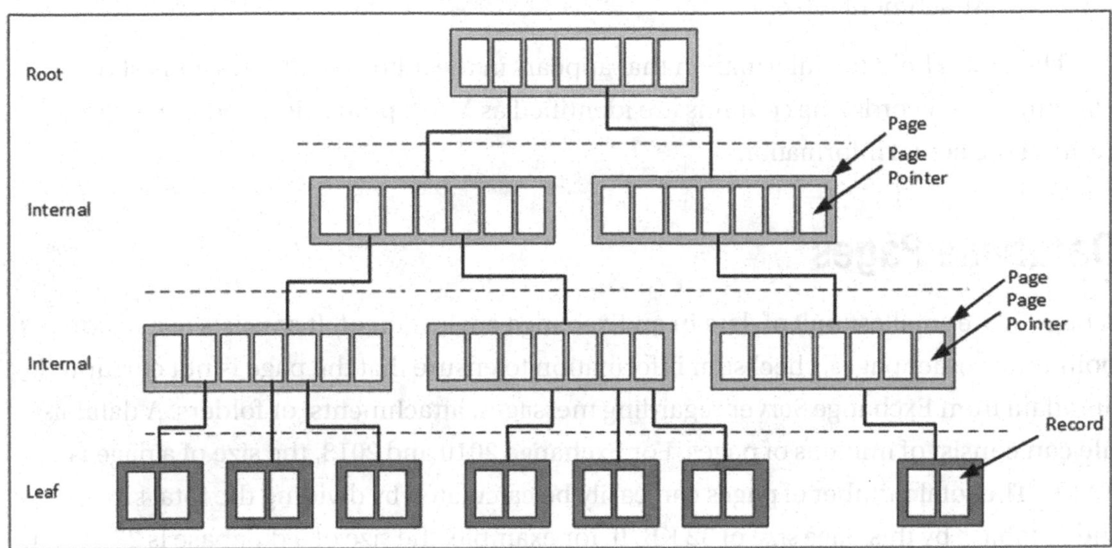

***Figure 4-2.** A balanced tree after a tree split*

If data is removed from the mailbox database, the leaves are emptied, and the parent pages become available again. When too many adjacent parent pages become available, ESE can merge those pages. Eventually, when lots and lots of merges happen, even up to the root level, ESE can remove an entire layer of pages, thereby shrinking the tree. Note that this happens inside the database. The tree can shrink, but the size of the database will never shrink! ESE pages are freed up and filled as a continuous process; once they are freed up, they are reorganized, as explained in a later section regarding online defragmentation.

To read data from a particular leaf, ESE starts at the root level and follows the tree down to the leaf. To reach the data, only three or four read actions are needed. Since most of the pages and pointers are stored in memory, this happens extremely fast—even in a 2 TB database, for example. ESE stores over 1600 page pointers in a 32 KB page, making it possible to create a tree with a minimal number of parent/child levels.

One or more trees in a database make up a table. There are several kinds of tables in Exchange Server:

- Mailbox table
- Folders table
- Message table
- Attachment table

The tables hold the information that appears in the inbox. The tables consist of columns and records; the columns are identified as MAPI properties, and the records contain the actual information.

Database Pages

A page is the smallest unit of data in an Exchange environment. It consists of a header, pointers to other pages, checksum information to ensure that the page is not corrupted, and data from Exchange Server regarding messages, attachments, or folders. A database file can consist of millions of pages. For Exchange 2010 and 2013, the size of a page is 32 KB. The total number of pages can easily be calculated by dividing the total size of the database by this page size of 32 KB. If, for example, the size of a database is 250 GB, it consists of 250 GB times 32 KB, or approximately 8.2 million pages.

Each page is sequentially numbered. Whenever a new page is created, it gets a new, incremented number. When the pages are read from the database and altered, they also get new page numbers before being written to the log file and flushed to the database file. This sequential number must be very large. In fact, it is a 64-bit number, which means that 18 quintillion changes can be made to a database!

One question that is asked sometimes is if it is possible to read the actual pages to see if there's any content there, especially in a disaster recovery scenario when data seems to have been lost.

It is not that simple. It is true; there is content in all these pages, but it is not readable without sophisticated tools. It is possible to check the contents of individual pages inside a mailbox database using the ESEUTIL tool, but as shown in Figure 4-3, there's not much readable information there.

```
Administrator: C:\Windows\system32\cmd.exe

C:\ExchDbs\Disk1>eseutil /mh MDB01.edb /p30

Extensible Storage Engine Utilities for Microsoft(R) Exchange Server
Version 15.02
Copyright (C) Microsoft Corporation. All Rights Reserved.

Initiating FILE DUMP mode...
      Database: MDB01.edb
          Page: 30

HEADER checksum      = 0x3C903C9095024758:0x000000000000001E:0x000000000000001E:0x017E017E4B384956
                        logged data checksum = d4922bcbb438221d

                         checksum <0x000001B0F2A90000,  8>:  4364054630594922328 (0x3C903C9095024758)
                     dbtimeDirtied <0x000001B0F2A90008,  8>:  1045665 (0xFF4A1)
                         pgnoPrev <0x000001B0F2A90010,  4>:  0 (0x0)
                         pgnoNext <0x000001B0F2A90014,  4>:  0 (0x0)
                         objidFDP <0x000001B0F2A90018,  4>:  7 (0x7)
                           cbFree <0x000001B0F2A9001C,  2>:  31476 (0x7AF4)
                cbUncommittedFree <0x000001B0F2A9001E,  2>:  0 (0x0)
                        ibMicFree <0x000001B0F2A90020,  2>:  1176 (0x498)
                      itagMicFree <0x000001B0F2A90022,  2>:  9 (0x9)
                           fFlags <0x000001B0F2A90024,  4>:  43011 (0xA803)
                   rgChecksum[0] <0x000001B0F2A90028,  8>:  30 (0x1E)
                   rgChecksum[1] <0x000001B0F2A90030,  8>:  30 (0x1E)
                   rgChecksum[2] <0x000001B0F2A90038,  8>:  107525083042957654 (0x17E017E4B384956)
                             pgno <0x000001B0F2A90040,  4>:  30 (0x1E)
                Leaf page
                Root page
                FDP page
                        Single Extent Space (ParentFDP: 1)
                Primary page
                New record format
                New checksum format
                PageFlushType = 1


TAG   0: cb:0x0010,ib:0x0000                                                               offset:0x0050-0x0060 flags:0x0000 (   )
TAG   1: cb:0x0073,ib:0x016b prefix:cb=0x0000 suffix:cb=0x0037 data:cb=0x003a offset:0x01bb-0x022e flags:0x0001 (v  )
TAG   2: cb:0x0073,ib:0x01de prefix:cb=0x0000 suffix:cb=0x0037 data:cb=0x003a offset:0x022e-0x02a1 flags:0x0001 (v  )
TAG   3: cb:0x0075,ib:0x0251 prefix:cb=0x0000 suffix:cb=0x0037 data:cb=0x003c offset:0x02a1-0x0316 flags:0x0001 (v  )
TAG   4: cb:0x0073,ib:0x0010 prefix:cb=0x0000 suffix:cb=0x0037 data:cb=0x003a offset:0x0060-0x00d3 flags:0x0001 (v  )
TAG   5: cb:0x0073,ib:0x0083 prefix:cb=0x0000 suffix:cb=0x0037 data:cb=0x003a offset:0x00d3-0x0146 flags:0x0001 (v  )
TAG   6: cb:0x0075,ib:0x00f6 prefix:cb=0x0000 suffix:cb=0x0037 data:cb=0x003c offset:0x0146-0x01bb flags:0x0001 (v  )
TAG   7: cb:0x0161,ib:0x0337 prefix:cb=0x0000 suffix:cb=0x00b5 data:cb=0x00aa offset:0x0387-0x04e8 flags:0x0001 (v  )
TAG   8: cb:0x0071,ib:0x02c6 prefix:cb=0x0000 suffix:cb=0x0037 data:cb=0x0038 offset:0x0316-0x0387 flags:0x0001 (v  )

Nodes: 8
                     min,    ave,    max, total
 Logical Key Sizes:   55,   70.8,    181,   566
   Node Data Sizes:   56,   72.3,    170,   578


Operation completed successfully in 0.31 seconds.


C:\ExchDbs\Disk1>_
```

***Figure 4-3.** The contents of a page inside a mailbox database are not readable*

Note Special recovery tools like Kroll Ontrack PowerControls can open a mailbox database file (i.e., the actual MDB01.edb file) to retrieve content from the mailbox database without running an Exchange server. These tools have logic to read all the tables and convert them to actual mailbox content.

Transaction Log Files

Mailbox items are processed by the Mailbox server in what are termed "transactions." A transaction can be

- The creation of a new message or a new calendar item
- The storage of a message received from SMTP in the mailbox
- The creation of a new folder in the mailbox
- The deletion of a message in the mailbox
- The renaming of a folder in the mailbox
- The creation of a new mailbox database

And so on.

All processing—that is, the creation of transactions—takes place in the server memory, in the log buffers, the ESE cache (this is where the pages reside), and the version store. The version store is a small part in memory, tied to the ESE cache, that is used by ESE to keep track of all transactions while they are created. When something goes wrong with a transaction, ESE can create a new transaction and keep track of the various versions of those transactions, hence the name.

The log buffers, each 1 MB in size, contain the contents of a log file that is currently being created. When transactions are created, they are stored in a particular log buffer, and this log buffer represents a log file that belongs to a certain mailbox database.

When a log buffer is filled with transactions, the entire log buffer is flushed to disk (i.e., written to a log file), the log file is closed, and a new log buffer and accompanying transaction log file is created. Transaction log files are identified as E00.log, E00000008FF.log, E0000000900.log, E0000000901.log, and so on. Please note that the number is hexadecimal, so they count from 0 to F.

At this point, pages are flushed to disk as transaction log files, but pages are kept in memory, and no changes are made to the database. This mechanism is called write-ahead logging, so the data in the log files is always ahead of the data in the mailbox database. Eventually, transactions are written to disk, directly from the ESE cache. The checkpoint file keeps track of which transactions are already written to disk. It does this by pointing to the last written transaction in the transaction log files (remember that all transactions are stored in the transaction log files).

A graphic representation of this technology can be seen in Figure 4-4.

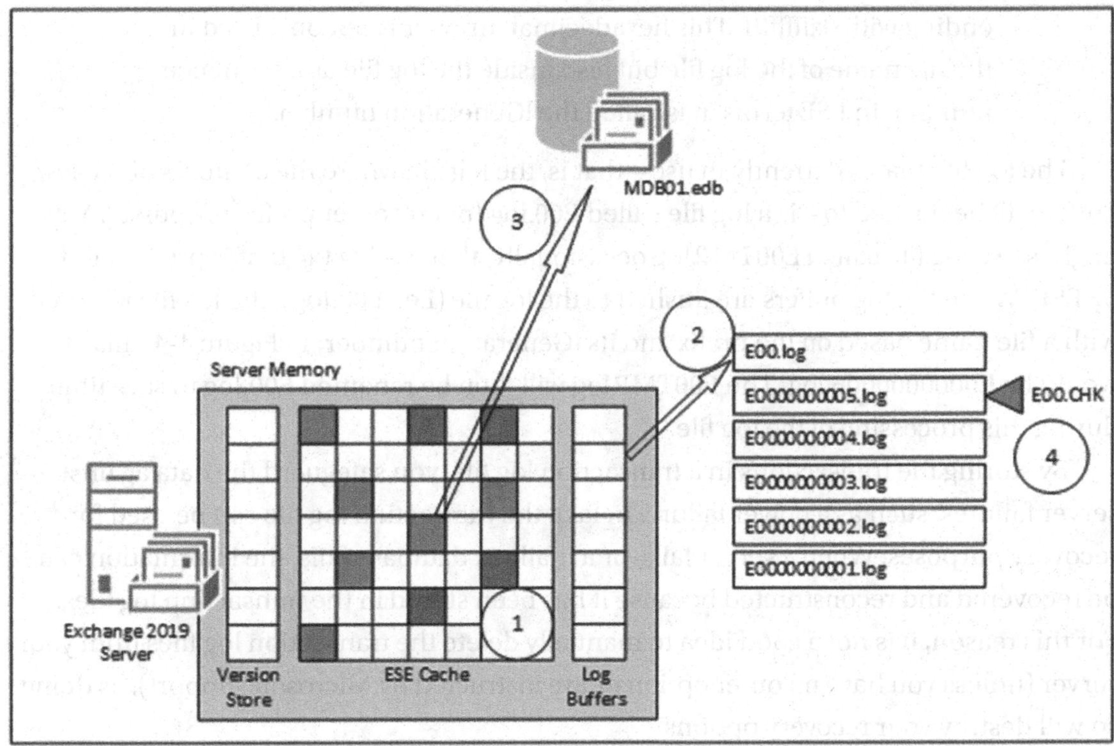

Figure 4-4. *The mailbox database, server memory, and log files*

Transactional logging is a sequential process, so subsequent transaction log files are numbered accordingly. Note that a hexadecimal notation is used, so after writing a transaction log file that ends with the number 9, the letter A is added. Only after writing a transaction log file ending with the letter F (the sixth letter of the alphabet) does Exchange Server start a new sequence.

The name of a log file can be split into two parts:

- **The prefix**—This is the first three characters of the name, in this example, E00. Every mailbox database has its unique set of log files, and the prefix is what differentiates one from another. The first mailbox database has prefix E00, while mailbox database number 100 has prefix E99. In contrast to the sequential hexadecimal numbering of the transaction log files, the prefix is in decimal notation.

- **The number**—This is an eight-character hexadecimal number that's generated sequentially, starting with 0x00000001 and theoretically ending with 0xffffffff. This hexadecimal number is not only used in the file name of the log file but also inside the log file as a sequence number. In ESE terms, it is called the lGeneration number.

The log file that is currently in use—that is, the log file where the contents of the log buffer will be flushed to—is a log file called E00.log (or any other prefix, of course). You might see a log file called E00TMP.log occasionally; that is a log file that is pre-created by ESE. When the log buffers are flushed to the log file (i.e., E00.log), the log file is stored with a file name based on the prefix and its lGeneration number; in Figure 4-4, this would be E0000000006.log. The E00TMP.log will then be renamed E00.log to save time during this processing of the log file.

By storing the transactions in a transaction log file, you safeguard the data against server failures, such as a power failure. In fact, the transaction log file can be used for recovery purposes. When a server fails, or a mailbox database fails, the information can be recovered and reconstructed because it has been stored in the transaction log files. For this reason, it is not a good idea to manually delete the transaction log files from your server (unless you have no other option or are instructed by Microsoft support), as doing so will destroy your recovery options.

Transaction log files are automatically removed from the Exchange Mailbox server when you run a backup solution, as will be explained later in this chapter.

Checkpoint File

As explained earlier, database pages remain in server memory after the transactions are flushed to the transaction log file. After some time, these pages are then stored in the mailbox database. At this point, they can also be removed from the server's memory. To keep track of which transactions are stored in the transaction log file and which are stored in the mailbox database, you need a checkpoint file.

The checkpoint file is an 8 KB file stored in the same location as the transaction log file, but it contains only a pointer. This pointer "points" to the transaction in the transaction log file that has just been stored in the mailbox database.

All pages in the transaction log file that are older than the pointer in the checkpoint file are stored in the mailbox database; all pages that are newer, therefore, remain in the server's memory and in the transaction log file. In case of a problem—for example, when the Exchange server is rebooted unexpectedly—the Exchange Server reads the location in the checkpoint file and knows which information is stored where, and thus it knows how it can start recovering information. This is a simple and safe solution for trouble-free processing of database information.

The amount of data that is still in server memory and not flushed to the mailbox database, and thus the amount of data "above" the checkpoint, is called the checkpoint depth. In Exchange 2019, the checkpoint depth can be 100 MB; this means that 100 MB of data can be in server memory but hasn't been flushed to the mailbox database, and so it is safely stored in the log files.

The checkpoint depth is per database; each database has its own set of log files, its own checkpoint file, and thus its own checkpoint depth. This means when you have, for example, 25 mailbox databases, you can have 25 × 100 log files, or 2.5 GB of mailbox data in server memory that has not been flushed to the mailbox database (but that is stored in the transaction log file, though!).

Why is this important to know? There are two reasons you want to know this:

- Exchange Server uses this technique for recovery purposes when mounting a mailbox database, after restoring a mailbox database from a backup, or by using the ESEUTIL tool.
- Mailbox data is dynamic, as data can be in server memory, in the mailbox database, or in the transaction log file. The backup application needs to be aware of this process so it can interact with the Exchange server while creating the backup. A regular file-level backup is not going to work when you are backing up mailbox databases.

How It Fits Together

A mailbox database that is running (i.e., it is mounted) is always in an inconsistent state. That is, there's mailbox data spread across the Exchange server's memory, the transaction log file, and the mailbox database. This inconsistent state is also known as dirty.

A graphic representation can be seen in Figure 4-5. Clearly visible in this figure is the part of the Mailbox databases that has been flushed to the transaction log files (and thus not yet to the mailbox database) and its relation to the checkpoint file.

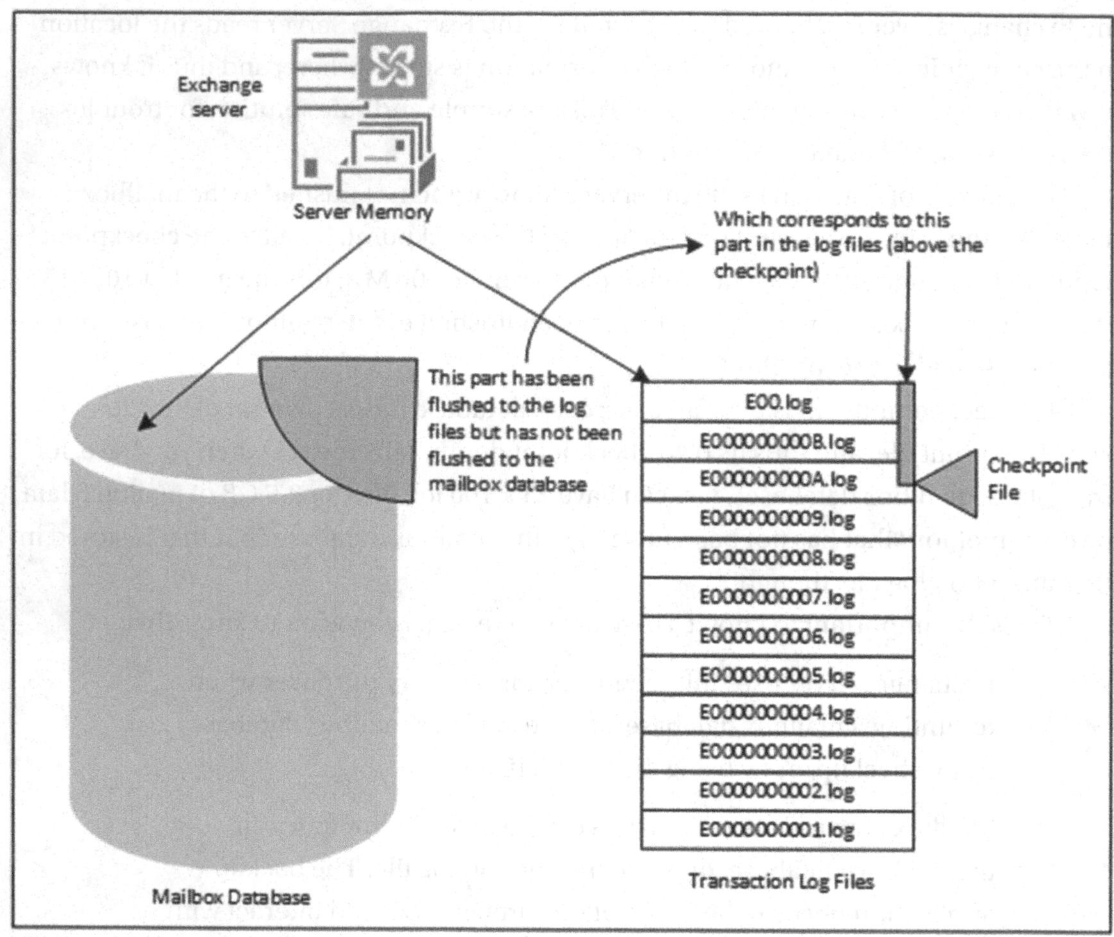

Figure 4-5. *The data that's not in the database is safely stored in the log files*

When you have a mailbox database on disk that is not mounted and is in a dirty shutdown state—for example, after a crash of the server—you need the corresponding transaction log file where the pages are stored that had not been previously written to the mailbox database. Only if you have these transaction log files is it possible to recover and bring the mailbox database to a consistent state. If you have a mailbox database in a dirty shutdown mode and you do not have the appropriate transaction log files, you are in trouble. The only thing that is left to do is to repair the mailbox database using the ESEUTIL tool, which will cause some data loss.

When a database is properly dismounted, it is brought into a consistent state. All data in server memory is flushed to the mailbox database, the checkpoint is moved to the last correct location, and all files are then closed. This is called a clean shutdown of the database.

Header Information

The transaction log files needed to get the database into a consistent state, and thus in a clean shutdown mode, are recorded in the header of the mailbox database. The header of the database is written into the first page of the database file, and it contains information regarding that mailbox database. The header information can be retrieved using the ESEUTIL tool. Just enter the following command in the directory where the database file resides:

ESEUTIL /MH MDB01

This will result in an output such as

```
Extensible Storage Engine Utilities for Microsoft(R) Exchange Server
Version 15.02
Copyright (C) Microsoft Corporation. All Rights Reserved.

Initiating FILE DUMP mode...
         Database: MDB1.edb

DATABASE HEADER:
Checksum Information:
Expected Checksum: 0x795a0c6b
  Actual Checksum: 0x795a0c6b

Fields:
        File Type: Database
         Checksum: 0x795a0c6b
   Format ulMagic: 0x89abcdef
   Engine ulMagic: 0x89abcdef
 Format ulVersion: 0x620,20,0  (attached by 0)
 Engine ulVersion: 0x620,60,140  (efvCurrent = 9060)
Created ulVersion: 0x620,20
     DB Signature: Create time:02/26/2019 16:44:58.029 Rand:2559253063
                   Computer:
         cbDbPage: 32768
           dbtime: 24287734 (0x17299f6)
            State: Dirty Shutdown
     Log Required: 36433-36645 (0x8e51-0x8f25)
    Log Committed: 0-36646 (0x0-0x8f26)
```

```
    Log Recovering: 0 (0x0)
    Log Consistent: 36433 (0x8e51)
   GenMax Creation: 05/05/2021 14:21:28.902 UTC
          Shadowed: Yes
        Last Objid: 3131
      Scrub Dbtime: 0 (0x0)
        Scrub Date: 00/00/1900 00:00:00.000 LOC
      Repair Count: 0
       Repair Date: 00/00/1900 00:00:00.000 LOC
  Old Repair Count: 0
   Last Consistent: (0x8797,99,770)  04/13/2021 18:58:53.752 UTC
       Last Attach: (0x8798,2,268)  04/13/2021 19:37:45.975 UTC
       Last Detach: (0x0,0,0)  00/00/1900 00:00:00.000 LOC
     Last ReAttach: (0x8AA4,2,268)  04/23/2021 10:42:52.940 UTC
              Dbid: 1
     Log Signature: Create time:02/26/2019 16:44:57.888 Rand:507225430
                    Computer:
        OS Version: (6.2.9200 SP 0 NLS ffffffff.ffffffff)

Previous Full Backup:
        Log Gen: 0-0 (0x0-0x0)
           Mark: (0x0,0,0)
           Mark: 00/00/1900 00:00:00.000 LOC

Previous Incremental Backup:
        Log Gen: 0-0 (0x0-0x0)
           Mark: (0x0,0,0)
           Mark: 00/00/1900 00:00:00.000 LOC

Previous Copy Backup:
        Log Gen: 0-0 (0x0-0x0)
           Mark: (0x0,0,0)
           Mark: 00/00/1900 00:00:00.000 LOC

Previous Differential Backup:
        Log Gen: 0-0 (0x0-0x0)
           Mark: (0x0,0,0)
           Mark: 00/00/1900 00:00:00.000 LOC
```

```
Current Full Backup:
        Log Gen: 0-0 (0x0-0x0)
           Mark: (0x0,0,0)
           Mark: 00/00/1900 00:00:00.000 LOC

Current Shadow copy backup:
        Log Gen: 0-0 (0x0-0x0)
           Mark: (0x0,0,0)
           Mark: 00/00/1900 00:00:00.000 LOC

     cpgUpgrade55Format: 0
    cpgUpgradeFreePages: 0
cpgUpgradeSpaceMapPages: 0

       ECC Fix Success Count: none
   Old ECC Fix Success Count: none
         ECC Fix Error Count: none
     Old ECC Fix Error Count: none
    Bad Checksum Error Count: none
Old bad Checksum Error Count: none

  Last Database Maintenance Finish Date: 00/00/1900 00:00:00.000 LOC
Current Database Maintenance Start Date: 04/23/2021 10:42:52.309 UTC
      Highest Continuous Database Maintenance Page: 0
      Highest Database Maintenance Page: 0

  Database Header Flush Signature: Create time:05/05/2021 14:21:28.907
  Rand:4254865283 Computer:
 Flush Map Header Flush Signature: Create time:00/00/1900 00:00:00.000
 Rand:0 Computer:

Operation completed successfully in 0.16 seconds.
```

There is quite a lot of information to retrieve from the mailbox database header:

- **DB Signature**—A unique value of creation date and time, plus a random integer that identifies this database. This value is also recorded in the transaction log file and the checkpoint files, and this ties them together. In this example, the DB signature is "Create time:02/26/2019 16:44:58.029 Rand:2559253063" which means the mailbox database was created on February 26, 2019, at 4:44 p.m.
- **cbDbPage**—The size of the pages used in this database; in Exchange 2016 and Exchange 2019, the page size is 32 KB.
- **Dbtime**—(Part of) the number of changes made to this database.
- **State**—The state of the database, that is, whether it is in a consistent state or not. The database in this example is in a dirty shutdown. It needs a certain number of transaction log files to get to a clean shutdown state.
- **Log Required**—If the database is not in a consistent state, these log files are needed to bring it into that consistent state. To make this database a consistent state again, the logfiles E0000008e51.log to E0000008f25.log are needed. Exchange Server will perform the recovery process automatically when mounting a database, so under normal circumstances no administrator intervention is needed at this point, but it is also possible to manually recover from a dirty shutdown using the ESEUTIL tool.
- **Last ObjID**—The number of B+ trees in this particular database. In this example, there are 3131 B+ trees in the database.
- **Log Signature**—A unique value of date, time, and an integer that uniquely identifies a series of log files. As with the database signature, this ties together the database file, the log files, and the checkpoint file.
- **Last Attach**—The date and time when the database was last mounted. "Mounting" is actually attaching the mailbox database to a stream of log files, hence the entry label "Last Attach."

- **Backup information**—Entries used by Exchange Server to keep track of the last full or incremental (VSS) backup that was made on this database. In this example, no backup was created since the initial creation of the Mailbox database.

The same kind of information is logged in the header of the transaction log file (ESEUTIL /ML E00.LOG) and in the header of the checkpoint file (ESEUTIL /MK E00.CHK). As these files are grouped together, you can match the files using the header information, for example:

```
ESEUTIL /ML E00.log
```

The output is something like the following:

```
Extensible Storage Engine Utilities for Microsoft(R) Exchange Server
Version 15.02
Copyright (C) Microsoft Corporation. All Rights Reserved.

Initiating FILE DUMP mode...
      Base name: e00
      Log file: e00.log
      lGeneration: 36646 (0x8F26)
      Checkpoint: (0x8E51,A0,0)
      creation time: 05/05/2021 14:21:28.902 UTC
      prev gen time: 05/05/2021 13:41:28.311 UTC
      prev gen accumulated segment checksum: 0x5bce24311c5cb937
      Format LGVersion: (8.4000.5.16) (generated by 9060)
      Engine LGVersion: (8.4000.20.60)
      Signature: Create time:02/26/2019 16:44:57.888 Rand:507225430
      Computer:
      Env SystemPath: F:\MDB01\LogFiles\
      Env LogFilePath: F:\MDB01\LogFiles\
      Env Log Sec size: 4096 (legacy, unknown actual)
      Env (CircLog,Session,Opentbl,VerPage,Cursors,LogBufs,LogFile,Buffers)
          (     off,   1000, 100000,  16384, 100000,   2048,    256,  63489)
      Using Reserved Log File: false
      Circular Logging Flag (current file): off
      Circular Logging Flag (past files): off
```

```
    Checkpoint at log creation time: (0x8E51,A0,0)
    1 F:\MDB01\MDB01.edb
            dbtime: 25878463 (0-25878463)
            objidLast: 3211
            Signature: Create time:02/26/2019 16:44:58.029
            Rand:2559253063 Computer:
            MaxDbSize: 0 pages
            Last Attach: (0x8798,2,268)
            Last Consistent: (0x8797,99,770)

    Last Lgpos: (0x8f26,4A,0)
    Accumulated segment checksum: 0x7e5e01a1e05146c8

Number of database page references:  198
Integrity check passed for log file: e00.log

Operation completed successfully in 0.47 seconds.
```

When you look at this output and compare it to the output of the mailbox database header, you'll notice that the mailbox database signature mentioned in the transaction log file is identical to the mailbox database signature in the mailbox database header. This means these files are tied together. Of course, the transaction log file was created recently, but in this header information, you'll also find information regarding the location of the checkpoint file on disk as stored in the Env SystemPath property. Also, the location of the transaction log files is recorded in the EnvLogFilePath property.

The last part to have a closer look at is the checkpoint file. As we now know, it references a page in one transaction log file. To look at the header information of the checkpoint file, this command is used:

```
C:\> ESEUTIL /MK E00.CHK
```

This generates output like the following:

```
Extensible Storage Engine Utilities for Microsoft(R) Exchange Server
Version 15.02
Copyright (C) Microsoft Corporation. All Rights Reserved.

Initiating FILE DUMP mode...
    Checkpoint file: e00.chk
```

```
    LastFullBackupCheckpoint: (0x0,0,0)
    Checkpoint: (0x8E51,A0,0)
    DbConsistency: (0x8E51,A0,0)
    FullBackup: (0x0,0,0)
    FullBackup time: 00/00/1900 00:00:00.000 LOC
    IncBackup: (0x0,0,0)
    IncBackup time: 00/00/1900 00:00:00.000 LOC
    Signature: Create time:02/26/2019 16:44:57.888 Rand:507225430
    Computer:
    Env (CircLog,Session,Opentbl,VerPage,Cursors,LogBufs,LogFile,Buffers)
        (    off,   1000, 100000,  16384, 100000,   2048,    256,  63489)
    1 F:\MDB01\MDB01.edb LogOff VerOn RW
      dbtime: 25860708 (0-25860708)
      objidLast: 3211
      Signature: Create time:02/26/2019 16:44:58.029 Rand:2559253063
      Computer:
      MaxDbSize: 0 pages
      Last Attach: (0x8798,2,268)
      Last Consistent: (0x8797,99,770)
Operation completed successfully in 0.16 seconds.
```

This checkpoint file was created during the creation of the mailbox database, as can be derived from the signature of the mailbox database. If you examine these examples closely, you'll find that the three files are closely related.

Single Instance Storage

Up until the 2007 version, Exchange Server had a feature called single instance storage (SIS). Using SIS, Exchange Server stored items in the mailbox database only one time per mailbox database. When an item had to be delivered to multiple mailboxes, it was stored only once, and the other mailboxes contained a pointer to this particular item. In the early days, when expensive 9 GB SCSI disks were used, this method could save valuable disk space and would increase performance dramatically. It made sense, since writing a large item takes much more time than writing a pointer.

Microsoft started to move away from SIS beginning with Exchange Server 2007, and starting with Exchange Server 2010, SIS is not used at all anymore. Newer disk technology and improved ESE technology make it possible to use large 4 TB SATA disks (or larger) without impacting disk performance—that is, of course, if the disk subsystem is not overcommitted. Microsoft's getting rid of SIS made it possible for the Exchange developers to create a less complex mailbox database structure, which in turn lowered the IOPS requirements.

Microsoft Exchange Information Store

While ESE is just the database engine, it stores the transactions in the transaction log file and in the mailbox database, as explained in the previous section. If you open this database file with some sort of binary editor, however, there's absolutely no readable information. The same is true for the transaction log file—no readable information.

The Information Store is the process running on the Mailbox server that's responsible for the logical part of the database processing. It transforms the information read from the mailbox database into something readable, like your inbox, the folders in the inbox, or the individual message items. In essence, this process hasn't changed since the original release of Exchange Server 4.0 in 1997. Of course, there have been improvements, such as the introduction of the 64-bit version of Exchange 2007, increasing the number of mailbox databases, and expanding the page size to 8 KB in 2007 and to 32 KB in 2010, but the overall concept hasn't changed.

In Exchange 2013, however, the Information Store process was rewritten in managed code. In other words, it is a .NET application, and in Exchange 2016 and Exchange 2019, this has not changed. More interesting, for every mailbox database that is mounted on an Exchange 2013 or higher, a new Information Store worker process is spawned and responsible for this database (see Figure 4-6). The huge advantage of this system is that all mailbox databases and the accompanying processes are fully independent of each other. That is, if you have an Exchange server with 25 mailbox databases mounted, and one of those databases crashes, including the Store worker process, the other 24 mailbox databases are not affected.

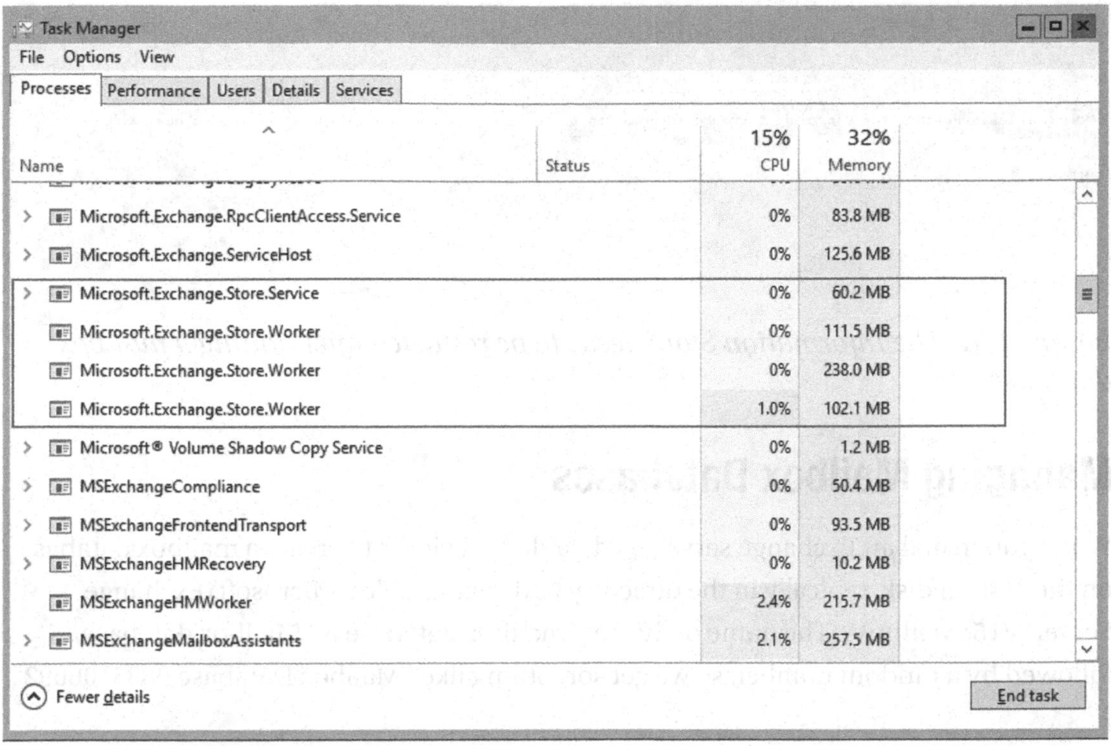

***Figure 4-6.** Multiple databases mean multiple Information Store worker processes*

Database Caching

For optimal performance, the Information Store wants to do only one thing: cache as much information as possible.

Reading and writing in memory is much faster than reading and writing on disk. The more information that is kept in the server's memory, the better the server's performance will be.

The amount of memory assigned to a particular mailbox database is determined at the start time of the Information Store process. This also means that when additional mailbox databases are added, the server's memory used for database caching needs to be redistributed. This is the reason a warning message such as "Please restart the Microsoft Exchange Information Store service on server EXCH01 after adding new Mailbox databases" appears; this is shown in Figure 4-7.

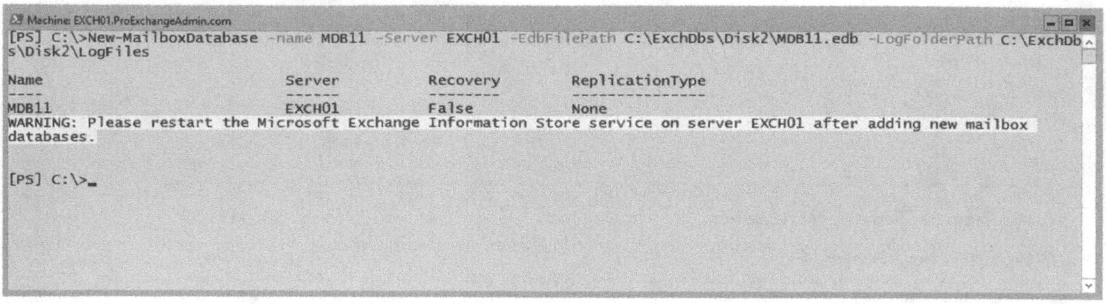

```
Machine: EXCH01.ProExchangeAdmin.com
[PS] C:\>New-MailboxDatabase -name MDB11 -Server EXCH01 -EdbFilePath C:\ExchDbs\Disk2\MDB11.edb -LogFolderPath C:\ExchDb
s\Disk2\LogFiles

Name                         Server          Recovery        ReplicationType
----                         ------          --------        ---------------
MDB11                        EXCH01          False           None
WARNING: Please restart the Microsoft Exchange Information Store service on server EXCH01 after adding new mailbox
databases.

[PS] C:\>_
```

Figure 4-7. *The Information Store needs to be restarted after adding a mailbox database*

Managing Mailbox Databases

When you install an Exchange server, its default behavior is to create a mailbox database on the system disk, typically in the directory C:\Program Files\Microsoft\Exchange Server\V15\Mailbox\. The name of the new mailbox database is "Mailbox database," followed by a random number, so we get something like "Mailbox Database 0833106092".

Note This random numbering can be avoided by using the /MdbName, /DbFilePath, and /LogFolderPath options during the unattended setup. This was explained in more detail in Chapter 2.

Although this mailbox database can be used in a production environment, most likely it does not fit into your company's naming convention, and it is not stored in a proper location. Therefore, the things you might want to do after the initial installation are

1. Rename the mailbox database to match your company's naming convention.

2. Move the mailbox database and the accompanying log files to a more suitable location—for example, an external disk, whether it be direct-attached storage (DAS) or some sort of SAN storage solution. Be aware that you can only do this before you create a DAG with additional mailbox database copies!

3. When you are following Exchange Native Data Protection and use a DAG, you can enable circular logging.

4. Change quotas for the mailbox database or change the retention times for deleted items.

5. Assign an Offline Address Book (OAB) to a mailbox database.

Rename a Mailbox Database

Renaming a mailbox database in Exchange server 2019 is not a big deal; it's just a matter of one PowerShell command.

To change a mailbox database name from Mailbox database 0833106092 to MDB01, enter the following command in EMS:

```
[PS] C:\> Get-MailboxDatabase -Identity "Mailbox database 0833106092" |
Set-MailboxDatabase -Name "MDB01"
```

Note In the previous example, the logical name of the mailbox database is renamed as they show up in EMS or in EAC. The actual EDB file or the directory on disk is not renamed. To rename these, you need to move the EDB file to another directory and give it a new file name.

Move a Mailbox Database

It is strongly recommended that you move mailbox databases to a separate location, preferably a dedicated disk. To move a mailbox database named MDB01 and its log files to a different location, just enter the following command in EMS:

```
[PS] C:\> Move-DatabasePath -Identity MDB01 -EdbFilePath C:\ExchDbs\Disk1\
MDB01.edb -LogFolderPath C:\ExchDbs\Disk1\LogFiles
```

An interesting option is the -ConfigurationOnly parameter. Normally, when you use the Move-DatabasePath cmdlet, the mailbox database settings in Active Directory are changed, and the mailbox database and its log files are moved to the assigned location. When the -ConfigurationOnly parameter is used, the settings are changed in Active Directory, but the actual file move does not occur. This can be useful in a disaster recovery scenario, where a mailbox database is recovered in another location and the

Mailbox server needs to use this mailbox database. This will be explained in more detail in the backup, restore, and disaster recovery section later in this chapter.

Circular Logging

As explained earlier in the chapter, circular logging is a technique whereby only a very limited number of transaction log files are kept on the server. Normally, transaction log files are kept until a backup has successfully run, but when circular logging is enabled, the transaction log files are removed from the server once all the transactions have been successfully committed to the mailbox database and shipped to the passive copies of that mailbox database when using a DAG.

In a single-server scenario, circular logging is not recommended because of its lack of recovery options, but in a DAG environment, circular logging poses less risk of data loss. Recovery options are provided by the DAG itself, so if a mailbox database is lost, another server in the DAG takes over.

To enable circular logging on a mailbox database named MDB01, enter the following command in EMS:

```
[PS] C:\> Set-MailboxDatabase -Identity MDB01 -CircularLoggingEnabled:$TRUE
```

If you enable circular logging on a server that's not a DAG member, you'll get a warning message that the circular logging will become active only when the mailbox database is dismounted and mounted again. When the Mailbox server is a DAG member, the circular logging option is applied immediately, and there's no need for remounting the mailbox database.

To disable the circular logging, the -CircularLoggingEnabled option should be set to $FALSE.

Quota Settings

When a new mailbox database is installed, the default quotas are set on the mailbox database. Quotas are limits set on a mailbox; if they are not explicitly set on the mailbox itself, the mailbox database quotas are enforced on the mailboxes.

The following quota settings are set by default:

- **Issue Warning at 1.9 GB**—This value determines when Exchange starts sending warning messages to the user about the fact that they're reaching their mailbox limit. By default, this limit is 100 MB lower than the next limit, whereby the user cannot send email anymore.
- **Prohibit Send at 2.0 GB**—This value determines when the user cannot send email anymore.
- **Prohibit Send and Receive at 2.1 GB**—This value determines when the user cannot send email but at the same time cannot receive email either. By default, this value is 100 MB higher than the previous limit—the Prohibit Send quota. Some customers prefer to leave this quota setting open, especially on mailboxes that receive email from customers, so as to prevent bouncing back email to the customers.

While these settings are sufficient for most users, they can be extended to a very large level. In Exchange 2019, a mailbox of 100 GB is not a problem at all on a server level; the only thing you must be aware of is that the storage sizing must be able to accommodate these large mailboxes.

To change the default quota settings on a mailbox database called MDB01 to 19, 20, and 22 GB, you can use the following command in EMS:

```
[PS] C:\> Set-MailboxDatabase -Identity MDB01 -IssueWarningQuota
19GB -ProhibitSendQuota 20GB -ProhibitSendReceiveQuota 22GB
```

Note Having a 20 GB mailbox on an Exchange server is not a problem, but complications may arise when using Outlook in cached mode. Outlook will cache mailbox contents in an .OST file on the local hard disk. Outlook 2013 by default will cache only one year of data using "the slider" in the user's Outlook profile. When a larger time window is selected, the .OST file can grow dramatically. When using a computer with a 5400 RPM hard drive, this will result in performance issues.

Exchange periodically sends warning messages to users who have almost hit their quota (the Issue Warning), who have hit their quota and cannot send (the Prohibit Send), or who have hit their quota and cannot send and receive (the Prohibit Send and Receive limit). The frequency of these warning messages is set using the QuotaNotificationSchedule property on a mailbox database, which you can check using EMS:

```
[PS] C:\> Get-MailboxDatabase -Identity MBB01 | fl
Name,QuotaNotificationSchedule
```

Besides the name of the mailbox database, it will also show the quota notification schedule, which by default is set to this:

```
QuotaNotificationSchedule : {Sun.1:00 AM-Sun.1:15 AM, Mon.1:00 AM-Mon.1:15
AM, Tue.1:00 AM-Tue.1:15 AM, Wed.1:00 AM-Wed.1:15 AM, Thu.1:00 AM-Thu.1:15
AM, Fri.1:00 AM-Fri.1:15 AM, Sat.1:00 AM-Sat.1:15 AM}
```

Mailboxes inherit their quotas from the mailbox database where they reside. It is possible to override these limits by setting the quotas directly on the mailbox. The quota can be higher or lower than the mailbox database setting.

To change the quota settings for a user named Clint to 9, 10, and 11 GB, execute the following command in EMS:

```
[PS] C:\> Set-Mailbox -identity Clint -UseDatabaseQuotaDefaults $False -Issue
WarningQuota 9GB -ProhibitSendQuota 10GB -ProhibitSendReceiveQuota 11GB
```

Assign an Offline Address Book

When a mailbox database is created, an Offline Address Book (OAB) is not assigned to it. In a typical environment, this is not needed, but there are situations where you can put one set of mailboxes in one mailbox database and another set of mailboxes in another mailbox database, and then you can assign a specific OAB to a specific mailbox database and thus to the mailboxes in these databases.

You can use the following command to assign an Offline Address Book called Custom Department OAB to a mailbox database called MDB01:

```
[PS] C:\> Set-MailboxDatabase -Identity MDB01 -OfflineAddressBook "Custom
Department OAB"
```

Create a New Mailbox Database

If you have a larger environment, then it's likely that you will need some additional mailbox databases besides the default mailbox database. When you have multiple mailbox databases, you can spread your mailboxes across these mailbox databases. Even better, when provisioning the mailboxes, you do not assign a mailbox database; Exchange Server will look for a mailbox database to host this new mailbox.

To create a new mailbox database MDB02 hosted on Server EXCH01, execute the following command in EMS:

```
[PS] C:\> New-MailboxDatabase -Name MDB02 -Server EXCH01 -EdbFilePath C:\
ExchDbs\Disk2\MDB02.edb -LogFolderPath C:\ExchDbs\Disk2\LogFiles
```

After the creation of the mailbox database, you can mount it using the following command:

```
[PS] C:\> Mount-Database -Identity MDB02
```

Note When you create a new mailbox database, this information is stored in Active Directory. The information needs to be replicated across all domain controllers. It can happen that, when creating a new mailbox database, this information is not replicated across all domain controllers when you enter the Mount-Database command. If that happens, the Mount-Database command fails, and an error is shown on the console. Nothing to worry about; just wait a couple of minutes and retry the Mount-Database command.

Delete a Mailbox Database

Before a mailbox database can be deleted, all the mailboxes in it need to be either deleted or moved to another mailbox database. When the mailbox database is empty, you can remove it. To remove a Mailbox database, execute the following command in EMS:

```
[PS] C:\> Remove-MailboxDatabase -Identity MDB01 -Confirm:$false
```

When the mailbox database is deleted, it is only deleted from Active Directory. The files themselves still exist on the Exchange server and must be manually deleted.

But one day you will run into the following snag. Suppose you've moved all the mailboxes to another mailbox database, and you want to delete the mailbox database. An error message says: "This mailbox database contains one or more mailboxes, mailbox plans, archive mailboxes, public folder mailboxes, or arbitration mailboxes."

When you check again, the mailbox database looks empty because nothing shows up in EAC, and nothing is shown when you enter a Get-Mailbox -Database MDB01 command in EMS. This situation is caused by system mailboxes in this mailbox database, and these system mailboxes are not shown by default. They can only be shown in the EMS by using the Get-Mailbox in combination with the following options:

- -Arbitration
- -Archive
- -AuditLog
- -AuxAuditLog
- -Migration
- -Monitoring

For example:

```
[PS] C:\> Get-Mailbox -Database MDB01 -Arbitration
[PS] C:\> Get-Mailbox -Database MDB01 -Archive
[PS] C:\> Get-Mailbox -Database MDB01 -Monitoring
```

To move these mailboxes to another mailbox database called MDB02, execute the following command in EMS:

```
[PS] C:\> Get-Mailbox -Database MDB01 -Arbitration | New-MoveRequest -Target
Database MDB02
```

When these system mailboxes are moved and the mailbox database is empty, it is possible to remove the mailbox database.

Online Maintenance

Maintenance is a broad term and describes several tasks. Discussed here are

- The deleted item retention settings
- The online maintenance

Deleted Item Retention

When items are removed from the mailbox database (messages, folders, mailboxes), they are not immediately deleted from the mailbox or the mailbox database; they are kept in the background for a particular amount of time called the retention time, and it is set by default to 14 days for individual mailbox items and 30 days for mailboxes.

The deleted item retention time and the Mailbox retention time are properties of a mailbox database and can be retrieved using the following command in EMS:

```
[PS] C:\> Get-MailboxDatabase -Identity DB01 | select
MailboxRetention,DeletedItemRetention
```

The retention time is shown as a time span: dd.hh:mm:ss, where d=days, h=hours, m=minutes, and s=seconds. This is shown in Figure 4-8.

```
Machine: EXCH01.ProExchangeAdmin.com
[PS] C:\>Get-MailboxDatabase -Identity MDB01 | Select MailboxRetention,DeletedItemRetention

MailboxRetention DeletedItemRetention
---------------- --------------------
30.00:00:00      14.00:00:00

[PS] C:\>_
```

Figure 4-8. *The default retention time settings of a mailbox database*

Changing the retention times of a mailbox database is like retrieving these settings, but instead of using "Get," you use "Set" in the PowerShell command.

To change the deleted item retention time to 90 days, for example, you use the following command:

```
[PS] C:\> Set-MailboxDatabase -Identity MDB01 -DeletedItemsRetention
90.00:00:00
```

When deleted items are past their retention time, they are permanently deleted from the mailbox database. When this happens, there's no way to get these items back.

There's an option in Exchange that only deletes these items permanently after they have been backed up. This option is called RetainDeletedItemsUntilBackup and is set to FALSE by default, so you must set it explicitly. To set this in combination with the 90-day deleted item retention time that was set in the previous example, you can use the following PowerShell command:

```
[PS] C:\> Set-MailboxDatabase -Identity AMS-DB01 -DeletedItemsRetention
90.00:00:00 -RetainDeletedItemsUntilBackup $TRUE
```

So, what actually happens? When a user deletes a message and purges it from the Deleted Items folder in their mailbox, or when an administrator deletes a mailbox, it is moved to the Recoverable Items folder. This is a special location in the mailbox database, not visible for users, where items are stored for as long as stipulated by the retention time.

Online Maintenance

Online maintenance is a process in Exchange Server that maintains the internal structure of the mailbox database, and it consists of two parts:

1. **Content maintenance**—Responsible for purging deleted items, purging indexes, purging deleted mailboxes, and checking for orphaned messages. This part focuses on content maintenance—that is, it is responsible for purging old content and keeping the mailbox database as accurate as possible.

2. **ESE maintenance**—Keeps track of all database pages and indexes inside the mailbox database and performs checksum checks of all individual pages inside the database. Single-bit errors can be fixed on the fly by ESE maintenance. ESE maintenance also performs online defragmentation to optimize the internal structure of the mailbox database. Online defragmentation reads all pages and indexes in the database and reorganizes these pages. The idea is to free up pages inside the database so new items can be written in the free space inside the database, preventing unnecessary growth of the database.

Content maintenance can finish in a couple of hours, even on the largest mailbox databases. By default, content maintenance runs from 1 a.m. until 5 a.m. on the Mailbox server. This maintenance schedule is also a property of a mailbox database and can be retrieved using the following PowerShell command:

```
[PS] C:\> Get-MailboxDatabase -Identity MDB01 | Select MaintenanceSchedule
```

This is shown in Figure 4-9.

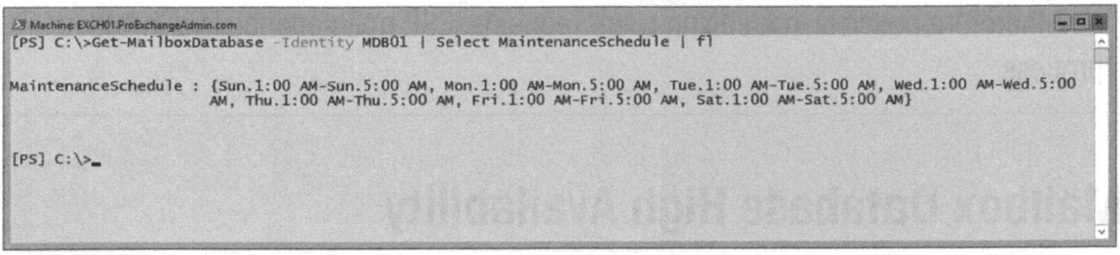

```
Machine: EXCH01.ProExchangeAdmin.com
[PS] C:\>Get-MailboxDatabase -Identity MDB01 | Select MaintenanceSchedule | fl

MaintenanceSchedule : {Sun.1:00 AM-Sun.5:00 AM, Mon.1:00 AM-Mon.5:00 AM, Tue.1:00 AM-Tue.5:00 AM, Wed.1:00 AM-Wed.5:00
                      AM, Thu.1:00 AM-Thu.5:00 AM, Fri.1:00 AM-Fri.5:00 AM, Sat.1:00 AM-Sat.5:00 AM}

[PS] C:\>_
```

***Figure 4-9.** The online maintenance schedule of a mailbox database*

If you want to change this time span, you must use all different times as input for the Set-MailboxDatabase command using the –MaintenanceSchedule parameter, for example:

```
Set-MailboxDatabase -Identity MDB01 -MaintenanceSchedule "Sun.00:00 AM-
Sun.04:00 AM","Mon.00:00-Mon.04:00","Tue.00:00-Tue.04:00","Wed.00:00-
Wed.04:00","Thu.00:00-Thu.04:00","Fri.00:00-Fri.04:00","Sat.00:00-
Sat.04:00"
```

If you run this command, the time spans are set, but you are also presented a warning message that this parameter is being deprecated. The reason is understandable; for large Mailbox databases, the time frame for online maintenance was not sufficient, and there was just not enough time to complete the online maintenance. It often conflicts with a backup schedule, ending up in an overloaded Exchange server in the middle of the night.

However, the warning saying it is deprecated was shown in Exchange server 2013, and it is still shown in Exchange server 2019. It is unknown if this ever gets removed from Exchange.

The second part of online maintenance is the ESE maintenance. This is a 24/7 background process. It is enabled by default, and it is recommended that you leave this enabled. If for some reason you want to disable ESE maintenance, you can set the -BackgroundDatabaseMaintenance parameter to $FALSE by executing the following command in EMS:

```
[PS] C:\> Set-MailboxDatabase -Identity AMS-DB01 -
BackgroundDatabaseMaintenance $FALSE
```

Note To prevent overwhelming the Mailbox server with checksum requests, and therefore possibly influencing client requests, ESE maintenance is a throttled process.

Mailbox Database High Availability

When you have a single Exchange server, you have a single point of failure, or SPOF. When this server fails, it is not available anymore, and your users are without their messaging service until you have restored or rebuild the Exchange server. Unfortunately, this can take a considerable amount of time.

To overcome this problem, you must implement a high availability solution; in short, that means implementing more servers offering the same service. In the case of Exchange, there are three distinct services affected:

- **Client Access**—To achieve high availability for clients, multiple Exchange servers must be configured in a load-balanced array. This was discussed in detail in Chapter 3.
- **Edge Transport**—To achieve high availability for SMTP on Edge Transport servers, multiple servers must be configured. This is discussed in Chapter 6.
- **Mailboxes**—To achieve high availability for mailboxes, a Database Availability Group or DAG must be implemented. This is discussed in this section.

Mailbox Service High Availability

A Database Availability Group or DAG is a logical grouping of a set of Exchange servers that can hold copies of each other's mailbox databases. So, when there are three Mailbox servers in a DAG, mailbox database MBX01 can be active on the first server in the DAG, but it can have a copy on the second and third servers in the DAG. When the first server in the DAG fails, the mailbox database copy on the second server becomes active and continues servicing the user requests with minimal downtime for the user.

Under the hood, a DAG is using components of Windows failover clustering, and as such we must discuss some of these components in more detail.

Cluster Nodes and the File Share Witness

A DAG consists of at least two Exchange Mailbox servers. It is possible to have a DAG with only one Exchange 2019 Mailbox server, but in this case there is no redundancy of course. Another server is involved in a DAG as well, and this is the witness server.

Under the hood, the DAG uses Windows failover clustering software, and there are two options to discuss here:

- **Dynamic quorum**—In Windows, the quorum majority is determined by the nodes that are active members of the cluster at a given time. This means that a cluster can dynamically change from an eight-node cluster to a seven- or six-node cluster, and in case of issues, the majority changes accordingly. In theory, it is possible to dynamically bring down a cluster to only one (1) cluster node, also referred to as the "last man standing." Besides changing automatically, an administrator can also change a member manually by setting the cluster's NodeWeight property to zero. The official Exchange product team's best practice is to leave the dynamic quorum enabled, but not to take it into account when designing an Exchange environment.
- **Dynamic witness**—In Windows, when a cluster is configured with dynamic quorum, a new feature called dynamic witness becomes available. The witness vote with a dynamic witness is automatically adjusted, based on the status of the FSW. If it is offline and not available, its witness vote is automatically set to zero, thereby eliminating the chances of an unexpected shutdown of the cluster.

Just as with dynamic quorum, the recommendation is to leave the dynamic witness enabled (by default). Exchange 2016 and 2019 are not aware of the dynamic witness, but it can take advantage of this cluster behavior.

From an Exchange Server point of view, the failover clustering software and its new features are fully transparent, so there is no need to start worrying about clusters, and there is no need to start managing the DAG with the failover cluster manager. All management of the DAG is performed using the Exchange Management Shell or the Exchange Admin Center. In fact, I strongly recommend not using the Windows failover cluster management tool in that case.

The witness server and the file share witness (the latter which is a shared directory on the witness server) are used only when there is an even number of Mailbox servers in the DAG, but as explained before, it is automatically adjusted. Furthermore, the witness server stores no mailbox information; it has only a cluster quorum role.

The following are the prerequisites for the witness server:

- The witness server cannot be a member of the DAG.
- The witness server must be in the same Active Directory forest as the DAG.
- The witness server must be running Windows Server 2008 or later.
- A single server can serve as a witness for multiple DAGs, but each DAG has its own witness directory.

Note If your organization has two data centers with DAG members, the witness server can be in either data center, but it can also be placed in a third data center or in Microsoft Azure.

The witness server plays an important role when problems arise in the DAG—for example, when an Exchange server is not available anymore. The underlying principle is based on an N/2+1 number of servers in the DAG. This means that for a DAG to stay alive when disaster strikes, at least half the number of Mailbox servers plus one need to be up and running. So, if you have a six-node DAG, the DAG can survive the loss of two Exchange servers (6/2+1).

The file share witness, however, is an additional server or vote in this process. So, if there are six Exchange servers in the DAG and three servers fail, the file share witness is the +1 server or vote, and the DAG will survive with four members: three Mailbox servers plus the additional file share witness.

Microsoft recommends you use an Exchange server as a file share witness, which of course cannot be a Mailbox server that is part of the DAG. The reason for this is that an Exchange server is always managed by the Exchange administrators in the organization, and the Exchange Trusted Subsystem Universal Security Group has control over all Exchange servers in Active Directory.

It is also possible to use another Windows server as the file share witness. The only prerequisite is that the Exchange Trusted Subsystem has full control over the Windows server, so the Exchange Trusted Subsystem needs to be a member of the local Administrators Security Group of the Windows server. As domain controllers do not have local groups, it would be necessary to add the Exchange Trusted Subsystem to the Domain Administrators Security Group. However, this imposes a security risk, and it is therefore not recommended.

Note There is no reason to configure the file share witness in a high availability configuration such as on a file cluster.

Exchange Server periodically checks for the file share witness—by default, every four hours—to see if the file share witness is still alive. If it is not available at that moment, the DAG continues to run without any issues. The only time the file share witness needs to be available is during DAG changes, when an Exchange server fails, or when Exchange servers are added to or deleted from the DAG.

A question that pops up on a regular basis is whether to store the file share witness on a DFS share, especially when the company is using a server with multiple locations. This is not a good idea. Imagine this: There are two locations, A and B, and the Exchange location has three Exchange servers configured in one DAG. The file share witness is located on a DFS share, and thus potentially available in both locations. Now, suppose the network connection between locations A and B fails for some reason. The DAG will notice the connection loss, and in both locations, Exchange will try to determine the number of available Mailbox servers and attempt to contact the file share witness. In location A, this will succeed and the DAG will continue to run with four nodes (three Exchange servers plus the file share witness). In location B, the same will happen, so

Exchange will try to contact the file share witness as well. Since the file share witness is available via the DFS share in location B also, the DAG will claim the file share witness in location B and continue to run as well. And Exchange in each location will assume that the DAG members in the other location have been shut down—which of course is not the case. This is called a split-brain scenario, a highly undesirable situation that will lead to unpredictable results, and it is a situation that is not supported at all.

Cluster Administrative Access Point

When a Windows failover cluster is created, an access point for the cluster is created as well. An access point is a combination of a name and an IP address. This IP address can be IPv4 or IPv6; it can be statically assigned or dynamically assigned using DHCP.

The first access point that gets created is the cluster administrative access point, sometimes also referred to as the cluster name and cluster IP address.

In Exchange, this cluster administrative access point is the name of the DAG and its IP address. As the name implies, this is only used for management purposes. Important to note is that clients connect to the Exchange Client Access Front End, and the Client Access Front End connects to a mailbox database where the mailbox resides.

Besides a cluster with an administrative access point, it is also possible to configure a cluster without an administrative access point, something that was introduced years ago in Windows server 2012 R2. In Exchange Server, this means that you create a DAG with a name and without an IP address. Is this bad? No, not at all, since nothing connects to the cluster administrative access point, except for the failover cluster manager. But since all cluster management is performed using the Exchange Management Shell, this is not needed for Exchange. In the section about the DAG creation process, we will show how to create a DAG without an administrative access point.

Note Be aware when using this. There are still third-party backup solutions that require a regular (old-fashioned) administrative access point.

Replication

A database availability group consists of several Exchange servers, and these Mailbox servers have multiple mailbox databases (see Figure 4-10). There is only one copy of a given mailbox database on a given Mailbox server in a DAG, so the total number of copies of a specific mailbox database can never exceed the number of Mailbox servers in the DAG.

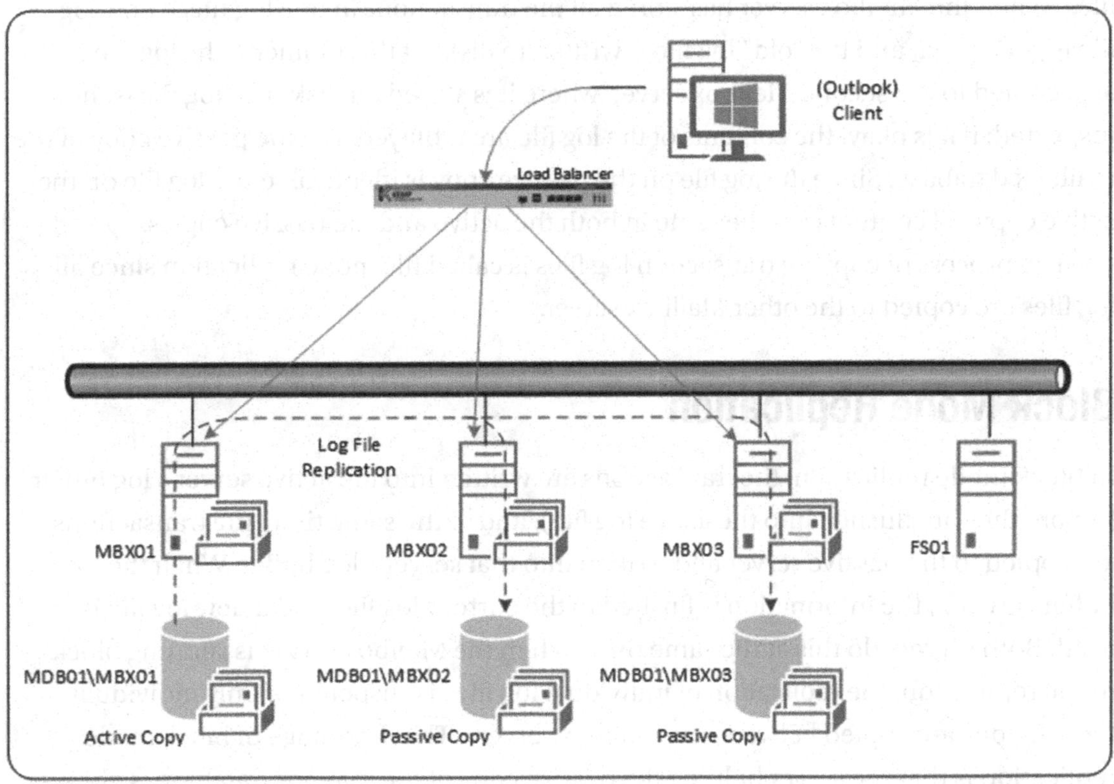

***Figure 4-10.** Schematical overview of a database availability group (DAG)*

The mailbox databases can be either active or passive copies. The active copy is where all the mailbox data processing takes place, and it is no different from a normal Exchange server that is not part of a DAG.

Now, another Exchange server in the DAG can host another copy of this same database; this is called a passive copy. A regular passive copy should be close to 100% identical to the active copy, and it is kept up to date by a technology called log shipping or log file replication.

There are two ways of replicating data from one Mailbox server to another:

- File mode replication
- Block mode replication

File Mode Replication

As explained earlier in this chapter, all transactions are logged in the transaction log files. When the Mailbox server has stored all the transactions in one log file, a new log file is generated, and the "old" log file is written to disk. At this moment, the log file is also copied to the second Mailbox server, where it is stored on disk. The log file is then inspected; if it is okay, the contents of the log file are replayed into the passive copy of the mailbox database. Since the log file on the passive copy is identical to the log file on the active copy, all contents are the same in both the active and the passive copies.

The process of copying transaction log files is called file mode replication since all log files are copied to the other Mailbox server.

Block Mode Replication

In block mode replication, the transactions are written into the active server's log buffer (before they are flushed into the active log file), and at the same time, the transactions are copied to the passive server and written into that server's log buffer. When the log buffers are full, the information is flushed to the current log file, and a new log file is used. Both servers do this at the same time. When the Mailbox server is running block mode replication, the replication of individual log files is suspended; only individual transactions are copied between the Mailbox servers. The advantage of block mode replication is that the server holding the passive copy of the mailbox database is always 100% up to date, and therefore failover times are greatly reduced.

The default process is block mode replication, but the Exchange server falls back to file mode replication when that server is too busy to cope with replicating individual transactions. If this happens, the Exchange server can replicate the individual transaction log files at its own pace, and even queue some log files when there are not enough resources.

An active mailbox database copy can have multiple passive copies on multiple Mailbox servers (remember that one server can hold only one copy of a specific mailbox database, active or passive). The active copy of a mailbox database is where all the processing takes place, and all the replication, whether it is file mode or block mode, takes place from this active copy to all passive copies of the mailbox database. There is absolutely no possibility that one passive copy will replicate log files to another passive copy. The only exception to this is when a new copy of a mailbox database is created from another passive copy, but that is only the initial creation, which is seeding.

Seeding

Creating the passive copy of an active mailbox database is called seeding. In this process, the mailbox database is copied from one Mailbox server to another Mailbox server. When seeding, the complete mailbox database (the actual mailbox database.edb) is copied from the first Mailbox server hosting the active copy of this mailbox database to the second Mailbox server. This is not a simple NTFS file copy, the Information Store streams the file from one location to another.

Here is how it works: The Information Store reads the contents of the mailbox database page by page, automatically checking them. If there's an error on a particular page (i.e., a corrupt page), the process stops and the error is logged. This way, Exchange prevents copying a mailbox database to another location that has corrupted pages. When seeding, you can select which mailbox database acts as the source of the seeding. This can be the active mailbox database, but it can also be a passive mailbox database.

Since the pages of the mailbox database are copied from one Exchange server to another Exchange server, the passive copy is identical to the active copy. When the entire mailbox database is copied to the other Exchange server, the remaining log files are copied to the other Mailbox server as well. When a new mailbox database is seeded, the process takes only a couple of minutes because there is not too much data to copy. But imagine a mailbox database of 1 TB in a normal production environment. When that must be seeded, it can take hours. And not only is the timing an important factor but also the process puts additional load on the servers. The 1 TB of data needs to be read and checked, copied via the network, and written to disk on the other Mailbox server.

AutoReseed

An interesting feature in Exchange is automatic reseed, or AutoReseed. In a typical environment when a disk in an Exchange server fails, it is replaced by IT staff, and an Exchange administrator creates a new copy of a mailbox database on the new disk.

AutoReseed is basically the same process, but automated; the idea behind AutoReseed is to get a mailbox database up and running again immediately after a disk failure. To achieve this, Exchange can use the Windows feature of multiple mount points per volume.

When AutoReseed is configured, the Exchange server has one or more spare disks in its disk cabinet. When a disk containing a mailbox database fails, the Microsoft Exchange Replication service automatically allocates a spare disk and automatically creates a new copy of this mailbox database.

The DAG has three properties that are used for the AutoReseed feature:

- **AutoDagVolumesRootFolderPath**—This is a link to the mount point that contains all available volumes, for example, C:\ExchVols. Volumes that host mailbox databases, as well as spare volumes, are located here.
- **AutoDagDatabasesRootFolderPath**—This is a link to the mount point that contains all mailbox databases, for example, C:\ExchDBs.
- **AutoDagDatabaseCopiesPerVolume**—This property contains the number of mailbox database copies per volume.

Important to note is that although there is one mailbox database on a particular location, it can be located through two possible ways. The first is via the C:\ExchVols mount point; the second is via the C:\ExchDBs mount point.

AutoReseed is regularly monitoring to come into action by using the following steps:

1. The Microsoft Exchange Replication service constantly scans for mailbox database copies that have failed—that is, that have a copy status of "FailedAndSuspended."
2. If a mailbox database is in a "FailedAndSuspended" status, the Microsoft Exchange Replication service does some prerequisite checks to see if AutoReseed can be performed.
3. If the checks are passed successfully, the Replication service automatically allocates a spare disk and configures it into the production disk system.

4. When the disk is configured, a new seeding operation is started, thus creating a new copy of the mailbox database.

5. When seeding is done, the Replication service checks if the new copy is healthy and resumes operation.

There is one manual step left at this point: the Exchange administrator has to replace the faulty disk with a new one and format the new disk appropriately.

Note For the AutoReseed to function correctly, the disks need to be configured in a mount point configuration. You cannot use dedicated drive letters.

In the section about the DAG creation process, implementing and configuring the AutoReseed is explained in detail.

Replication (Copy) Queue and Replay Queue

In an ideal situation, transaction log files are replicated to another Exchange server directly after the log files are written to disk, and they are processed immediately after being received by the other Exchange server. Unfortunately, we do not live in an ideal world, so there might be some delay somewhere in the system.

When the Exchange servers are busy, it can happen that more transaction log files are generated than the replication process can handle and transmit. If this is the case, the log files are queued on the Exchange server holding the active copy of the mailbox database. This queue is called the replication queue. Queuing always happens, and it is normally not a reason for concern if the number of log files in the queue is low and the log files do not stay there too long. However, if there are thousands of messages waiting in line, it is time to do some further investigation.

When the transaction log files are received by the Exchange server holding the passive copy of the mailbox database, those transaction log files are stored in the replay queue. Queuing up in the replay queue happens as well and is also not a reason for concern when the number of transaction log files is low. There can be spikes in the number of transaction log files in the replay queue, but when the number of transaction log files is constantly increasing, there is something wrong. It can happen that the disk holding the mailbox database is generating too many read and write operations. Or there may not be enough resources to flush the queue, and so the queue will grow. If the system can flush the queue in a reasonable time, and there are not thousands of messages in the queue, you should be fine.

Lagged Copies

Regarding the replay queue, there is one exception to note: lagged copies. If you have implemented lagged copies in your DAG, and you experience many log files in the replay queue, then there is nothing to worry about.

Lagged copies are passive copies of a mailbox database that are not kept up to date. This means that log files are replicated to the Exchange server holding the lagged copy, but the log files themselves are kept in the replay queue. This lag time between replication and writing to the server can be as little as 0 second (the log file is replayed immediately) or up to 14 days. A very long lag time will have a serious impact on scalability, of course. A full 14 days' worth of log files can mean a tremendous amount of data being stored in the replay queue; also, replaying the transaction log files of a lagged copy can take quite some time when longer time frames are used.

Note Lagged copies are not a high availability solution; rather, they are a disaster recovery solution.

Active Manager

The Active Manager is a component of Exchange, and it runs inside the Microsoft Exchange Replication services on all Exchange servers. The Active Manager is the component that is responsible for the high availability inside the database availability group.

There are several types of Active Managers:

- **Primary Active Manager (PAM)**—The PAM is the role that decides which copy of a mailbox database is the active copy and which ones are the passive copies; as such, PAM reacts to changes in the DAG, such as DAG member failures. The DAG member that holds the PAM role is always the server that also holds the quorum resource or the default cluster group.

- **Standby Active Manager (SAM)**—The SAM is responsible for providing DAG information, for example, which mailbox database is an active copy and which copies are passive copies, to other Exchange components like the Client Access service or the Hub Transport service. If the SAM detects a failure of a mailbox database, it requests a failover to the PAM. The PAM then decides which copy to activate.
- **Standalone Active Manager**—The Standalone Active Manager is responsible for mounting and dismounting databases on that particular server. This Active Manager is available only on Exchange servers that are not members of a DAG.

DAG Across (Active Directory) Sites

In the previous examples, the DAG has always been installed in one Active Directory site. However, there is no such boundary in the DAG, so it is possible to create a DAG that spans multiple Active Directory sites, even in different physical locations. For instance, it is possible to extend the DAG for anticipating two potential scenarios:

- **Database disaster recovery**—In this scenario, mailbox databases are replicated to another location exclusively for off-site storage. These databases are safe there, should disasters, like a fire or flood, strike at the primary location.
- **Site resiliency**—In this scenario, the DAG is (most likely) evenly distributed across two locations (see Figure 4-11). The second location, however, also has multiple Exchange servers with a full-blown Internet connection. When disaster strikes and the primary site is no longer available, the second site can take over all functions.

When using a Geo-DNS solution, only one FQDN (i.e., webmail.proexchangeadmin.com) can be used. For example, in Figure 4-11, there are two Active Directory sites, one location in Amsterdam and another in London. When a user tries to contact webmail.proexchangeadmin.com when traveling in the UK, they are automatically connected to the London site.

When they try to access webmail.proexchangeadmin.com in the Netherlands, they are connected to the Amsterdam site. In either case, after authentication the client is automatically proxied to the correct Mailbox server to get the mailbox information.

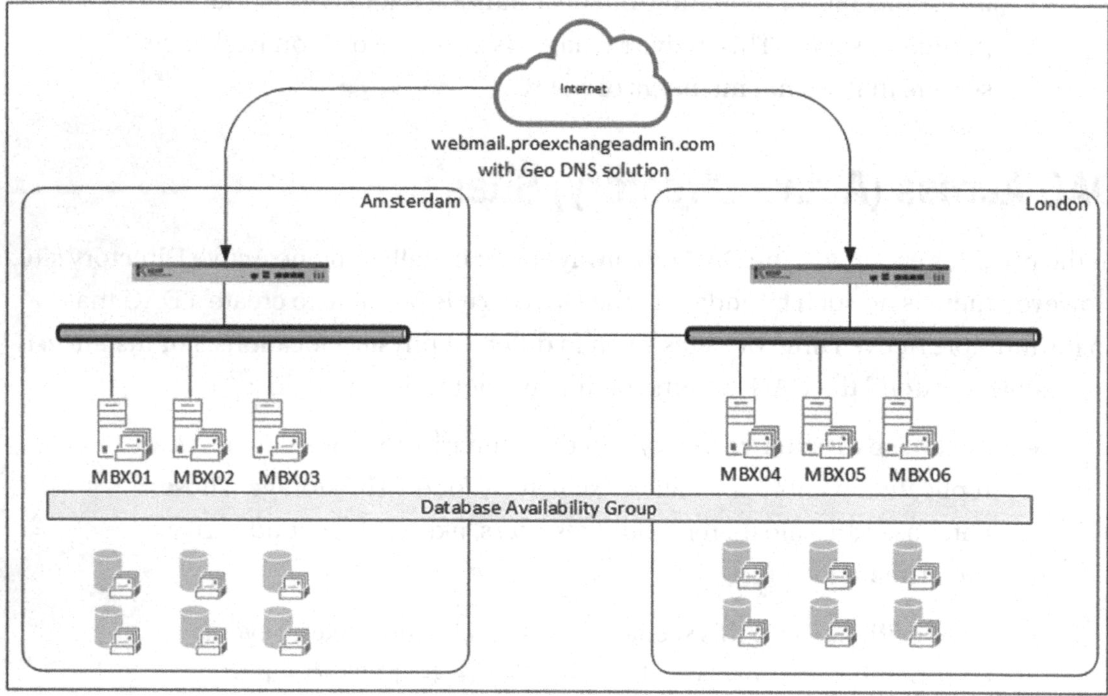

Figure 4-11. *A DAG stretched across two locations*

By default, a site failover is not an automated process. If a data center failover needs to happen, especially when the site holding the file share witness is involved, administrative action is required. However, it is possible to work around this limitation by placing the file share witness in a third Active Directory site.

It is possible to create an active/active scenario whereby both data centers are active, servicing users and processing mail data. In this case, two DAGs must be created; each DAG is active in one data center, and its passive copies are in the other data center. Note, however, that an Exchange server can be a member of only one DAG at a time.

This could mean that you need more servers in an active/active scenario, a downside of having two DAGs.

Creating a site-resilient configuration with multiple DAGs requires careful planning, plus asking yourself a lot of questions, both technical and organizational. Typical questions are

- What level of service is required?
- What level of service is required when one data center fails?
- What are the objectives for recovery point and recovery time?
- How many users are on the system and which data centers are these users connecting to?
- Is the system designed to service all users when one data center fails?
- How are services moved back to the original data center?
- Are there any resources available (like IT staff) for these scenarios?

These are just basic planning questions to be answered before you even think about implementing a site-resilient configuration. And remember: the more requirements there are and the stricter they are, the more expensive the solution will be!

DAG Networks

A DAG uses one or more networks for client connectivity and for replication. Each DAG contains at least one network for client connectivity, which is created by default, and zero or more replication networks. In Exchange 2010, this default DAG network was called the MAPI network. The MAPI protocol is no longer used in Exchange as a native client protocol, but the default DAG network is still called MapiDagNetwork.

For years, Microsoft has been recommending the use of multiple networks to separate the client traffic from the replication traffic. With the current 10 GB networks, separating client traffic from replication traffic is no longer an issue. Also, the use of a Serverblade infrastructure with its 10 GB backbone separation of traffic was more of a logical separation than a physical separation. Therefore, Microsoft moves away from the recommendation of separating network traffic, thereby simplifying the DAG network configuration.

When you still want to separate client traffic from replication traffic, you can do so in a supported manner. In Exchange, the network is automatically configured by the system. If additional networks need to be configured, you set the DAG to manual configuration, then create the additional DAG networks.

When using multiple networks, it is possible to designate a network for client connectivity and the other networks for replication traffic. When multiple networks are used for replication, Exchange automatically determines which network to use for replication traffic. When all the replication networks are offline or not available, Exchange automatically switches back to the MAPI network for the replication traffic.

Default gateways need to be considered when you are configuring multiple network interfaces in Windows Server. The only network that needs this configuring with a default gateway is the client connectivity network; all other networks should not be configured with a default gateway.

Other recommendations important for replication networks are the following:

- Disabling the DNS registration on the TCP/IP properties of the respective network interface
- Disabling the protocol bindings, such as the client for Microsoft networks and file and printer sharing for Microsoft networks, on the properties of the network interface
- Rearranging the binding order of the network interfaces so that the client connectivity network is at the top of the connection order

When using an iSCSI storage solution, make sure that the iSCSI network is not used at all for replication purposes. Remove any iSCSI network connection from the replication network list.

DAG Creation

Creating a database availability group consists of several steps:

- Creating the DAG object
- Adding the Exchange servers to the DAG
- Creating additional Mailbox database copies

Creating the Database Availability Group Object

The first step in the process is to create the DAG object using Exchange Management Shell. In this step, only an object in Active Directory is created. As explained earlier in this chapter, a computer name object (CNO) and a cluster IP address are no longer needed in Exchange 2016 and Exchange 2019. To create a new DAG object, execute the following command in EMS:

```
[PS] C:\> New-DatabaseAvailabilityGroup -Name DAG01 -WitnessServer FS01.
proexchangeadmin.com -WitnessDirectory C:\DAG01_FSW -Database
AvailabilityGroupIPAddresses ([System.Net.IPAddress])::None
```

Creating the DAG is straightforward—it is only an entry written in the configuration partition of Active Directory. If you want to check it, you can use ADSI Edit and navigate to CN=DAG01, CN=Database Availability Groups, CN=Exchange Administrative Group (FYDIBOHF23SPDLT), CN=Administrative Groups, CN=ProExchange, CN=Microsoft Exchange, CN=Services, CN=Configuration, DC=Proexchangeadmin, DC=com.

This is shown in Figure 4-12.

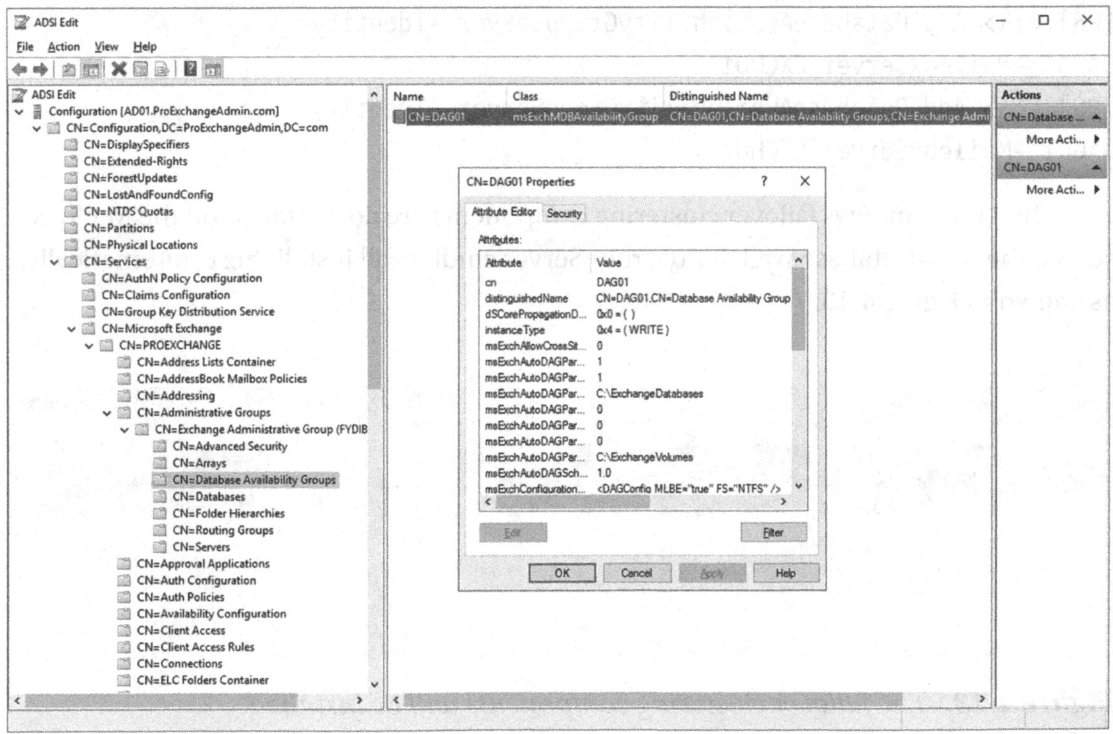

Figure 4-12. The newly created DAG in Active Directory

The information that's returned when running a Get-DatabaseAvailabilityGroup command is just a representation of this object in Active Directory, combined with information taken from the local registry (when using the -status parameter).

Note Microsoft recommends that the file share witness best be another Exchange server. This Exchange server cannot be a member of the same DAG. However, it can be a member of another DAG, or any other server in the same Active Directory site.

In this example, a file server called FS01 is used. Since Exchange cannot control a non-Exchange Server, the Active Directory's security group Exchange Trusted Subsystem should be added to the local administrator's security group on the file share witness server.

Adding Exchange Servers

Once the DAG exists, the Exchange servers can be added to it, which is also a straightforward process; just run the following commands to add the servers EXCH01 and EXCH02 to the DAG created in the previous step:

```
[PS] C:\> Add-DatabaseAvailabilityGroupServer -Identity
DAG01 -MailboxServer EXCH01
[PS] C:\> Add-DatabaseAvailabilityGroupServer -Identity
DAG01 -MailboxServer EXCH02
```

When the Windows failover clustering components are not installed on the Mailbox server, the Add-DatabaseAvailabilityGroupServer cmdlet will install these automatically, as shown in Figure 4-13.

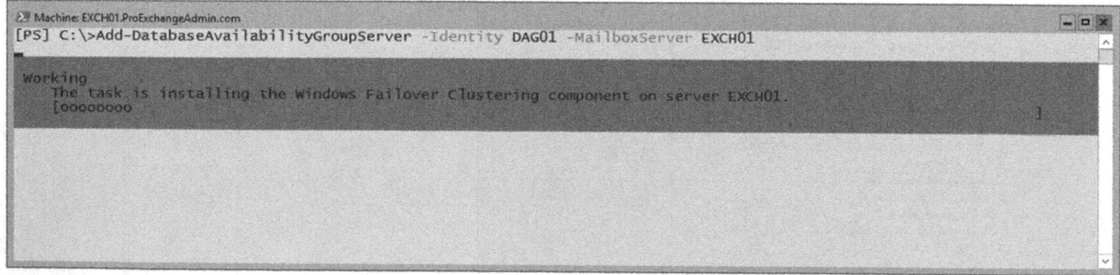

Figure 4-13. *The failover clustering components will be installed automatically*

At this point, a DAG is created with two members using a file server as a witness server.

Adding the Mailbox Database Copies

Now that the DAG is fully up and running, it is time for the last step: creating additional copies of the mailbox databases. Initially, there's only one copy of the mailbox database, but you can create redundancy when you add multiple copies on other Mailbox servers in the DAG.

It is important to note that the location of the mailbox database is identical on all Mailbox servers holding a copy of a particular mailbox database. So, if you have a mailbox database C:\ExchDbs\Disk1\MDB01\MDB01.edb of server EXCH01, the copy of the mailbox database on server EXCH02 is on C:\ExchDbs\Disk1\MDB01\MDB01.edb as well. This might sound obvious, but every now and then, I talk to people who are not aware of this.

To create additional copies of a mailbox database in a DAG, you can use the Add-MailboxDatabaseCopy cmdlet. To add copies of mailbox databases called MDB01 on Exchange server EXCH02 and MDB02 on Exchange server EXCH01, you can use the following commands:

```
[PS] C:\> Add-MailboxDatabaseCopy -Identity MDB01 -MailboxServer
EXCH02 -ActivationPreference 2
[PS] C:\> Add-MailboxDatabaseCopy -Identity MDB02 -MailboxServer
EXCH01 -ActivationPreference 2
```

The activation preference is meant for administrative purposes and for planned switchovers. It is not used by an automatic failover. In case of an automatic failover, a process called the best copy selection on the Mailbox server is used to determine the optimal passive copy for activation.

Configuring the DAG Networks

In our example, the DAG is now configured with two Mailbox servers; by default, only one DAG network is configured, the default MapiDagNetwork. You can quickly see this in the EAC, in the lower-right part of the DAG view, as shown in Figure 4-14.

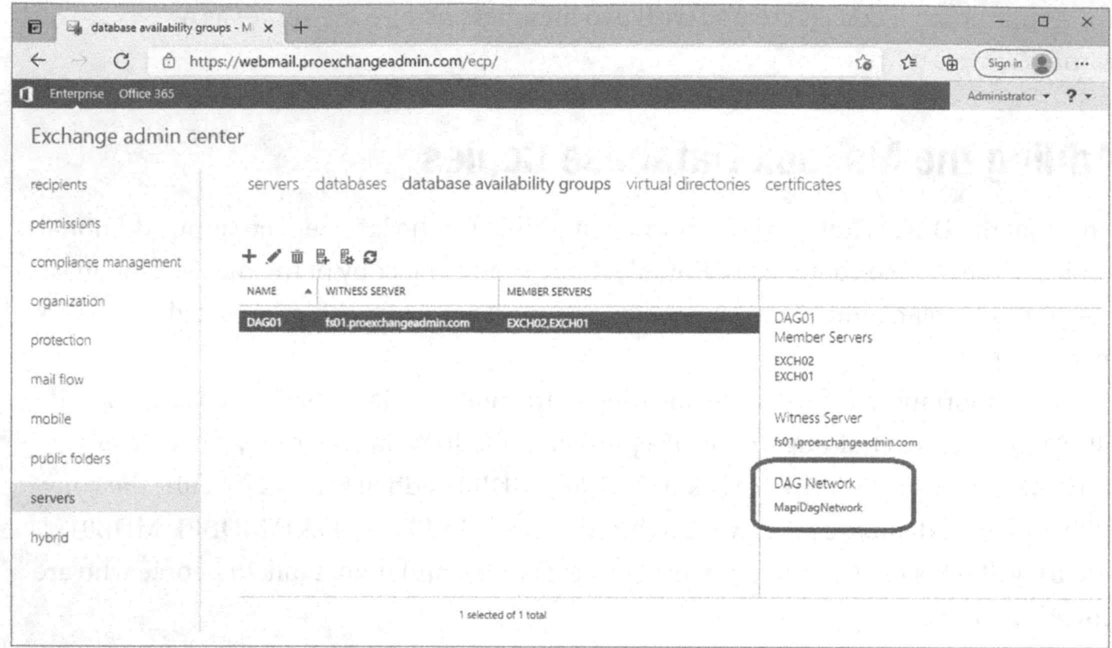

***Figure 4-14.** Only one network is configured by default in a DAG*

To add an additional DAG network (if the servers have multiple network interfaces, of course), the DAG itself should be set to manual configuration, as mentioned earlier. This can only be done using the EMS with the following command:

```
[PS] C:\> Set-DatabaseAvailabilityGroup -Identity
DAG01 -ManualDagNetworkConfiguration $true
```

To create a new additional network for replication purposes, you can use the following command:

```
[PS] C:\> New-DatabaseAvailabilityGroupNetwork -DatabaseAvailabilityGroup
DAG01 -Name "ProExchange Replication Network" -Subnets
192.168.0.0/24 -ReplicationEnabled:$ true
```

To designate this new network as a dedicated replication network, you must disable the replication feature of the regular MapiDagNetwork in the DAG. To disable this, you can use the following command:

```
[PS] C:\> Set-DatabaseAvailabilityGroupNetwork -Identity DAG01\
MapiDagNetwork -ReplicationEnabled:$false
```

After running these commands, you have created a separate network in the DAG specifically for replication traffic.

AutoReseed Configuration

As explained earlier in this chapter, you can use AutoReseed to have Exchange automatically reseed a mailbox database when one mailbox database or a disk containing mailbox databases in a DAG fails, assuming you have configured multiple copies, of course. AutoReseed is using the "multiple mountpoints per volume" option of Windows server.

Configuring AutoReseed involves several steps:

- Configure the database availability group.
- Install and configure database disks.
- Create the mailbox databases.
- Create mailbox database copies.

These steps are explained in the next sections.

Configuring the Database Availability Group

The AutoReseed feature uses several properties on the database availability group that need to be populated:

- AutoDagDatabasesRootFolderPath, which will be C:\ExchDbs, is the location where our regular mailbox database mount points are located.
- AutoDagVolumesRootFolderPath, which will be C:\ExchVols, is the location where all available volumes are located, including the spare volumes.
- AutoDagDatabaseCopiesPerVolume, contains the number of mailbox database copies per volume; in our example, this will be two mailbox databases per volume.

You can use the following command to set these:

```
[PS] C:\> Set-DatabaseAvailabilityGroup DAG01 -AutoDagDatabasesRootFolderPath
"C:\ExchDbs" -AutoDagVolumesRootFolderPath
"C:\ExchVols" -AutoDagDatabaseCopiesPerVolume 2
```

For simplicity, we are only using two volumes. One volume contains two mailbox database copies; the other volume is the spare volume.

Installing and Configuring Database Disks

To implement AutoReseed, you must create multiple disks on your Exchange 2019 server where the disks are configured using mount points. In this example, we have two Exchange 2019 servers, each configured with two disks, Vol1 and Vol2. Vol1 has two mailbox databases called MDB11 and MDB12; Vol2 is a spare disk that will be used if Vol1 fails.

These two disks will be mounted in a directory C:\ExchVols, but they will also be mounted in a directory C:\ExchDbs, as shown in Figure 4-15.

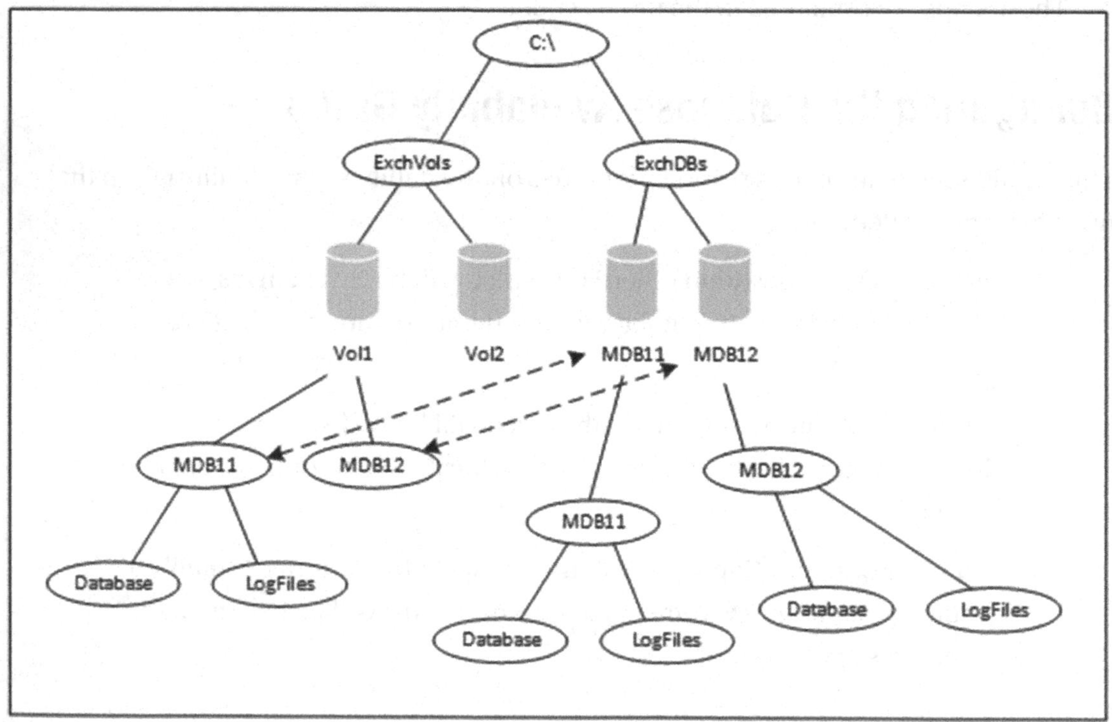

Figure 4-15. *Schematical overview of an AutoReseed configuration*

When the disks are installed, you can create the root directories for the volumes and mailbox database mount points:

```
C:\> MD C:\ExchVols
C:\> MD C:\ExchDBs
```

You format the disks and mount them into the appropriate volume folders:

- C:\ExchVols\Vol1
- C:\ExchVols\Vol2

Then you create the mailbox database folders in the appropriate location:

```
C:\> MD C:\ExchDBs\MDB01
C:\> MD C:\ExchDBs\MDB02
```

Creating the mount points for the mailbox databases is a bit trickier. You can use the Disk Management MMC snap-in, or you can use the command-line tool Mountvol.exe to achieve this.

When using the Disk Management MMC snap-in, you must select a disk that was created in the previous step—for example, C:\ExchVols\Vol1. To add an additional mount point, right-click the disk and select "Change Drive Letter and Path." Use the Add button to select a mailbox database directory—for example, C:\ExchDBs\MDB11.

Repeat this step for the second mailbox database directory as well, as shown in Figure 4-16.

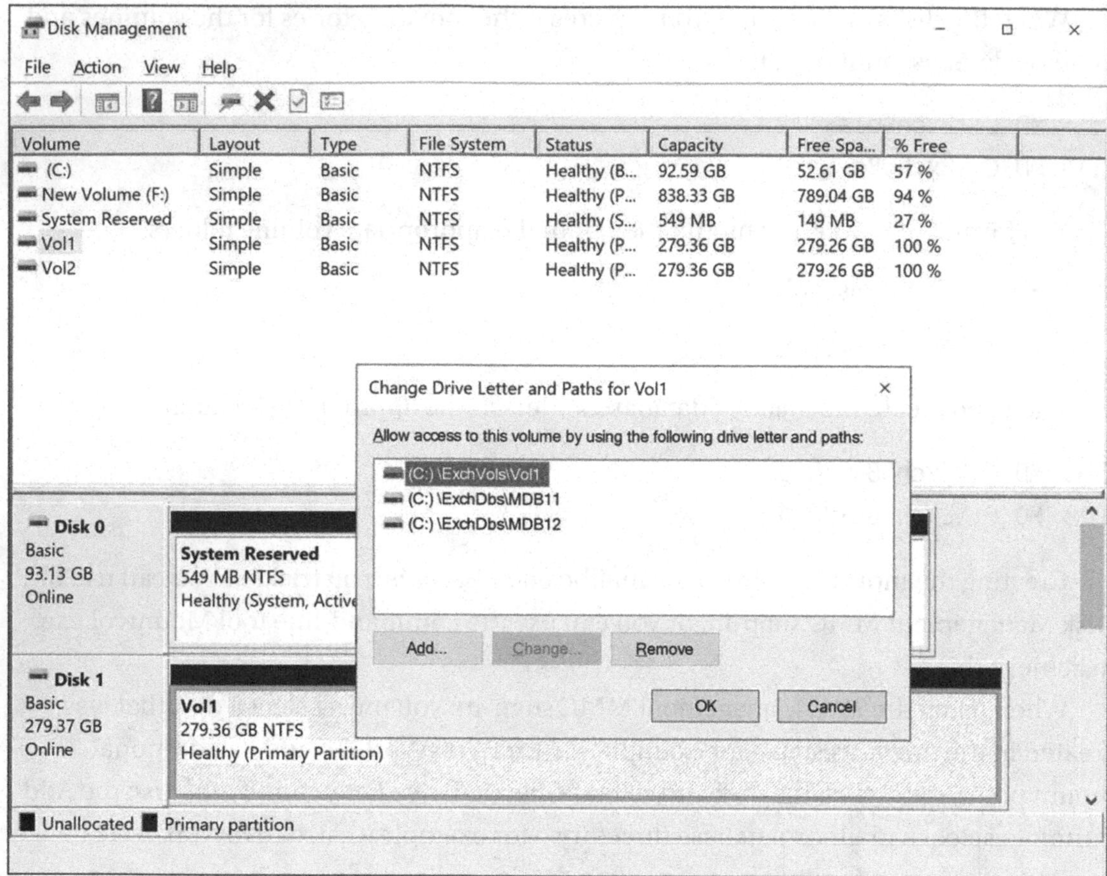

***Figure 4-16.** Mount the disk in the database directories*

The steps as shown in Figure 4-16 need to be repeated for the remaining two directories for mailbox databases MDB03 and MDB04. The second volume should be mounted in these two directories.

Instead of using the Computer Management MMC snap-in, it is possible to use the Mountvol.exe command-line utility. The Mountvol.exe utility is used as follows:

```
C:\> Mountvol.exe c:\ExchDbs\MDB01 \\?\Volume (GUID)
C:\> Mountvol.exe c:\ExchDbs\MDB02 \\?\Volume (GUID)
```

You can retrieve the GUIDs of the individual volumes using Mountvol.exe as well; just use a command like Mountvol.exe C:\ExchVols\ and you will see something like what is shown in Figure 4-17.

```
Administrator: Command Prompt

Possible values for VolumeName along with current mount points are:

    \\?\Volume{e3e14036-0000-0000-0000-100000000000}\
        *** NO MOUNT POINTS ***

    \\?\Volume{93f86827-e088-423e-a0ba-c359ef732c97}\
        C:\ExchVols\Vol1\

    \\?\Volume{3f2ba2b3-0aed-42a7-8d04-aced628131fd}\
        C:\ExchVols\vol2\

    \\?\Volume{607955c3-0000-0000-0000-100000000000}\
        F:\

    \\?\Volume{e3e14036-0000-0000-0000-602200000000}\
        C:\

C:\>
```

***Figure 4-17.** Retrieve the disk GUIDs using Mountvol.exe*

To add the disk as an additional mount point to both mailbox database directories, you can use the following commands:

```
C:\> Mountvol.exe C:\ExchDbs\MDB11 \\?\Volume{93f86827-e088-423e-a0ba-
c359ef732c97}\
C:\> Mountvol.exe C:\ExchDbs\MDB12 \\?\Volume{93f86827-e088-423e-a0ba-
c359ef732c97}\
```

You can check the results by running the Mountvol.exe utility without any parameters. The output is shown in Figure 4-18.

```
Administrator: Command Prompt

Possible values for VolumeName along with current mount points are:

    \\?\Volume{e3e14036-0000-0000-0000-100000000000}\
        *** NO MOUNT POINTS ***

    \\?\Volume{93f86827-e088-423e-a0ba-c359ef732c97}\
        C:\ExchVols\Vol1\
        C:\ExchDbs\mdb11\
        C:\ExchDbs\mdb12\

    \\?\Volume{3f2ba2b3-0aed-42a7-8d04-aced628131fd}\
        C:\ExchVols\vol2\

    \\?\Volume{607955c3-0000-0000-0000-100000000000}\
        F:\

    \\?\Volume{e3e14036-0000-0000-0000-602200000000}\
        C:\

C:\>
```

***Figure 4-18.** The disk is mounted in three different locations*

These steps must be executed on all Exchange servers that are part of the DAG.

Creating Mailbox Databases

The next step is to create the directory structure on both Mailbox servers where the mailbox database files will be stored. This depends on your own naming convention, of course, but it could look something like this:

```
C:\> md c:\ExchDBs\MDB11\MDB11.db
C:\> md c:\ExchDBs\MDB11\MDB11.log
C:\> md c:\ExchDBs\MDB12\MDB12.db
C:\> md c:\ExchDBs\MDB12\MDB12.log
```

Note The transaction logfile directory must be like the MDB12.log notation. If not, the AutoReseed workflow will fail.

The mailbox database file itself will be stored in the AMS-MDB01.DB subdirectory, while the accompanying transaction log files will be stored in the AMS-MDB01.log subdirectory.

New mailbox databases will be created in the directories you just created; just use the following commands in the Exchange Management Shell:

```
[PS] C:\> New-MailboxDatabase -Name MDB11 -Server EXCH11 -EdbFilePath C:\
ExchDbs\MDB11\MDB11.db\MDB11.edb -LogFolderPath C:\ExchDbs\MDB11\MDB11.log
[PS] C:\> New-MailboxDatabase -Name MDB12 -Server EXCH11 -EdbFilePath C:\
ExchDbs\MDB12\MDB12.db\MDB12.edb -LogFolderPath C:\ExchDbs\MDB12\MDB12.log
```

Creating Mailbox Database Copies

Of course, you need to create an additional copy of the mailbox database on the second Exchange 2019 server. As explained in the previous section, you can create copies of the mailbox databases by using the following commands:

```
[PS] C:\> Add-MailboxDatabaseCopy -Identity MDB01 -MailboxServer EXCH02 -
ActivationPreference 2
```

```
[PS] C:\> Add-MailboxDatabaseCopy -Identity MDB02 -MailboxServer EXCH02 -
ActivationPreference 2
[PS] C:\> Add-MailboxDatabaseCopy -Identity MDB03 -MailboxServer EXCH01 -
ActivationPreference 2
[PS] C:\> Add-MailboxDatabaseCopy -Identity MDB04 -MailboxServer EXCH01 -
ActivationPreference 2
```

At this point, you have created a DAG with the AutoReseed option. If Vol1 fails, it should automatically reseed the mailbox databases to another disk. The best way to test this is to set Vol1 offline in the Computer Management MMC snap-in.

The AutoReseed Process

When a disk fails and goes offline, Exchange will notice almost immediately and activate the copy of the mailbox databases on the second Exchange server as expected. This is clearly visible when we execute a Get-MailboxDatabaseCopyStatus command, as shown in Figure 4-19. The mailbox databases on EXCH01 are in a FailedAndSuspended state while they are mounted on server EXCH02.

```
Machine: EXCH11.ProExchangeAdmin.com
[PS] C:\>Get-MailboxDatabaseCopyStatus -server exch11

Name                      Status           CopyQueue ReplayQueue LastInspectedLogTime  ContentIndex
                                           Length    Length                            State
----                      ------           --------- ----------- --------------------  ------------
MDB11\EXCH11              FailedAndSuspen  551       0                                 NotApplicabl
                          ded                                                          e
MDB12\EXCH11              FailedAndSuspen  17        1           7/2/2021 7:28:15 PM   NotApplicabl
                          ded                                                          e

[PS] C:\>_
```

Figure 4-19. *The mailbox databases on the first Mailbox server are FailedAndSuspended*

What happens next is that a repair workflow is started. The workflow will try to resume the failed mailbox database copy, and if this fails, the workflow will assign the spare volume to the failed disk. This is the exact workflow:

1. The workflow will detect a mailbox database copy that is in a Failed and Suspended state for 15 minutes.

2. Exchange will try to resume the failed mailbox database copy three times with a five-minute interval.

3. If Exchange cannot resume the failed copy, Exchange will try to assign a spare volume five times with a one-hour interval.

4. Exchange will try an InPlaceSeed with the SafeDeleteExistingFiles option five times with a one-hour interval.

5. If all retries are completed with no success, the workflow will stop. If it is successful, Exchange will finish the reseeding.

6. When everything fails, Exchange will wait three days and see if the mailbox database copy is still in the Failed and Suspended state, then it will restart the workflow from step 1.

All events are logged in the event log. There is a special crimson channel for this, which you can find in Applications and Services Logs ➤ Microsoft ➤ Exchange ➤ HighAvailability ➤ Seeding.

The first event that's logged is Event ID 1109 from the AutoReseed manager, indicating that something is wrong and that no data can be written to location C:\ExDbs\MDB01\MDB01.log. This makes sense because the disk has actually "failed" and is no longer available. This event is shown in Figure 4-20.

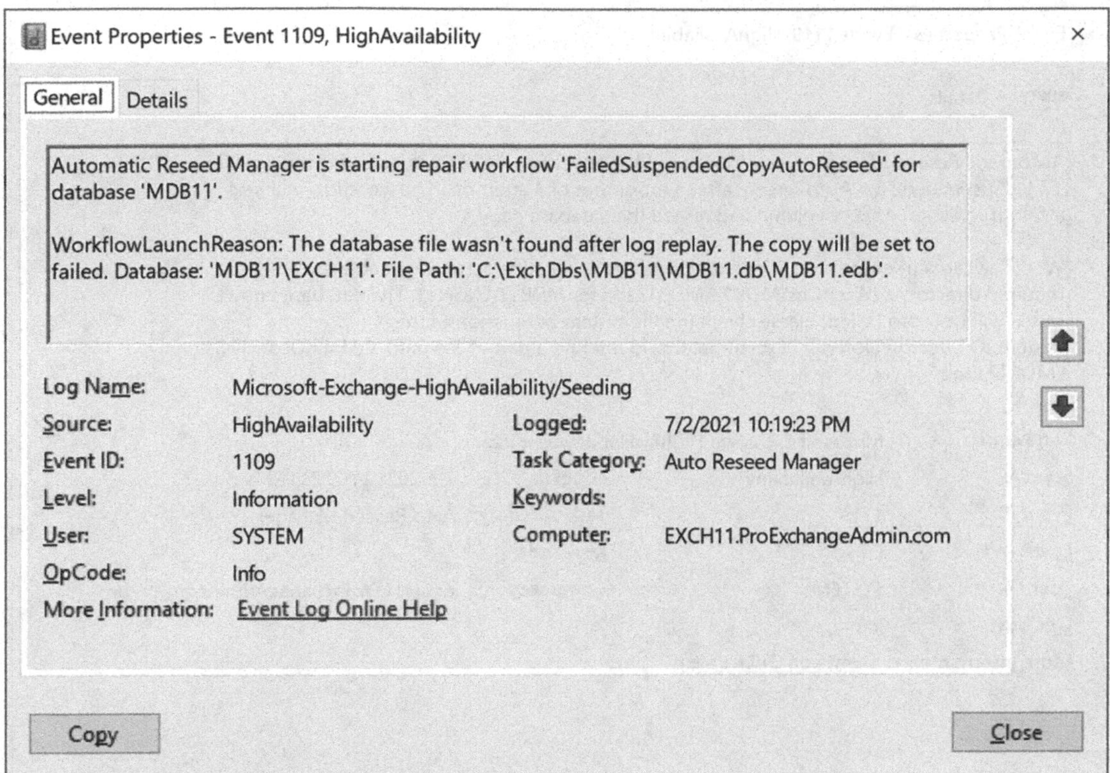

***Figure 4-20.** The first AutoReseed event indicating something is wrong with the disk containing the mailbox database*

Subsequent events in the event log will indicate the AutoReseed manager attempting to resume the copy of the mailbox database. As outlined earlier, it will try this three times, followed by an attempt to reassign a spare disk.

This event is shown in Figure 4-21. Please note that it takes almost an hour before Exchange moves to this step.

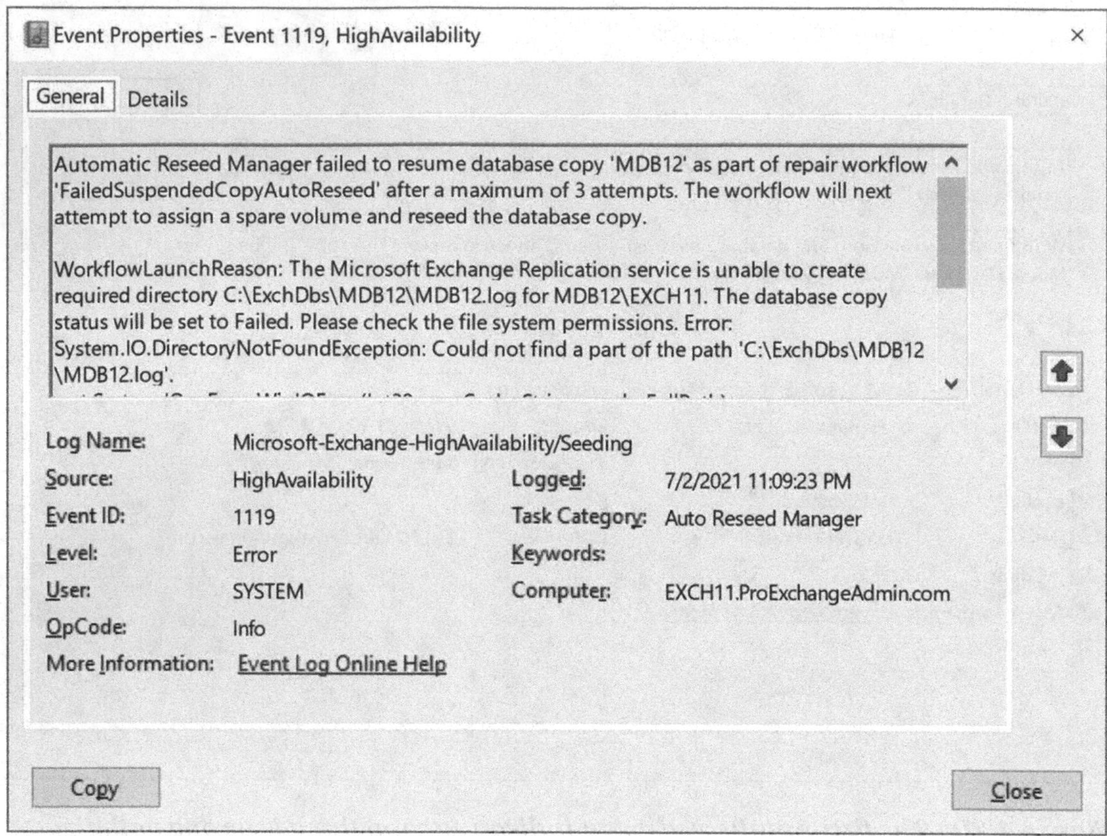
Event Properties - Event 1119, HighAvailability
General
Details
Automatic Reseed Manager failed to resume database copy 'MDB12' as part of repair workflow 'FailedSuspendedCopyAutoReseed' after a maximum of 3 attempts. The workflow will next attempt to assign a spare volume and reseed the database copy.
WorkflowLaunchReason: The Microsoft Exchange Replication service is unable to create required directory C:\ExchDbs\MDB12\MDB12.log for MDB12\EXCH11. The database copy status will be set to Failed. Please check the file system permissions. Error: System.IO.DirectoryNotFoundException: Could not find a part of the path 'C:\ExchDbs\MDB12\MDB12.log'.
Log Name: Microsoft-Exchange-HighAvailability/Seeding
Source: HighAvailability
Logged: 7/2/2021 11:09:23 PM
Event ID: 1119
Task Category: Auto Reseed Manager
Level: Error
Keywords:
User: SYSTEM
Computer: EXCH11.ProExchangeAdmin.com
OpCode: Info
More Information: Event Log Online Help
Copy
Close

***Figure 4-21.** Exchange is reassigning a spare disk*

When the disk is successfully reassigned, Exchange will automatically start reseeding the replaced disk, indicated by Event ID 1127 (still logged by the AutoReseed manager), as shown in Figure 4-22.

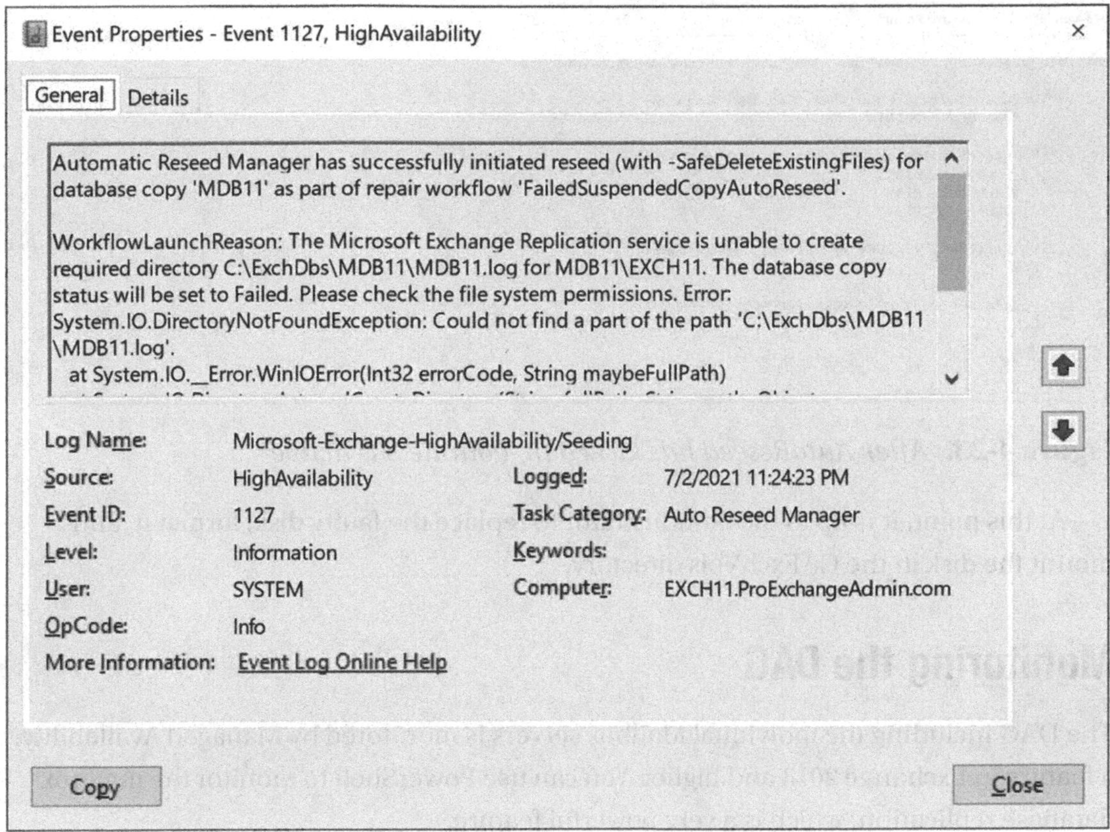
Event Properties - Event 1127, HighAvailability
General
Details
Automatic Reseed Manager has successfully initiated reseed (with -SafeDeleteExistingFiles) for database copy 'MDB11' as part of repair workflow 'FailedSuspendedCopyAutoReseed'.
WorkflowLaunchReason: The Microsoft Exchange Replication service is unable to create required directory C:\ExchDbs\MDB11\MDB11.log for MDB11\EXCH11. The database copy status will be set to Failed. Please check the file system permissions. Error: System.IO.DirectoryNotFoundException: Could not find a part of the path 'C:\ExchDbs\MDB11\MDB11.log'.
at System.IO.__Error.WinIOError(Int32 errorCode, String maybeFullPath)
Log Name: Microsoft-Exchange-HighAvailability/Seeding
Source: HighAvailability
Logged: 7/2/2021 11:24:23 PM
Event ID: 1127
Task Category: Auto Reseed Manager
Level: Information
Keywords:
User: SYSTEM
Computer: EXCH11.ProExchangeAdmin.com
OpCode: Info
More Information: Event Log Online Help
Copy
Close

***Figure 4-22.** Exchange automatically reseeds the new disk*

Depending on the size of your mailbox databases, it can take quite a long time for this step to finish.

You can use the Mountvol utility again to check the new configuration. If all went well, you will see the mailbox databases now on volume 3, as shown in Figure 4-23.

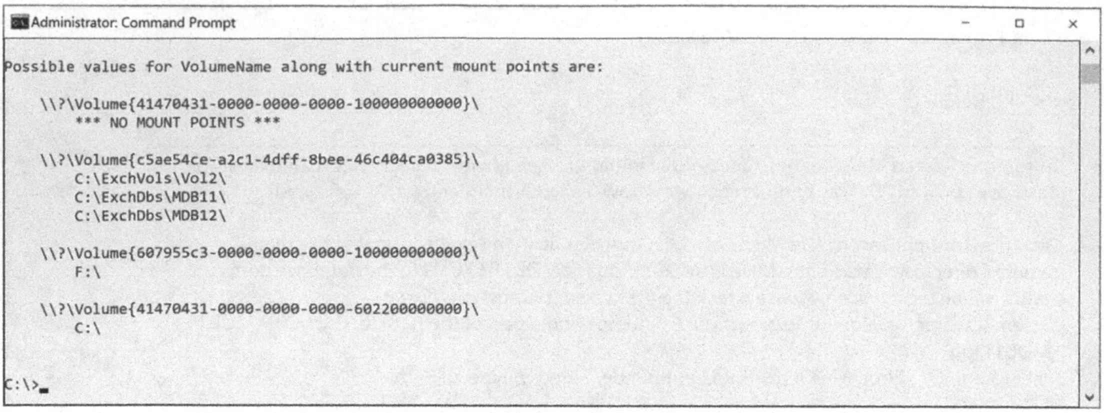

```
Administrator: Command Prompt

Possible values for VolumeName along with current mount points are:

    \\?\Volume{41470431-0000-0000-0000-100000000000}\
        *** NO MOUNT POINTS ***

    \\?\Volume{c5ae54ce-a2c1-4dff-8bee-46c404ca0385}\
        C:\ExchVols\Vol2\
        C:\ExchDbs\MDB11\
        C:\ExchDbs\MDB12\

    \\?\Volume{607955c3-0000-0000-0000-100000000000}\
        F:\

    \\?\Volume{41470431-0000-0000-0000-602200000000}\
        C:\

C:\>_
```

Figure 4-23. *After AutoReseed has kicked in, volume 3 is active*

At this point, it is up to the administrator to replace the faulty disk, format it, and mount the disk in the C:\ExchVols directory.

Monitoring the DAG

The DAG including the individual Mailbox servers is monitored by Managed Availability, a feature in Exchange 2013 and higher. You can use PowerShell to monitor the mailbox database replication, which is a very powerful feature.

Mailbox Database Replication

Mailbox database replication is a key service for determining if the servers are performing as expected. When the performance of an Exchange server or related service degrades, you will see the replication queues start growing.

There are two types of queues available for mailbox database replication:

- **Copy queue**—This is the queue where transaction log files reside before they are replicated (over the network) to other Mailbox servers holding passive copies of a mailbox database.
- **Replay queue**—This queue resides on the Mailbox server holding a passive copy of the mailbox database. It holds transaction log files that are received from the active mailbox database copy but haven't yet been replayed into the passive mailbox database copy.

Both queues fluctuate constantly, and it is no big deal when they are momentarily increasing as long as they start decreasing in minutes.

Note When you have lagged copies in your DAG, especially when the lag time is long, you can expect many items in the replay queues. If so, there is no need to worry since this is expected behavior.

You can monitor the replication queues in EMS using the Get-MailboxDatabaseCopyStatus command:

1. To monitor all copies of a particular mailbox database, you can use the following command: Get-MailboxDatabaseCopyStatus -Identity MDB1 | Format-List.
2. To monitor all mailbox database copies on a given server, you can use the following command:

   Get-MailboxDatabaseCopyStatus -Server EXCH01 | Format-List.
3. To monitor the status and network information for a given mailbox database on a given server, you can use the following command: Get-MailboxDatabaseCopyStatus -Identity MDB3\EXCH03 -ConnectionStatus | Format-List.
4. To monitor the copy status of a given mailbox database on a given server, you can use the following command: Get-MailboxDatabaseCopyStatus -Identity MDB1\EXCH02 | Format-List.

Note The syntax of the identity of the mailbox database copy looks a bit odd, but it is the name of the mailbox database located on the Mailbox server holding the passive copy. In this case, it is mailbox database MDB3 located on Mailbox server EXCH03, thus MDB3\EXCH03.

I often combine the Get-MailboxDatabaseCopyStatus command with the Get-MailboxDatabase command to get a quick overview of all mailbox databases, their passive copies, and the status of the replication queues (see Figure 4-24). To do this, use the following command:

```
[PS] C:\> Get-MailboxDatabase | Get-MailboxDatabaseCopyStatus
```

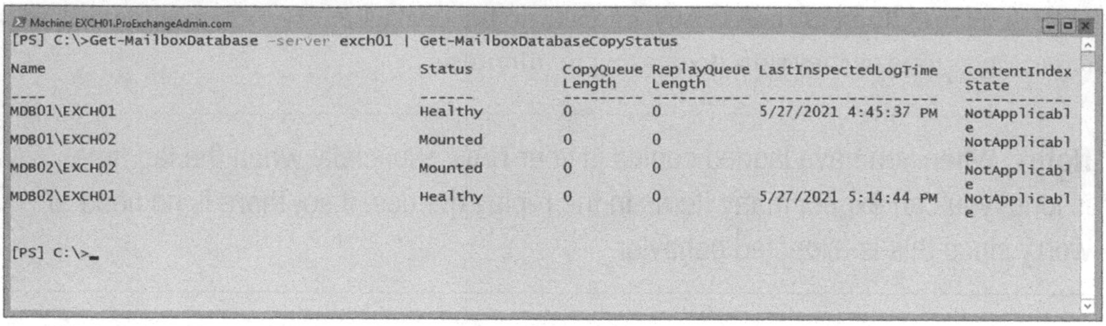

```
Machine: EXCH01.ProExchangeAdmin.com
[PS] C:\>Get-MailboxDatabase -server exch01 | Get-MailboxDatabaseCopyStatus

Name                          Status      CopyQueue ReplayQueue LastInspectedLogTime    ContentIndex
                                          Length    Length                              State
----                          ------      --------- ----------- --------------------    ------------
MDB01\EXCH01                  Healthy     0         0           5/27/2021 4:45:37 PM    NotApplicabl
                                                                                        e
MDB01\EXCH02                  Mounted     0         0                                   NotApplicabl
                                                                                        e
MDB02\EXCH02                  Mounted     0         0                                   NotApplicabl
                                                                                        e
MDB02\EXCH01                  Healthy     0         0           5/27/2021 5:14:44 PM    NotApplicabl
                                                                                        e

[PS] C:\>_
```

Figure 4-24. *Monitoring the status of mailbox database copies*

Note When you are moving mailboxes from one Mailbox server to another Mailbox server, a lot of transaction log files are generated. It is quite common that, under these circumstances, replication cannot keep up with demand, and you will see a dramatic increase in the replication queues. Things can get even worse when you are using circular logging in a DAG, since the log files will be purged only when the transaction log files are replayed into the mailbox database and all the DAG members agree on purging the log files. When there are too many log files, replication will slow down, the disk holding the log files will fill up, and the mailbox database can potentially dismount. The only way to avoid this situation is to throttle down the mailbox moves so that replication can keep up with demand.

Health Check Commands

Another way in EMS to check for mailbox replication is to use the Test-ReplicationHealth command. This command tests the continuous replication, the availability of the Active Manager, the status of the underlying failover cluster components, the cluster quorum, and the underlying network infrastructure. To use this command against server AMS-EXCH01, you can enter the following command:

```
[PS] C:\> Test-ReplicationHealth -Identity EXCH01
```

The output of this command is shown in Figure 4-25.

```
Machine: EXCH01.ProExchangeAdmin.com
[PS] C:\>Test-ReplicationHealth -Identity EXCH01

Server          Check                          Result      Error
------          -----                          ------      -----
EXCH01          ClusterService                 Passed
EXCH01          ReplayService                  Passed
EXCH01          ActiveManager                  Passed
EXCH01          TasksRpcListener               Passed
EXCH01          TcpListener                    Passed
EXCH01          ServerLocatorService           Passed
EXCH01          DagMembersUp                   Passed
EXCH01          MonitoringService              Passed
EXCH01          ClusterNetwork                 Passed
EXCH01          QuorumGroup                    Passed
EXCH01          FileShareQuorum                Passed
EXCH01          DatabaseRedundancy             Passed
EXCH01          DatabaseAvailability           Passed
EXCH01          DBCopySuspended                Passed
EXCH01          DBCopyFailed                   Passed
EXCH01          DBInitializing                 Passed
EXCH01          DBDisconnected                 Passed
EXCH01          DBLogCopyKeepingUp             Passed
EXCH01          DBLogReplayKeepingUp           Passed

[PS] C:\>_
```

***Figure 4-25.** The Test-ReplicationHealth command checks the entire replication stack*

Microsoft has written two health metric scripts, which are in the C:\Program Files\Microsoft\Exchange Server\v15\Scripts directory, that gather information about mailbox databases in a DAG. These scripts are

- CollectOverMetrics.ps1
- CollectReplicationMetrics.ps1

The CollectOverMetrics.ps1 script reads DAG member event logs to gather information regarding mailbox database operations for a specific time. Database operations can be mounting, dismounting, database moves (switchovers), or failovers. The script can generate an HTML file and a CSV file for later processing in Microsoft Excel, for example.

To show information in a DAG called DAG01, as well as all mailbox databases in this DAG, you can navigate to the scripts directory and use a command like the following:

```
.\CollectOverMetrics.ps1 -DatabaseAvailabilityGroup DAG01 -Database:"DB*"
-GenerateHTMLReport -ShowHTMLReport
```

The CollectReplicationMetric.ps1 is a more advanced script since it gathers information in real time while the script is running. Also, it gathers information from performance monitor counters related to mailbox database replication. The script can be run to

1. Collect data and generate a report (CollectAndReport, the default setting)

2. Collect data and store it (CollectOnly)

3. Generate a report from earlier stored data (ProcessOnly)

The scripts start PowerShell jobs that gather all information, and, as such, it is a time- and resource-consuming task. The final stage of the script, when all data is processed to generate a report, can also be time and resource intensive.

To gather one hour of performance data from a DAG using a one-minute interval and generate a report, the following command can be used:

```
.\CollectReplicationMetrics.ps1 -DagName DAG1 -Duration "01:00:00" -Frequency
"00:01:00" -ReportPath
```

To read data from all files called CounterData* and generate a report, the following command can be used:

```
.\CollectReplicationMetrics.ps1 -SummariseFiles (dir CounterData*) -Mode
ProcessOnly -ReportPath
```

Note Do not forget to navigate to the scripts directory before entering this command. This can be easily done by entering cd $exscripts in EMS.

Not directly related to monitoring an Exchange server is the RedistributeActiveDatabases.ps1 script. It can happen, especially after a failover, that the mailbox databases are not properly distributed among the Mailbox servers.

For example, in such a scenario, one Mailbox server may be hosting only active copies of mailbox databases, while another Mailbox server is hosting only passive copies. To redistribute the mailbox database copies over the available Mailbox servers, you can use the following command:

```
.\RedistributeActiveDatabases.ps1 -DagName
DAG1 -BalanceDbsByActivationPreference -ShowFinalDatabaseDistribution
```

This command will distribute all mailbox databases by their activation preference, which was set during the creation of the mailbox database copies. If you have a multi-site DAG, you can use the -BalanceDbsBySiteAndActivationPreference parameter. This will balance the mailbox databases to their most preferred copy, but also try to balance mailbox databases within each Active Directory site.

Backup and Restore

One of the things a typical Exchange Server administrator does not want to talk about is restoring information or disaster recovery, because those can be so very difficult to do in Exchange, regardless of its version. The first matter, backing up data, is not that difficult; you just install a backup application and run it on a regular basis. So far, no need to worry.

But what happens if a Mailbox database crashes, it will not mount again, and you've got users and managers complaining they cannot work? What do you do then? What is a good time to start looking at tools like ESEUTIL? Or when do you decide to restore a mailbox database from your backup?

Even worse, what happens when an entire Exchange server crashes and is completely lost? Do you rebuild the server? Do you restore it from backup? Or maybe you rely on snapshot technology, which you have been told is a good thing?

In this chapter, we're going to explore backup technologies in Exchange server, and we will cover

- VSS backups, or Volume Shadowcopy Service, sometimes also referred to as "snapshot backup." We'll explore the default Windows Server Backup (WSB) and a low-level tool called DiskShadow, which shows you what's happening when you're creating a VSS backup.
- Restoring techniques, to both a standard location and an alternative location.
- Recovery techniques, using ESEUTIL.
- Disaster recovery techniques, to rebuild an entire server.
- Exchange Native Data Protection, sometimes also referred to as "backupless environment."

When your Exchange server crashes beyond repair, it is time to recover your Exchange server, and we are going to explore your options there as well. In short, we are going to rebuild and recover the entire Exchange server, but we will also have a look at rebuilding and recovering a mailbox database.

The last topic that we will explore in this section is a solution called Exchange Native Data Protection. This is also sometimes referred to as a "backupless" Exchange environment.

This backupless thing scares a lot of IT administrators, but in fact it is possible to recover from all major outages without having a backup. The only thing you must do is evaluate the requirements for implementing this Exchange Native Data Protection solution to determine if it fits your needs.

All solutions, procedures, and commands are equal for Exchange 2013, Exchange 2016, and Exchange 2019, so let's get started.

Backing Up an Exchange Server

Backing up Exchange server 2019 is a process of storing your Exchange server data, like the mailbox databases, on another medium. This medium, in turn, can be stored on another location as a safeguard if you face the loss of an entire location.

But not only mailbox databases need to be backed up; you can also back up information like your transport log files or protocol log files, SSL certificates, or maybe even the entire Exchange 2019 Server.

Although explained earlier in this chapter, a mailbox database consists of the following components:

- The mailbox database, where the actual data is stored
- The transaction log files, where the transactions are stored as soon as processing of a transaction is finished in memory
- The checkpoint file, which keeps track of which transactions are stored in the transaction log files but have not yet been flushed to the mailbox database
- Reserved transaction log files, which are stored as reserved transaction log files in case a disk where these transaction log files are stored becomes full

It is important to remember that all transactions are always stored in the transaction log files before they are flushed into the mailbox database. You need to understand the workings of the mailbox database and its database technologies to understand the backup and restore technologies used in Exchange server, but it also is useful to know for recovery purposes.

Backup Technologies

The Exchange mailbox databases are backed up using snapshots. Microsoft utilizes a framework for this called the Volume Shadowcopy Service (VSS). Let's look at what VSS is and how it works with Exchange server.

VSS Backup

Windows Server 2003 was the first Microsoft operating system capable of creating snapshot backups using the Volume Shadowcopy Service (VSS) framework. Unfortunately, in those days it was not possible to create VSS backups of Exchange Server itself. Exchange Server 2007 running on Windows Server 2008 was the first version of Exchange Server capable of using the VSS technology, and VSS backups have been in use in Exchange Server ever since.

There are two kinds of snapshot backups:

- **Clone**—This is a full copy or split mirror. In this scenario, a complete copy, or mirror image, is maintained until an application or administrator effectively "breaks" the mirror. From this point on, the original and the clone are fully independent of each other. The mirror copy is effectively frozen in time.
- **Copy on write**—This is a differential copy. A shadow copy is created that is different from a full copy of the original data, made before the original data has been overwritten. Effectively, the backup copy consists of the data in the shadow copy combined with the data in the original location. Both copies need to be available to reconstruct the original data.

The VSS consists of the VSS service itself, as well as requestors, writers, and providers. The central part is the VSS running on the computer. It is responsible for coordinating all activities concerning backups and restores.

The requestor typically is the backup application. This can be the default out-of-the-box Windows Server Backup, or it can be any third-party backup solution or a Windows tool like DiskShadow.

The writer is the application-specific part of VSS. Writers exist for Microsoft Exchange, Active Directory, IIS, NTFS, SQL Server, and so on. The Exchange writer is responsible for coordinating all Exchange-related activities, such as flushing data to the mailbox database, freezing the mailbox database during the VSS snapshot, and so on.

The provider works with storage. It can be the Windows provider, which can create copy-on-write snapshots of a disk, or it can be a vendor-specific hardware provider.

Thus, the VSS is at the core, as can be seen in Figure 4-26. The arrows show the communication paths within the VSS function.

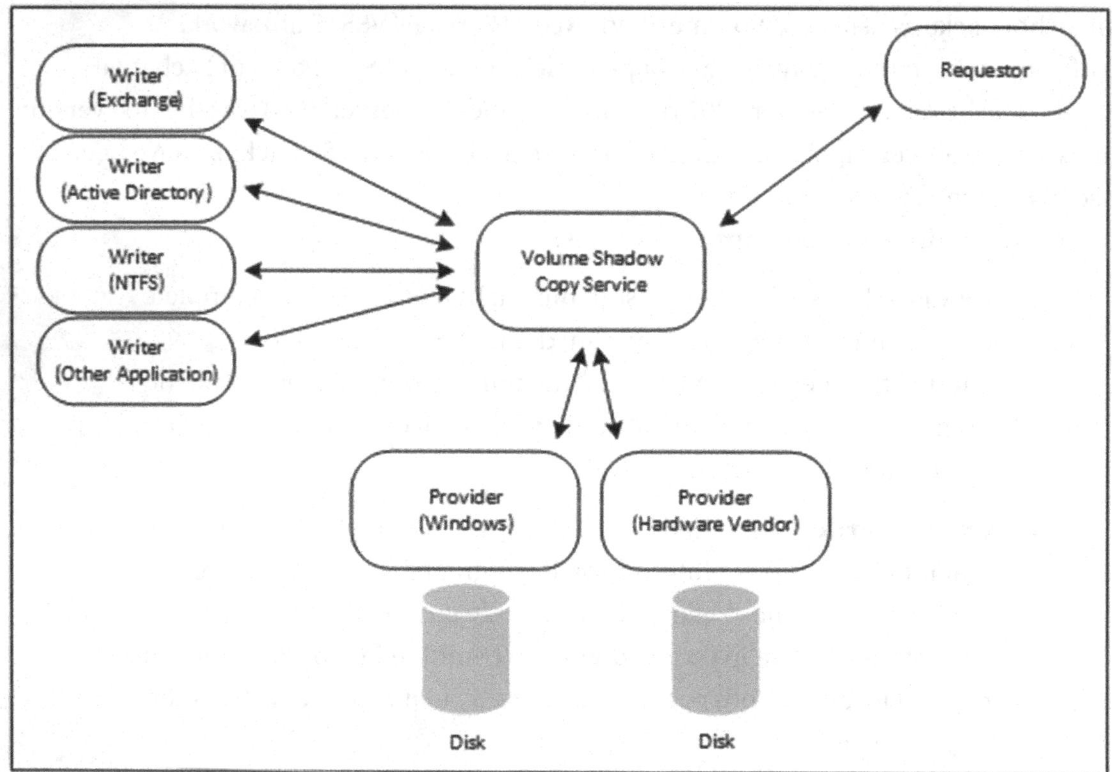

Figure 4-26. *VSS with its requestor, writers, and providers*

For a VSS backup to be created, the following steps occur sequentially:

1. The backup application or requestor sends a command to the VSS to make a shadow copy of the mailbox database.

2. The VSS sends a command to the Exchange writer to prepare for a snapshot backup.

3. The VSS sends a command to the appropriate provider to create a shadow copy of the mailbox database. (The storage provider can be a hardware storage provider provided by the hardware vendor or the default Windows storage provider.)

4. The Exchange writer temporarily stops or pauses the mailbox database and puts it into read-only mode; all data in the server memory is then flushed to the mailbox database. Also, a log file rollover is performed to make sure that all data will be in the backup set. This holds for a couple of seconds while the snapshot is taken. All write IOs are queued at this point.

5. The shadow copy is created.

6. The VSS releases the Exchange server to resume ordinary operations, and all queued write IOs are completed.

7. The VSS queries the Exchange writer to confirm that the write IOs were successfully held while the snapshot was taken. If the write operations were not successfully held, there could potentially be an inconsistent shadow copy. If this is the case, the shadow copy is deleted and the requestor is notified of the failed snapshot.

8. If the snapshot was successful, the requestor verifies the integrity of the backup set (the clone). If the clone integrity is good, the requestor informs Exchange Server that the snapshot was successful.

9. The snapshot can now be transferred to a backup device.

10. When all data is successfully moved to the backup device, the requestor informs VSS that the backup was successful and that the log files can be purged.

In contrast to the streaming backup, where consistency is checked by ESE, the Exchange writer itself does not perform this consistency check.

Steps 1 through 6 usually take between 10 and 15 seconds. Note that this is the time it takes to take the actual snapshot; it does not include the time needed to write all the data to the backup device which is step 9 in the preceding list. Depending on the size of the mailbox database, this step can take up to several hours to complete.

You might be familiar with a VSS administrative tool called VSSADMIN. You can use VSSADMIN to quickly check the various components in the VSS infrastructure. For example, to list all the VSS writers on a server, simply use the VSSADMIN List Writers command in a command prompt window. For Exchange Server 2019, the output will be something like that shown in Figure 4-27.

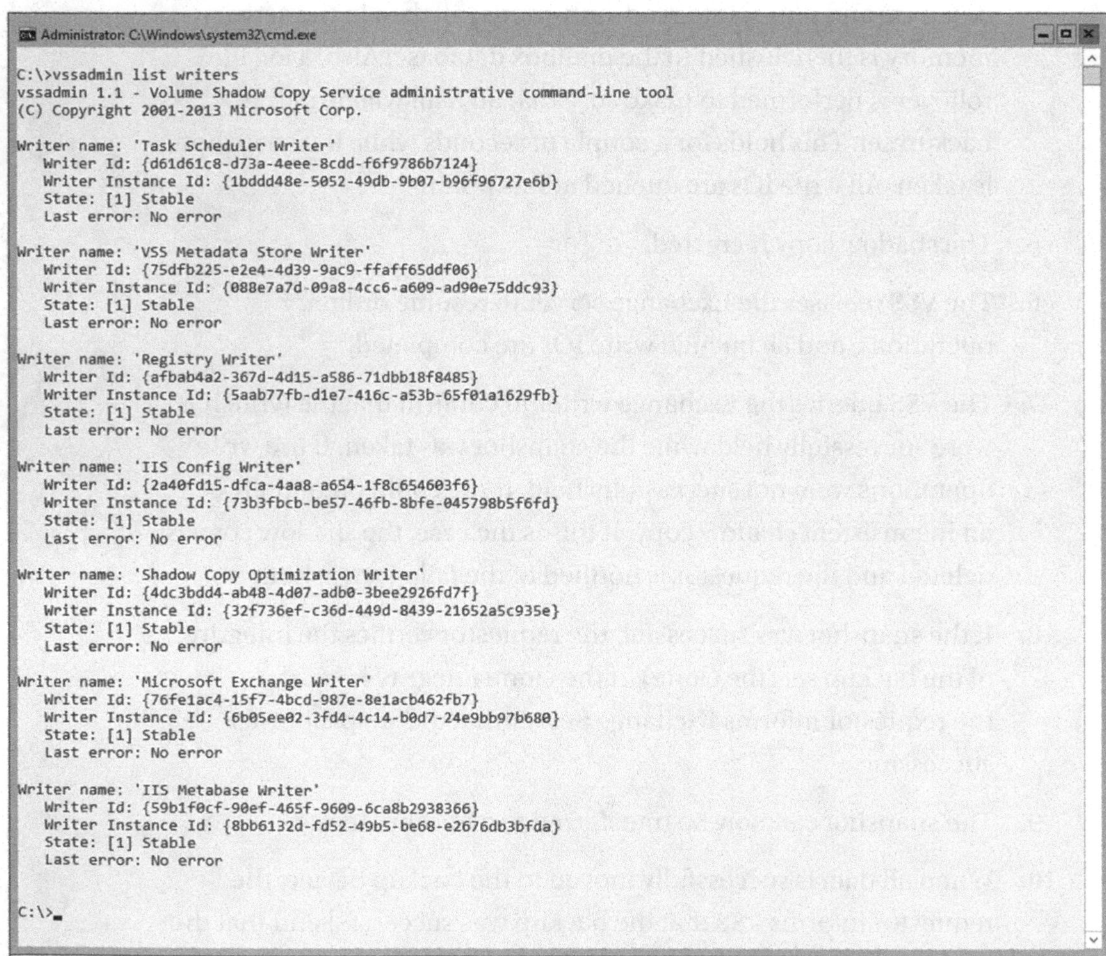

Figure 4-27. *A subset of VSS writers on an Exchange 2019 server*

Similarly, you can list the VSS providers, existing shadow copies, or volumes eligible for creating shadow copies.

VSSADMIN is an old (but still useful) tool and is replaced by a tool called DiskShadow. DiskShadow is more powerful, reveals more information about the VSS infrastructure, and can even create backups.

Both tools are available on Windows server 2019.

Back Up a Mailbox Database

For backing up your mailbox databases, there are various applications available. Which one you use is a matter of personal experience or company license, but the most important factor in making your choice is that the application be "Exchange aware." Windows Server comes with Windows Server Backup (WSB), which is also capable of backing up Exchange 2019 mailbox databases.

It is a simple but limited backup application, but it is used quite often. DiskShadow is a low-level tool you can use for backing up your Exchange mailbox databases, but I do not recommend it for daily use because it is quite complex. Let us discuss both applications.

Using Windows Server Backup in PowerShell

Exchange server 2019 contains a VSS plug-in that can be used with WSB. Although WSB has limited functionality, it can create backups and restore them if needed. Another advantage of WSB is that it is free and comes with Windows Server.

To install Windows Server Backup, execute the following command in PowerShell:

```
PS C:\> Add-WindowsFeature Windows-Server-Backup
```

Note To get an overview of all available WSB cmdlets, you can use the following URL: `http://bit.ly/WSBCommands`. You can also run Get-Command *wb* in PowerShell; this will show all Windows Server Backup–related commands directly on the console.

Windows Server Backup is policy based. To create a new policy, we first create a variable $WBPolicy and populate it with all the options that are needed.

This policy now needs to be populated with the following configuration options:

- **Schedule**—When the backup will be running
- **VSS options**—Whether a full backup or a copy backup will be created
- **Volumes to backups**—The volumes containing the mailbox databases
- **Target disk**—A disk where the backup will be stored

The first step is to create a variable with the new Windows Server Backup policy. To do this, execute the following command in PowerShell:

```
PS C:\> $WBPolicy = New-WBPolicy
```

To add the schedule, the VSS full backup option, the volumes to backup, and the disk to write backup to, execute the following commands in PowerShell:

```
PS C:\> $Schedule = Set-Date "05/07/2021 01:30:00"
PS C:\> Set-WBSchedule -Policy $WBPolicy -Schedule $Schedule
PS C:\> Set-WBVssBackupOptions -Policy $WBPolicy -VssFullBackup
PS C:\> $Volumes = Get-WBVolume -AllVolumes | Where-Object {$_.MountPath -like
"C:\ExchDbs\*"}
PS C:\> Add-WBVolume -Policy $WBPolicy -Volume $Volumes
PS C:\> $Disks = Get-WBDisk
PS C:\> $Target = New-WBBackupTarget -Disk $Disks[4] -Label "Backup"
PS C:\> Add-WBBackupTarget -Policy $WBPolicy -Target $Target
```

To store the policy on the Exchange server, execute the following command in PowerShell:

```
PS C:\> Set-WBPolicy -Policy $WBPolicy -Force
```

This Windows Server Backup policy will create a VSS full backup of both mount points (where the Exchange databases and log files are located) daily; it will run every day at 01:30 a.m. The data will be stored on an additional disk, dedicated for backup purposes.

The backup will start automatically during the next cycle that has been configured with the schedule option, but to start the backup immediately, execute the following command in PowerShell:

```
PS C:\> Get-WBPolicy | Start-WBBackup
```

When this command is executed, a full VSS backup of the volumes containing the mailbox databases will be created. It will start with a VSS snapshot of these volumes, followed by a consistency check of the mailbox databases to ensure the mailbox database's integrity.

When the consistency check is finished successfully, the data is backed up to the backup location; the backup can take a couple of hours if you have a large mailbox database.

If you check the application log in the event viewer, you'll see the following entries:

- **Event ID 2021 (MSExchangeRepl)**—Successfully collected metadata document in preparation for backup.
- **Event ID 2110 (MSExchangeRepl)**—Successfully prepared for a full or a copy backup of database MDB01.
- **Event ID 2023 (MSExchangeRepl)**—VSS writer successfully prepared for backup.
- **Event ID 2005 (ESE)**—Shadow copy instance started. This will be a full shadow copy.
- **Event ID 2025 (MSExchangeRepl)**—VSS successfully prepared for a snapshot.
- **Event ID 2001 (ESE)**—MDB01 shadow copy freeze started.
- **Event ID 2027 (MSExchangeRepl)**—VSS writer instance has successfully frozen the databases.
- **Event ID 2003 (ESE)**—MDB01 shadow copy freeze ended.
- **Event ID 2029 (MSExchangeRepl)**—VSS writer instance has successfully thawed the databases.
- **Event ID 2035 (MSExchangeRepl)**—VSS writer has successfully processed the post-snapshot event.

- **Event ID 2021 (MSExchangeRepl)**—VSS writer has successfully collected the metadata document in preparation for backup.
- **Event ID 224 (ESE)**—MDB01 deleting log files C:\ExchDbs\Disk1\LogFiles\E0000000001.log to C:\ExchDbs\Disk1\LogFiles\E0000000644.log.
- **Event ID 2046 (MSExchangeRepl)**—VSS writer has successfully completed the backup of database MDB01.
- **Event ID 2006 (ESE)**—MDB01 shadow copy completed successfully.
- **Event ID 2033 (MSExchangeRepl)**—VSS writer has successfully processed the backup completion event.
- **Event ID 2037 (MSExchangeRepl)**—VSS writer backup has been successfully shut down.

When you check the location of the log files using Windows Explorer, you'll notice that most of the log files have indeed been purged. The information in the mailbox database itself has also been updated with backup information.

You can use the Get-MailboxDatabase command with the -Status option to retrieve information regarding the backup status of a Mailbox database:

```
[PS] C:\> Get-MailboxDatabase -identity MDB01 -Status | Select
Name,*backup*
Name                           : MDB01
BackupInProgress               : False
SnapshotLastFullBackup         : True
SnapshotLastIncrementalBackup  :
SnapshotLastDifferentialBackup :
SnapshotLastCopyBackup         :
LastFullBackup                 : 5/6/2021 1:53:46 PM
LastIncrementalBackup          :
LastDifferentialBackup         :
LastCopyBackup                 :
RetainDeletedItemsUntilBackup  : False
```

You can also use the ESEUTIL /MH MDB01.edb command to check the header for backup information; be aware that the Mailbox database needs to be dismounted for this. If you use ESEUTIL, you will see something like this:

```
Previous Full Backup:
        Log Gen: 1605-1629 (0x645-0x65d) - OSSnapshot
           Mark: (0x65E,1,0)
           Mark: 05/06/2021 11:53:46.986 UTC

Current Full Backup:
        Log Gen: 0-0 (0x0-0x0)
           Mark: (0x0,0,0)
           Mark: 00/00/1900 00:00:00.000 LOC
```

You might ask yourself why this information is written under Previous Full Backup, while the entry under Current Full Backup is empty. This is because when you create a backup, the entry Current Full Backup is written with information regarding the backup as it runs. When the backup is finished, the entries are moved from the Current Full Backup section to the Previous Full Backup section, and the Current Full Backup is emptied. When a backup is restored to disk, and you check the header information after a restore, you can always identify the database as a backup that has been restored instead of a "normal" mailbox database because it will show as Previous Full Backup.

Using Windows Server Backup GUI

I can imagine that, for backup purposes, you do not want to use PowerShell. Still a lot of Exchange administrators think that PowerShell is complex and difficult. Let us look at the graphical user interface (GUI) as well, assuming you have Exchange server 2019 running on Windows 2019 Desktop Experience, or Exchange server 2016.

To create a backup of your Exchange databases, you use the following steps:

1. In the administrative tools section, select Windows Server Backup. This is an MMC snap-in. In the Actions pane, select Backup Once.

2. In the Backup Options page, select Different Options and click Next to continue.

3. In this example, we want only to back up the mailbox database, so select the Custom option and click Next to continue.

4. The mailbox database is located on mount point C:\ExchDbs\Disk1; use the Add Items button to select this disk.

5. To change the type of backup that is being created, click the Advanced Settings button, select the VSS Settings tab, and select the VSS Full Backup radio button. Click OK to return to the previous page and click Next to continue.

6. WSB has the option of backing up to a remote share or to a local disk, whichever you prefer. On our server, there is an additional backup disk (disk X), so select Local Drives and click Next to continue.

7. In the Backup Destination drop-down box, select the disk where the backup needs to be stored; on our server, this would be disk X. Click Next to continue.

8. The selection is now complete. Click Backup to start the actual backup process.

Note By default, WSB will create a copy backup instead of a full backup. This is understandable, as it will not interfere with a normal backup cycle when you are using another backup solution and you want to test using WSB. If you want to make a regular backup using WSB, make sure you change this setting. This is a common pitfall with WSB.

The backup will now start with the creation of the VSS snapshot, and it will perform a consistency check of the mailbox data, as shown in Figure 4-28. Be aware that this information can be visible for a small amount of time, especially when the mailbox database is not that large, and the consistency check takes only a few seconds. This backup status check is the only visual indication you have that an Exchange-aware backup is running.

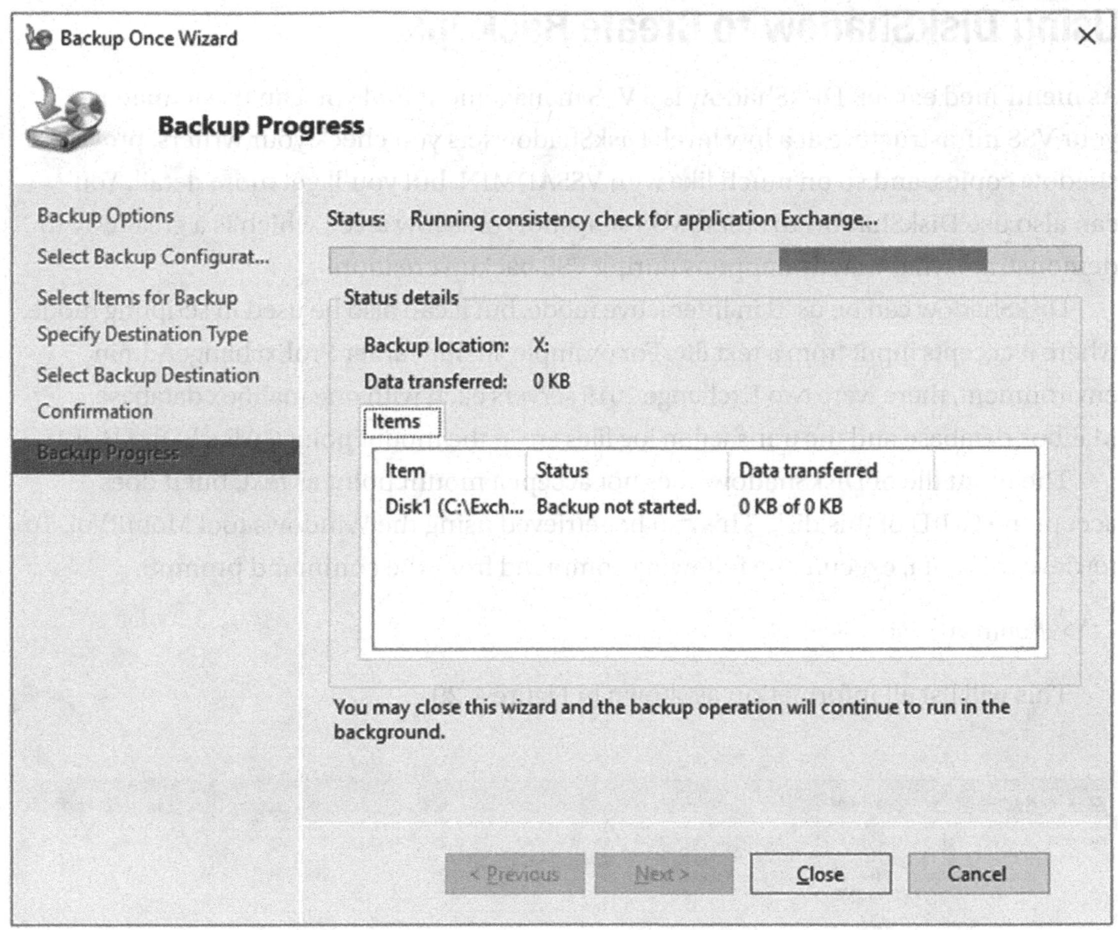

Figure 4-28. *Windows Server Backup automatically checks for database consistency*

When the consistency check is finished successfully, the data is backed up to the backup location, and after a while (which can take a couple of hours if you have a large mailbox database), the backup is completed.

Note Another common pitfall I see regularly is that admins think they are creating an Exchange-aware backup, but instead create a file-level backup of an Exchange database. While this creates a backup of the mailbox database, it does not perform a consistency check, and it does not purge the transaction log files. As such, it is extremely difficult, if not even impossible, to gracefully restore such a backup.

Using DiskShadow to Create Backups

As mentioned earlier, DiskShadow is a VSS management tool you can use to manage your VSS infrastructure at a low level. DiskShadow lets you check your writers, providers, shadow copies, and so on much like with VSSADMIN, but you'll get more detail. You can also use DiskShadow to create VSS snapshots on a low level, which is a great way to demonstrate what exactly happens during VSS backup creation.

DiskShadow can be used in interactive mode, but it can also be used in scripting mode, where it accepts input from a text file. For example, in our earlier ProExchangeAdmin environment, there were two Exchange 2019 servers each with one mailbox database. Mailbox database and the transaction log files are in the mount point C:\ExchDbs\Disk1.

The input file of DiskShadow does not accept a mount point as text, but it does accept the GUID of this disk. This can be retrieved using the Windows tool MountVol. To retrieve this data, execute the following command from the command prompt:

```
C:\> MountVol /L
```

This will list all information as shown in Figure 4-29.

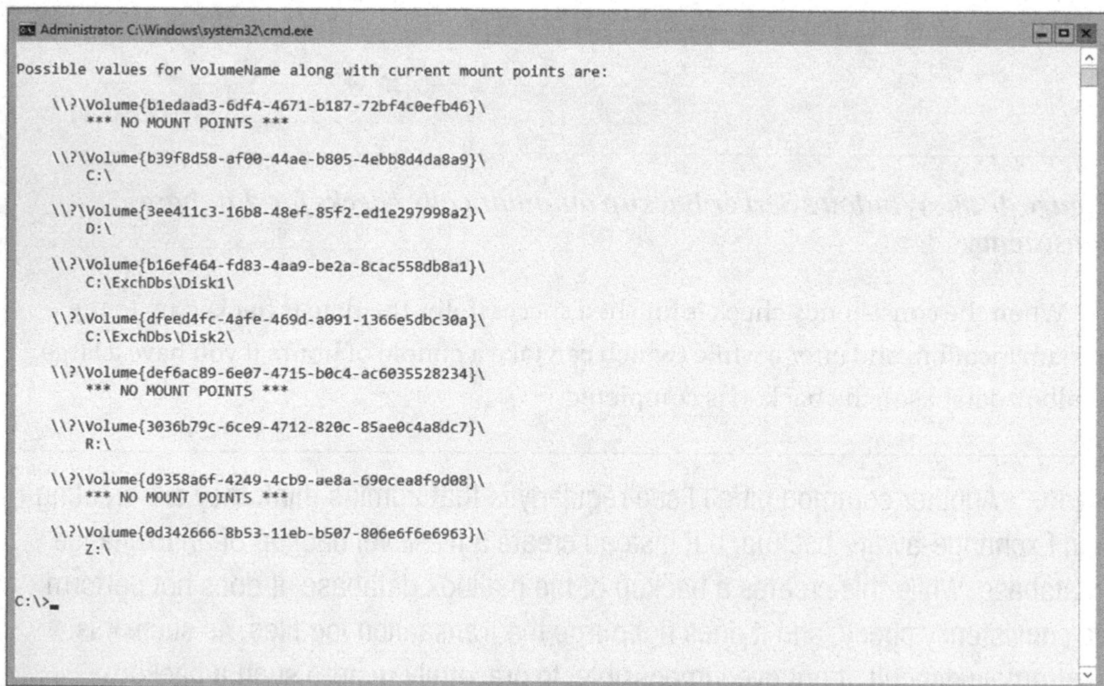

Administrator: C:\Windows\system32\cmd.exe
Possible values for VolumeName along with current mount points are:
\\?\Volume{b1edaad3-6df4-4671-b187-72bf4c0efb46}\
*** NO MOUNT POINTS ***
\\?\Volume{b39f8d58-af00-44ae-b805-4ebb8d4da8a9}\
C:\
\\?\Volume{3ee411c3-16b8-48ef-85f2-ed1e297998a2}\
D:\
\\?\Volume{b16ef464-fd83-4aa9-be2a-8cac558db8a1}\
C:\ExchDbs\Disk1\
\\?\Volume{dfeed4fc-4afe-469d-a091-1366e5dbc30a}\
C:\ExchDbs\Disk2\
\\?\Volume{def6ac89-6e07-4715-b0c4-ac6035528234}\
*** NO MOUNT POINTS ***
\\?\Volume{3036b79c-6ce9-4712-820c-85ae0c4a8dc7}\
R:\
\\?\Volume{d9358a6f-4249-4cb9-ae8a-690cea8f9d08}\
*** NO MOUNT POINTS ***
\\?\Volume{0d342666-8b53-11eb-b507-806e6f6e6963}\
Z:\
C:\>

***Figure 4-29.** MountVol output for mount points*

To create an input file for DiskShadow to create a VSS backup of MDB1, the following input file can be used:

```
SET verbose on
SET context persistent
# Exclude other writers on Exchange Server
# Can be retrieved using VSSADMIN List Writers
Writer Exclude {d61d61c8-d73a-4eee-8cdd-f6f9786b7124}
Writer Exclude {75dfb225-e2e4-4d39-9ac9-ffaff65ddf06}
Writer Exclude {0bada1de-01a9-4625-8278-69e735f39dd2}
Writer Exclude {e8132975-6f93-4464-a53e-1050253ae220}
Writer Exclude {be000cbe-11fe-4426-9c58-531aa6355fc4}
Writer Exclude {afbab4a2-367d-4d15-a586-71dbb18f8485}
Writer Exclude {4dc3bdd4-ab48-4d07-adb0-3bee2926fd7f}
Writer Exclude {542da469-d3e1-473c-9f4f-7847f01fc64f}
Writer Exclude {a6ad56c2-b509-4e6c-bb19-49d8f43532f0}
Writer Exclude {2a40fd15-dfca-4aa8-a654-1f8c654603f6}
Writer Exclude {7e47b561-971a-46e6-96b9-696eeaa53b2a}
Writer Exclude {59b1f0cf-90ef-465f-9609-6ca8b2938366}
Writer Exclude {e8132975-6f93-4464-a53e-1050253ae220}

Writer Exclude {1072ae1c-e5a7-4ea1-9e4a-6f7964656570}
Writer Exclude {4969d978-be47-48b0-b100-f328f07ac1e0}
Writer Exclude {41e12264-35d8-479b-8e5c-9b23d1dad37e}

# Exchange writer is required
Writer Verify {76fe1ac4-15f7-4bcd-987e-8e1acb462fb7}
# Take the actual snapshot
begin backup
add volume \\?\Volume{b16ef464-fd83-4aa9-be2a-8cac558db8a1}\ alias
VSS_Backup_Disk1
create
# Expose the snapshot as additional drive S:
expose %VSS_Backup_Disk1% S:
End backup
```

The first two entries are to turn on verbose logging and set the context to persistent, so the information will not be lost. Then, all VSS writers on the Exchange servers are disabled except the VSS Exchange writer. The GUIDs of the VSS writers can be retrieved by using the VSSADMIN List Writers command.

Volume C:\ExchDbs\Disk1 is used for creating the VSS snapshot and an alias VSS_Backup_Disk1. This alias can be any readable name you like.

At this point, the actual snapshot is created using the CREATE command. In Windows, this is a copy-on-write snapshot whereby the snapshot information is written on the same disk and on the mailbox database, but it is not visible for a regular user or administrator. (All the steps as explained in the previous section are performed here, and all the events are recorded in the event log as well.) This step usually takes between 15 and 30 seconds, depending on the hardware that is used.

When the snapshot is created, it is exposed using the EXPOSE command. This way, it is visible as a regular disk to the operating system, and thus accessible, as shown in Figure 4-30.

The backup is started by using the following command on a command line:

```
C:\> DiskShadow.exe /S C:\Install\inputfile.txt
```

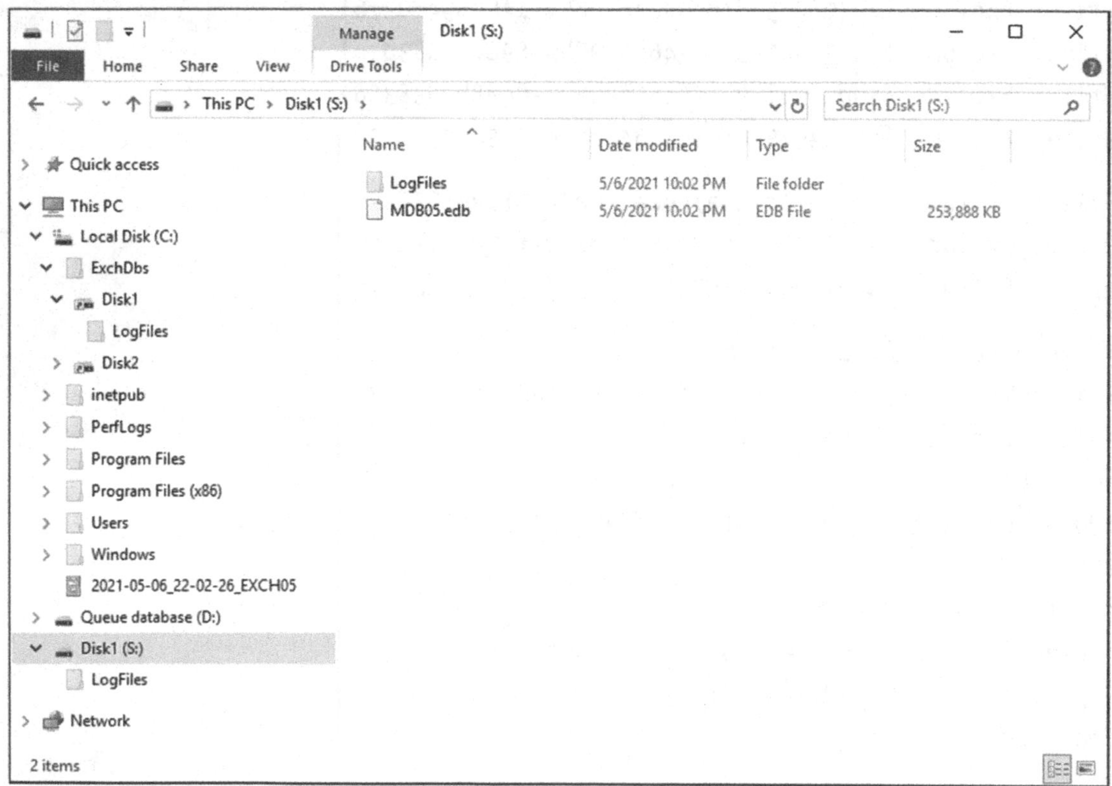

Figure 4-30. *The VSS snapshots are published as additional drives in Windows*

When the backup in DiskShadow is ended using the End Backup command, a request is sent to ESE to purge any log files that are no longer needed for recovery purposes. If the VSS snapshot was created on a single Exchange server, or a DAG member with active copies of the mailbox database, then the request is processed locally. If the snapshot was created using a passive copy of a mailbox database, the request is automatically sent to the Mailbox server that is hosting the active copy of the mailbox database. The log files are purged on that Exchange server, and the truncation itself is replicated to the Mailbox servers hosting the passive copies of the mailbox database. This means that you no longer need to know which mailbox database in a DAG you back up; the appropriate log files are automatically purged.

This is the pure VSS snapshot function: a snapshot of the mailbox database is created, and its log files are purged (when successful, of course). But remember that the mailbox database has not been checked for consistency, nor has it been backed up to a safe location. To check the consistency of a mailbox database, you use the ESEUTIL tool again, but now with the /k switch:

```
S:\> ESEUTIL /K MDB05.edb
```

This command will read all the pages in the database and check the consistency of all those pages, as shown in Figure 4-31.

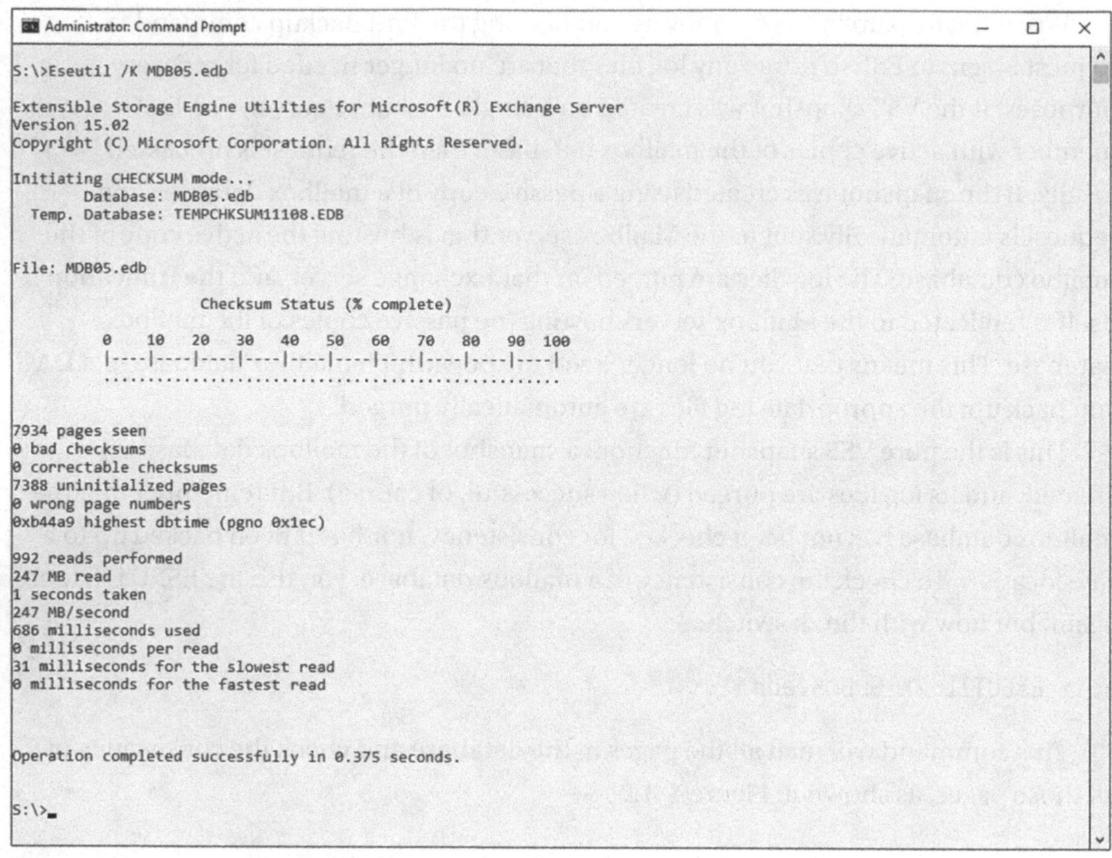

Administrator: Command Prompt
S:\>Eseutil /K MDB05.edb
Extensible Storage Engine Utilities for Microsoft(R) Exchange Server
Version 15.02
Copyright (C) Microsoft Corporation. All Rights Reserved.
Initiating CHECKSUM mode...
Database: MDB05.edb
Temp. Database: TEMPCHKSUM11108.EDB
File: MDB05.edb
Checksum Status (% complete)
0 10 20 30 40 50 60 70 80 90 100
7934 pages seen
0 bad checksums
0 correctable checksums
7388 uninitialized pages
0 wrong page numbers
0xb44a9 highest dbtime (pgno 0x1ec)
992 reads performed
247 MB read
1 seconds taken
247 MB/second
686 milliseconds used
0 milliseconds per read
31 milliseconds for the slowest read
0 milliseconds for the fastest read
Operation completed successfully in 0.375 seconds.
S:\>

***Figure 4-31.** Checking the database consistency using the ESEUTIL tool*

The final step in a backup, then, is to copy the mailbox database snapshots from the published locations (drive S: and drive T:) to another safe location using, for example, Explorer. Once this is done, you have been successful in manually creating a full backup.

Note Do not forget to remove the exposed VSS snapshots using the UNEXPOSE command in DiskShadow and remove the actual VSS shadow copies using the DELETE SHADOWS command. The easiest way to do this is using DiskShadow in interactive mode.

Back Up Other Configuration Information

The previous section discussed how to back up mailbox databases in Exchange, since this is the most important aspect of an Exchange server's role. There are more things that need to be backed up, however, either in a regular backup sequence or maybe after there have been configuration changes, for example:

- Log files (not transaction log files), as Exchange logs quite a lot of information in log files—for instance, in IIS log files located in C:\inetpub\logs\logfiles, which contain logging from all HTTPS-based clients like Outlook Web App, Exchange Web Services, Autodiscover, Outlook Anywhere, and ActiveSync.
- SMTP Transport Protocol logs, located in C:\Program Files\Microsoft\Exchange Server\V15\TransportRoles\Logs\Hub\ProtocolLog. These are disabled by default, but when enabled these might be included in a daily backup routine.
- Message tracking information, located in C:\Program Files\Microsoft\Exchange Server\V15\TransportRoles\ Logs\MessageTracking.
- Entire directory, depending on the (legal) backup requirements of your company; it might be necessary to back up the entire logging directory in C:\Program Files\Microsoft\Exchange Server\V15\Logging.
- CONFIG files, such as transport configuration files located in C:\Program Files\Microsoft\ Exchange Server\V15\Bin. This file is used to relocate the SMTP message database and log files to another location. No need to include this in a daily backup sequence, but it is necessary to back up after configuration changes.
- SSL certificate. No need to back up this daily, but you should back up after the initial installation of the certificate. It is needed when rebuilding an Exchange server or maybe when adding additional Exchange servers. Make sure that when you create a backup of your SSL certificate, you also include the private key in the certificate backup. If not, it is useless when rebuilding your Exchange server.

- System state or entire server, depending on your disaster recovery plan. You might want to back up the server's system state, or maybe the entire server, for rebuilding purposes. (We will get back to this later in this chapter.)

When using server virtualization, it is an option to back up the entire virtual machine using a backup solution.

Veeam, for example, is a third-party vendor that offers backup solutions in a virtual environment. Veeam can back up the VMs, and using the Hyper-V Integration Components or VMware tools, the VSS backup information is sent to the operating system inside the VM. This way, the virtual machine is also aware that a snapshot is being made.

Restoring Exchange Server

Backing up your Exchange environment does make sense, but restoring the backup is even more important. In all my years as an Exchange consultant, I have regularly met customers who thought that their backup solutions were fine, but they did not have any idea how to restore them if needed. The worst way to find out is during a disaster, when you must restore information rapidly, as there likely are hundreds of users and managers complaining. Most often, the restoration will fail at this moment because of the lack of experience.

In this section, I will focus on restoring mailbox databases, since these are where all the data is. Later in this chapter, I will explain how to restore the Exchange servers as part of a disaster recovery operation.

There are two options for restoring mailbox databases:

- Restore the mailbox database to its original location. In this scenario, the original mailbox database is taken offline and is overwritten by the mailbox database in the backup set. Since all the information is also stored in the log files, the information processed by the Mailbox server since the last backup was created will automatically be replayed by the Mailbox server. If all goes well, no information, or almost no information, will be lost and the mailbox database will be in the same state as before.

- Restore the mailbox database to another location. In this scenario, the mailbox database from the backup set is restored to another location, most likely a dedicated restore disk on your Mailbox server. When the mailbox database is restored to another location, the original mailbox database can continue running and thus continue servicing client requests.

A recovery mailbox database can be used as well. This is a special mailbox database, not visible for regular clients (only for the Exchange administrator), that can be used to restore a particular mailbox; you can move this mailbox into the production mailbox database or export it to a PST file.

Restoring to an Original Location

A lot of interesting technologies are used to make the mailbox database backup process as smooth as possible without interrupting any users. Restoring a mailbox database to its original location is straightforward work.

The mailbox database must be taken offline, and thus users will face some downtime because Exchange Server is not available anymore. The mailbox database is then restored from the backup set, additional log files are replayed automatically, and the mailbox database can then be mounted again. There is nothing fancy to do when restoring a mailbox database.

In the previous section, WSB was used to back up the mailbox database, so you must use WSB again to restore the mailbox database. For testing purposes, you can log on to the mailbox before the restore action and send some messages around to see if these are replayed after the backup is restored. To restore a previous backup using WSB, you can use these steps:

1. Log on to the EAC as an administrator and navigate to Servers ➤ Databases. Select the appropriate Mailbox database and dismount it.
2. When the Mailbox database is still selected, open its properties and select maintenance. Check the “This database can be overwritten by a restore” checkbox as shown in Figure 4-32.

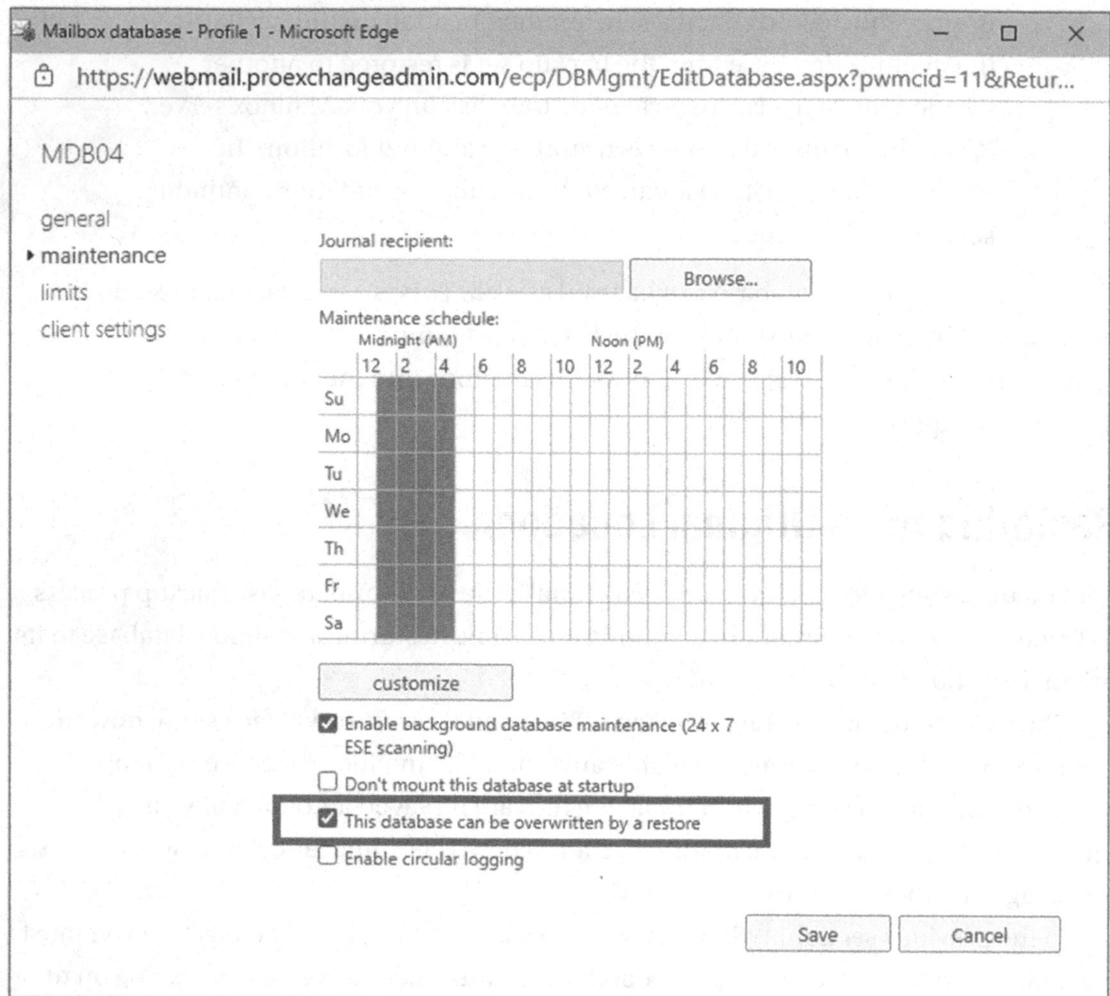

***Figure 4-32.** Setting the option "This database can be overwritten by a restore"*

Note This option can be set in PowerShell by using the command Set-MailboxDatabase –Identity MDB01 –AllowFileRestore $true.

---

3. Open WSB, and in the Actions pane, select Recover.
4. In the Recovery wizard that starts, select where the backup is located. This can be on a disk attached to the server itself, or it can be a remote location. Select "This server" and click Next to continue.

5. In the Select Backup Date window, select the backup set you want to restore to this server. Once selected, click Next to continue.

6. Next is the Select Recovery Type window, which is very important. WSB is Exchange aware, and thus an Exchange backup is an application backup. This way, the backup is restored as the Exchange writer would like it to be. If you select Volumes, for example, the backup is restored as an ordinary file backup, and this is useless from an Exchange perspective. Select Applications as shown in Figure 4-33 and click Next to continue.

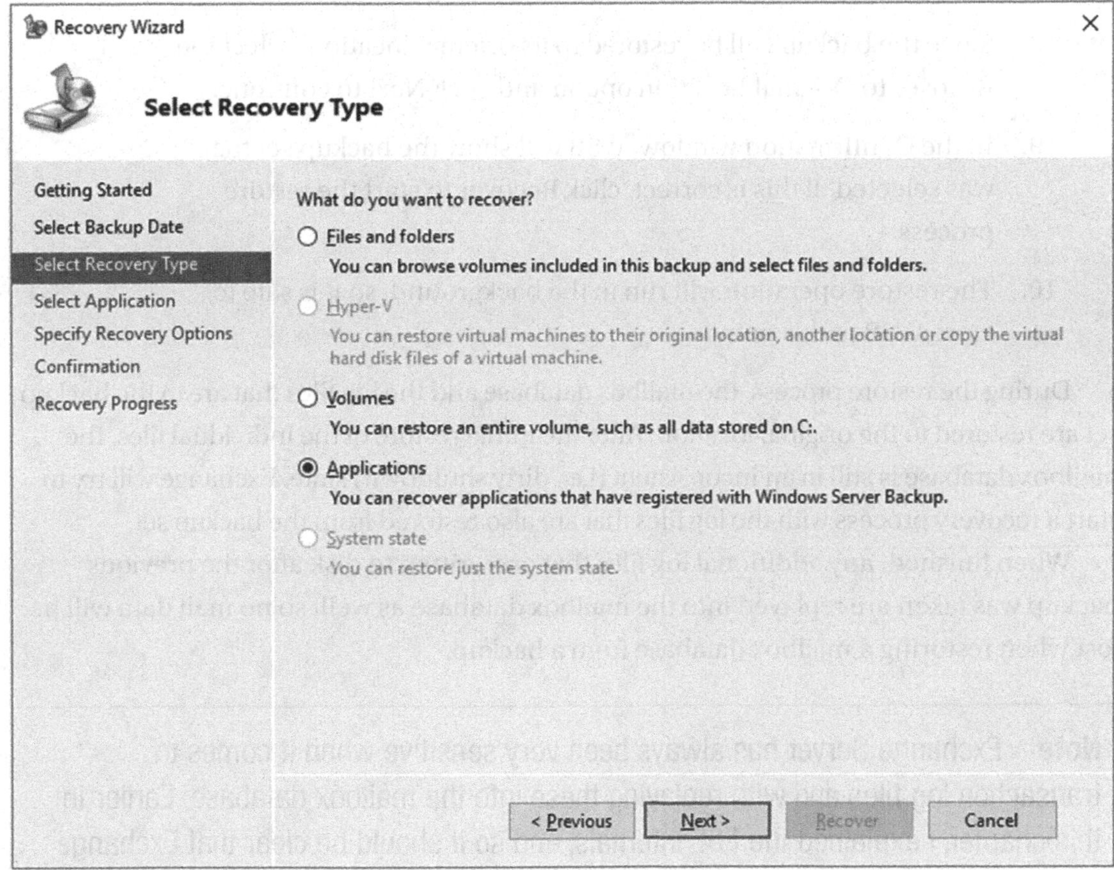

***Figure 4-33.** Select the Applications radio button when restoring a mailbox database*

7. In the Select Application window, make sure Exchange is selected. The remaining log files since the last backup was taken can be automatically replayed into the Mailbox database; this is the default behavior. If you do not want this to happen, check the "do not perform a roll-forward recovery" checkbox. Click Next to continue.

Note This option is only available when the mailbox database is not located on the system drive and boot drive, typically drive C:\. That is, it is only available when the mailbox database is on a separate drive.

---

8. Since the backup will be restored to its original location, select the Recover to Original Location option and click Next to continue.
9. In the Confirmation window, WSB will show the backup set that was selected. If this is correct, click Recover to start the restore process.
10. The restore operation will run in the background, so it is safe to close WSB at this point.

During the restore process, the mailbox database and the log files that are in the backup set are restored to the original location. After the initial restore of the individual files, the mailbox database is still in an inconsistent (i.e., dirty shutdown) state. Exchange will try to start a recovery process with the log files that are also restored from the backup set.

When finished, any additional log files that are written to disk after the previous backup was taken are replayed into the mailbox database as well, so no mail data will be lost when restoring a mailbox database from a backup.

Note Exchange Server has always been very sensitive when it comes to transaction log files and with replaying these into the mailbox database. Earlier in this chapter, I explained the ESE internals, and so it should be clear that Exchange Server is 100% dependent on all transaction log files. If only one log file is missing, the replay of the log files will fail. Therefore, you should never delete any of the log files manually; or do so only if you are 150% sure of what you are doing, or if Microsoft support instructs you to do so!

During the restore process, several events are written to the event log, indicating the progress of the restore operation or if any problems have arisen during the process, for example:

- **Event ID 4347 (MSExchangeRepl)**—Exchange Replication Service VSS writer will restore a backup set to database MDB04\EXCH04, which is the same database from which the backup was originally taken.
- **Event ID 4367 (MSExchangeRepl)**—Exchange Replication Service VSS writer successfully restored the backup set. To bring the restored databases to a clean shutdown state, database recovery will be performed using the information in the restore environment document MDB04\EXCH04.
- **Event ID 4370 (MSExchangeRepl)**—Exchange Replication Service VSS writer will perform database recovery on database MDB04.edb as part of the restore process for MDB04\EXCH04, followed by several events from ESE, indicating the recovery steps for the restored Mailbox database.
- **Event ID 40008 (MSExchangeIS)**—Mount completed successfully for database <<GUID>>.
- **Event ID 3156 (MSExchangeRepl)**—Active Manager successfully mounted database MDB04 on server EXCH04.proexchangeadmin.com.
- **Event ID 737 (Backup)**—The operation to recover component(s) 'e3c4d2b5-678e-443e-9f55-777c447eb220' has completed successfully at '2021-05-10T11:04:34.488000000Z.'

If you log on to your mailbox and check any messages that were sent after the last backup was taken, you will see that these are still available in the mailbox and thus successfully recovered.

Restoring to Another Location

Restoring a mailbox database to its original location is only useful when the original mailbox database is lost, for whatever reason. Restoring to its original location means you must dismount the mailbox database, resulting in an outage for users. So, in a normal production situation, you do not want to dismount your mailbox database for restoring purposes unless there's no other option.

Restoring a backup to another location has the advantage of leaving the original mailbox mounted, allowing users to continue working. Also, when using this method, there is no risk in accidentally overwriting the mailbox database with a database that is restored, since the original database is still mounted and thus reports as "file in use."

The procedure for restoring the mailbox database to another location does not differ that much from restoring the mailbox to its original location.

The Restore Process

If you want to restore to another location, you follow these steps:

1. Log on to the Exchange server, open WSB, and in the Actions pane, select Recover.

2. In the Recovery wizard that starts, select where the backup is located. This can be on a disk attached to the server itself, or it can be a remote location. Select the appropriate option here and click Next to continue.

3. In the Select Backup Date window, select the backup set you want to restore to this server. Once selected, click Next to continue.

4. Next, the Select Recovery Type window is very important. WSB is Exchange aware, and thus an Exchange backup is an application backup. This way, the backup is restored as the Exchange writer would like it to be. If you select Volumes, for example, the backup will be restored as an ordinary file backup, and this is useless from an Exchange perspective. Select Applications and click Next to continue.

5. In the Select Application window, make sure Exchange is selected and click Next to continue.

6. Since the backup will be restored to another location, select the Recover to Another Location option, and use the Browse button to select a disk and directory where you want to restore the mailbox database. Typically, a dedicated restore LUN is used for this purpose. In our example, we use G:\RestoreDB to restore the mailbox database from backup. This is shown in Figure 4-34.

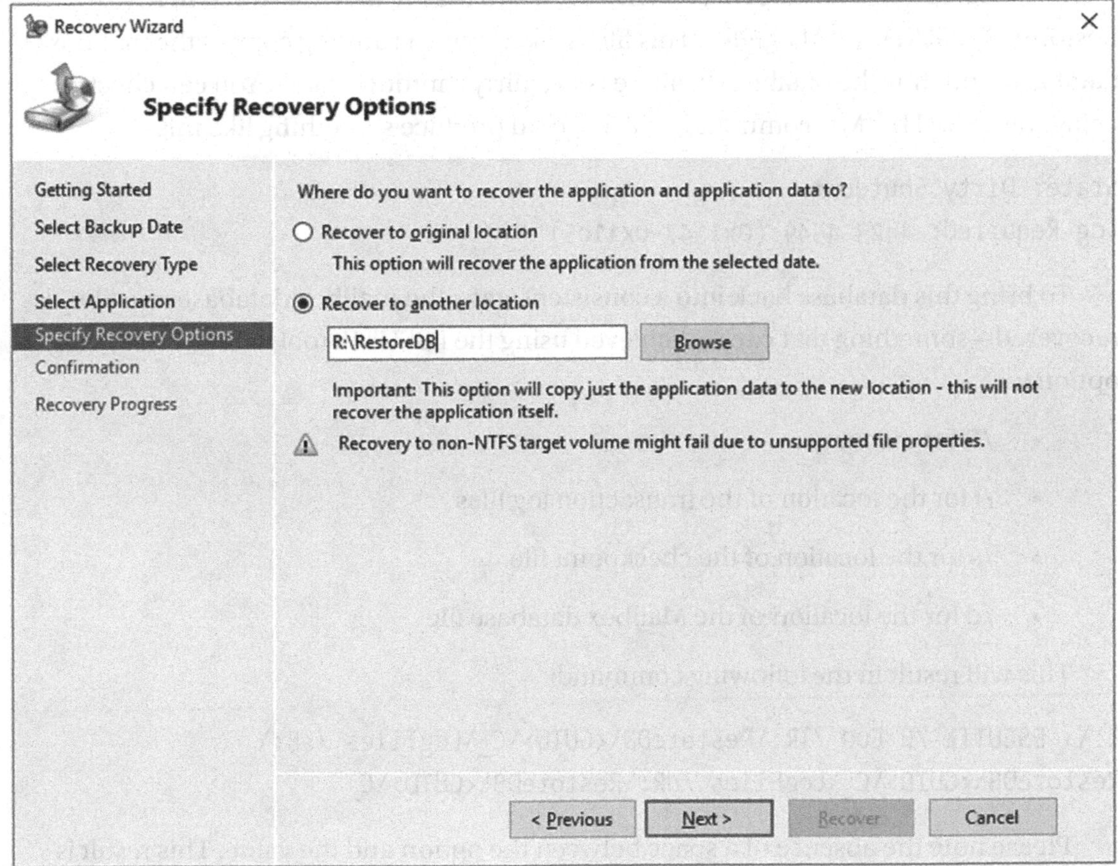

***Figure 4-34.** Restoring a mailbox database to an alternative location*

7. The selection is shown in the confirmation window. If all is okay, then click the Restore button to start the recover process.

8. Since only the mailbox database and its log files are restored from backup, the process finishes much faster than when restoring to its original location. In this process, no additional recovery steps are performed, so you must do this manually.

The mailbox database and the accompanying log files are now restored from the backup set. The file location is also restored, so now there is a mailbox database MDB04 located in R:\RestoreDB\<GUID>\C_\, and the log files are stored in R:\RestoreDB\<GUID>\C_\LogFiles. This file is taken from a running copy of the mailbox database, and thus the mailbox database is in a dirty shutdown state. You can check this using the ESEUTIL /MH command, which would produce something like this:

```
State: Dirty Shutdown
Log Required: 4423-4549 (0x1147-0x11c5)
```

To bring this database back into a consistent state, the mailbox database must be recovered—something that can be achieved using the ESEUTIL tool with the following options:

- /R for recovery
- /l for the location of the transaction log files
- /s for the location of the checkpoint file
- /d for the location of the Mailbox database file

This will result in the following command:

```
R:\> ESEUTIL /R E00 /lR:\RestoreDB\<GUID>\C_\Logfiles /sR:\
RestoreDB\<GUID>\C_\LogFiles /dR:\RestoreDB\<GUID>\C_
```

Please note the absence of a space between the option and the value. This result is shown in Figure 4-35.

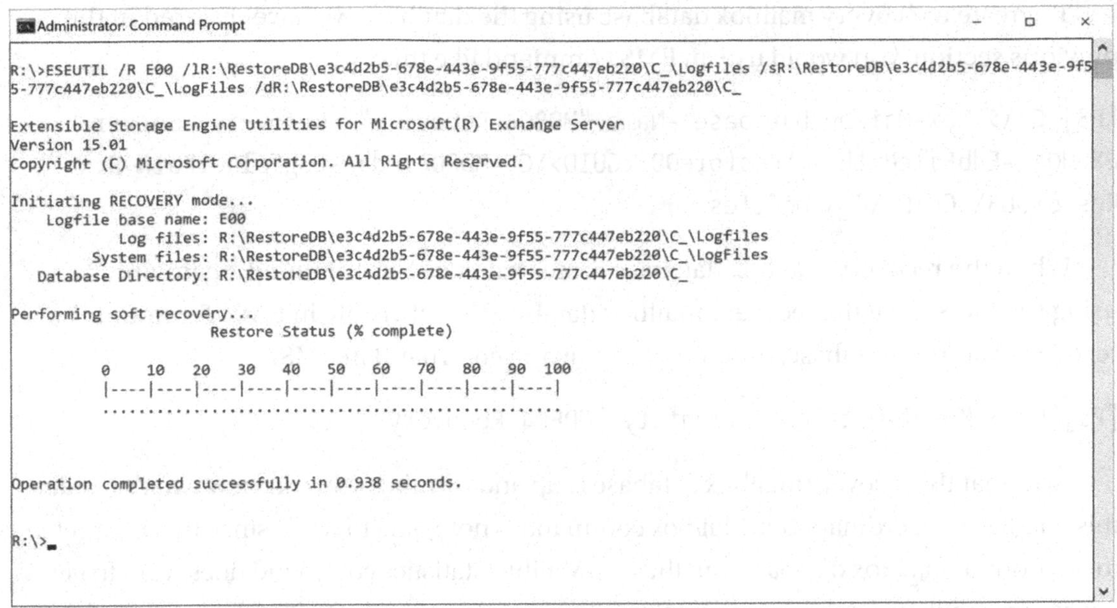

```
Administrator: Command Prompt

R:\>ESEUTIL /R E00 /lR:\RestoreDB\e3c4d2b5-678e-443e-9f55-777c447eb220\C_\Logfiles /sR:\RestoreDB\e3c4d2b5-678e-443e-9f5
5-777c447eb220\C_\LogFiles /dR:\RestoreDB\e3c4d2b5-678e-443e-9f55-777c447eb220\C_

Extensible Storage Engine Utilities for Microsoft(R) Exchange Server
Version 15.01
Copyright (C) Microsoft Corporation. All Rights Reserved.

Initiating RECOVERY mode...
    Logfile base name: E00
            Log files: R:\RestoreDB\e3c4d2b5-678e-443e-9f55-777c447eb220\C_\Logfiles
         System files: R:\RestoreDB\e3c4d2b5-678e-443e-9f55-777c447eb220\C_\LogFiles
   Database Directory: R:\RestoreDB\e3c4d2b5-678e-443e-9f55-777c447eb220\C_

Performing soft recovery...
                      Restore Status (% complete)

          0    10   20   30   40   50   60   70   80   90  100
          |----|----|----|----|----|----|----|----|----|----|
          ...................................................


Operation completed successfully in 0.938 seconds.

R:\>
```

Figure 4-35. *Recovering the mailbox database after a restore to an alternative location*

Now when you check the database again using the ESEUTIL /MH command, the database will be in a clean shutdown state and ready to use. A use case for this kind of restore is the recovery database as discussed in the next section.

Recovery Database

A recovery database in Exchange is a special mailbox database, invisible to normal users, where you can mount a normal database restored from backup. This means that you will have one normal mailbox database MDB04 running in its original location and one recovery mailbox MDB04 running in recovery mode.

Creating a recovery mailbox database is not very different from creating a regular mailbox database, but it can be managed only by using EMS. When creating the recovery mailbox database, you have to use the -Recovery switch to tell Exchange that a recovery mailbox database is created.

To create a recovery mailbox database using the database we have restored in the previous section, you would use an EMS command like this:

```
[PS] C:\> New-MailboxDatabase -Name "MDB04 Recovery" -Recovery -Server
EXCH04 -EdbFilePath R:\RestoreDB\<GUID>\C_\MDB04.edb -LogFolderPath R:\
RestoreDB\<GUID>\C_\LogFiles
```

When the recovery mailbox database is created, it can be mounted, again only using the EMS since the recovery mailbox database is not visible in EAC. To mount the recovery Mailbox database, execute the following command in EMS:

```
[PS] C:\> Mount-Database -Identity "MDB04 Recovery"
```

Now that the recovery mailbox database is up and running, you can view what's inside this database. An ordinary Get-Mailbox command is not going to work, since this is targeted to the normal mailbox database, but the Get-MailboxStatistics command does work to get a recovery mailbox database. Just use the following command to retrieve the mailbox data from the recovery mailbox database. Figure 4-36 shows the output from this command:

```
[PS] C:\> Get-MailboxStatistics -Database "MDB04 Recovery" | Select-Object
DisplayName,ItemCount |-Format-Table -AutoSize
```

```
Machine: EXCH04.ProExchangeAdmin.com
[PS] C:\>Get-MailboxStatistics -Database "MDB04 Recovery" | Select-Object DisplayName,ItemCount | Format-Table -AutoSize

DisplayName                                          ItemCount
-----------                                          ---------
SystemMailbox{e3c4d2b5-678e-443e-9f55-777c447eb220}         46
HealthMailbox-EXCH04-MDB04                                 186
In-Place Archive -HealthMailbox-EXCH04-002                 183
In-Place Archive -HealthMailbox-EXCH04-MDB04                28
HealthMailbox-EXCH04-002                                   177
Boardroom                                                   21
HealthMailbox-EXCH02-003                                   183
HealthMailbox-EXCH02-007                                    20
In-Place Archive -HealthMailbox-EXCH02-003                 197
HealthMailbox-EXCH01-003                                   173
HealthMailbox-EXCH01-007                                    20
In-Place Archive -HealthMailbox-EXCH01-003                 179
In-Place Archive -HealthMailbox-EXCH02-007                  28
In-Place Archive -HealthMailbox-EXCH01-007                  44
HealthMailbox-EXCH05-001                                   169
HealthMailbox-EXCH05-006                                    20
In-Place Archive -HealthMailbox-EXCH05-001                 177
In-Place Archive -HealthMailbox-EXCH05-006                  33
Jaap Wesselius                                             371
DMARC Reports                                               21
Marina Baggus                                              251

[PS] C:\>
```

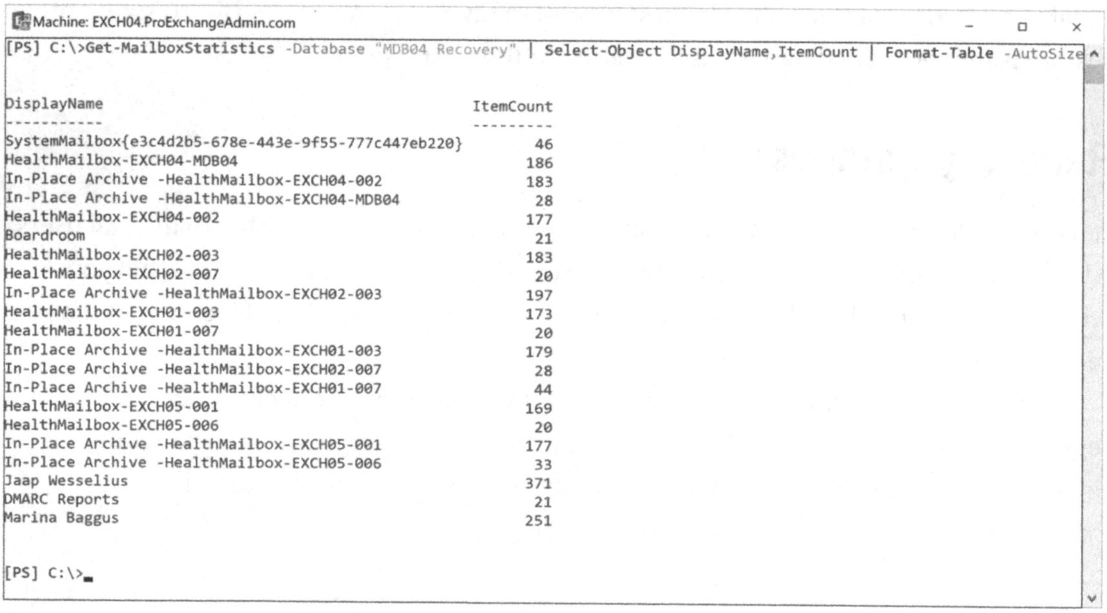

Figure 4-36. *Using the Get-MailboxStatistics command to view what's inside the recovery mailbox database*

This information can be used to restore mailbox content from the recovery mailbox database into the normal production mailbox database by using the New-MailboxRestoreRequest command in the EMS.

To retrieve mailbox content from the administrator mailbox inside the recovery mailbox database into the normal administrator mailbox, you can use the following command:

```
[PS] C:\> New-MailboxRestoreRequest -SourceDatabase
"MDB04 Recovery" -SourceStoreMailbox Jaap -TargetMailbox Jaap
```

The content will be imported into the normal mailbox, but content will not be overwritten. If items already exist in the target mailbox, an additional copy of the item is created so that no information gets lost.

Note If you are uncertain what will happen during a command like the New-MailboxRestoreRequest, you can always use the -WhatIf switch. The command will be the same, but it will not be executed. The results, however, will be shown on the console. If you are satisfied with the results, you can then rerun the command but without the -WhatIf parameter.

The preceding example will restore the entire mailbox from the recovery mailbox database, but it is possible to use a more granular approach. For instance, you can use the -IncludeFolders parameter to specify the folder in the mailbox that needs to be restored. To include the contents from the inbox, the option -IncludeFolders “Inbox/*” can be used; or in the case of restoring only the Deleted Items folder, the option -IncludeFolders “DeletedItems/*” can be used, for example:

```
[PS] C:\> New-MailboxRestoreRequest -SourceDatabase
"MDB04 Recovery" -SourceStoreMailbox Jaap -TargetMailbox Jaap -IncludeFolders
"DeletedItems/*"
```

Note There is a dependency here on the regional settings of the mailbox. In English, you have an “inbox,” while in Dutch the same folder is called “Postvak In”; in Spanish, it is “bandeja de entrada.” You must be aware of the regional setting of the mailbox when performing this command.

For certain purposes, it is possible to restore mailbox content from the mailbox in the recovery mailbox database to another mailbox that's not the original mailbox—for example, a legal mailbox. Suppose there's a mailbox called "Legal," and this mailbox is used to gather information from a mailbox from a backup. A command similar to this can be used:

```
[PS] C:\> New-MailboxRestoreRequest -SourceDatabase "MDB04 Recovery"
-SourceStoreMailbox Jaap -TargetMailbox legal -TargetRootFolder "Recovery
Items"
```

Dial-Tone Recovery

A recovery database is also used in a process called dial-tone recovery. In this recovery scenario, you get the users back online as quickly as possible after a mailbox database crash, and you work on mailbox database recovery in the background.

Suppose a mailbox database has crashed beyond repair, but you need to get users back online immediately. In this case, you can remove all corrupted files from the disk and mount the mailbox database again. Since Exchange does not find any mailbox database files, it creates a new mailbox database and new log files (after showing a warning message).

Users who had their mailboxes in the crashed mailbox database can now start their mail client, and new mailboxes will automatically be created in the new mailbox database. Of course, that database is empty, but users are online again. They can send mail, but more importantly, they can receive mail again. The last thing you want to have happened is for external customers to send email to your organization, and they receive error messages like "Mailbox info@contoso.com is not available."

Since users are online, they can continue to work, and you can work in the background on restoring the last mailbox database backup to a recovery mailbox database. When the mailbox database is restored and all remaining log files are replayed into the recovered mailbox database, you can swap the two mailbox databases. The recovered mailbox database is then moved to the production location, while the newly created mailbox database, which now also has items in it, is moved to the recovery mailbox database location.

The trick you perform at this point is to mount the newly created mailbox database as a recovery mailbox database and move the new content, using the New-MailboxRestoreRequest command as explained in the previous section, into the restored mailbox database. Once finished, you will have the mailbox database up and running again, without having lost any data.

The good part here is that you can restore the mailbox database from a backup, but your users are able to log on again and continue sending and receiving email. Yes, at that moment they will not have their "old" mailbox content available (not only email items but also the temporary mailbox does not contain any information or additional permissions), but at least they are online during the restore procedures.

Note Some third-party backup applications use a granular restore technology, whereby it is possible to restore individual items directly from the VSS backup. What happens is that the VSS backup is completely indexed after the backup, indexing all individual email messages. These messages can then be restored directly from the backup, where the MAPI/HTTP is used for storing directly into the mailbox.

Recovering an Exchange Server

The previous section discussed mailbox database technologies: how they work, how to back them up, and how to restore them. It showed how it is possible to restore a mailbox database to its original location or to an alternative location. In the last scenario, you created a recovery mailbox database, restored data from this recovery mailbox database, and used it in a dial-tone scenario.

But what happens if an entire server is lost and beyond repair? Then you need to rely on your disaster recovery skills.

Rebuilding an Exchange Server

When the Exchange server is lost, it needs to be rebuilt, and the services, configuration, and data need to be restored. Earlier in this chapter, I described where all the information is stored that is needed to rebuild an Exchange server, for example:

- Mailbox data is stored in the mailbox database, which should be on additional disks. If you are in luck, these are still safe after losing your Exchange server.

- Configuration data is sometimes stored in config files, located somewhere in the C:\Program Files\Microsoft\Exchange Server\v15 directory.
- All kinds of log files are also stored in the C:\Program Files\Microsoft\Exchange Server directory.
- SSL certificates are stored somewhere safe.
- Server configuration is stored in Active Directory.

Now, if you have taken care of the first four items listed earlier, the last one about Active Directory is interesting. All configuration data that is not in the config files is stored in Active Directory, and that can be used when rebuilding the Exchange server. But instead of entering all the details manually during setup, this information is retrieved from Active Directory during installation.

Rule number 1 in a crisis situation is: Don't panic and don't destroy any data—not from disks and not from Active Directory. Otherwise, this action will backfire on you at some point!

To successfully rebuild an Exchange server, you can use the following steps:

1. Reset the computer account. When the server has crashed beyond repair and you must rebuild your server, do not remove the Computer object from Active Directory. Instead, reset the Computer object in Active Directory, as follows:

   a. Log on to a domain controller, or any other member server that has the Active Directory tools installed, and open the Active Directory Users and Computers MMC snap-in.

   b. Locate the Computer object, right-click it, and select Reset Account (see Figure 4-37). This will reset the Computer object so you can join a new Windows Server (using the same name) to Active Directory.

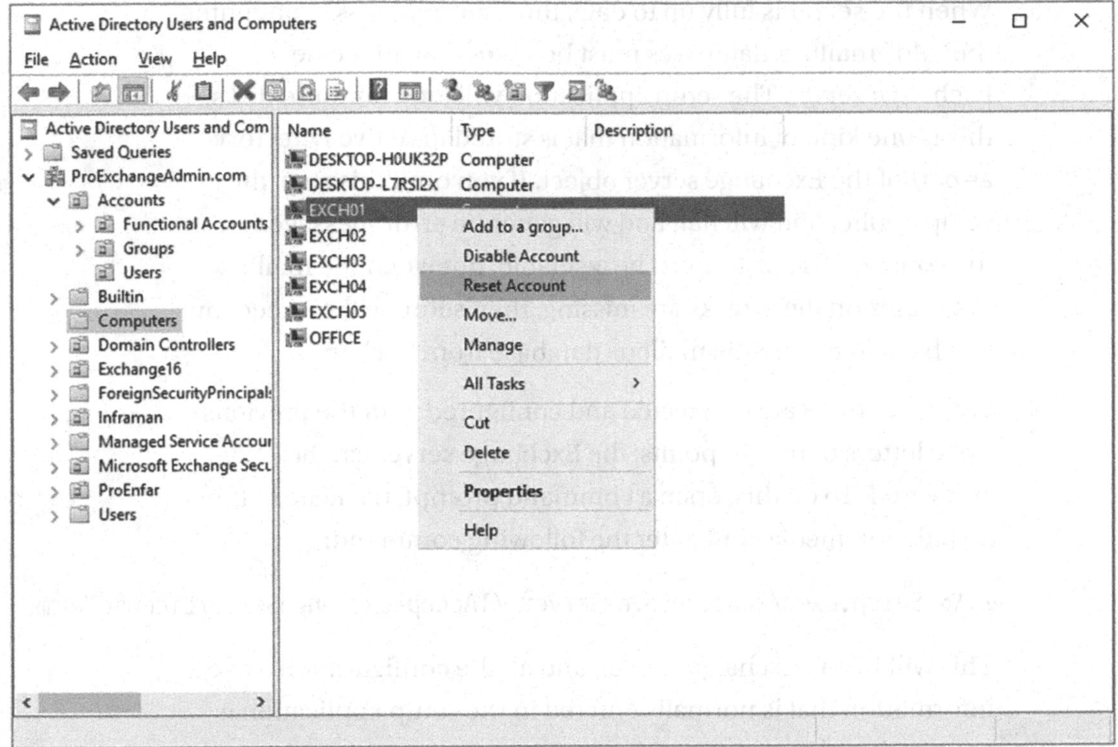

***Figure 4-37.** Resetting the Computer object in a disaster recovery scenario*

2. Install a new Windows server with the same specifications as the "old" Mailbox server. Use the same operating system and bring it up to date with the same hot fixes and service packs as were applied to the old Exchange server. Very important: Use the same server name as was for the old Exchange server. That is, when the old server name was EXCH01, the new server name needs to be EXCH01 as well.

3. Join the new server, using the original name, to the Active Directory domain. When joined, reboot the server and log on to the new server as a domain administrator.

4. When logged on as an administrator with sufficient permissions, install the prerequisite software. This is explained in Chapter 2.

5. When the server is fully up to date, the (external) disks containing the "old" mailbox databases must be accessible to the new Exchange server. The setup application will look for these disks; this is one kind of information that is stored in Active Directory as part of the Exchange server object. If you omit this step, the setup application will halt and will generate error messages on the console. The disks must be available, but when the mailbox databases on these disks are missing, then setup will succeed, but you have to restore the mailbox database from backup.

6. When the disks are connected and configured with the previous drive letters or mount points, the Exchange server can be recovered. To do this, open a command prompt, navigate to the installation media, and enter the following command:

   ```
   Z:\> Setup.exe /mode:RecoverServer /IAcceptExchangeServerLicenseTerms
   ```

   This will install Exchange server, and all the configuration information that is normally entered in the setup application is now retrieved from Active Directory.

7. When the setup application is finished and the server is reinstalled, shown in Figure 4-38, reboot the server.

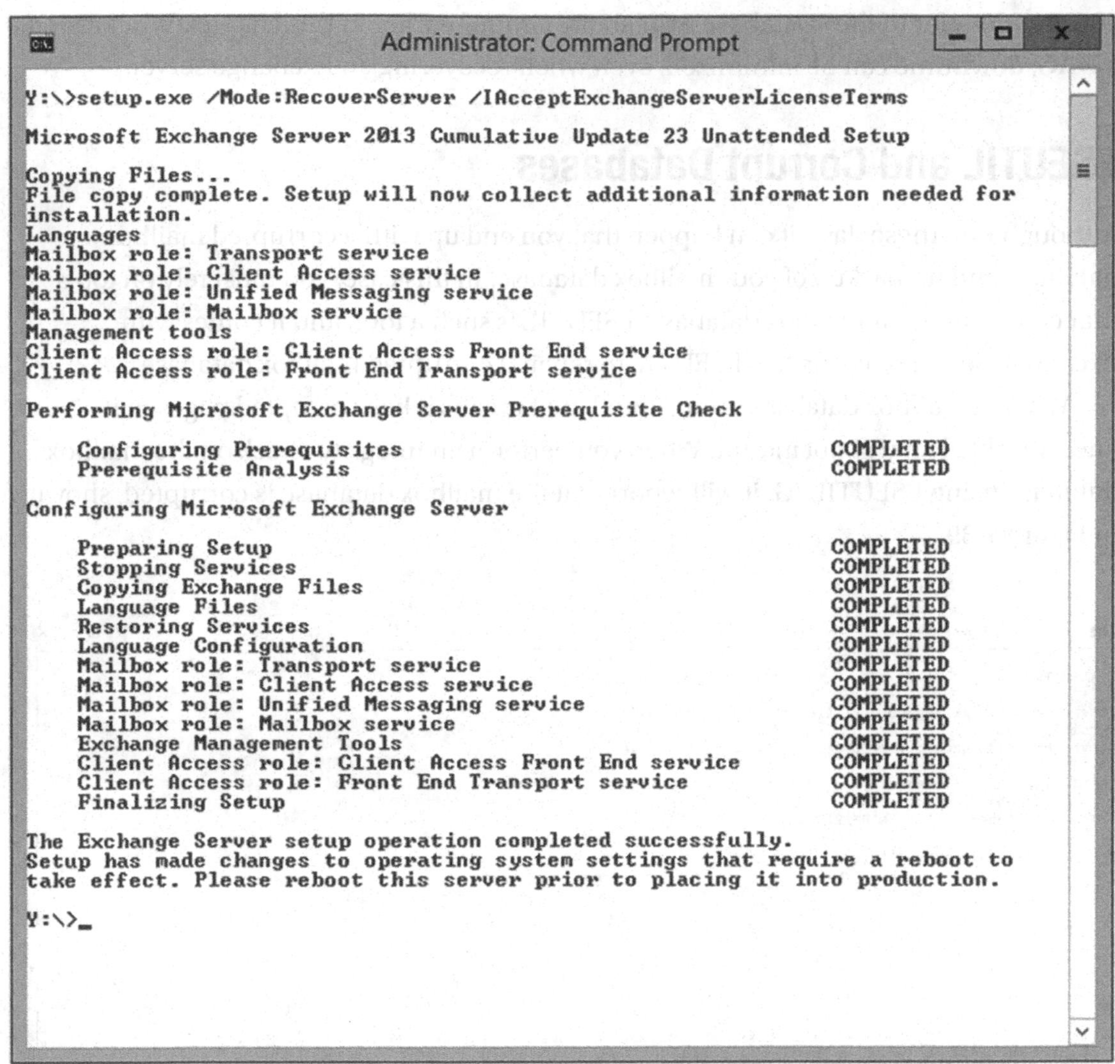
```
Y:\>setup.exe /Mode:RecoverServer /IAcceptExchangeServerLicenseTerms

Microsoft Exchange Server 2013 Cumulative Update 23 Unattended Setup

Copying Files...
File copy complete. Setup will now collect additional information needed for
installation.
Languages
Mailbox role: Transport service
Mailbox role: Client Access service
Mailbox role: Unified Messaging service
Mailbox role: Mailbox service
Management tools
Client Access role: Client Access Front End service
Client Access role: Front End Transport service

Performing Microsoft Exchange Server Prerequisite Check

    Configuring Prerequisites                                   COMPLETED
    Prerequisite Analysis                                       COMPLETED

Configuring Microsoft Exchange Server

    Preparing Setup                                             COMPLETED
    Stopping Services                                           COMPLETED
    Copying Exchange Files                                      COMPLETED
    Language Files                                              COMPLETED
    Restoring Services                                          COMPLETED
    Language Configuration                                      COMPLETED
    Mailbox role: Transport service                             COMPLETED
    Mailbox role: Client Access service                         COMPLETED
    Mailbox role: Unified Messaging service                     COMPLETED
    Mailbox role: Mailbox service                               COMPLETED
    Exchange Management Tools                                   COMPLETED
    Client Access role: Client Access Front End service         COMPLETED
    Client Access role: Front End Transport service             COMPLETED
    Finalizing Setup                                            COMPLETED

The Exchange Server setup operation completed successfully.
Setup has made changes to operating system settings that require a reboot to
take effect. Please reboot this server prior to placing it into production.

Y:\>_
```

***Figure 4-38.** Recovering an Exchange server with information from Active Directory*

After rebooting, you can check the mailbox databases that were on the (external) disk drives; they should be good, although dismounted. When you mount the mailbox databases on the recovered server, you are good to log in to your mailbox using OWA. The last steps are to restore or reconfigure additional items like the SSL certificate, virtual directories, additional config files, or other log files, as explained earlier in this chapter.

When done, though your server has been unavailable for some time, it is now restored to its original location. If you (and your users) are unhappy with the downtime, you should refer to the “Database Availability Group” earlier in this chapter. When using a DAG, downtime can be minimized, even when recovering an Exchange server.

ESEUTIL and Corrupt Databases

Although rare these days, it can happen that you end up with a corrupted mailbox database and no backup of your mailbox database. In this case, you must rely on tools that can repair your mailbox database. ESEUTIL is such a tool, and it comes with Exchange Server; you can use ESEUTIL to repair a corrupted mailbox database.

When a mailbox database is corrupted, that means it has corrupted pages in it, and most likely it will not mount. When you perform an integrity check on the mailbox database using ESEUTIL /G, it will report that the mailbox database is corrupted, shown in Figure 4-39.

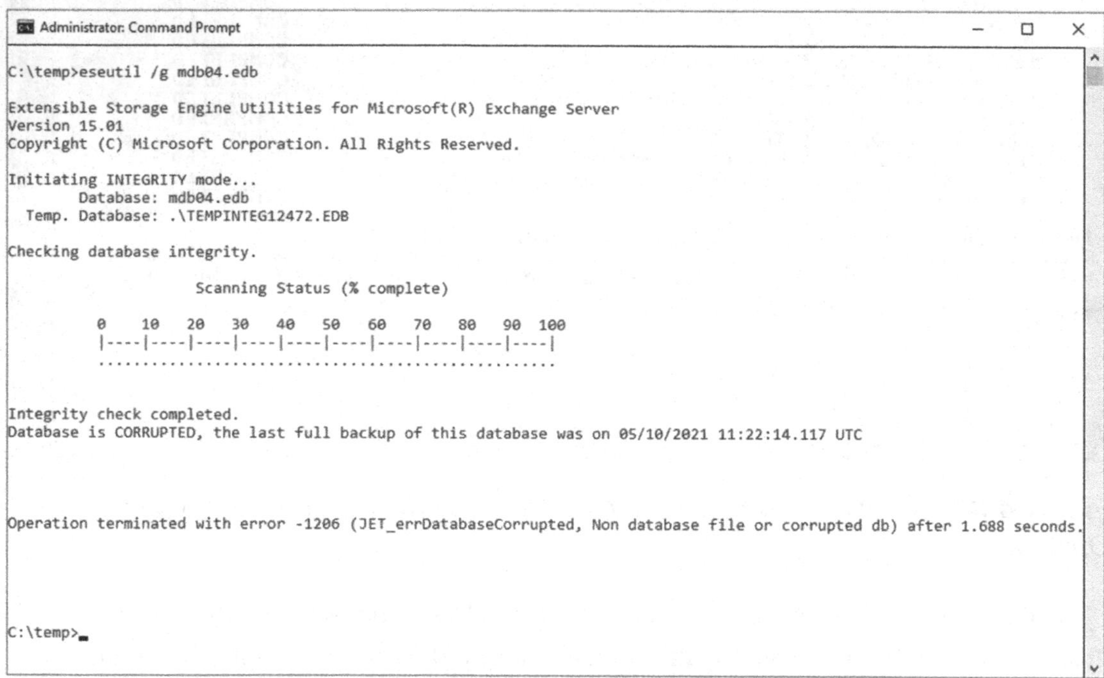

Figure 4-39. *ESEUTIL report of mailbox database as corrupted*

ESEUTIL also has an option to repair a mailbox database, but it is a very destructive way of repairing. What it does is open the mailbox database and check all the pages in the database. When a page is found to contain corrupted pointers (i.e., pointers to other pages containing data), it will remove these pointers from the page. The result is that no pages contain invalid pointers anymore, but the data that was referenced using those pages is automatically lost.

It is not possible to predict which pages and pointers are corrupted, and thus it is not possible to anticipate what data you will be missing. Unfortunately, your users will find this out in the end.

You can start a repair with ESEUTIL /P MDB01.edb. A warning message is shown saying that you should only run Repair on damaged or corrupted databases. The caution is that Repair will not apply information in the transaction log files to the database and may cause information to be lost. And it will ask you if you want to continue.

If you do, click the OK button to continue. ESEUTIL will perform a consistency check first, then scan the database and repair any damaged information that it found. This is shown in Figure 4-40.

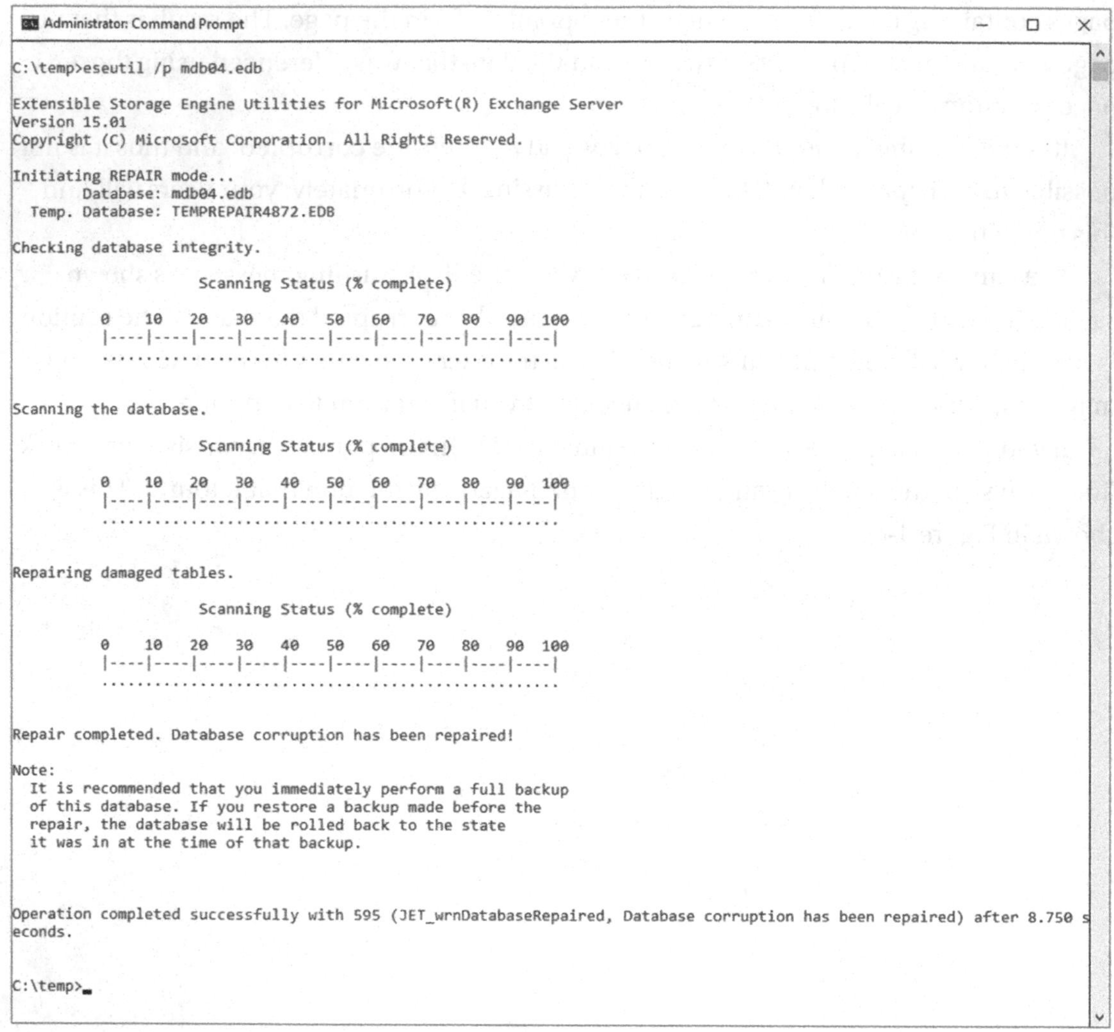

***Figure 4-40.** ESEUTIL /P does several checks before repairing damaged information*

One question that always pops up is how long it takes for a mailbox database repair to be completed. As a rule of thumb, I use 10 GB per hour for processing. So, if you have a 250 GB mailbox database you must repair, it will take approximately 25 hours to complete. There is no need to panic when you do not see any dots moving on the console; ESEUTIL just needs time to do its work.

This is the reason Microsoft recommends not using large mailbox databases (i.e., larger than 200 GB) when a DAG is not used. If you are using a 500 GB mailbox database in a single Mailbox server environment, and you run into a situation like this, you will have a hard time ensuring service delivery (which should be documented in the SLA).

It is recommended that you create a new mailbox database after a corrupted mailbox database has been repaired.

This can be done in two ways:

- Create a new mailbox database on the Exchange server and move all the mailboxes from the old and repaired mailbox database to the new mailbox database. Once they are moved, the old mailbox database can be removed. Do not forget to create a new backup of the new mailbox database when done.
- Use ESEUTIL /D to perform an offline defragmentation. The net effect of this is that a new mailbox database is created with the old name. When you use ESEUTIL /D to perform an offline defragmentation, it will create a new mailbox database file next to the old mailbox database file. Then it will read all information from the old file and merge it into the new file. However, to do this you first have to dismount the mailbox database, and it can only be mounted after ESEUTIL has finished. Again, this can take a considerable amount of time.

This way, not only is a new file created but also new indices, new tables, new pointers, and so on—so basically you end up with a new mailbox database. When the copy process is complete, the old (and previously corrupted) mailbox database will be deleted.

Exchange Native Data Protection

Exchange Native Data Protection is a solution that was first introduced in Exchange Server 2010, sometimes also referred to as a "backupless environment." This is an Exchange server environment where a traditional backup solution is not used and where native Exchange functions are the replacement—when possible, of course. Exchange Native Data Protection is not only used in Exchange on-premises, but it is also used in Exchange Online.

Note In some market segments, such as legal, finance, or health care, there are (legal) requirements that dictate how to create regular backups, keep them for a certain amount of time, and/or store them on a separate location. For these, Exchange Native Data Protection is not a solution.

Exchange Native Data Protection can help you in scenarios where

- Users have unintentionally deleted items from their mailboxes and need them urgently.
- You need to restore items from a user's mailbox for legal purposes.
- A mailbox was deleted unintentionally.
- Hardware failures caused loss of a mailbox database or maybe loss of an entire server.
- There has been failure or loss of an entire data center.

Exchange server has a lot of built-in features that can take care of some of these items; for example, there are deleted item retention, in-place hold, single item recovery, archive mailboxes, retention policies, and a database availability group (DAG).

Using these features, it is possible to create an environment where a traditional backup is not used, but where the disasters mentioned earlier would be fully covered. The advantage of this arrangement is that the total cost of ownership of a full-fledged Exchange environment is most likely lower than that of a regular Exchange environment with a traditional backup solution.

Microsoft recommends evaluating your various requirements and the available options before deciding whether this is a viable solution for your organization. For more information, visit the Exchange Native Data Protection site on Microsoft docs at `http://bit.ly/NativeProtection`.

In the following sections, we will discuss the various components of Native Data Protection.

Delete Item Retention

When users delete items from their mailboxes, the items are not visible to the users anymore, but they are still in the users' mailboxes. They are stored in hidden folders in their mailboxes, which is part of the "dumpster."

Deleted items are kept in the Recoverable Items folder for a time called the deleted item retention period.

By default, the retention time for deleted items is 14 days, while for a deleted mailbox it is 30 days. This means that after these times, the items are deleted from the server. Deleted item retention is a property of the mailbox database and can be set using the Set-MailboxDatabase command with the – DeletedItemRetention parameter and is specified as a time span: dd.hh:mm:ss. To set the deleted item retention time to 60 days, for example, you can use the following command:

```
[PS] C:\> Set-MailboxDatabase -Identity MDB01 -DeletedItemRetention
60.00:00:00
```

To set the deleted item retention time for mailboxes, the same command is used but with the MailboxRetention option. For example, to change the deleted mailbox retention time to seven days, you can use the following command:

```
[PS] C:\> Set-MailboxDatabase -Identity MDB01 -MailboxRetention 7.00:00:00
```

Within this deleted item retention time, users can recover deleted items themselves in Outlook. In Outlook 2013 and higher, you select the Folders tab and then click the Recover Deleted Items button. A new window will pop up showing all messages that are not in the Deleted Items folder but can still be recovered from the Recoverable Items folder (see Figure 4-41).

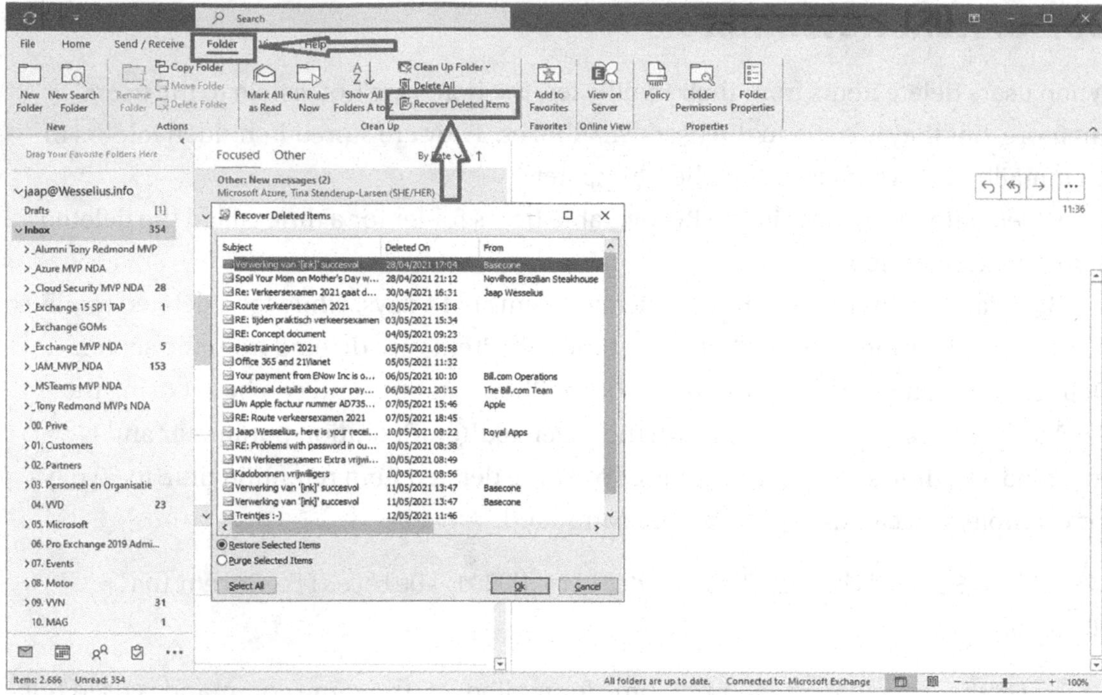

***Figure 4-41.** End users can recover deleted items*

In OWA, the deleted items can be recovered as well. In the OWA navigation pane, right-click the Deleted Items folder and select the Recover Deleted Items option.

When the user permanently deletes a message (i.e., purges the Deleted Items folder), the message can no longer be recovered—not even by administrators—unless the Single Item Recovery option is enabled. Single Item Recovery is covered later in this section.

In-Place Hold

Although you now know it is possible to stretch the deleted item retention period, it is not really a good idea to stretch this time to a couple of years; doing so would have a disastrous effect on the size of the mailbox database. The solution for this in Exchange is "in-place hold."

With in-place hold, you have the possibility of

- Placing user mailboxes on hold and preserving mailbox content from any possible alteration
- Preserving delete items, that is, items that can be deleted manually by the user or by an automated process like messaging records management (MRM)
- Searching for and retaining items matching specified criteria
- Preserving items indefinitely or for a specific duration
- Keeping in-place hold transparent from the user by not having to suspend MRM
- Enabling in-place eDiscovery searches of items placed on hold

In short, items can be on hold in a user's mailbox without the user knowing it.

Litigation hold allowed putting all items on hold for an indefinite amount of time. In-place hold is more granular, with the following possible parameters:

- **What to hold**—It is possible to specify which items to put on hold by using parameters such as keywords, recipients, senders, start and end dates, and type of items, such as messages, calendar items, and so forth.
- **How long to hold**—It is possible to specify how long these items should be on hold.

To place a mailbox on in-place hold, you need to have specific permissions. These permissions are granted to users who are members of the Discovery Management RBAC group or users who are assigned the Legal Hold and Mailbox Search management roles.

Note In-place hold is a premium feature that requires an Enterprise Client Access License (CAL). You only need the Enterprise CAL for mailboxes that use this feature.

To create a new in-place hold using PowerShell, you can use the following command:

```
[PS] C:\> New-MailboxSearch -Name "In-place hold John Smith Mailbox"
-SourceMailboxes J.Smith -InPlaceHoldEnabled $true
```

When a new mailbox search is started, an informational warning message is shown saying that the new Mailbox server will not be effective immediately and that it can take up to 60 minutes before becoming active (see Figure 4-42).

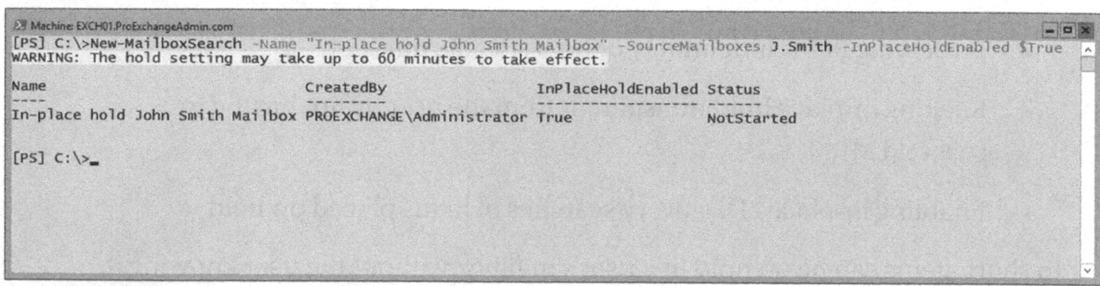

***Figure 4-42.** Creating a new mailbox search using the EMS*

For example, all items in Joe's mailbox will now be on hold for an indefinite period. When Joe deletes items and purges his deleted items manually, they will be stored. If Joe receives a message and deliberately makes changes to this message, the original and the changed messages will both be kept. It is good practice to monitor the deleted items quota in the mailboxes for which you have enabled in-place hold.

Single Item Recovery

When a message is deleted from a mailbox, it is stored in the Recoverable Items folder of that mailbox. Items stay in this folder until the deleted item retention period expires. Only then are they fully removed from the Exchange server by the server's online maintenance. When a user permanently deletes a message, it is removed immediately from the Recoverable Items folder, and the user is no longer able to recover that message—not even the administrator is able to recover it. One exception, however, is when the mailbox is on in-place hold. Then, deleted items are retained until the in-place hold is removed.

To be able to recover these deleted items when they have been permanently deleted by the user, you can enable single item recovery on the mailbox. When this is enabled, permanently deleted messages are retained in the Recoverable Items folder until the deleted item retention period is passed, and then the message is fully removed from the Recoverable Items folder.

Single item recovery can be enabled only with PowerShell and by using the following command:

```
[PS] C:\> Set-Mailbox -Identity "Sarah Summertime"
-SingleItemRecoveryEnabled $true
```

For mailboxes that have single item recovery enabled, it is also possible to set a different deleted item retention time using the -RetainDeletedItemsFor option, as follows:

```
[PS] C:\> Set-Mailbox -Identity "Glenn Kendall" -SingleItemRecoveryEnabled
$true -RetainDeletedItemsFor 30
```

Recovering items when single item recovery is enabled consists of two steps:

1. Searching for the missing items and recovering them
2. Restoring the recovered items

Searching for deleted items in mailboxes that have single item recovery enabled or mailboxes that are on in-place hold is part of in-place eDiscovery. As such, you need special permissions to search for these deleted items or to search in these mailboxes. This makes sense since you are looking into somebody else's potentially private information. With the permission stipulation in place, it is impossible to "accidentally" search others' mailboxes.

Permission is granted to members of the Discovery Management RBAC role group. To perform a search, you follow these steps:

1. Select Compliance Management in the Feature pane and select the In-Place eDiscovery and Hold tab. In the toolbar, click the New icon.
2. In the New In-Place eDiscovery and Hold wizard, enter a name and a description for the new hold you are creating. Click Next to continue.

3. The next window lets you choose if you want to search all mailboxes or only specific mailboxes. Assuming the latter, select the Specify Mailboxes to Search radio button and use the Add button to select a mailbox that needs to be added to the new search. Select the mailbox, use the Add button, and click OK to return to the previous window. This mailbox should now be listed in the Results pane. Click Next to continue.

4. In the Search Query window, you can define the query that needs to be used. Enter the keywords, start and end dates, recipient and sender, and the item type, like email, meeting, notes, and so forth. Select the options you need and click Next to continue.

5. If needed, you can opt to place the content matching the search query on hold. It can be on hold indefinitely or for a certain number of days. Click Finish to continue.

   The search is not executed immediately, but an estimate of the search results is shown in the Details pane, including the number of items returned by the search and its size (see Figure 4-43).

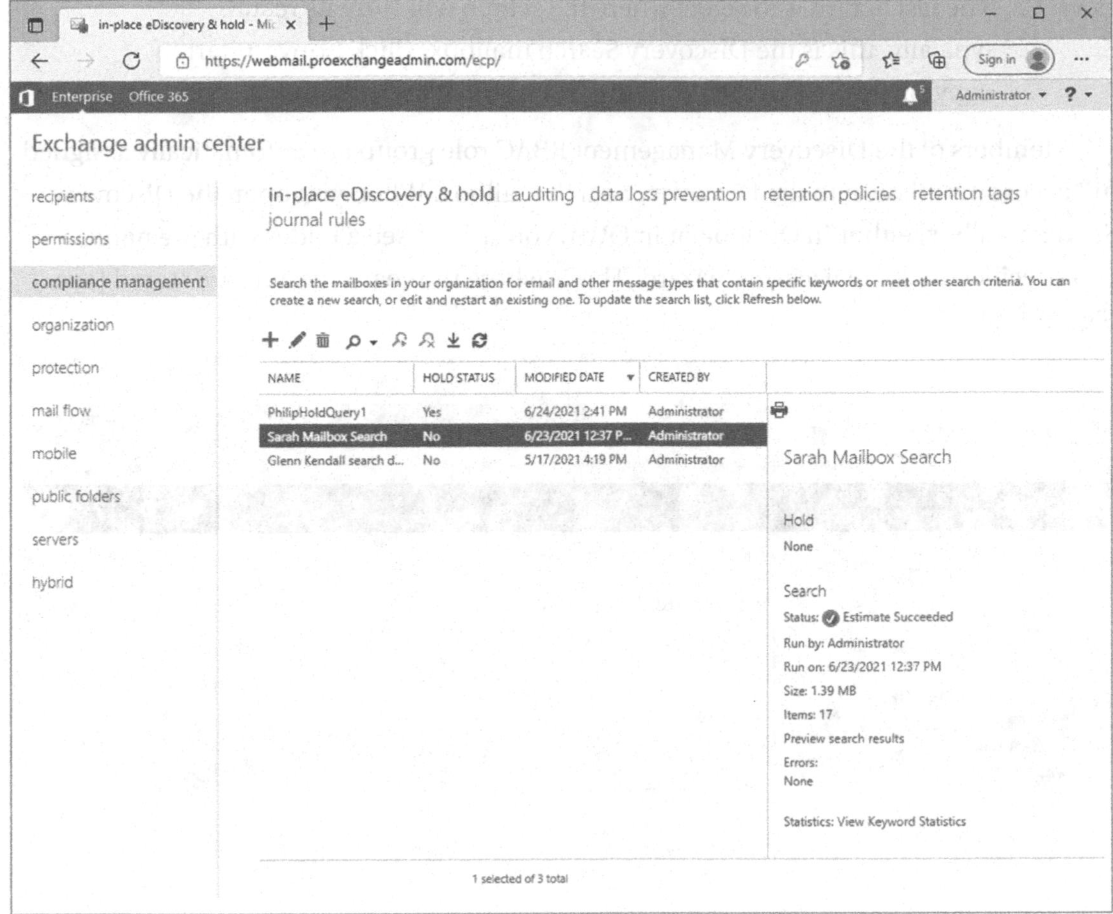

***Figure 4-43.** The new search that was just created*

6. When the results are satisfactory, the search can be executed. Click the Down arrow next to the search icon and select the Copy Search Results option. You can select which options can be enabled, such as

    - Include unsearchable items.
    - Enable de-duplication.
    - Enable full logging.
    - Send me mail when the copy is completed.

7. The last action is to select where the search will store its results; typically, this is the Discovery Search mailbox. Click Copy to start copying the search results to the Discovery Search mailbox.

Members of the Discovery Management RBAC role group are automatically assigned full access permission to the Discovery Search mailbox. When you open the Discovery Search mailbox, either in Outlook or in OWA, you should see a folder with the name you specified in the eDiscovery wizard. This is where the search results are stored (see Figure 4-44).

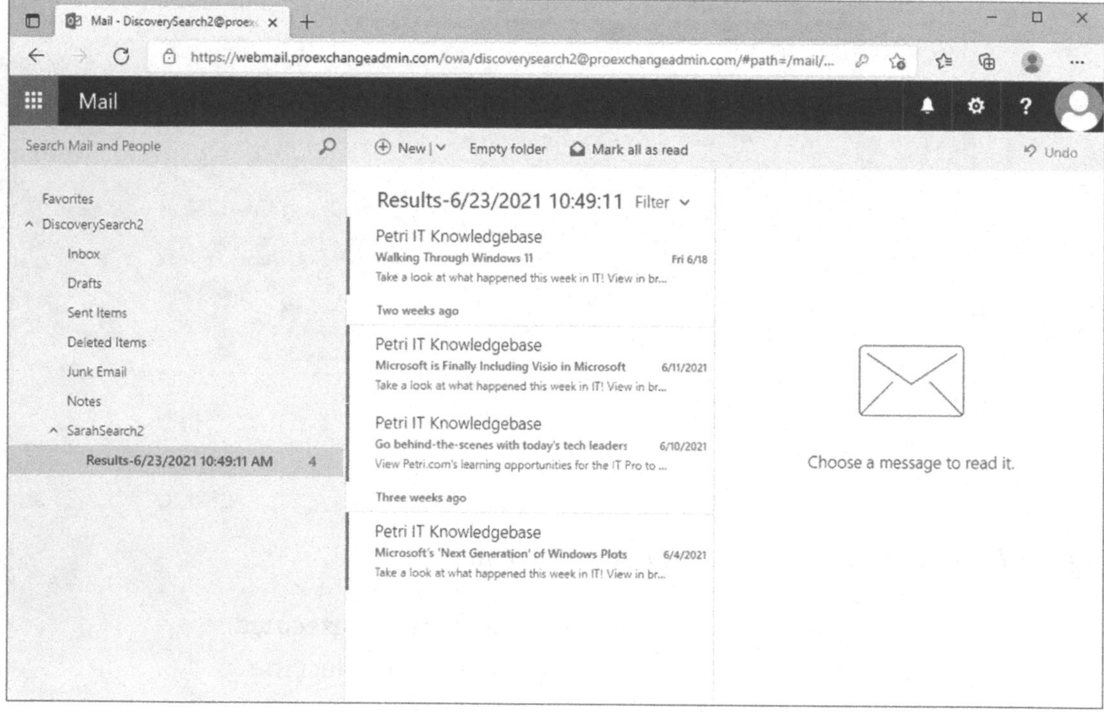

***Figure 4-44.** Search results are stored in the Discovery Search mailbox*

When the results are stored in the Discovery Search mailbox, it is possible to export those results to the user's mailbox using the Search-Mailbox command:

```
[PS] C:\> Search-Mailbox "Discovery Search Mailbox" -SearchQuery
"Glenn's Search" -TargetMailbox "Glenn Kendall" -TargetFolder "Recovered
Messages" -LogLevel Full -DeleteContent
```

For example, this command moves the items from the search results into Kim Akers' mailbox in a folder called Recovered Messages. When this is done, the items in the Discovery Search mailbox are deleted.

Using New-MailboxExportRequest, it is also possible to export the search results to a PST file. The same prerequisites apply as when using a normal export request. The MRS processes the request, so the PST file needs to be stored to a file share where the Exchange Trusted Subsystem USG has permission for full access.

For example, the following command will start a new export request of the folder called Kim Akers in the Discovery Search mailbox, where the subject of the items is "Exchange" and will store the PST file on a file share called HelpDeskPst on a server called FS01:

```
[PS] C:\> New-MailboxExportRequest -Mailbox "Discovery Search
Mailbox" -SourceRootFolder "Glenn Kendall" -ContentFilter {Subject -eq
"Exchange"} -FilePath \\ FS01\HelpDeskPst\KimAkersRecovery.pst
```

Archive Mailboxes

An archive mailbox is just a normal mailbox, but it is connected to a user as a secondary mailbox and is used for archiving purposes. The archive mailbox, however, is separate from the user's primary mailbox and can be located on additional storage, on a separate server, or even in Exchange Online.

An archive mailbox is visible from Outlook and from Outlook on the Web; it appears as an additional mailbox in the client. The only snag is that if you do not have Autodiscover configured correctly, it might not show up in Outlook. In Outlook on the Web, it always shows up.

Important Note The Archive mailbox is not cached in an Outlook .OST file and thus only accessible when connected to an Exchange server.

To create an archive mailbox for a user called Joe and locate this archive mailbox in a mailbox database called MDB01, you can use the following command (see Figure 4-45):

```
[PS] C:\> Enable-Mailbox -Identity "Glenn Kendall" -Archive -ArchiveDatabase
MDB02
```

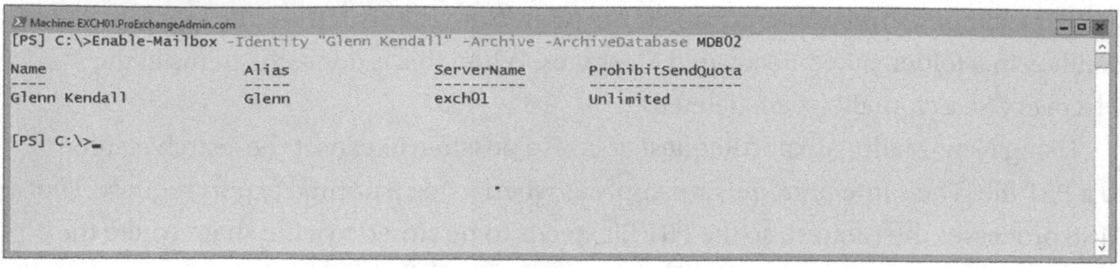

```
[PS] C:\>Enable-Mailbox -Identity "Glenn Kendall" -Archive -ArchiveDatabase MDB02

Name                    Alias             ServerName        ProhibitSendQuota
----                    -----             ----------        -----------------
Glenn Kendall           Glenn             exch01            Unlimited

[PS] C:\>_
```

***Figure 4-45.** Creating an archive mailbox using EMS*

Note In-place archiving is a premium feature and requires an Exchange Enterprise Client Access License (CAL).

By default, an archive mailbox has an archive quota of 100 GB and an archive quota warning at 90 GB. This means that a warning message will be sent to the user when the archive reaches 90 GB, but this is sufficient to store tons of information.

Note Archive mailboxes are a perfect "PST killer." By nature, PST files are stored on the user's workstation or laptop, where they are not backed up and are prone to getting lost when the laptop is stored. Storing PST files on a network share is not supported and can give erratic results in Outlook. Also, a backup application can skip these files when they are still open in Outlook. But when they are moved to archive mailboxes, they are stored safely, available for the user, and backed up frequently. It is a perfect solution for getting rid of your PST files.

The user can manually move data to the archive mailbox, but an administrator can also import data into that archive mailbox. The New-MailboxImportRequest command can be used to import PST files from a file share directly into an archive mailbox. To achieve this in EMS, use a command like this example:

```
[PS] C:\> New-MailboxImportRequest -Mailbox "Glenn Kendall" -FilePath \\
FS01\PSTFiles\Glenn-Archive.pst -IsArchive
```

Another way to automatically move data from the user's mailbox into the archive mailbox is by using retention policies. Retention policies are discussed in detail in Chapter 11.

Summary

The Mailbox service in Exchange server 2016 and Exchange server 2019 is identical to the Mailbox server role in Exchange server 2013. The Mailbox service in Exchange is responsible for hosting copies of the Mailbox databases.

To achieve high availability on mailbox databases, Exchange server can be combined in a Database Availability Group or DAG. A DAG can host multiple copies of a Mailbox database; if one copy of a Mailbox database fails, or when one server hosting a Mailbox database fails, another server can take over Mailbox services for users. This reduces the downtime for users when a server fails. Mailbox database copies can be hosted in one or more data centers in multiple locations. The latter gives the option to create data center redundancy when configured properly.

Mailbox databases must be backed up. The native tool in Windows is Windows Server Backup. It can back up Mailbox databases or entire Exchange servers, but third-party tools are better solutions. Often, these are combined with storage solutions, making it possible to create high-performance backups. Creating backups is not a problem; restoring a backup can be more challenging. Also, recovering mailbox databases using a recovery database or a dial-tone recovery can be cumbersome. This must be properly documented and tested regularly. You should question yourself if you want to rely on restore technologies or want to implement a DAG for more reliability and availability.

Microsoft also offers a "backupless solution" with Exchange where no backups are created. This solution is built on DAGs, including lagged copies and multiple compliance solutions. When configured correctly, this is a viable solution for traditional backups. Exchange Online is running completely without backups, and the underlying DAGs and compliance features take care of everything.

The first four chapters have been about the Exchange infrastructure; the next chapter is about what is using Exchange and thus about Recipients.

CHAPTER 5

Managing Recipients

In Exchange 2019, multiple types of recipients are available:

- User mailboxes
- Resource Mailboxes
- Linked Mailboxes
- Mail-Enabled Users
- Remote Mailboxes
- Site Mailboxes
- Public Folders
- Contacts

Recipients are grouped in address lists of which multiple are available in Exchange:

- Global Address Lists
- Custom Address Lists
- Offline Address Books
- Address Book Policies

These are all discussed in this chapter.

M. de Rooij and J. Wesselius, *Pro Exchange 2019 and 2016 Administration*,
https://doi.org/10.1007/978-1-4842-7331-9_5

User Mailboxes

There are a couple of ways to create new user mailboxes in Exchange:

- Create a new mailbox in EMS or EAC and have the accompanying user account in Active Directory created automatically.
- Mailbox-enable an existing user account.
- Bulk management, for example, by importing a CSV file with mailbox information.

We will discuss this in more detail.

Create a User Mailbox

It is possible to create a new user mailbox with the accompanying user account using the New-Mailbox command in EMS. To do this, execute the following command in EMS:

```
[PS] C:\> New-Mailbox -Name "David Honeychurch" -FirstName David
-LastName Honeychurch -Alias David -DisplayName "David Honeychurch"
-OrganizationalUnit "OU=Users,OU=Accounts,DC=Proexchangeadmin,DC=com"
-Database MDB01 -UserPrincipalName david@proexchangeadmin.com
```

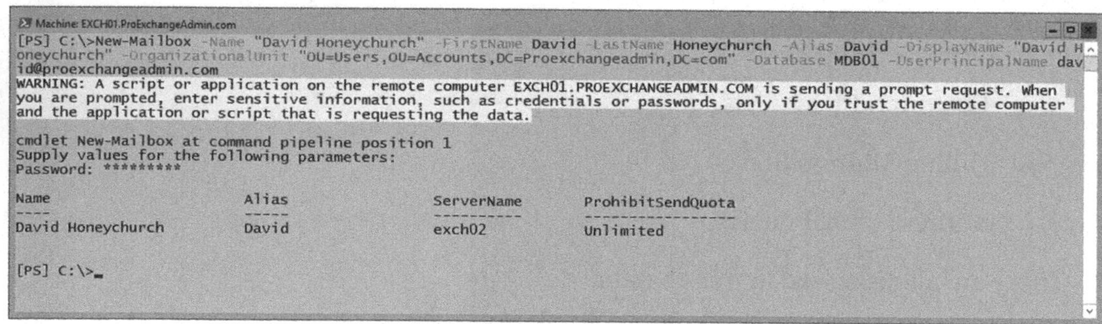

Figure 5-1. Creating a new Mailbox in EMS

As shown in Figure 5-1, this command will create a new user account called "David Honeychurch" in the OU=Users Organizational Unit OU=Accounts container in Active Directory. The user principal name will be set to david@proexchangeadmin.com, and the mailbox will be created in the MDB01 mailbox database.

It is not possible to enter a password on the command line because passwords are only accepted as a secure string in Active Directory. Therefore, you are prompted for a new password for this user account.

To work around this, you can use the ConvertTo-SecureString function in PowerShell. This will convert a clear text string like P@$$w0rd1 into a secure string that will be accepted by PowerShell when creating a new user. The command for creating a new user with a mailbox and for setting the password will be something like this:

```
[PS] C:\> New-Mailbox -Name "Percy Blake" -OrganizationalUnit "OU=Users,OU=
Accounts,DC=Proexchangeadmin,DC=com" -Password (ConvertTo-SecureString -String
'P@$$w0rd1' -AsPlainText -Force) -Database MDB01 -FirstName Percy -LastName
Blake -DisplayName "Percy Blake" -UserPrincipalName "percy@proexchangeadmin.com"
```

In the preceding example, a mailbox database is explicitly set. It is also possible to omit the –Database option when creating a new mailbox. If you do this, the Mailbox server automatically determines the best location for the new mailbox.

The algorithm used here first determines which mailbox databases are available in Active Directory and are not excluded for provisioning. Then it looks at the number of mailboxes in each mailbox database and picks the mailbox database with the lowest number of mailboxes.

By default, when a mailbox is created, a new email address is assigned using an Email Address Policy. It is also possible to bypass this using the -PrimarySmtpAddress option. When you use this option, the EmailAddressPolicyEnabled property of the new mailbox is set to false, and an email address policy is never applied. To do this, execute the following command in EMS:

```
[PS] C:\> New-Mailbox -Name "Jeronimo Ramirez" -FirstName Jeronimo -LastName
Ramirez -Alias Jeronimo -DisplayName "Jeronimo Ramirez" -Password
(ConvertTo-SecureString -String 'P@$$w0rd1' -AsPlainText -Force) -Database
MDB01 -UserPrincipalName Jeronimo@proexchangeadmin.com -PrimarySmtpAddress
Jeronimo@proexchangeadmin.com
```

Note The official name for a mailbox in Exchange is a mailbox-enabled user.

Mailbox-Enabling an Existing User Account

It is possible that an account in Active Directory already exists; it could have been created by the Active Directory team, for example. If so, you can mailbox-enable this user account. When mailbox-enabling an existing user account, a mailbox is added to it.

If you have an existing user account in Active Directory called "William Gray" and you want to assign a mailbox to him located in the Mailbox Database MDB02, you can execute the following command in EMS:

```
[PS] C:\> Enable-Mailbox -Identity "William Gray" -Alias William -Database
MDB02
```

Personally, I like to use a Get-User cmdlet first to see if it retrieves the correct user account from Active Directory. If it does, I repeat the command and pipe it into the Enable-Mailbox cmdlet:

```
[PS] C:\> Get-User -Identity "William Gray" | Enable-Mailbox -Alias
William -Database MDB02
```

The advantage of creating a user account in Active Directory in advance is that you can add a lot more properties using the New-ADUser command in PowerShell or in the Active Directory Users and Computers MMC snap-in. For example, to create a new user account in Active Directory, and populate additional properties, execute the following command in PowerShell:

```
[PS] C:\> New-ADUser -Name "Jessie Wingo" -SAMAccountName Jessie -Server
AD01 -UserPrincipalName Jessie@proexchangeadmin.com -GivenName
Jessie -Surname Wingo -DisplayName "Jessie Wingo" -Path "OU=Users,OU=
Accounts,DC=proexchangeadmin,DC=com" -AccountPassword (ConvertTo-
SecureString "Pass1word" -AsPlainText -Force) -Company "Les
Aventures" -StreetAddress "1, Longway" -PostalCode "X3B 84W" -City
London -Country "GB" -OfficePhone "+44 123 456 789" -Title "Managing
Consultant" -HomePage "www.proexchangeadmin.com" -Fax "+44 123 456
789" -MobilePhone "+44 123 456 789"  -Enabled:$TRUE
```

Note You can visit the `https://countrycode.org/` site to find a complete list of all country codes.

Using variables in combination with the New-ADUser and Enable-Mailbox commands makes an IT admin file much easier.

Bulk Management

If you have a lot of mailboxes that need to be created, you can use a PowerShell script to do this. This PowerShell script can read the accounts from a CSV or XLSX file and import it into Active Directory and create the mailboxes. Especially when you have a lot of mailboxes to create, it is a convenient way to use PowerShell.

Suppose you have several Mailboxes to create in your environment; a CSV that is supplied to you can be formatted as follows:

```
FirstName,LastName,DisplayName,Alias,Password,OU
Basam,Damdu,"Basam Damdu",Basam,Pass1word,"Proexchangeadmin.com/Accounts/
Users"
Commissioner,Pradier,"Commissioner Pradier",Commissioner,Pass1word,"Proexch
angeadmin.com/Accounts/Users"
Professor,Labrousse,"Professor Labrousse",Professor,Pass1word,"Proexchangea
dmin.com/Accounts/Users"
Ahmed,Nasir,"Ahmed Nasir",Pass1word,"Proexchangeadmin.com/Accounts/Users"
```

The password is supplied in clear text in the CSV file. Like the previous example, the ConvertTo-SecureString command is used to convert it to a secure string so Active Directory will accept it.

A PowerShell script that reads this CSV file can be like this:

```
Param([string]$Users)
$Database="MDB01"
$UPNsuffix="proexchangeadmin"
$Users = Import-Csv -Path C:\install\users.csv

ForEach ($user in $users)
{
  $sp = $NULL
  $upn = $NULL
  $sp = ConvertTo-SecureString -String $user.password -AsPlainText -Force
       $user.password
```

```
  $upn = $user.FirstName + "@"+ $upnSuffix
  New-Mailbox -Password $sp -Database $Database -UserPrincipalName
  $UPN -Alias $User.alias -Name $User.DisplayName -FirstName $User.
  FirstName -LastName $User.LastName -OrganizationalUnit $user.OU
}
```

The first three commands are obvious. The variables are created where the mailbox database is defined, the user principal name is created, and an array is created containing all the accounts from the CSV file.

The second step is a function that converts the clear text password into a secure string that is accepted by the New-Mailbox cmdlet.

The last step is where a new user account and mailbox are created for every user in the array. Script execution is shown in Figure 5-2.

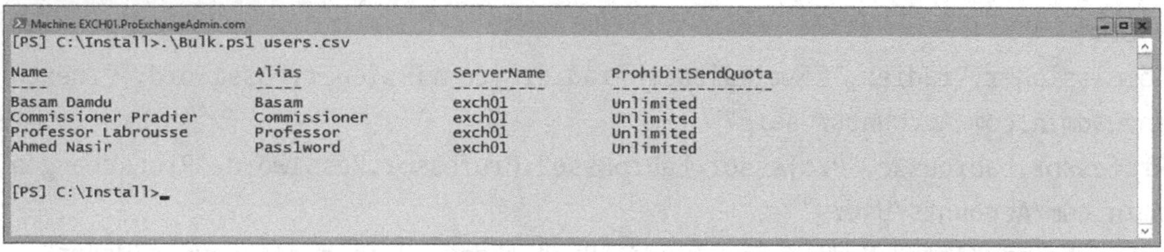

```
Machine: EXCH01.ProExchangeAdmin.com
[PS] C:\Install>.\Bulk.ps1 users.csv

Name                    Alias           ServerName      ProhibitSendQuota
----                    -----           ----------      -----------------
Basam Damdu             Basam           exch01          Unlimited
Commissioner Pradier    Commissioner    exch01          Unlimited
Professor Labrousse     Professor       exch01          Unlimited
Ahmed Nasir             Passlword       exch01          Unlimited

[PS] C:\Install>_
```

Figure 5-2. *Creating new users using a PowerShell script can be very efficient*

Remove a Mailbox

Mailboxes need to be created, and at some point, mailboxes need to be removed as well. When it comes to removing mailboxes, there are two options:

1. **The mailbox is disabled**—In this case, the mailbox is deleted, and the values of the Exchange-related properties are removed from the user account. Important to note here is that the user account in Active Directory continues to exist, so the user can still log on to Windows and Active Directory and can continue to access other resources on the network. A resource mailbox has a disabled user account associated with it, and as such a resource mailbox cannot be disabled.

2. **The mailbox is removed**—In this case, the mailbox is deleted, including the user account, from Active Directory. An archive mailbox cannot be deleted; it can only be disabled.

When a mailbox is deleted, it remains in the mailbox database until the retention time for the deleted mailbox expires. Up until this point, this mailbox is referred to as a disconnected mailbox.

To disable a mailbox, the following command can be used:

```
[PS] C:\> Disable-Mailbox -Identity "Jessy Wingo"
```

When you perform this command, a confirmation is requested. You can avoid this question by adding the `-Confirm:$false` option to the `Disable-Mailbox` cmdlet.

Removing a mailbox is like disabling a mailbox. To remove a mailbox and its accompanying user account, you enter the following command:

```
[PS] C:\> Remove-Mailbox -Identity " Jeronimo Ramirez" -Confirm:$false
```

To check if the mailbox has been deleted (or actually disconnected), you can run the following commands:

```
[PS] C:\> Get-MailboxDatabase | Get-MailboxStatistics | ?{$_.DisplayName -eq
"Jessy Wingo" } | fl DisconnectReason,DisconnectDate
```

When a mailbox is properly deleted, the DisconnectReason property will show "Disabled." Another value for the DisconnectReason is "SoftDeleted." A mailbox is soft deleted when it is moved from one mailbox database to another mailbox database. Just as when removing a mailbox, the source mailbox is deleted in the source mailbox database, and it remains there until the retention period expires.

Tip To avoid any issues with accidental removal of mailboxes, or any Exchange recipient, I always recommend enabling the Active Directory recycle bin. When enabled and an object is accidentally deleted, you can always restore it easily from the recycle bin.

Managing Mailboxes

When the new mailbox is created and during normal operation, there are certain things you must do for managing the mailboxes. Managing mailboxes can include

- Set additional properties like Company or Department.
- Set quota setting on a mailbox.
- Set regional configuration properties.
- Assign a policy to the mailbox.
- Add additional email address.
- Create an archive mailbox.
- Implement cmdlet extension agents.
- Move mailboxes.
- Import and export mailboxes to PST files.

Active Directory Properties

Properties like Company or Department are Active Directory properties and not Exchange specific. Therefore, you cannot use the Set-Mailbox cmdlet to set these. Instead, you can use the Set-User cmdlet to set them, for example:

```
PS C:\> Set-User -Identity JBrown -Company "Bookworkx" -Department "Sales"
```

Quota Settings

In Chapter 4, I explained that quota settings are put on a mailbox database. It is also possible to put quota settings on a mailbox, and these quota settings will override the mailbox database quotas. To change the quota settings for all users in, say, the BookWorkxOrganizational Unit, you can use the following command:

```
[PS] C:\> Get-Mailbox -OrganizationalUnit "BookWorkx" |
Set-Mailbox -IssueWarningQuota 10GB -ProhibitSendQuota
11GB -ProhibitSendReceiveQuota 15GB -UseDatabaseQuotaDefaults $false
```

It is important to set the `-UseDatabaseQuotaDefaults` property to $false. If you do not do this, the mailbox database quota settings are not overridden.

Regional Settings

The first time you log on to OWA, you are requested to set the time zone and to select a language. In a typical environment, these will be identical across all mailboxes. An exception could be if you are living in a dual-language country like Belgium. You would set the default time zone to "W. Europe Standard Time" and set the language to French or Dutch, depending on the location of the user. For example, for Brussels-based users, you would set it to

```
[PS] C:\> Set-MailboxRegionalConfiguration -Identity Pascal -Language
fr-FR -LocalizeDefaultFolderName  $TRUE -Timezone "W. Europe Standard Time"
```

And for Antwerp-based users, you would set it to

```
[PS] C:\> Set-MailboxRegionalConfiguration -Identity Johan -Language
nl-NL -LocalizeDefaultFolderName  $TRUE -Timezone "W. Europe Standard Time"
```

Tip If you want to get the time zone you are currently in, you can use the TZUTIL utility. Run this in a command prompt, and it will show you the current time zone of the Windows machine you are logged on to.

Assign Address Book Policies

An Exchange-specific Address Book Policy can be assigned to a mailbox using the Set-Mailbox cmdlet. If you have an Address Book Policy called "BookWorkx ABP" and you want to assign it to the JBrown mailbox, you can use the following command:

```
[PS] C:\> Set-Mailbox -Identity JBrown -AddressBookPolicy "BookWorkx ABP"
```

Note Address Book Policies are discussed in more detail later in this chapter.

Adding Email Addresses

Adding email addresses to a mailbox is a little more difficult because the EmailAddress property of a mailbox is a multivalued property; that is, this particular property can have more than one value.

If you add a value to a property, the original value is overwritten, which is something to be avoided when using multivalued properties. To change a multivalued property, add an Add or Remove option to the value. For example, to add two additional email addresses to John's mailbox, you can use the following command:

```
[PS] C:\> Set-Mailbox -Identity JBrooks -EmailAddresses @{Add="John.Brooks@
contoso.com", "John.A.Brooks@contoso.com"}
```

Removing a value from a multivalued property is similar:

```
[PS] C:\> Set-Mailbox -Identity JBrooks -EmailAddresses
@{Remove=John.A.Brooks@contoso.com}
```

Archive Mailboxes

An archive mailbox is a secondary mailbox connected to a user's primary mailbox. To create an archive mailbox, you can use the Enable-Mailbox cmdlet with the -Archive option. For example, to enable the archive mailbox to John Brook's mailbox, you can use the following command:

```
[PS] C:\> Enable-Mailbox -Identity JBrooks -Archive
```

Exchange Server will automatically provision the archive mailbox in one of the available mailbox databases; it uses the same algorithm when creating a normal mailbox. If you want to set the mailbox database manually, you can use the -ArchiveDatabase option, for example:

```
[PS] C:\> Enable-Mailbox -Identity JBrooks -Archive -ArchiveDatabase MB10
```

Cmdlet Extension Agents

Not directly related to the creation of new mailboxes but interesting enough to discuss here are the cmdlet extension agents. Using cmdlet extensions, it is possible to expand the functionality of PowerShell cmdlets and tailor them to your organizational needs.

An example of such an extension could be the automatic creation of an archive mailbox whenever a normal user mailbox is created. The scripting agent configuration is stored in the file called ScriptingAgentConfig.xml, which is stored in a directory `C:\Program Files\Microsoft\Exchange Server\V15\Bin\CmdletExtensionAgents` on the Exchange server.

Note There is a ScriptingAgentConfig.xml.sample file located in this directory that you can use as a reference.

To create a cmdlet extension that is executed when the New-Mailbox cmdlet has finished ("onComplete"), and create a new archive mailbox in the same mailbox database as the original user mailbox, you create a ScriptingAgentconfig.xml that contains the following code and store this file in the directory, as mentioned earlier:

```
<?xml version="1.0" encoding="utf-8" ?>
<Configuration version="1.0">
  <Feature Name="MailboxProvisioning" Cmdlets="New-Mailbox">
    <ApiCall Name="OnComplete">
    If($succeeded) {
      $Name= $provisioningHandler.UserSpecifiedParameters["Name"]
      If ((Get-Mailbox $Name).ArchiveDatabase -eq $null) {
        $ArchiveDatabase= (Get-Mailbox $Name).Database
        Enable-Mailbox $Name -Archive -ArchiveDatabase $ArchiveDatabase
        }
      }
    </ApiCall>
  </Feature>
</Configuration>
```

To enable the cmdlet extension agent, you run the following PowerShell command on each Mailbox server:

```
[PS] C:\> Enable-CmdletExtensionAgent "Scripting Agent"
```

The actual provisioning of the mailbox and the archive mailbox takes place on the Mailbox server, so you must copy the XML files to all Exchange servers in your Exchange environment because you never know where a specific command is executed.

When you run the New-Mailbox command, an archive mailbox is automatically created. It is not shown when the mailbox is created, but when you request the properties after creating it, they are visible as shown in Figure 5-3.

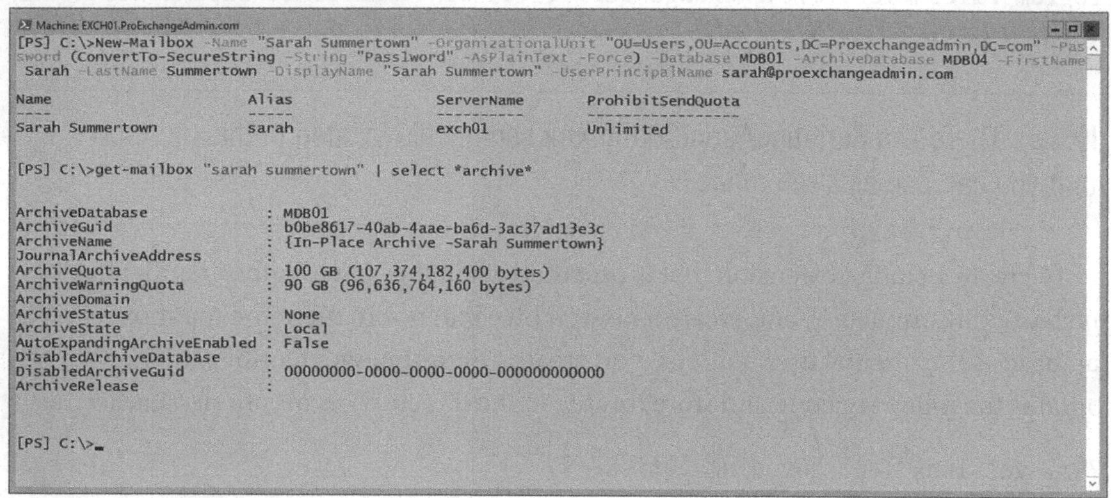

***Figure 5-3.** With the cmdlet extension, an archive mailbox is automatically created*

Mailbox Delegation

Another important item to be aware of is the *mailbox delegation,* a feature that is widely used in a manager and assistant scenario where the manager needs to grant their assistant access to their mailbox. There are three types of mailbox delegation in Exchange:

1. **Send As permission**—The assistant can send a message from the manager's mailbox. The recipient will see only the manager as the sender of the email message.

2. **Send on Behalf permission**—The assistant can send email on behalf of the manager. The recipient of the message will see that the message was sent on behalf of the manager, and the sender of the message will be shown as "Assistant on behalf of manager."

3. **Full Access permission**—The assistant has full access (read, write, edit, and delete) to all items in the manager's entire mailbox.

For example, if Philip Mortimer is a manager at BookWorkx and Sarah Summertown is his assistant, you can follow these commands to set the different permissions:

1. To grant Full Access permissions to user Sarah on Philip's mailbox using the EMS, you can use the following command:

```
[PS] C:\> Add-MailboxPermission -Identity Philip -User
Sarah -AccessRights FullAccess -InheritanceType all
```

2. To grant the Send As permission to user Sarah on Philip's mailbox using the EMS, you can use the following command:

```
[PS] C:\> Add-ADPermission -Identity Philip -User
Sarah -ExtendedRights "Send As"
```

3. To grant the Send on Behalf permission to user Sarah on Philip's mailbox using the EMS, you can use the following command:

```
[PS] C:\> Set-Mailbox -Identity Philip -GrantSendOnBehalfTo Sarah
```

When Sarah has Full Access on Philip's mailbox and opens her mailbox, Philip's mailbox will automatically appear as an additional mailbox in her Outlook. The process that is responsible for this automatic appearance is called "automapping" and is part of the Autodiscover process. Now Sarah can use her own mailbox, but when she sends an email, she can select her manager (i.e., Philip Mortimer) in the From field. When she does, and he sends a message to Professor Labrousse, the Professor sees in his mailbox the sender information as shown in Figure 5-4.

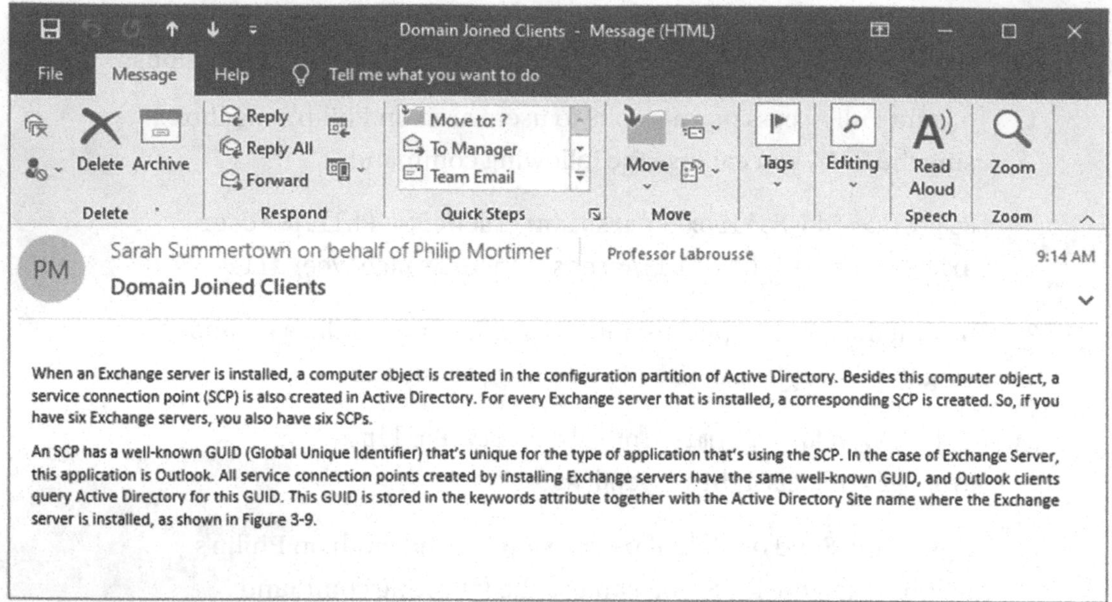

Figure 5-4. *The message Professor Labrousse sees when Sarah sends a message on behalf of her manager*

Note When a user is only granted Full Access permission to a mailbox, this user cannot send email messages from the mailbox they have been granted permission to. To achieve this, the user must have Send As or Send on Behalf permission.

Instead of assigning permissions to a Mailbox-Enabled user directly, it is also possible to assign permissions to a Security Group. When a Mailbox-Enabled user or a Mail-Enabled user is added to the Security Group, the permissions are automatically assigned.

For example, suppose there is a shared mailbox for HR staff called "HR@Proexchangeadmin.com" and there is a Security Group called "All HR Employees" where all HR staff is a member of. To assign Full Access permissions to this Security Group, execute the following command:

```
[PS] C:\> Add-MailboxPermission -Identity HR -User "All HR
Employees" -AccessRights FullAccess -InheritanceType all
```

Now when user Peter is added to this Security Group, he automatically inherits the Full Access permission on the HR mailbox.

Moving Mailboxes

There are situations where you want to move mailboxes between Exchange servers. Moving mailboxes is an online process and has little or no impact on users.

Moving mailboxes is a process taken care of by the Mailbox Replication Service or MRS, and MRS runs on every Exchange server. The name of the service is MSExchangeMailboxReplication.exe, not to be confused with the server MSExchangeRepl.exe, which is part of the Database Availability Group. This service has nothing to do with the Mailbox Replication Service.

Moving mailboxes can be

- **Local mailbox moves**—Mailboxes are moved between mailbox databases in the same Exchange organization.
- **Cross-forest moves**—Mailboxes are moved between Exchange servers in a different Exchange organization in a different Active Directory forest. Often referred to as a cross-forest migration.
- **Remote mailbox moves**—Mailboxes are moved between on-premises mailbox databases and mailbox databases in Exchange Online. This kind of mailbox move is only available in an Exchange hybrid configuration.

Moving mailboxes using the MRS can be across multiple Exchange versions as shown in Figure 5-5. Please note that Exchange 2010 can only exist in an environment with Exchange 2013 or Exchange 2016. Exchange 2010 cannot exist in an organization with Exchange 2019.

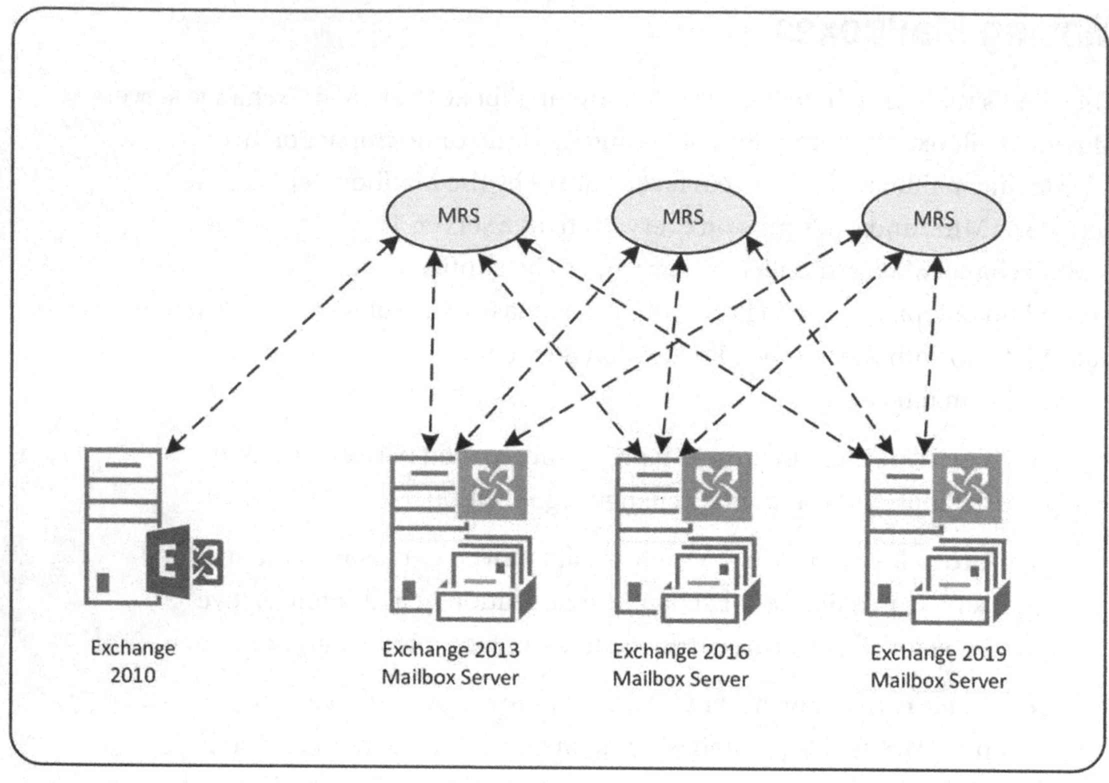

Figure 5-5. *The Mailbox Replication Service*

Besides moving mailboxes, MRS is also the process that can export and import mailboxes to PST files, and it can move public folders between different mailbox databases.

Moving mailboxes is an asynchronous process. It is triggered by the `New-MoveRequest` command and is running in the background on an Exchange server in the organization. The `New-MoveRequest` command moves mailboxes individually. It is possible to create batches with move requests, making it possible to process large amounts of mailbox moves in just one batch.

When a `New-MoveRequest` command is executed, a move request is registered in the system of the active copy of the mailbox database. MRS periodically scans this system mailbox, and when found, the MRS starts moving the mailbox. When the move request has not been picked up by the MRS, it shows the status "queued" when executing the `Get-MoveRequest` command.

While the move requests are registered in the system mailbox of the source mailbox databases, MRS itself writes status information to the Migration system mailbox (Migration.8f3e7716-2011-43e4-96b1-aba62d229136, found in every Exchange organization) to keep track of all mailbox moves, even when the original source mailbox database has been deleted.

MRS copies the mailbox content from the source database to the target database. As such, the user can continue to work with the mailbox in the source database. This is extremely useful when moving mailboxes of several gigabytes in size.

When the move reaches 95%, MRS locks the mailbox and checks the mailbox for any changes like new messages or changed messages. If any changes are found, they are copied to the new location. MRS changes the Active Directory attributes and deletes the mailbox in the source database, and Outlook continues to work with the mailbox in the new mailbox database.

Finalizing the mailbox move can be fully automatic, but it can also be scheduled using the `-CompleteAfter` option when executing a `New-MoveRequest` command. What I normally recommend is moving mailboxes during office hours but finalize the moves off-business hours. This way, the move is finalized overnight, Active Directory replication can take place, and the next morning when the user logs on, Outlook automatically connects to the "new" mailbox.

To move the mailbox of user Glenn from mailbox database MDB01 to mailbox database MDB04 on another Exchange server, and finalize it overnight, execute the following command:

```
[PS] C:\> New-MoveRequest -Identity "Glenn Kendall" -TargetDatabase
MDB04 -AllowLargeItems -BadItemLimit 10 -CompleteAfter "06/05/2021 02:00 AM"
```

When executing the `New-MoveRequest` command, a warning message is displayed:

```
WARNING: When an item can't be read from the source database or it can't be
written to the destination database, it
will be considered corrupted. By specifying a non-zero BadItemLimit, you
are requesting Exchange not copy such items to  the destination mailbox.
At move completion, these corrupted items will not be available at the
destination mailbox.
```

This is shown in Figure 5-6.

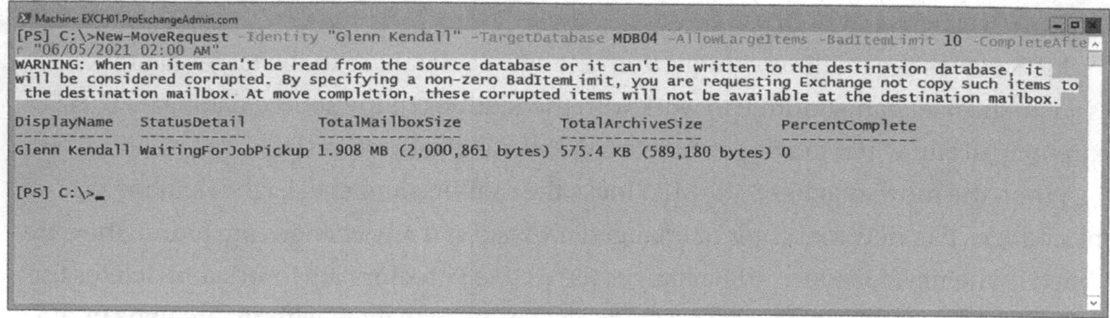

```
[PS] C:\>New-MoveRequest -Identity "Glenn Kendall" -TargetDatabase MDB04 -AllowLargeItems -BadItemLimit 10 -CompleteAfter "06/05/2021 02:00 AM"
WARNING: When an item can't be read from the source database or it can't be written to the destination database, it
will be considered corrupted. By specifying a non-zero BadItemLimit, you are requesting Exchange not copy such items to
 the destination mailbox. At move completion, these corrupted items will not be available at the destination mailbox.

DisplayName   StatusDetail         TotalMailboxSize             TotalArchiveSize           PercentComplete
-----------   ------------         ----------------             ----------------           ---------------
Glenn Kendall WaitingForJobPickup 1.908 MB (2,000,861 bytes) 575.4 KB (589,180 bytes) 0

[PS] C:\>
```

Figure 5-6. *Starting a new mailbox move*

What happens is that when MRS finds a corrupt message, it will stop moving the mailbox. When using the `-BadItemLimit` option, MRS will skip corrupted messages and continue moving the mailbox. But when the threshold is reached and another corrupt item is found, it will stop moving mailboxes.

Instead of using the `-CompleteAfter` option, it is also possible to use the `-SuspendWhenReadyToComplete` option. When this option is used and the move reaches 95%, it is automatically suspended. It can be resumed using the `Resume-MoveRequest` command. However, Microsoft does not recommend using this, and uses the `-CompleteAfter` option.

To view the status of a move request, you can use the `Get-MoveRequest` and `Get-MoveRequestStatistics` commands. When combining with the `select` command, it is possible to retrieve only specific values, for example:

```
[PS] C:\> Get-MoveRequest | Get-MoveRequestStatistics | select DisplayName,
status, BadItemsEncountered, BytesTransferred, PercentComplete
```

This will retrieve only the name of the mailbox being moved, the status of the move, the number of corrupt items that have been encountered, the number of bytes that have been moved, and the percentage of the move. This is shown in Figure 5-7.

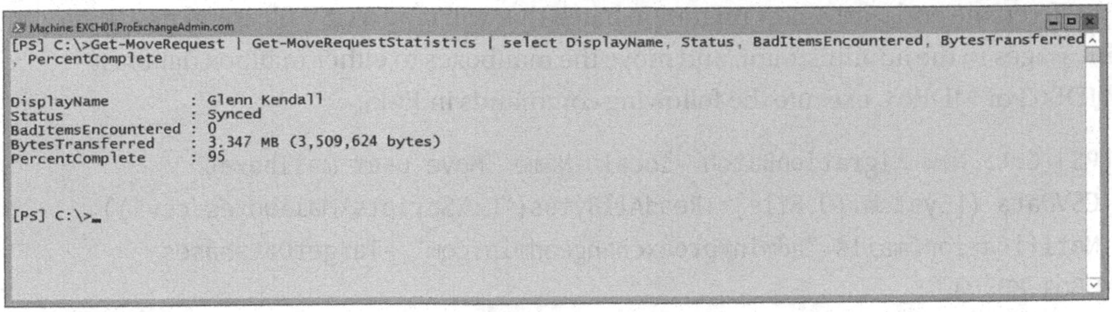

```
Machine: EXCH01.ProExchangeAdmin.com
[PS] C:\>Get-MoveRequest | Get-MoveRequestStatistics | select DisplayName, Status, BadItemsEncountered, BytesTransferred
, PercentComplete

DisplayName         : Glenn Kendall
Status              : Synced
BadItemsEncountered : 0
BytesTransferred    : 3.347 MB (3,509,624 bytes)
PercentComplete     : 95

[PS] C:\>_
```

Figure 5-7. *Retrieving statistics of a move request*

When moving mailboxes, both the primary mailbox and the archive mailbox are moved to the target database. It is possible to move the archive mailbox only using the -ArchiveOnly option. The -ArchiveTargetDatabase option can be used to locate the archive mailbox on a different mailbox database.

Note The Exchange Admin Center does not work with individual mailbox moves. Instead, migration batches are used. So, the previous example of moving one mailbox using the New-MoveRequest command does not show up in EAC.

Starting in Exchange 2013, Microsoft introduced the concept of migration batches. A migration batch is a batch of move requests that are managed as a whole. You can create a CSV file containing the individual mailboxes that must be moved and start and stop the batch with just one command. Also, the migration batch can send out notification messages with detailed information regarding the moves.

The CSV file can contain one or two columns. The first column indicates the mailbox that must be moved; the second column indicates the Mailbox type. A typical CSV file can look like this:

```
EmailAddress,MailboxType
user1@proexchangeadmin.com,Primary
user2@proexchangeadmin.com,Archive
user3@proexchangeadmin.com,PrimaryAndArchive
user4@proexchangeadmin.com,PrimaryAndArchive
```

To create and start a new migration batch that will read a CSV file, send notification messages to the administrator, and move the mailboxes to either mailbox database MDB03 or MDB04, execute the following commands in EMS:

```
[PS] C:\> New-MigrationBatch -local -Name "Move user mailboxes"
-CSVData ([System.IO.File]::ReadAllBytes("C:\Scripts\Mailboxes.csv"))
-NotificationEmails "admin@proexchangeadmin.com" -TargetDatabases
MDB03,MDB04
[PS] C:\> Start-MigrationBatch -Name "Move user mailboxes"
```

This is shown in Figure 5-8.

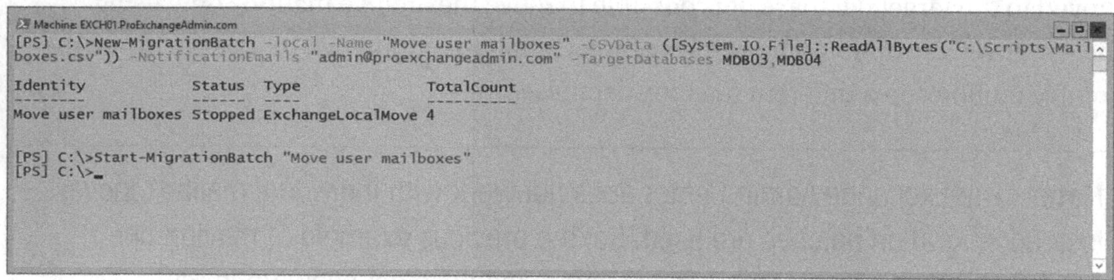

***Figure 5-8.** Create and start a new migration batch*

The replication service will send out status request messages to the recipients mentioned in the `-NotificationEmails` option. This notification message will show how long the batch is running, the number of mailboxes, and a CSV file containing details about the status of the individual mailboxes being moved. Such a notification email is shown in Figure 5-9.

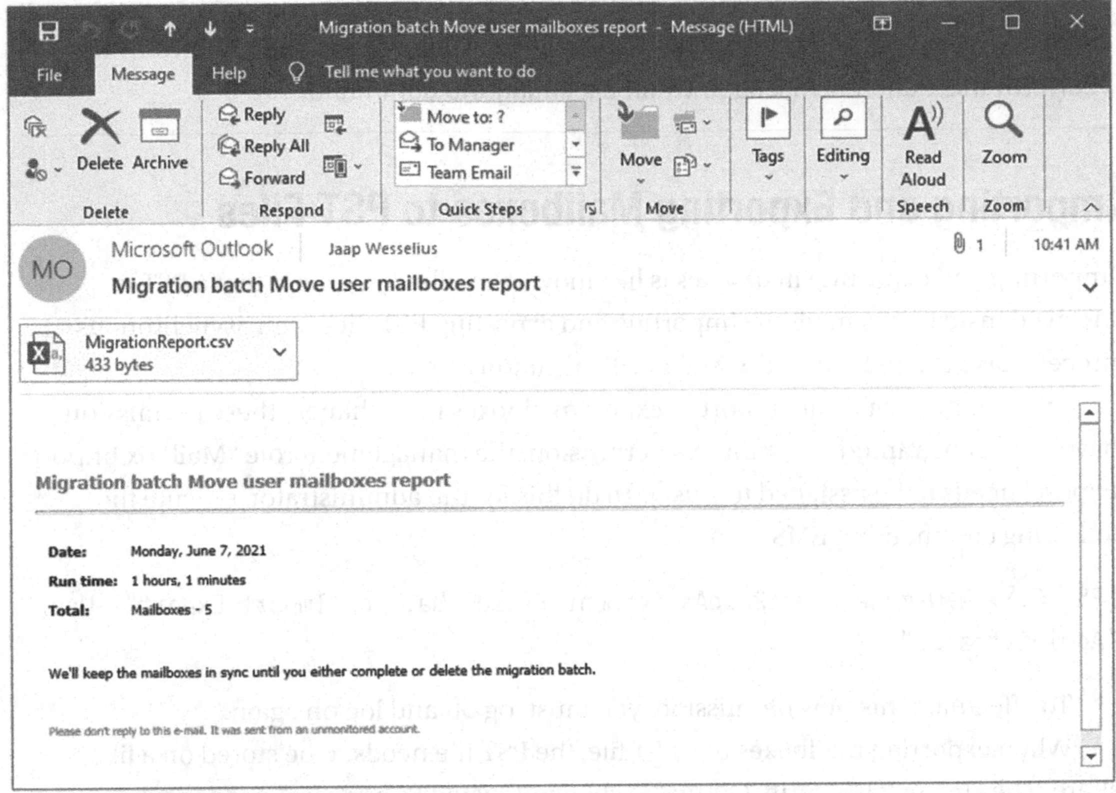

***Figure 5-9.** A notification mail is sent by the replication service*

The migration batch will trigger individual move requests, so you can check the status of the migration batch using the `Get-MigrationBatch` command, and you can check the individual moves using the `Get-MoveRequest` command. You can finalize the migration batch using the `Complete-MigrationBatch` command, which completes the entire batch, but you can also finalize individual move requests using the `Resume-MoveRequest` command.

To finalize the entire migration batch, execute the following command in EMS:

```
[PS] C:\> Complete-MoveRequest -Identity "Move user mailboxes" -Confirm:$false
```

To finalize an individual move request as part of a migration batch, use the Get-MoveRequest command to check the move you want to finalize and execute the following command in EMS:

```
[PS] C:\> Resume-MoveRequest -identity "Percy Blake" -confirm:$false
```

Note The -confirm:$false option is to suppress the "Are you sure you want to perform this action?" message when executing the command.

Importing and Exporting Mailboxes to PST Files

Importing and exporting mailboxes is like moving mailboxes, except that a PST is involved instead of a mailbox. Importing and exporting PST files is an asynchronous process, also carried out by the Mailbox Replication Service.

By default, no one can import or export mailboxes in Exchange; these permissions have not been granted. To grant this permission, the management role "Mailbox Import Export" needs to be assigned to a user. To do this for the administrator, execute the following command in EMS:

```
[PS] C:\> New-ManagementRoleAssignment -Role "Mailbox Import Export" -User
"Administrator"
```

To effectuate this new permission, you must log off and log on again.

When exporting mailboxes to a PST file, the PST file needs to be stored on a file share. The Universal Security Group "Exchange Trusted Subsystem" needs permissions on this file share. To export a mailbox to this file share, this group must have a read/write permission; to import a PST from this file share, this group must have a read permission.

To export a mailbox to the file share, execute the following command in EMS:

```
[PS] C:\> New-MailboxExportRequest -Mailbox Jaap -FilePath \\FS01\PSTFiles\
Jaap.pst
```

The `New-MailboxExportRequest` command accepts the `-BadItemLimit` and `-LargeItemItemLimit` option, like moving mailboxes to prevent halting the export when corrupt items or large items are encountered.

An interesting option when exporting mailboxes to a PST file is the `-ContentFilter` option. This option uses an OPATH filter to filter out and thus export only a specific subset of the mailbox. An example of an export where only Exchange 2016 and author information before January 1, 2018, is filtered could be

```
[PS] C:\> New-MailboxExportRequest -Mailbox Jaap -ContentFilter
"(Body -like 'Exchange 2016') -and (body -like 'author') -and (Received -lt
'01/01/2018')" -FilePath \\FS01\PSTFiles\Jaap-Exchange2016.pst
```

To export an archive mailbox to a PST file, the `-IsArchive` option can be used.

To import a PST file in a mailbox, the `New-MailboxImportRequest` command can be used. Like exporting a mailbox and moving a mailbox, this is also a functionality that is performed by the Mailbox Replication Service. To import a PST file from a file share, execute the following command in EMS:

```
[PS] C:\> New-MailboxImportRequest -Mailbox Jerome -FilePath \\FS01\
PSTFiles\Jerome.pst
```

It is possible to monitor the progress of a mailbox import or export by using the `Get-MailboxImportRequestStatistics` or `Get-MailboxExportRequestStatistics` command. By default, it does not reveal much information, but when using the Format-List command, all parameters are returned on the console. A subset of this can be returned by using the `-Select` option. To request the statistics of the previous mailbox import request, execute a command similar to

```
[PS] C:\>Get-MailboxImportRequest | Get-MailboxImportRequestStatistics | select
TargetAlias, status, BadItemsEncountered, BytesTransferred, PercentComplete
```

This is shown in Figure 5-10.

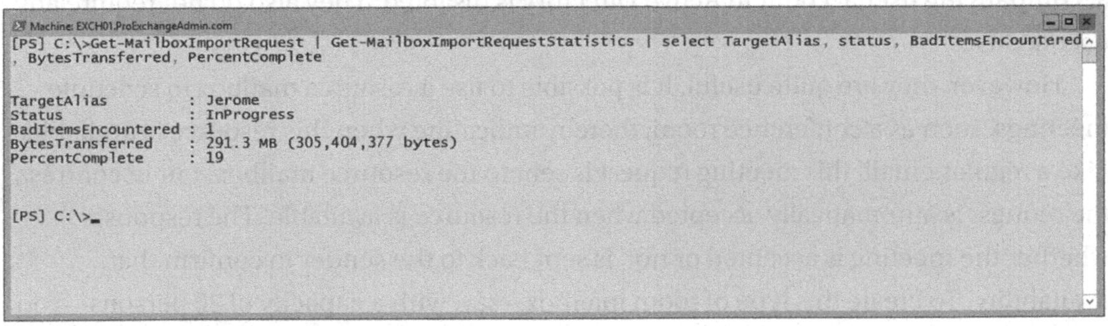

```
Machine: EXCH01.ProExchangeAdmin.com
[PS] C:\>Get-MailboxImportRequest | Get-MailboxImportRequestStatistics | select TargetAlias, status, BadItemsEncountered
, BytesTransferred, PercentComplete

TargetAlias         : Jerome
Status              : InProgress
BadItemsEncountered : 1
BytesTransferred    : 291.3 MB (305,404,377 bytes)
PercentComplete     : 19

[PS] C:\>_
```

***Figure 5-10.** Request statistics of a mailbox import request*

Importing, exporting, and moving mailboxes are limited by the hardware resources available to Exchange. When there are not enough resources available, the import, export, or move is stalled, and a status detail is shown when executing a statistics command. Most common status details are

- StalledDueToTarget_Processor
- StalledDueToTarget_DiskLatency

- StalledDueToTarget_ContentIndexing
- StalledDueToTarget_MdbReplication

While annoying and not good for performance, this is not something to worry about immediately. When resources become available again, MRS will automatically resume where it was halted.

Resource Mailboxes

A resource mailbox is a normal mailbox with the exception that it does not belong to a normal user; instead, it belongs to a resource. In Exchange, there are two types of resource mailboxes:

- **Room mailbox**—Represents a (conference) room in your office
- **Equipment mailbox**—Represents some sort of equipment, like a beamer, that's not tied to a conference room

A resource mailbox represents something that can be booked by regular users when scheduling meetings. Since these resources cannot log on to the mailbox, the accompanying user account in Active Directory is disabled. They also do not require any user licenses.

However, they are quite useful. It is possible to use a resource mailbox to schedule meetings, such as a conference room, thereby indicating when this resource is available. Like a regular email, this meeting request is sent to the resource mailbox, but in contrast, the request is automatically accepted when the resource is available. The response, whether the meeting is accepted or not, is sent back to the sender to confirm that availability. To create this type of room mailbox—say, with a capacity of 20 persons—you use the following command:

```
[PS] C:\> New-Mailbox -Room -UserPrincipalName ConfRoom2ndFloor@
Proexchangeadmin.com -Alias ConfRoom2ndFloor -Name "Conference Room 2nd
Floor" -ResourceCapacity 20 -Database "MDB01" -ResetPasswordOnNextLogon
$true -Password (ConvertTo-SecureString -String 'P@$$w0rd1' -AsPlainText -Force)
```

Creating an equipment mailbox is similar; the only difference is that there is less to configure. There is no location, no phone number, and no capacity to enter, but otherwise the process is the same. To create an equipment mailbox for a Sony Beamer, you can use the following command:

```
[PS] C:\> New-Mailbox -Equipment -UserPrincipalName SonyBeamer@
Proexchangeadmin.com -Alias SonyBeamer -Name "Sony Beamer" -Database
"MDB01" -ResetPasswordOnNextLogon $true -Password (ConvertTo-SecureString -String
'P@$$w0rd1' -AsPlainText -Force)
```

Resource mailboxes do not show up in the Exchange Admin Center under the regular mailboxes. Instead, select the Resources tab to view all resource mailboxes.

Shared Mailboxes

A shared mailbox is a mailbox that has a user account, but the user account is disabled. As such, a user cannot log on to a shared mailbox directly. To access a shared mailbox, a user must have an appropriate permission (Full Access or Send As) to use this mailbox. Once the user has Full Access, they can log on to their own mailbox and open the shared mailbox as a secondary mailbox.

A shared mailbox for the BookWorkx Sales Department could be created using the following command:

```
[PS] C:\> New-Mailbox -Shared -UserPrincipalName Sales@
Proexchangeadmin.com -Alias Sales -Name "Sales" -DisplayName "BookWorkx
Sales Department" -Database "MDB01" -OrganizationalUnit "Functional
Accounts" -ResetPasswordOnNextLogon $true -Password (ConvertTo-Secure
String -String 'P@$$w0rd1' -AsPlainText -Force)
```

To grant all users in the Accounts Organizational Unit Full Access permission for this shared mailbox, you could use the following command:

```
[PS] C:\> Get-Mailbox -OrganizationalUnit Accounts | ForEach {Add-
MailboxPermission -Identity Sales -User $_.Identity -AccessRights
FullAccess -InheritanceType all}
```

To grant all users in the Accounts Organizational Unit Send As permission for this shared mailbox, you could use the following command:

```
[PS] C:\> Get-Mailbox -OrganizationalUnit Accounts | ForEach {Add-ADPermission -Identity Sales -User $_.Identity -ExtendedRights "Send As"}
```

To check if this command was successful, you can use the following command:

```
[PS] C:\> Get-Mailbox -Identity Sales | Get-MailboxPermission | Select Identity, User, AccessRights
```

This command will show a list of all users who have permission on this mailbox, as shown in Figure 5-11.

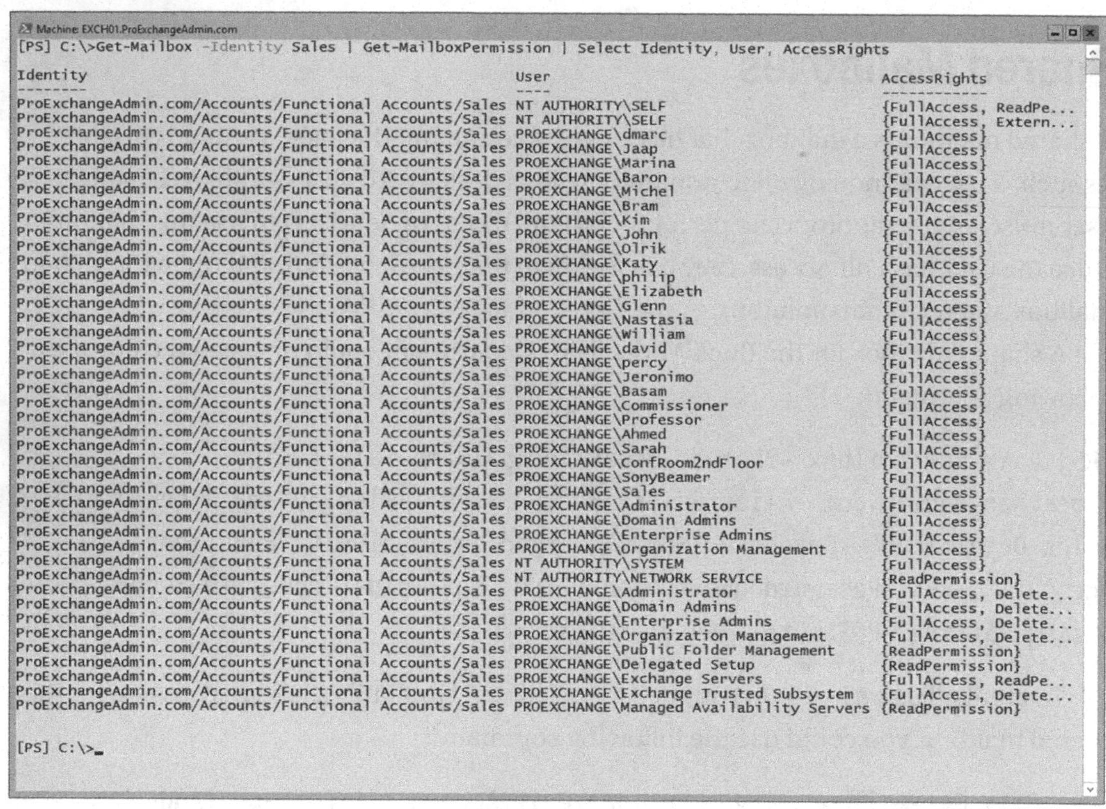

Figure 5-11. *All users who have permissions on the sales mailbox*

Linked Mailboxes

A linked mailbox differs from a regular mailbox in that it does not have an active user account in Active Directory. Instead, it is used by a normal user, and that user is created in another Active Directory forest. There is a forest trust between the forest holding the user account and the forest holding the mailboxes. Thus, the user account is linked to the mailbox. The forest that holds the Exchange servers, and thus the mailboxes, is sometimes also referred to as a resource forest. The other forest is referred to as the account forest.

A regular mailbox always has an accompanying user account, but when a linked mailbox is used, this accompanying user account is disabled. For this scenario, you need some sort of provisioning process. This is how the user account in forest A and the mailbox in forest B are linked, as can be seen in Figure 5-12. Note that the Active Directory forest A does not have any Exchange servers installed, and thus the user accounts do not have any Exchange-related properties. Since there is a trust relationship, users in forest A can log on and seamlessly access their mailboxes in forest B.

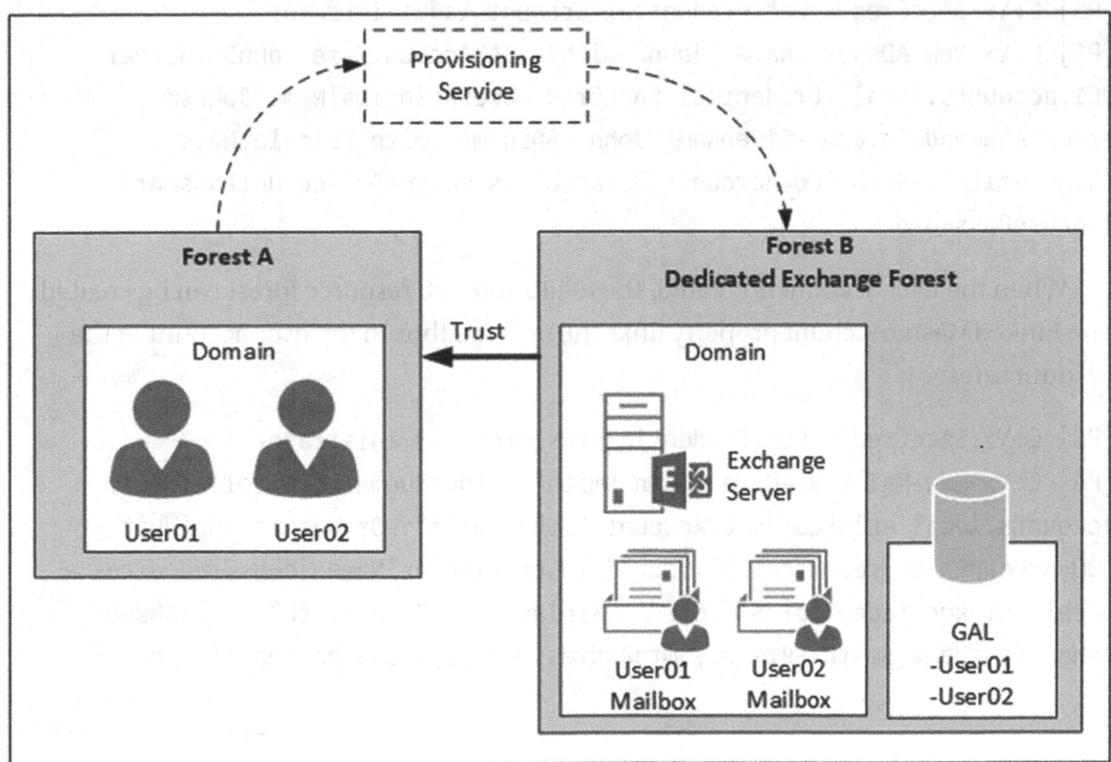

***Figure 5-12.** A linked mailbox scenario consists of an account forest A and an Exchange forest B*

The advantage of this arrangement is that it makes it possible to have multiple, fully separated Active Directory forests where the user accounts reside but have only one Exchange forest with all the mailboxes of all the (trusted) Active Directory accounts.

You may want to implement linked mailboxes if you have multiple Active Directory forests holding user accounts governed by strict security policies that do not allow multiple departments in one Active Directory forest. Using linked mailboxes makes it possible to create one Exchange environment for multiple, fully separated departments. While this might seem strange from an Active Directory point of view, when viewed from an Exchange perspective it is a fully supported scenario.

Provisioning linked mailboxes is a bit more work since it involves creating a user account in the account forest and a user account and mailbox in the resource forest.

In the following EMS commands, which are run from an Exchange 2019 server in the resource forest, a new resource mailbox is created for user John Smith. The account forest is "accounts.local", and the resource forest where Exchange 2019 is installed is "resources.local". The name of the domain controller is DC1.accounts.local.

```
[PS] C:\> $AccCred = Get-Credential accounts\administrator
[PS] C:\> New-ADUser -Name "John Smith" -SAMAccountName JohnS -Server
DC1.accounts.local -Credential $AccCred -UserPrincipalName Johns@
proexchangeadmin.com -GivenName John -Surname Smith -DisplayName
"John Smith" -Path "OU=Accounts,DC=accounts,DC=com" -AccountPassword
$SecurePassword
```

When the user account is created, the mailbox in the resource forest can be created. The LinkedMasterAccount property links the new mailbox to the user account in the account forest:

```
[PS] C:\> $AccCred = Get-Credential resources\administrator
[PS] C:\> New-Mailbox -Name "John Smith" -LinkedDomainController DC1.
accounts.local -LinkedMasterAccount "John Smith" -OrganizationalUnit
"OU=Accounts,DC=resources,DC=local" -UserPrincipalName johns@resources.
local -LinkedCredential $AccCred -DisplayName "John Smith" -FirstName
John -LastName Smith -PrimarySmtpAddress Johns@proexchangeadmin.com
```

Note These procedures have not been changed since Exchange 2010.

Distribution Groups

In Active Directory, there are two types of groups:

- **Security Group**—Used for granting permissions to users or other groups that are members of this group
- **Distribution Group**—Used for distributing email to users or other groups that are members of this group

Before Exchange can use these groups, the groups must be mail-enabled. When a group is mail-enabled, all Exchange-related properties are set, and you can start using the group for distributing email messages.

Note Both a Security Group and a Distribution Group can be mail-enabled. As such, you can use a Security Group for mail-related purposes. On the other hand, a Distribution Group cannot be used for granting permission to resources, as you can with a Security Group. If you want to grant permission to a Distribution Group, you must first convert it to a Security Group using PowerShell or the Active Directory Users and Computers (ADUC) MMC snap-in.

In Exchange, it is possible to create a new Distribution Group, as well as to mail-enable a Distribution Group or Security Group that exists in Active Directory.

In Active Directory, there are three types of groups:

- Domain local groups
- Global groups
- Universal groups

When it comes to Exchange, only universal groups are used. The primary subject of this section is the Universal Distribution Group.

Create a New Distribution Group

To create a new Distribution Group in Active Directory and automatically mail-enable it, you can use the following command:

```
[PS] C:\> New-DistributionGroup -Name "Management" -OrganizationalUnit Groups
```

To create a new Security Group in Active Directory and automatically mail-enable it, you can add the –Type Security option to the previous command:

```
[PS] C:\> New-DistributionGroup -Name "Management" -OrganizationalUnit
Groups -Type Security
```

Mail-Enable an Existing Group

An existing group in Active Directory (either Distribution Group or Security Group) can be mail-enabled as well. To do this, you can use the following command:

```
[PS] C:\> Enable-DistributionGroup -Identity AllEmployees -Alias
AllEmployees
```

If the existing group in Active Directory has a non-universal group scope, an error message is displayed saying "You can't mail-enable this group because it isn't a universal group. Only a universal group can be mail-enabled."

So, before an existing group can be mail-enabled, its group scope needs to be converted to universal. This can be achieved using the following command:

```
[PS] C:\> Set-ADGroup -Identity AllEmployees -GroupScope Universal
```

Once converted, the group can be mail-enabled.

Manage Group Membership

Adding or removing a member to a Distribution Group is straightforward. To add a member to a Distribution Group, just enter the following command:

```
[PS] C:\> Add-DistributionGroupMember -Identity AllEmployees -Member
"Colonel Olrik"
```

Removing a member from a Distribution Group is similar:

```
[PS] C:\> Remove-DistributionGroupMember -Identity AllEmployees -Member
"Colonel Olrik"
```

Instead of adding mailboxes as members of a Distribution Group, it is possible to add other Distribution Groups as a member, a process called nesting. The commands are identical. To add a Distribution Group called HR to the AllEmployees Distribution Group, you can use the following command:

```
[PS] C:\> Add-DistributionGroupMember -Identity AllEmployees -Member "HR"
```

Group Membership Approval

Users can decide whether they are members of a Distribution Group. This can be useful for special interest groups, but not for company-wide Distribution Groups. You do not want users to leave a Distribution Group like "All Employees" or to join certain Distribution Groups like "HR," for example.

The Distribution Group membership approval has the following options:

- **Open**—Anyone can join or leave the Distribution Group without approval of the group manager.
- **Closed**—No one can leave or join the group. All requests will automatically be rejected.
- **Owner approval**—The group manager must approve a request to join the group. This option is for joining only.

Note Mail-enabled Security Groups are closed.

The New-DistributionGroup cmdlet has the -MemberJoinRestriction and the -MemberDepartRestriction options to control group membership behavior. To create a new Distribution Group called "All Employees" where no users can automatically join or leave, you can use the following command:

```
[PS] C:\> New-DistributionGroup -Name "All Employees" -OrganizationalUnit
Groups -MemberDepartRestriction Closed -MemberJoinRestriction Closed
```

An interesting option is the ApprovalRequired. When this is used and a user wants to join the Distribution Group, a request message is sent to the manager or owner of the Distribution Group. For example, suppose we create a Distribution Group called "Exchange Authoring," with the ApprovalRequired set for the join restriction:

```
[PS] C:\> New-DistributionGroup -Name "Exchange Authoring" -OrganizationalUnit
Groups -MemberDepartRestriction Closed -MemberJoinRestriction
ApprovalRequired -ManagedBy proexchange\sarah
```

Now, when user Professor Labrousse wants to join this Distribution Group, a message is sent to the manager of the group, and the manager (Sarah in this example) must approve the membership request as shown in Figure 5-13.

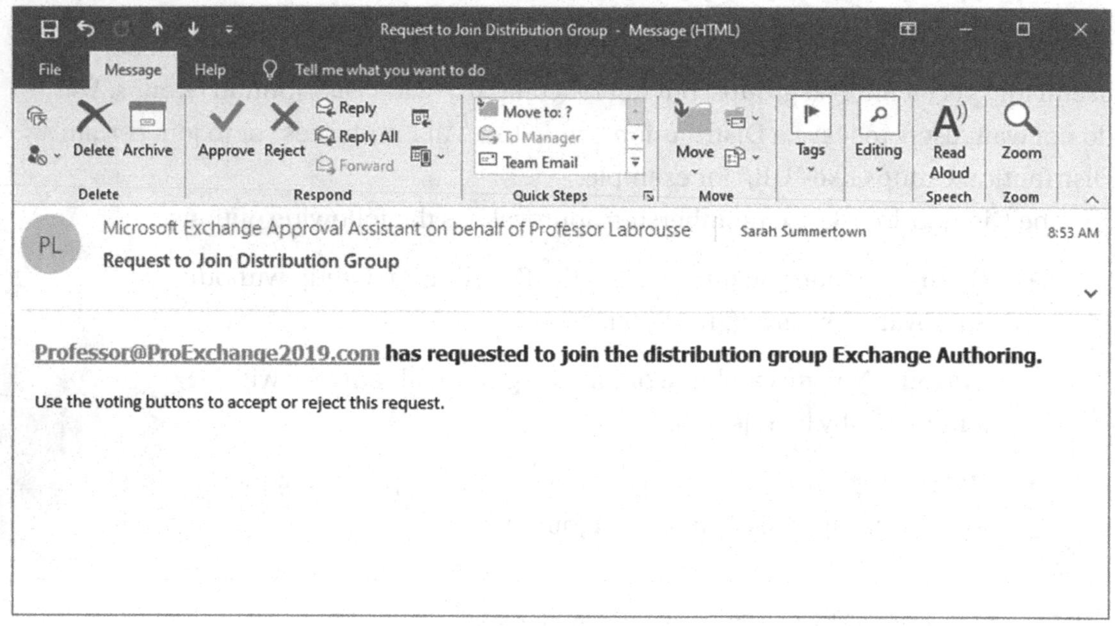

***Figure 5-13.** A request is sent to the owner of the distribution group*

Group membership for a regular Distribution Group is static: you must manually add or remove members. For large organizations, this can be quite some administrative work. Instead of using regular Distribution Groups, you can use Dynamic Distribution Groups.

Dynamic Distribution Groups

A Dynamic Distribution Group is like a regular Distribution Group, but group membership is dynamically determined, based on certain properties of the mailboxes.

For example, you can create a Dynamic Distribution Group called "All Employees" that contain all recipients (i.e., mailboxes, public folders, contacts, and other distribution groups) that have the value "ProExchangeAdmin" in their company attribute.

When the New-DynamicDistributionGroup is used, you cannot set the –ManagedBy option, although this option is shown on the console when the group is created. You must use the Set-DynamicDistributionGroup cmdlet to set this option.

To create a new Dynamic Distribution Group and set the ManagedBy option, execute the following commands in EMS:

```
[PS] C:\> New-DynamicDistributionGroup -Name "All Employees" -IncludedRecipients
AllRecipients -OrganizationalUnit Groups -ConditionalCompany
"ProExchangeAdmin"
[PS] C:\> Set-DynamicDistributionGroup -Identity "All Employees" -ManagedBy
ProExchange\Sarah
```

This is shown in Figure 5-14.

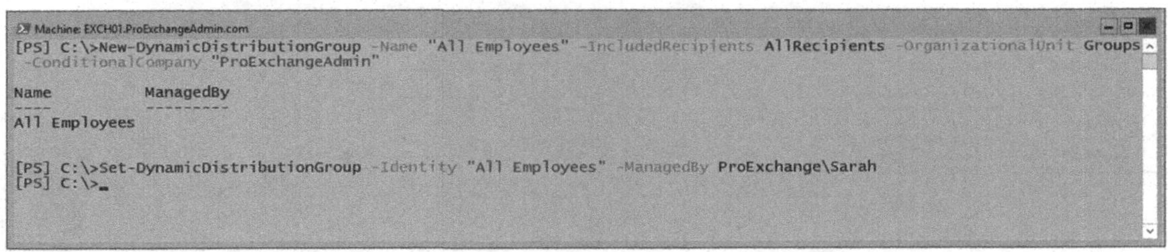

Figure 5-14. *Create a new Dynamic Distribution Group and assign a manager*

It is possible to include fewer recipients by using only the mailbox users in the –IncludedRecipients option and using the department filter instead of the company filter, for example:

```
[PS] C:\> New-DynamicDistributionGroup -Name "HR Employees" -IncludedRecipients
MailboxUsers -ConditionalDepartment "HR"
[PS] C:\> Set-DynamicDistributionGroup -Identity "HR Employees" -ManagedBy
Proexchange\Sarah
```

More granularities can be achieved by filtering on the custom attributes. In a migration scenario, you can stamp CustomAttribute1 with a value "Migrated" after a successful mailbox migration to Exchange 2019. To create a Dynamic Distribution Group that contains only mailboxes that are migrated to Exchange 2019, you can use something like this:

```
[PS] C:\> New-DynamicDistributionGroup -Name "Migrated
Mailboxes" -IncludedRecipients MailboxUsers - ConditionalCustomAttribute1
"Migrated"
[PS] C:\> Set-DynamicDistributionGroup -Identity "Migrated
Mailboxes" -ManagedBy Administrator
```

To check which mailboxes are members of a Dynamic Distribution Group, you must use the recipient filter functionality. Load the group into a variable and retrieve the recipients by using the filter, like this:

```
[PS] C:\> $HREmployees = Get-DynamicDistributionGroup "HR Employees"
[PS] C:\> Get-Recipient -RecipientPreviewFilter $HREmployees.RecipientFilter
```

This will provide a list of all recipients who are members of this Dynamic Distribution Group, as shown in Figure 5-15.

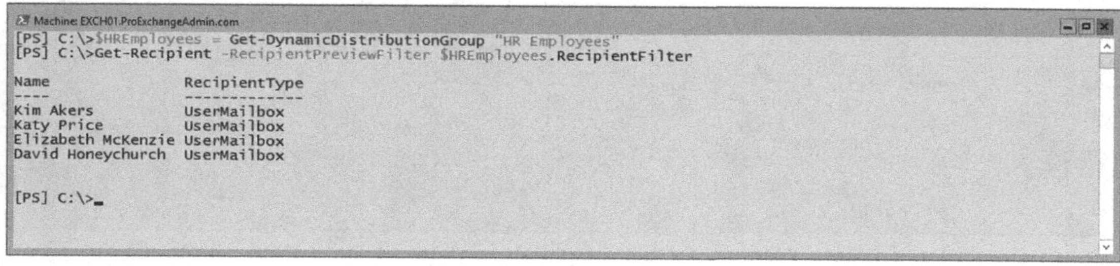

Figure 5-15. *Check dynamic group membership*

Moderated Distribution Group

A Moderated Distribution Group is a Distribution Group where messages that are intended for this group are first sent to a moderator, and the moderator approves or rejects the message. After approval, the message is sent to all members of the Distribution Group.

To use the moderation function, the Distribution Group must be enabled for moderation by employing the -ModerationEnabled option and using the -ModeratedBy option to set the moderator. These options are available on the New-DistributionGroup and the Set-DistributionGroup.

To enable moderation on a Distribution Group called "Finance" and set user Sarah Summertown as the moderator, you can use the following command:

```
[PS] C:\> Set-DistributionGroup -Identity Finance -ModerationEnabled:
$TRUE -ModeratedBy proexchange\sarah
```

When a user named Professor Labrousse, who is a member of the Finance Distribution Group, tries to send a message to members of this Distribution Group, a mail tip appears indicating the moderation of this Distribution Group, as shown in Figure 5-16.

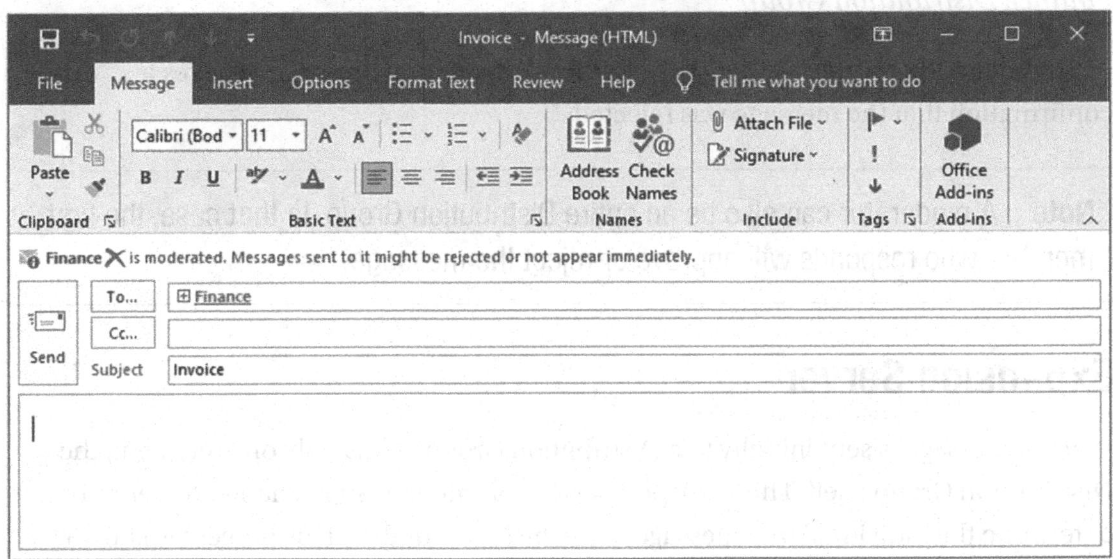

***Figure 5-16.** A mail tip is shown, indicating moderation of the message*

When the professor sends the message, a confirmation message is first sent to the moderator, that is, Sarah Summertown, who finds an approval request when she logs on to her mailbox, as shown in Figure 5-17. When Sarah approves the message, it is delivered to members of this Distribution Group.

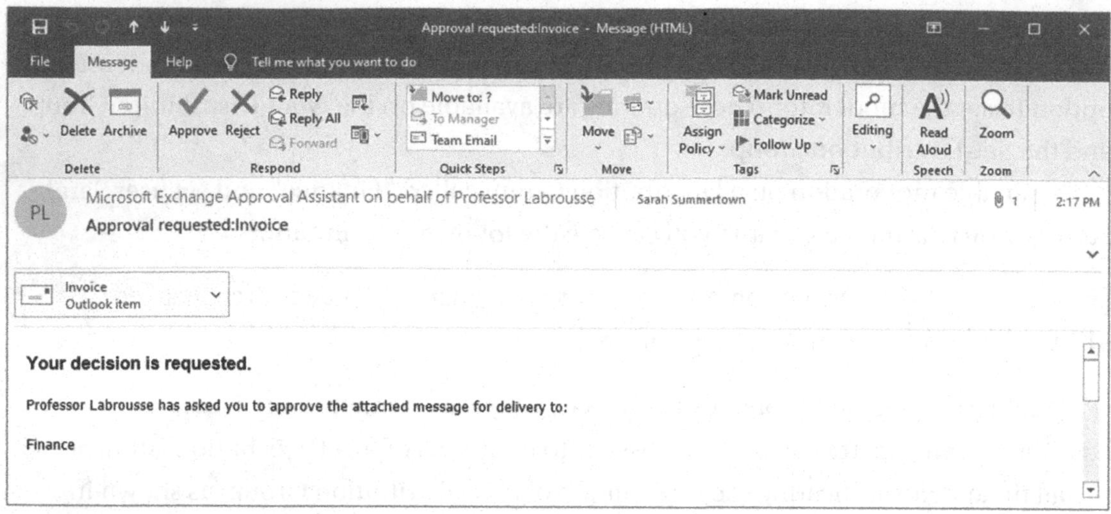

***Figure 5-17.** The moderator can either approve or reject the message sent to the Finance Distribution Group*

If the moderator rejects the message, the sender of that message receives a confirmation that the message was rejected.

Note A moderator can also be an entire Distribution Group. In that case, the first member who responds will approve or reject the message.

Expansion Server

When a message is sent initially to a Distribution Group, it has only one recipient, the Distribution Group itself. The Transport service running on an Exchange server must determine the individual that message has to be forwarded to. This process is known as expansion.

Distribution Group membership is static, based on the memberOf property of the mailboxes. Since a Dynamic Distribution Group has no membership the way a regular Distribution Group has, and thus there are no properties set, an Active Directory query is used for retrieving the members of a Dynamic Distribution Group.

An Expansion server is an Exchange 2013 Mailbox server that is responsible for expanding the Distribution Groups when it is processing messages. By default, no Expansion server is set for a Distribution Group, so any Mailbox server to which an email is delivered can perform the expansion.

Setting a dedicated Expansion server on a Distribution Group can be useful in a multi-site environment. Suppose Contoso.com has a Distribution Group in the UK with lots of members; it would make sense to use a Mailbox server at the local site for expansion purposes. This way, a message sent to this Distribution Group is dispatched to the UK before being expanded.

If the Expansion server is set, the Mailbox server accepting the message does not do any processing; it just routes the message to the Expansion server. If this server is, for some reason, not available, the message will not be delivered until the Expansion server again becomes available.

You can set the ExpansionServer property on a Distribution Group by using the following command:

```
[PS] C:\> Set-DistributionGroup -Identity "All Employees" -ExpansionServer
EXCH04
```

Note This command can be used for both Distribution Groups and Dynamic Distribution Groups.

Remove a Distribution Group

A Distribution Group can be removed as well as disabled. As with disabling mailboxes, disabling a Distribution Group retains the group in Active Directory but removes all Exchange properties, whereas removing a Distribution Group deletes the group from Active Directory as well.

To disable a Distribution Group, you can use the following command:

```
[PS] C:\> Disable-DistributionGroup -Identity "All Employees" -Confirm:$FALSE
```

To remove a Distribution Group, you can use the following command:

```
[PS] C:\> Remove-DistributionGroup -Identity "All Employees" -Confirm:$FALSE
```

Contacts

A contact in Active Directory is not a security principal, as is a user account. It cannot be used to log on to the network and access network resources, as you can with a normal user account. Instead, a contact in Active Directory can be compared to a business card in a Rolodex: you can use it to store contact information.

In Exchange, a contact can also be mail-enabled, and as such it becomes a recipient. However, a mail-enabled contact in Exchange does not have a mailbox; it does have an external email address. For internal purposes, it might also have a local address, but when messages are sent to this local address, they are routed to the contact's external address.

A mail-enabled contact also appears in the Exchange address lists, and thus it can be selected as a recipient by clients.

To create a mail-enabled contact, you can use the following command:

```
[PS] C:\> New-MailContact -ExternalEmailAddress Beau@hotmail.com -Name
"Beau Terham" -OrganizationalUnit Contacts -FirstName Beau -LastName Terham
```

When a contact already exists in Active Directory, it can be mail-enabled using the following command:

```
[PS] C:\> Enable-MailContact -Identity "Greg McGain" -ExternalEmailAddress
Greg@GMConsulting.com
```

When a user checks the All Contacts address list, all mail-enabled contacts show up, as shown in Figure 5-18. The contact can be selected for receiving an email message or for scheduling a meeting with the person, depending on the icon selected.

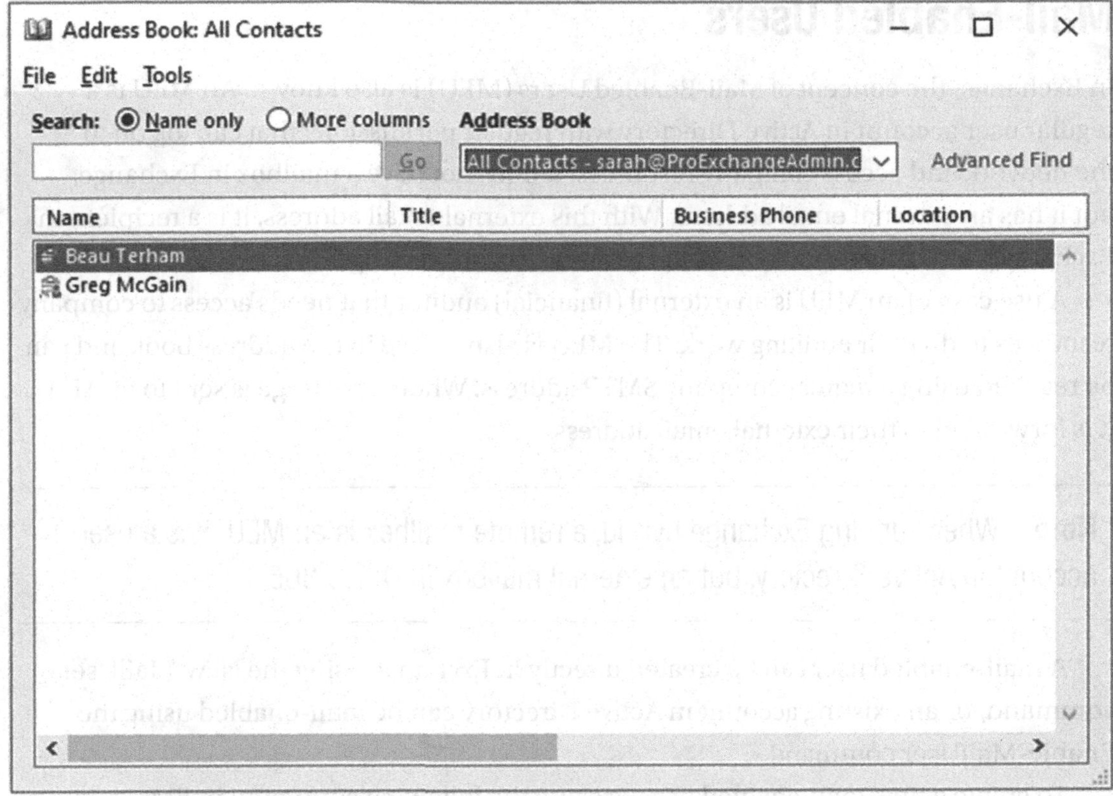

***Figure 5-18.** The mail-enabled contacts are listed in the All Contacts address list*

Mail-enabled contacts can be removed or disabled. When removed, the accompanying contact in Active Directory is deleted as well; when just disabled, the accompanying contact in Active Directory is preserved.

To disable a mail-enabled contact, you can use the following command:

```
[PS] C:\> Disable-MailContact -Identity "Beau Terham" -Confirm:$FALSE
```

To remove a mail-enabled contact, and remove the accompanying contact from Active Directory as well, you can use the following command:

```
[PS] C:\> Remove-MailContact -Identity "Greg McGain" -Confirm:$FALSE
```

Mail-Enabled Users

In Exchange, the concept of Mail-Enabled Users (MEU) is also known. An MEU is a regular user account in Active Directory with regular permissions that can log on to the network and access company resources. It does not have a mailbox in Exchange, but it has an external email address. With this external email address, it is a recipient in Exchange, and it also shows up in the address lists of Exchange.

A use case of an MEU is an external (financial) auditor that needs access to company resources to do their auditing work. The MEU is also visible in the address book and can be reached using a regular company SMTP address. When a message is sent to an MEU, it is forwarded to their external email address.

Note When running Exchange hybrid, a remote mailbox is an MEU. It is a user account in Active Directory, but an external mailbox in Office 365.

A mail-enabled user can be created directly in Exchange using the New-MailUser command, or an existing account in Active Directory can be mail-enabled using the Enable-MailUser command.

To create a new mail-enabled user, execute the following command in EMS:

```
[PS] C:\> New-MailUser -Name "External Auditor" -ExternalEmailAddress
ExternalAuditor@gmail.com -PrimarySMTPAddress ExternalAuditor@proexchangeadmin.
com -DisplayName "External Auditor" -FirstName External -LastName
Auditor -OrganizationalUnit "Functional Accounts" -Password
(ConvertTo-SecureString -String 'P@$$w0rd1' -AsPlainText -Force)
```

To mail-enable an existing Active Directory account, execute the following command in EMS:

```
[PS] C:\> Enable-MailUser -Identity "Financial Auditor"
-ExternalEmailAddress FinancalAuditor@gmail.com -PrimarySMTPAddress
FinancialAuditor@proexchangeadmin.com
```

Once created, the mail-enabled accounts appear in the Exchange address book as shown in Figure 5-19.

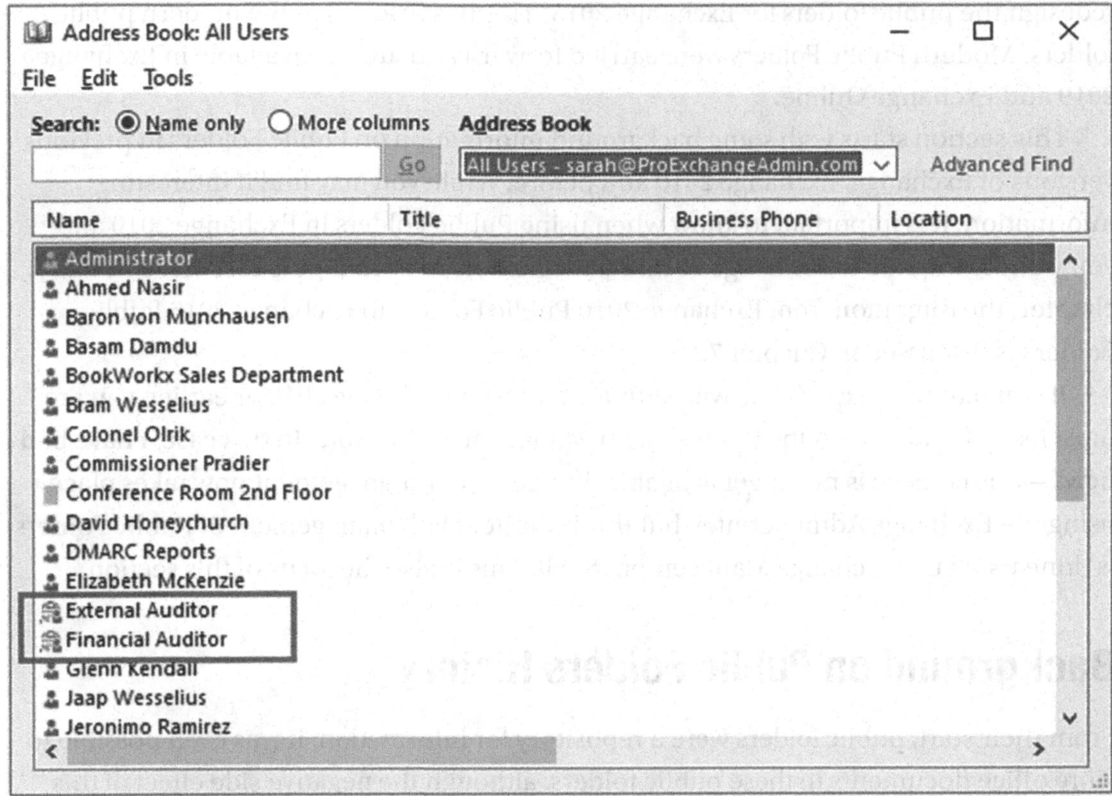

***Figure 5-19.** The mail-enabled users show up in the Address Book of Exchange*

Note The names mailbox-enabled user and mail-enabled user are often confusing. The first one is an account in Active Directory with a mailbox in Exchange; the second is an account in Active Directory without a mailbox but with an external email address.

Modern Public Folders

Public folders have been around since the first version of Exchange Server, back in 1996. These are another repository of information where messages, appointments, or contacts can be stored and shared among recipients. Starting with Exchange Server 2007, Microsoft decommissioned the public folders, a decision that was not popular with Exchange customers; after endless debate, Microsoft decided to restore and completely redesign the public folders for Exchange 2013. This has resulted in the modern public folders. Modern Public Folders were carried forward and are still available in Exchange 2019 and Exchange Online.

This section starts with some background information on Public Folders in previous versions of Exchange, Exchange 2010 and before. While you may find it interesting information, it is important to know when using Public Folders in Exchange 2010 and you want to migrate to Exchange 2016. Public Folders in Exchange is discussed in this chapter; the migration from Exchange 2010 Public Folders to Exchange 2016 Public Folders is discussed in Chapter 7.

If you have any experience with Public Folders in Exchange 2010 or earlier, you are most likely familiar with the Public Folder Management Console. In this case, I have bad news—this console is no longer available. Public Folder management now takes place using the Exchange Admin Center, but this is limited. Full management of Public Folders is done using the Exchange Management Shell. This is also the focus of this section.

Background on Public Folders History

From their start, public folders were a repository for information; it was even possible to store office documents in these public folders, although the negative side effect of this capability was the problem of ever-growing public folders.

These public folders used to have their own databases, called public folder databases. The databases were the same as mailbox databases, using the same ESE database technology and managed by the same Information Store. Only the database schema and the information inside the database were different. The public folder databases also had their own replication mechanism, making it possible to create multiple databases with the same information and thus offering database redundancy. And to make these folders even more compelling, they used a multi-master replication technology, so that it was possible to make changes to documents on different servers, with the two copies in sync.

The public folders consisted of two parts:

- **The hierarchy**—This is the structure of the items kept in the public folder database, or how and where the individual items are stored in the folders. The hierarchy is similar to a directory structure on a local hard disk, with all its folders and subfolders. In public folders, you can set permissions on the folders, making it possible to create a departmental information solution—for example, where only employees of the accompanying department can view the information contained in the designated folder.

- **The content**—This is the actual information that is stored in the public folders.

The hierarchy is an entity, and the entire folder structure is stored in the hierarchy. The hierarchy is then replicated across all public folder databases, including all public folders and their permissions. When a new public folder database is created, the hierarchy needs to be replicated to this new database before the database can be used.

There are two types of folders in a traditional public folder database:

- **System folders**—These are system-generated folders that contain free/busy information and the Offline Address Book. The system folders are used by older Outlook clients—Outlook 2003 and earlier. Without the system folders, these older Outlook clients would not even be able to get started! When using Outlook 2003 or earlier, the calendaring information is stored locally and published every 15 minutes to the free/busy folder on the Exchange server. The Offline Address Book is generated once a day, typically in the middle of the night, and stored in the Offline Address Book folder. Outlook clients then download a copy of the Offline Address Book during business hours.
- **Public folders**—These are the normal public folders where recipients can store information, where permissions are set, and whose contents can be replicated across multiple public folder databases.

Public folder replication is set on a per-folder basis; this means that data from one server can be replicated to a second Exchange server, while data from another server can be replicated to a third Exchange server, making it possible to create a flexible, distributed, and powerful information solution.

For accessing public folder information, Outlook would connect directly to the Exchange 2010 Mailbox server hosting the public folder database, whereas the same Outlook client would connect to the RPC Client Access service running on the Exchange 2010 CAS to retrieve information from the inbox. So, one Outlook client connects in two different ways. Using the RPC Client Access service running on multiple Exchange 2010 CAS servers created a redundant connection mechanism, something that was not possible for the public folders. There can be multiple copies of a particular public folder on multiple public folder databases, but there is no automatic failover mechanism built into the “old” public folder solution. However, this situation was corrected in Exchange Server 2010 SP2 RU2, when an alternative server tag was introduced. This alternative server tag introduced a public folder failover function.

The bad thing is that there was not much development involving public folders after the early 2000s. As mentioned earlier, by Exchange Server 2007, Microsoft had started to decommission the public folders. However, in the development phase of Exchange 2013, Microsoft decided to reinstate the public folders. At that point, they decided to completely rewrite the public folder architecture and bring it back to life.

Modern Public Folders in Exchange

The basic idea behind the public folders has not changed. There still is a hierarchy containing the public folder structure, and there still is the actual content that is stored in the public folders. However, the completely redesigned public folders no longer use a separate public folder database; the public folders are now stored in mailbox databases. This makes it possible to do the following:

- Use the Client Access Front End (CAFE) to access the public folder information, offering redundancy on the way clients connect to public folders.
- Use the database availability group (DAG) for redundancy on the public folder and mailbox database level, as discussed in the previous chapter.

The hierarchy in Exchange modern public folders is now stored in a new type of mailbox: the public folder mailbox. If new public folders are created, they are stored in the hierarchy in this public folder mailbox. It is possible to create multiple hierarchies in an Exchange environment, but there is only one primary or master public folder mailbox (also referred to as the primary hierarchy mailbox). The public folder mailbox is stored in a normal mailbox database, which can be identified during creation of the public folder database. For redundancy, this mailbox database can be in a database availability group, but it is important to note that there is only one writeable copy of the public folder mailbox.

Once the hierarchy mailbox is created, the public folders can be created, and permissions can be assigned to these new public folders.

Create Public Folders

By default, Public Folders are not configured on Exchange 2013, 2016, or 2019. When deploying Public Folders in your Exchange organization, the first step is to establish the public folder settings on the organizational level in Exchange, and then create a new hierarchy located in a public folder mailbox.

To check the Public Folder settings on an organizational level, execute the following command in EMS to retrieve a list of all settings:

```
[PS] C:\>Get-OrganizationConfig | select *public*

DefaultPublicFolderAgeLimit                  :
DefaultPublicFolderIssueWarningQuota         : Unlimited
DefaultPublicFolderProhibitPostQuota         : Unlimited
DefaultPublicFolderMaxItemSize               : Unlimited
DefaultPublicFolderDeletedItemRetention      : 30.00:00:00
DefaultPublicFolderMovedItemRetention        : 7.00:00:00
PublicFoldersLockedForMigration              : False
PublicFolderMigrationComplete                : False
PublicFolderMailboxesLockedForNewConnections : False
PublicFolderMailboxesMigrationComplete       : False
PublicFolderShowClientControl                : False
PublicFoldersEnabled                         : Local
PublicComputersDetectionEnabled              : False
RootPublicFolderMailbox                      :
RemotePublicFolderMailboxes                  : {}
```

By default, the sizing quotas for public folders are set to unlimited, and the deleted item retention and moved item retention are set to 14 days. Organizational settings can be set only using the EMS, so to change these settings and reflect your company's standards, open Exchange Management Shell and execute the following commands:

```
[PS] C:\> Set-OrganizationConfig -DefaultPublicFolderIssueWarningQuota
1.9GB -DefaultPublicFolderProhibitPostQuota 2.3GB -DefaultPublicFolderMaxItemSize
200MB -DefaultPublicFolderDeletedItemRetention 30.00:00:00 -Default
PublicFolderMovedItemRetention 30.00:00:00
```

The first step to create a public folder infrastructure is to create a primary hierarchy mailbox. In this example, the hierarchy mailbox will be in mailbox database MDB01, and the accompanying user account will be in the OU=Functional Accounts in Active Directory:

```
[PS] C:\> New-Mailbox -PublicFolder -Name PFHierarchy -OrganizationalUnit
"Functional Accounts" -Database MDB01
```

A warning message may appear that not all functionality is available immediately, but you can safely ignore this message and wait for some time for replication to complete.

When the public folder mailbox is created, you can create content public folders. To create a new public folder called "HQ," execute the following command:

```
[PS] C:\> New-PublicFolder -Name HQ -Path \
```

The Public Folder will be in the PFHierarchy mailbox that was created in the previous step. It is also possible to use dedicated mailboxes to distribute the Public Folders among. When using a large Public Folder infrastructure, this will have a positive effect on performance.

To create new public folders called "Marketing," "Sales," and "HR" under the HQ folder, execute the following commands:

```
[PS] C:\> New-PublicFolder -Name Marketing -Path \HQ
[PS] C:\> New-PublicFolder -Name Sales -Path \HQ
[PS] C:\> New-PublicFolder -Name HR -Path \HQ
```

Move Public Folders

In the previous section, the Public Folders were automatically created in the hierarchy mailbox. When hosting a lot of Public Folders or when Public Folders grow big, it makes sense to use dedicated mailboxes for this. When using multiple Public Folder mailboxes on multiple mailbox databases, maybe even on multiple Exchange servers, you can distribute the load among these servers, thereby improving performance.

Public Folders can be moved as individual Public Folders or as an entire subtree of Public Folders. For the first option, the `New-PublicFolderMoveRequest` can be used; for the latter, Microsoft supplies a script, available in the $Exscripts directory, to achieve this.

Like moving mailboxes and exporting/importing mailboxes, moving Public Folders is an asynchronous process executed by the Mailbox Replication Service.

To move a single Public Folder to a new Public Folder mailbox, execute the following command in EMS:

```
[PS] C:\> New-PublicFolderMoveRequest -Folders \Information\Newsletters\
Petri -TargetMailbox PF1
```

The -Folders option accepts multiple values, so to move two Public Folders to another Public Folder mailbox, execute the following command:

```
[PS] C:\> New-PublicFolderMoveRequest -Folders \Information\Newsletter\
Petri, \Information\Newsletter\Microsoft -TargetMailbox PF1
```

Like moving mailboxes, the New-PublicFolderMoveRequest command accepts the `-AllowLargeItems` and `-BadItemLimit` options. When the finalization should be done off business hours, you can use the `-SuspendWhenReady` to complete option. Once suspended, you can finalize the Public Folder move using the Resume-PublicFolderMoveRequest command. By default, a Public Folder move request gets a name "PublicFolderMove." However, when executing the New-PublicFolderMoveRequest, you can assign any name you like using the -Name option.

To finalize a Public Folder migration request, execute the following command:

```
[PS] C:\> Resume-PublicFolderMoveRequest -Identity PublicFolderMove
```

If you want to move an entire tree or branch of Public Folders to another Public Folder mailbox, you can use a Microsoft script for this. The `Move-PublicFolderBranch` script was created for this purpose, and this script can be found in the Exchange server script directory. To move a complete tree of Public Folders using this script, execute the following commands:

```
[PS] C:\> CD $ExScripts
.\Move-PublicFolderBranch.ps1 -FolderRoot \Information -TargetPublicFolder
Mailbox PF1
```

Public Folder Permissions

By default, users do not have permissions on Public Folders, so you need to grant these permissions using the `Add-PublicFolderClientPermission` command in EMS. This command takes the Public Folder, the user, and the permissions as input.

As for the permissions, the roles listed in Table 5-1 are available.

***Table 5-1.** Overview of Roles and Permissions for Public Folders*

Role	Create Items	Read Items	Create Folders	Folder Owner	Folder Contact	Folder Visible	Edit Owned Items	Edit All Items	Delete Owned Items	Delete All Items
None						X				
Owner	X	X	X	X	X	X	X	X	X	X
Publishing Editor	X	X	X			X	X	X	X	X
Editor	X	X				X	X	X	X	X
Publishing Author	X	X	X			X	X		X	X
Author	X	X				X	X		X	
Non-editing Author	X	X				X				
Reviewer		X				X				
Contributor	X					X				

So, full access to a public folder corresponds to the Publishing Editor role, so to grant user Sarah full access to the Marketing public folder, execute the following command:

```
[PS] C:\> Add-PublicFolderClientPermission -Identity \HQ\Marketing -User
Sarah -AccessRights PublishingEditor
```

Likewise, to remove these permissions, you can use the `Remove-PublicFolderClientPermission` command. To remove all access for user Sarah on the Marketing public folder, execute the following command:

```
[PS] C:\> Remove-PublicFolderClientPermission -Identity \HQ\Marketing -User
Sarah
```

Mail-Enable Public Folders

Public Folders appear automatically in Outlook, and when granted appropriate permissions, users can post items in Public Folders. It is also possible to mail-enable Public Folders so users can send messages to a Public Folder. Public Folders will accept both internal and external messages.

To mail-enable a Public Folder, execute the following command in EMS:

```
[PS] C:\> Enable-MailPublicFolder -Identity \HQ\Marketing
```

When executing this command, a special Public Folder object is created in the OU=Microsoft Exchange System Objects container in Active Directory as shown in Figure 5-20.

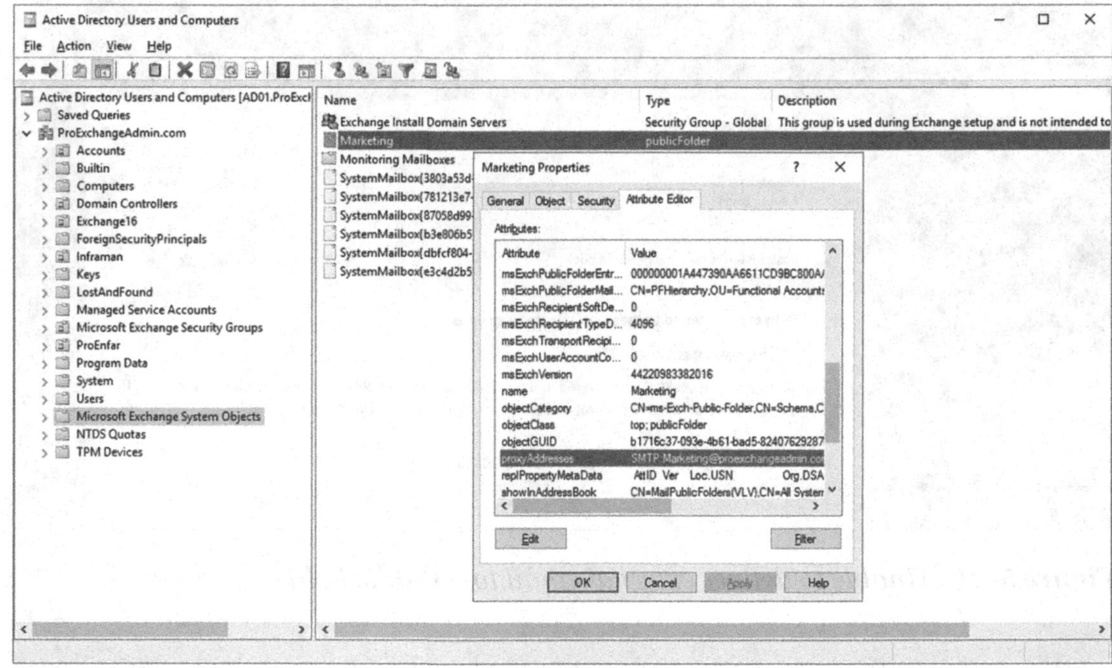

Figure 5-20. *An object is created in Active Directory when mail-enabling a Public Folder*

Note You must enable "Advanced Features" under the "View" menu in Active Directory Users and Computers MMC snap-in to see the hidden objects.

This object holds all Exchange-specific attributes for the Public Folder and is shown using the `Get-MailPublicFolder` command. Be aware that when a Public Folder is mail-enabled, the `Get-PublicFolder` no longer works for this Public Folder. Instead, the `Get-MailPublicFolder` must be used.

By default, when a Public Folder is mail-enabled, it only accepts internal messages. External messages are blocked with the following message: "Your message could not be delivered to a public folder because delivery to this address is restricted to authenticated senders" as shown in Figure 5-21.

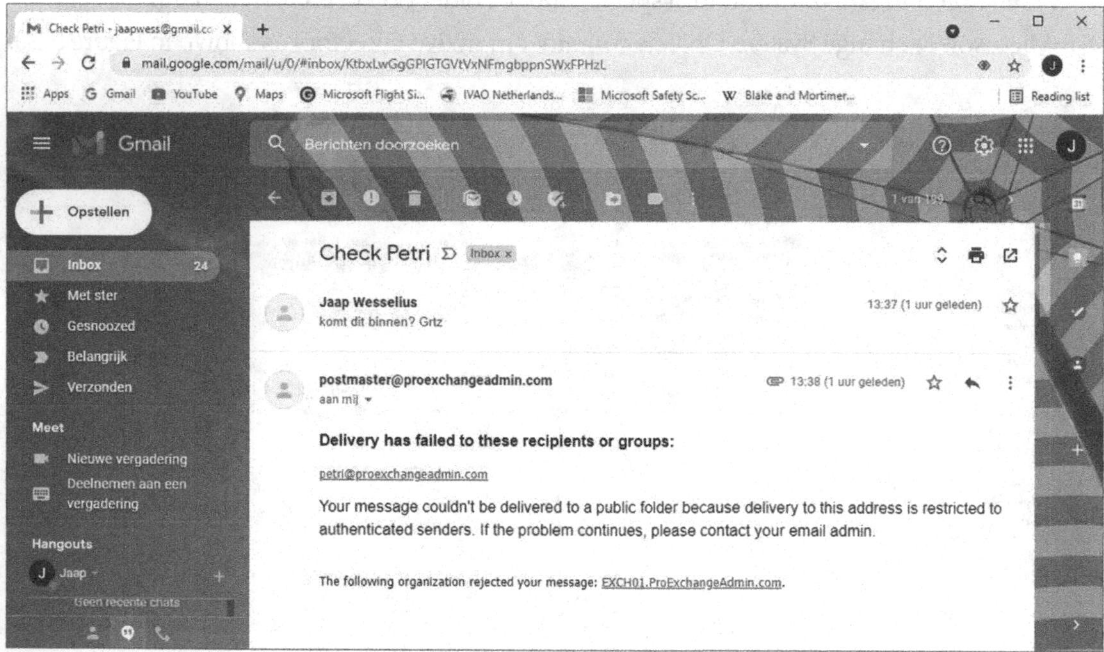

***Figure 5-21.** Unable to deliver external email to a Public Folder*

Anonymous delivery is restricted on Public Folders. To solve this, anonymous must have the minimum set of permissions to deliver messages to the Public Folder, which is the "create items" set. To set these permissions, execute the following command in EMS:

```
[PS] C:\ >Get-MailPublicFolder Petri | Add-PublicFolderClientPermission -User
Anonymous -AccessRights CreateItems
```

After executing, the Public Folder will also accept external email.

Public Folders and Clients

Public Folders appear semi-automatic in Outlook clients. Outlook will discover public folders automatically, but they are not shown by default. When you click the three dots in the left-hand pane and select folders, Public Folders will appear as shown in Figure 5-22.

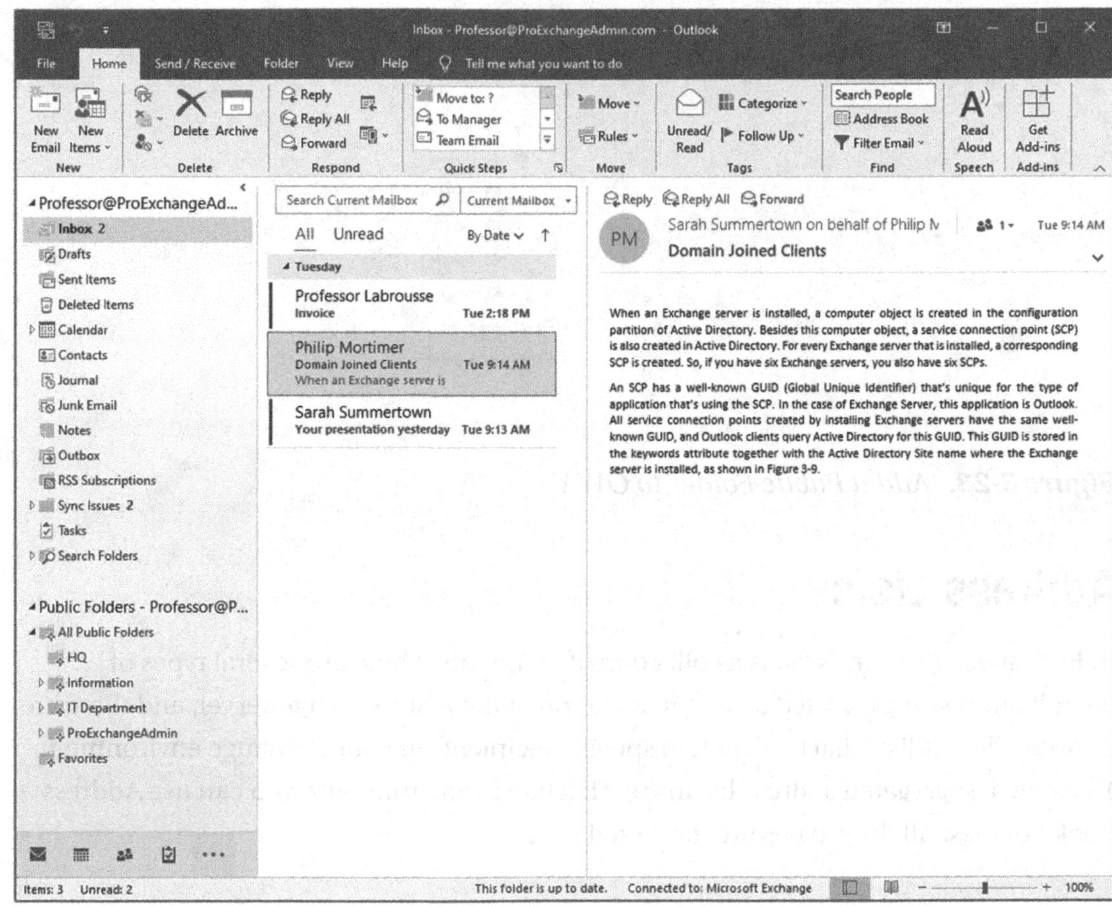

Figure 5-22. *Public Folders appear semi-automatic in Outlook*

Public Folders and OWA

To access Public Folders in OWA, right-click Favorites and click "Add Public Folders to Favorites." An additional window is shown in OWA, listing the available Public Folders as shown in Figure 5-23. Select a Public Folder and click "Add to favorites." The folder is now added to favorites and ready to use.

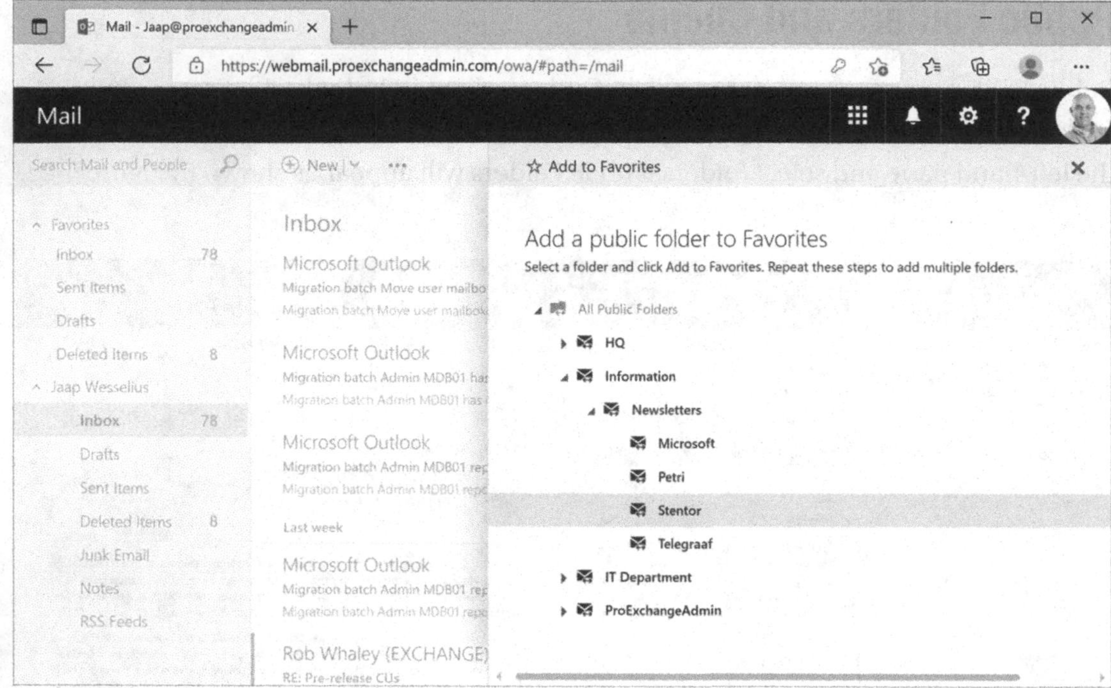

Figure 5-23. Add a Public Folder to OWA

Address Lists

In Exchange, an address list is a collection of recipients. There are several types of default address lists created during installation of the first Exchange server, and there are custom address lists that can contain specific recipients in your Exchange environment. To create a segregated address list in your Exchange environment, you can use Address Book Policies. All three types are discussed next.

Default Address Lists

There are multiple types of default address lists:

- **All Users**—An address list that contains all mailbox-enabled users in the Exchange environment.
- **All Rooms**—An address list that contains all resource mailboxes of the type "Room" in the Exchange environment.

- **All Distribution Lists**—An address list that contains all mail-enabled Distribution Groups in the Exchange environment. This includes both Distribution Groups and Security Groups.
- **All Contacts**—An address list that contains all mail-enabled contacts in the Exchange environment.
- **Default Global Address List (GAL)**—An address list that contains all recipients in the Exchange environment. The GAL is automatically created by Exchange during installation.
- **Public Folders**—An address list that contains all public folders in the Exchange environment.

Address lists are dynamically generated, so clients need to be online with the Exchange server to view the various address lists. To overcome this obstacle, especially for Outlook clients running in cached mode, there is an Offline Address Book (OAB) that contains the information in the Default Global Address List. Outlook clients can download this OAB to use when they are not connected to the network and thus are not connected to the Exchange server.

Custom Address Lists

It is possible to create custom address lists, tailored to the needs of your organization. Very large organizations with large departments can especially benefit from having custom address lists. One example that comes to mind is a large university, where custom address lists exist for every department's faculty. Similarly, large corporations use multiple customer address lists.

For example, suppose ProExchangeAdmin.com has three large departments: RND, Production, and Sales. A manager might want to create an address list for each department. Custom address lists can be based on organizational units in Active Directory, but it is recommended that you use an Active Directory attribute to differentiate the address lists. To create address lists based on the department attribute, you can use the following commands:

```
[PS] C:\> New-AddressList -Name "RND All Users Address List"
-ConditionalDepartment RND -IncludedRecipients MailboxUsers
```

```
[PS] C:\> New-AddressList -Name "Production All Users Address
List" -ConditionalDepartment Production -IncludedRecipients MailboxUsers
[PS] C:\> New-AddressList -Name "Sales All Users Address
List" -ConditionalDepartment Sales -IncludedRecipients MailboxUsers
```

The -ConditionalDepartment and -IncludedRecipients options are automatically converted to a recipient filter, as shown in Figure 5-24.

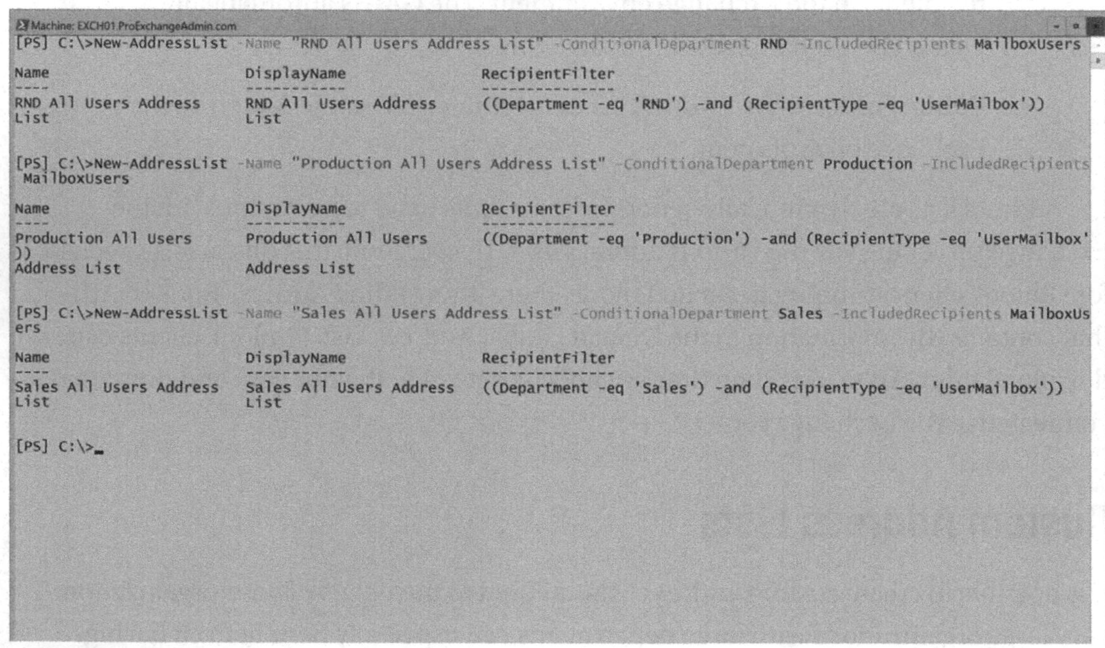

***Figure 5-24.** Creating an address list of the RND Department*

Checking the membership of an address list is similar to checking the membership of a Dynamic Distribution Group. You read the address list into a variable and filter out the recipients:

```
[PS] C:\> $AL = Get-AddressList "RND All Users Address List"
[PS] C:\> Get-Recipient -RecipientPreviewFilter $AL.RecipientFilter
```

All members in the address list are shown on the console, as can be seen in Figure 5-25.

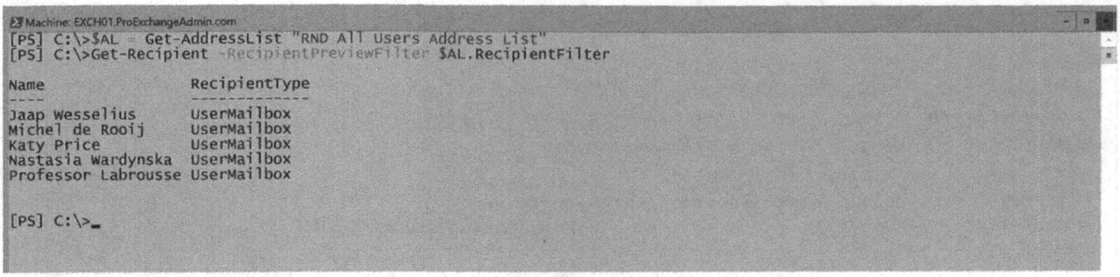

```
Machine: EXCH01.ProExchangeAdmin.com
[PS] C:\>$AL = Get-AddressList "RND All Users Address List"
[PS] C:\>Get-Recipient -RecipientPreviewFilter $AL.RecipientFilter

Name                 RecipientType
----                 -------------
Jaap Wesselius       UserMailbox
Michel de Rooij      UserMailbox
Katy Price           UserMailbox
Nastasia Wardynska   UserMailbox
Professor Labrousse  UserMailbox

[PS] C:\>_
```

Figure 5-25. *Members of a custom address list*

The newly created custom address lists haven't been applied or updated yet; this means they exist in Active Directory, are shown in a client like OWA, but they do not return any mailboxes yet. To apply these new address lists, you enter the following commands:

```
[PS] C:\> Update-AddressList -Identity "RND All Users Address List"
[PS] C:\> Update-AddressList -Identity "Production All Users Address List"
[PS] C:\> Update-AddressList -Identity "Sales All Users Address List"
```

Now, when a user in the RND Department checks the RND address list, they will see all users with this department property correctly displayed, as shown in Figure 5-26.

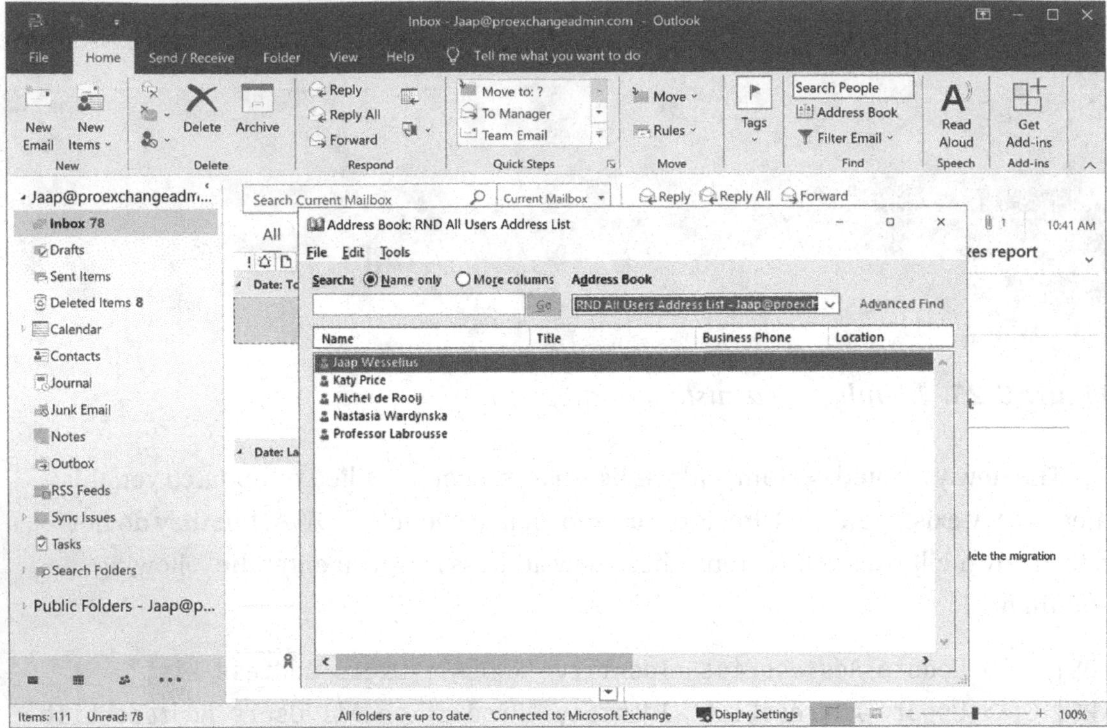

***Figure 5-26.** The department address list shows the correct recipients*

It is possible to create address lists that contain other recipients than mailboxes; you can do this using the `-IncludedRecipients` option. The following values are available for the `-IncludedRecipients` option:

- None
- MailboxUsers
- MailUsers
- Resources
- MailGroups
- MailContacts
- AllRecipients

Instead of using the `-IncludedRecipients` option, you can use the `-RecipientFilter` option. Using the `-RecipientFilter` option gives you more flexibility because you can also build powerful filters.

For example, to create an address list that contains all "room" mailboxes in your organization that have an alias and for which the department attribute is set to "RND," you can use the following command:

```
[PS] C:\> New-AddressList -Name "RND All Rooms AL" -Container "\" -DisplayName
"RND All Rooms AL" -RecipientFilter "((Alias -ne '`$NULL') -and (Department -eq
'RND') -and ((RecipientDisplayType -eq 'ConferenceRoomMailbox') -or
(RecipientDisplayType -eq 'SyncedConferenceRoomMailbox')))"
```

Note The -RecipientFilter option cannot be used with the -Conditional Company, -ConditionalDepartment, -ConditionalStateOrProvince, or -IncludedRecipients options.

If you need to create address lists that span multiple departments, the standard `-ConditionalDepartment` (or department property) won't work. However, you can use a custom attribute for the search filter in an address list, which gives you even more flexibility. The downside of doing this is that you need to stamp this custom attribute during provisioning, of course.

To create an address list that is targeted to all employees across all departments, you can stamp the CustomAttribute1 with "Finance" and create the following address list:

```
[PS] C:\> New-AddressList -Name "ProExchangeAdmin Finance
Employees" -DisplayName "ProExchangeAdmin Finance Employees Address
List" -RecipientFilter "((Alias -ne '`$NULL') -and (objectClass -eq
'user') -and (CustomAttribute1 -eq 'Finance'))"
```

Offline Address Books

As mentioned in the beginning of this section, address lists are only available for online clients. For Outlook clients who can work offline, the Offline Address Book (OAB) is available.

The OAB is a collection of address lists that is generated typically once a day, available for download on the Exchange server. For this download, there's a virtual directory called "OAB" available on the Exchange server.

To create a dedicated Offline Address Book for the RND Department, and that includes the "RND All Users Address List" and the "RND All Rooms AL" address lists (created in the previous section), you can use the following command:

```
[PS] C:\> New-OfflineAddressBook -Name "RND OAB" -AddressLists "\RND All
Users Address List","RND All Rooms AL" -VirtualDirectories "EXCH01\OAB
(Default Web Site)" -GeneratingMailbox "CN=SystemMailbox{bb558c35-97f1-
4cb9-8ff7-d53741dc928c},CN=Users,DC=Proexchangeadmin,DC=com"
```

The arbitration mailbox, as defined in the `-GeneratingMailbox` option, is the mailbox responsible for generating the OAB. If you omit the `-GeneratingMailbox` option, the OAB is created but it is never generated and thus is not available for download.

This Offline Address Book will be available for download on Exchange server EXCH01. If you have multiple Exchange servers, and you want to use all Exchange servers for OAB downloads, you can use the `-GlobalWebDistributionEnabled $TRUE` option. When used, the `-VirtualDirectories` option must be omitted.

Address Book Policies

In the previous section, multiple address lists were created, based on all kinds of filtering techniques and properties. While this works fine, it has one drawback: all address lists are visible for everybody in the organization. If someone has a mailbox and can log on to it, they are able to view all the address lists.

Large companies or hosting companies may want to segregate their address lists so that every department, division, or tenant has its own address lists, and only users included in those address lists can view their own address lists and cannot view the address lists of other departments.

In Exchange 2003 and Exchange 2007, this was possible by explicitly granting or denying permissions on objects in Active Directory. While this worked great in these versions of Exchange, it is not feasible in Exchange 2010 and higher. To achieve such segregation of address lists, Microsoft introduced the Address Book Policy (ABP) in Exchange 2010, and Address Book Policies are still used in Exchange 2019. The ABP is applied to a mailbox and represents a view on the address lists. That is, via the ABP you define which address lists are available for mailboxes.

Suppose that the RND Department has the following address lists:

- RND Global Address List
- RND All Rooms
- RND All Users
- RND All Contacts
- RND All Groups
- RND OAB

To create an ABP that includes all these address lists, you can use the following command:

```
[PS] C:\> New-AddressBookPolicy -Name "RND ABP" -GlobalAddressList "\RND
Global Address List" -OfflineAddressBook "\RND OAB" -RoomList "\RND All
Rooms" -AddressLists "\RND All Users","\RND All Groups","\RND All Contacts"
```

When the ABP is created, it can be applied to a mailbox:

```
[PS] C:\> Set-Mailbox -Identity Professor -AddressBookPolicy "RND ABP"
```

Now, when user Professor Labrousse logs in to his mailbox and checks the address lists, he will see only the RND Department address lists, as shown in Figure 5-27.

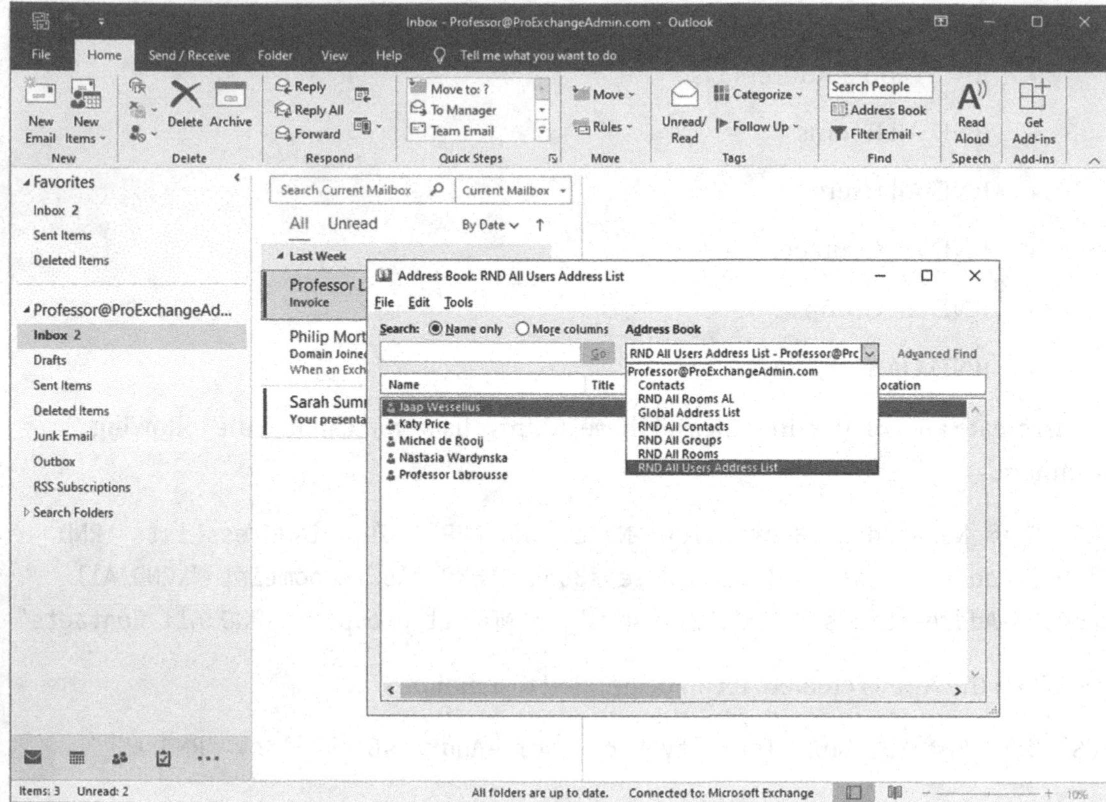

***Figure 5-27.** After applying the ABP, only the proper address lists are visible*

Note Using Address Book Policies is the only supported and properly functioning way to achieve segregation of address lists.

Summary

In Exchange, there are multiple types of recipients. The most common of course are user mailboxes. But besides user mailboxes, there are shared mailboxes, mailboxes that are shared between multiple other users. Typical shared mailboxes in every organization are "sales," "support," "info," etc. A mail is delivered in the shared mailbox, and other users can process these messages.

Resource mailboxes are for planning purposes. Room mailboxes are an example; you can book a room for a meeting, and when possible it is automatically accepted. Another type of resource mailbox is an equipment mailbox. This can be a beamer for a meeting room, but a company car is another example.

Mailboxes are grouped in address lists, both online and offline. The latter for Outlook clients running in cached mode. Address lists can be for users, rooms, contacts, etc. and can be organized into an Address Book Policy. An Address Book Policy can be applied to a mailbox so that only the address lists in the Address Book Policy are visible.

Public Folders have been around in Exchange since the beginning. In 2007, Microsoft wanted to decommission Public Folders, but customers were thinking differently. In Exchange 2013, Microsoft introduced "Modern Public Folders." The usage is like the old Public Folders, but modern Public Folders can use all new features of Exchange 2013 and higher. And Public Folders are still available in Exchange 2019, and there are no signs that they will be decommissioned anytime soon. As a side note, Public Folders are available in Exchange Online as well.

Recipients are for processing messages. The next chapter is about Exchange Transport, or how messages get in and out of Exchange.

CHAPTER 6

Exchange Transport

Exchange Transport is an integral part of any Exchange server, whether it be a Mailbox server or an Edge Transport server. Exchange Transport consists of several components that are responsible for

- Sending and receiving messages to and from the Internet
- Sending and receiving messages to other Exchange servers
- Picking up and delivering messages to mailboxes
- Relaying SMTP messages from other devices or applications
- Delivering message hygiene
- Providing redundancy in message delivery

To achieve this, any Exchange server has multiple services that are responsible for transport:

- Microsoft Exchange Transport
- Microsoft Exchange Transport Log Search
- Microsoft Exchange Front-end Transport
- Microsoft Exchange Mailbox Transport Submission
- Microsoft Exchange Mailbox Transport Delivery
- Microsoft Exchange anti-spam update
- Microsoft Exchange EdgeSync

M. de Rooij and J. Wesselius, *Pro Exchange 2019 and 2016 Administration*,
https://doi.org/10.1007/978-1-4842-7331-9_6

These seven services combined make up Exchange Transport, and all are discussed in detail in this chapter. This chapter is about Exchange 2019, but it is also valid for Exchange 2016. It also applies to an Exchange 2013 multi-role server, but with some creativity, it also applies to separate Exchange 2013 Client Access and Exchange 2013 Mailbox servers.

Transport Pipeline

The complete, end-to-end mail delivery process, from accepting external SMTP messages on the Exchange server to delivering the actual message to the mailbox, is called the *transport pipeline*. The transport pipeline consists of several individual components:

1. **Front-End Transport service (FETS)**—FETS is responsible for accepting SMTP messages from external SMTP hosts. FETS can also be configured as a front-end proxy on send connectors.

2. **Transport service**—The Transport service is responsible for processing all inbound and outbound SMTP messages. It receives messages on the receive connector from the FETS, from the Transport server running on other Exchange servers, or from any down-level Hub Transport servers when running Exchange 2016 and Exchange 2010 in coexistence. When the messages are received, they are queued in the submission queue.

3. The **submission queue** also receives messages from the pickup directory and from the replay directory. When messages are properly formatted (in an .EML format), you can drop them into the pickup directory, and they will be automatically processed.

4. From the submission queue, the messages are sent to the **categorizer**. This is the process whereby the Transport server determines whether the message must be delivered locally or remotely, whether it is on an internal Exchange server or an external server on the Internet. When categorized, the messages are delivered to a send connector. It is important to note that the Transport server never communicates directly with the mailbox databases.

5. **Mailbox Transport service**—The Mailbox Transport service, not to confuse with the Transport service, consists of two parts:

6. **Mailbox Transport Submission service**—This is responsible for picking up messages from a user's drafts or outbox folder. Remote procedure calls (RPC) are used to communicate with the Information Store to pick up messages, and then the SMTP is used to deliver messages to the local Transport server or to the Transport server running on other Exchange 2013 Mailbox servers in the organization.

7. **Mailbox Transport Delivery service**—This is responsible for receiving messages from the Transport server and delivering those messages to the user's inbox or underlying folder. Messages are accepted from the local Transport server or from the Transport server running on other Exchange 2013 Mailbox servers in the organization. Next, RPC is used to communicate with the Information Store to deliver the messages to the inbox, and the SMTP is used to communicate with the Exchange 2013 Transport server.

The transport pipeline is shown in Figure 6-1.

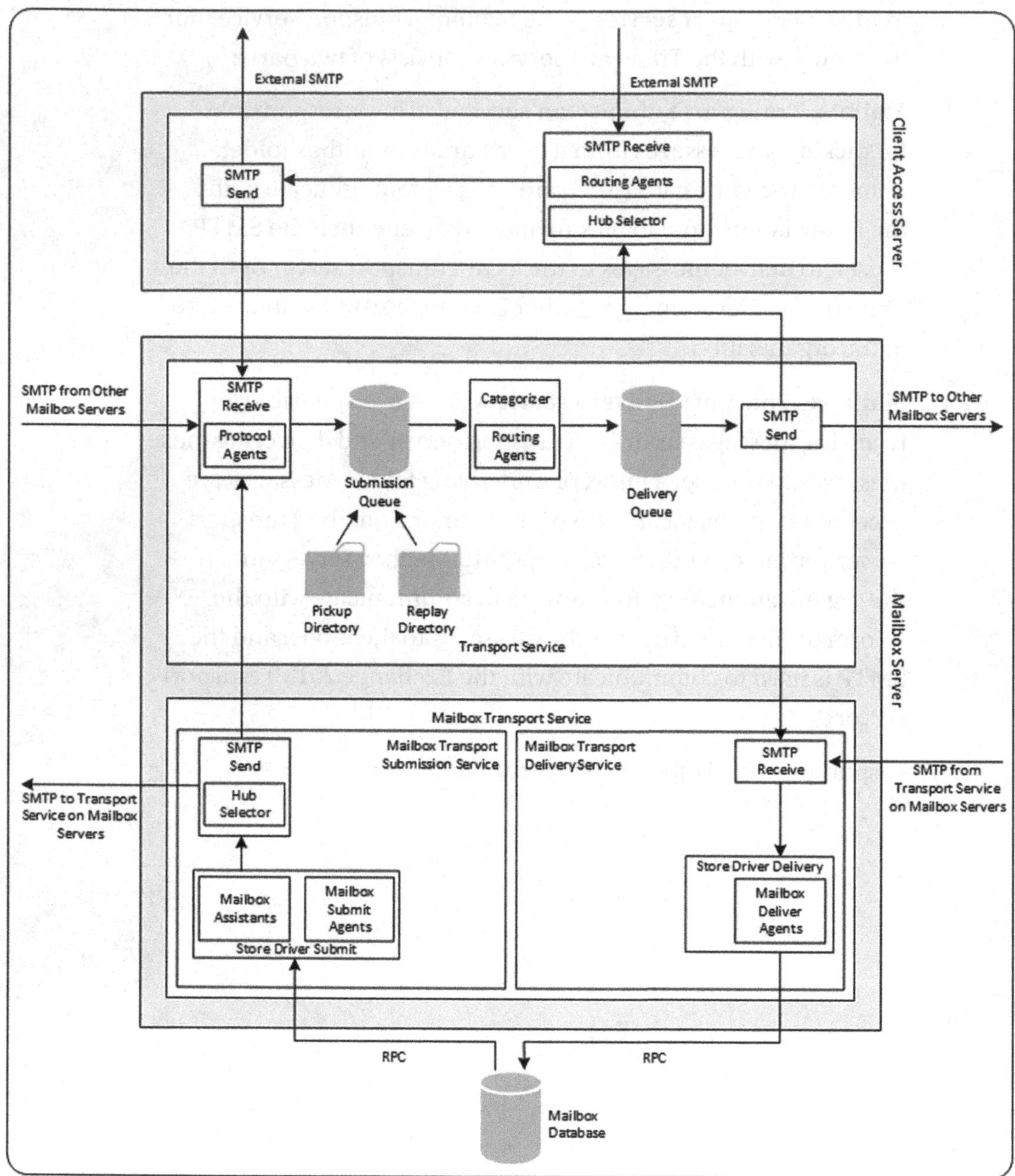

Figure 6-1. *The transport pipeline in Exchange server*

Routing Destinations

When a message arrives at the Transport service on an Exchange server, it must be categorized. In other words, the recipient or recipients need to be determined. Once Exchange knows the list of recipients, the server knows where to route the message.

The destination for a message is called the *routing destination*. Routing destinations can be

- A mailbox database containing a mailbox or a public folder
- A send connector responsible for sending a message to another Active Directory site with an Exchange server or to an external SMTP server
- A Distribution Group Expansion server, or an Exchange server that is responsible for extracting recipients from a Distribution Group if the message destination is a Distribution Group

Delivery Groups

The concept of delivery groups was created in Exchange 2013. A *delivery group* is a collection of Exchange servers. These servers are responsible for delivering SMTP messages within this group of servers. The following delivery groups can be identified in Exchange:

- **Routable DAG**—These are all the Exchange servers that are members of a DAG. The mailbox databases in this DAG are the routing destinations of the delivery group. A message can be delivered to one Exchange server in a DAG, and this Exchange server is responsible for routing the message to the Exchange server that holds the active copy of the mailbox database in the DAG. Since the DAG can span multiple Active Directory sites, the routing boundary for the routable DAG is the DAG itself, not the Active Directory site.
- **Mailbox delivery group**—This is a collection of Exchange servers in one Active Directory site that is *not* a member of a DAG. In a mailbox delivery group, the routing boundary is the Active Directory site itself.

- **Connector source server**—This is a collection of Exchange servers that act as the source server for a particular send connector. These are only the source servers of a particular send connector; Exchange servers that are not defined as source servers of the send connector, but that are in the same Active Directory site, are *not* part of this delivery group.
- **Active Directory site**—This is an Active Directory site that is not the final Active Directory site, which means the message is in transit through this Active Directory site. For example, it can be a hub site or a connecting Active Directory site for an Exchange Edge Transport server. An Exchange server cannot contact an Edge Transport server that has an Edge subscription in another Active Directory site, so the message must pass through this Active Directory site to be relayed to the Edge Transport server.
- **Server list**—This is one or more Exchange servers that are configured as Distribution Group Expansion servers.

Queues

In Exchange Server, a queue is a destination for a message, as well as a temporary storage location on the Exchange server. For every destination, there is a queue, so there are queues for submissions, for message delivery to the mailbox, for routing to other Exchange servers in the organization, or for routing to an external destination.

When messages arrive at the Transport service, they are immediately stored on the local disk of the Exchange server. The storage technology used is the extensible storage engine (ESE), which is the same engine as used for the mailbox databases. By default, the mail queue database and its accompanying log files and checkpoint file can be found on C:\Program Files\Microsoft\Exchange Server\V15\TransportRoles\data\Queue (see Figure 6-2). The ESE database has circular logging enabled. This means that log files no longer needed are automatically deleted, and, as such, there is no recovery method, such as replay of log files.

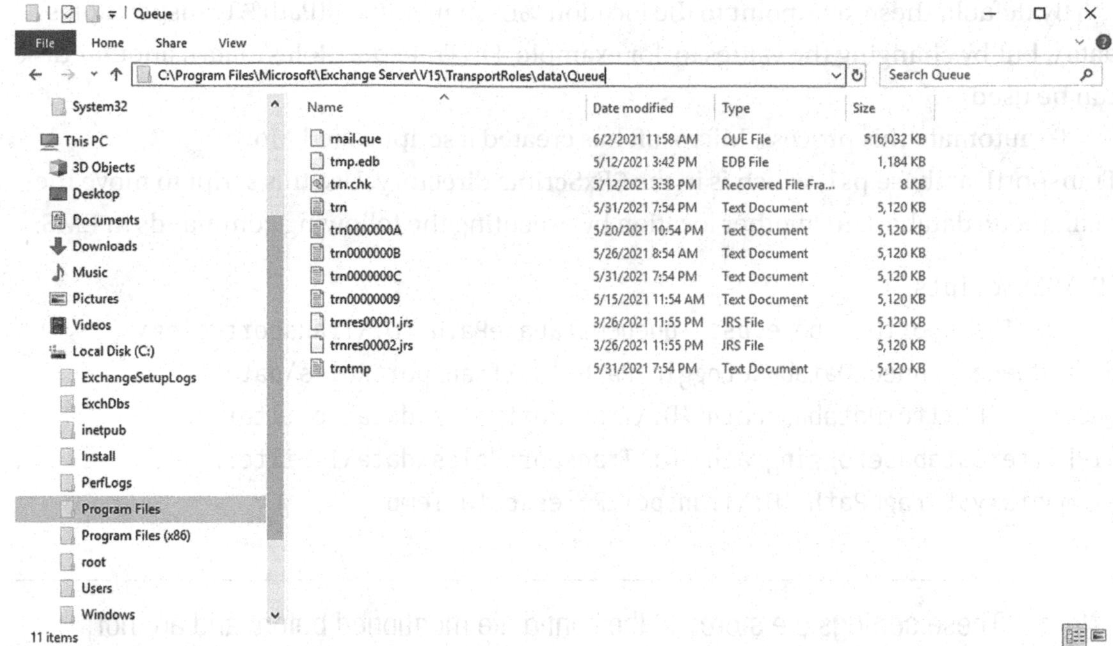

***Figure 6-2.** The mail queue database is a normal ESE database*

It is possible to change some of the configuration options of the mail queue database. When Exchange is installed in the default location, all configuration settings are stored in the EdgeTransport.exe.config file, which can be found in C:\Program Files\Microsoft\Exchange Server\V15\bin. Most settings in this file can be left at their default values, but it is possible to change the location of all mail queue-related files and directories to another disk. The advantage of doing this is that, if there's unexpected growth in these files, it will not affect the normal system and boot drives. If these fill up, there is always the possibility that the services running on this server will gradually stop working; worse, the entire server might stop working. This is an undesirable situation for any Exchange Server.

If you open the EdgeTransport.Config.Exe file and browse through the file, you will see the following keys:

- QueueDatabasePath
- QueueDatabaseLoggingPath
- IPFilterDatabasePath
- IPFilterDatabaseLoggingPath
- TemporaryStoragePath

By default, these keys point to the location %ExchangeInstallPath%TransportRoles\data\, but by changing the values to, for example, D:\TransportRoles\data\, another disk can be used.

To automate this process, Microsoft has created a script called Move-TransportDatabase.ps1, which is in the $ExScripts directory. Use this script to move the mail queue database to another location by executing the following commands in EMS:

```
CD \$ExScripts
.\Move-TransportDatabase.ps1 -queueDatabasePath 'D:\TransportRoles\
data\Queue' -queueDatabaseLoggingPath 'D:\TransportRoles\data\
Queue' -iPFilterDatabasePath 'D:\TransportRoles\data\IpFilter'
-iPFilterDatabaseLoggingPath 'D:\TransportRoles\data\IpFilter'
-temporaryStoragePath 'D:\TransportRoles\data\Temp'
```

Note These settings are stored in the config file mentioned before and are not stored in Active Directory. This means that there is always the risk that the config file is overwritten when installing a new Cumulative Update. You must be aware of this.

Shadow Redundancy

There is one type of queue that always raises questions. At first look, there are always messages in this queue, and they do not seem to disappear quickly. Shadow queues, also referred to as shadow redundancy, are there for message redundancy: messages are stored in shadow queues until the next hop in the message path reports a successful delivery. Only then is the message deleted from the shadow queue.

Imagine an Exchange server in London that is sending messages to the Internet but has no Internet connection of its own. There are also two Exchange servers in Amsterdam, and Amsterdam has its own Internet connection. A network connection exists between the two locations:

1. The Exchange server in London sends an SMTP message to Exchange server (A) in Amsterdam, EXCH01. As soon as the message is delivered in Amsterdam, it is stored in the shadow queue on the server in London.

2. Exchange server (A) in Amsterdam sends the message to server (B) in Amsterdam, EXCH02. As soon as the message is accepted, it is stored in the shadow queue on server (A).

3. Server (A) knows the message was successfully delivered and reports back to the server in London. At this moment, the message can safely be deleted from the London shadow queue because there still is a backup message, but now it's on server (A).

4. Server (B) sends the message to the Edge Transport server in the perimeter network, and when delivered, server (B) reports back to server (A), which can now delete the message from its shadow queue.

Sending a message from the Exchange server to the Internet is difficult, of course, because not all SMTP servers on the Internet support shadow queues. If not supported, the messages are automatically deleted from the sender's shadow queue after some time.

Shadow queue redundancy is built into Exchange 2013 for messages that are in transit. If one server fails, for whatever reason, and the server is no longer available, the previous Exchange server in the message path can retry delivering the message via a different available path.

Managing Queues

Most of Exchange server queues exist for only a limited time. When the Transport server cannot deliver a message, the message stays in the queue until the server can successfully deliver the message (it keeps trying) or until the message expires; the default message expiration time is two days.

These queues can be managed by using the Queue Viewer, which is a graphic tool, or by using the EMS. The Queue Viewer can be found in the toolbox, an MMC snap-in that is automatically installed during the installation of Exchange Server.

Open the Exchange toolbox and select "Queue Viewer" under mail flow tools. The Queue Viewer shows the queues on the server currently operating, but if you select "Connect to Server" in the actions pane, you can use it to view information on other Exchange servers as well (see Figure 6-3).

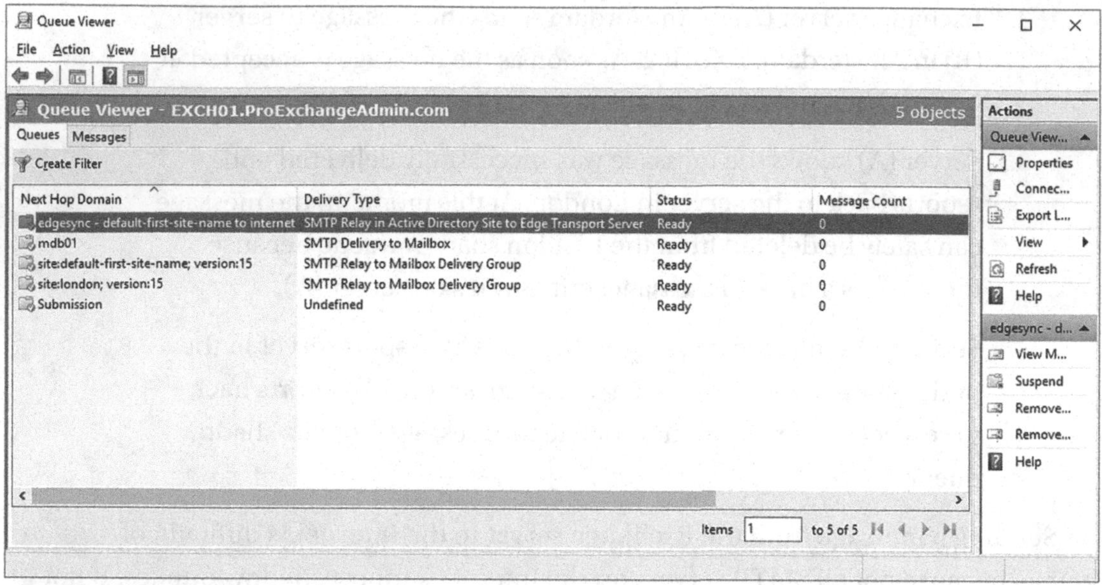

***Figure 6-3.** Queue information using the Queue Viewer*

The Queue Viewer is an incredibly valuable tool for troubleshooting purposes. It shows messages that are in a queue, of course, but if you open the message, it also shows the reason why the messages cannot be delivered. The tool also gives you the option of suspending a queue or removing messages from a queue, either with or without generating a nondelivery report (NDR).

It is also possible to manage the queues using the EMS. This method is more complex, but it offers many more granular options. The basic command to get queue information is the `Get-Queue` cmdlet. The Get-Queue cmdlet will show the queues on the server where the cmdlet is executed (see Figure 6-4). Using the identity of the queue, you can obtain more information by using the `Get-Queue -Identity EXCH01\6` cmdlet, for example. The actual error is not shown when using this cmdlet, but you can use the `Get-Queue -Identity NYC-EXCH01\6 | FL` cmdlet for all information regarding the queue or the `Get-Queue -Identity NYC-EXCH01\6 | select Identity,DeliveryType,Status,MessageCount,NexthopDomain,LastError` to show the actual error message the transport service is experiencing.

```
Machine: EXCH01.ProExchangeAdmin.com
[PS] C:\>Get-Queue -Server EXCH03 | ft -a

Identity             DeliveryType                     Status MessageCount Velocity RiskLevel OutboundIPPool NextHopDomain
--------             ------------                     ------ ------------ -------- --------- -------------- -------------
EXCH03\6019          SmtpRelayWithinAdSiteToEdge      Ready  0            0        Normal    0              edgesync - ...
EXCH03\6209          SmtpDeliveryToMailbox            Ready  0            0        Normal    0              mdb03
EXCH03\6210          SmtpDeliveryToMailbox            Ready  0            0        Normal    0              mdb04
EXCH03\6213          SmtpRelayToDag                   Ready  0            0        Normal    0              dag01
EXCH03\6215          SmtpRelayToMailboxDeliveryGroup  Retry  1            -0.02    Normal    0              site:london...
EXCH03\Submission    Undefined                        Ready  0            0        Normal    0              Submission
EXCH03\Shadow\6020   ShadowRedundancy                 Ready  0            0        Normal    0              edge01.proe...

[PS] C:\>Get-Queue -Identity EXCH03\6215 | select LastError | fl


LastError : [{LRT=6/2/2021 4:05:28 PM};{LED=441 4.4.1 Error encountered while communicating with primary target IP
            address: "Failed to connect. Winsock error code: 10060, Win32 error code: 10060." Attempted failover to
            alternate host, but that did not succeed. Either there are no alternate hosts, or delivery failed to all
            alternate hosts. The last endpoint attempted was 10.83.4.222:2525};{FQDN=site:london;
            version:15};{IP=10.83.4.222}]


[PS] C:\>_
```

***Figure 6-4.** Use the Get-Queue cmdlet to get information about messages stuck in the queue*

The Get-Queue cmdlet will only show results from the Exchange server where the cmdlet is executed. You can also use the Get-TransportService cmdlet to get a list of all Transport services running on all Exchange servers and pipe this output into the Get-Queue cmdlet: `Get-TransportService | Get-Queue`. This will show all queues on all Transport services in the organization.

When a message cannot be delivered, it will stay in the queue, and it can stay there for up to two days, which is the default wait time. When this happens, there is no need for any concern; Exchange will keep trying to deliver the message. Also, the number of messages in a queue can vary over time; for example, you could have 20–30 messages in a queue for an Internet send connector. But the messages must be delivered after some time, of course. If there is a steady increase in the number of messages in a queue, or if many queues are created and the messages get stuck in there, then it's time to dig deeper into the cause of the excessive queuing.

Safety Net

Safety Net is a redundancy feature in Exchange 2013 and higher for the Transport service. Safety Net stores messages in a queue that were successfully delivered to the mailboxes. Safety Net is redundant by itself; there's a primary Safety Net and a shadow Safety Net. The primary Safety Net exists on the Exchange server where the message originates, while the shadow Safety Net exists on the Exchange server where the message is delivered. As soon as the message is delivered, it is stored in the Safety Net queue. Messages are kept in the Safety Net queue for 48 hours, which is the default time.

Safety Net and shadow redundancy are complementary. That is, shadow redundancy is responsible for messages in transit, while Safety Net is responsible for messages that have been delivered to mailboxes. The cool thing is that Safety Net is a fully automated feature; there is no need for any manual action. All coordination is done by the Active Manager, which is also responsible for failover scenarios in the DAG.

When something happens on the Exchange server, Active Manager requests a resubmission from Safety Net. For large organizations, these messages most likely exist on multiple Mailbox servers, so (a lot of) duplicate messages can occur. Exchange server however has a mechanism that detects duplicate messages; it finds and eliminates those duplicate messages, preventing the recipient from receiving multiple copies. Unfortunately, resubmitted messages from Safety Net are also delivered to mail servers outside the Exchange organization. Since these servers do not have the duplicate message detection mechanism, external users can receive multiple identical messages.

When the primary Safety Net is not available, Active Manager tries requesting a resubmit for 12 hours. If unsuccessful after this time, Active Manager then contacts the other Mailbox servers and requests a resubmit of messages for the mailbox database.

Send and Receive Connectors

For sending and receiving SMTP messages, Exchange uses the concept of connectors:

- **Send Connector**—This is used to send messages. This can be to another SMTP host on the Internet, to an Edge Transport server or to an Exchange server in another Active Directory site, or to Exchange Online Protection.

- **Receive Connector**—This is used to receive messages from other SMTP hosts, applications, multifunctional devices, or Exchange Online Protection.

A receive connector can also be used to relay SMTP messages from devices or applications. These messages can be delivered to mailboxes on Exchange, but also to the Internet. This requires some additional configuration and caution since it is easy to create an open relay to the Internet.

Send and Receive connectors are discussed in the following sections.

Send Connectors

A send connector in Exchange is a connector that is responsible for sending SMTP messages. A well-known send connector is an Internet send connector that will send messages to the Internet.

A send connector is known in the entire organization, so all Exchange servers in all Active Directory sites have knowledge about send connectors and can use them.

To create a new Send Connector to send messages from Exchange to the Internet, execute the following command in EMS:

```
[PS] C:\> New-SendConnector -Name "To Internet" -Internet
-SourceTransportServer EXCH01 -AddressSpaces *
```

This will create a new Send Connector of type "Internet." The `-SourceTransportServer` option indicates which Exchange server can use this connector to send mail via this connector. In this example, it is only EXCH01, but it is a multivalue property, so your multiple servers can be added here. The address space value "*" means that all domains can be sent via this connector.

By default, MX routing is used for Send Connectors. It is also possible to use a smarthost for outbound email and have this smarthost deliver to the Internet. To create a Send Connector to send email to the Internet, but use a smarthost with FQDN smtphost.proexchangeadmin.com instead and use two Exchange servers, execute the following command in EMS:

```
[PS] C:\> New-SendConnector -Name "To Internet" -Internet
-SourceTransportServer EXCH01,EXCH02 -AddressSpaces * -DNSRoutingEnabled
$False -SmartHosts smtphost.proexchangeadmin.com
```

A typical use case for sending email via a smarthost is when using a cloud-based message hygiene solution like Exchange Online Protection, Trend Micro Hosted Email Security, or Mimecast Email Security. The Send Connector will send out all email to the cloud provider, and they will deliver the email to its destination.

By default, a Send Connector can be used by all Exchange servers in the entire organization. A US-based Send Connector can be used by Exchange servers in Australia. To prevent this, it is possible to scope a Send Connector to only an Active Directory where the source transport servers are located using the `-IsScopedConnector` option.

The default value of this option is $False, but when set to $True, only the local Exchange servers can use this Send Connector. For other Active Directory sites, dedicated Send Connectors need to be created in that Active Directory site.

It is also possible to create a Send Connector for specific domains and route messages for this domain via another path. For example, if we want to route messages for a domain @exchangelabs.nl not via the regular Internet Send Connector, but directly to the Edge Transport server for this domain, we can create such a Send Connector using the following command:

```
[PS] C:\> New-SendConnector -Name "Exchangelabs" -Partner
-SourceTransportServer EXCH01,EXCH02 -AddressSpaces "*.exchangelabs.nl"
-DNSRoutingEnabled $False -SmartHosts ams-edge03.exchangelabs.nl
```

This is especially interesting if you want to route mail to a trusted partner, and you want to secure this traffic using IPSEC or Mutual TLS.

The Send Connectors mentioned earlier are all external connectors; this means that messages sent via these connectors have a destination outside of our Exchange organization. There is no need to worry about message routing between Exchange servers, not even if there are multiple Active Directory sites in the Exchange organization. For internal routing, an implicit connector called intra-organization Send Connector is automatically created in each Exchange organization. This intra-organization is invisible, requires no maintenance, and is automatically available.

For troubleshooting purposes, it can be useful to disable a Send Connector for some time. To achieve this, the `Set-SendConnector` command accepts the `-Enabled` option. By default, a Send Connector is enabled; to disable it, the `-Enabled` option must be set to false. To disable the Send Connector that was previously created, execute the following command in EMS:

```
[PS] C:\> Set-SendConnector -Identity "To Internet" -Enabled $False
```

To reenable the Send Connector, execute the command again with the `-Enabled` option set to $True.

A Send Connector can log information to a protocol logfile. This logs quite some information, so it is disabled by default. The Microsoft recommendation is to enable protocol logging only for troubleshooting purposes.

To enable logging on the previously created Send Connector, execute the following command in EMS:

```
[PS] C:\> Set-SendConnector -Identity "To Internet" -ProtocolLoggingLevel
Verbose
[PS] C:\> Restart-Service MSExchangeTransport
```

The default location for the transport protocol logfiles is `C:\Program Files\Microsoft\Exchange Server\V15\TransportRoles\Logs\Hub\ProtocolLog\SMTPSend`. Tons of information are written into these logfiles, and they are easy to get lost. Several logfiles are created per day; the date and time plus a sequence number are in the name of the logfile. Be aware that transport logging happens with UTC time stamp, so this can differ several hours with your local time zone, depending on your location of course.

The following is an excerpt from the Send Connector's logfile, when sending a message via the Exchangelabs connector that was created earlier. Some information was deleted from this excerpt, like the time stamp, name of the connector, and source and target IP addresses:

```
attempting to connect
"220 AMS-EDGE03.exchangelabs.nl Microsoft ESMTP MAIL Service ready at Tue,
8 Jun 2021 16:42:24 +0200",
EHLO EXCH02.ProExchangeAdmin.com,
250  AMS-EDGE03.exchangelabs.nl Hello [10.38.96.232] SIZE 37748736
PIPELINING DSN ENHANCEDSTATUSCODES STARTTLS X-ANONYMOUSTLS X-EXPS NTLM
8BITMIME BINARYMIME CHUNKING XEXCH50 XSHADOW,
STARTTLS,
220 2.0.0 SMTP server ready,
CN=EXCH02 CN=EXCH02 520250EA1B13D08B47B5E45D5476FDCD
D4FA1A0243A929AEEBF4D77DE93D50B691DB0A79 2021-03-24T19:11:23.000Z
2026-03-24T19:11:23.000Z EXCH02;EXCH02.ProExchangeAdmin.com,Sending
certificate Subject Issuer name Serial number Thumbprint Not before Not
after Subject alternate names
CN=ams-edge03.exchangelabs.nl CN=GeoTrust RSA CA 2018, OU=www.
digicert.com, O=DigiCert Inc, C=US 0F5DFD821512AD3D39F446D05337C7F7
94D3DEB2BC4F09430AEC7E20B822850F3A52F7C1 2020-03-09T01:00:00.000Z
2022-03-10T13:00:00.000Z ams-edge03.exchangelabs.nl",Remote certificate
Subject Issuer name Serial number Thumbprint Not before Not after Subject
alternate names
```

```
TLS protocol SP_PROT_TLS1_2_CLIENT negotiation succeeded using bulk
encryption algorithm CALG_AES_256 with strength 256 bits, MAC hash
algorithm CALG_SHA_384 with strength 0 bits and key exchange algorithm
CALG_ECDH_EPHEM with strength 256 bits"
94D3DEB2BC4F09430AEC7E20B822850F3A52F7C1,Received certificate Thumbprint
EHLO EXCH02.ProExchangeAdmin.com,
250  AMS-EDGE03.exchangelabs.nl Hello [10.38.96.232] SIZE 37748736
PIPELINING DSN ENHANCEDSTATUSCODES X-EXPS NTLM 8BITMIME BINARYMIME CHUNKING
XEXCH50 XSHADOW,
sending message with RecordId 7821135446026 and InternetMessageId
<21ed6e00639c4807af45313a5cbd7e25@ProExchangeAdmin.com>
MAIL FROM:<Professor@ProExchangeAdmin.com> SIZE=7057,
RCPT TO:<j.wesselius@exchangelabs.nl>,
250 2.1.0 Sender OK,
250 2.1.5 Recipient OK,
BDAT 3242 LAST,
"250 2.6.0 <21ed6e00639c4807af45313a5cbd7e25@ProExchangeAdmin.com>
[InternalId=92651034509316, Hostname=AMS-EDGE03.exchangelabs.nl] 4610 bytes
in 0.214, 20.942 KB/sec Queued mail for delivery",
QUIT,
221 2.0.0 Service closing transmission channel,
```

Clearly visible are the different steps that take place in SMTP communication. It starts with opening the connection, followed by a handshake and a certificate exchange. This is for TLS purposes. Exchange is using opportunistic TLS, which means it always tries to use TLS, even with the local self-signed certificate. The certificate is only used for encryption and not for server validation, so even when a certificate has expired, it can still be used for opportunistic TLS.

The last part is the actual sending of the message, in this example, from Professor Labrousse at ProExchangeAdmin to Jaap Wesselius at Exchangelabs.

The default location of the protocol log files is on the same disk as where the Exchange binaries are installed; in most cases, this will be the c:\ drive. To prevent filling up the disk with protocol logfiles and causing the server to halt, I always recommend placing the logfiles on a different disk. This is a setting of the Transport service on the Exchange server.

To retrieve the current settings for the logfiles, execute the following command:

```
[PS] C:\> Get-Transportservice -Identity EXCH01 | Select *logpath*
```

This is shown in Figure 6-5.

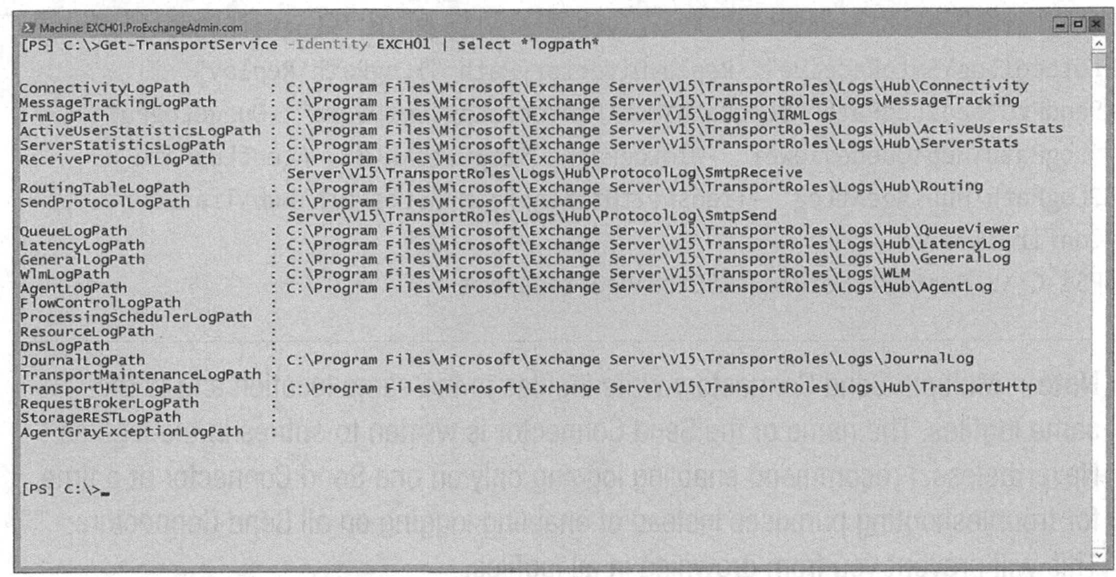

Figure 6-5. *Several locations are used for transport logging*

To relocate the logfiles, the `Set-TransportService` command can be used with the appropriate options. To relocate the logfiles for the Send Connector, execute the following command:

```
[PS] C:\> Set-TransportService -Identity EXCH01 -SendProtocolLogPath
"D:\Program Files\Microsoft\ExchangeServer\V15\TransportRoles\Logs\Hub\
Connectivity\SMTPSend"
```

Changing one setting does not make much sense; when changing multiple settings, it makes sense to use a variable with the location of the logfiles, and if you want to change this for multiple servers, use another variable with the name of the Exchange server, for example:

```
[PS] C:\> $ServerName = "EXCH01"
[PS] C:\> $LogPath = "D:\Program Files\Microsoft\Exchange Server\V15\
TransportRoles\Logs"
```

```
[PS] C:\> Set-TransportService -Identity $ServerName -IrmLogPath "$LogPath\
IRMLogs" -ActiveUserStatisticsLogPath "$LogPath\ActiveUsersStats"
-ServerStatisticsLogPath "$LogPath\ServerStats" -PickupDirectoryPath
"$LogPath\Pickup" -RoutingTableLogPath "$LogPath\Routing"
-PipelineTracingPath "$LogPath\PipelineTracing" -ConnectivityLogPath
"$LogPath\Hub\Connectivity" -ReceiveProtocolLogPath "$LogPath\Hub\
ProtocolLog\SmtpReceive" -ReplayDirectoryPath "$LogPath\Replay"
-SendProtocolLogPath "$LogPath\Hub\ProtocolLog\SmtpSend" -QueueLogPath
"$LogPath\Hub\QueueViewer" -WlmLogPath "$LogPath\WLM" -AgentLogPath
"$LogPath\Hub\AgentLog" -TransportHttpLogPath "$LogPath\Hub\TransportHttp"
-Confirm:$false
[PS] C:\> Restart-Service MSExchangeTransport
```

Note Multiple Send Connectors write logfiles to the same location and to the same logfiles. The name of the Send Connector is written to entries in the logfiles. Nevertheless, I recommend enabling logging only on one Send Connector at a time for troubleshooting purposes instead of enabling logging on all Send Connectors. This will prevent you from drowning in all logfiles.

Receive Connectors

In contrast to Send Connectors that are created manually, Exchange also has Receive Connectors that are automatically created during installation. As the name implies, Receive Connectors are responsible for receiving messages. These can be internal messages between Exchange servers within the organization (which are automatically authenticated) and external messages from outside the organization. These are anonymous connections. Be aware that if you have a Cisco IronPort in front of your Exchange server, it is also treated as external mail and thus requires anonymous access.

During the installation of Exchange server EXCH01, five Receive Connectors are created:

- **Client Frontend EXCH01**—Listening on port 587, this receive connector is used by clients like Mozilla Thunderbird that want to use authenticated SMTP to send email. This port needs users to authenticate to use the service.

- **Client Proxy EXCH01**—Listening on port 465, this connector receives the client's messages from the Client Access services on the Exchange server 2019 server or any other Exchange server 2019 server in the same Active Directory site.
- **Default EXCH01**—Listening on port 2525, this is the SMTP service accepting messages from the Default Frontend Receive Connector on the Exchange server 2019 server or any other Exchange server 2019 server in the same Active Directory site. This connector is not scoped for regular clients to be used.
- **Default Frontend EXCH01**—Listening on port 25, this is the receive connector for regular inbound SMTP messages. Servers that connect to this port can be other SMTP servers, Exchange 2010 Hub Transport services, other Exchange 2013/2016/2019 servers in the organization, or applications or devices that need to submit messages to mailboxes.
- **Outbound Proxy Frontend EXCH01**—Listening on port 717, this connector accepts messages from the Transport service on the Exchange server and relays the messages to external hosts. This only takes place on Send Connectors that have the front-end proxy option enabled.

All SMTP servers, applications, devices, or appliances always connect to the Default Frontend receive connector on port 25. All messages delivered to this connector can be delivered to mailboxes anywhere in the Exchange organization.

So, if you have a multifunctional "scan to mail" device, it will scan a document and connect to this Default Frontend Receive Connector, and the mail will be delivered to a mailbox without a problem.

To demonstrate this, we can use telnet from any computer in the network and set up a connection on port 25 to the Exchange server by running the following command from a command prompt:

```
C:> Telnet EXCH01.proexchangeadmin.com 25
```

And the Exchange server will return something like

```
220 EXCH01.ProExchangeAdmin.com Microsoft ESMTP MAIL Service ready at Wed,
9 Jun 2021 14:11:19 +0200
```

This is an interactive session, so it is now possible to enter any SMTP command to mimic a sending SMTP server. To send an email from any sender to a recipient in Exchange, enter the following commands in the telnet session:

```
HELO server.local
Mail from: sender@gmail.com
Rcpt to: professor@proexchangeadmin.com
Data
Hello world
.
```

This is the most basic form of sending an email using telnet, and it will be delivered as well. The email will be delivered, but since it is not formatted well, it will not be a readable message in Outlook.

A better version would be something like this:

```
Set localecho
Set logfile c:\temp\telnet.txt
Open exch01.proexchangeadmin.com 25
HELO mytelnet.local
mail from: jaapwess@hotmail.com
rcpt to: professor@proexchangeadmin.com
data
From: "Jaap Wesselius" <jaapwess@hotmail.com>
To: "Professor Labrousse" <professor@proexchangeadmin.com>
Subject: Sent using telnet
Date: Wed, 9 Juni 2021 14:17:00 +0200

Hi Professor,

welcome to Telnet magic

Kind regards
SMTP Admin Jaap
.
```

It is important to close with the dot; this is for the SMTP server to signal that the message has ended and that it can be delivered.

Using the telnet command Set `logfile c:\temp\telnet.txt`, all information is automatically logged, so when opening the logfile, we can see the following:

```
220 EXCH01.ProExchangeAdmin.com Microsoft ESMTP MAIL Service ready at Wed,
9 Jun 2021 14:19:22 +0200
HELO mytelnet.local
250 EXCH01.ProExchangeAdmin.com Hello [fe80::e409:afe5:1909:75fa%7]
mail from: jaapwess@hotmail.com
250 2.1.0 Sender OK
rcpt to: professor@proexchangeadmin.com
250 2.1.5 Recipient OK
data
354 Start mail input; end with <CRLF>.<CRLF>
From: "Jaap Wesselius" <jaapwess@hotmail.com>
To: "Professor Labrousse" <professor@proexchangeadmin.com>
Subject: Sent using telnet
Date: Wed, 9 Juni 2021 14:17:00 +0200
Hi Professor,
welcome to Telnet magic
Kind regards
SMTP Admin Jaap
.
250 2.6.0 <9d9a6c11-68ce-485d-94ff-1bd5633e0b0d@EXCH01.ProExchangeAdmin.
com> [InternalId=7915624726530, Hostname=EXCH02.
ProExchangeAdmin.com] 1774 bytes in 0.163, 10.568 KB/sec Queued mail for
delivery
quit
221 2.0.0 Service closing transmission channel
```

The email is accepted by the Receive Connector and delivered to the mailbox. When checking the mailbox with Outlook, a readable message appears as shown in Figure 6-6.

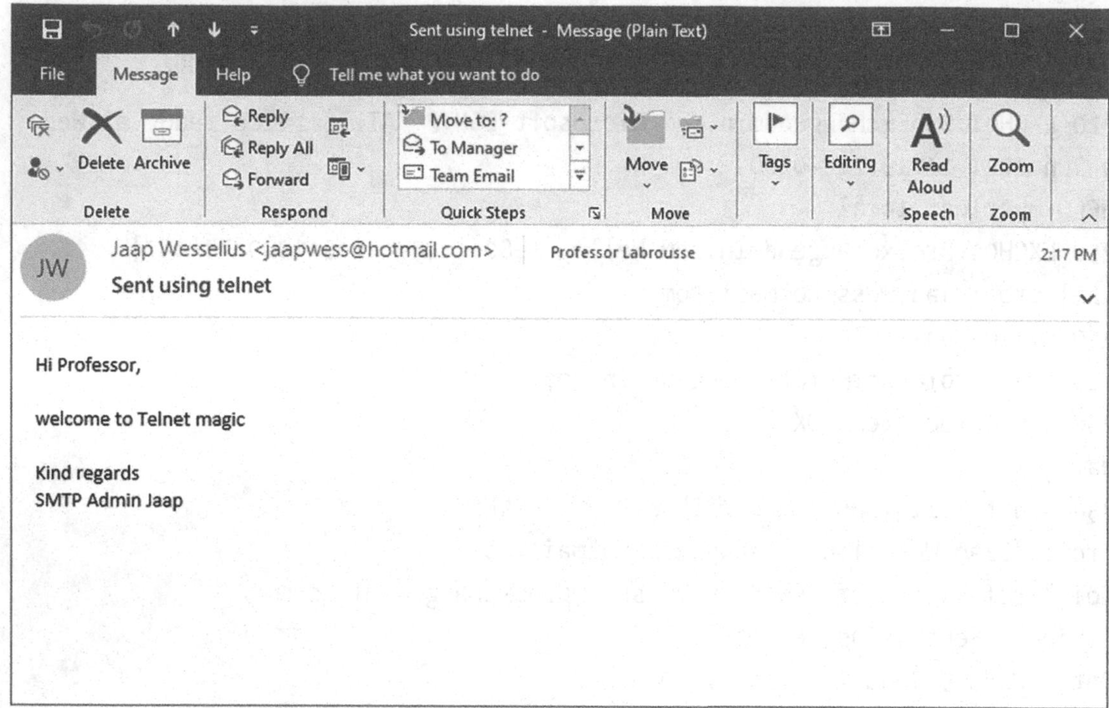

***Figure 6-6.** A properly formatted email sent from the command line using telnet*

Just like Send Connectors, Receive Connectors can perform protocol logging as well. Protocol logging should be used for troubleshooting purposes only since it generates a lot of information and can quickly fill up the local hard disk.

By default, the Default Receive Connector protocol logfile is in C:\Program Files\Microsoft\Exchange Server\V15\TransportRoles\Logs\FrontEnd\ProtocolLog\SmtpReceive. Please note that these logfiles are in a very different location than the previously mentioned Send Connector logfiles. The Default Receive Connector is part of the Front-End Transport Service. This is a completely different service and logs its information in another location.

When checking the Receive Connector protocol logfile, the previously sent email can be identified quickly as shown in the following excerpt:

```
"220 EXCH01.ProExchangeAdmin.com Microsoft ESMTP MAIL Service ready at Wed,
9 Jun 2021 14:38:07 +0200",
Tarpit for '0.00:00:05' due to '500 5.3.3 Unrecognized command 'unknown'',
500 5.3.3 Unrecognized command 'unknown',
HELO mytelnet.local,
```

```
250 EXCH01.ProExchangeAdmin.com Hello [fe80::e409:afe5:1909:75fa%7],
mail from: jaapwess@hotmail.com,
08D92B4309EB1B3D;2021-06-09T12:38:07.639Z;1,receiving message
250 2.1.0 Sender OK,
rcpt to: professor@proexchangeadmin.com,
250 2.1.5 Recipient OK,
data,
354 Start mail input; end with <CRLF>.<CRLF>,
```

It contains some interesting additional information. The second line contains tarpitting information. Tarpitting is an anti-spam measure in Exchange to frustrate malicious SMTP servers (or malicious telnet clients). In this example, it will halt the connection for five seconds; this will frustrate scripts that are trying to send out malicious email.

The third line contains a "`500 5.3.3 Unrecognized command 'unknown'`", most likely caused by a copy-and-paste issue into the telnet session.

After the mail from: line, a message ID can be identified; this is assigned by Exchange when a message is received and will remain the same during the lifetime of the message.

To change the location of the protocol logfiles, the `Set-FrontendTransportService` command can be used with the `-ReceiveProtocolLogPath` option. To change the location of the logfiles to an additional disk D:\, execute the following commands:

```
[PS] C:\> Set-FrontEndTransportService -Identity EXCH01
-ReceiveProtocolPath D:\Program Files\Microsoft\Exchange Server\V15\
TransportRoles\Logs\FrontEnd\ProtocolLog\SmtpReceive
[PS] C:\> Restart-Service MSexchangeFrontendTransport
```

To change all FETS logging options in just one command, execute the following commands in EMS:

```
[PS] C:\> $ServerName = "EXCH01"
[PS] C:\> $LogPath = "D:\Program Files\Microsoft\Exchange Server\V15\
TransportRoles\Logs\FrontEnd\"
[PS] C:\> Set-FrontendTransportService -Identity $ServerName
-AgentLogPath "$LogPath\ AgentLog" -ConnectivityLogPath "$LogPath\
Connectivity" -ReceiveProtocolLogPath "$LogPath\ ProtocolLog\SmtpReceive"
-SendProtocolLogPath "$LogPath\\ProtocolLog\SmtpSend"
[PS] C:\> Restart-Service MSExchangeFrontEndTransport
```

SMTP Relay

When trying to relay SMTP messages to external hosts (on the Internet, for example), you will receive an error message like `unable to relay` or more detailed `550 5.7.54 SMTP; Unable to relay recipient in non-accepted domain`. Relaying to external hosts is only possible for authenticated users or servers.

I always recommend to not configure the Default Receive Connectors for relaying SMTP messages, but instead create a dedicated connector for SMTP relay purposes. The reason for this is when something happens, you can disable the relay connector and continue working with the default connector.

Creating an SMTP relay connector consists of the following steps:

1. Create a Receive Connector. This should be created on the Front-End Transport service.
2. Specify the IP addresses of hosts that are allowed to use the new Receive Connector.
3. Modify the permissions on the Receive Connector to allow anonymous relay.

Note Sometimes, I get the understandable question of why a Receive Connector for relay purposes is used and not a Send Connector. It is all about accepting the message; Exchange must accept the message to relay it using the available Send Connector. Once accepted, Exchange will take care of delivering the message, internal or external.

Create a New Receive Connector

Creating a new Receive Connector is straightforward. To create a new Receive Connector for SMTP relay purposes, execute the following command in EMS:

```
[PS] C:\> New-ReceiveConnector -Name "SMTP Anonymous Relay" -Server
EXCH01 -TransportRole FrontendTransport -Custom -Bindings 0.0.0.0:25
-RemoteIpRanges 127.0.0.1
```

This is shown in Figure 6-7.

```
Machine: EXCH01.ProExchangeAdmin.com
[PS] C:\>New-ReceiveConnector -Name "SMTP Anonymous Relay" -Server EXCH01 -TransportRole FrontendTransport -Custom -Bindings 0.0.0.0:25 -RemoteIPRanges 127.0.0.1

Identity                     Bindings       Enabled
--------                     --------       -------
EXCH01\SMTP Anonymous Relay {0.0.0.0:25}    True

[PS] C:\>_
```

Figure 6-7. *Create a new Receive Connector for relay purposes*

This will create a new Receive Connector on the Front-End Transport service that listens on port 25, but only accepts connections from the "localhost."

To make it identifiable when opening a connection, the banner can be changed. To do this, execute the following command in EMS:

```
[PS] C:\> Set-ReceiveConnector -Identity "EXCH01\SMTP Anonymous Relay"
-Banner "220 EXCH01 SMTP Relay Connector"
```

Note The banner must always start with "220" followed by a string.

To add more IP addresses that are allowed to use the Receive Connector, execute the following commands in EMS:

```
[PS] C:\> $RemIPs = Get-ReceiveConnector "EXCH01\SMTP Anonymous Relay"
[PS] C:\> $RemIPs.RemoteIPRanges += "10.38.96.235","10.38.96.236","10.38.96.225"
[PS] C:\> Set-ReceiveConnector "EXCH01\SMTP Anonymous Relay"
-RemoteIPRanges $RemIPs.RemoteIPRanges
```

An obvious mistake would be to use `-RemoteIPRanges "10.38.96.235","10.38.96.225","10.38.96.226"` in the previous example. While it does add the IP addresses to the RemoteIPRanges, it also overwrites existing IP addresses.

To remove an IP address, execute the following commands in EMS:

```
[PS] C:\> $RemIPs = Get-ReceiveConnector "EXCH01\SMTP Anonymous Relay"
[PS] C:\> $RemIPs.RemoteIPRanges -= "127.0.0.1"
[PS] C:\> Set-ReceiveConnector "EXCH01\SMTP Anonymous Relay"
-RemoteIPRanges $RemIPs.RemoteIPRanges
```

Modify Permissions on the Receive Connector

For modifying permissions on the Receive Connector, two options are available:

1. Configure the connections as externally secured.
2. Configure the connections as anonymous.

When configured as "externally secured," the network hosts are considered as authenticated senders. Messages that are submitted bypass anti-spam features and message size limit checks. The sender's name must be resolved to a display name in Exchange. Permissions to submit messages are granted as if they originate from internal senders within the Exchange organization.

To configure the Receive Connector as externally secured, execute the following command in EMS:

```
[PS] C:\> Set-ReceiveConnector "EXCH01\SMTP Anonymous Relay" -AuthMechanism
ExternalAuthoritative -PermissionGroups ExchangeServers
```

The advantage of this approach is that it is easy to configure, easier than the anonymous logon options as described in the following paragraph.

When **configured as anonymous**, the hosts are considered anonymous senders. Messages do not bypass anti-spam, and message size limits are applied. Permissions to NT AUTHORITY\ANONYMOUS LOGON are granted to relay messages. Again, only IP addresses in the -RemoteIPRanges are allowed to submit messages and therefore relay messages.

To configure the Receive Connector as anonymous, execute the following commands in EMS:

```
[PS] C:\> Set-ReceiveConnector "EXCH01\SMTP Anonymous Relay"
-PermissionGroups AnonymousUsers
[PS] C:\> Get-ReceiveConnector "EXCH01\SMTP Anonymous Relay" | Add-
ADPermission -User "NT AUTHORITY\ANONYMOUS LOGON" -ExtendedRights "Ms-Exch-
SMTP-Accept-Any-Recipient"
```

The advantage of this second approach is that it grants the minimum required permissions to allow anonymous relay.

Is there an advantage of one way over another? The first one is easier to configure; a purist would say that the second is more secure. Since anti-spam and message limits are not bypassed, one can truly say it is more secure.

You can test the SMTP relay using telnet. Open telnet on port 25 and enter the commands as mentioned in the general Receive Connector section. One thing to look for is the banner; this should return the string as previously entered. This is shown in Figure 6-8.

```
Command Prompt
220 EXCH01 SMTP Relay Connector
helo windows
250 EXCH01.ProExchangeAdmin.com Hello [10.38.96.225]
mail from:professor@proexchangeadmin.com
250 2.1.0 Sender OK
rcpt to:jaapwess@gmail.com
250 2.1.5 Recipient OK
data
354 Start mail input; end with <CRLF>.<CRLF>
subject: check my mail
mail from: "Professor" <professor@proexchangeadmin.com>
hoi
.
250 2.6.0 <b634e21d-ffc2-4fd3-875a-77e6ce0a7779@EXCH01.ProExchangeAdmin.com> [InternalId=8018703941633, Hostname=EXCH01.
ProExchangeAdmin.com] 1703 bytes in 0.258, 6.430 KB/sec Queued mail for delivery
quit
221 2.0.0 Service closing transmission channel


Connection to host lost.

C:\Users\professor>
```

***Figure 6-8.** Test the anonymous relay functionality*

How does Exchange determine which Receive Connector to use? In this example, both the Default Receive Connector and the SMTP relay connector listen on the same IP address and the same port number. When a connection is set up with the Exchange server on port 25, Exchange determines based on the source IP address which connector's RemoteIPRanges setting best matches. In our example, the source IP address is in the RemoteIPRanges property of the SMTP relay connector, and it will connect to this Receive Connector. If there is no match, the Default Receive Connector is used.

Protocol Logging

Like the Mailbox server role, the Edge Transport server role logs protocol information as well. When enabled, both the Send Connector and Receive Connector log information on the disk where the Exchange binaries are installed. The location of the protocol logfiles can be retrieved using the `Get-TransportService` command. To achieve this, execute the following command in EMS:

```
[PS] C:\> Get-TransportService | select *ProtocolLogPath | fl

ReceiveProtocolLogPath : C:\Program Files\Microsoft\Exchange Server\V15\
TransportRoles\Logs\Edge\ProtocolLog\SmtpReceive
```

```
SendProtocolLogPath        : C:\Program Files\Microsoft\Exchange Server\V15\
TransportRoles\Logs\Edge\ProtocolLog\SmtpSend
```

To change the location of the protocol logfiles to (dedicated) drive d:\, execute the following commands in EMS:

```
[PS] C:\> $LogPath = "D:\Program Files\Microsoft\Exchange Server\V15\
TransportRoles\Logs\Edge\ProtocolLog"
[PS] C:\> Set-TransportService -Identity Edge01 -ReceiveProtocolLogPath
"$LogPath\SmtpReceive"
[PS] C:\> Set-TransportService -Identity Edge01 -SendProtocolLogPath
"$LogPath\SmtpSend"
[PS] C:\> Restart-Service MSExchangeTransport
```

Message Tracking

As an Exchange administrator, you are most likely familiar with users that complain they have never received a certain message or that they have sent an email, but it was never received by the recipient. Naturally, they blame Exchange for this behavior. Of course, this can be the case, but it is also possible that the recipient deleted the message or that it was somehow lost in transit when the recipient is located elsewhere. This is impossible to trace, but it is possible to see that the message left the Exchange organization and thus is out of our reach.

To track sending, receiving, and delivering of messages, Exchange keeps track of all activity of the message flow in the Exchange Transport pipeline. Message tracking can be used for troubleshooting purposes, for mail flow analysis, or for message forensics.

Message tracking logfiles are circular logging. Logfiles are deleted when

- They reach their maximum age; the default setting is 30 days.
- The message tracking log folder reaches its maximum size. Individual logfiles are 10 MB; the default log folder size is 1000 MB.

Note Only the metadata of messages are stored. The messages themselves are not kept.

Message tracking can be done using the `Get-MessageTrackingLog` command in the Exchange Management Shell. It accepts options like the server, start and end dates, sender and recipient, eventID, or subject of the message.

To find details of a message sent by Professor to Sarah in the first week of June, and list only information regarding sending or receiving, execute the following command in EMS:

```
[PS] C:\> Get-MessageTrackingLog -Server EXCH01 -Start "06/01/2021" -End
"06/07/2021" -Sender professor@proexchangeadmin.com -Recipient sarah@
proexchangeadmin.com -EventID Send,Receive
```

If you are not interested in the EventIDs, but are interested in getting information regarding a specific message, you can use the `-MessageSubject` option, for example:

```
[PS] C:\> Get-MessageTrackingLog -Server EXCH01 -Start "06/01/2021" -End
"06/07/2021" -Sender professor@proexchangeadmin.com -MessageSubject Invoice
```

This is shown in Figure 6-9.

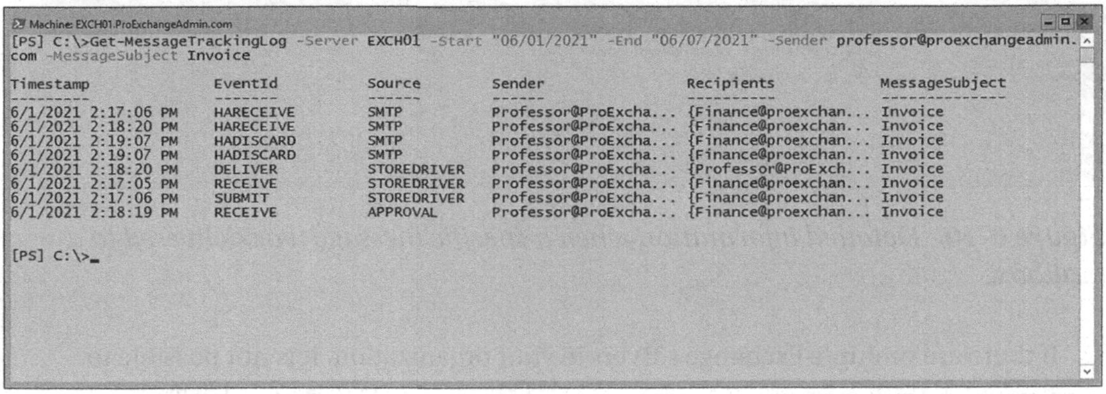

```
Machine: EXCH01.ProExchangeAdmin.com
[PS] C:\>Get-MessageTrackingLog -Server EXCH01 -Start "06/01/2021" -End "06/07/2021" -Sender professor@proexchangeadmin.
com -MessageSubject Invoice

Timestamp              EventId      Source       Sender                    Recipients                MessageSubject
---------              -------      ------       ------                    ----------                --------------
6/1/2021 2:17:06 PM    HARECEIVE    SMTP         Professor@ProExcha...     {Finance@proexchan...     Invoice
6/1/2021 2:18:20 PM    HARECEIVE    SMTP         Professor@ProExcha...     {Finance@proexchan...     Invoice
6/1/2021 2:19:07 PM    HADISCARD    SMTP         Professor@ProExcha...     {Finance@proexchan...     Invoice
6/1/2021 2:19:07 PM    HADISCARD    SMTP         Professor@ProExcha...     {Finance@proexchan...     Invoice
6/1/2021 2:18:20 PM    DELIVER      STOREDRIVER  Professor@ProExcha...     {Professor@ProExch...     Invoice
6/1/2021 2:17:05 PM    RECEIVE      STOREDRIVER  Professor@ProExcha...     {Finance@proexchan...     Invoice
6/1/2021 2:17:06 PM    SUBMIT       STOREDRIVER  Professor@ProExcha...     {Finance@proexchan...     Invoice
6/1/2021 2:18:19 PM    RECEIVE      APPROVAL     Professor@ProExcha...     {Finance@proexchan...     Invoice

[PS] C:\>_
```

***Figure 6-9.** Retrieve transport information regarding a specific message*

To get more detailed information when this message was delivered, use the `-EventID Deliver` option, and use the Format-List command, for example:

```
[PS] C:\> Get-MessageTrackingLog -Server EXCH01 -Start "06/01/2021" -End
"06/07/2021" -Sender professor@proexchangeadmin.com -MessageSubject Invoice
-EventID Deliver | Format-List
```

The results with detailed information are shown in Figure 6-10.

```
Machine: EXCH01.ProExchangeAdmin.com

[PS] C:\>Get-MessageTrackingLog -Server EXCH01 -Start "06/01/2021" -End "06/07/2021" -Sender professor@proexchangeadmin.
com -MessageSubject Invoice -eventid Deliver | fl


RunspaceId              : ead31739-5e77-4339-96d8-bffec74a92d5
Timestamp               : 6/1/2021 2:18:20 PM
ClientIp                :
ClientHostname          : EXCH02.ProExchangeAdmin.com
ServerIp                :
ServerHostname          : EXCH01
SourceContext           : 08D924CCB931FEE0;2021-06-01T12:18:20.175Z;ClientSubmitTime:2021-06-01T12:17:05.465Z
ConnectorId             :
Source                  : STOREDRIVER
EventId                 : DELIVER
InternalMessageId       : 7090991005703
MessageId               : <aaa9a2a273114cf69da4f8584523b804@ProExchangeAdmin.com>
NetworkMessageId        : bc1e4136-0750-4817-054f-08d924f72ba3
Recipients              : {Professor@ProExchangeAdmin.com}
RecipientStatus         : {}
TotalBytes              : 14198
RecipientCount          : 1
RelatedRecipientAddress :
Reference               :
MessageSubject          : Invoice
Sender                  : Professor@ProExchangeAdmin.com
ReturnPath              : Professor@ProExchangeAdmin.com
Directionality          : Originating
TenantId                :
OriginalClientIp        : 10.38.96.225
MessageInfo             : 2021-06-01T12:18:19.876Z;SRV=EXCH01.ProExchangeAdmin.com:TOTAL-SUB=0.302|SA=0.202|MTSS-PEN=0.
                          101(MTSSD-PEN=0.100(MTSSDA=0.030|MTSSDC=0.004|SDSSO-PEN=0.050 (SMSC=0.029(X-SMSDR=0.013)|MTSS
                          DM-PEN=0.006)));SRV=EXCH02.ProExchangeAdmin.com:TOTAL-HUB=0.299|SMR=0.134(SMRDI=0.010|SMRC=0.
                          123(SMRCL=0.101|X-SMRCR=0.122))|CAT=0.061(CATOS=0.002 (CATSM=0.002(CATSM-Malware
                          Agent=0.001))|CATRESL=0.027(X-CATRESLX=0.005)|CATORES=0.009 (CATRS=0.009(CATRS-Index Routing
                          Agent=0.008))|CATBIF=0.018)|QDM=0.104;SRV=EXCH01.ProExchangeAdmin.com:TOTAL-DEL=0.082|SMR=0.0
                          28(SMRDI=0.028)|SDD=0.053(SDDSPCR=0.006(SDDCC=0.006)|SDDSPCS=0.002(SDDOS=0.001)|SDDPM=0.015(S
                          DDPM-Conversations Processing Agent=0.011|SDDPM-Mailbox Rules Agent=0.002)|SDDSCMG=0.001(SDDC
                          MM=0.001)|SDDCM=0.001|SDDSDMG=0.024(SDDR=0.024)|X-SDDAD=0.003|X-SDDS=0.010)
MessageLatency          : 00:00:00.3530000
MessageLatencyType      : EndToEnd
EventData               : {[IncludeInSla, True], [MailboxDatabaseGuid, 781213e7-cf6b-4a4f-979c-baf9a2e08231],
                          [Mailboxes, 3cb8738a-005b-4c15-8e45-6cc9ff748c69], [StoreObjectIds, AAAAAHIAwc4GfTBNmAyUTFuhK
                          mIHABEehGKc+7pLmIvTzrwkEZkAAAAAAQwAABEehGKc+7pLmIvTzrwkEZkAAAAACXEAAA==], [FromEntity,
                          Hosted], [ToEntity, Hosted], [P2RecipStat, 0.006/1], [MsgRecipCount, 1], [SubRecipCount, 1],
                          [DeliveryLatency, 0.352], [AttachCount, 0], [E2ELatency, 0.353], [DeliveryPriority, Normal],
                          [AccountForest, ProExchangeAdmin.com]}
TransportTrafficType    : Email
SchemaVersion           : 15.02.0858.012


[PS] C:\>_
```

***Figure 6-10.** Detailed information when a specific message was delivered to a mailbox*

If there are multiple Exchange servers in your organization, it is not possible to predict which Exchange server is processing a message and in what order. To use message tracking across all Exchange servers, execute a command similar to this one in EMS:

```
[PS] C:\> Get-TransportService | Where{$_.Name -like "EXCH*"} | Get-
MessageTrackingLog
```

All transport services will be retrieved with a server name starting with "EXCH"; in our example, this includes all Exchange servers, but excludes the Edge Transport server.

SSL Certificates

For securing messages in transit, Exchange always tries to use TLS or Transport Layer Security. Exchange 2019 uses TLS 1.2 by default; older versions of TLS are disabled. Exchange 2013 and Exchange 2016 use TLS 1.0 and TLS 1.1, but can use TLS 1.2 as well.

Note TLS 1.3 is not supported by Windows 2019, so Exchange 2019 cannot use TLS 1.3. Windows Server 2022 will support TLS 1.3 by default.

As mentioned before, Exchange Transport supports opportunistic TLS. This way, Exchange Transport can use the default self-signed certificate or an expired certificate. The certificate is only used for encryption purposes and not for server validation purposes.

So, you can safely use the default self-signed certificate, but you can also opt for using a normal, third-party SSL certificate on the Exchange server. When you do, this certificate can also be used for validation purposes.

To request a new certificate, execute the following commands in EMS on the Edge Transport server:

```
[PS] C:\> $RequestData = New-ExchangeCertificate -GenerateRequest
-Server EDGE01 -SubjectName "c=NL, S=Noord-Holland, L=Amsterdam,
O=ProExchangeAdmin, OU=RND, CN=Edge01.Proexchangeadmin.com" -DomainName
edge01.exchangelabs.nl -PrivateKeyExportable $true
[PS] C:\> Set-Content -path C:\Install\ssl-request.req -value $RequestData
```

The contents of the ssl-request.req file must be used with the certificate authority to request a new certificate. Once the certificate is issued and downloaded to c:\install, execute the following commands in EMS on the Edge Transport server:

```
[PS] C:\> $Data = [Byte[]]$(Get-Content -Path "c:\install\edge01_
proexchangeadmin_com.p7b" -Encoding byte -ReadCount 0)
[PS] C:\> Import-ExchangeCertificate -Server EDGE01 -FileData $Data
[PS] C:\> Get-ExchangeCertificate -Thumbprint
94D3DEB2BC4F09430AEC7E20B822850F3A52F7C1 | Enable-ExchangeCertificate
-Services SMTP
```

A warning message appears, asking if you want to overwrite the default self-signed certificate. Choose No; do not overwrite the default certificate. This default certificate is used by the Edge Synchronization. This is shown in Figure 6-11.

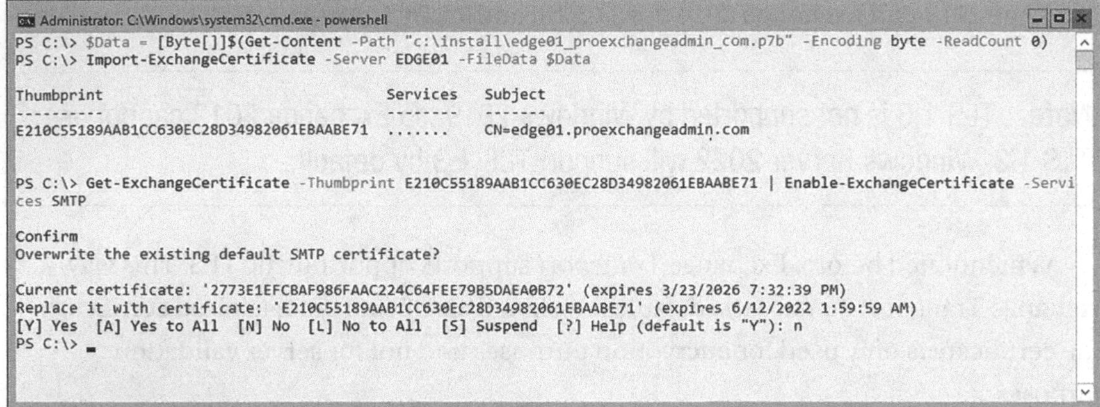

Figure 6-11. *Importing the new certificate on the Edge Transport server*

Note One use case for a third-party certificate on the Edge Transport server is when using this in combination with Exchange Online Protection for message hygiene purposes.

To check the certificate status on an Internet-facing Exchange server, or any email server, I normally use the `https://checktls.com` site. CheckTLS can, as the name implies, check TLS possibilities of a mail server. Navigate to the site, enter the FQDN of the Edge Transport server, and check the results as partially shown in Figure 6-12.

```
[000.250]         We can use this server
[000.250]         TLS is an option on this server
[000.250] -->STARTTLS
[000.332] <--220 2.0.0 SMTP server ready
[000.333]         STARTTLS command works on this server
[000.519]         Connection converted to SSL
                  SSLVersion in use: TLSv1_2
                  Cipher in use: ECDHE-RSA-AES256-GCM-SHA384
                  Perfect Forward Secrecy: yes
                  Certificate #1 of 3 (sent by MX):
                  Cert signed by: #2
                  Cert VALIDATED: ok
                  Cert Hostname VERIFIED (edge01.proexchangeadmin.com = edge01.proexchangeadmin.com | DNS:edge01.proexchangeadmin.com)
                  Not Valid Before: Jun 11 00:00:00 2021 GMT
                  Not Valid After: Jun 11 23:59:59 2022 GMT
                  subject= /CN=edge01.proexchangeadmin.com
                  issuer= /C=US/O=DigiCert Inc/CN=GeoTrust TLS DV RSA Mixed SHA256 2020 CA-1
                  Certificate #2 of 3 (sent by MX):
                  Cert signed by: #3
                  Cert VALIDATED: ok
                  Not Valid Before: Jul 16 12:21:44 2020 GMT
                  Not Valid After: May 31 23:59:59 2023 GMT
                  subject= /C=US/O=DigiCert Inc/CN=GeoTrust TLS DV RSA Mixed SHA256 2020 CA-1
                  issuer= /C=US/O=DigiCert Inc/OU=www.digicert.com/CN=DigiCert Global Root CA
                  Certificate #3 of 3 (added from CA Root Store):
                  Cert signed by: #3
                  Cert VALIDATED: ok
                  Not Valid Before: Nov 10 00:00:00 2006 GMT
                  Not Valid After: Nov 10 00:00:00 2031 GMT
                  subject= /C=US/O=DigiCert Inc/OU=www.digicert.com/CN=DigiCert Global Root CA
                  issuer= /C=US/O=DigiCert Inc/OU=www.digicert.com/CN=DigiCert Global Root CA
```

Figure 6-12. *CheckTLS.com for checking TLS options on your mail server*

Message Hygiene

Message hygiene is a part of any Exchange deployment that has changed dramatically the last couple of years. Ten years or so ago, multiple vendors were offering on-premises solutions for message hygiene. Nowadays, most message hygiene solutions are cloud based.

The Exchange Edge Transport server is often used as an SMTP gateway between the internal Exchange environment and any cloud-based message hygiene solution. The Exchange Edge Transport server does offer some basic functionality for message hygiene. I will discuss the Edge Transport server and its message hygiene features.

Edge Transport Server

Microsoft introduced the Exchange Edge Transport server years ago, in Exchange 2007 to be precise, and it is still available in Exchange 2019. In the early days, the Edge Transport server was positioned as a message hygiene solution, especially when Microsoft Forefront Protection for Exchange was installed. But, Forefront Protection for Exchange is discontinued years ago, and in 2021, the Microsoft solution for message hygiene is Exchange Online Protection. So, the Edge Transport service is typically installed in the perimeter network as a gateway between the internal Exchange servers and Exchange Online Protection. Using an Edge Transport Server in the perimeter network avoids publishing your internal Exchange server to the Internet for SMTP purposes.

You can however use an Edge Transport server as a first line of defense in a test environment, and it does a decent job when it comes to connection filtering. It is suited for a test environment, but for a production environment, I recommend using a cloud service.

Besides message hygiene, the Edge Transport servers can be used for mail flow rules and address rewriting.

Located in the perimeter network, the Edge Transport servers are not a member of the internal Active Directory domain. In fact, you can have multiple Edge Transport servers in your perimeter network. The positive side of this is that when the Edge Transport server gets compromised, the internal Active Directory is untouched. The downside, however, is that there is no shared configuration, and so you must configure all the Edge Transport servers manually, although there's an export and import utility to keep all the Edge Transport servers identical; the mechanism it uses is called cloning (more about this later in this chapter).

The Edge Transport servers need to have some knowledge of the Exchange configuration on the internal network; it would be hard to route messages to the correct Mailbox server on that internal network or to perform recipient filtering. Therefore, there exists a synchronization mechanism between the Mailbox servers on the internal network and the Edge Transport server on the perimeter network. This mechanism is called edge synchronization. Using edge synchronization, the Mailbox servers push (limited) information to the Edge Transport servers on a regular basis. There is no pull mechanism, so the Edge Transport server never pulls information from the internal Exchange server. When it comes to firewalling, only port 50636 needs to be opened outbound. Naturally, port 25 for SMTP needs to be open in both directions.

So, the Edge Transport servers act as your primary defense when it comes to Simple Mail Transfer Protocol (SMTP) traffic, and all inbound messages are routed via your Edge Transport servers. The MX records in the public Domain Name Service (DNS) point to your Edge Transport servers. You can have multiple MX records whereby each MX record points to a particular Edge Transport server.

A simple representation of a network of two Edge Transport servers and two Mailbox servers is shown in Figure 6-13.

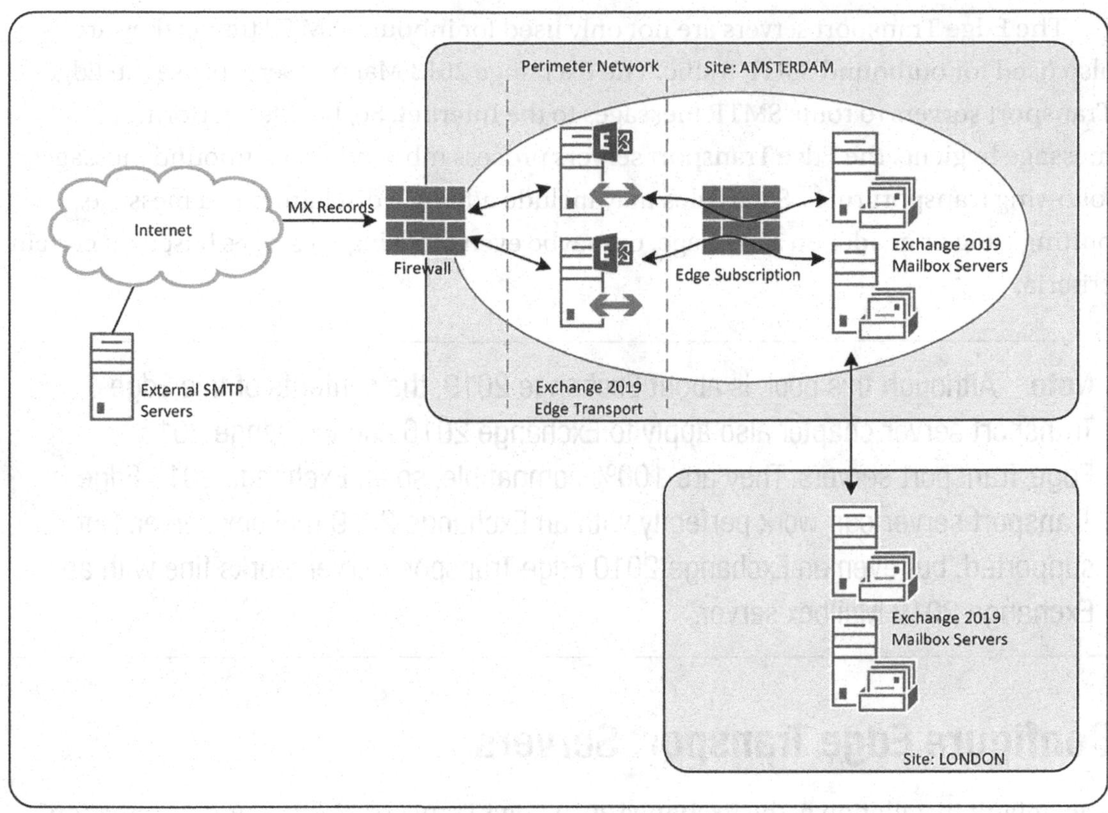

***Figure 6-13.** The Edge Transport servers are located in the perimeter network*

The installation of Edge Transport servers is not bound to a particular site, but edge synchronization is bound to a particular site in Active Directory. So, if you have two Edge Transport servers at a site called Amsterdam, as shown in Figure 6-13, the two Edge Transport servers are synchronized with the two Mailbox servers at this site. If you have an additional site in London, the Edge Transport servers will not send information directly to the Mailbox servers in London, but route messages via the Exchange 2019 mailbox servers in the Amsterdam site.

If you want to implement two Edge Transport servers in the London Active Directory site, you must create an edge synchronization there as well, and then this edge synchronization is bound to the Mailbox servers in that London Active Directory site.

There must be separate MX records pointing to these Edge Transport servers as well. When building a configuration like this, you automatically get site redundancy for inbound SMTP traffic.

The Edge Transport servers are not only used for inbound SMTP traffic; they are also used for outbound SMTP traffic. The Exchange 2013 Mailbox servers use the Edge Transport servers to route SMTP messages to the Internet. So, besides performing message hygiene, the Edge Transport servers process inbound and outbound messages, following transport rules. Such rules may include adding a disclaimer to a message, putting a tag or header on a message, or maybe even blocking messages based on certain criteria.

Note Although this book is about Exchange 2019, the contents of this Edge Transport server chapter also apply to Exchange 2016 and Exchange 2013 Edge Transport servers. They are 100% compatible, so an Exchange 2013 Edge Transport server can work perfectly with an Exchange 2019 mailbox server. Not supported, but even an Exchange 2010 Edge Transport server works fine with an Exchange 2019 Mailbox server.

Configure Edge Transport Servers

The default installation of the Exchange 2019 Edge Transport Servers and the creation of an Edge Subscription are already covered in Chapter 2, so I will only discuss the configuration options of the Edge Transport server.

Relocate Transport Database

Like any Exchange server, the Transport database is installed on the same disk as where the Exchange binaries are installed; by default, this is the c:\ drive. The Transport database is where all inbound and outbound messages are always stored.

When an Edge Transport server is used, all inbound and outbound messages are always routed via this Edge Transport server. As such, the Transport database can grow very rapidly. To prevent the disk filling up, it is recommended to use a separate disk for this Transport database.

When Exchange is installed, a script is automatically stored in the Exchange scripts directory that will relocate the Transport database. To move this database from the default c:\ drive to the d:\ drive, execute the following commands in EMS:

```
[PS] C:\> CD $ExScripts
[PS] C:\> $LogPath = "D:\Program Files\Microsoft\Exchange Server\V15\
TransportRoles\data"
[PS] C:\> .\Move-TransportDatabase.ps1 -queueDatabasePath "$LogPath\
Queue" -queueDatabaseLoggingPath "$LogPath\Queue" -iPFilterDatabasePath
"$LogPath\IpFilter" -iPFilterDatabaseLoggingPath "$LogPath\IpFilter"
-temporaryStoragePath "$LogPath\Temp"
```

The script will stop the Transport service, move the database to another location, change the appropriate configuration files, and start the Transport service again.

Anti-spam Settings

Inbound SMTP messages from the Internet are delivered to the Edge Transport server and are processed for message hygiene in a certain order:

1. Connection filtering
    - IP Allow list
    - IP Block list
    - Real-time Block List (RBL)
2. Sender filtering
3. Recipient filtering
4. Sender ID filtering
5. Content filtering
    - Outlook safe sender
    - SCL threshold
6. Sender Reputation
7. Attachment filtering

When processing is complete, the message is sent to the internal Exchange 2019 Mailbox server. This is shown in Figure 6-14.

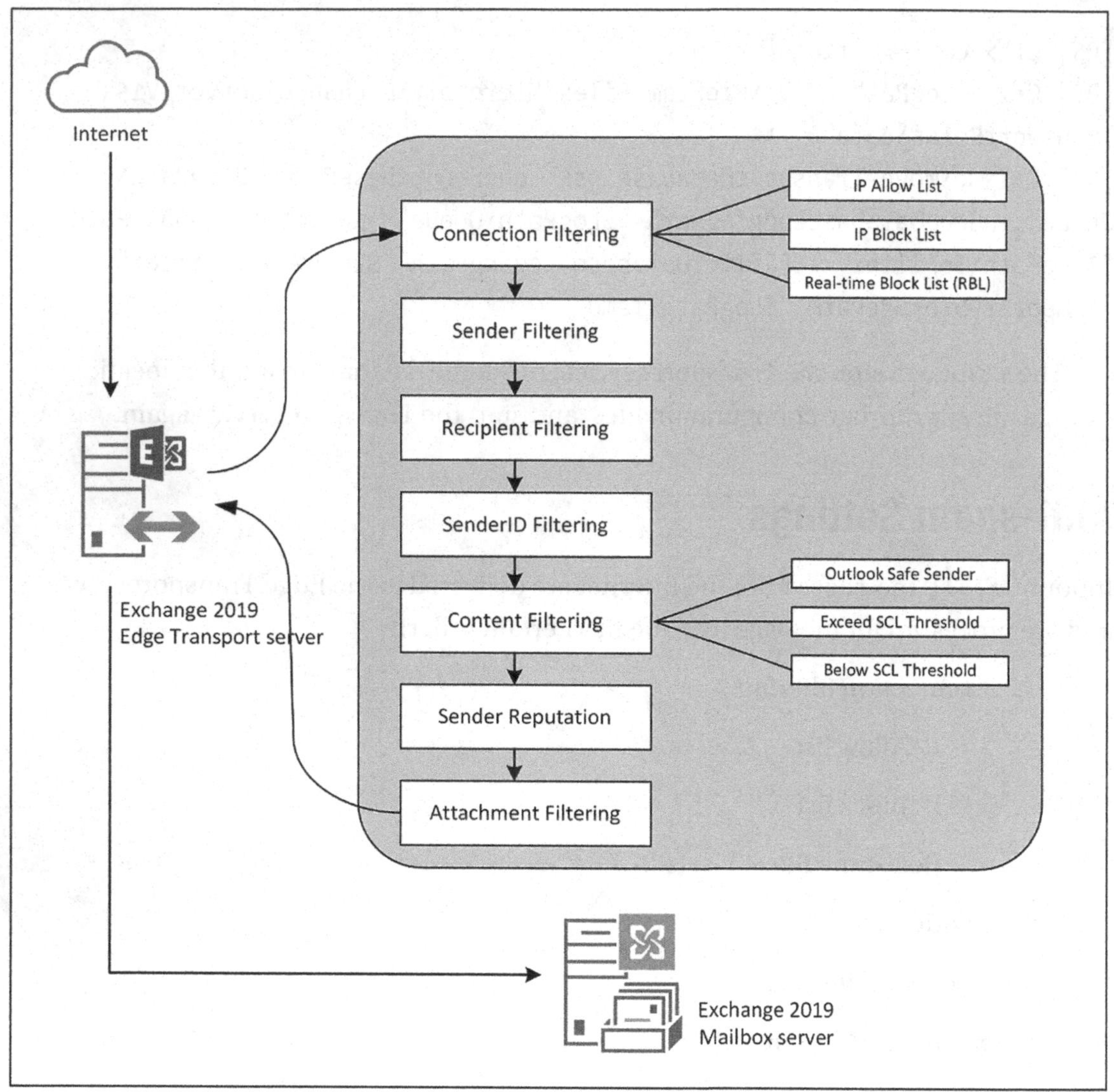

***Figure 6-14.** The order of message processing on an Exchange 2019 Edge Transport server*

The Edge Transport server works with transport agents. The following transport agents are available on the Edge Transport server:

- Connection filtering agents
- Sender Filter agent
- Recipient Filter agent
- Sender ID agent
- Content Filter agent
- Sender Reputation agent
- Attachment Filter agent

You can retrieve a list of transport agents by running the `Get-TransportAgent` cmdlet in the Exchange Management Shell on the Edge Transport server, as shown in Figure 6-15. Note that all transport agents are enabled by default and are configured with default settings.

```
Administrator: C:\Windows\system32\cmd.exe - powershell
PS C:\> Get-TransportAgent

Identity                              Enabled       Priority
--------                              -------       --------
Connection Filtering Agent            True          1
Address Rewriting Inbound Agent       True          2
Edge Rule Agent                       True          3
Content Filter Agent                  True          4
Sender Id Agent                       True          5
Sender Filter Agent                   True          6
Recipient Filter Agent                True          7
Protocol Analysis Agent               True          8
Attachment Filtering Agent            True          9
Address Rewriting Outbound Agent      True          10


PS C:\> _
```

***Figure 6-15.** Transport agents available on an Edge Transport server*

As can be seen in Figure 6-15, the first and most important step in message hygiene is connection filtering. This is where messages that come from IP addresses or ranges that are on block lists are filtered out. In fact, this constitutes most of all email entering the Edge Transport server.

Connection Filtering Agents

Connection filtering is the first default layer of defense when SMTP messages access the Exchange 2013 Edge Transport server. When a sending SMTP server on the Internet sets up a connection on port 25 to the Edge Transport server, the server checks this sending SMTP server. If there's something wrong, the connection is closed, even before any mail data is sent to the Edge Transport server.

There are four ways to configure the connection filtering:

- IP Allow list
- IP Allow list providers
- IP Block list
- IP Block list providers

IP Allow List

When a remote SMTP server sets up a connection with the Edge Transport server to send a message, the Edge Transport server checks to see if the IP address this remote SMTP server is using is whitelisted. In general, a whitelist is a list of server names or IP addresses of SMTP servers that are trusted. If it is, this remote SMTP server is assumed to be safe, and the connection is allowed; the message is accepted.

To add an IP address to the IP Allow list, you can use the Add-IPAllowListEntry, followed by the IP address of the remote SMTP server, for example:

```
[PS] C:\> Add-IPAllowListEntry -IPAddress 178.251.192.4
```

The output is shown in Figure 6-16.

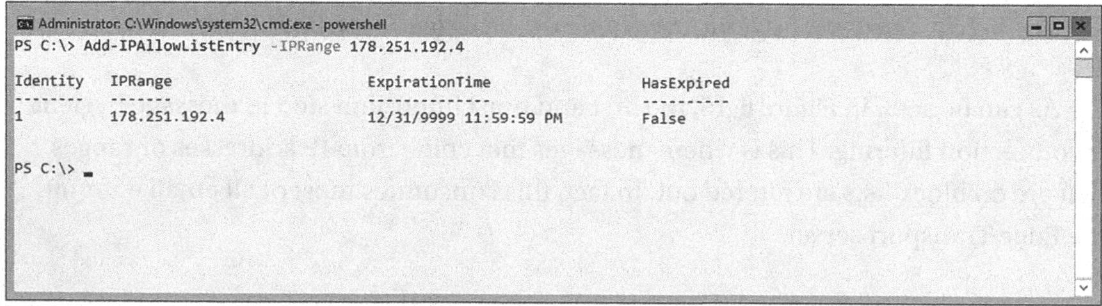

Figure 6-16. *Adding an IP address to the IP Allow list*

When a remote SMTP server is whitelisted by the Edge Transport server, a spam confidence level (SCL) rating of -1 is stamped on the message; more specifically, an X-header is added to the message. This way, Exchange knows the message is safe and treats it as such, and this message is not processed by any other anti-spam agent on the Edge Transport server.

When checking the header of a message originating from this host, you will see something like this:

Return-Path: j.wesselius@exchangelabs.nl

```
X-MS-Exchange-Organization-Antispam-Report: IPOnAllowList
X-MS-Exchange-Organization-SCL: -1
X-MS-Exchange-Organization-AuthSource: ams-edge03.exchangelabs.nl
```

IP Allow List Providers

Instead of adding IP addresses manually to the IP Allow list, it is possible to use IP Allow list providers. These providers have lists of trusted SMTP servers, servers that are definitely not associated with any spam activity.

You must be careful when implementing these providers. As explained in the previous section, messages sent by allowed SMTP hosts are automatically tagged an SCL of -1, which means these messages flow through the Exchange organization without being inspected by any other anti-spam agent; therefore, the provider needs to be completely trustworthy.

There are several providers, sometimes referred to as whitelist providers, available on the Internet; for example, there is Spamhaus Whitelist (`www.spamhauswhitelist.com`) or the DNS WhiteList organization (`www.dnswl.org`).

Be aware that this is a matter of getting what you pay for; there are no free and reliable IP Allow list providers.

Therefore, I suggest not using an IP Allow list provider and instead relying on the IP Block lists and IP Block list providers.

IP Block List

An IP Block list is the exact opposite of an IP Allow list. When an external SMTP server sets up a connection with the Exchange Edge Transport server, and this SMTP server is on the Edge Transport server's Block list, the connection is automatically voided.

To add an IP address to the Edge Transport server's Block list, you can use the `Add-IPBlockListEntry` command followed by the IP address of the SMTP server you want to block, for example:

```
[PS] C:\> Add-IPBlockListEntry -IPAddress 192.168.10.100
```

It is also possible to add a range of IP addresses to the Block list, for example:

```
[PS] C:\> Add-IPBlockListEntry -IPRange 192.168.10.0/24
```

To add an IP address to the Block list temporarily, you use the -ExpirationTime parameter. To add the SMTP server to the Block list but have it automatically removed on September 1, 2021, you would use the following command:

```
[PS] C:\> Add-IPBlockListEntry -IPAddress 192.168.10.100 -ExpirationTime
"9/1/2021 00:00"
```

To get an overview of all IP addresses that are on the Edge Transport server's Block list, you can use the `Get-IPBlockListEntry` command, without any parameters.

To review the IP Block list configuration of the Edge Transport server, you can use the `Get-IPBlockListConfig` command.

Note The IP Block list is configured on a per-server basis. If you have multiple Edge Transport servers, you must configure them individually, but this is prone to error. When deploying the Edge Transport servers, you can also configure one Edge Transport server and export the configuration to subsequent Edge Transport servers. However, remember that changes also need to be made to lists on all Edge Transport servers.

Configuring and maintaining the IP Block lists is quite some work, so it is better to automate this task by using an IP Block list provider.

IP Block List Providers

To automate maintenance of the IP Block list, you can use an IP Block list provider. The process is identical to a regular IP Block list as discussed in the previous section, but instead of you maintaining the IP Block list entries manually, the entries are maintained by a provider.

One well-known provider is Spamhaus (`www.spamhaus.org`), in particular their Zen Combined Block List.

To configure this provider, you open the Exchange Management Shell on the Edge Transport server and enter the following command:

```
[PS] C:\> Add-IPBlockListProvider -Name SpamHaus -LookupDomain zen.
spamhaus.org -Enabled $true -BitmaskMatch $null -Priority 1 -AnyMatch $true
-RejectionResponse 'Message blocked due to black listing'
```

This is shown in Figure 6-17.

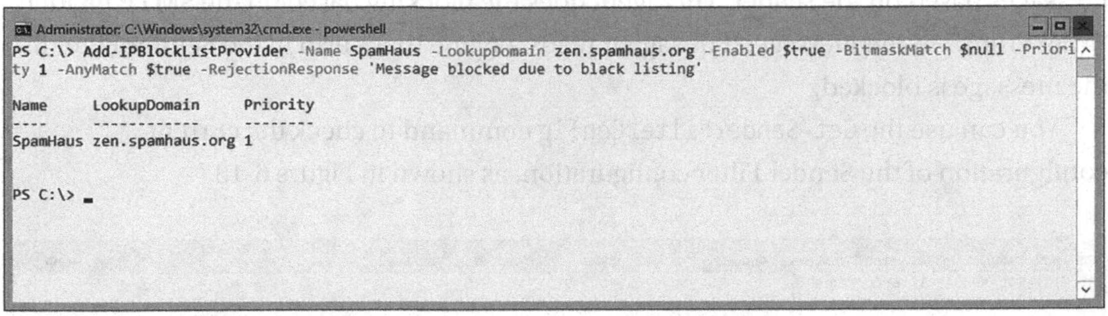

```
Administrator: C:\Windows\system32\cmd.exe - powershell
PS C:\> Add-IPBlockListProvider -Name SpamHaus -LookupDomain zen.spamhaus.org -Enabled $true -BitmaskMatch $null -Priori
ty 1 -AnyMatch $true -RejectionResponse 'Message blocked due to black listing'

Name     LookupDomain     Priority
----     ------------     --------
SpamHaus zen.spamhaus.org 1

PS C:\>
```

Figure 6-17. *Adding Spamhaus as a Block list provider*

You can use the –RejectionResponse parameter of the `Add-IPBlockListProvider` command to add a customer message that's returned to the sender of the message, but the message cannot exceed 240 characters.

It is possible to disable the IP Block list function on a per-user basis. This way, it is always possible for recipients to receive email messages, regardless of any IP Block list provider. To set this, you can use the `Set-IPBlockListProvidersConfig` command with the `-ByPassedRecipients` parameter. For example, to bypass the IP Block list filtering for a user named sarah@proexchangeadmin.com, you can use the following command:

```
[PS] C:\> Set-IPBlockListProvidersConfig -ByPassedRecipients "sarah@
proexchangeadmin.com"
```

To add or remove multiple recipients at the same time as when the IP Block list provider is configured, you can use the @{Add="recipient"} syntax:

```
[PS] C:\> Set-IPBlockListProvidersConfig -ByPassedRecipients @{Add="jaap@
proexchangeadmin.com","professor@proexchangeadmin.com"; Remove="sarah@
proexchangeadmin.com"}
```

The IP Block list typically works for connections coming from the Internet or external connections. It is also possible to configure the IP Block list for internal use; you use the -InternalMailEnabled parameter. By default, this function is turned off, but you can enable it using the following command:

```
[PS] C:\> Set-IPBlockListProvidersConfig -InternalMailEnabled $true
```

Sender Filtering

Sender filtering is a default feature in the Edge Transport server that enables you to filter messages based on the sender. This agent does the blocking based on the SMTP header "Mail From:" in the message. If the agent reads a name that's also in the Sender Filter list, the message is blocked.

You can use the `Get-SenderFilterConfig` command to check the current configuration of the Sender Filter configuration, as shown in Figure 6-18.

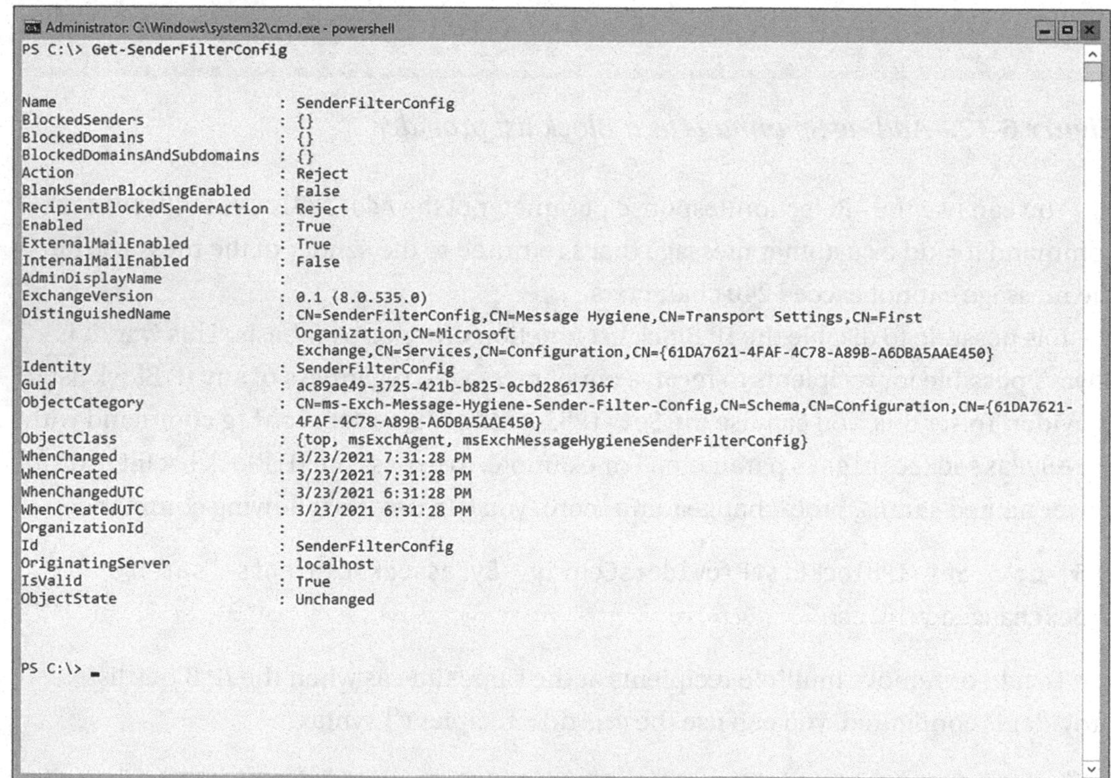

Figure 6-18. *The configuration of the Sender Filter*

To add a particular sender to the Sender Filter configuration, you can use the Set-SenderFilterConfig command. This command takes the -BlockedSenders parameter to add specific senders, but you can also use the -BlockedDomains and -BlockedDomainsAndSubdomains parameters to add complete domains to the Sender Filter configuration. For example, to add a user called john@alpineskihouse.com to the blocked senders list and to add the cheapwatches.com domain to the list of blocked senders, you can use the following command:

```
[PS] C:\> Set-SenderFilterConfig -BlockedSenders "John@alpineskihouse.com"
-BlockedDomains "cheapwatches.com"
```

If you want to block senders from the northwindtraders.com and all its subdomains, you can use the following command:

```
[PS] C:\> Set-SenderFilterConfig -BlockedDomainsAndSubdomains
northwindtraders.com
```

These properties are multivalue, which means they can contain more than one value. If you want to add multiple senders to the Sender Filter configuration later on, you must use the @{Add="sender"} syntax. If you want to remove senders from the Sender Filter configuration, you must use the @{Remove="sender"} syntax, for example:

```
[PS] C:\> Set-SenderFilterConfig -BlockedSenders @{Add="onlinecasino@gmail.
com","enlargement@hotmail.com"; Remove="john@alpineskihouse.com"}
```

You must use the same syntax if you want to add or remove domains from the BlockedDomains and BlockedDomainsAndSubDomains properties.

To get an overview of all blocked senders and domains on your Edge Transport server, you can use the `Get-SenderFilterConfig` again, for example:

```
[PS] C;\> Get-SenderFilterConfig | Format-List BlockedSenders,BlockedDomains,
BlockedDomainsAndSubdomains
```

Note Only anonymous connections are processed by the Sender Filter agent.

It is possible to configure the Sender Filter agent to filter out messages that do not have anything listed in the “Mail From” header of a message. This safeguards your organization from NDR attacks from the Internet. To configure this, you use

```
[PS] C:\> Set-SenderFilterConfig -BlankSenderBlockingenabled $true
```

Note It is relatively easy to spoof the Mail From header in an email message. Therefore, it is not recommended you rely exclusively on the Sender Filter agent.

Recipient Filtering

Recipient filtering on the Edge Transport server gives you the opportunity to accept messages only for existing recipients in your Exchange environment. As its name implies, the Recipient Filter agent on the Edge Transport server only accepts messages with a valid recipient in your Exchange organization.

The accepted domains configured in an Exchange environment have a property called AddressBookEnabled. This property enables or disables recipient filtering for an accepted domain. By default, the Recipient Filter agent is enabled for authoritative accepted domains and is disabled for accepted domains that are configured as internal relay domains or as external relay domains.

To check the value of the AddressBookEnabled property, and thus the status of the Recipient Filter agent, you can use the following command:

```
[PS] C:\> Get-AcceptedDomain | Format-List Name,AddressBookEnabled
```

If you want to disable the Recipient Filter agent, you can use the following command:

```
[PS] C:\> Set-RecipientFilterConfig -Enabled $false
```

You can use recipient filtering not only to block messages to unknown recipients but also to block individual recipients in your Exchange organization; you do this by adding them individually, using the following command:

```
[PS] C:\> Set-RecipientFilterConfig -BlockedRecipients joe@
proexchangeadmin.com
```

Just as described for sender filtering, you can use the @{Add="<recipient>" syntax to add other recipients to the blocked recipients list. This adds john@proexchangeadmin.com and blake@proexchangeadmin.com and removes joe@proexchangeadmin.com at the same time:

```
[PS] C:\> Set-RecipientFilterConfig -BlockedRecipients @{Add="john@
proexchangeadmin.com","blake@proexchangeadmin.com"; Remove="joe@
proexchangeadmin.com"}
```

You can use the -RecipientValidationEnabled parameter to enable recipient validation, which blocks messages to recipients in your Exchange organization who do not exist. To enable recipient validation, you can use the following command:

```
[PS] C:\> Set-RecipientFilterConfig -RecipientValidationEnabled $true
```

When you enable the recipient validation, the Recipient Filter agent does a recipient lookup. Since the Edge Transport server does not have access to the internal Active Directory, it performs this lookup in the local Active Directory Lightweight Directory Service (AD LDS), which contains a list of internal users. To prevent any information from being exposed when the Edge Transport server is compromised, the user information is stored directly in AD LDS, but only a one-way hash is used with a secure hash algorithm (SHA)-256.

Sender ID Filtering

Sender ID filtering is a DNS-based technique whereby the receiving SMTP server (in our case, this is the Exchange Edge Transport server) checks for certain DNS records (called SPF records) of the sending organization. Sender ID filtering is Microsoft's implementation (or naming) of SPF.

This SPF record in DNS, which is the responsibility of the sending organization, defines which SMTP servers are allowed to send SMTP messages on behalf of this SMTP domain. When properly configured, the IP address of the sending SMTP record matches the SPF record in the public DNS. When this does not match, it might signal spoofing of the SMTP domain and thus be a spamming technique. To make it more difficult, it can also indicate a misconfigured SPF entry in DNS.

When the Edge Transport server performs the Sender ID check, there are two potential results:

- **Pass**—The IP address of the remote SMTP server matches the information in the SPF record, and a header indicating the successful test is added to the message. This also contributes to the sender's reputation data. (Sender reputation is explained later in this chapter.)

- **Fail**—The IP address of the remote SMTP server does not match the information in the SPF record, or an SPF record was not found. The first can indicate a malicious message or SMTP server. It is also possible that the SPF is not configured or is misconfigured owing to some changes in the sender's messaging infrastructure. A failed Sender ID test contributes to the sender's reputation data, but in a negative way, of course.

The reputation data contributes to the spam confidence level (SCL) of an email message; in turn, this determines what happens to a message, as shown in Figure 6-19.

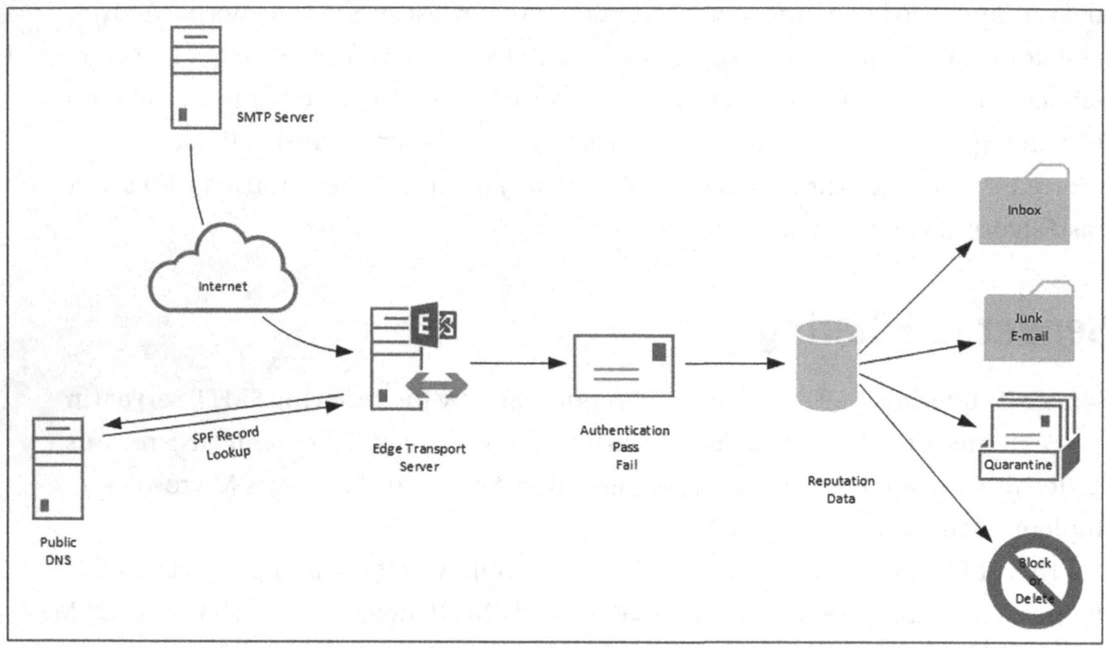

Figure 6-19. *Overview of the Sender ID framework*

The SPF record (a TXT record can be used as well) is registered in the public DNS of the sending organization, and this is checked by the receiving Mail server, your Edge Transport server.

When you open the EMS and enter the `Get-SenderIDConfig` cmdlet, you'll see the default settings for the Sender ID agent. You might want to change the SpoofedDomainAction setting; this setting determines what the agent needs to do when the Sender ID check returns an error (wrong IP on sending SMTP server and possibly a spoofed domain).

There are multiple options:

- **StampStatus**—This is the default setting. It stamps an additional header on the message, and the server continues processing.
- **Reject**—This option returns an NDR to the sender, notifying them that something is wrong.
- **Delete**—This option deletes the message without returning an NDR to the sender. In this case, when it is a legitimate sender, they never know the message got lost.

It is also possible to bypass certain sending SMTP domains using the BypassedSenderDomains parameter. To change the Sender ID setting to Reject and add the Microsoft.com SMTP domain to the bypassed sender domains, you can use the following command:

```
[PS] C:\> Set-SenderIDConfig -SpoofedDomainAction Reject -
BypassedSenderDomains Microsoft.com
```

If you want external recipients to perform a Sender ID check on the email messages sent by your organization, and thus contribute to a higher success rate for your messages, you must implement an SPF record in your public DNS domain as well.

To create an SPF record, you can check the `http://openspf.org` website; the SPF Record Syntax page on this site explains all the details on how to set up an SPF record in public DNS.

As an example, the Edge Transport server edge01.proexchangeadmin.com has two public IP addresses:

- **IPv4**—176.62.196.248
- **IPv6**—2a02:20b0:112:1::1

All email messages are always coming from these IP addresses. In the future, it might also be possible to create a hybrid situation with Microsoft Exchange Online (which is discussed in Chapter 9), and in that scenario, mail can also be sent from Office 365.

The corresponding SPF record must contain the IPv4, IPv6, and Microsoft FQDN, and the record must look like this:

```
v=spf1 ip4:176.62.196.248 ip6:2a02:20b0:112:1::1 include:spf.protection.
outlook.com -all
```

You can check your SPF record on the MXToolbox site at `https://mxtoolbox.com/spf.aspx`, which will show your SPF record, if there are any misconfigurations, and an explanation of all entries.

Content Filtering

Content filtering is another important feature of the Edge Transport server. Using content filtering, it's possible to filter and delete incoming messages based on certain keywords like "online casino," "cheap watches," "Viagra," or whatever other words you want to target. You can use the Add-ContentFilterPhrase cmdlet to add specific words to the Content Filter agent, for example:

```
$Phrases = 'Bitcoin',' WING HANG BANK','Helly my dear'
$Phrases | ForEach-Object {Add-ContentFilterPhrase -Phrase $_ -Influence
BadWord}
```

This is shown in Figure 6-20.

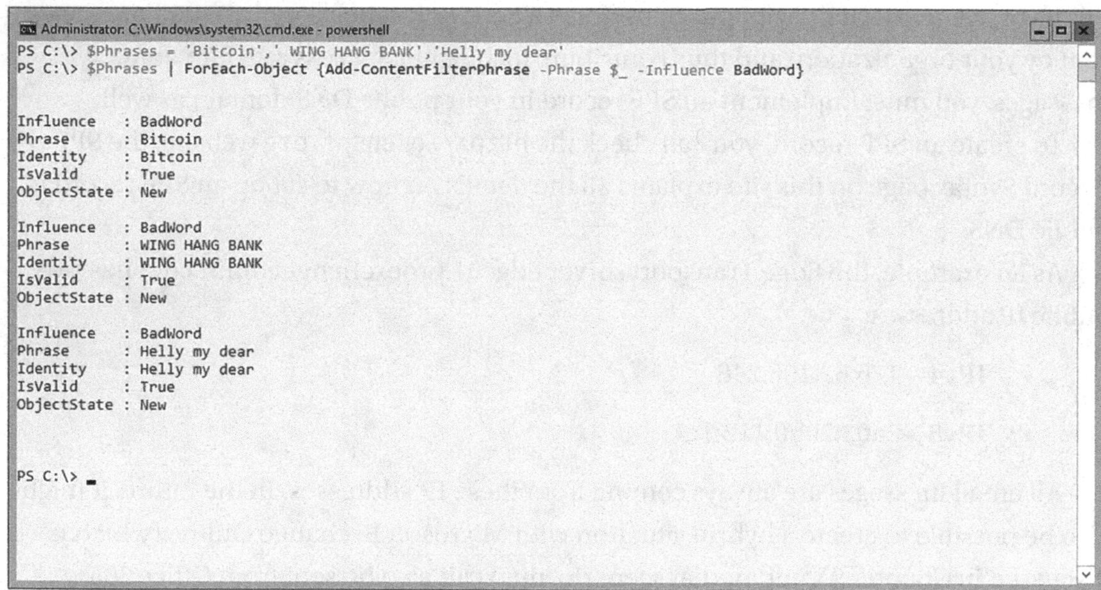
Administrator: C:\Windows\system32\cmd.exe - powershell

```
PS C:\> $Phrases = 'Bitcoin',' WING HANG BANK','Helly my dear'
PS C:\> $Phrases | ForEach-Object {Add-ContentFilterPhrase -Phrase $_ -Influence BadWord}

Influence   : BadWord
Phrase      : Bitcoin
Identity    : Bitcoin
IsValid     : True
ObjectState : New

Influence   : BadWord
Phrase      : WING HANG BANK
Identity    : WING HANG BANK
IsValid     : True
ObjectState : New

Influence   : BadWord
Phrase      : Helly my dear
Identity    : Helly my dear
IsValid     : True
ObjectState : New


PS C:\> _
```

Figure 6-20. *Setting specific words for content filtering*

Content filtering also works with the spam confidence level (SCL). This number identifies the likelihood of an email message being spam. An SCL rating of 9 means the message is most likely spam, while an SCL rating of 1 indicates the message is likely legitimate.

Based on the SCL rating, you can block messages, reject messages (and NDR is returned to the sender), or send the messages to a quarantine mailbox. My personal preference is to block no. 9 messages, reject no. 8 messages, and forward no. 7 messages to a quarantine mailbox.

These settings are set using the `Set-ContentFilterConfig` cmdlet on the Edge Transport server:

```
[PS] C:\> Set-ContentFilterConfig -QuarantineMailbox quarantaine@
proexchangeadmin.com -SCLQuarantineEnabled $true -SCLQuarantineThreshold 7
[PS] C:\> Set-ContentFilterConfig -SCLDeleteEnabled $true -
SCLDeleteThreshold 9
[PS] C:\> Set-ContentFilterConfig -SCLRejectEnabled $true -
SCLRejectThreshold 8
```

This is shown in Figure 6-21.

```
Administrator: C:\Windows\system32\cmd.exe - powershell
PS C:\> Set-ContentFilterConfig -QuarantineMailbox quarantaine@proexchangeadmin.com -SCLQuarantineEnabled $true -SCLQuar
antineThreshold 7
PS C:\> Set-ContentFilterConfig -SCLDeleteEnabled $true -SCLDeleteThreshold 9
PS C:\> Set-ContentFilterConfig -SCLRejectEnabled $true -SCLRejectThreshold 8
PS C:\>
```

***Figure 6-21.** Using the spam confidence level ratings*

It is also possible to bypass certain recipients from content filtering. A common candidate for this is the email address postmaster@proexchangeadmin.com or abuse@proexchangeadmin.com. These settings are also made using the `Set-ContentFilterConfig` cmdlet:

```
[PS] C:\> Set-ContentFilterConfig -BypassedRecipients postmaster@
proexchangeadmin.com, abuse@proexchangeadmin.com
```

There are a couple of best practices you can take into consideration:

1. Use a dedicated mailbox and user account for the quarantine mailbox and remove the quota limits from this mailbox. If there is a quota on the mailbox and the contents exceed this limit, the mail will get lost.

2. Use a dedicated mailbox database for the quarantine mailbox.
3. Configure Outlook so that the original sender, recipient, and BCC fields are shown in the Message view.

To get an overview of all Content Filter agent settings, you can use the `Get-ContentFilterConfig` command, as shown in Figure 6-22.

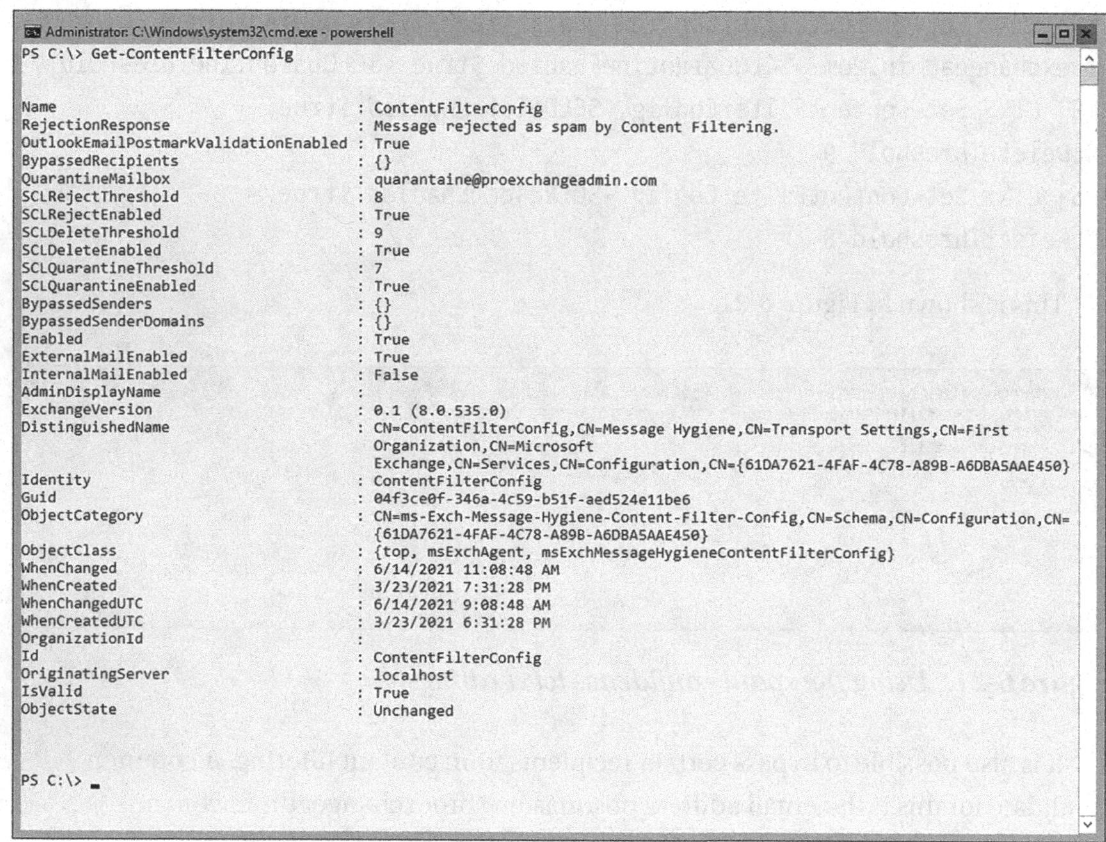

```
Administrator: C:\Windows\system32\cmd.exe - powershell
PS C:\> Get-ContentFilterConfig

Name                                   : ContentFilterConfig
RejectionResponse                      : Message rejected as spam by Content Filtering.
OutlookEmailPostmarkValidationEnabled  : True
BypassedRecipients                     : {}
QuarantineMailbox                      : quarantaine@proexchangeadmin.com
SCLRejectThreshold                     : 8
SCLRejectEnabled                       : True
SCLDeleteThreshold                     : 9
SCLDeleteEnabled                       : True
SCLQuarantineThreshold                 : 7
SCLQuarantineEnabled                   : True
BypassedSenders                        : {}
BypassedSenderDomains                  : {}
Enabled                                : True
ExternalMailEnabled                    : True
InternalMailEnabled                    : False
AdminDisplayName                       :
ExchangeVersion                        : 0.1 (8.0.535.0)
DistinguishedName                      : CN=ContentFilterConfig,CN=Message Hygiene,CN=Transport Settings,CN=First
                                         Organization,CN=Microsoft
                                         Exchange,CN=Services,CN=Configuration,CN={61DA7621-4FAF-4C78-A89B-A6DBA5AAE450}
Identity                               : ContentFilterConfig
Guid                                   : 04f3ce0f-346a-4c59-b51f-aed524e11be6
ObjectCategory                         : CN=ms-Exch-Message-Hygiene-Content-Filter-Config,CN=Schema,CN=Configuration,CN=
                                         {61DA7621-4FAF-4C78-A89B-A6DBA5AAE450}
ObjectClass                            : {top, msExchAgent, msExchMessageHygieneContentFilterConfig}
WhenChanged                            : 6/14/2021 11:08:48 AM
WhenCreated                            : 3/23/2021 7:31:28 PM
WhenChangedUTC                         : 6/14/2021 9:08:48 AM
WhenCreatedUTC                         : 3/23/2021 6:31:28 PM
OrganizationId                         :
Id                                     : ContentFilterConfig
OriginatingServer                      : localhost
IsValid                                : True
ObjectState                            : Unchanged

PS C:\> _
```

Figure 6-22. *Retrieving all content filtering settings*

Sender Reputation

On the Edge Transport server, a Protocol Analysis agent is running which analyzes statistics from SMTP senders. The Protocol Analysis agent is a nonconfigurable agent, and Sender Reputation relies on persistent data that's received from this Protocol Analysis agent.

A Sender Reputation Level (SRL) is calculated based on the following characteristics:

- EHLO/HELO analysis of the sending SMTP server
- Reverse DNS lookup
- SCL ratings of a particular sender
- Open proxy test on the sending SMTP server

Based on the outcome of these tests, an SRL is calculated, and this SRL is an indication of the likelihood of a spammer; it is somewhat like the SCL ratings for individual messages. An SRL rating of 0 indicates that the sending SMTP server is probably not a spamming server, while a value of 9 for the SRL indicates it is a spamming server.

Based on the SRL rating, actions can be taken on the messages as follows:

- Rejected
- Deleted and archived
- Accepted and marked as a blocked sender

By default, all senders start with an SRL rating of 0. Only after receiving 20 messages does Sender Reputation start calculating the SRL. If a sender is registered as a blocked sender, Sender Reputation signals the Sender Filter agent to block this sender.

Note The SRL is kept in memory. When the Transport service is restarted on the Edge Transport servers, all SRL data is lost and Sender Reputation restarts with 0.

The SRL threshold is set to 7 by default, and this is sufficient for most organizations. However, you should monitor the effectiveness of this setting and, if needed, adjust the threshold using the `Set-SenderReputationConfig` command. This command takes the -SrlBlockThreshold parameter to change the SRL setting.

Another interesting parameter is the -SenderBlockinPeriod, which defines the number of hours a particular sender is blocked when this sender exceeds the threshold. To change the SRL threshold to a value of 6 and set the blocking period to 36 hours, for example, you can use the following command:

```
[PS] C:\> Set-SenderReputationConfig -SrlBlockThreshold 6
-SenderBlockingPeriod 36
```

When the Transport Edge server's anti-spam configuration is fully configured, you can continue with the other settings, such as the SSL certificates (which is optional), and can start testing the Transport Edge server.

Test of the Edge Transport Server

The easiest way to test the installation of your Edge Transport server is to start sending email. You can also use the Remote Connectivity Analyzer (RCA) (`www.testexchangeconnectivity.com`) to test the environment. To use the analyzer, you open the RCA in your browser, select Exchange server, and select Outbound SMTP mail. Then, you enter the IP address of the outbound SMTP server, select the options you want to check, and enter your email address, as shown in Figure 6-23.

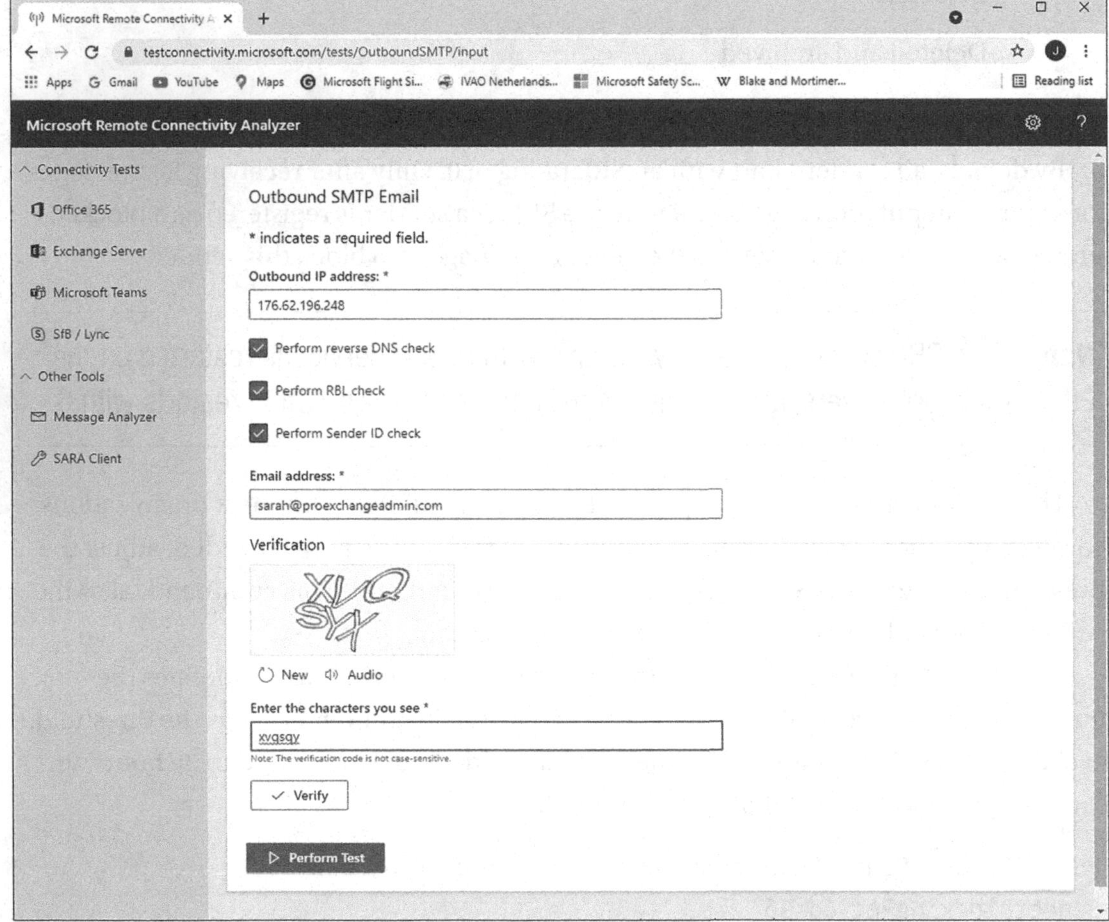

Figure 6-23. *Testing the Outbound SMTP email configuration*

When all is well, you will see the results in seconds; all options should show the green balls with the white checkmark, as shown in Figure 6-24.

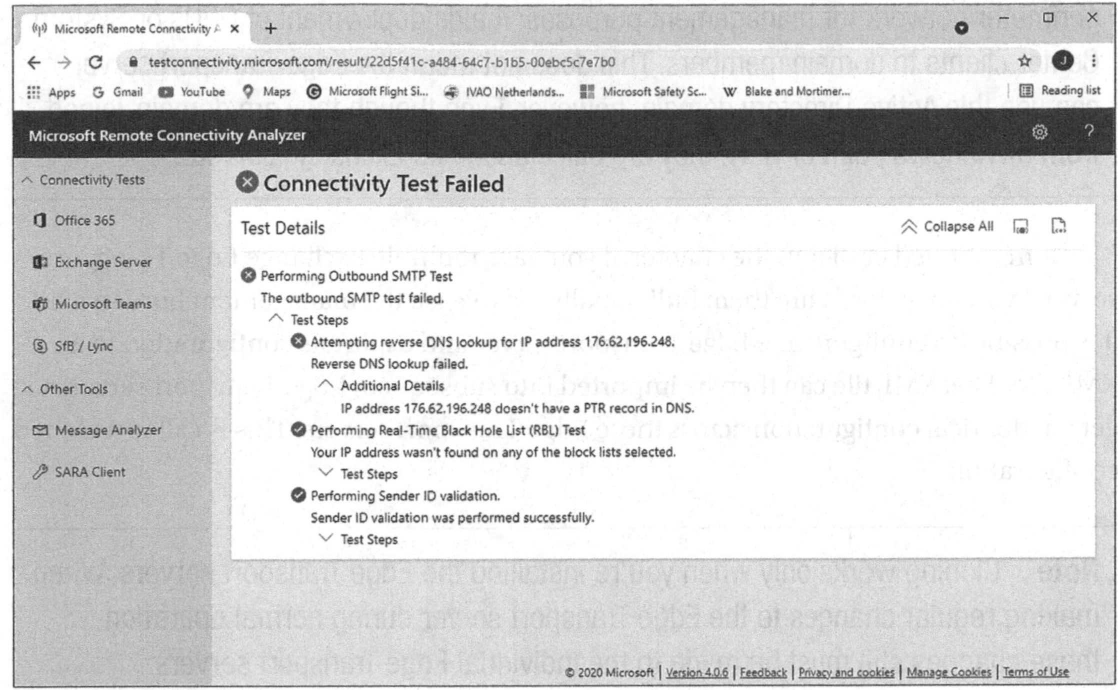

Figure 6-24. *Results that show the outbound SMTP test was successful*

In Figure 6-24, the first test fails. This is the reverse DNS check which is not configured for the Edge Transport server in the ProExchangeAdmin environment.

Export and Import Edge Configuration

Exchange Mailbox servers are domain-joined, and almost all configuration is stored in Active Directory. This means that configuration information can be shared among multiple Exchange servers.

For example, information regarding transport rules on Exchange Mailbox servers is stored in Active Directory, and it is used by all Exchange Mailbox servers in the organization. The Exchange Edge Transport server, however, is not a member of the Active Directory domain, and therefore configuration information cannot be shared among multiple Edge Transport servers.

Note Joining the Edge Transport servers to an Active Directory domain is supported. For example, some customers have an Active Directory domain in their perimeter network for management purposes; it aids deployment of GPOs or System Center clients to domain members. This does not mean the Edge Transport server can use this Active Directory domain, however. Even though they are domain-joined from a Windows point of view, they are still standalone Exchange servers.

As mentioned earlier in the chapter, if you have multiple Exchange Edge Transport servers, you must configure them individually. To release the management burden a bit, it is possible to configure one Edge Transport server and export its configuration to an XML file. This XML file can then be imported into subsequent Edge Transport servers to get an identical configuration across these Edge Transport servers. This is called a cloned configuration.

Note Cloning works only when you're installing the Edge Transport servers. When making regular changes to the Edge Transport server during normal operation, these changes still must be made to the individual Edge Transport servers.

Microsoft has written a script that can be used for multiple installations, located in the $ExScripts directory on the Edge Transport server and called ExportEdgeConfig.ps1. To export the Edge Transport server configuration, you open the Exchange Management Shell, navigate to the $ExScripts directory, and enter the following command:

```
[PS] C:> .\ExportEdgeConfig.ps1 -CloneConfigData:"C:\Temp\EdgeClonedConfig.xml"
```

This command will generate a configuration file that contains the individual settings of the Edge Transport server. You copy this XML file to another Edge Transport server. To do so, on the other Edge Transport server, you open the Exchange Management Shell and enter the following command:

```
[PS] C:\> .\ImportEdgeConfig.ps1 -CloneConfigData:"C:\Temp\
EdgeClonedConfig.xml" -IsImport $false -CloneConfigAnswer:"C:\Temp\
CloneAnswerFile.xml"
```

This command will run a trial import of the configuration file, and any settings that are not valid for this Edge Transport server are logged into the answer file. Any errors that are logged in the answer file can be edited in the clone answer file, as shown in Figure 6-25. When no changes are needed, the answer file will be empty!

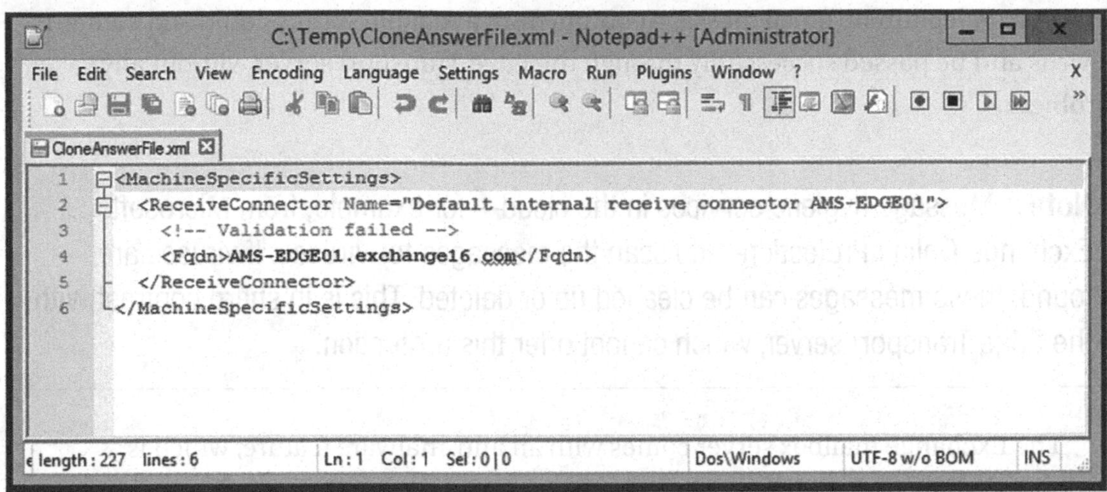

Figure 6-25. *The answer files show any problems that need to be fixed when cloning*

To run a full import to the subsequent Edge Transport server, you can run the same command but change the value of the -IsImport parameter to $True, for example:

```
[PS] C:\> .\ImportEdgeConfig.ps1 -CloneConfigData:"C:\Temp\
EdgeClonedConfig.xml" -IsImport $true -CloneConfigAnswer:"C:\Temp\
CloneAnswerFile.xml"
```

Note You cannot run the ImportEdgeConfig.ps1 script on an Edge Transport server that's subscribed to the internal Exchange servers; therefore, you must do this in advance of creating the edge subscription.

Mailbox Server

The Edge Transport server is all about anti-spam and filtering out messages received from malicious senders. It can do content inspection, but only on certain keywords, to filter out unsolicited email. It does not do content inspection to filter out viruses, for example. A legitimate email message coming from a reliable source could still contain a virus and be passed successfully through the Edge Transport server without any problem.

Note Message hygiene services in the cloud—for example, from Microsoft Exchange Online Protection—do scan the messages for viruses. If viruses are found, these messages can be cleaned up or deleted. This is in sharp contrast with the Edge Transport server, which cannot offer this protection.

The Exchange mailbox server comes with an anti-malware feature, which is described in the next section.

Mailbox Server Anti-malware

The Exchange Mailbox server comes with an anti-malware engine which is enabled by default. This anti-malware engine can perform content scanning for viruses. The Exchange anti-malware service is a single engine (whereas the old Forefront Protection for Exchange consisted of four separate engines), and it scans all inbound and outbound messages in transit. There's no option to scan messages that are already in the Mailbox database, it is only scanning messages in transit.

Malware definition files are downloaded once per hour from the Microsoft download site. This means that the Exchange Mailbox servers need to be able to access the Internet on port 80. The URL of this download location is `http://amupdatedl.microsoft.com/server/amupdate`.

When the definition files are updated, events are logged in the event log from source FIPFS. Event ID 6033 shows detailed information when the update is downloaded and what version it is, as shown in Figure 6-26.

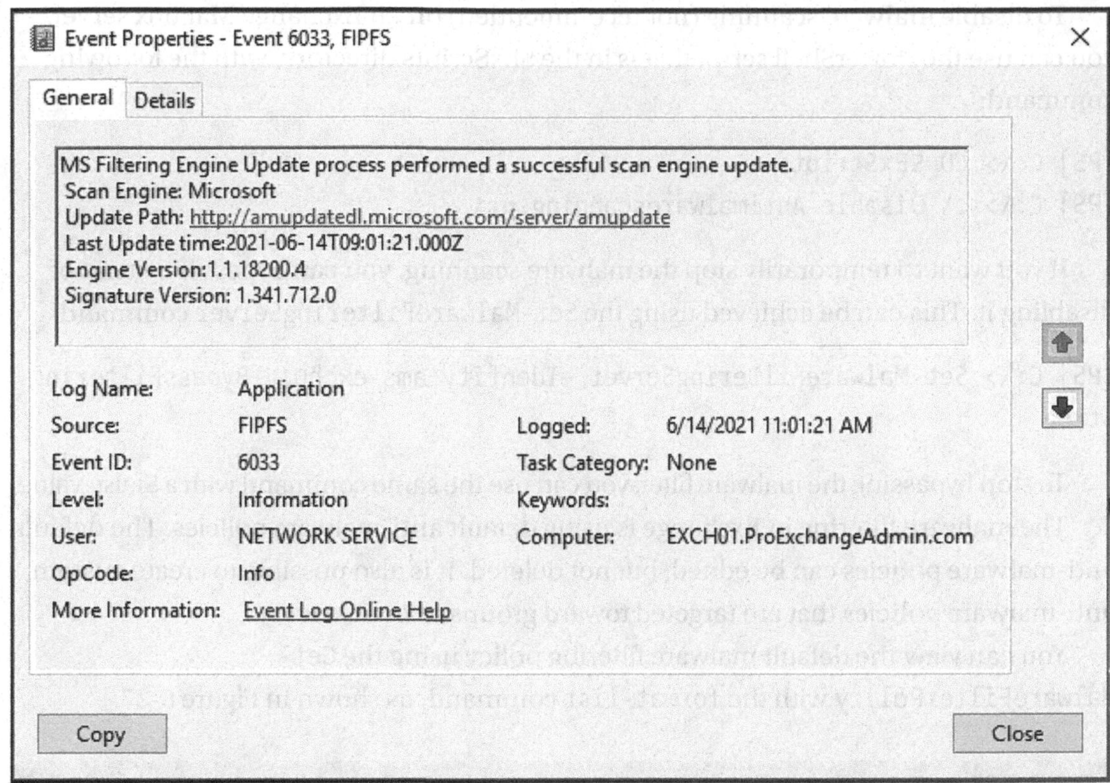

***Figure 6-26.** Signature file updates are logged in the application event log*

It is possible to manually update these definition files. Microsoft has written a script that can be found in the $ExScripts directory, which you can use with the following command:

```
[PS] C:\> CD $ExScripts
[PS] C:\> .\Update-MalwareFilteringServer.ps1 -Identity exch01.
proexchangeadmin.com
```

Another option is to manually download the definition files and store them on a file share. To update the Mailbox server with the definition files stored on a file share, you use the following command:

```
[PS] C:\> CD $ExScripts
[PS] C:\> .\Update-MalwareFilteringServer.ps1 -Identity exch01.
proexchangeadmin.com -EngineUpdatePath \\FS01\UpdateShare
```

To disable malware scanning (not recommended) on an Exchange Mailbox server, you can use the PowerShell script that is in the $ExScripts directory, with the following command:

```
[PS] C:\> CD $ExScripts
[PS] C:\> .\ Disable-Antimalwarescanning.ps1
```

If you want to temporarily stop the malware scanning, you can bypass it instead of disabling it. This can be achieved using the `Set-MalwareFilteringServer` command:

```
[PS] C:\> Set-MalwareFilteringServer -Identity ams-exch01 -BypassFiltering
$true
```

To stop bypassing the malware filter, you can use the same command with a $false value.

The malware filtering in Exchange is using default anti-malware policies. The default anti-malware policies can be edited, but not deleted. It is also possible to create custom anti-malware policies that are targeted toward groups of mailboxes.

You can view the default malware filtering policy using the `Get-MalwareFilterPolicy` with the `format-list` command, as shown in Figure 6-27.

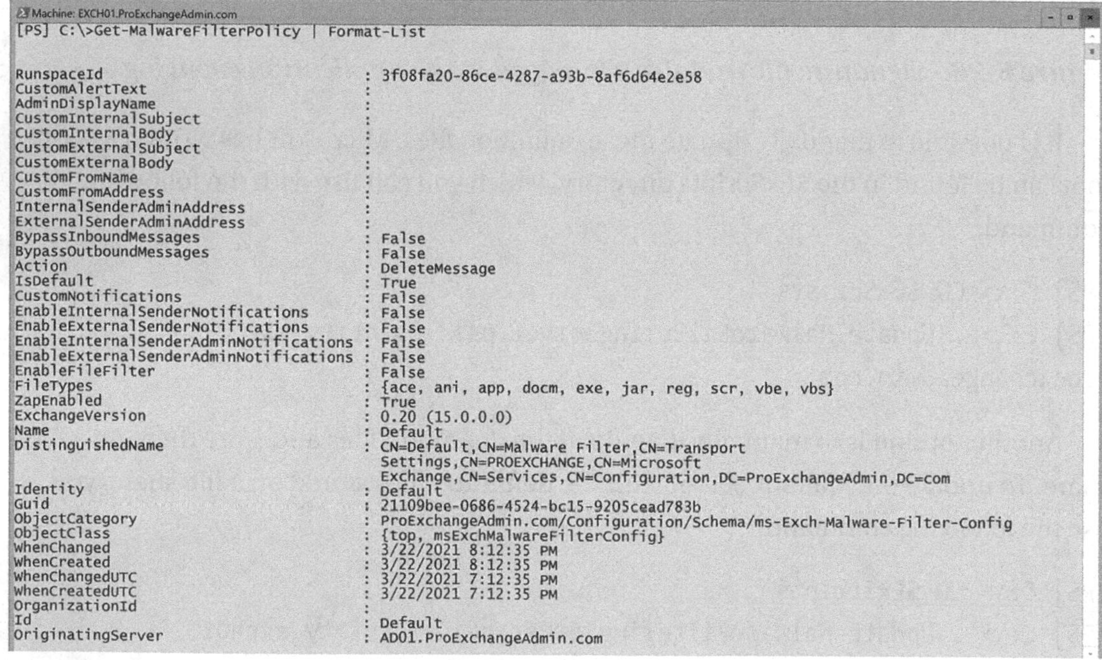

Figure 6-27. *The default malware filter policy in Exchange*

You can also create custom alert messages for both internal and external alerts, as well as what should happen when an infected message is found. New malware filter policies can be created using the New-MalwareFilterPolicy command. The following example creates a new malware filter policy named "ProExchangeAdmin Malware Filter Policy" that enables notifications to the administrator mailbox. Messages that contain malware are blocked, and the sender of the message is not notified.

```
[PS] C:\> New-MalwareFilterPolicy -Name "ProExchangeAdmin Malware
Filter Policy" -EnableInternalSenderAdminNotifications $true
-InternalSenderAdminAddress admin@proexchangeadmin.com
```

If you want to use a custom notification, you must use the `-CustomNotifications` parameter and set it to $true. At the same time, you must configure the following options:

- CustomFromAddress
- CustomFromName
- CustomExternalSubject
- CustomExternalBody
- CustomInternalSubject
- CustomInternalBody

A malware filter rule contains one or more malware filter policies; a malware filter rule can be assigned to a mailbox. For example, to create a new malware filter rule that contains the ProExchangeAdmin malware filter policy created in the previous example, you can use the `New-MalwareFilterRule` command as follows:

```
[PS] C:\> New-MalwareFilterRule -Name "ProExchangeAdmin Recipients
Rule" -MalwareFilterPolicy "ProExchangeAdmin Malware Filter Policy"
-RecipientDomainIs proexchangeadmin.com
```

You can use the `-SentTo` parameter to select the recipients to whom the malware filter rule is applied. For a broader scope, you can use the `-SentToMemberOf` parameter to define the members of a distribution group where the malware filter rule will be applied.

You can test the anti-malware settings using the EICAR test virus. This is a small text file that contains unharmful test virus pattern and is used by anti-virus and anti-malware vendors for testing purposes. To do so, you create a new text file and copy this exact line into the text file:

```
X5O!P%@AP[4\PZX54(P^)7CC)7}$EICAR-STANDARD-ANTIVIRUS-TEST-FILE!$H+H*
```

Make sure that this is the only string in the file. When done, you will have a 68-byte file that can be stored as EICAR.TXT. Be careful with local virus scanners on your workstation, as these scanners will pick up the EICAR pattern as well. Send a new message to yourself, attach the EICAR.TXT file, and see what happens.

Load-Balancing the Edge Transport Servers

When you have multiple Exchange Edge Transport servers, most likely you want to load-balance the SMTP traffic. The good thing is that you only have to worry about load-balancing the incoming SMTP traffic; traffic between the Edge Transport servers and the internal Exchange Mailbox servers is automatically load balanced.

An Edge Transport server is bound to an Active Directory site through the edge subscription. This means that all Exchange Mailbox servers will use this Edge Transport server. Going the other way, this one Edge Transport server will use all the Exchange Mailbox servers so that SMTP traffic will be load balanced across those Mailbox servers using a round-robin mechanism.

If you have multiple Edge Transport servers in your perimeter network, then each Edge Transport server will have its own edge subscription. Of course, each Edge Transport server will automatically load-balance the inbound SMTP traffic across all available Exchange Mailbox servers. The Mailbox servers in turn automatically use all the edge subscriptions and therefore automatically load-balance their outbound SMTP traffic across the multiple Edge Transport servers.

Inbound SMTP traffic originating from external hosts (i.e., from the Internet) is a different story, though. If you have multiple Edge Transport servers, you will have multiple external IP addresses and multiple FQDNs, so you must distribute that inbound SMTP traffic across these servers. The easiest way to do this is to use multiple MX records in the public DNS. These MX records are used by sending SMTP hosts, and by using multiple MX records, the inbound connections are automatically distributed.

Another option is to use a (hardware) load balancer for inbound SMTP traffic. In the load balancer, you create a virtual IP (VIP), and this IP address is used in an MX record. This way, only one MX record is used, and this MX record points to the load balancer.

In the load balancer, you can use layer 4 (L4) load balancing to distribute the incoming requests across all available Edge Transport servers. If for some reason one server fails, the load balancer will automatically disable this server so it is no longer used by the VIP in the load balancer.

So, balancing the load to the Edge Transport servers is not a big deal and is relatively easy to implement.

Note If you have multiple Edge Transport servers, you can also use Windows Network Load Balancing (NLB) as a load balancing solution. However, the official Microsoft recommendation is to use a (hardware) load balancer for load-balancing your Exchange traffic.

Summary

The transport pipeline in Exchange 2013/2016/2019 is the name of all SMTP transport–related services. The transport pipeline consists of the Front-End Transport service (FETS); this is the service where SMTP clients and hosts connect to. The back end of the transport pipeline consists of the transport service and transport delivery services.

Clients connect to a Receive Connector to drop messages, and a Send Connector is used to send messages to external hosts. Each and every client can connect to a Receive Connector to deliver messages to local mailboxes, but to relay messages to external hosts, an additional Receive Connector with relay permissions must be created.

An additional server role in Exchange Transport is the Edge Transport server, typically located in the perimeter network as an SMTP gateway between the Internet and the internal Exchange server. Originally developed with message hygiene in mind, but this server has been taken over by message hygiene cloud services like Exchange Online Protection. However, the anti-spam features are still available in the Edge Transport server, and knowledge about this is still important when using an Edge Transport server, even in combination with a cloud service.

PART 2

Upgrading Exchange Server

CHAPTER 7

Upgrading from Exchange 2010 to Exchange 2016

The primary focus of this book is on Exchange 2019, but it contains a lot of content about Exchange 2016 and even Exchange 2013. In the beginning of 2021, a lot of customers are still running on Exchange 2010, and when not moving to Office 365, they are moving to Exchange 2016. Hard-coded limitations in the Exchange setup application prevent an upgrade from Exchange 2010 directly to Exchange 2019. The reason for this is that Microsoft only supports n-2 versions. So, Exchange 2019 is only supported in combination with Exchange 2016 or Exchange 2013 in one environment. Exchange 2016 is supported with Exchange 2013 or Exchange 2010 in one environment.

The only way to directly move from Exchange 2010 to Exchange 2019 is by building a brand-new Active Directory with Exchange 2019 and moving all resources to Exchange 2019. This is referred to as an interorg migration.

This chapter focuses on a regular move from Exchange 2010 to Exchange 2016, where the latter is introduced in the existing environment.

Moving to Exchange 2016

Moving from Exchange 2010 is relatively easy because Exchange 2016 is simply introduced into the current Exchange Server environment. This saves you the hassle of building a new Active Directory environment, moving all your resources to that new Active Directory, and working around any problems that might occur when you're keeping both directories in sync during the coexistence phase.

I deliberately say "relatively easy" because it still takes quite some time and effort to accomplish this task and to work around some difficulties caused by incompatibilities between the two. It is all about upward and downward compatibility.

M. de Rooij and J. Wesselius, *Pro Exchange 2019 and 2016 Administration*,
https://doi.org/10.1007/978-1-4842-7331-9_7

Exchange 2016 front-end services can work perfectly with mailboxes stored on Exchange 2010, but the Exchange 2010 Client Access server cannot work with mailboxes stored on Exchange 2016.

When a client accesses the Exchange 2016 Client Access Front-End services and the mailbox is still on Exchange 2010, the request is simply proxied to the Exchange 2010 server, and the client keeps its connection with the Exchange 2016 server. Maybe you remember migrations from Exchange 2003 to Exchange 2010 where a legacy namespace was used, and client requests were redirected from the Exchange 2010 namespace to the Exchange 2003 namespace. Utterly complex and prone to error. This is not the case with an Exchange 2010/2016 coexistence.

Upgrading from Exchange 2010 to Exchange 2016 consists of the following steps:

1. Prepare Active Directory.
2. Install and configure the Exchange 2016 servers.
3. Change client access to Exchange 2016.
4. Change SMTP routing via Exchange 2016.
5. Move resources to Exchange 2016.
6. Decommission Exchange 2010.

Note When upgrading the environment to Exchange 2016, the new Exchange servers must be properly designed. Use the Requirements Calculator for Exchange as discussed in Chapter 2 to design the new Exchange environment.

Prerequisites

Installing Exchange 2016 into an existing Exchange 2010 environment does not differ much from a greenfield installation as discussed in Chapter 2, but there are some differences:

- Exchange 2016 is only supported on Windows Server 2012 R2 and Windows Server 2016. I always recommend using Windows Server 2016.
- Windows Server 2016 Server Core is not supported.

- Windows Server 2019 Domain Controllers are supported by Exchange 2016, but these are not supported by Exchange 2010. So, you can only introduce Windows Server 2019 Domain Controllers after decommissioning Exchange 2010.
- Active Directory Forest Functional Level (FFL) of Windows 2016 is supported by Exchange 2016 and Exchange 2010.
- Exchange 2010 should be running Service Pack 3 and the latest Update Rollup available; at the time of writing, this is Update Rollup 32. An earlier version may be supported by Exchange 2010, but from a security point of view, you must be running Update Rollup 32 anyway.

The prerequisite software for Exchange 2016 on Windows 2016 is identical to Exchange 2019 running on Windows 2019:

- .NET Framework 4.8
- Visual C++ Redistributable Package for Visual Studio 2012
- Visual C++ Redistributable Package for Visual Studio 2013
- Microsoft Unified Communications Managed API 4.0 Core Runtime 64-bit

---

Note Sometimes, the Microsoft **December 13, 2016 (KB3206632) security update** is mentioned as well, but this is already available when running an up-to-date Windows 2016 server.

Use the following commands to download and install the prerequisite Windows Servers and Roles on Windows 2016:

```
PS C:\> Install-WindowsFeature NET-Framework-45-Features, Server-Media-
Foundation, RPC-over-HTTP-proxy, RSAT-Clustering, RSAT-Clustering-
CmdInterface, RSAT-Clustering-Mgmt, RSAT-Clustering-PowerShell,
WAS-Process-Model, Web-Asp-Net45, Web-Basic-Auth, Web-Client-Auth, Web-
Digest-Auth, Web-Dir-Browsing, Web-Dyn-Compression, Web-Http-Errors,
Web-Http-Logging, Web-Http-Redirect, Web-Http-Tracing, Web-ISAPI-Ext,
Web-ISAPI-Filter, Web-Lgcy-Mgmt-Console, Web-Metabase, Web-Mgmt-Console,
```

```
Web-Mgmt-Service, Web-Net-Ext45, Web-Request-Monitor, Web-Server, Web-
Stat-Compression, Web-Static-Content, Web-Windows-Auth, Web-WMI, Windows-
Identity-Foundation, RSAT-ADDS, Telnet-Client
```

To download the .NET Framework 4.8:

```
PS C:\> Start-BitsTransfer -Source "https://download.visualstudio.
microsoft.com/download/pr/7afca223-55d2-470a-8edc-6a1739ae3252/
abd170b4b0ec15ad0222a809b761a036/ndp48-x86-x64-allos-enu.exe" -Destination
C:\Install
```

To download Visual C++ Redistributable Package for Visual Studio 2012:

```
PS C:\> Start-BitsTransfer -Source "https://download.microsoft.com/
download/1/6/B/16B06F60-3B20-4FF2-B699-5E9B7962F9AE/VSU_4/vcredist_x64.exe"
-Destination c:\Install\VS2012
```

To download Visual C++ Redistributable Package for Visual Studio 2013:

```
PS C:\> Start-BitsTransfer -Source "https://download.microsoft.com/
download/2/E/6/2E61CFA4-993B-4DD4-91DA-3737CD5CD6E3/vcredist_x64.exe"
-Destination c:\Install\VS2013
```

And finally, to download the Microsoft Unified Communications Managed API 4.0, Core Runtime 64-bit:

```
PS C:\> Start-BitsTransfer -Source "http://download.microsoft.com/
download/2/C/4/2C47A5C1-A1F3-4843-B9FE-84C0032C61EC/UcmaRuntimeSetup.exe"
-Destination c:\Install
```

For an unattended installation of the prerequisite software, use the following commands in a PowerShell window with elevated privileges:

```
PS C:\> Start-Process -FilePath "C:\Install\ndp48-x86-x64-allos-enu.exe"
-ArgumentList "/q" -Wait
PS C:\> Start-Process -FilePath "C:\Install\VS2012\vcredist_x64.exe"
-ArgumentList "/q" -Wait
PS C:\> Start-Process -FilePath "C:\Install\VS2013\vcredist_x64.exe"
-ArgumentList "/q" -Wait
```

```
PS C:\> Start-Process -FilePath "C:\Install\UcmaRuntimeSetup.exe"
-ArgumentList "-q" -Wait
```

The last command will automatically reboot the server when needed.

Prepare Active Directory

When all requirements are met, Active Directory can be prepared for the introduction of Exchange 2016 using the following commands:

```
Z:\> Setup.exe /PrepareSchema /IAcceptExchangeServerLicenseTerms
Z:\> Setup.exe /PrepareAD /IAcceptExchangeServerLicenseTerms
Z:\> Setup.exe /PrepareDomain /IAcceptExchangeServerLicenseTerms
```

Or, if you are using multiple Active Directory domains, you can replace this last command with the following command for easy deployment:

```
Z:\> Setup.exe /PrepareAllDomains /IAcceptExchangeServerLicenseTerms
```

Note Please note the absence of the /OrganizationName in the second command. This is because an Exchange organization already exists in Active Directory, so there is no need for a new organization name.

When preparing the Active Directory configuration partition using the /PrepareAD switch, the following warning message is shown:

```
Setup will prepare the organization for Exchange Server 2016 by using
'Setup /PrepareAD'. No Exchange Server 2013 roles have been detected in
this topology. After this operation, you will not be able to install any
Exchange Server 2013
roles.
For more information, visit: https://docs.microsoft.com/Exchange/plan-and-
deploy/deployment-ref/readiness-checks?view=exchserver-2016
```

This is shown in Figure 7-1.

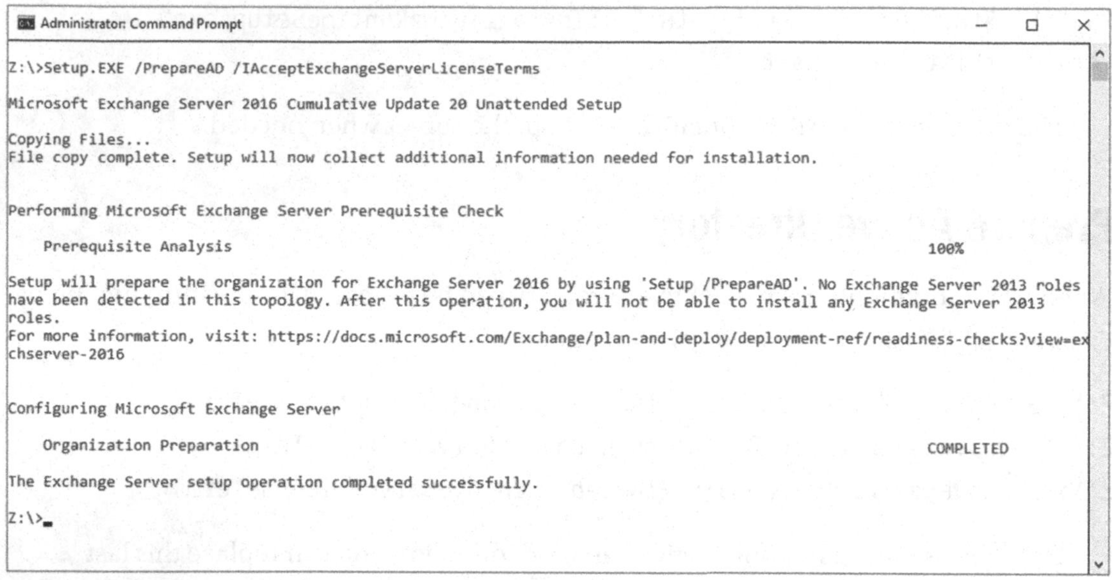

Administrator: Command Prompt
Z:\>Setup.EXE /PrepareAD /IAcceptExchangeServerLicenseTerms
Microsoft Exchange Server 2016 Cumulative Update 20 Unattended Setup
Copying Files...
File copy complete. Setup will now collect additional information needed for installation.
Performing Microsoft Exchange Server Prerequisite Check
Prerequisite Analysis 100%
Setup will prepare the organization for Exchange Server 2016 by using 'Setup /PrepareAD'. No Exchange Server 2013 roles have been detected in this topology. After this operation, you will not be able to install any Exchange Server 2013 roles.
For more information, visit: https://docs.microsoft.com/Exchange/plan-and-deploy/deployment-ref/readiness-checks?view=exchserver-2016
Configuring Microsoft Exchange Server
Organization Preparation COMPLETED
The Exchange Server setup operation completed successfully.
Z:\>

***Figure 7-1.** During the preparation of Active Directory, an Exchange 2013–related warning is shown.*

If for some reason you need an Exchange 2013 server, you cancel the operation and repeat the same step from an Exchange 2013 installation media.

After preparations with Exchange 2016 CU20, the Active Directory schema should be at level 15333, while the Exchange organization stored in the configuration partition of Active Directory should be at level 16620. Details about version numbering can be found in Table 2-4 in Chapter 2.

Installing Exchange 2016

When the server is properly designed, Windows is installed, and all prerequisite software is installed, Exchange 2016 can be installed. This can be a tricky process when performed during business hours.

When the Client Access components of an Exchange 2016 server are installed, a new service connection point (SCP) is created in Active Directory. As explained earlier, this SCP is used by Outlook clients to find an Exchange server that can be used to retrieve Exchange and mailbox configuration, a process called "Autodiscover." When this SCP is created, it contains the URL of the Exchange server, for example, `https://exch11.proexchangeadmin.com/autodiscover/autodiscover.xml`, where a more typical URL would be the autodiscover.proexchangeadmin.com version. Another issue is that the

Exchange server is configured with a self-signed certificate, not trusted by any client. So, when an Outlook client accidentally finds this local URL and tries to connect to it, it detects the self-signed certificate and generates a certificate warning as shown in Figure 7-2.

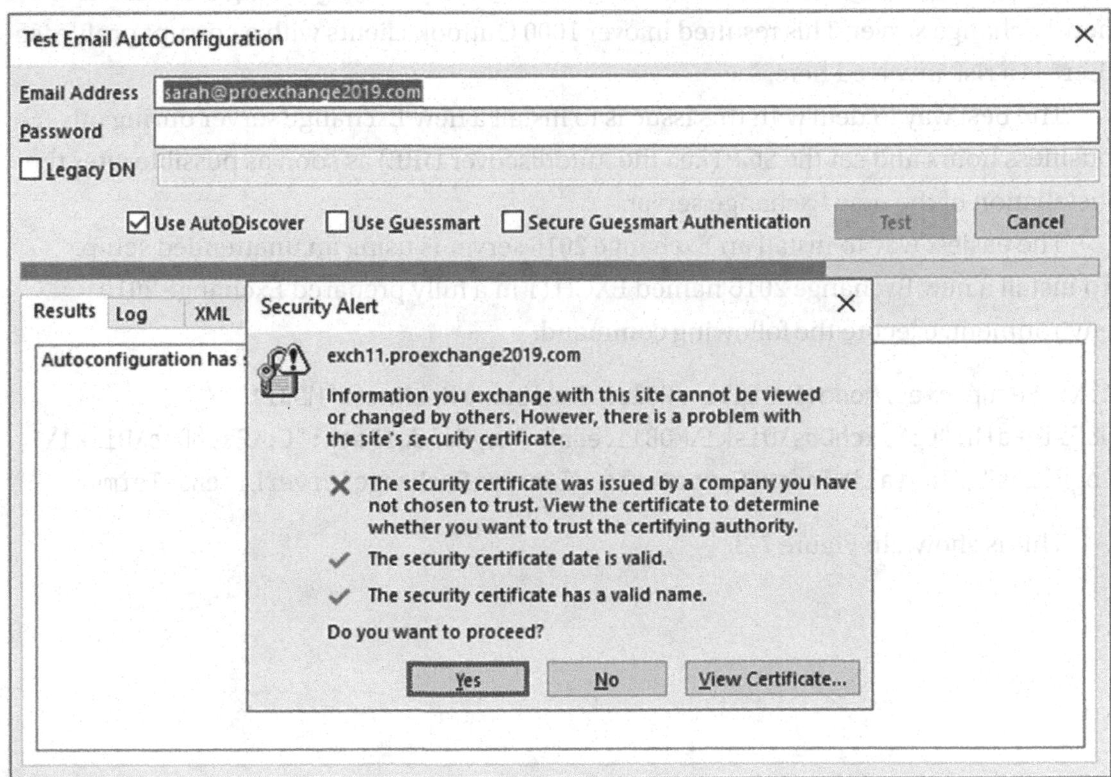

***Figure 7-2.** A certificate warning in Outlook, caused by a self-signed certificate during installation*

This will generate help desk calls and frustrated users, something we would all like to avoid.

To avoid this, Microsoft recommends installing new Exchange servers in a separate Active Directory site. Outlook clients will find SCP records in their own site, and not in such a dedicated installation site.

Another option is of course to install Exchange off business hours or to change the SCP to the normal value as soon as the installation of the new Exchange 2016 has finished and take the risk of Outlook clients finding this wrong SCP. Mind you, it can go wrong. I have faced such an issue in a large enterprise environment with 32 Exchange servers and 40,000 clients where the SCP turned out to be wrong during installation of a new Exchange server. This resulted in over 1000 Outlook clients with a corrupt profile, so there is a risk involved here.

The best way to deal with this issue is to install a new Exchange server during off-business hours and set the SCP (i.e., the Autodiscover URL) as soon as possible after the installation of the new Exchange server.

The easiest way to install an Exchange 2016 server is using an unattended setup. To install a new Exchange 2016 named EXCH11 in a fully prepared Exchange 2010 environment, execute the following command:

```
Z:\> Setup.exe /Mode:Install /Roles:Mailbox /MdbName:"MDB11" /
DbFilePath:"C:\ExchDbs\Disk1\MDB11.edb" /LogFolderPath:"C:\ExchDbs\Disk1\
LogFiles" /InstallWindowsComponents /IAcceptExchangeServerLicenseTerms
```

This is shown in Figure 7-3.

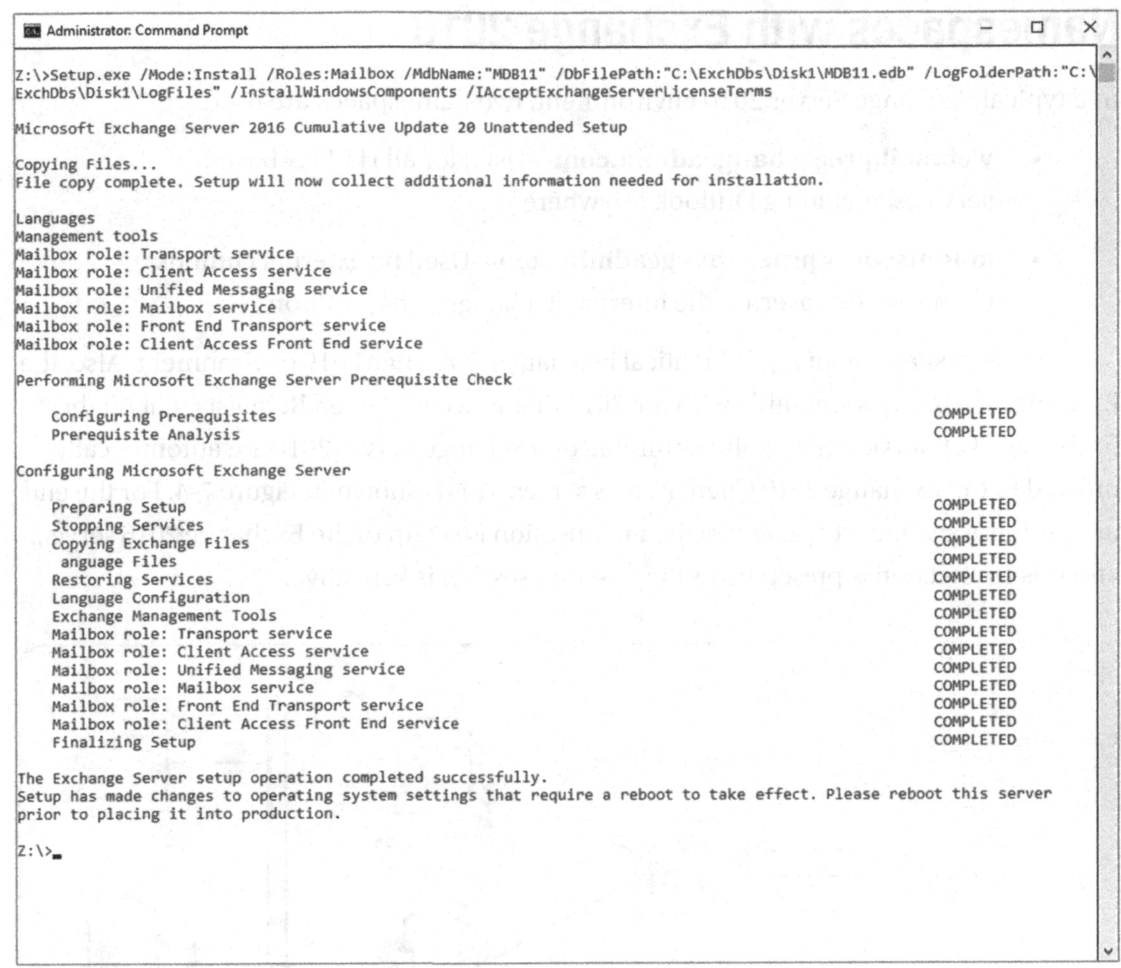
Administrator: Command Prompt
Z:\>Setup.exe /Mode:Install /Roles:Mailbox /MdbName:"MDB11" /DbFilePath:"C:\ExchDbs\Disk1\MDB11.edb" /LogFolderPath:"C:\ExchDbs\Disk1\LogFiles" /InstallWindowsComponents /IAcceptExchangeServerLicenseTerms
Microsoft Exchange Server 2016 Cumulative Update 20 Unattended Setup
Copying Files...
File copy complete. Setup will now collect additional information needed for installation.
Languages
Management tools
Mailbox role: Transport service
Mailbox role: Client Access service
Mailbox role: Unified Messaging service
Mailbox role: Mailbox service
Mailbox role: Front End Transport service
Mailbox role: Client Access Front End service
Performing Microsoft Exchange Server Prerequisite Check
Configuring Prerequisites COMPLETED
Prerequisite Analysis COMPLETED
Configuring Microsoft Exchange Server
Preparing Setup COMPLETED
Stopping Services COMPLETED
Copying Exchange Files COMPLETED
anguage Files COMPLETED
Restoring Services COMPLETED
Language Configuration COMPLETED
Exchange Management Tools COMPLETED
Mailbox role: Transport service COMPLETED
Mailbox role: Client Access service COMPLETED
Mailbox role: Unified Messaging service COMPLETED
Mailbox role: Mailbox service COMPLETED
Mailbox role: Front End Transport service COMPLETED
Mailbox role: Client Access Front End service COMPLETED
Finalizing Setup COMPLETED
The Exchange Server setup operation completed successfully.
Setup has made changes to operating system settings that require a reboot to take effect. Please reboot this server prior to placing it into production.
Z:\>

Figure 7-3. *Unattended install of Exchange 2016 in an Exchange 2010 environment*

When an Exchange 2016 server is installed in an existing Exchange 2010 environment, you will have two management interfaces. One for Exchange 2010 and one for Exchange 2016. These are one way compatible. In the Exchange 2010 management console or management shell, you will not see any Exchange 2016 information. You may think something is wrong when running the `Get-ExchangeServer` command in the Exchange 2010 management shell and the Exchange 2016 server does not show up, but this is not the case. It is by design that this does not show up; the Exchange 2016 server can only be managed from Exchange 2016 EAC or management shell.

After installing the Exchange 2016 server, the server can be configured. Namespaces in this respect are imported in a coexistence scenario, so we will continue with that first.

Namespaces with Exchange 2010

In a typical Exchange Server 2010 environment, two namespaces are used:

- **webmail.proexchangeadmin.com**—Used for all HTTPS-based services, including Outlook Anywhere
- **autodiscover.proexchangeadmin.com**—Used by external Outlook clients for discovering the internal Exchange configuration

The namespace planning is identical in a native Exchange 2016 environment. Also, the Exchange 2016 works smoothly with the 2010 Client Access server. Requests that hit the Exchange 2016 server for a mailbox running on Exchange Server 2010 are automatically proxied to the Exchange 2010 Client Access server. This is shown in Figure 7-4. For the end user, this is a seamless experience; their connection is set up to the Exchange 2016 server, and this connection is preserved as long as their session is kept alive.

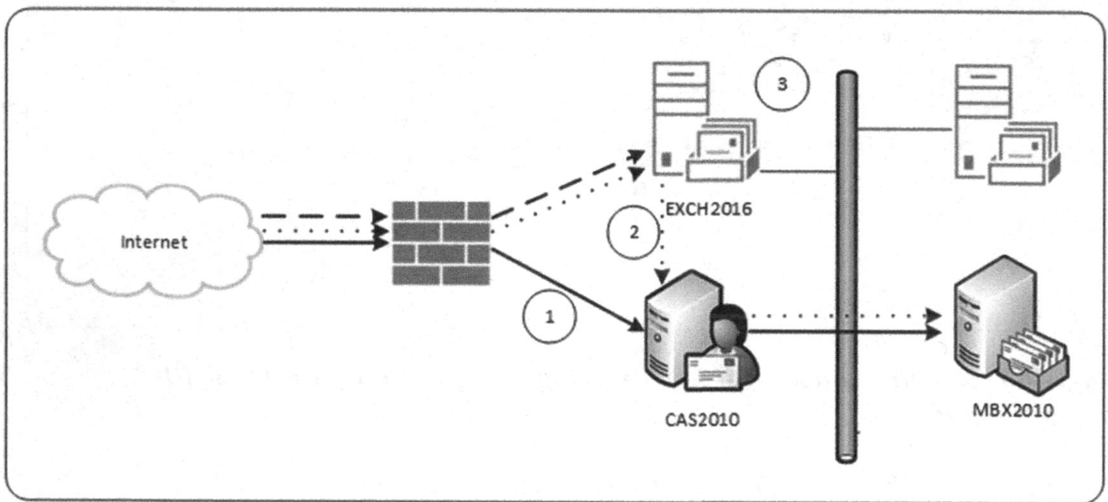

***Figure 7-4.** Coexistence scenario with Exchange 2010*

Figure 7-4 shows what happens in an Exchange Server 2010/2013 coexistence scenario:

1. The solid line is the original situation, where clients connect via webmail.proexchangeadmin.com and autodiscover.proexchangeadmin.com to the Exchange Server 2010 CAS. The CAS retrieves the information from the 2010 Mailbox server.

2. The dotted line is the coexistence scenario. Clients connect using webmail.proexchangeadmin.com and autodiscover.proexchangeadmin.com to the Exchange 2016 server. Requests are proxied to the 2010 CAS, which retrieves the information from the 2010 Mailbox server and returns the information via the Exchange 2016 server to the client. No connection is set up between the client and the 2010 CAS; this is fully transparent for the end user.

3. The dashed line is the final situation. Clients connect to the Exchange 2016 server using the webmail.proexchangeadmin.com and autodiscover.proexchangeadmin.com FQDN, and the requests are proxied directly to the Exchange 2016 server hosting the mailbox. This can be the same server as where the client connects to or any other Exchange 2016 server.

In an Exchange Server 2010/2016 coexistence scenario, the following are true for all protocols:

- Outlook Web App is proxied from the Exchange 2016 server to the 2010 CAS when the mailbox is still on the 2010 Mailbox server. The interface for those mailboxes is still 2010 and will not benefit from the new 2016 Outlook Web App features.

- Autodiscover requests are proxied from the Exchange 2016 server to the 2010 CAS when the user mailbox is still on the 2010 Mailbox server. This is true for both internal and external clients. Internal clients get the Exchange 2016 server via the service connection point (SCP), while external clients construct the URL from the SMTP email address of the user.

- Outlook Anywhere connections (HTTPS) from Outlook clients are proxied from the Exchange 2016 server to the 2010 CAS as long as the mailbox is on the 2010 Mailbox server.

- Exchange ActiveSync and Exchange Web Services are proxied from the Exchange 2016 server to the 2010 CAS as long as the mailbox is running on the 2010 Mailbox server.

- POP3 and IMAP4 are proxied from the Exchange 2016 server to the 2010 CAS when the mailbox is still on Exchange 2010.

So, all requests are proxied from the Exchange 2016 server to the 2010 CAS. If there are multiple Exchange 2016 servers, they are load-balanced using a (hardware) load balancer. This load balancing solution can either be layer 4 or layer 7, whichever you prefer.

If there are multiple 2010 Client Access servers, there is no need for a load balancer solution on Exchange Server 2010. The Exchange 2016 server picks a (healthy, available) 2010 CAS randomly from Active Directory, so the load is automatically distributed across all 2010 Client Access servers in this site.

Outlook clients in an existing Exchange Server 2010 environment connect to the RPC Client Access service running on the Exchange Server 2010 Client Access server. If multiple Exchange 2010 Client Access servers are used, a load-balanced array of Client Access servers is used; this configuration is called the CAS array. When Exchange 2016 is introduced into the existing Exchange Server 2010 environment, nothing changes in the way internal Outlook clients connect to the CAS array. Only if the mailbox is moved from Exchange Server 2010 to Exchange 2016 does the Outlook client no longer connect to the CAS array. Instead, the client starts using Outlook Anywhere or MAPI/HTTP and then connects to the Exchange 2016.

Coexistence with Exchange Server 2010 and SSL Certificates

In an Exchange Server 2010/2016 coexistence scenario, there is no need to worry about SSL certificates. The existing SSL certificate on the 2010 CAS in a typical environment should have domain names webmail.proexchangeadmin.com and autodiscover.proexchangeadmin.com. At one point, the clients connect to the 2016 servers using the same domain names, so it is just a matter of exporting the SSL certificate from the 2010 CAS to the Exchange 2016 server.

Client requests are proxied to the 2010 CAS, but the information is only encrypted using the SSL certificate; the SSL certificate is not used for server authentication. Since the 2010 CAS is a member of the same Active Directory environment, it is automatically trusted by the Exchange 2016 server.

To use an existing SSL certificate from the 2010 CAS, you follow these steps:

1. On the 2010 CAS, you use the Exchange Management Console to export the SSL certificate to a .pfx file and store this .pfx file on a network share like \\fs01\management\exported-certificate.pfx.

2. On the Exchange 2016 server, you open EMS and enter the following command to import the .pfx file:

```
[PS] C:\> Import-ExchangeCertificate -Server EXCH11 -FileData
([Byte[]]$(Get-Content -Path "\\fs01\management\exported-certificate.pfx"
-Encoding byte -ReadCount 0)) | Enable-ExchangeCertificate -Server EXCH11
-Services IIS
```

The same SSL certificate is now ready for use on Exchange 2016.

Exchange Server 2010 and Virtual Directories

Now that there are two separate and different Exchange server versions, you need to take special care when it comes to configuring the virtual directories that are part of those Exchange servers.

In Exchange 2016, all virtual directories should point to the Exchange 2016 server, so this is no different from a normal greenfield installation. All mailboxes that have been moved to Exchange 2016 will use these settings (see Table 7-1).

Table 7-1. *Virtual Directory Settings on the Exchange 2016 Client Access Server*

Virtual Directory	Internal URL	External URL
OWA Virtual Directory	https://webmail.proexchangeadmin.com/owa	https://webmail.proexchangeadmin.com/owa
ECP Virtual Directory	https://webmail.proexchangeadmin.com/ecp	https://webmail.proexchangeadmin.com/ecp
ActiveSync Virtual Directory	https://webmail.proexchangeadmin.com/Microsoft-Server-ActiveSync	https://webmail.proexchangeadmin.com/Microsoft-Server-ActiveSync
EWS Virtual Directory	https://webmail.proexchangeadmin.com/EWS/Exchange.asmx	https://webmail.proexchangeadmin.com/EWS/Exchange.asmx

(*continued*)

Table 7-1. (*continued*)

Virtual Directory	Internal URL	External URL
OAB Virtual Directory	https://webmail.proexchangeadmin.com/OAB	https://webmail.proexchangeadmin.com/OAB
PowerShell Virtual Directory	https://webmail.proexchangeadmin.com/PowerShell	https://webmail.proexchangeadmin.com/PowerShell
MAPI Virtual Directory	https://webmail.proexchangeadmin.com/Mapi	https://webmail.proexchangeadmin.com/Mapi
Outlook Anywhere	https://webmail.proexchangeadmin.com/	https://webmail.proexchangeadmin.com/

Just as in Chapter 2, the best way to configure the virtual directories is to use the `change_vdir_settings.ps1` PowerShell script to minimize the risk for errors. This script will set all the virtual directories and configure Outlook Anywhere as well.

If a mailbox has not been moved to the Exchange 2016 server, the Exchange 2016 will detect this when the user is authenticated during the initial client request, and the request will be proxied to the 2010 CAS. In this situation, the same settings (see Table 7-2) are used, as all client requests are proxied from the Exchange 2016 server to the 2010 CAS. For the client, what happens on the Exchange Server level is fully transparent, so the same virtual directory settings apply as for mailboxes that are already on Exchange 2016. In the original environment, the namespaces used were the same as in the coexistence scenario, so if all is correct, there is no need to change anything on the Exchange Server 2010 virtual directory settings.

Table 7-2. *Virtual Directory Settings on the Exchange 2010 Client Access Server*

Virtual Directory	Internal URL	External URL
OWA Virtual Directory	`https://webmail.proexchangeadmin.com/owa`	`https://webmail.proexchangeadmin.com/owa`
ECP Virtual Directory	`https://webmail.proexchangeadmin.com/ecp`	`https://webmail.proexchangeadmin.com/ecp`
ActiveSync Virtual Directory	`https://webmail.proexchangeadmin.com/Microsoft-Server-ActiveSync`	`https://webmail.proexchangeadmin.com/Microsoft-Server-ActiveSync`
EWS Virtual Directory	`https://webmail.proexchangeadmin.com/EWS/Exchange.asmx`	`https://webmail.proexchangeadmin.com/EWS/Exchange.asmx`
OAB Virtual Directory	`https://webmail.proexchangeadmin.com/OAB`	`https://webmail.proexchangeadmin.com/OAB`
PowerShell Virtual Directory	`https://webmail.proexchangeadmin.com/PowerShell`	`https://webmail.proexchangeadmin.com/PowerShell`
MAPI Virtual Directory	`https://webmail.proexchangeadmin.com/Mapi`	`https://webmail.proexchangeadmin.com/Mapi`
Outlook Anywhere	`https://webmail.proexchangeadmin.com/`	`https://webmail.proexchangeadmin.com/`

Note Outlook Anywhere in a coexistence scenario is like Outlook Anywhere in a native Exchange 2010 environment, so no additional changes are necessary.

It is not possible to manage Exchange Server 2010 settings from the EMS running on the Exchange 2016 environment. Exchange Server 2010 settings should be managed from the 2010 Exchange Management Console or 2010 Exchange Management Shell.

Making the Change for Clients

If all servers have been installed and configured, it is time to make the change in how clients access the Exchange platform. This is an important moment; one mistake here can potentially have an impact on all clients.

Although this change is important, the effect is different for every client. Outlook clients, including Outlook 2019, will connect to the Exchange 2010 CAS array, and this will not change when the switch to the Exchange 2016 server is made. But those same Outlook clients also use Autodiscover and the Exchange Web Services, and these protocols are impacted during the change. Figure 7-5 shows an Outlook 2019 client connected to an Exchange 2010 server. Clearly visible is the CAS array with FQDN outlook.proexchange2019.com.

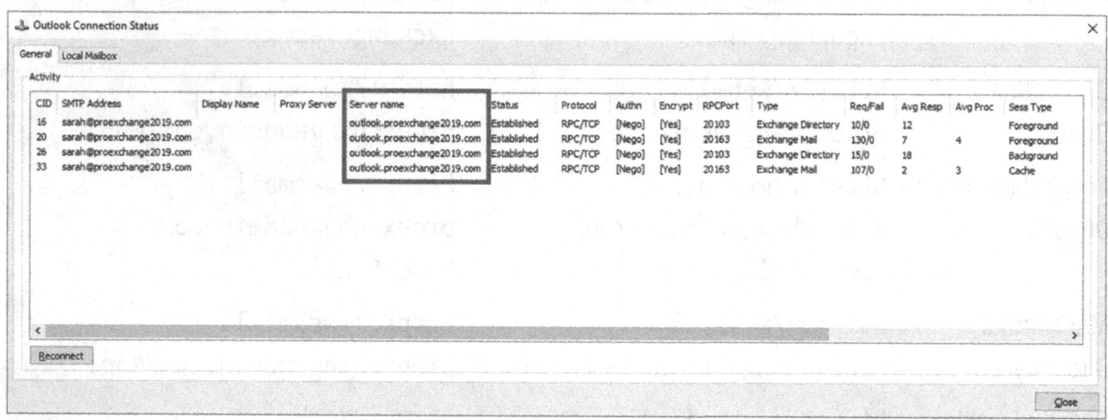

***Figure 7-5.** Outlook 2019 connected to the CAS array on Exchange 2010*

For internal clients, it is just a matter of changing the internal DNS records for webmail.proexchange.com and autodiscover.proexchange.com to the Exchange 2016 server. If there are multiple Client Access servers in a load-balanced array, you must create a new VIP for the Exchange 2016 server since the Exchange 2010 VIP is a completely different configuration. When done and tested, change the VIP from Exchange 2010 to Exchange 2016. However, this is the case only for HTTP services; the CAS array IP address should not be changed, of course.

For external clients, the forwarding address on the firewall needs to be changed from the 2010 CAS to the Exchange 2016 server.

The client now uses the webmail.proexchangeadmin.com FQDN to connect to the Exchange 2016 server, and the Exchange 2016 OWA logon form is presented, and this is the first change for users! When the user's mailbox is on the Exchange 2016 Mailbox server, the mailbox is shown directly after authentication. When the user's mailbox is still on Exchange Server 2010, the request is proxied to the 2010 CAS, and the mailbox data is retrieved. No second logon attempt is needed. The end user with their mailbox does not see any difference at this point until their mailbox is moved to Exchange 2016.

SMTP Mail in a Coexistence Scenario

During the coexistence phase, the SMTP mail flow must be changed from the previous version of Exchange Server to Exchange 2016. It does not matter when the mail flow is changed, however. It can be changed in the beginning of the transition process, halfway through the process, or just before the previous version of Exchange Server is decommissioned. The Edge Transport server from the previous versions can also play a role in the Exchange 2016 environment.

Changing the SMTP Mail Flow

Initially, SMTP messages are delivered to the Exchange 2010 Hub Transport servers, and inbound SMTP messages are delivered to the recipients' mailboxes. When mailboxes are moved to Exchange 2016, the Exchange 2010 Hub Transport server sends inbound messages using SMTP to the Exchange 2016 server, where they are delivered to the recipients' mailboxes.

Specifically, an inbound SMTP message is delivered to the Exchange 2016 Front-End Transport service, which proxies the inbound SMTP connection to an Exchange 2016 Mailbox server hosting the mailbox. An inbound SMTP message intended for a recipient still on Exchange Server 2010 is sent from the Exchange 2016 Front-End Transport service using SMTP to an Exchange 2010 Hub Transport server. From there, it is delivered to the recipient's mailbox. If the mailbox is moved to Exchange 2016, the Transport service on the Exchange 2016 server delivers the message to the Exchange 2016 server hosting the recipient's mailbox.

Is there a guideline or best practice for when to change the mail flow? Opinions may vary here. I have seen customers change the SMTP mail flow as their first step in the transition process so that they know their platform is running fine. At the same time,

I have seen customers change the mail flow after the last mailbox move, a step that concludes their transition process. It depends on your own preferences.

Using an Edge Transport Server

As explained in previous chapters, there is an additional server role called the Edge Transport server. This server is typically installed in the perimeter zone of the network, and its role is to act as an SMTP gateway between the Internet and the internal Exchange servers.

The MX records on the public DNS point to the Edge Transport servers, and therefore these Edge Transport servers accept messages from the Internet. They apply a set of anti-spam rules to the inbound messages, ensuring that only legitimate messages are sent to the internal Exchange organization. After this, the messages are delivered to the internal Exchange servers, which deliver the messages to the recipients' mailboxes. The Edge Transport server is tied to the internal Exchange servers using the Edge subscription, a mechanism whereby information from the internal Exchange organization is pushed to the Edge Transport server.

In a coexistence scenario with an Exchange 2010 Edge server, a mail continues to be delivered to the Exchange 2010 Hub Transport server, and this server delivers the messages to an Exchange 2016 Mailbox server when the recipients' mailboxes are moved to Exchange 2016.

The good news is that the Exchange 2010 Edge Transport servers continue to work with the 2016 Mailbox server, including the Edge synchronization. The only thing you must do is to create a new Edge subscription.

Another option is to introduce a new Exchange 2016 Edge Transport server into your organization and decommission the previous Edge Transport server. Here are the two options.

Continuing with the Previous Edge Transport Server

If you opt for the first option, using the previous Edge Transport server with the Exchange 2016 Mailbox server, it is just a matter of removing the existing Edge subscription between the Edge Transport server and the Exchange 2010 Hub Transport server, then creating a new Edge subscription between the Edge Transport server and the 2016 Mailbox server. Mail from the Internet will then be delivered to the Exchange 2010 Edge Transport server and sent to the Exchange 2016 server. This is shown in Figure 7-6.

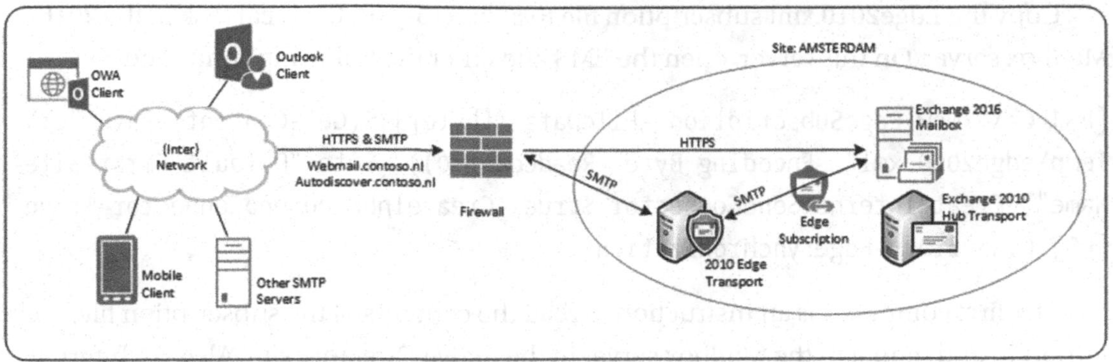

***Figure 7-6.** The Exchange 2010 Edge Transport with an Exchange 2016 Mailbox server*

To change the Edge synchronization from an Exchange 2010 Hub Transport server to a new Exchange 2016 Mailbox server, you must remove the existing Edge subscription and create a new one, then bind it to the Exchange 2016 Mailbox server.

To remove an existing Edge Subscription, open EMS on the Exchange 2010 Edge Transport server and enter the following command:

```
[PS] C:\> Get-EdgeSubscription -Identity EXCH2010 | Remove-EdgeSubscription
```

Repeat this command on the internal Exchange 2010 Hub Transport server.

Please note that at this stage you do not have any connection left between the Exchange 2010 Edge Transport server and the internal Exchange organization, so you must act quickly to minimize downtime.

To create a new Edge Subscription, log on to the previous Edge Transport server, open EMS, and enter the following command:

```
[PS] C:\> New-EdgeSubscription -FileName C:\Temp\Edge2010.xml
```

A warning message is shown, saying the subscription file is valid for 1440 minutes (which equals 24 hours). (If the subscription file is not processed within this time frame, a new subscription must be created.) Enter "Y" to confirm your knowledge of the warning message, and the subscription file will be created.

Copy the Edge2010.xml subscription file to a directory on the local disk of the 2016 Mailbox server. On this server, open the EMS and enter the following commands:

```
[PS] C:\> New-EdgeSubscription -FileData ([byte[]]$(Get-Content -Path "C:\
Temp\edge2010.xml" -Encoding Byte -ReadCount 0)) -Site "Default-First-Site-
Name" -CreateInternetSendConnector $true -CreateInboundSendConnector $true
[PS] C:\> Start-EdgeSynchronization
```

The first command is an instruction to read the contents of the subscription file, import it, and bind it to the Mailbox server in the Active Directory site. Also, an Internet send connector and an inbound send connector are created. The second command starts the Edge synchronization process. It is as easy as that.

It can take some time before you can successfully run the `Start-EdgeSynchronization` command. If it fails directly after importing the Edge Subscription file, please wait a couple of minutes and try again.

Note The Exchange 2010 Edge Transport server should be able to resolve the Exchange 2016 Mailbox server, and vice versa. This can be achieved using DNS, but using a HOSTS file for resolving an Edge Transport server is quite common as well.

Introducing a New Exchange 2016 Edge Transport Server

The second option when working with Edge Transport servers is to introduce a new Exchange 2016 Edge Transport server next to the existing Edge Transport server.

You install a brand-new Exchange 2016 Edge Transport server in the perimeter network and make sure you have Internet connectivity (at least on port 25), and that name resolution works fine, both to the Internet and to the internal network, then you install the Exchange 2016 Edge Transport server role.

Note Installing and configuring the Exchange 2016 Edge Transport server role is explained in detail in Chapter 2.

When the Exchange 2016 Edge Transport server is installed, you can create a new Edge Subscription. Log on to the Exchange 2016 Edge Transport server, open EMS, and enter the following command:

```
[PS] C:\> New-EdgeSubscription -FileName C:\Temp\Edge2016.xml
```

When the file is created, you copy it to the local hard disk of the Exchange 2016 Mailbox server. On this server, you open EMS and enter the following commands:

```
[PS] C:\> New-EdgeSubscription -FileData ([byte[]]$(Get-Content -Path "C:\
Temp\edge2016.xml" -Encoding Byte -ReadCount 0)) -Site "Default-First-Site-
Name" -CreateInternetSendConnector $true -CreateInboundSendConnector $true
[PS] C:\> Start-EdgeSynchronization
```

This will create the subscription between the Exchange 2016 Edge Transport server and the Exchange 2016 Mailbox server and initiate the synchronization process. You now have a situation as shown in Figure 7-7.

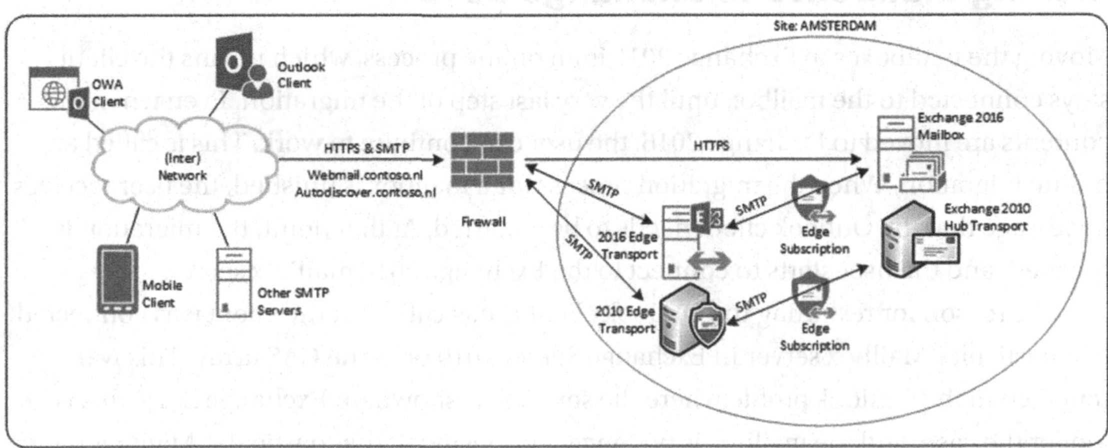

***Figure 7-7.** Introducing a new Exchange 2016 Edge Transport server next to the down-level Edge Transport server*

When you have rerouted incoming SMTP traffic from the firewall to the Exchange 2016 Edge Transport server, you can decommission the Exchange 2010 Edge Transport server. To remove the Edge Subscription between the Exchange 2010 Hub Transport server and the Exchange 2010 Edge Transport server, you log on to the Exchange 2010 Hub Transport server, open EMS, and enter the following command:

```
[PS] C:\> Get-EdgeSubscription -Identity <<Name>> | Remove-EdgeSubscription
```

where <<Name>> is the NetBIOS name of the Exchange 2010 Edge Transport server. When the old Edge Subscription is removed, you can decommission the Exchange 2010 Edge Transport server.

Moving Resources to Exchange 2016

The most important step in the transition process is to move the mailboxes and other resources from Exchange 2010 to the new Exchange 2016 server. “Other resources” in this respect are the address lists and the offline address book.

Moving Mailboxes to Exchange 2016

Moving the mailboxes to Exchange 2016 is an online process, which means the client stays connected to the mailbox until the very last step of the migration. Even when the contents are moved to Exchange 2016, the user can continue to work. This is called an online migration. When the migration process for a mailbox is finished, the user receives a message that the Outlook client needs to be restarted. At that point, the migration is finished, and the user starts to connect to the Exchange 2016 mailbox server.

The reason for restarting the Outlook client is basically that the client was connected to a particular Mailbox server in Exchange Server 2010 or to the CAS array. This was reflected in the Outlook profile where the server was shown. In Exchange 2016, this is no longer the case, and the mailbox is no longer connected to that particular Mailbox server. You can see this in the Outlook profile, where there is no longer a server or CAS array shown; instead, the GUID of the mailbox is followed by the end user’s primary SMTP address.

The process responsible for moving the Mailboxes is the Mailbox Replication Service (MRS), a service that is running on the Exchange 2016 server. Or better, on every Exchange 2016 server. This is shown in Figure 7-8.

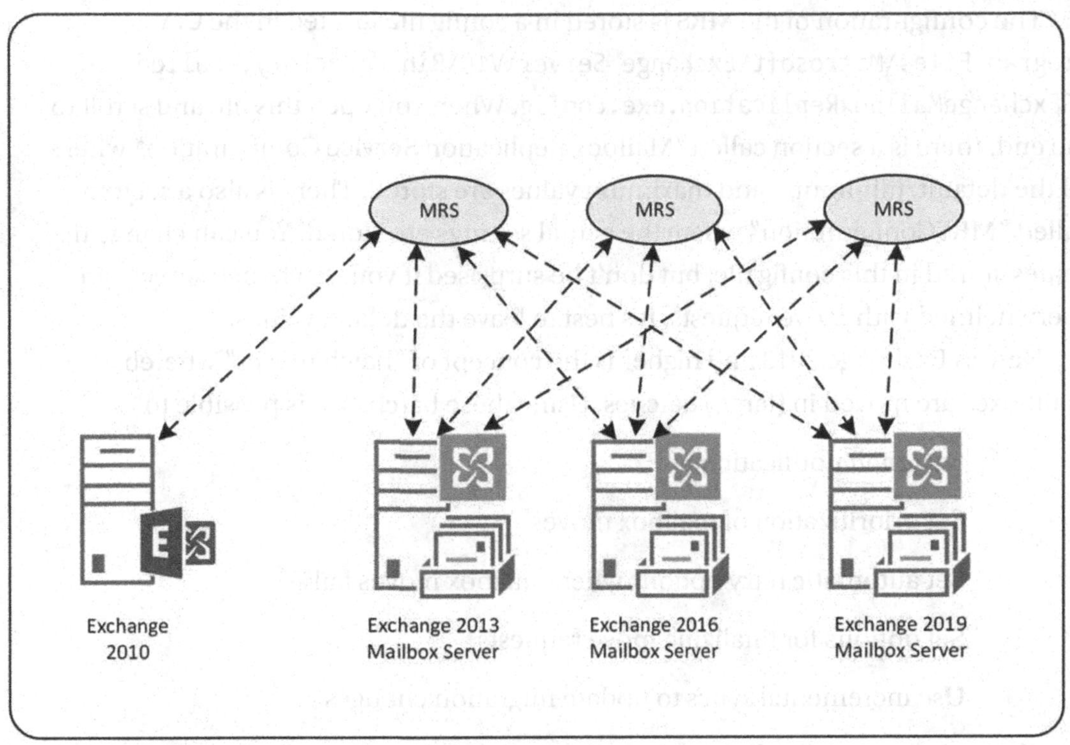

***Figure 7-8.** The Mailbox Replication Service (MRS)*

When a mailbox needs to be moved from one mailbox database to another mailbox database, the actual mailbox move is initiated with a move request. With a move request, a flag is set in the system mailbox of the source mailbox database, and this flag is picked up by the MRS. The MRS then creates a copy of that mailbox in the target mailbox database, and it starts moving the mailbox data from the source to the target. This is an online and fully transparent mechanism; the recipient can be online and will not notice anything about moving data. When the MRS is about to finish the migration of data, the source mailbox is closed, and all remaining data is written into the target mailbox; the properties in Active Directory are updated as well.

The MRS is running on every Exchange 2016 server, so if there are five Exchange 2016 servers, there are also five instances of MRS running in the Exchange environment. It is possible to tune the MRS on the Exchange 2016 server. By default, very few mailboxes are moved concurrently, to prevent the Mailbox server from becoming overwhelmed as mailboxes are moved. This otherwise tremendous amount of traffic might impact users when mailboxes are being moved during business hours.

The configuration of the MRS is stored in a config file located in the `C:\Program Files\Microsoft\Exchange Server\V15\Bin directory, called MSExchangeMailboxReplication.exe.config`. When you open this file and scroll to the end, there is a section called "Mailbox Replication Service Configuration" where all the default, minimum, and maximum values are stored. There is also a section called "MRSConfiguration" where the actual settings are stored. You can change the values stored in this config file, but don't be surprised if your Exchange servers are overwhelmed with move requests; it's best to leave the default values.

New in Exchange 2013 and higher is the concept of "batch moves" whereby mailboxes are moved in (large) batches. Using these batches, it is possible to

- Set email notifications
- Set prioritization of mailbox moves
- Set automatic retry options when mailbox moves fail
- Set options for finalizing move requests
- Use incremental syncs to update migration changes

The move request finalization is an interesting feature that was also available in Exchange Server 2010. It makes it possible to move mailboxes from a source mailbox database to a target mailbox database, but without finalizing the actual move. When the move is around 95% finished, the synchronization of mailbox data stops, and the source and the target are kept in sync. It is then possible to finalize the actual move later, for example, during off-business hours. This way, the user does not receive the (disruptive) message about restarting the Outlook client at an inconvenient time.

Note Moving mailboxes is a "pull" mechanism, so the move process is initiated from the Exchange 2016 server. To initiate a move request, the EAC or the 2016 Exchange Management Shell must be used.

To initiate a mailbox move for a user called joe@proexchangeadmin.com, you log on to an Exchange 2016 server, open EMS, and execute the following command:

```
[PS] C:\> New-MoveRequest -Identity joe@proexchangeadmin.com -
TargetDatabase MDB01
```

You can also get a list of mailboxes on the previous Exchange Mailbox server, for example, based on a mailbox database called MBX2010, and use the pipeline feature to move all mailboxes to a mailbox database called MDB01. This will result in a command like

```
[PS] C:\> Get-Mailbox -Database "MBX2010" | New-MoveRequest -TargetDatabase
MDB01
```

You can monitor the move of the mailboxes with the Get-MoveRequest command; if needed, you can add the Get-MoveRequestStatistics command, like this:

```
[PS] C:\> Get-MoveRequest | Get-MoveRequestStatistics
```

This will give you a quick overview of all move requests that are currently available and whether their status is queued, in progress, or completed. To get an overview of all move requests that are running at a particular moment, you can make a selection based on the status of the move request, like this:

```
[PS] C:\> Get-MoveRequest | Where {$_.Status -eq "InProgress"}
```

Exchange Server 2010 has a mailbox for discovery search purposes. To move this mailbox, you need to use the EMS on Exchange 2016 with the following command:

```
[PS] C:\> get-mailbox -Identity discovery* | New-MoveRequest -
TargetDatabase MDB01
```

Exchange Server also uses system mailboxes and arbitration mailboxes for approval functionality, for example, when messages need to be moderated before they are sent out. Messages that need moderation are stored temporarily in these mailboxes. The mailboxes are hidden, but they can be migrated only by using the EMS.

To retrieve a list of all system mailboxes on Exchange Server 2010, execute the following command in EMS:

```
[PS] C:\> Get-Mailbox -Server EX2010SRV -Arbitration
```

This action will return all system mailboxes on Exchange Server 2010. To move these mailboxes, you simply pipe the output of the Get-Mailbox command into the New-MoveRequest command:

```
[PS] C:\> Get-Mailbox -Server EX2010SRV -Arbitration | New-MoveRequest -
TargetDatabase MDB01
```

If you do not specify a target database, Exchange 2016 will select a mailbox database automatically, based on the availability of mailbox resources.

When the regular mailboxes, the discovery mailbox, and the system mailboxes are moved to Exchange 2016, then the mailbox databases on the previous version of Exchange Server should be empty and are ready for removal.

Moving Address Lists to Exchange 2016

When all the mailboxes are moved to Exchange 2016, it is time to move the other resources. Regular address lists reside in Active Directory, so when moving them to Exchange 2016, there is no need to pay extra attention; they will be used automatically by Exchange 2016.

Since the address lists were created in the previous version of Exchange Server, they should also be managed with the previous EMS or the Exchange Management Console. But to make them "ready" for Exchange 2016, just touch the address lists and store them without changing any values. To do this, use the `Get-AddressList | Set-AddressList` command in the 2016 Exchange Management Shell. The commands will show something like this on the console:

```
[PS] C:\> Get-AddressList | Set-AddressList
WARNING: The command completed successfully but no settings of '\All
Contacts' have been modified.
WARNING: The command completed successfully but no settings of '\All
Groups' have been modified.
WARNING: The command completed successfully but no settings of '\All Rooms'
have been modified.
WARNING: The command completed successfully but no settings of '\All Users'
have been modified.
WARNING: The command completed successfully but no settings of '\Public
Folders' have been modified.
[PS] C:\ >
```

Moving the Offline Address Book to Exchange 2016

A nice feature for Outlook clients is that they can work offline, also referred to as cached mode. When working in cached mode, clients need an address book, and so the offline address book (OAB) is used. This is a list of addresses aggregated in files that can be downloaded by the Outlook client for offline use. This way, clients can always use the address lists, even when they are not connected to the network.

Exchange 2010 uses an offline address book called Default Offline Address Book. Its format is version 3 or version 4, and it is distributed to clients using public folders or web distribution—that is, it is a virtual directory on the Exchange 2010 CAS.

Exchange 2016 uses a new offline address book. It is based on version 4 and exclusively uses web distribution. The name of Exchange 2016 Offline Address Book is Default Offline Address Book (2013). This is a cosmetic bug in Exchange 2016; the OAB still has "2013" in its name. You can use the 2016 Exchange Management Shell to view the available offline address books via the Get-OfflineAddressBook command:

```
[PS] C:\> Get-OfflineAddressBook
Name                                  Versions                AddressLists
----                                  --------                ------------
Default Offline Address Book          {Version3, Version4}    {\Default
                                                              Global Address
                                                              List}
Default Offline Address Book (Ex2013) {Version4}              {\Default
                                                              Global Address
                                                              List}
[PS] C:\>
```

Outlook clients will automatically detect the new default offline address book, so there is no need to change anything here.

If you have custom Offline Address Books in your organization, you cannot move them to Exchange Server 2016. Instead, you must recreate them on Exchange Server 2016 using the `New-OfflineAddress` book command in the EMS.

When all the mailboxes are moved to Exchange 2016, the previous version's default Offline Address Book is no longer needed and can be removed using the Exchange 2010 Management Console. You will find the old default offline address book by opening the Management Console, expanding the Organization Configuration, and selecting the Mailbox option. In the Results pane, select the tab for the Offline Address Book and remove that address book by right-clicking it.

Decommissioning the Previous Exchange Server

When all resources have been moved or removed, you can decommission the Exchange 2010 Server. This is not really a big deal at all, and it involves the following steps:

1. Make sure the Exchange 2010 Hub Transport server is not responsible anymore for any mail traffic. This not only includes SMTP from and to the Internet but also third-party appliances or (custom) applications that might have been using the Hub Transport server for receiving or relaying messages. Caution: You don't want to remove the Exchange 2010 Server and find out that your multifunctional devices cannot send out messages anymore.

   To achieve this, you can enable SMTP protocol logging on both the receive connector and the send connector, and check the corresponding log files. By default, you can find these log files at the following locations:

   - SMTP receive

     C:\Program Files\Microsoft\Exchange Server\V14\TransportRoles\Logs\ ProtocolLog\SMTPReceive

   - SMTP send

     C:\Program Files\Microsoft\Exchange Server\V14\TransportRoles\Logs\ ProtocolLog\SMTPSend

2. Remove the mailbox databases from the Exchange 2010 Server by using the Exchange Management Console or the Exchange Management Shell on the old Exchange Server.

3. Remove the previous Exchange Mailbox server role. This can be done by opening the control panel on the Exchange server and selecting "Uninstall Exchange Server." Uncheck the mailbox server roles and the Exchange management tools option in the setup application. This will remove the Mailbox server role for this server.
4. Remove the previous Exchange CAS and Hub Transport server roles. Again, this can be achieved by opening the control panel and uninstalling the Exchange Server. Uncheck the Client Access server role, the Hub Transport server role, and the Exchange management tools to completely remove these from the Exchange 2010 Server.

If an Exchange 2010 multi-role server is used, steps 3 and 4 can be combined by deselecting all server roles in one step.

When all these steps are successfully executed, the previous Exchange Server is now fully removed, and only the Exchange 2016 servers remain in the Exchange organization.

Important Note Decommissioning the previous version is not simply a matter of turning it off. Now this may sound silly, but it happens frequently in a virtualized server environment. It is tempting to turn off the virtual machines and just delete them, but this is absolutely wrong. When you do this, all information regarding previous versions of Exchange Server remains in Active Directory. From an Exchange 2016 point of view, "they" are still there (but not responding, of course). This can lead to erratic behavior. So, fully uninstall the previous Exchange Server!

Summary

Although this book is about Exchange 2019 and Exchange 2016, there are still a lot of customers running Exchange 2010. Exchange 2010 is out of support, but Exchange 2016 is not, and a coexistence scenario with Exchange 2010 and Exchange 2016 is also still supported.

When running on Exchange 2010, you must move your environment as soon as possible to Exchange 2016. Why not Exchange 2019? Microsoft only supports n-2 versions in any Exchange version, so Exchange 2019 is only supported with Exchange 2016 and Exchange 2013. Exchange 2016 is only supported with Exchange 2013 and Exchange 2010 in one environment.

Moving or transitioning from Exchange 2010 to Exchange 2016 is not really a big deal. Maybe you remember moving from Exchange 2003 to Exchange 2010, where you had this redirection solution and you had to use a legacy namespace... this is no longer the case, and Exchange 2016 can proxy all connections directly to Exchange 2010 without any issues. This makes life much easier.

The only big step in an Exchange 2010 to Exchange 2016 migration is where the accessing of the platform is changed. At one point, clients must connect to Exchange 2016 instead of Exchange 2010. When not configured properly, this may result in disruption of the service. As such, it should always be performed off business hours.

If you are lucky enough to have Exchange 2013 running in your organization, the migration from Exchange 2013 to Exchange 2016 or Exchange 2019 is even simpler than the migration from Exchange 2010 to Exchange 2019. The migration of Exchange 2013 to Exchange 2019 is covered in the next chapter.

CHAPTER 8

Upgrading from Exchange 2013 to Exchange 2019

When Microsoft was moving Exchange Online from Exchange 2010 to Exchange 2013, it was clear that this was utterly complex for large organizations, although it was still much better than previous migrations.

One of the design goals for Exchange 2013 and higher is to simplify the migration to new versions. This pays off since the migration from Exchange 2013 or Exchange 2016 to Exchange 2019 is straightforward. It is still not as easy as an in-place upgrade or installing a Cumulative Update, but it is getting close.

The front-end services between the three versions are 100% compatible, which means you install an Exchange 2016 server in a load-balanced array of Exchange 2013 servers, and the same is true for Exchange 2019.

The mailbox services in the back end are different; these are not compatible when it comes to Mailbox database engines, and they cannot be matched and mixed in a DAG unfortunately as Windows versions are different between the Exchange versions.

In this chapter, I will write Exchange 2013 to Exchange 2019, but everything is the same for Exchange 2016. If there are major changes in moving from Exchange 2016 to Exchange 2019, I will make an additional note.

But in the end, upgrading from Exchange 2013 to Exchange 2019 is not a daunting task. Here it goes.

Moving to Exchange 2019

Moving from Exchange 2010 is easy because Exchange 2016 is simply introduced into the current Exchange Server environment. A long story short, the only thing you have to worry about is the storage.

M. de Rooij and J. Wesselius, *Pro Exchange 2019 and 2016 Administration*,
https://doi.org/10.1007/978-1-4842-7331-9_8

From a protocol perspective, Exchange 2013 and Exchange 2019 are 100% compatible. If a client connects to Exchange 2013 and the client's mailbox is on Exchange 2016, the connection is proxied to the Exchange 2016 server. If the mailbox is on Exchange 2019, the connection is proxied to Exchange 2019. Proxying means the client keeps the connection with Exchange 2013. This up-level proxy is scenario 1 with the solid line in Figure 8-1.

When the client connects to Exchange 2016 and the client's mailbox is on Exchange 2013, the connection is proxied to Exchange 2013 (down-level proxy). If the mailbox is on Exchange 2019, the connection is proxied to Exchange 2019 (up-level proxy). This is scenario 2 with the dashed line in Figure 8-1.

The last one is when the client connects to Exchange 2019. If the mailbox is on another (down-level) server, the connection is proxied to this server. This is scenario 3 with the dotted line in Figure 8-1.

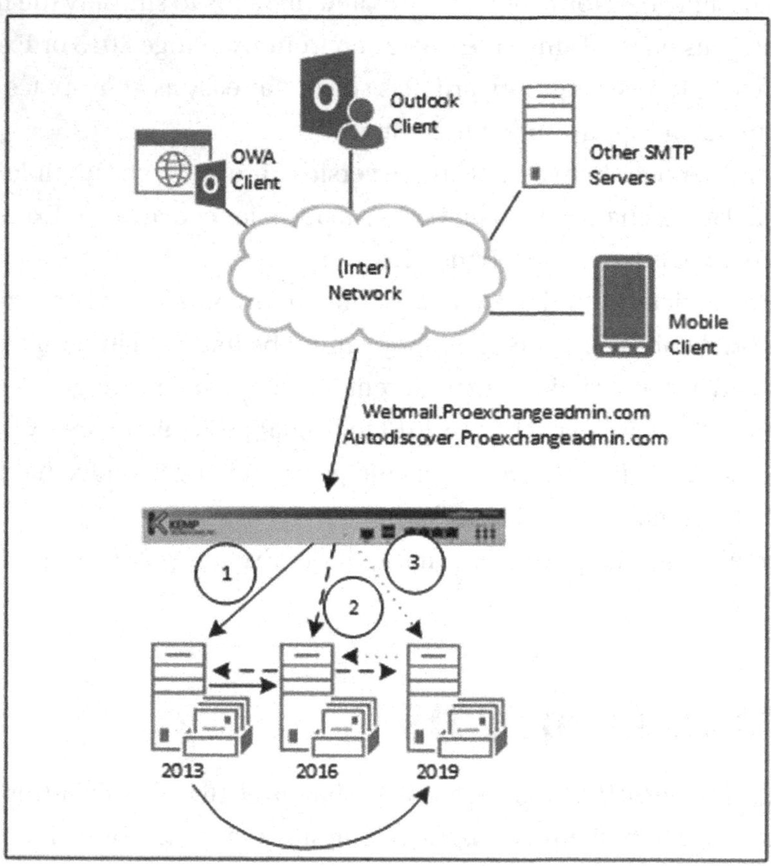

***Figure 8-1.** Protocol proxying in Exchange*

In the back end, things are a bit less compatible. When upgrading from Exchange 2013 to Exchange 2016 or Exchange 2019, you must build a new storage solution. From a mailbox database perspective, the different versions of Exchange are not compatible. This means for every version of Exchange, you must build a new Database Availability Group.

In Figure 8-2, there are four Exchange servers in a load-balanced array, and this works as explained in the previous section. But, two Exchange 2013 have their own Database Availability Group (DAG1) and so does Exchange 2019 (DAG2). If you also had two Exchange 2016 servers in this scenario, you would have a third Database Availability Group.

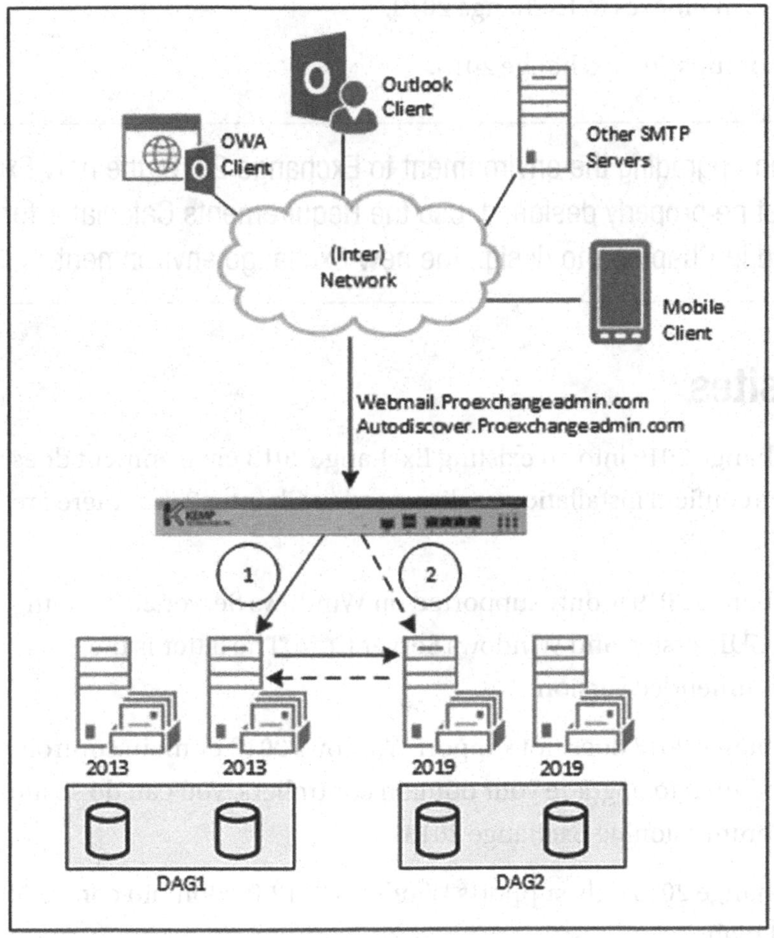

***Figure 8-2.** Multiple DAGs in one Exchange environment*

After adding Exchange 2019 into the existing Exchange 2013 environment, you must move all mailboxes from DAG1 to DAG2 before you can decommission Exchange 2013.

Upgrading from Exchange 2013 to Exchange 2019 consists of the following steps:

1. Prepare Active Directory.
2. Install and configure the Exchange 2019 servers.
3. Add the Exchange 2019 servers to the load balancer.
4. Change SMTP routing via Exchange 2019.
5. Move mailboxes to Exchange 2019.
6. Decommission Exchange 2013.

Note When upgrading the environment to Exchange 2019, the new Exchange servers must be properly designed. Use the Requirements Calculator for Exchange as discussed in Chapter 2 to design the new Exchange environment.

Prerequisites

Installing Exchange 2019 into an existing Exchange 2013 environment does not differ much from a greenfield installation as discussed in Chapter 2, but there are some differences:

- Exchange 2019 is only supported on Windows Server 2019, both the GUI version and Windows Server Core. The latter is the recommended version.
- Exchange 2013 does not support Windows 2019 domain controllers. If you plan to upgrade your domain controllers, you can do so after decommissioning Exchange 2013.
- Exchange 2019 only supports Windows 2012 R2 domain controllers and higher.
- Exchange 2013, Exchange 2016, and Exchange 2019 all support Windows 2016 Forest Functional Level.
- Exchange 2013 must be running Cumulative Update 23 with the latest Security Update installed.

The following prerequisite software for Exchange 2019 needs to be installed on the Windows 2019 server:

- .NET Framework 4.8
- Visual C++ Redistributable Package for Visual Studio 2012
- Visual C++ Redistributable Package for Visual Studio 2013
- Microsoft Unified Communications Managed API 4.0 Core Runtime 64-bit

Use the following commands to install the prerequisite Windows Server Roles and Features on Windows 2019:

```
PS C:\> Install-WindowsFeature Server-Media-Foundation, NET-Framework-
45-Features, RPC-over-HTTP-proxy, RSAT-Clustering, RSAT-Clustering-
CmdInterface, RSAT-Clustering-Mgmt, RSAT-Clustering-PowerShell,
WAS-Process-Model, Web-Asp-Net45, Web-Basic-Auth, Web-Client-Auth, Web-
Digest-Auth, Web-Dir-Browsing, Web-Dyn-Compression, Web-Http-Errors,
Web-Http-Logging, Web-Http-Redirect, Web-Http-Tracing, Web-ISAPI-Ext,
Web-ISAPI-Filter, Web-Lgcy-Mgmt-Console, Web-Metabase, Web-Mgmt-Console,
Web-Mgmt-Service, Web-Net-Ext45, Web-Request-Monitor, Web-Server, Web-
Stat-Compression, Web-Static-Content, Web-Windows-Auth, Web-WMI, Windows-
Identity-Foundation, RSAT-ADDS, Telnet-Client
```

To download the .NET Framework 4.8:

```
PS C:\> Start-BitsTransfer -Source "https://download.visualstudio.
microsoft.com/download/pr/7afca223-55d2-470a-8edc-6a1739ae3252/
abd170b4b0ec15ad0222a809b761a036/ndp48-x86-x64-allos-enu.exe" -Destination
C:\Install
```

To download Visual C++ Redistributable Package for Visual Studio 2012:

```
PS C:\> Start-BitsTransfer -Source "https://download.microsoft.com/
download/1/6/B/16B06F60-3B20-4FF2-B699-5E9B7962F9AE/VSU_4/vcredist_x64.exe"
-Destination c:\Install\VS2012
```

To download Visual C++ Redistributable Package for Visual Studio 2013:

```
PS C:\> Start-BitsTransfer -Source "https://download.microsoft.com/
download/2/E/6/2E61CFA4-993B-4DD4-91DA-3737CD5CD6E3/vcredist_x64.exe"
-Destination c:\Install\VS2013
```

And finally, to download the Microsoft Unified Communications Managed API 4.0, Core Runtime 64-bit:

```
PS C:\> Start-BitsTransfer -Source "http://download.microsoft.com/
download/2/C/4/2C47A5C1-A1F3-4843-B9FE-84C0032C61EC/UcmaRuntimeSetup.exe"
-Destination c:\Install
```

For an unattended installation of the prerequisite software, use the following commands in a PowerShell window with elevated privileges:

```
PS C:\> Start-Process -FilePath "C:\Install\ndp48-x86-x64-allos-enu.exe"
-ArgumentList "/q" -Wait
PS C:\> Start-Process -FilePath "C:\Install\VS2012\vcredist_x64.exe"
-ArgumentList "/q" -Wait
PS C:\> Start-Process -FilePath "C:\Install\VS2013\vcredist_x64.exe"
-ArgumentList "/q" -Wait
PS C:\> Start-Process -FilePath "C:\Install\UcmaRuntimeSetup.exe"
-ArgumentList "-q" -Wait
```

The last command will automatically reboot the server when needed.

Prepare Active Directory

When all requirements are met, Active Directory can be prepared for the introduction of Exchange 2019 using the following commands:

```
Z:\> Setup.exe /PrepareSchema /IAcceptExchangeServerLicenseTerms
Z:\> Setup.exe /PrepareAD /IAcceptExchangeServerLicenseTerms
Z:\> Setup.exe /PrepareDomain /IAcceptExchangeServerLicenseTerms
```

Or, if you are using multiple Active Directory domains, you can replace this last command with the following command for easy deployment:

```
Z:\> Setup.exe /PrepareAllDomains /IAcceptExchangeServerLicenseTerms
```

When preparing the Active Directory configuration partition using the /PrepareAD switch, the following warning message is shown:

```
Setup will prepare the organization for Exchange Server 2019 by using
'Setup /PrepareAD'. No Exchange Server 2016 roles have been detected in
this topology. After this operation, you will not be able to install any
Exchange Server 2016
roles.
For more information, visit: https://docs.microsoft.com/Exchange/plan-and-
deploy/deployment-ref/readiness-checks?view=exchserver-2019
```

This is shown in Figure 8-3.

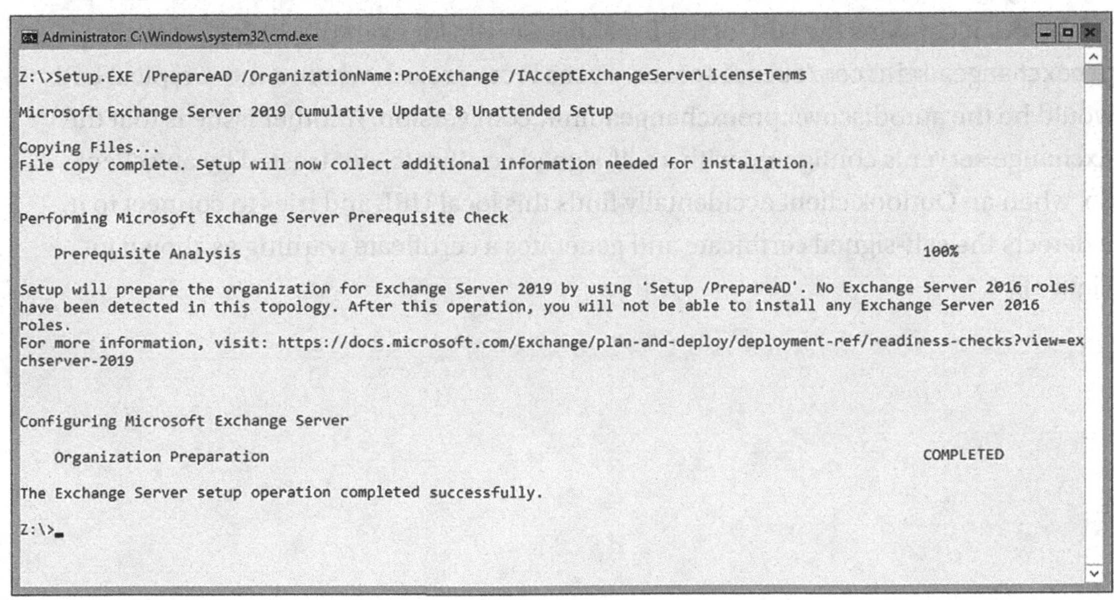
Administrator: C:\Windows\system32\cmd.exe
Z:\>Setup.EXE /PrepareAD /OrganizationName:ProExchange /IAcceptExchangeServerLicenseTerms
Microsoft Exchange Server 2019 Cumulative Update 8 Unattended Setup
Copying Files...
File copy complete. Setup will now collect additional information needed for installation.
Performing Microsoft Exchange Server Prerequisite Check
Prerequisite Analysis 100%
Setup will prepare the organization for Exchange Server 2019 by using 'Setup /PrepareAD'. No Exchange Server 2016 roles have been detected in this topology. After this operation, you will not be able to install any Exchange Server 2016 roles.
For more information, visit: https://docs.microsoft.com/Exchange/plan-and-deploy/deployment-ref/readiness-checks?view=exchserver-2019
Configuring Microsoft Exchange Server
Organization Preparation COMPLETED
The Exchange Server setup operation completed successfully.
Z:\>

***Figure 8-3.** During the preparation of Active Directory, an Exchange 2016–related warning is shown*

If for some reason you need an Exchange 2016 server, you must cancel the operation and repeat the same step from an Exchange 2016 installation media.

After preparations with Exchange 2019 CU9, the Active Directory schema should be at level 17002, while the Exchange organization stored in the configuration partition of Active Directory should be at level 16757. Details about version numbering can be found in Table 2-3 in Chapter 2.

Installing Exchange 2019

When the server is properly designed, Windows is installed, and all prerequisite software is installed, Exchange 2019 can be installed. This can be a tricky process when performed during business hours.

When the Client Access components of an Exchange 2019 server are installed, a new service connection point (SCP) is created in Active Directory. As explained earlier, this SCP is used by Outlook clients to find an Exchange server that can be used to retrieve Exchange and mailbox configuration, a process called "Autodiscover." When this SCP is created, it contains the URL of the Exchange server, for example, `https://exch11.proexchangeadmin.com/autodiscover/autodiscover.xml`, where a more typical URL would be the autodiscover.proexchangeadmin.com version. Another issue is that the Exchange server is configured with a self-signed certificate, not trusted by any client. So, when an Outlook client accidentally finds this local URL and tries to connect to it, it detects the self-signed certificate and generates a certificate warning as shown in Figure 8-4.

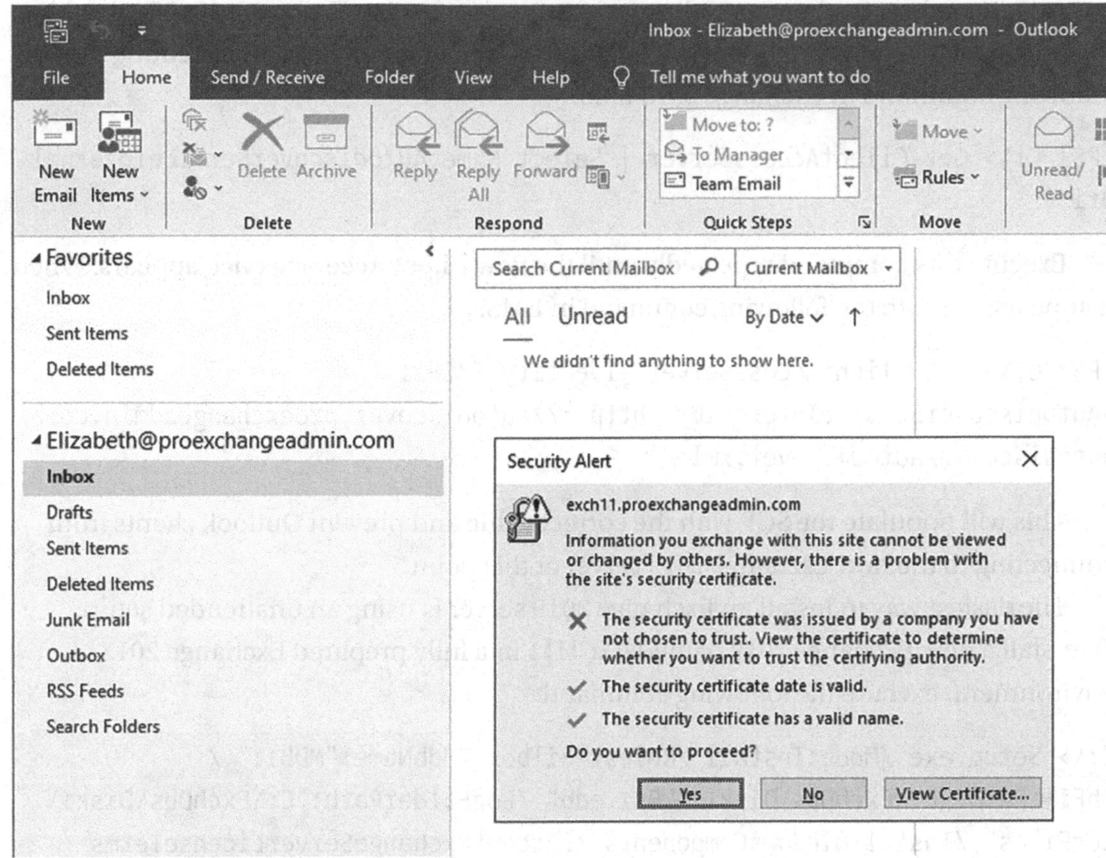

***Figure 8-4.** A certificate warning in Outlook, caused by a self-signed certificate during installation*

This will generate help desk calls and frustrated users, something we would all like to avoid.

To avoid this, Microsoft recommends installing new Exchange servers in a separate Active Directory site. Outlook clients will find SCP records in their own site, and not in such a dedicated installation site.

Another option is of course to install Exchange off business hours or to change the SCP to the normal value as soon as the installation of the new Exchange 2019 has finished and take the risk of Outlook clients finding this wrong SCP. Mind you, it can go wrong. I have faced such an issue in a large enterprise environment with 32 Exchange servers and 40,000 clients where the SCP turned out to be wrong during installation of a new Exchange server. This resulted in over 1000 Outlook clients with a corrupt profile, so there is a risk involved here.

Another solution when upgrading from Exchange 2013 to Exchange 2019 is checking the existence of a new SCP in the Exchange 2013 Management Shell by executing the following command in Exchange 2013 EMS:

```
[PS] C:\> Get-ClientAccessServer | Select Name,AutodiscoverServiceInternal
Uri
```

Execute this command repeatedly until the new Client Access Service appears. When it appears, execute the following command in EMS:

```
[PS] C:\> Set-ClientAccessServer -Identity EXCH11
-AutodiscoverServiceInternalUri https://autodiscover.proexchangeadmin.com/
autodiscover/autodiscover.xml
```

This will populate the SCP with the correct value and prevent Outlook clients from connecting to the new Exchange 2019 server at this point.

The easiest way to install an Exchange 2019 server is using an unattended setup. To install a new Exchange 2019 named EXCH11 in a fully prepared Exchange 2013 environment, execute the following command:

```
Z:\> Setup.exe /Mode:Install /Roles:Mailbox /MdbName:"MDB11" /
DbFilePath:"C:\ExchDbs\Disk1\MDB11.edb" /LogFolderPath:"C:\ExchDbs\Disk1\
LogFiles" /InstallWindowsComponents /IAcceptExchangeServerLicenseTerms
```

This is shown in Figure 8-5.

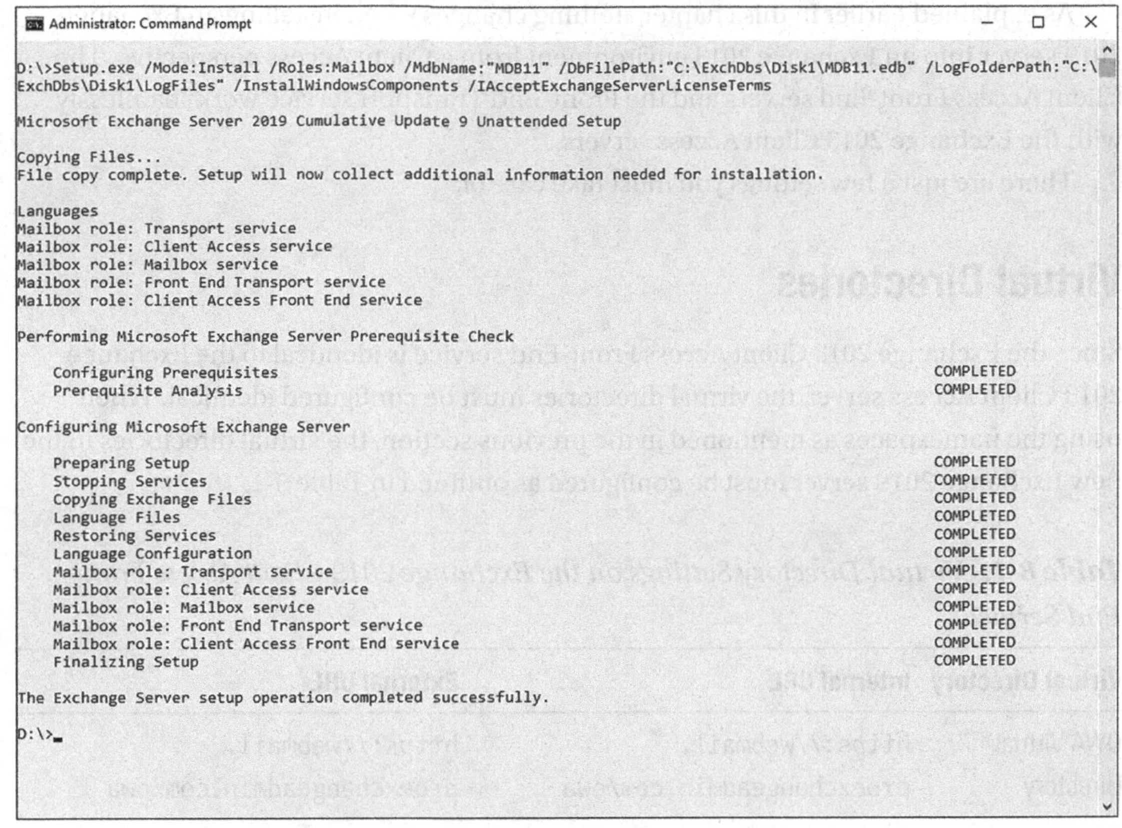
Administrator: Command Prompt
D:\>Setup.exe /Mode:Install /Roles:Mailbox /MdbName:"MDB11" /DbFilePath:"C:\ExchDbs\Disk1\MDB11.edb" /LogFolderPath:"C:\ExchDbs\Disk1\LogFiles" /InstallWindowsComponents /IAcceptExchangeServerLicenseTerms
Microsoft Exchange Server 2019 Cumulative Update 9 Unattended Setup
Copying Files...
File copy complete. Setup will now collect additional information needed for installation.
Languages
Mailbox role: Transport service
Mailbox role: Client Access service
Mailbox role: Mailbox service
Mailbox role: Front End Transport service
Mailbox role: Client Access Front End service
Performing Microsoft Exchange Server Prerequisite Check
Configuring Prerequisites COMPLETED
Prerequisite Analysis COMPLETED
Configuring Microsoft Exchange Server
Preparing Setup COMPLETED
Stopping Services COMPLETED
Copying Exchange Files COMPLETED
Language Files COMPLETED
Restoring Services COMPLETED
Language Configuration COMPLETED
Mailbox role: Transport service COMPLETED
Mailbox role: Client Access service COMPLETED
Mailbox role: Mailbox service COMPLETED
Mailbox role: Front End Transport service COMPLETED
Mailbox role: Client Access Front End service COMPLETED
Finalizing Setup COMPLETED
The Exchange Server setup operation completed successfully.
D:\>

***Figure 8-5.** Unattended install of Exchange 2019 in an Exchange 2013 environment*

When running a mixed Exchange environment with server versions 2013 and higher, it is recommended to use the management interface of the newest version. So, after installing Exchange 2019 into an existing Exchange 2013 environment, use the Exchange Admin Center and Exchange Management Shell of Exchange 2019.

Namespaces with Exchange

In a typical Exchange Server 2013 environment, three namespaces are used:

- **webmail.proexchangeadmin.com**—Used for all HTTPS-based services, including Outlook Anywhere
- **autodiscover.proexchangeadmin.com**—Used by external Outlook clients for discovering the internal Exchange configuration
- **Mail.proexchangeadmin.com**—Used for SMTP mail purposes

As explained earlier in this chapter, nothing changes when installing an Exchange 2019 server into an Exchange 2013 environment from a Client Access perspective. The Client Access Front-End servers and the Front-End Transport service work seamlessly with the Exchange 2013 Client Access servers.

There are just a few settings you must take care of.

Virtual Directories

Since the Exchange 2013 Client Access Front-End service is identical to the Exchange 2013 Client Access server, the virtual directories must be configured identical. When using the namespaces as mentioned in the previous section, the virtual directories in the new Exchange 2019 server must be configured as outlined in Table 8-1.

Table 8-1. *Virtual Directory Settings on the Exchange 2019 Client Access Front-End Service*

Virtual Directory	Internal URL	External URL
OWA Virtual Directory	`https://webmail.proexchangeadmin.com/owa`	`https://webmail.proexchangeadmin.com/owa`
ECP Virtual Directory	`https://webmail.proexchangeadmin.com/ecp`	`https://webmail.proexchangeadmin.com/ecp`
ActiveSync Virtual Directory	`https://webmail.proexchangeadmin.com/Microsoft-Server-ActiveSync`	`https://webmail.proexchangeadmin.com/Microsoft-Server-ActiveSync`
EWS Virtual Directory	`https://webmail.proexchangeadmin.com/EWS/Exchange.asmx`	`https://webmail.proexchangeadmin.com/EWS/Exchange.asmx`
OAB Virtual Directory	`https://webmail.proexchangeadmin.com/OAB`	`https://webmail.proexchangeadmin.com/OAB`

(*continued*)

Table 8-1. (*continued*)

Virtual Directory	Internal URL	External URL
PowerShell Virtual Directory	https://webmail.proexchangeadmin.com/PowerShell	https://webmail.proexchangeadmin.com/PowerShell
MAPI Virtual Directory	https://webmail.proexchangeadmin.com/Mapi	https://webmail.proexchangeadmin.com/Mapi
Outlook Anywhere	https://webmail.proexchangeadmin.com/	https://webmail.proexchangeadmin.com/

Just as in Chapter 2, the best way to configure the virtual directories is to use the `change_vdir_settings.ps1` PowerShell script to minimize the risk for errors. This script will set all the virtual directories and configure Outlook Anywhere as well.

SSL Certificates

Since the virtual directories on the Exchange 2019 server are configured identical to the virtual directories on Exchange 2013, the same SSL certificate can be used on Exchange 2019.

To use an existing SSL certificate from the Exchange 2013 Client Access server, you follow these steps:

1. On the Exchange 2013 Client Access server, execute the following command in EMS to export the SSL certificate to a .pfx file:

    ```
    C:\> Export-ExchangeCertificate -Thumbprint
    4952E8C42A8279D16999A85400CE9F3DD4EC7458 -FileName
    "\\FS01\Install\webmail_proexchangeadmin_com.pfx"
    -BinaryEncoded -Password (ConvertTo-SecureString
    -String "Pass1word" -AsPlainText -Force)
    ```

    The thumbprint value can be retrieved from the Exchange 2013 server using the Get-ExchangeCertificate command.

2. On the Exchange 2019 server, you open EMS and enter the following command to import the .pfx file:

```
[PS] C:\> Import-ExchangeCertificate -Server EXCH11
-FileData ([Byte[]]$(Get-Content -Path "\\FS01\Install\webmail_
proexchangeadmin_com.pfx" -Encoding byte -ReadCount 0))
| Enable-ExchangeCertificate -Server EXCH11 -Services IIS
```

The same SSL certificate is now ready for use on Exchange 2019.

SMTP Mail in a Coexistence Scenario

During the coexistence phase, the SMTP mail flow is not changing dramatically. The Exchange 2013 will gladly accept the new Exchange 2019 servers, and these servers will automatically take part in message routing.

For outbound messaging, the only thing you must do is add the new Exchange 2019 server to existing Send Connectors.

For inbound messaging, the firewall or anti-spam appliance need to be changed so that inbound messages are also delivered to the Exchange 2019 server.

If you have any SMTP relay Receive Connectors, you must reconfigure these to use the Exchange 2019 server.

Using an Edge Transport Server

As explained before, the Edge Transport server is typically used as an SMTP gateway located in the demilitarized zone of the network. As such, it exchanges mail between the Internet and the internal Exchange servers.

Just with the internal mailbox servers, the Exchange 2013 Edge Transport server can work seamlessly with new Exchange 2019 mailbox servers. Vice versa, Exchange 2019 Edge Transport server with older Exchange 2013 or Exchange servers works seamlessly as well.

During coexistence, there are two options:

- Continue with the Exchange 2013 Edge Transport Server.
- Introduce a new Exchange 2019 Edge Transport Server.

Continuing with the Previous Edge Transport Server

If you opt for the first option, using the Exchange 2013 Edge Transport server with the Exchange 2013 and Exchange 2019 servers in coexistence, it is just a matter of recreating the Edge Subscription. The Exchange 2013 Edge Transport server will continue working with both the Exchange 2013 and Exchange 2019 Mailbox server. This is shown in Figure 8-6.

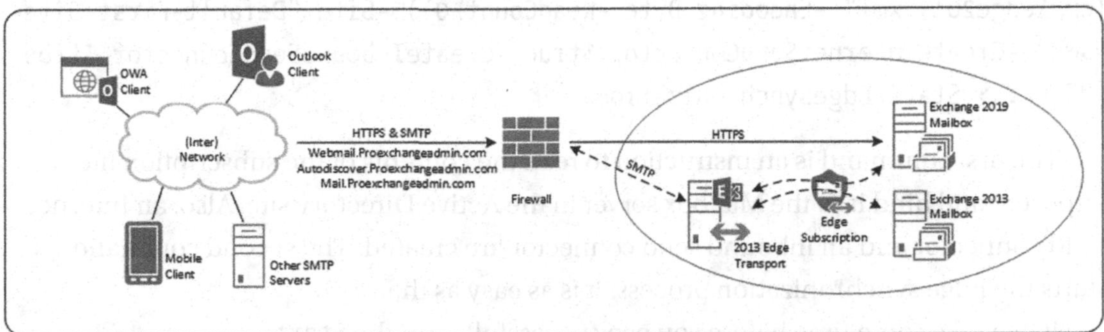

***Figure 8-6.** The Exchange 2013 Edge Transport with an Exchange 2013 and Exchange 2019 Mailbox server*

When you opt for this scenario and you only have one Exchange 2013 Edge Transport server, this will cause some downtime for inbound and outbound mail flow.

The Edge Subscription must be removed from both the Exchange 2013 Edge Transport server and the Exchange 2013 Mailbox server. To remove the Edge Subscription, execute the following command in EMS on both servers:

```
[PS] C:\> Get-EdgeSubscription -Identity EXCH2013 | Remove-EdgeSubscription
```

At this stage, you do not have any connection left between the Exchange 2013 Edge Transport server and the internal Exchange organization, so you must act quickly to minimize downtime.

To create a new Edge Subscription, execute the following command on the Exchange 2013 Edge Transport server:

```
[PS] C:\> New-EdgeSubscription -FileName C:\Temp\Edge2013.xml
```

A warning message is shown, saying the subscription file is valid for 1440 minutes (which equals 24 hours). (If the subscription file is not processed within this time frame, a new subscription must be created.) Enter "Y" to confirm your knowledge of the warning message, and the subscription file will be created.

Copy the Edge2013.xml subscription file to a directory on the local disk of the 2019 Mailbox server. On this server, execute the following commands in EMS:

```
[PS] C:\> New-EdgeSubscription -FileData ([byte[]]$(Get-Content -Path "C:\
Temp\edge2013.xml" -Encoding Byte -ReadCount 0)) -Site "Default-First-Site-
Name" -CreateInternetSendConnector $true -CreateInboundSendConnector $true
[PS] C:\> Start-EdgeSynchronization
```

The first command is an instruction to read the contents of the subscription file, import it, and bind it to the Mailbox server in the Active Directory site. Also, an Internet send connector and an inbound send connector are created. The second command starts the Edge synchronization process. It is as easy as that.

It can take some time before you can successfully run the `Start-EdgeSynchronization` command. If it fails directly after importing the Edge Subscription file, please wait a couple of minutes and try again.

Note The Exchange 2013 Edge Transport server should be able to resolve the Exchange 2013 and the Exchange 2019 Mailbox server, and vice versa. This can be achieved using DNS, but using a HOSTS file for resolving an Edge Transport server is quite common as well.

Introducing a New Exchange 2019 Edge Transport Server

The second option when working with Edge Transport servers is to introduce a new Exchange 2019 Edge Transport server next to the existing Edge Transport server.

You install a brand-new Windows 2019 server in the perimeter network and make sure you have Internet connectivity (at least on port 25), and that name resolution works fine, both to the Internet and to the internal network, then you install the Exchange 2019 Edge Transport server role.

Note Installing and configuring the Exchange 2019 Edge Transport server role is explained in detail in Chapter 2.

When the Exchange 2019 Edge Transport server is installed, you can create a new Edge Subscription. Log on to the Exchange 2019 Edge Transport server and execute the following command:

```
[PS] C:\> New-EdgeSubscription -FileName C:\Temp\Edge2019.xml
```

When the file is created, you copy it to the local hard disk of the Exchange 2019 Mailbox server. On this server, execute the following commands:

```
[PS] C:\> New-EdgeSubscription -FileData ([byte[]]$(Get-Content -Path "C:\
Temp\edge2019.xml" -Encoding Byte -ReadCount 0)) -Site "Default-First-Site-
Name" -CreateInternetSendConnector $true -CreateInboundSendConnector $true
[PS] C:\> Start-EdgeSynchronization
```

This will create the Edge Subscription between the Exchange 2019 Edge Transport server and the Exchange 2013 and Exchange 2019 Mailbox server and initiate the synchronization process. You now have a situation as shown in Figure 8-7.

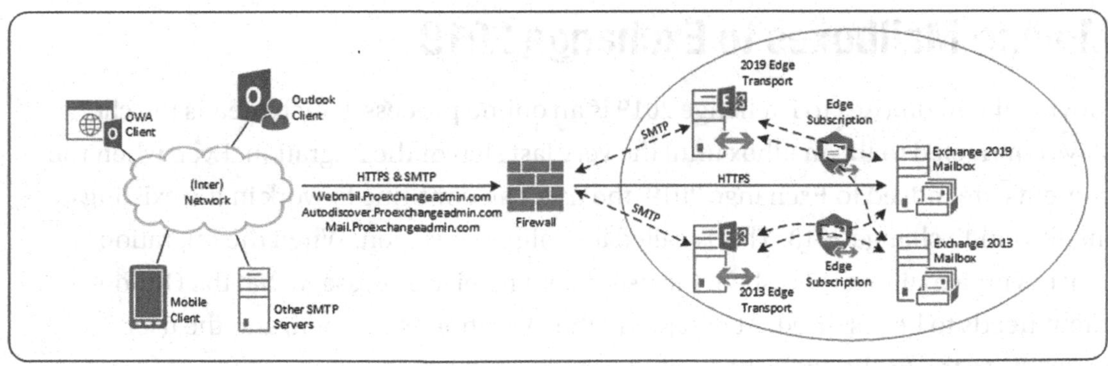

Figure 8-7. *Introducing a new Exchange 2019 Edge Transport server next to the down-level Edge Transport server*

To initiate proper communication between the "old" Exchange 2013 Edge Transport server and the internal Exchange 2013 and Exchange 2019 mailbox server, the Edge Subscription for this server should be replaced as well. You can use the procedure as described in the previous section.

After this, you will have two Edge subscriptions in the internal Exchange organization, one for every Edge Transport server. At this point, you can continue with two different Exchange Edge Transport servers, or you can choose to decommission the old Exchange 2013 Edge Transport server. But, before you can decommission the old Exchange 2013 Edge Transport server, do not forget to remove the Edge Subscription for this Edge Transport server. To do this, execute the following command on the Exchange 2019 Mailbox server:

```
[PS] C:\> Get-EdgeSubscription -Identity <<Name>> | Remove-EdgeSubscription
```

where <<Name>> is the NetBIOS name of the Exchange 2013 Edge Transport server.

Moving Resources to Exchange 2019

The most important step in the transition process is to move the mailboxes and other resources from Exchange 2013 to the new Exchange 2019 server.

Moving Mailboxes to Exchange 2019

Moving the mailboxes to Exchange 2019 is an online process, which means the client stays connected to the mailbox until the very last step of the migration. Even when the contents are moved to Exchange 2019, the user can continue to work in the existing mailbox in Exchange 2013. This is called an online migration. When the migration process for a mailbox is finished, the user might receive a message that the Outlook client needs to be restarted. At that point, the migration is finished, and the user connects to the Exchange 2019 mailbox server.

The process responsible for moving the Mailboxes is the Mailbox Replication Service (MRS), a service that is running on the Exchange 2019 server. Or better, on every Exchange server as shown in Figure 8-8.

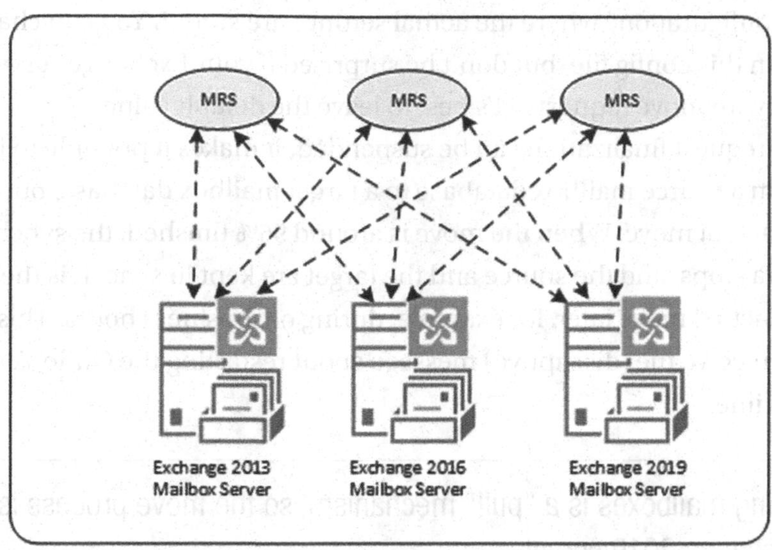

Figure 8-8. *The Mailbox Replication Service (MRS)*

When a mailbox needs to be moved from one mailbox database to another mailbox database, the actual mailbox move is initiated with a move request. With a move request, a flag is set in the system mailbox of the source mailbox database, and this flag is picked up by the MRS. The MRS then creates a copy of that mailbox in the target mailbox database, and it starts moving the mailbox data from the source to the target. This is an online and fully transparent mechanism; the recipient can be online and will not notice anything about moving data. When the MRS is about to finish the migration of data, the source mailbox is closed, and all remaining data is written into the target mailbox; the properties in Active Directory are updated as well.

The MRS is running on every Exchange server, so if there are five Exchange servers, there are also five instances of MRS running in the Exchange environment. It is possible to tune the MRS on the Exchange server. By default, very few mailboxes per database and per server are moved concurrently, to prevent the Mailbox server from becoming overwhelmed as mailboxes are moved. This otherwise tremendous amount of traffic might impact users when mailboxes are being moved during business hours.

The configuration of the MRS is stored in a config file located in the `C:\Program Files\Microsoft\Exchange Server\V15\Bin directory, called MSExchangeMailboxReplication.exe.config`. When you open this file and scroll to the end, there is a section called "Mailbox Replication Service Configuration" where all the default, minimum, and maximum values are stored. There is also a section called "MRSConfiguration" where the actual settings are stored. You can change the values stored in this config file, but don't be surprised if your Exchange servers are overwhelmed with move requests; it's best to leave the default values.

The move request finalization can be suspended. It makes it possible to move mailboxes from a source mailbox database to a target mailbox database, but without finalizing the actual move. When the move is around 95% finished, the synchronization of mailbox data stops, and the source and the target are kept in sync. It is then possible to finalize the actual move later, for example, during off-business hours. This way, the user does not receive the (disruptive) message about restarting the Outlook client at an inconvenient time.

Note Moving mailboxes is a "pull" mechanism, so the move process is initiated from the Exchange 2019 server.

To initiate a mailbox move for a user called joe@proexchangeadmin.com, you log on to an Exchange 2019 server, open EMS, and execute the following command:

```
[PS] C:\> New-MoveRequest -Identity joe@proexchangeadmin.com -
TargetDatabase MDB11
```

You can also get a list of mailboxes on the previous Exchange Mailbox server, for example, based on a mailbox database called MBX01, and use the pipeline feature to move all mailboxes to a mailbox database called MDB11. This will result in a command like

```
[PS] C:\> Get-Mailbox -Database "MBX01" | New-MoveRequest -TargetDatabase
MDB11
```

You can monitor the move of the mailboxes with the Get-MoveRequest command; if needed, you can add the Get-MoveRequestStatistics command, like this:

```
[PS] C:\> Get-MoveRequest | Get-MoveRequestStatistics
```

This will give you a quick overview of all move requests that are currently available and whether their status is queued, in progress, or completed. To get an overview of all move requests that are running at a particular moment, you can make a selection based on the status of the move request, like this:

```
[PS] C:\> Get-MoveRequest | Where {$_.Status -eq "InProgress"}
```

Exchange uses special system mailboxes, arbitration mailboxes, and the discovery search mailbox. I recommend migrating these first from Exchange 2013 to Exchange 2019. This way, features like arbitration, eDiscovery, and Audit logging become available on Exchange 2019.

To move these mailboxes, use the following commands:

```
[PS] C:\> Get-Mailbox -Arbitation | New-MoveRequest -TargetDatabase MDB11
[PS] C:\> get-mailbox -Identity discovery* | New-MoveRequest -
TargetDatabase MDB11
```

If you do not specify a target database with the New-MoveRequest command, Exchange will select a mailbox database automatically, based on the availability of resources.

When the regular mailboxes, the discovery mailbox, and the system mailboxes are moved to Exchange 2019, then the mailbox databases on the previous version of Exchange Server should be empty and are ready for removal.

Address Lists in Exchange 2019

When all the mailboxes are moved to Exchange 2019, it is time to move the other resources. Regular address lists reside in Active Directory, so there is no need to "move" them to Exchange 2019. From a management perspective, Address Lists can be managed both from Exchange 2013 and Exchange 2019. There is no need to pay extra attention to Address Lists.

Moving the Offline Address Book to Exchange 2019

Prior to Exchange 2013 CU5, the Offline Address Book (OAB) was generated by an Exchange server. When the server was not available, OAB changes could not be generated and distributed to clients.

In Exchange 2013 CU5, Microsoft changed the way how OABs were generated, and now they are generated using a generation mailbox. To view which generation mailbox is generating the OAB, execute the following command:

```
[PS] C:\> Get-Mailbox -Arbitration | where {$_.PersistedCapabilities -like
"*oab*"} | ft name,servername
```

This is shown in Figure 8-9.

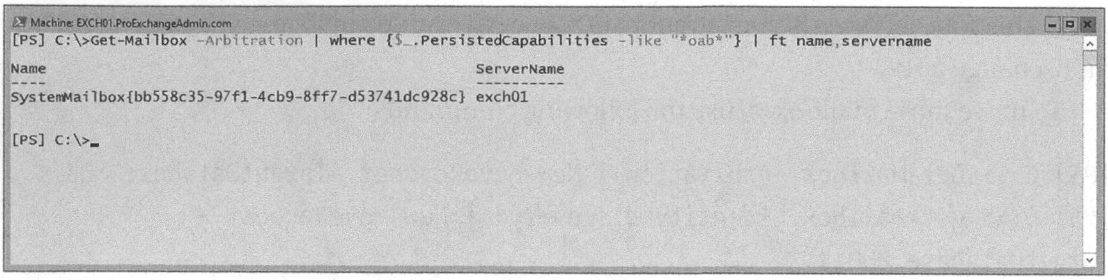

```
Machine: EXCH01.ProExchangeAdmin.com
[PS] C:\>Get-Mailbox -Arbitration | where {$_.PersistedCapabilities -like "*oab*"} | ft name,servername

Name                                              ServerName
----                                              ----------
SystemMailbox{bb558c35-97f1-4cb9-8ff7-d53741dc928c} exch01

[PS] C:\>_
```

***Figure 8-9.** The arbitration mailbox responsible for generating the OAB*

The advantage of moving from a generating server to a generating mailbox is that the mailbox can take advantage of the high availability features in a Database Availability Group. When a server is not available, another copy of the mailbox database takes over the OAB generation service.

When moving from Exchange 2013 to Exchange 2019, the only thing you must do regarding the OAB is moving the arbitration mailbox to Exchange 2019.

To move all arbitration mailboxes in just one command to a mailbox called MBX11 on Exchange 2019, execute the following command:

```
[PS] C:\> Get-Mailbox -Arbitration | New-MoveRequest -TargetDatabase MDB11
```

To move only the arbitration mailbox that is responsible for the OAB generation to this mailbox database, execute the following command:

```
[PS] C:\> Get-Mailbox -Arbitration | where {$_.PersistedCapabilities -like
"*oab*"} | New-MoveRequest -TargetDatabase MDB11
```

Decommissioning the Previous Exchange Server

When all resources have been moved or removed, you can decommission the Exchange 2013 Server. This is not really a big deal at all, and it involves the following steps:

1. Make sure the Exchange 2013 server is not responsible anymore for any mail traffic. This not only includes SMTP from and to the Internet but also third-party appliances or (custom) applications that might have been using the Hub Transport server for receiving

or relaying messages. Caution: You don't want to remove the Exchange 2013 Server and find out that your multifunctional devices cannot send out messages anymore.

To achieve this, you can enable SMTP protocol logging on both the receive connector and the send connector, and check the corresponding log files. By default, you can find these log files at the following locations:

- SMTP receive

  C:\Program Files\Microsoft\Exchange Server\V15\TransportRoles\Logs\ ProtocolLog\SMTPReceive

- SMTP send

  C:\Program Files\Microsoft\Exchange Server\V15\TransportRoles\Logs\ ProtocolLog\SMTPSend

2. Remove the mailbox databases from the Exchange 2013 Server. This can be achieved by using the Exchange Management Shell or Exchange Admin Center in Exchange 2013 or Exchange 2019.

3. Uninstall the Exchange 2013 server. This can be done by opening the control panel on the Exchange 2013 server and selecting "Uninstall Exchange Server." Uncheck the server roles and the Exchange management tools option in the setup application. This will remove the Exchange 2013 server roles for this server.

   Another option is to use the unattended setup by executing the following command from a command prompt with elevated privileges:

   ```
   Z:\> Setup.exe /Mode:Uninstall /Roles:Mailbox,
   ClientAccess /IAcceptExchangeServerLicenseTerms
   ```

4. When uninstalled, the Windows server can be removed from the Active Directory domain and turned off.

When all these steps are successfully executed, the Exchange 2013 Server is now fully removed, and only the Exchange 2019 servers remain in the Exchange organization.

Important Note Decommissioning the previous version is not simply a matter of turning it off. This still happens in a virtualized server environment. It is tempting to turn off the virtual machines and just delete them, but this is wrong. When you do this, all information regarding previous versions of Exchange Server remains in Active Directory. From an Exchange 2016 point of view, "they" are still there (but not responding, of course). This can lead to erratic behavior. So, fully uninstall the previous Exchange Server!

Summary

Exchange 2013 was introduced in January 2013, and mainstream support ended in April 2013. Extended support ends in April 2023, so at the time of writing, it still is in extended support. Microsoft does not release any Cumulative Updates anymore, but only Security Updates when security issues classified as "critical" are fixed.

Exchange 2013, 2016, and 2019 are very similar, so migrating from Exchange 2013 to Exchange 2016 or Exchange 2019 is not difficult. From a client access perspective, all three Exchange versions can be part of the same load-balanced array of Exchange servers. The only requirement is that they are all configured identical.

From a mailbox database point of view, it is a bit more work. Every Exchange version needs its own storage solution and its own Database Availability Group, so you must build a new Exchange server farm for this.

Moving resources is not difficult. When hosting a lot of mailboxes on Exchange 2013, it can take a lot of time, but that's about it. Hence a small chapter on moving from Exchange 2013 to Exchange 2019.

PART 3

Integration with Office 365

CHAPTER 9

Exchange Hybrid

While there are companies out there still running Exchange Server on-premises as part of a standalone email infrastructure, an increasing number of customers operate Exchange Server complementary to Exchange Online, the email infrastructure that is part of the Microsoft 365. Microsoft 365 and thus Exchange Online are subscription-based offerings built around Office- and Windows-related software and services.

While many consider today's Microsoft 365 and Exchange Online programs well established, they were officially launched around June 2011. Microsoft 365, which is the branding for Office 365 with the addition of Windows 10 and security products, is the successor to Business Productivity Online Suite (BPOS). BPOS was launched in 2008 as a package of individually hosted Microsoft products, such as Exchange and Live Meeting.

At the time of writing, Microsoft 365 offers software and cloud-based services founded on workloads such as

- Microsoft Exchange Online for email, with Exchange Online Protection and Defender for cloud-based email filtering
- Microsoft Teams for communications and conferencing
- Microsoft SharePoint for social networking and collaboration
- Microsoft Office Web Apps for online Microsoft Office Suite
- OneDrive for cloud file storage
- Yammer for social networking
- Microsoft Office desktop application licenses
- Planner, Power Apps, and Power Automate for workflow and process automation
- Power BI for analytics and data visualization

M. de Rooij and J. Wesselius, *Pro Exchange 2019 and 2016 Administration*,
https://doi.org/10.1007/978-1-4842-7331-9_9

What products and services are available to your organization depends on your subscription plan. The Microsoft 365 subscriptions and packages change quite frequently; current subscriptions for businesses can be compared at `https://bit.ly/M365Bplans` and enterprise plans at `https://bit.ly/M365Eplans`. This is also the location to start your Microsoft 365 journey by selecting one of the subscription plans. Most plans offer the option of a trial, where you can try out its features.

Note Since Office 365 is available as a subscription plan, without the addition of Windows 10 or Enterprise Mobility + Security (EMS), we will refer to **Office 365**. Statements made with regard to Office 365 will also apply to Microsoft 365, unless noted otherwise. Also, with **Exchange Online** (EXO), we will refer to the Exchange Online environment that is part of Office 365, as Exchange Online is also the name of a specific Office 365 business plan offering hosted Exchange email services.

Since 2014, Microsoft has adopted a cloud-first strategy. This means that changes and new features will be introduced in Office 365 first. Contrary to customer environments, the high level of standardization in the Office 365 service enables introducing or rolling back small, gradual changes. When they are deemed suitable for on-premises usage, changes might get propagated to the on-premises Exchange Server product in the form of a cumulative update or service pack. However, owing to scale, some features never make it to the on-premises world, such as Microsoft Teams. Where Teams' predecessor Skype for Business was available as an on-premises deployable product, Teams could never run on-premises due to its architecture, depending on Exchange for user and group mailboxes, SharePoint for sites and file storage, (Azure) Active Directory, Enterprise Voice, and integration with Power Platform, to name a few.

Because of the nature of Outlook Web App and the Outlook client, this cloud-first strategy also means feature changes usually become available in Outlook Web App first. Web apps are closely followed by Microsoft 365 Apps for enterprise, also known as Office 365 ProPlus, the Click-to-Run (C2R) version of the Microsoft Office desktop product. The standalone Office 2019 product (MSI) will require a hotfix or service pack for every new or changed feature. In some cases, the MSI will not even receive the same features as the C2R version, such as support for more than 500 folders per mailbox.

When considering moving to Office 365, full or in hybrid, organizations need to be aware of the consequences and potential impact of this switch. For example, while you can configure aspects of your cloud-based tenant, some limitations are set in stone by the provider, such as the maximum mailbox size.

Caution Organizations using Office 365 services, in full or partially like with Exchange Hybrid deployments, will need to keep track of changes in the cloud service; these changes might affect their business in the mid or long term, such as deprecation of Basic Authentication or the termination of support for TLS versions below 1.2 for mail flow.

This chapter will focus on the deployment of Exchange Hybrid, where companies utilize a mixed model, integrating their on-premises Exchange infrastructure with Exchange Online. Note that your organization needs to select the Exchange Hybrid model, mainly driven by time frames and required interoperability during migration.

The first choice organizations need to make when deploying Exchange Hybrid is Classic or Modern topology:

- **Classic** topology will require more configuration, is more feature-rich, and requires publishing of Exchange on-premises to the outside world.

- **Modern** topology uses one or more Hybrid agents which need to be deployed. These agents will manage mailbox migrations (MRS) and Free/Busy requests. It will utilize an Azure App Proxy for these tasks and therefore only requires outbound connections to the Internet for this functionality.

The second choice is related to Full or Minimal configuration:

- **Full Hybrid**—Best fit for large organizations, which require integration between Exchange on-premises and Exchange Online during the migration period. This option is also the most flexible, offering migrating mailboxes back on-premises, exchange of Free/Busy information, and additional mail flow controls.

– **Minimal Hybrid**—Best suited for small- to medium-sized organizations that are more time constraint and do not require cross-premises integration during the migration. Additionally, this option requires the least configuration and resources.

Note You can switch from Modern to Classic topology. This is useful when it turns out migration executing takes longer than expected, and lack of cross-premises functionality becomes a problem. To switch, select the Classic topology when running the Hybrid Configuration Wizard to reconfigure.

It might be helpful to understand what the exact technical differences are between Classic and Modern, Full and Minimal. For this purpose, Table 9-1 contains an overview of all differences for these topologies and modes with regard to features and configuration elements.

Table 9-1. *Exchange Hybrid, Classic vs. Modern, Full and Minimal*

	Classic		**Modern**	
	Minimal	**Full**	**Minimal**	**Full**
Feature				
Cross-premises Free/Busy		Yes		Yes
Organization Configuration Transfer (OCT)	Yes	Yes	Yes	Yes
Hybrid Modern Auth Support		Yes		
Cross-Premises Feature				
eDiscovery		Yes		
Message Tracking		Yes		
Delegates		Yes		Yes
Folder Access		Yes		
Retention to Archive (EXO)		Yes		Yes

(*continued*)

Table 9-1. (*continued*)

	Classic		Modern	
	Minimal	**Full**	**Minimal**	**Full**
Required Configuration				
Send/Receive Connectors		Yes		Yes
Federation Trust		Yes		Yes
Organizational Relationship		Yes		Yes
OAuth		Yes		Yes
Autodiscover + certificate	Yes	Yes	Yes	Yes
SMTP certificate		Yes		Yes
EWS certificate	Yes	Yes		
Publishing				
TCP/443 Internet > Exchange	Yes	Yes	Yes[1]	Yes[1]
TCP/443 Exchange > EXO + Office 365 Common	Yes	Yes	Yes[2]	Yes[2]
TCP/25 EXO > Exchange		Yes		Yes
TCP/25 Exchange > EXO		Yes		Yes
TCP/80 Exchange > Internet (Certificate CRL)	Yes	Yes	Yes	Yes
TCP/5985 Hybrid Agent > Exchange (CAS, WinRM)			Yes	Yes
TCP/5986 Hybrid Agent > Exchange (CAS, WinRM)			Yes	Yes

Note Office 365 Common in Table 9-1 refers to the common Office 365 services. Which URLs and IP addresses are involved with which part of Office 365 is published at https://bit.ly/O365UrlsIps. Some vendors offer built-in functionality to allow components to automatically reconfigure themselves using this information.

[1] Only when required for Autodiscover, not required for Hybrid Agent

[2] Includes Hybrid Agent for *.msappproxy.net

To assist organizations in determining their migration path, Microsoft published an Exchange deployment assistant. After answering a few basic questions, such as what version of Exchange is currently used and what deployment option you will be using, the tool generates step-by-step instructions. The Exchange deployment assistant can be found at **http://bit.ly/exchangeda**. It gets updated regularly to reflect changes in the migration process.

The remaining of this chapter will focus on the Exchange Full Hybrid/Classic deployment, which is what most organizations choose. It is also the deployment that offers most flexibility and rollback options and is usually the end situation after onboarding of mailboxes has been completed. Where appropriate, specific details on those other scenarios will be highlighted.

Hybrid Identity

In Exchange Hybrid, the main directory of Office 365 holding security principles such as users and groups, Azure Active Directory, is kept in sync with the local Active Directory. When it comes to synchronizing objects between on-premises infrastructure and Azure Active Directory, there are two topologies to choose from:

- **Azure AD Connect** is the de facto topology for Exchange Hybrid and requires installing one or more synchronization servers in your local infrastructure. Multiple AD Connect servers can be used for availability, with one being the designated main server propagating changes and others functioning as staging servers. During long outages or maintenance, staging servers can be promoted to become main servers.
- **Azure AD Connect Cloud Sync** differs from AD Connect in that it does not require installing additional infrastructure. The synchronization of objects is achieved using agents which need to be deployed in your local infrastructure. Availability can be increased by deploying multiple agents. However, some features are not supported by Azure AD Connect Cloud Sync, most notably the lack of Exchange Hybrid support.

To authenticate against Office 365 services such as Exchange Online, there are a few models organizations can choose from:

1. **Cloud authentication**—In this model, the identity is stored in Azure Active Directory, and authentication is performed against Azure Active Directory as well. Authentication leverages the synchronized password hashes (Password Hash Synchronization or PHS), or when organizations do not desire this, authentication can be relayed from Office 365 to Active Directory using agent technology (Pass-Through Authentication or PTA). Identities authenticating this way are known as managed identities.

2. **Federated authentication**—In this model, the identity is stored in Azure Active Directory, but the actual authentication is performed by solutions such as Active Directory Federation Services or AD FS. This solution will perform authentication against the local Active Directory. Identities authenticating this way are known as federated identities.

Deployments using AD FS are becoming rare and usually are more complex as other services are often plugged in to perform additional third-party services. AD FS is complementary to AD Connect, as AD FS only provides authentication services; it does not populate identities in Office 365. For this reason, the remainder of this Exchange Hybrid chapter will focus on cloud authentication.

Tip Prior to deploying AD Connect, it is recommended to use a tool called IdFix to identify problems with users, contacts, or groups in your Active Directory that may lead to synchronization problems. IdFix is available from GitHub at **`https://github.com/microsoft/idfix`**.

The component synchronizing identities and optionally password hashes in cloud authentication is the directory synchronization server, or Azure AD Connect. Originally named DirSync, and still commonly referred to by this name, AD Connect is a software component that needs to be installed on the local infrastructure. It periodically updates its database, the metaverse, with information from Active Directory and Azure Active

Directory and determines which changes it needs to propagate to Active Directory or Azure Active Directory. The main elements in play at this type of deployment are shown in Figure 9-1.

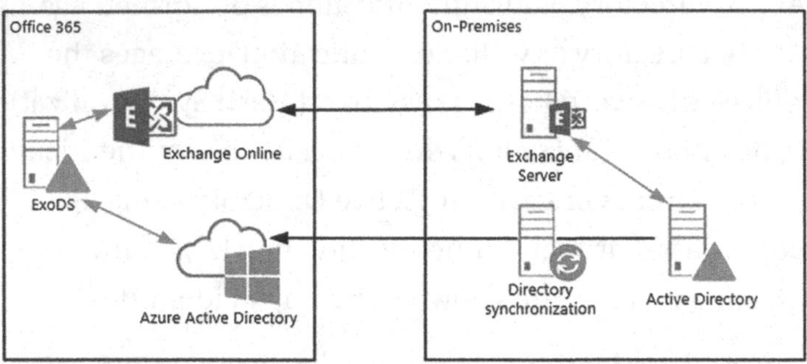

Figure 9-1. *Hybrid deployment with AD Connect*

AD Connect manages objects that are in scope and synchronizes Exchange-related attributes such as email addresses. Synchronization is one-way for most attributes; some attributes like publicDelegates can be written back when writeback is configured (more on that later). The implication of this model is that the management of those synchronized objects and attributes, such as mailboxes and distribution groups, needs to be performed on-premises and more precisely using an on-premises Exchange Server.

A local Exchange server is required for managing synchronized objects. Changing attributes directly or using third-party tools is not supported. Also, in most cases, changing attributes of synchronized objects is actively blocked in Office 365. Organizations that want to go all in on Office 365 and Exchange Online are sometimes surprised when they discover they need to keep a minimal Exchange on-premises infrastructure, only for managing mail-enabled objects.

Tip AD Connect can synchronize objects from one or more local Active Directories to Azure Active Directory. For an overview of supported Azure AD Connect topologies, see **`https://bit.ly/ADConnectTopologies`**.

Figure 9-1 also depicts ExoDS, which is the directory utilized by Exchange Online. This directory is a totally different directory from Azure Active Directory and contains Exchange-related objects and information. A background process (backsync) synchronizes objects and attributes between Azure Active Directory and ExoDS. This process is something to be aware of, as it could happen that changes in Azure Active Directory are not instantly visible in Exchange Online. In some way, it can be seen as Active Directory replication latency.

Caution When using AD Connect, the source of authority for objects synchronized is on-premises. These objects need to be managed using Exchange on-premises, even when you have migrated all mailboxes to Exchange Online.

Another feature of AD Connect is that it can also synchronize password hashes (Password Hash Synchronization or PHS). This means the hash of your on-premises user is synchronized to Office 365, so that you can use the same credentials on-premises as well as in Office 365. This creates a same sign-on experience and, when using AD FS, can also function as a fallback authentication mechanism when AD FS is unavailable. When selected, AD Connect can also sync those password hashes back, for example, to accommodate changing your password in Office 365 instead of locally.

AD Connect can selectively synchronize objects, for domains, OU, groups, or attribute filters. Do note that some functionality may require synchronizing all mail-related objects, such as Global Address List generation in Exchange Online, or population of dynamic distribution groups (DDG). Not synchronizing a potential member of a dynamic distribution group to Azure Active Directory means that mail sent to that recipient will never get delivered, as the DDG's underlying filter will never contain that destination.

Note Hybrid Server is a term frequently used for Exchange servers which are used in Hybrid deployments, especially when deployed for the purpose of interoperability with Exchange Online, such as Exchange 2016 in existing Exchange 2010 deployments. However, they are "just Exchange servers" that are functionally identical to any Exchange server.

Also, when you are deploying Exchange 2019 servers as part of the migration to Office 365, and are not going to host mailboxes on them, you need a license key for Exchange 2019. This policy has changed in comparison with Exchange 2016 and earlier versions. For earlier versions of Exchange, you could request a free Hybrid License Key. This functionality still exists for organizations that are coming from older Exchange versions, choosing Exchange 2016 as their Exchange Hybrid server. If you are deploying Exchange Hybrid using Exchange 2016, the Hybrid Configuration Wizard (HCW) can check if your organization is eligible for free license and acquire and license the server for you.

Tip To monitor and report on AD Connect health, you can deploy an Azure AD Connect Health agent on your local infrastructure. This will monitor on-premises health conditions, depending on whether you deployed AD Connect with or without AD FS, and report to Azure AD Connect Health service in Azure portal. Additional benefits are that any synchronization issues will also be logged in the portal, and you can set alerting options.

Deploying Exchange Hybrid

Regarding the deployment of Exchange 2019 in Exchange Hybrid, support for coexistence between Exchange versions on-premises and Exchange Hybrid servers is shown in Table 9-2. In principle, you can position an Exchange server in front of a down-level Exchange server. It is beyond the scope of this book, but when you are still running an Exchange 2010 environment, you need to use an Exchange 2013- or 2016-based Exchange Hybrid server. This version can manage client traffic for these older Exchange versions, as well as redirect or proxy requests to Office 365. Exchange 2019 cannot be used in combination with any Exchange version below Exchange 2013 CU21.

Table 9-2. *Hybrid Deployment Supportability Matrix*

On-Premises	Hybrid Server			
	Exchange 2019	**Exchange 2016**	**Exchange 2013**	**Exchange 2010**
Exchange 2019	Yes	No	No	No
Exchange 2016	Yes	Yes	No	No
Exchange 2013	Yes	Yes	Yes	No
Exchange 2010	No	Yes	Yes	Yes

Note Exchange 2010 is out of support. When planning to onboard all mailboxes, you can deploy designated Exchange Hybrid 2016 servers on-premises in the end, before decommissioning Exchange 2010. When mailboxes are kept on-premises, at some point you need to perform an upgrade, which includes migrating those mailboxes from Exchange 2010 to Exchange 2016. Eventually, when all Exchange 2010 servers have been removed, you can introduce Exchange 2019 in the organization.

The actual deployment of AD Connect is straightforward. After selecting the designated system, you need to decide if you want to use SQL Server Express for storage or a SQL Server 2012 or later instance (case-sensitive collation) depending on the number of objects you expect to synchronize. This is not an exact calculation, but approximately 100,000 objects can be managed using SQL Server Express, which also happens to have a 10 GB database size limit. Needless to say, the system running AD Connect contains copies of personal data and therefore must be secure properly. In essence, treat it as any domain controller. Also, make sure the operating system supports TLS 1.2, which is now mandatory.

Tip Depending on your environment, AD Connect may require proper sizing. For sizing recommendations, see **https://bit.ly/ADConnectSizing**.

Deploying AD Connect

Download the AD Connect package via the **Azure AD portal ➤ Azure AD Connect**, or go to **https://bit.ly/ADConnectDownload**. During installation, the AD Connect setup will ask a few questions regarding your deployment. Note that you can choose an **Express** or **Custom** setup. An Express setup is meant for organizations running a single Active Directory forest that are going to use Password Hash Synchronization. In other scenarios or when you want full control over the configuration, select the Custom setup. Note that the AD Connect setup will fetch required dependencies such as SQL Server Express during setup.

Tip During a Custom setup, AD Connect contains an option to **Import synchronization settings**. This allows you to quickly deploy additional AD Connect staging servers.

During setup, you can configure AD Connect to use a global Managed Service Account (gMSA) for its services. To configure this, create the gMSA account first, and select it when setting up AD Connect. The benefit of using a gMSA account over a regular Active Directory service account is that Active Directory will manage the account, including periodically changing the password. During setup which type of account is going to be used; if you wish to switch, you need to deploy a new AD Connect server in staging mode, promote it, and decommission the old AD Connect server. More background on Managed Service Accounts can be seen at **https://bit.ly/ADConnectMSA**.

After installing AD Connect and its services, the Custom setup proceeds with its initial configuration by starting to ask what sign-on method it needs to configure. Enable single sign-on when you want users to have a single sign-on experience working with Office 365 services. Note that this only works when AD Connect is configured to use PHS or Pass-Through Authentication (PTA). More about PHS, PTA, and federation using Active Directory Federation Services (AD FS) and their differences at **https://bit.ly/ADConnectSingleSignOn**.

Next, provide the account to connect to your Office 365 tenant. The setup will verify the connection to your tenant. It will create the account (prefixed ...) in your tenant which will be used for its synchronization process. Proceed by specifying which Active Directories it needs to synchronize with. Select the UPN suffix it needs to use to synchronize identities for (only suffixed which match verified domains in your tenant can be selected), and pick the attribute which needs to be synchronized as the user principal name in your tenant. This then also becomes the account which users need to log on to Office 365 services, except when using federation as authentication.

Caution When installing AD Connect, the setup will ask about **SourceAnchor**, the attribute to uniquely identify users from your organization. By default, this will be objectGuid, which is fine for small, single forest organizations. However, when you have multiple forests, there is a chance objectGuids (which are random) may overlap. In those cases, select ms-DS-Consistency-Guid to prevent these issues. The ms-DS-ConsistencyGuid attribute needs to be populated to sync, and your provisioning process or IDM solution should fill it with something unique. AD Connect will translate your on-premises ms-DS-ConsistencyGuid (Byte Array) back and forth to ImmutableId in your tenant. To do this yourself, use something like

```
#ms-DS-ConsistencyGuid to ImmutableId
$Guid= [GUID]((Get-ADUser -Identity UserA -Properties
MS-DS-ConsistencyGuid).'ms-DS-ConsistencyGuid')
$ImmutableId= [system.convert]::ToBase64String( $Guid.
ToByteArray())
#ImmutableId to ms-DS-ConsistencyGuid:
[GUID]([System.Convert]::FromBase64String((Get-AzureADUser
-ObjectId UserA).ImmutableID))
```

In the next screens, you can select to synchronize objects from all domains and Organizational Units or narrow down the selection to specific domains, Organizational Units, or other filtering options such as groups. The Optional Features screen shows an option which is important for Exchange Hybrid, which is **Exchange Hybrid deployment**. Enabling it allows AD Connect to sync back the attributes mentioned in Table 9-3 from your tenant to Active Directory.

Table 9-3. AD Connect Exchange Hybrid Deployment Attribute Writeback

Attribute	Description
msDS-ExternalDirectoryObjectId	This attribute correlates to the object in Azure Active Directory.
msExchArchiveStatus	Personal archive status for users using cloud-based personal archives—i.e., Exchange Online Archiving.
msExchUserHoldPolicies	In-place hold status of mailboxes.
ProxyAddresses	The legacyExchangeDN of the User, Contact, or Group in Exchange Online is added as an X500 address to the proxyAddresses attribute in the local Active Directory. This makes sure replies or cached name entries still work after migrating mailboxes to Exchange Online.
SafeSendersHash BlockedSendersHash SafeRecipientHash	Filtering and online safe and blocked sender information.
msExchUCVoiceMailSettings	Voice mail status for users having cloud-based voice mail configured.
publicDelegates	Allows mailboxes in Exchange Online to be granted SendOnBehalfTo permissions to mailboxes in Exchange on-premises.

To see the complete list of which attributes get synchronized or synchronized back, see **https://bit.ly/ADConnectAttributes**.

Tip To prevent nondelivery reports when replying to old email messages after offboarding mailboxes, the legacyExchangeDN is written back as an X500 address to on-premises objects.

After deployment, depending on your environment, your AD Connect server is set to automatically perform upgrades. The default synchronization schedule will be set to run every 30 minutes. You can view these settings by opening a local PowerShell session on the AD Connect server and running `Get-ADSyncAutoUpgrade` or `Get-ADSyncScheduler`, respectively. The results can be seen in Figure 9-2.

```
PS C:\Program Files\Microsoft Azure Active Directory Connect> Get-ADSyncAutoUpgrade
Enabled
PS C:\Program Files\Microsoft Azure Active Directory Connect> Get-ADSyncScheduler

AllowedSyncCycleInterval               : 00:30:00
CurrentlyEffectiveSyncCycleInterval    : 00:30:00
CustomizedSyncCycleInterval            :
NextSyncCyclePolicyType                : Delta
NextSyncCycleStartTimeInUTC            : 6/26/2021 4:29:12 PM
PurgeRunHistoryInterval                : 7.00:00:00
SyncCycleEnabled                       : True
MaintenanceEnabled                     : True
StagingModeEnabled                     : False
SchedulerSuspended                     : False
SyncCycleInProgress                    : False
```

***Figure 9-2.** Default AD Connect AutoUpgrade and Scheduler settings*

Disabling AutoUpgrade is generally not recommended, but if the need occurs, you can adjust this setting using `Set-ADSyncAutoUpgrade Enabled or Set-ADSyncAutoUpgrade Disabled`. Depending on your environment and things like number of objects, you do might wish to adjust the default synchronization schedule. To accomplish this, from PowerShell, run the `Set-ADSyncScheduler -CustomizedSyncCycleInterval hh:mm:ss`, where hh:mm:ss is the interval in hours, minutes, and seconds. Note that you cannot use an interval less than 30 minutes.

Tip If your environment consists of a large number of objects or contains large groups with up to 250,000 members, consider switching to the Azure AD Connect v2 endpoint for enhanced performance. This procedure is described in **`https://bit.ly/ADConnectV2Endpoint`**.

Autodiscover in Hybrid

Chapter 3 already covered Autodiscover and explained how this process works in an on-premises Exchange environment. In general, you configure an Autodiscover DNS record autodiscover.<domain> in public DNS which points to your Exchange on-premises environment. Now, by doing so, not only can clients configure themselves properly, but services like Exchange Online can also figure out which endpoint to talk to when querying Free/Busy information or when migrating your mailbox, for example.

During migrations, when mailboxes exist in Exchange Online on-premises as well as in Exchange Online, your Autodiscover record can stay pointing to the Exchange on-premises environment. But when all user mailboxes have finished migrating to Exchange

Online, the question arises if you perhaps can switch Autodiscover to point to Exchange Online. The answer to this question depends on whether you want to keep configuring clients for mailboxes which are still hosted on-premises or not. If not, and all user mailboxes have moved to Exchange Online, you can replace the current Autodiscover record with a CNAME record pointing to Exchange Online, for example:

```
autodiscover.contoso.com    CNAME    autodiscover.outlook.com
```

If you still have a few application mailboxes residing on-premises for which you may want to perform Free/Busy lookups, for example, you need to perform an additional step. This step is reconfiguring the organizational relationship, so that it does not use Autodiscover, but points directly to your Exchange environment. More on that later in this chapter.

For mailboxes which have been migrated, the MRS will leave behind a Mail-Enabled User (MEU), also known as a Remote Mailbox object, in the on-premises environment. This way, the on-premises Global Address List will still contain an entry, and mail will still route properly as your legacyExchangeDN, Exchange's internal addressing, will be retained and stamped on your migrated mailbox. The targetAddress property of the MEU however will be pointing to one of the secondary proxy addresses stamped on the MEU and mailbox. This address will be in the format <alias>@<tenant>.mail.onmicrosoft.com and gets stamped by the default email address policy which will be modified by the Hybrid Configuration Wizard.

Note The Remote Routing address in the Remote Mailbox cmdlets is identical to targetAddress in Exchange or Active Directory.

With targetAddress pointing to <alias>@tenant.mail.onmicrosoft.com, the continuation of mail flow is covered, as mail gets routed to Exchange Online. Important for Autodiscover is that Exchange on-premises supports Autodiscover redirection. When Exchange is asked to perform an Autodiscover lookup, sometimes referred to as Autodiscover Plain Old XML (POX) or SOAP as it is XML based, and the targetAddress is set, its value will be used for redirection. Instead of endpoint configuration, clients or services will receive response similar to the following excerpt:

```
<Account>
  <Action>redirectAddr</Action>
  <RedirectAddr>alias@tenant.mail.contoso.com</RedirectAddr>
</Account>
```

Note that the opposite is also true: for mailboxes which are located on-premises, AD Connect will provision MEUs in your tenant. Their "targetAddress" will point to their regular email address, as that still resolves to the Exchange on-premises endpoint for Autodiscover and mail flow. A visual example of this setup is shown in Figure 9-3.

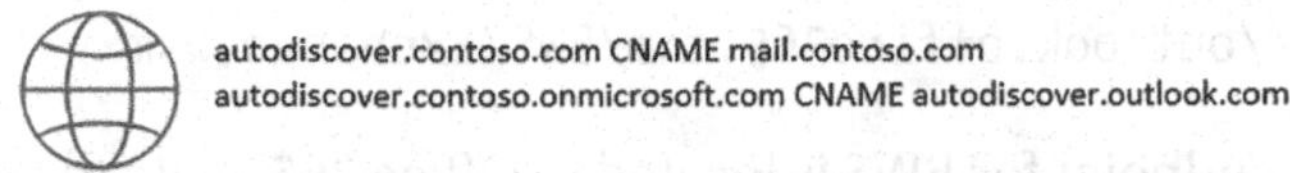

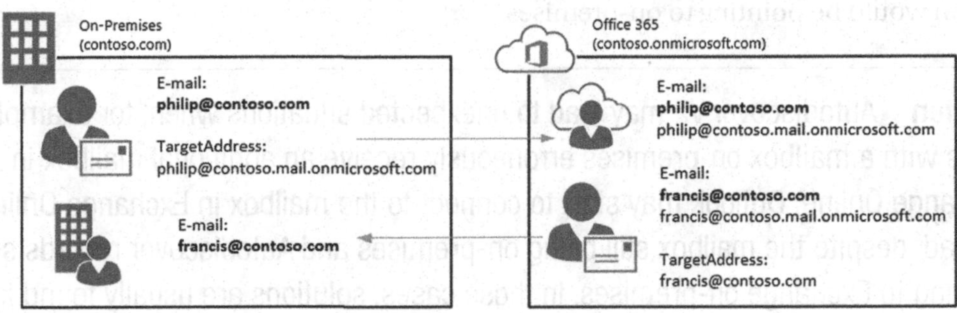

***Figure 9-3.** Autodiscover redirection*

In this figure, Philip is a user with a mailbox in Office 365. His email address is philip@contoso.com. When Outlook does an Autodiscover lookup, it contacts contoso.com for Autodiscover information. That request is processed by their Exchange on-premises infrastructure, which finds a mail-enabled user object with that address. It also discovers that its target address is configured as philip@contoso.mail.onmicrosoft.com, and it will return that value to the client. The client can now try to use the provided philip@contoso.mail.onmicrosoft.com address for Autodiscover, and this request will successfully be processed by Exchange Online.

Be advised clients such as Outlook or Teams may perform an AutodiscoverV2 lookup. In those cases, REST calls are performed initially against Office 365 to determine endpoints. Apart from the email address of the target, the requestor also needs to specify the protocol or service, such as AutodiscoverV1 (to fetch an original XML response with endpoint information) or EWS. The goal is to increase the performance of the lookup process for onboarded users, but be aware it may interfere with the expected process as it may take some shortcuts.

An example of a REST Autodiscover V2 call for EWS services and returned output:

```
Invoke-RestMethod 'https://autodiscover-s.outlook.com/autodiscover/
autodiscover.json?Email=michel@myexchangelabs.com&Protocol=Ews'

Protocol Url
-------- ---
Ews      https://outlook.office365.com/EWS/Exchange.asmx
```

As shown, the endpoint for EWS is located in Office 365. Note that if the recipient was known in Office 365, and had an MEU pointing on-premises, the returned endpoint location would be pointing to on-premises.

Caution Autodiscover V2 may lead to unexpected situations when, for example, users with a mailbox on-premises erroneously receive an additional mailbox in Exchange Online. Outlook may start to connect to the mailbox in Exchange Online instead, despite the mailbox still being on-premises and Autodiscover records still pointing to Exchange on-premises. In those cases, solutions are usually found in AD Connect synchronization or inadvertent licensing.

Federation with Azure Active Directory

Another configuration aspect to briefly mention before configuring Exchange Hybrid is the federation with Azure Active Directory. At some point, your organization and users might wish to exchange information with other organizations. For example, companies agreeing to a form of partnership or preparing for an upcoming merger might want to share their calendaring information. Another example is contractors or vendors who want to share product information with the organizations they work for or with.

Exchange versions prior to Exchange 2007 used a tool called the inter-organization replication tool (IORepl) for exchanging information with other organizations. It was a public folder and replication based, and consequentially there were some downsides to it, such as the information shared was not delayed because of replication. Exchange 2007 introduced Exchange Web Services (EWS) together with an Availability Service, which offered a web-based exchange of information. Using a service account for authenticated access, organizations could look up information from a remote organization. Unfortunately, mail-enabled users with a properly set targetAddress attribute were still required to direct requests to the proper organization and endpoints, identical to the process Autodiscover follows for redirection as mentioned in the previous section. These setups lead to directory tools providing so-called GALsync functionality, where recipients from one organization are provisioned as mail-enabled users in another organization, not only for the purpose of providing address book-related information but also to direct Free/Busy requests.

Starting with Exchange 2010, federation was introduced. Federation allows the secure sharing of information between Exchange organizations, and the mechanism is displayed in Figure 9-4. After configuration, the federation delegation uses organizational relationships between partners. For organizations to federate, they establish a trust relationship with Azure Active Directory, which then can function as an online trust broker for authentication and authorization. This approach does away with the earlier requirement of having to configure trusts and set up accounts for web-based sharing information. If you trust Azure Active Directory, and if you have registered and verified your domains in Office 365, you are good to go. It is then up to the organization to configure sharing of information with other organizations. Sharing of information between the Exchange Online and Exchange on-premises in Exchange Hybrid is configured by default. More on configuring organization-level sharing of information later in this chapter.

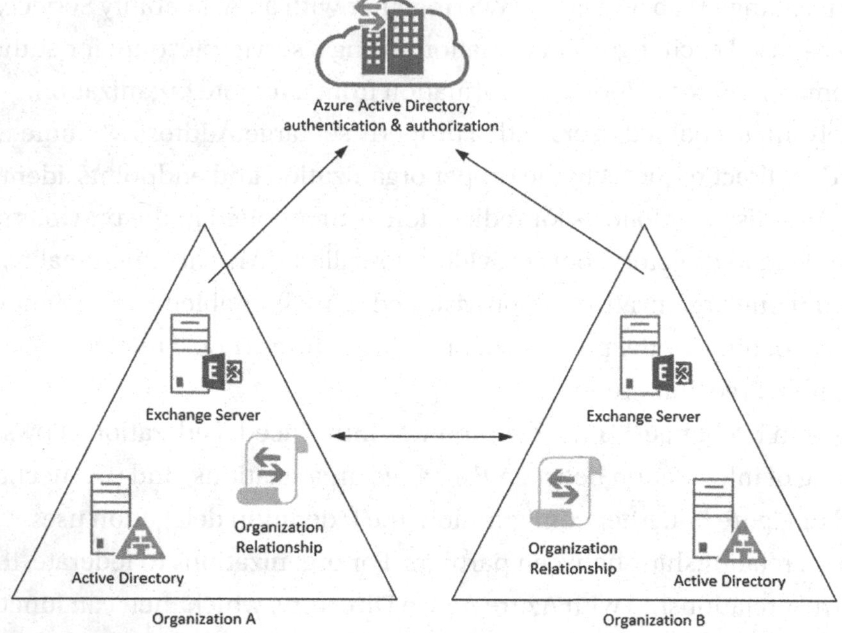

Figure 9-4. Federation with Azure Active Directory

Note Azure Active Directory for authentication and authorization, sometimes also referred to as Azure SSO, was previously called MFG or Microsoft Federation Gateway. Also, federation with Azure Active Directory (authorization and authentication) should not be confused with Active Directory Federation Services or AD FS, which is an identity provider.

Hybrid Configuration Wizard

Configuring Exchange Hybrid consists of setting up federation with Azure Active Directory, secure mail flow, remote domains, connectors, and validation. There used to be 50 manual steps involved in setting up Exchange Hybrid before the Hybrid Configuration Wizard came available for Exchange 2010 Service Pack 2 in September 2015. Today, many people only know the HCW process. At one point, this is good (why make things more complex than necessary). On the other hand, during troubleshooting you may have to dive in, at which point knowing what goes on behind the scenes can be helpful.

Note Per mid-2020, the HCW can configure hybrid deployment up to five tenants simultaneously, provided synchronization does not overlap synchronizing objects to more than one tenant. Also, every tenant will have its own namespaces for routing and authentication, and you need individual certificates to secure mail flow for proper attribution of messages.

The Hybrid Configuration Wizard, or HCW, is an app which you run via the Exchange admin portal or via **`https://aka.ms/HybridWizard`**. This way, you are always guaranteed to run the latest version when (re)configuring your Exchange Hybrid setup. The HCW has become a fully evolved tool to set things up, for Exchange hybrid deployments using Exchange 2010 and up. In fact so much evolved, that for configuring Exchange Hybrid using Exchange 2019 is only supported using the HCW. While the HCW is web app based, it runs PowerShell commands against your local Exchange infrastructure and Exchange Online as well.

Caution The HCW must run successfully for your Exchange hybrid deployment to be supported. Also, after upgrading your Exchange version, you officially need to rerun the HCW to anticipate any changes in the Exchange on-premises version. This also applies to when you have upgraded your Exchange on-premises hybrid servers from Exchange Server 2016 to 2019, for example. To stay supported in Exchange Hybrid, you need to stay current; your Exchange on-premises may only run one version behind the current release.

The HCW performs the following global steps:

1. Using the HCW, you define the desired state. Part of the process is proving ownership of the domain names you want to enable for federation by creating TXT records in the public DNS containing secrets. So, be prepared to make changes in the public DNS when running the HCW, or provide network administrators with the information they need to register.

2. Behind the scenes, the desired hybrid configuration is then stored in Active Directory using the cmdlet `Set-HybridConfiguration`. The location of the information is below the Configuration container at **CN=Hybrid Configuration,CN=<Exchange Organization Name>,CN=Microsoft Exchange,CN=Services**.
3. At the completion of the HCW, you run `Update-HybridConfiguration`. This triggers the hybrid configuration engine.
4. The engine reads the desired state.
5. The engine collects the current Exchange on-premises and Exchange Online configuration.
6. Based on the desired state and the current state, the engine determines the delta and tasks it needs to execute. Depending on the delta, these tasks may include
    a. Managing accepted domains for mail flow and Autodiscover requests. Your Office 365 tenant will have a domain in the form of **<domain name>.onmicrosoft.com**. This address space is added to the default email address policy, and secondary email addresses are stamped with this address for internal routing between on-premises and Exchange Online.
    b. Picking and configuring an on-premises certificate for secure mail flow between Exchange on-premises and Exchange Online using TLS.
    c. Configuring federation and defining the organizational relationships between the Exchange on-premises and Exchange Online, and vice versa.
    d. Configuring secure mail flow between Exchange on-premises Mailbox servers, via Edge servers when available and desired, and Exchange Online Protection (EOP). Here, you also have

the option to always route outbound messages through your on-premises organization using the Centralized Mail Transport (CMT) option. There's more on mail flow later in this chapter.

e. Configuring the OAuth Authentication. More on OAuth later.

Note The HCW does not configure your public DNS MX records. If at some point in your migration project, you want to start routing inbound messages through Exchange Online Protection, you need to reconfigure the MX record, pointing it to <domain>.mail.protection.outlook.com, replacing dots in your domain with a dash, for example, myexchangelabs-com.mail.protection.outlook.com.

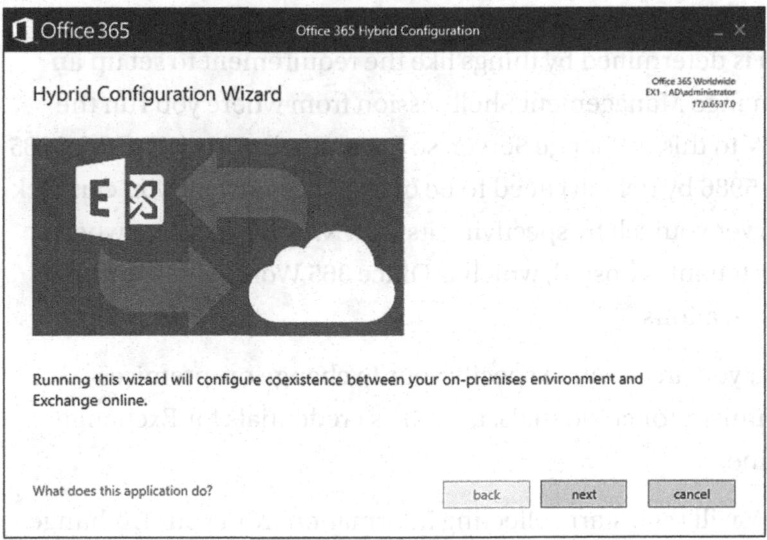

Figure 9-5. Hybrid Configuration Wizard

Tip When you press F12 in the HCW, you will get a small menu with shortcuts to certain functions, such as opening the log file, or the folder with the HCW logs. This can be helpful during troubleshooting.

We will now show a quick run-through of the HCW, of which the start screen is displayed in Figure 9-5. Just be advised that the HCW is a live application and may be subject to change at any time.

1. To run the HCW, you need a supported browser, and TLS 1.2 needs to be supported by the operating system you are going to run the HCW on. Microsoft Internet Explorer is end of life, so its successor Microsoft Edge is a good option; see **www.microsoft.com/edge**. Start Edge on one of your Exchange Mailbox servers or a member server with Exchange Management Tools installed. Navigate to **aka.ms/HybridWizard**, and install the app from **Microsoft Office 365 Hybrid Configuration Wizard**.

2. After clicking Next, the HCW will check your Exchange on-premises environment and try to detect one of your on-premises Exchange servers suitable for configuring Exchange Hybrid. This is determined by things like the requirement to set up an Exchange Management Shell session from where you run the HCW to this Exchange Server, so PowerShell ports (WinRM, 5985 and 5986 by default) need to be open. Alternatively, you can pick a server yourself by specifying its FQDN. You can select where your tenant is hosted, which is Office 365 Worldwide for most organizations.

3. Next, you are asked to specify your Exchange on-premises administrator credentials, as well as credentials for Exchange Online.

4. HCW will then start collecting information from your Exchange on-premises environment, as well as your Exchange Online environment.

5. Next, the question is asked which Exchange Hybrid model you wish to deploy. As mentioned in the beginning of this chapter, options here are **Minimal** and **Full Hybrid Configuration**. As mentioned earlier, we will select the **Full** option as an example. Optionally, you can select Organization Configuration Transfer (OCT) here. The purpose of the OCT is to port certain settings

from your Exchange on-premises environment to Exchange Online. The policies and configuration elements that are covered are shown in Table 9-4. Note that OCT is a one-time transfer; it does not synchronize existing configuration elements.

***Table 9-4.** Organization Configuration Transfer Information*

Policy or Attributes from Configuration			
ActiveSync Device Access Rule	DLP Policy	OWA Mailbox Policy	Retention Policy Tags
ActiveSync Mailbox Policy	Malware Filter Policy	Policy Tip Config	Sharing Policy
ActiveSync Organization Settings	Mobile Device Mailbox Policy	Remote Domains	Smime Config
Address List	Organization Config	Retention Policy	Transport Config

6. Then, you need to specify which domains you want to include in hybrid deployment at the Hybrid Domains step.

Note When you only have one accepted domain, the Hybrid Domains section is skipped. The accepted domain will be included in hybrid deployment.

---

7. The HCW will then ask about configuring secure mail flow between your Exchange on-premises environment and Exchange Online. When you have no Edge Transport servers, choose Mailbox servers to configure; when you are using Edge Transport servers in your organization, you can select that option after which HCW will configure the necessary connectors through the Edge Transport subscription. Clicking Advanced will display an additional option, which you can select to configure Centralized Mail Transport.

8. You then need to specify which Exchange servers are going to host inbound connections. Click the drop-down box, and check the Mailbox servers which should get a receive connector.

9. Now is the time to also specify which Exchange servers are going to be hosts that are allowed to send mail to Exchange Online through the outbound send connector which the HCW is going to configure. Click the drop-down box, and check the Mailbox servers which should be eligible.

10. One of the last steps is selecting the certificate which should be used to securing mail flow. This certificate should be installed on the Exchange servers which you have selected for inbound and outbound mail flow in the previous steps.

11. Enter the FQDN which should be configured on the outbound connector in Exchange Online to access your Exchange on-premises environment, for example, mail.contoso.com.

12. Now the HCW has collected all the information it needs to know to configure, or reconfigure, your Exchange Hybrid deployment.

Once the HCW finished successfully, your Exchange Hybrid deployment should be ready. Should issues occur, the Hybrid Configuration Wizard log is an invaluable source of information mentioning the configuration steps that have been performed against your Exchange on-premises and Exchange Online environments. It will also show you potentially what went wrong or provide clues thereabout.

By default, the name of the HCW log file is the time stamp of starting the HCW (YYYYMMDD_HHMMSS.log) and is stored in the **%APPDATA%\Microsoft\Exchange Hybrid Configuration** folder, located on the Exchange server which was hosting the HCW session. In addition to the HCW log, you can also use the Remote Connectivity Analyzer (RCA) to troubleshoot connectivity issues that might be preventing you from successfully setting up Exchange Hybrid. You can find the RCA at **`http://exrca.com`**.

Tip To track log entries while running the HCW, open a PowerShell session while the HCW has started, navigate to the log folder (you can use the F12 trick to open the folder and get its name), and enter `Get-Content <LogFile.log> -Wait` to display lines as they are added to the log, similar to the tail in Linux.

Connecting to Office 365

While PowerShell is really powerful for the management of Exchange environments, on-premises and online, most administrators still use the Exchange Admin Center when administering Office 365 for one-off tasks. But, as with on-premises Exchange, using PowerShell sometimes provides a better option, as repetitive tasks might become tedious when performed through the EAC. In some situations, using PowerShell might even be required, for example, elements cannot be configured through the EAC or when you want to automate tasks, either by yourself or using one of the many community scripts available (of course, after careful inspection).

Knowing how to connect to Exchange Online, Azure Active Directory or one of the other methods to manage Office 365 using PowerShell is there for essential. Unfortunately, every workload, be it Exchange Online or Azure Active Directory or Teams, requires its own PowerShell session. That would not be a problem if every workload was consistent in the way to connect. Unfortunately, that is not yet always the case. Workloads often have their own PowerShell module which needs to be installed, and every module can have small deviations in connect parameters or things like naming of parameters.

In the following sections, you will get to know how to set up PowerShell sessions to Exchange Online and Azure Active Directory.

Connecting to Exchange Online

When you connect to Exchange Online using PowerShell, you need to be aware of the fact that the session you will create will be subject to Role-Based Access Controls (RBAC). These controls determine what cmdlets and parameters you will have at your disposal, and which ones you do not. For example, by default Exchange administrators cannot use the New-MailboxImportRequest cmdlet. More on RBAC in Chapter 10.

After connecting to Exchange Online, you might also notice some cmdlets are similar to their Exchange on-premises counterpart. Cmdlets might carry a different name, such as Get-OutboundConnector instead of Get-SendConnector or Get-MessageTrace instead of Get-MessageTracking. Cmdlets might also be absent, such as Get-MailboxDatabase, or they are missing parameters, such as Server or ADSite, as these do not make a lot of sense for tenant administrators in a cloud service such as Office 365. Output might also differ, as internal information might be omitted from output, such as server names.

Connecting to Exchange Online using PowerShell is performed using the Exchange Online Management module. PowerShell Remoting is still an option, but as most organizations have disabled Basic Authentication or require Multi-factor Authentication, the usage of this module is highly recommended. The module is available from the PowerShell Gallery, a public repository for PowerShell modules. The installation is straightforward:

1) Open a PowerShell session in elevated mode.
2) Run `Install-Module ExchangeOnlineManagement` to install the module.
3) Use `Import-Module ExchangeOnlineManagement` to explicitly load the module.
4) Run `Connect-ExchangeOnline` to initiate connection to Exchange Online. After connecting, your session is set up. You will have received an authentication token which has a certain lifetime. This locally cached token can be reused in your current security context during reconnection or when you are using the same UPN, for example:

   ```
   Connect-ExchangeOnline -UserPrincipalName admin@contoso.
   onmicrosoft.com
   ```

Note The PowerShell Gallery is a public repository containing PowerShell modules, scripts, and Desired State Configuration resources. It is installed by default in recent Windows versions (Windows Server 2016, Windows 10 or later), and you can check for its presence using `Get-PSRepository`. You can also browse by pointing your browser to **`https://powershellgallery.com`**.

```
> connect-exchangeonline -UserPrincipalName michel@myexchangelabs.com

----------------------------------------------------------------------------
The module allows access to all existing remote PowerShell (V1) cmdlets in addition to the 9 new, faster, and more reliable
cmdlets.

|--------------------------------------------------------------------------|
|    Old Cmdlets                        |    New/Reliable/Faster Cmdlets    |
|--------------------------------------------------------------------------|
|    Get-CASMailbox                     |    Get-EXOCASMailbox              |
|    Get-Mailbox                        |    Get-EXOMailbox                 |
|    Get-MailboxFolderPermission        |    Get-EXOMailboxFolderPermission |
|    Get-MailboxFolderStatistics        |    Get-EXOMailboxFolderStatistics |
|    Get-MailboxPermission              |    Get-EXOMailboxPermission       |
|    Get-MailboxStatistics              |    Get-EXOMailboxStatistics       |
|    Get-MobileDeviceStatistics         |    Get-EXOMobileDeviceStatistics  |
|    Get-Recipient                      |    Get-EXORecipient               |
|    Get-RecipientPermission            |    Get-EXORecipientPermission     |
|--------------------------------------------------------------------------|

To get additional information, run: Get-Help Connect-ExchangeOnline or check https://aka.ms/exops-docs

Send your product improvement suggestions and feedback to exocmdletpreview@service.microsoft.com. For issues related to the
module, contact Microsoft support. Don't use the feedback alias for problems or support issues.
----------------------------------------------------------------------------
```

***Figure 9-6.** Connecting to Exchange Online using PowerShell*

Beyond the scope of this book but interesting to note is that at the moment of writing, the ExchangeOnlineManagement module contains nine cmdlets which use the Graph API to query Office 365, instead of their "regular" counterpart which uses remote PowerShell. The Graph API cmdlets can be identified using their EXO noun prefix. To list them, use `Get-Command -Module ExchangeOnlineManagement -Noun EXO*`. The cmdlets and their counterparts are shown in Figure 9-6.

The EXO cmdlets have a performance benefit. They also have some peculiarities, such as the requirement to explicitly specify properties or property sets to retrieve, which is why they cannot be interchanged with their non-Graph API counterparts without checking first. In the end, the adoption is worth the effort, especially if you use these cmdlets in scripts or routines which process larger sets of data (mailboxes, permissions, etc.).

The **Connect-ExchangeOnline** cmdlet contains an optional **Prefix** parameter, which can be used to prefix nouns of imported cmdlets. For example, `Connect-ExchangeOnline -Prefix Cloud` will result in **Get-Recipient** being imported as **Get-CloudRecipient**. Note that "Cloud" can be any textual label. While -Prefix Super will work, Get-SuperMailbox does not make a lot of sense, so referring to the context is recommended. This makes prefixes ideal when working with multiple Exchange environments, for example, Exchange on-premises and Exchange Online or the Exchange on-premises environment of a remote organization. It allows you to identify which environment you are addressing, the local Exchange on-premises without a prefix, "cloud" for Exchange Online or "partner" for a subsidiary. The only thing to keep in mind is that when used in scripts or procedures, you need to make sure you are connected to the proper environment using the same prefix.

Note The Microsoft Graph API is a unified method to access Microsoft 365 resources such as Azure Active Directory, Exchange Online, and Enterprise Mobility + Security services. To get an idea of Graph, have a look at Graph Explorer, at **https://developer.microsoft.com/graph/graph-explorer**.

Connecting to Azure Active Directory

Connecting to Azure Active Directory using PowerShell requires installing the related Azure Active Directory module, available from the PowerShell Gallery. Installing and using follows the same basic principles of the ExchangeOnlineManagement module:

1) Open a PowerShell session in elevated mode.
2) Run `Install-Module AzureAD` to install the module.
3) Use `Import-Module AzureAD` to explicitly load the module.
4) Run `Connect-AzureAD` to initiate connection to Azure AD. After connecting, your session is set up. You will have received an authentication token which has a certain lifetime. This locally cached token can be reused in your current security context during reconnection or when you are using the same UPN, for example:

```
Connect-AzureAD -AccountId admin@contoso.onmicrosoft.com
```

As you may notice, and as mentioned earlier, here is one of those small inconsistencies, as Connect-AzureAD uses AccountId to specify the UPN to log on with, where Connect-ExchangeOnline uses UserPrincipalName.

Tip When you cannot download or install required PowerShell modules, you can export the module files using another workstation with access and copy the files. Then, you can import the module directly from the copied file set. In short `Save-Module -Name ExchangeOnlineManagement -Path C:\PSModules -Repository PSGallery`, then, after copying the exported module from C:\PSModules, import the module using the explicit path, `Import-Module -Name C:\PSModules\ExchangeOnlineManagement`

Now the Azure AD module requires a bit of historical context. The Azure AD module is the official successor to a module named MSOnline. The MSOnline module was released a long time ago and at that time was available as an MSI. It was labeled "Microsoft Online Services Module for Windows PowerShell x64" and also required another package to facilitate sign-in, the "Microsoft Online Services Sign-In Assistant." While less easy to maintain back in the days, the MSOnline module contained nearly every function to manage every aspect of Azure AD.

Then came the Azure AD module in 2016, which was new and used the Graph API to interact with Azure AD. This is also the reason why the MSOnline module is version v1.x, and Azure AD immediately started with version v2.x to mark its evolution. However, it quickly came to light not all functionality offered in MSOnline (since then sometimes referred to as AzureADv1) was available in the new AzureADv2 module, or configuration elements were more difficult to manage. In fact, even to date, not all functionality offered by MSOnline is available via the Graph API and thus also not available in AzureADv2. And perhaps never will be. In the instructions from vendors, you also might encounter references to the MSOnline module and its *-MSOL* commands for the exact same reason.

Some of the functions not available in AzureADv2, offered by MSOnline:

- Converting domains in the tenant from federated to managed (and back), which may be required when using AD FS, and you wish to fall back to synchronized password hashes for authentication.
- Configuring multi-factor (strong) authentication settings for users.

To install the MSOnline module, just `Install-Module MSOnline`, `Import-Module MSOnline`, and then run `Connect-MSOLService` to connect. A quick note that the MSOnline module currently does not work on PowerShell 7.x, but that might change in the future.

Sharing of Information

Sharing information is possible on two levels in Exchange and Office 365:

- **Organization relationships**, or organizational sharing as it is named in Office 365, allow federated organizations to share calendar information with other federated organizations.
- **Sharing policies** allow user-level sharing of calendar information, within the boundaries of the policy.

An organizational relationship is tied to a namespace. For Exchange on-premises, this is usually the regular domain, for example, contoso.com. For Exchange Online, this is the routing email domain, for example, contoso.mail.onmicrosoft.com. With Autodiscover pointing to Exchange on-premises, requests for contoso.com will get a redirection instruction to Exchange Online via the targetAddress attribute set on migrated mailboxes.

Caution Federation for on-premises Exchange with other organizations running Exchange Hybrid does not work for cloud-based mailboxes. Because the Exchange server on-premises performing the availability lookup has an organizational relationship with the on-premises Exchange organization of the partner, it will not proxy the request to Office 365 after receiving the `targetAddress` redirect to `@<tenant>.mail.onmicrosoft.com` address. The trick is to create an organizational relationship with `<tenant>.mail.onmicrosoft.com` for partners. Ideally, those routing addresses are set as `targetAddress` on locally stored contacts, which makes the lookup more efficient, but is far from ideal as it requires you to know which partner mailboxes are cloud based and which are not. A third-party product providing GALsync functionality might be helpful in those cases.

Because Exchange on-premises is a different organization than your Exchange Online environment, you will have two locations where organizational relationships and sharing policies are defined. The Organization Configuration Transfer option in the Hybrid Configuration Wizard can assist in creating the initial sharing policies in Exchange Online using the definitions found in Exchange on-premises.

You can inspect and configure the current sharing policy by using the EAC, navigating to **Organization ➤ Sharing**, as shown in Figure 9-7.

Note If your organization has not been enabled for federation yet, EAC will notify you and give you the option to perform this step at this location.

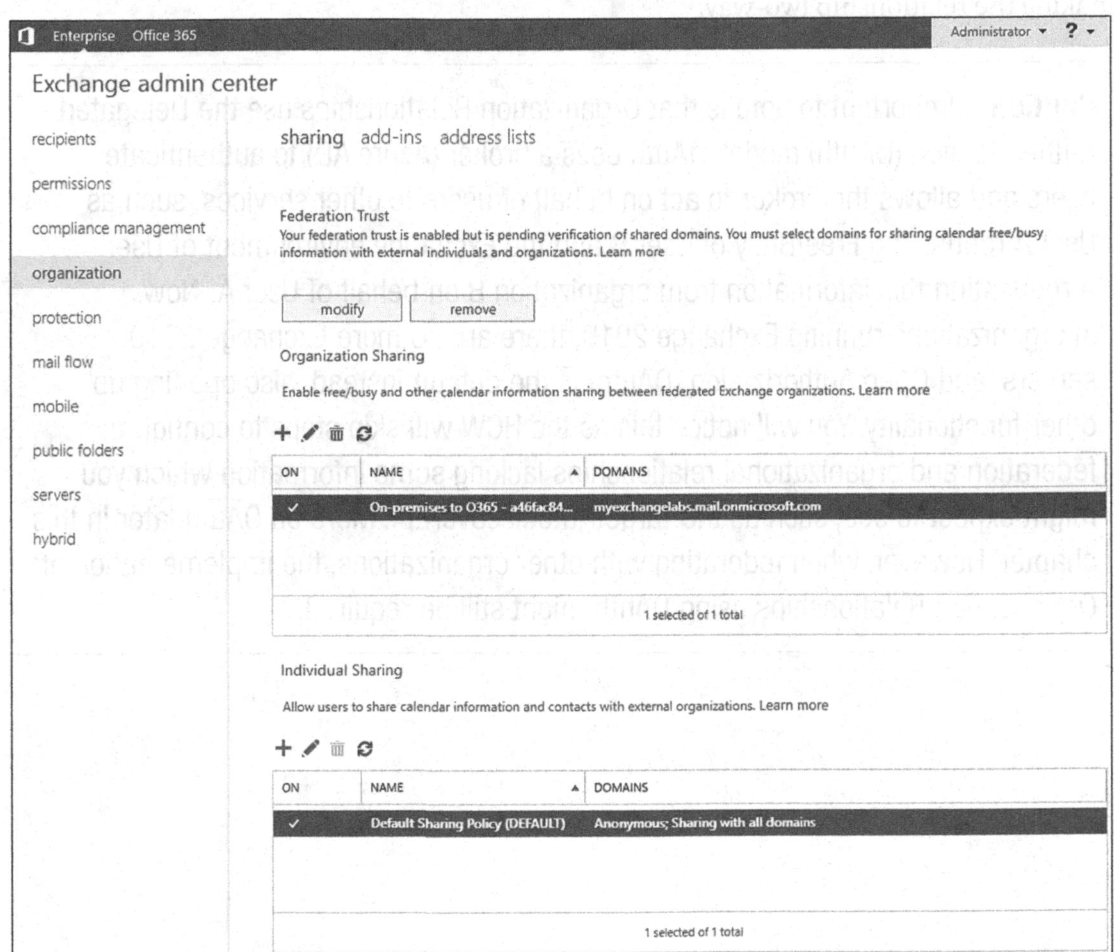

***Figure 9-7.** Organization Sharing and Individual Sharing options in EAC*

As visible, the HCW has created an organizational relationship in Exchange on-premises “On-Premises to Office 365 - <GUID>” for the domain myexchangelabs.mail.onmicrosoft.com. The GUID in the name is the GUID of your organization in Office 365, as can be found using `(Get-OrganizationConfig).Guid` in Exchange Online.

Organizational Relationships

Federating information with other organizations is configured through so-called organizational relationships. You can view the configured organizational relationship by using the cmdlet `Get-OrganizationRelationship`. If you run this cmdlet in an Exchange Online Management session, you will see the organizational relationship created by the HCW. This is the counterpart of the organizational relationship created on-premises, making the relationship two-way.

Caution Important to note is that Organization Relationships use the Delegated Authentication (DAuth) model. DAuth uses a broker (Azure AD) to authenticate users and allows the broker to act on behalf of users to other services, such as User A requesting Free/Busy of User B and the Exchange environment of User A requesting this information from organization B on behalf of User A. Now, in organizations running Exchange 2019, there are no more Exchange 2010 servers, and Open Authorization (OAuth) is the default instead, also opening up other functionality. You will notice this as the HCW will skip steps to configure federation and organizational relationships lacking some information which you might expect to see, such as the TargetAutodiscoverEpr. More on OAuth later in this chapter. However, when federating with other organizations, the implementation of Organization Relationships using DAuth might still be required.

```
> Get-OrganizationRelationship | fl

RunspaceId                   : e7e755f9-910c-45da-a2f9-084889683d2b
DomainNames                  : {myexchangelabs.com}
FreeBusyAccessEnabled        : True
FreeBusyAccessLevel          : LimitedDetails
FreeBusyAccessScope          :
MailboxMoveEnabled           : False
MailboxMoveCapability        : None
MailboxMovePublishedScopes   : {}
IdentityMoveEnabled          : False
IdentityMoveCapability       : None
IdentityMovePublishedScopes  : {}
PeopleSearchEnabled          : False
PeopleSearchCapability       : None
PeopleSearchPublishedScopes  : {}
OAuthApplicationId           :
DeliveryReportEnabled        : True
MailTipsAccessEnabled        : True
MailTipsAccessLevel          : All
MailTipsAccessScope          :
PhotosEnabled                : True
TargetApplicationUri         :
TargetSharingEpr             :
TargetOwaURL                 : https://mail.myexchangelabs.com/owa
TargetAutodiscoverEpr        :
OrganizationContact          :
Enabled                      : True
ArchiveAccessEnabled         : False
AdminDisplayName             :
ExchangeVersion              : 0.10 (14.0.100.0)
Name                         : O365 to On-premises - b94fdb6a-84c4-44e4-9a36-18e3741d5b02
DistinguishedName            : CN=O365 to On-premises - b94fdb6a-84c4-44e4-9a36-18e3741d5b02,CN=Federation,CN=Configurat
                               ion,CN=myexchangelabs.onmicrosoft.com,CN=ConfigurationUnits,DC=EURPR05A002,DC=prod,DC=out
                               look,DC=com
Identity                     : O365 to On-premises - b94fdb6a-84c4-44e4-9a36-18e3741d5b02
ObjectCategory               : EURPR05A002.prod.outlook.com/Configuration/Schema/ms-Exch-Fed-Sharing-Relationship
ObjectClass                  : {top, msExchFedSharingRelationship}
WhenChanged                  : 30/06/2021 19:07:48
WhenCreated                  : 30/06/2021 19:07:27
WhenChangedUTC               : 30/06/2021 17:07:48
WhenCreatedUTC               : 30/06/2021 17:07:27
ExchangeObjectId             : 0b97cd9f-ca9c-4640-863b-8622ed621ebb
OrganizationId               : EURPR05A002.prod.outlook.com/Microsoft Exchange Hosted
                               Organizations/myexchangelabs.onmicrosoft.com - EURPR05A002.prod.outlook.com/Configuration
                               Units/myexchangelabs.onmicrosoft.com/Configuration
Id                           : O365 to On-premises - b94fdb6a-84c4-44e4-9a36-18e3741d5b02
Guid                         : 0b97cd9f-ca9c-4640-863b-8622ed621ebb
OriginatingServer            : DB3PR05A02DC002.EURPR05A002.prod.outlook.com
IsValid                      : True
ObjectState                  : Changed
```

***Figure 9-8.** Organization Relationship definition*

In Figure 9-8, you can see that from Exchange Online's viewpoint, sharing information for the myexchangelabs.com address space has been defined. This information exchange for address spaces mentioned in `DomainNames` is defined by the following properties:

- `FreeBusyAccessEnabled` defines if the organization wants to share free/busy information to the other organization.
- `FreeBusyAccessLevel` sets the amount of detail that is shared. Options are
    - *None* when no free/busy information is to be shared
    - *AvailabilityOnly* when only availability is shared
    - *LimitedDetails* when free/busy is shared with time, subject, and location information
- `FreeBusyAccessScope` can be used to limit the information sharing to a certain security group. When this is not set, the free/busy settings in the organizational relationship apply to the whole organization.
- `MailboxMoveEnabled` defines if mailboxes can be moved to the external organization.
- `DeliveryReportEnabled` defines if the organization wants to share delivery report information. This needs to be enabled in both organizations when they want to perform cross-organization message tracking.
- `ArchiveAccessEnabled` defines whether the organization has been configured to provide access to remote personal archives. This needs to be enabled in your on-premises organizational relationship setting when using Exchange Online Archiving (EOA), for example.
- `MailTipsAccessEnabled` defines if mail tips information is provided to the external organization.
- `MailTipsAccessLevel` sets the level of mail tips provided to the external organization. Options are

- *None* when no mail tips information is to be provided.
- *Limited* when only mail tips are to be provided that can prevent nondelivery reports (NDR) or automatic replies such as out-of-office notifications (OOF). Other mail tips such as large audience are not returned.
- *All* when all mail tips are to be provided.

- `MailTipsAccessScope` can be used to return mail tips only for certain security groups. When this is not set, the mail tips settings in the organizational relationship are applied to the whole organization.
- `PhotosEnabled` defines if photo data is returned to the external organization.

To customize organizational relationships, use `Set-OrganizationRelationship`. To create a new one, use `New-OrganizationRelationship`, or use the functions from the EAC interface.

Caution Before you can customize specific sharing details in your tenant, you might be required to enable tenant customization; to accomplish this, run `Enable-OrganizationCustomization` in an Exchange Online session. You will be notified when you need to perform this step.

Note that when you modify an existing organizational relationship, you will have additional configuration options, for the Application URI and Autodiscover endpoint. These settings and an additional one which you should be aware of are also available as parameters to `New-OrganizationRelationship` and `Set-OrganizationRelationship`. These parameters and their usage are

- **TargetAutodiscoverEpr**—When set, it defines the Autodiscover endpoint to use to look up endpoints for resources defined by the domains specified in DomainNames. For example, **`https://autodiscover.contoso.com/autodiscover/autodiscover.svc/wssecurity`**. When not set, public DNS is used.
- **TargetOWAURL**—When set, it defines the URL used for OWA redirection after logging in to a migrated mailbox.

- **TargetSharingEpr**—When set, it overrides the Exchange Web Services endpoint to use for resources defined by the domains in DomainNames, for example, **`https://mail.contoso.com/EWS/exchange.asmx/wssecurity`**. When not set, the endpoint for EWS provided by the Autodiscover process will be used for directing availability lookups.

Tip If your organization does not like the default OWA redirection URL **`https://outlook.com/OWA/contoso.com`**, you can use a CNAME record to perform the redirection. First, create a CNAME in public DNS pointing to **outlook.com**. Second, reconfigure the **TargetOWAUrl**, pointing it to the CNAME followed by **/owa**. For example, when a CNAME has been defined named **cloudmail.contoso.com**, redefine the **TargetOWAUrl** using `Set-OrganizationRelationship -Identity 'On-premises to O365 - <GUID>' -TargetOwaUrl http://cloudmail.contoso.com/owa`.

If at any point you want to validate your organizational relationships,, use Test-OrganizationRelationship, specifying the name of the organizational relationship object as Identity and the mailbox to initiate the test request, for example: `Test-OrganizationRelationship -UserIdentity francis@myexchangelabs.com -Identity 'On-premises to O365 - <GUID>'`

Tip If your Free/Busy lookups stop working at some point, check if the federation trust is still in working order by using **Test-FederationTrust**. If it reports "Failed to validate delegation token," try to refresh the metadata of the on-premises federation trust by using `Get-FederationTrust | Set-FederationTrust -RefreshMetaData:$true`.

Sharing Policies

Whereas organizational relationships define how information is shared on the organizational level, sharing policies, or individual sharing as it is called in EAC, define the user-level calendar sharing options. This includes sharing calendar or contact information with users of both federated organizations and non-federated organizations. In the latter case, Internet publishing is used to publish the information.

The sharing policies define what users are allowed to share. The action of sharing that information is initiated by the user. When you want to manage the sharing policies through the EAC, you navigate to **Organization ➤ Sharing**. In the bottom section named "Individual Sharing," you will find the currently configured sharing policies, as shown in Figure 9-7.

When using an Exchange Online Management session, you can retrieve the list of current sharing policies by using the SharingPolicy cmdlets. You will see that by default one sharing policy is already configured: the default sharing policy. To inspect this policy, use `Get-SharingPolicy | fl Name, Domains, Enabled` as shown in Figure 9-9.

```
[PS] C:\>Get-SharingPolicy | fl Name, Domains, Enabled

Name    : Default Sharing Policy
Domains : {Anonymous:CalendarSharingFreeBusyReviewer, *:CalendarSharingFreeBusySimple}
Enabled : True
```

Figure 9-9. *Default sharing policy*

In Figure 9-9, you can see that there are two entries configured in the default sharing policy: **Anonymous:CalendarSharingFreeBusyReviewer** and ***:CalendarSharingFreeBusySimple**. The format of these entries is **Domain:Action[,Action]**, whereby

- The domain "**Anonymous**" applies to everyone outside your organization.
- The domain "*****" represents everyone inside your organization.
- Action can be one of the following values:
  - `CalendarSharingFreeBusySimple` enables sharing of Free/Busy hours only.
  - `CalendarSharingFreeBusyDetail` enables sharing of Free/Busy hours, subject, and location.

- `CalendarSharingFreeBusyReviewer` enables sharing of Free/Busy hours, subject, location, and the body of the message or calendar item.
- `ContactsSharing` enables sharing of contacts.

So, the default policy is configured to allow users to individually share Free/Busy hours, subject, location, and the body of the message or calendar item with external users, and to share Free/Busy hours with any internal domain.

Caution For anonymous calendar and contact sharing features to work, verify that `AnonymousFeaturesEnabled` is set to `$True` on the OWA virtual directory.

Let us create a new sharing policy named "Custom Sharing Policy" and allow users to share `CalendarSharingFreeBusyReviewer` and contact information with the domain litware.com. For this, you need to run

```
New-SharingPolicy -Name 'Custom Sharing Policy'
 -Domains 'litware.com:CalendarSharingFreeBusyReviewer,ContactsSharing'
```

Now, suppose you want to allow `CalendarSharingFreeBusySimple` sharing with all other external domains as well. You need to run `Set-SharingPolicy` adding this configuration to the Domains attribute:

```
Set-SharingPolicy -Identity 'Custom Sharing Policy'
 -Domains @{Add='Anonymous:CalendarSharingFreeBusySimple'}
```

The instruction **Add** makes sure the entry gets added to any existing entries on the Domains attribute. Only thing remaining now is configuring this sharing policy on mailboxes which are allowed this new policy. Each mailbox is assigned one sharing policy. This will be the default sharing policy. To assign a mailbox a different sharing policy, use Set-Mailbox with the SharingPolicy parameter:

```
Set-Mailbox -Identity francis@contoso.com -SharingPolicy 'Custom Sharing
Policy'.
```

Now, if this user wants to share their calendar or contacts folder, they can use the Share Calendar or Share Contacts folder options from Outlook. For calendar sharing, they may choose a lower level of detail than set by the policy. Note that Outlook is unaware of the sharing policy settings; when the user tries to share more details than permitted, they will receive an error message as soon as they try to send the email with the sharing link. Also, when the intended recipient is not part of a federated organization, the user is notified and they will need to use Internet Calendar Publishing instead.

Note The link sent to recipients to access the calendar or contacts is obfuscated but is not password protected.

Internet Calendar Publishing

To share calendar information with non-federated or non-Exchange recipients, users can be allowed to publish their calendar online, depending on the effective sharing policy configuration. This requires external publishing of OWA, as well as calendar publishing, which is enabled by default. You can inspect current configuration using

```
Get-OWAVirtualDirectory | Select Identity,ExternalUrl,CalendarEnabled.
```

When allowed and configured, users can publish their calendar. The location will be based on OWA's ExternalURL configuration. The calendar is published as an iCalendar .ics file and as an HTML page. Apart from the publication window, users can also pick the access level when publishing, as shown in Figure 9-10.

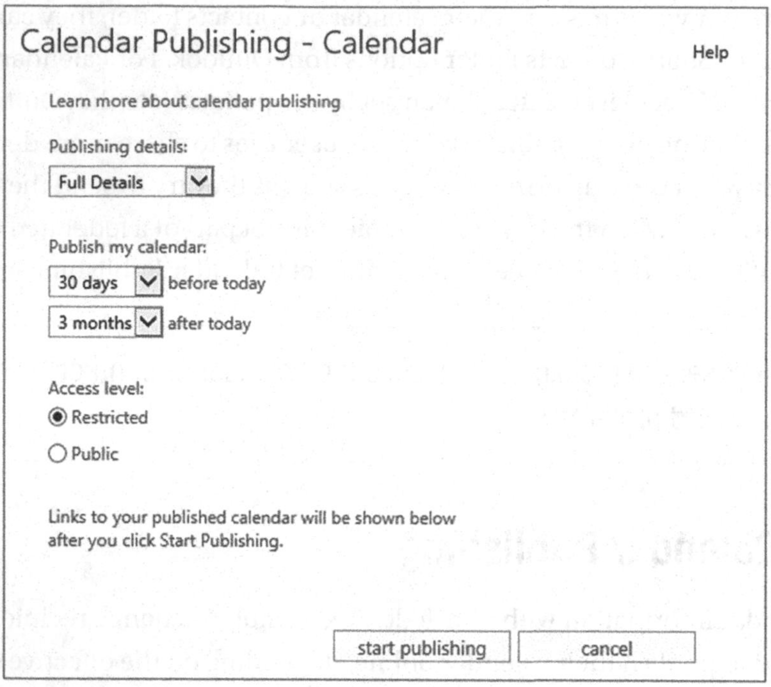

Figure 9-10. *Internet Calendar Publishing*

- **Public** results in a relatively simple URL, for example, `http://mail.myexchangelabs.com/owa/calendar/philip@myexchangelabs.com/Calendar/calendar.ics`.
- **Restricted** results in a less obvious URL, as GUIDs and hashes are added, for example, `http://mail.myexchangelabs.com/owa/calendar/58b843d23d124ae2af0fc1e338e1357f@myexchangelabs.com/865a2dcb67814672b2e9fec0240a4f9c9679842447551712479/calendar.ics`.

Although less likely to be guessed or memorized, the URL is not secure because HTTP is used. But when it is needed, there are options to publish calendars publicly. Note that the ICS (iCal) format is a calendar file format that is compatible with many applications, including Outlook. These can also be added manually to Outlook, opening the Calendar view, right-clicking **Other Calendars**, and selecting **Add Calendar ➤ From Internet**.

Modern Authentication

In the section about organizational relationships, we briefly touched on these relationships using the Delegated Authentication (DAuth) model. Modern Authentication (OAuth) is an authentication protocol that provides applications or services a secure way to delegate access to their resources. For Exchange 2019, this means allowing applications such as Exchange Online or Microsoft Teams to authenticate to Exchange on-premises, or vice versa, using OAuth. For this purpose, applications or the services which they represent are configured as partner applications. Additional benefits of OAuth over DAuth are, among other things

- Exchange delegation, honoring the configured folder permissions instead of being bound by the organization sharing configuration
- In-Place eDiscovery of messages spread over both locations
- Cross-premises message tracking making it easier to track messages flowing through both locations
- Retention policies on mailboxes hosted in Exchange on-premises archiving directly to Exchange Online Archives
- Microsoft Teams integrating with mailboxes hosted in Exchange on-premises for calendaring

---

Caution When configuring Hybrid deployment using the HCW and Exchange 2016 or 2013, and Exchange 2010 is still present in the organization, the HCW will not configure OAuth. The manual process can be found at **`http://bit.ly/OAuthConfig`**.

After HCW set up OAuth, you can test it from the on-premises environment to Office 365 and vice versa by using `Test-OAuthConnectivity`, specifying the mailbox you want to use for testing. You also need to specify the application or protocol to test, using TargetUri to specify the endpoint. Services supported for the Test cmdlet are

- EWS for Exchange Web Services
- AutoD for Autodiscover
- Generic

So, for example, to test OAuth from on-premises to Exchange Online with EWS:

```
Test-OAuthConnectivity -Service EWS -TargetUri https://outlook.office365.
com/EWS/Exchange.asmx
 -Mailbox <onpremmailbox@contoso.com>
```

To test OAuth from Exchange Online to Exchange on-premises for Autodiscover:

```
Test-OAuthConnectivity -Service AutoD -TargetUri https://autodiscover.
contoso.com/Autodiscover/Autodiscover.svc/WSSecurity
 -Mailbox <cloudmailbox@contoso.com>
```

When successful, the command will return ResultType Success for Task "Checking EWS API Call Under Oauth." When not successful, you need to investigate the issue. In that case, perform the same command but pipe the output to fl. It will show detailed output on the calls performed and the results. For example, make sure you use an account which is synchronized between the two organizations; otherwise, you may encounter 401 Unauthorized errors. Note that when you want to manually check the configuration, the manual OAuth setup process mentioned earlier can provide helpful guidance.

With OAuth configured, organizations that have configured relationships with other organizations or between Exchange on-premises and Exchange Online, Exchange will first try OAuth before trying DAuth authentication. That is, if there is a definition of a possible OAuth-enabled relationship, which is where the **Intra-Organization Connector** (IOC) and **Intra-Organization Configuration** come in view. Configuration-wise, the IOC connector looks similar to Organization Relationship: it defines the domains to use with the IOC, what the discovery endpoint is (Autodiscover), etc.

The Intra-Organization Configuration contains the IOC details of the current environment, so the information in Exchange on-premises differs from Exchange Online, also with Exchange Hybrid configured. Details of the IOC connector should match the IOC configuration of the partner organization. For example, the discovery endpoint of the IOC connector in Exchange Online pointing to on-premises should match the IOC discovery endpoint attribute of Exchange on-premises.

```
[PS] C:\>Get-IntraOrganizationConfiguration
WARNING: Please check that the Autodiscover endpoint of "https://mail.myexchangelabs.com/autodiscover/autodiscover.svc" is correct and can be
accessed externally. If it's incorrect or can't be accessed externally, use an existing Autodiscover endpoint that can be accessed externally
for the configuration of the intra-organization connector.

OnlineDiscoveryEndpoint                         :
OnlineTargetAddress                             :
OnPremiseTargetAddresses                        : {}
OnPremiseDiscoveryEndpoint                      : https://mail.myexchangelabs.com/autodiscover/autodiscover.svc
OnPremiseWebServiceEndpoint                     : https://mail.myexchangelabs.com/EWS/Exchange.asmx
DeploymentIsCompleteIOCReady                    : True
HasNonIOCReadyExchangeCASServerVersions         : False
HasNonIOCReadyExchangeMailboxServerVersions     : False
```

Figure 9-11. *Intra-Organization Configuration*

Let us have a look at the IOC configuration. Figure 9-11 shows the output of `Get-IntraOrganizationConfiguration` when run in Exchange on-premises. The IOC configuration is not configurable; values are determined when setting up Exchange Hybrid:

- **OnlineDiscoveryEndpoint** is the Exchange Online Autodiscover endpoint. When run in Exchange Online, this attribute is **`https://autodiscover-s.outlook.com/autodiscover/autodiscover.svc`**.
- **OnlineTargetAddress** is the Exchange Online default address space. In Exchange Online, this attribute is the default mail routing address associated with Exchange Online, for example, **contoso.mail.onmicrosoft.com**.
- **OnPremiseTargetAddresses** are the email domains associated with the on-premises environment, for example, **contoso.com**.
- **OnPremiseDiscoveryEndpoint** is the Exchange on-premises Autodiscover URI. In Exchange Online, this attribute is not set.
- **OnPremiseWebServiceEndpoint** is the Exchange on-premises EWS URI. In Exchange Online, this attribute is not set.

Tip If you ever run into the problem of having on-premises organization configuration lingering in your tenant, you can view currently configured on-premises organizations in your tenant using `Get-OnPremisesOrganization`. When needed, you can use `Remove-OnPremisesOrganization -Identity <Guid>` to remove the orphaned configuration object of the organization identified by the GUID.

To watch the configuration of IOC connectors, use `Get-IntraOrganizationConnector`. Figure 9-12 shows the default IOC connector created on-premises by HCW. Its name is HybridIOC, followed by the GUID of the remote organization, in this case the tenant.

```
[PS] C:\>Get-IntraOrganizationConnector | fl Identity,TargetAddressDomains,DiscoveryEndpoint,Enabled

Identity             : HybridIOC - ██6fac84-50d1-████-8e4c-c924f████a5b
TargetAddressDomains : {myexchangelabs.mail.onmicrosoft.com}
DiscoveryEndpoint    : https://autodiscover-s.outlook.com/autodiscover/autodiscover.svc
Enabled              : True
```

Figure 9-12. *Intra-Organization Connector*

IOC connectors are configurable, but in principle should be left under the management of the HCW. They do provide the actual endpoints and domain names that apply, so can be used to validate theoretical federation path during troubleshooting:

- **TargetAddressDomains** are the email domains associated with the remote organization. In this case, we are running the cmdlet on-premises, so we see the default email routing domain associated with Exchange Online.
- **DiscoveryEndpoint** is the Autodiscover endpoint of the remote organization. We run this on-premises, so it contains the Exchange Online Autodiscover URI. When running in Exchange Online, we will see the Autodiscover URI for on-premises here.
- **TargetSharingEpr** is the EWS endpoint. This is only available in Exchange Online and can be used to override the EWS endpoint. When not set, the EWS endpoint provided by the Autodiscover process will be used.

Mailbox Migration

After configuring your Exchange Hybrid deployment, your population of mailboxes will be residing in Exchange on-premises. AD Connect will have provisioned Mail-Enabled Users in your tenant, provided there are no synchronization issues and objects are in scope of the synchronization process. Now, how to get mailboxes moved to Exchange Online, often referred to as onboarding?

Caution Before you can start using mailboxes in Exchange Online, make sure you have applied a proper license including an Exchange Online Plan. If not, mailboxes will be inaccessible. Furthermore, unlicensed mailboxes will have a 30-day grace period. After this grace period, mailbox data will be removed. Permanently.

To move mailboxes, a process is followed which is somewhat similar to cross-forest mailbox moves performed on-premises. It is shown in Figure 9-13. In this case, the target MEU has already been provisioned by AD Connect; on-premises we would have used the infamous Prepare-MoveRequest.ps1 script or a tool offering GALsync-like functionality for this step.

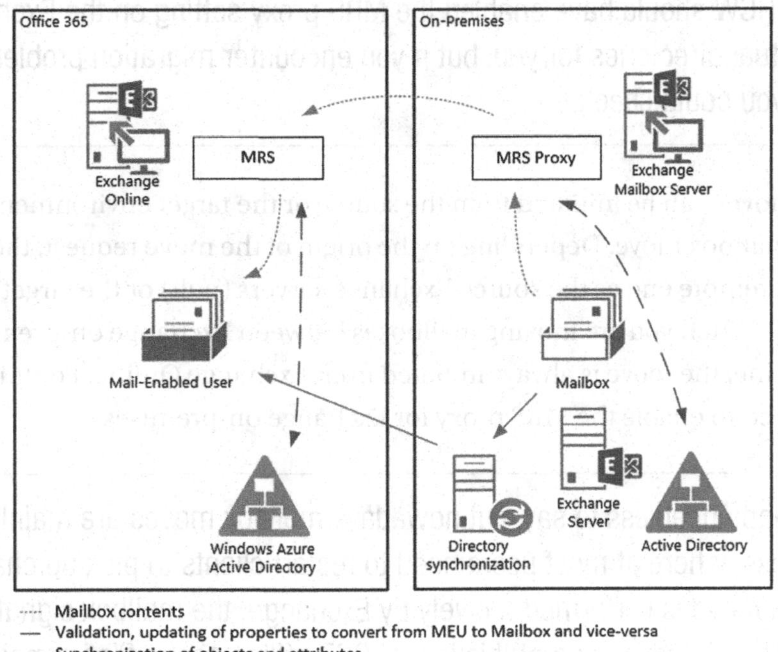

***Figure 9-13.** Onboarding mailboxes to Exchange Online*

When you perform regular mailbox moves within the Exchange on-premises organization, a service called Microsoft Exchange Mailbox Replication will coordinate the move. When you are performing cross-forest moves or moves between Exchange on-premises and Exchange Online (also known as remote moves), something called the MRS proxy proxies the traffic related to the move, acting as the counterpart to the MRS. Both MRS and MRS proxy update the Active Directory in their respective environments with information such as the database hosting the mailbox. Eventually, MRS will convert the mailbox user objects to mail-enabled user objects, and vice versa in the destination, when the move has been successfully completed.

By default, the MRS proxy functionality is disabled, so before you can perform any remote moves, you need to enable the MRS proxy. This can be performed via the EAC (**Servers ➤ Virtual Directories ➤ EWS (default website)** entries), or you can use EMS for a specific Exchange server or just for all available servers:

```
Get-WebServicesVirtualDirectory | Set-WebServicesVirtualDirectory
-MRSProxyEnabled $true
```

Note The HCW should have enabled the MRS proxy setting on the Exchange Web Services virtual directories for you, but if you encounter migration problems, this is something you could check.

Remote moves can be initiated from the source or the target environment, effecting a push or pull mailbox move. Depending on the origin of the move request, the MRS proxy is used on the remote end as the source Exchange servers (pull) or the target Exchange servers (push). When you are moving mailboxes between Exchange on-premises and Exchange Online, the move is always initiated from Exchange Online. For this reason, you always need to enable the MRS proxy for Exchange on-premises.

Note Perhaps needless to say, but nowadays mailbox moves are mainly an online process, where at most users need to restart clients to pick up changes. Because the move is performed natively by Exchange, the mailbox signature is preserved. The big advantage of this is that OST offline cache files remain valid and do not require resynchronization.

First, let us briefly introduce some terms that are related to onboarding (and offboarding) mailboxes to Exchange Online:

– A **Migration Endpoint** defines the FQDN to be used for migration, together with credentials for authentication and tuning information such as how many moves and mailbox syncs can be performed in parallel. Note that when modifying these last parameters, your environment needs to be able to handle. In general, it is best to use the defaults as a starting point. When needed, organizations can introduce additional migration endpoints via additional Internet breakouts to improve overall throughput.

– A **Migration Batch** is a batch of identities whose mailboxes need to be migrated. You configure it with the identities of the users, hand-picked or provided using a CSV file, together with the migration endpoint. You also configure it to automatically complete after finishing or not and what email domain should be used to pick the address to stamp as targetAddress on the mailbox on-premises after it gets converted to MEU after completion. A recipient needs to be selected which will receive mail reports on the progress of the migration.

– A **Migration User** is an entity representing the mailbox being moved. Note that for mailboxes with online archives, there will be migration user objects for the mailbox and the archive as well. Parameters are taken from the attached Migration Batch; you cannot create a separate "Migration User."

– A **Move Request** is the underlying job for MRS that moves mailbox contents from location to location. It inherits its settings from the Migration User object.

To verify if requirements for a successful migration are in place, you can use the `Test-MigrationServerAvailability` cmdlet. You can optionally add the `-Verbose` switch to add extra information to the output, which might prove useful when you are troubleshooting:

```
Test-MigrationServerAvailability -ExchangeRemoteMove -EmailAddress henk@
myexchangelabs.com -Autodiscover -Credentials (Get-Credential)
```

Caution Migration endpoints are authenticated against using Basic Authentication. If you disable Basic Authentication or the underlying authentication methods such as NTLM, mailbox moves will fail.

When you have used the HCW to set up Exchange Hybrid, there should already be a Migration Endpoint configured in your Exchange Online organization. To inspect it, open its EAC, and navigate to **Recipients ➤ Migration ➤ … ➤ Migration Endpoints**, or just use `Get-MigrationEndpoint` in an Exchange Online Management session.

With the Migration Endpoint in place, you are ready to start onboarding mailboxes. How is mainly dictated by frequency and scale. For incidental moves, the EAC will suffice. It's easy and rather self-explaining:

1) In the EAC from Exchange Online, navigate to **Recipients ➤ Migration.** Click the + sign and you will have the option to Migrate to or from Exchange Online.

2) After selecting **Migrate to Exchange Online**, you can start defining the parameters of your Migration Batch. You are asked what type of move you want to perform. Since the source is Exchange, pick **Remote Move Migration**.

3) The next screen allows you to pick the identities of the mailboxes you would like to move. You can pick them manually with + or provide a CSV file containing a column **EmailAddress** and the identities of the mailboxes to move.

4) Next, you need to pick the Migration Endpoint to use for this move.

5) You are then asked to provide a name for the migration job, as well as provide the target delivery domain. This is the email domain name which is going to be used to configure the targetAddress on the MEU after migration completes, effectively forwarding mail and routing requests like Free/Busy. By default, this is set to the OnlineTargetAddress of the IOC configuration, for example, **contoso.mail.onmicrosoft.com**. If needed, you can move the primary mailboxes and any archives together or only move the archives of those mailboxes. This can be useful when you want to move to an Exchange Online Archiving plan, for example.

6) The last screen will ask a few things. First, you can set the recipient who will receive mail on the progress of the migration job. You also can specify when the job needs to start and when the job needs to finish. Note that you can choose to manually complete the migration. The benefit of this mechanism is that you can stage mailbox contents early and complete the migration at a later point. In the meantime, Exchange will incrementally synchronize mailbox contents every 24 hours, so that the delta of changes when completion is required is minimal.

7) Click **New** to create the Migration Batch.

The migration page should now contain your newly created Migration Batch. You can check its progress, inspecting per mailbox progress or issues clicking the Mailbox status, or click Complete when you have configured the job to manually complete.

To successfully migrate mailboxes, the secondary email addresses of that mailbox need to contain an entry using the domain specified at step 5. If not, MRS cannot set the targetAddress post-migration, and the operation for that mailbox will fail. Also, addresses which are not configured as Accepted Domain in Office 365 may cause the migration of a mailbox to fail, reporting "You can't use the domain because it's not an accepted domain for your organization."

Caution When staging mailboxes using non-autocompleting migrations, be advised that those staged mailboxes are subject to mailbox deletion retention time, which is 30 days in Office 365. After this period, mailboxes for which the move has not been completed will be removed. When a mailbox is removed, it is recreated when the move is resumed. In this case, all items that were already transferred are copied again.

When the move is successful, you might be prompted to restart the Outlook client ("The administrator made a change."), depending on the authentication methods used on-premises and single sign-on configuration. If you are unable to successfully connect, make sure you check if the Autodiscover app pool in IIS on your Exchange servers has been reconfigured; by default, it caches Autodiscover information for an hour. You might with to set the recycle interval during migration periods to something shorter, for example, 15 minutes, as shown in Figure 9-14.

You may also be required to reenter your credentials when you are not using a modern authentication or a single sign-on solution. The reason for this is that when you are saving the password in Outlook, it is stored for the endpoint Outlook uses. After onboarding mailboxes, the endpoint is switched from the Exchange on-premises endpoint to office365.outlook.com, causing existing stored passwords not to work.

***Figure 9-14.** Configuring the MSExchangeAutodiscoverAppPool recycling interval*

Tip It is best practice to configure the recycling interval of the Autodiscover app pool in IIS during migration projects. This makes sure clients get current Autodiscover information.

In addition to moving mailboxes using the EAC, you can also use the Exchange Online Management session to create and manage the migration batches and users. To perform a migration using New-MigrationBatch, you can use the following parameters:

- **Name** is the Name of the Migration Batch. Note that the underlying MigrationUser and MoveRequests jobs created from MigrationBatch will carry this name as well, for easy reference and selection. The MoveRequest BatchName will however get a prefix "MigrationService:", as will be shown later.
- **SourceEndpoint** is the Identity of the Migration Endpoint to use.
- **TargetDeliveryDomain** is the email domain that will determine which secondary email address will be stamped as targetAddress post-migration.

- **AutoComplete** determines if the mailbox move should automatically complete (**$true**) or not (**$false**). Alternatively, CompleteAfter can be used to specify a time stamp to start move completion, similar to the options provided in EAC.
- **AutoStart** determines if the mailbox move should start immediately. When AutoComplete is set to $false, setting this to $true will start validation and staging immediately.
- **BadItemLimit** is optional and increases the tolerance for bad items by allowing migration to skip this maximum number of corrupt items. BadItemLimit is to be deprecated in favor of Data Consistency Scoring.
- **LargeItemLimit** is optional and allows migration of the specified number of messages that are larger than the current message size limit. The default message size limit in Office 365 is 35 MB (25 MB + MIME overhead). Like BadItemLimit, LargeItemLimit is deprecated in favor of Data Consistency Scoring.
- **CSVData** contains the raw content of the CSV of the mailboxes to migrate. Use `[System.IO.File]::ReadAllBytes( $Filename)` to import its contents.
- If identities are not provided via a CSV file, you can use the **Users** parameter to specify one or more identities on the command line.
- **NotificationEmails** can be used to specify one or more recipients who will receive periodic move reports.

Tip Data Consistency Scoring, as mentioned at BadItemLimit and LargeItemLimit, attempts to provide administrators an overall grade of the data moved, qualifying it as **Perfect**, **Good**, **Investigate**, or **Poor**. This is opposed to these limit parameters, which usually are set during migration, increased when moves get stuck because the BadItemLimit threshold is reached, and eventually are never looked at again. When problems are encountered, administrators are required to actively approve skipping of items. To use Data Consistency Scoring, leave BadItemLimit and LargeItemLimit blank. More on DCS at **`https://bit.ly/DataConsistencyScore`**.

For example, assume we have a CSV file "Users.csv" containing identities of mailboxes we are going to move. Note that the following example uses a splatting technique, which can improve readability when using multiple parameters with commands by offering them as a hashtable:

```
$UsersFile= '.\Users.csv'
$BatchParam= @{
    Name= 'TestBatch'
    SourceEndpoint= 'mail.myexchangelabs.com'
    TargetDeliveryDomain= 'myexchangelabs.mail.onmicrosoft.com'
    AutoComplete= $false
    AutoStart= $true
    CSVData= [System.IO.File]::ReadAllBytes( $UsersFile)
    NotificationEmails= 'jaap@myexchangelabs.com'
}
New-MigrationBatch @BatchParam
```

Tip Exchange Online mailbox moves are throttled. When planning mailbox moves, use an average 0.3–1 GB/hour rate per mailbox, but an exact number is impossible to determine, owing to the many variables, such as MRS proxy hardware, bandwidth, and latencies, or the number of items in mailboxes. To enhance throughput, you can increase the number of concurrent moves, which is a configuration item of the Migration Endpoint. When MRS proxy servers become the bottleneck, add more MRS proxy servers. In conjunction with disabling AutoComplete, starting staging of moving mailbox contents early and completing at a later date, you can improve on delivery. To make a calculated estimation, it is recommended to perform trial migrations and check those for throughput rates to be expected.

Your Migration Batch should now be submitted and also be visible in the EAC, for example. Note that there is a limit of 100 Migration Batch objects, so when you are reaching the limit, you need to clear up old, finished Migration Batches. You can view current Migration Batches using Get-MigrationBatch; to view Migration, use Get-MigrationUser, optionally specifying the Batch name. Also interesting to know is that you can use Get-MigrationUserStatistics to retrieve statistics related to the mailbox move, as shown in Figure 9-15.

```
> Get-MigrationBatch

Identity Status    Type               TotalCount
-------- ------    ----               ----------
Test     Completed ExchangeRemoteMove 2

mdero@TAURUS  C:
> Get-MigrationUser -BatchId Test

Identity                    Batch    Status     LastSyncTime
--------                    -----    ------     ------------
Jaap@myexchangelabs.com     Test     Completed  02/07/2021 00:03:36
Marina@myexchangelabs.com   Test     Completed  02/07/2021 00:45:53

mdero@TAURUS  C:
> Get-MigrationUser -BatchId Test | Get-MigrationUserStatistics

Identity                    Batch    Status     Items Synced   Items Skipped
--------                    -----    ------     ------------   -------------
Jaap@myexchangelabs.com     Test     Completed  24             0
Marina@myexchangelabs.com   Test     Completed  21             0
```

***Figure 9-15.** Monitoring mailbox onboarding using Get-Migration* cmdlets*

Tip When issues arise during mailbox moves, use the command `Get-MigrationUser <ID> | Get-MigrationUserStatistics -Report | fl Report` to retrieve a detailed mailbox synchronization report.

Mentioned earlier were Move Request objects, which are the "real" jobs performing the mailbox moves. Move Requests are created from their related MigrationUser. When needed, you can manage Move Requests directly, but this is generally not recommended:

- Move Requests are more difficult to manage.
- Move Requests require more configuration per mailbox move, such as endpoints and credentials; The Migration User "inherits" this information from the Migration Endpoint.
- While Move Requests are more direct, you need to manage every move individually; the Migration Batch allows to manage the set as one configuration item.
- Status is not always aligned between MigrationUser and MoveRequest; there can be a delay before this attribute gets updated.
- Move Requests cannot be managed from the EAC.

Tip When migrating a mailbox has failed and MRS will not resume it, you can suspend a batch using `Stop-MigrationBatch -Identity <Name>`, remove the move request that has failed using `Remove-MoveRequest -Identity <UserID>`, and restart the Migration Batch using `Resume-MigrationBatch -Identity <Name>`. This process should recreate the move request, but note that this is unsupported.

Offboarding

Finally, to offboard mailboxes to Exchange on-premises, basically the same process can be followed as onboarding mailboxes. In EAC, select Migrate from Exchange Online. The dialogs that follow are identical, except for the following differences:

- **TargetDeliveryDomain** should be the on-premises email domain, for example, contoso.com. This will be used to select an entry from the secondary addresses and stamp it as targetAddress on the MEU in Exchange Online after completing offboarding.
- **RemoteTargetDatabase** to enter the mailbox database(s) where the mailboxes need to be migrated to on-premises. You can enter multiple database names, separated by a comma. Mailbox requests created will be spread by MRS over these databases.
- **RemoteArchiveTargetDatabase** (optional) to specify the name of the mailbox database to move personal archives to, when applicable.

Remote Mailboxes

After a mailbox is onboarded, the on-premises Mail-Enabled User will become known as a "Remote Mailbox." It functions identical to a Mail-Enabled User, and its recipient type is also MailUser. Remote mailboxes should be managed using RemoteMailbox cmdlets, such as Get-RemoteMailbox. Note that this also applies to Remote Mailboxes that are of type Shared, Equipment, or Room. For Remote Mailboxes, Get-MailUser will not work, and will result in a "recipient not found" error.

In the on-premises EAC, these remote mailboxes appear in **Recipients ➤ Mailboxes** as mailboxes of the type Office 365, as shown in Figure 9-16. This could be confusing but simplifies the management of the mix of on-premises and Exchange Online mailboxes using a single EAC.

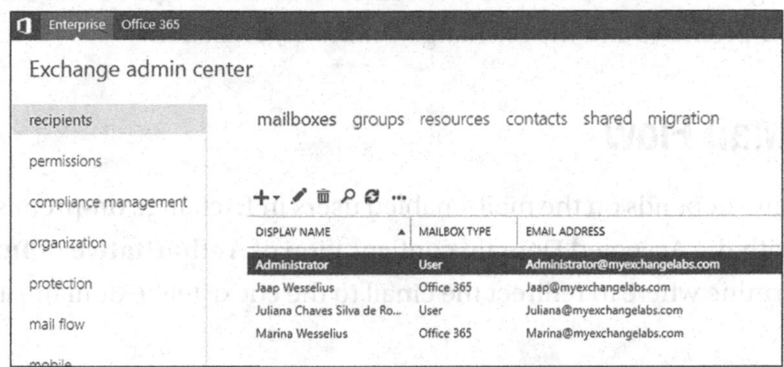

Figure 9-16. *Managing mixed set of mailboxes using EAC*

With Active Directory, Exchange, and Exchange Online, it can be confusing sometimes. It becomes complex when commands use different parameters for the same attribute. With regard to Remote Mailboxes, RemoteRoutingAddress is used to specify the address to route messages and federation requests to. In Exchange Online, for Mail-Enabled Users, this is the externalEmailAddress. In Active Directory, this is targetAddress. When used, all three configure the same Active Directory attribute.

Mail Flow

Mail flow describes how email is routed in an organization and between the organization and external destinations, such as the Internet and partners. With Office 365, you need to configure routing between your organization and Exchange Online, especially with Exchange hybrid deployments where you want communications between on-premises mailboxes and cloud-based mailboxes to be secure.

Chapter 6 discussed mail flow and how to configure it for Exchange on-premises deployments by using send and receive connectors. In Office 365, you also can define connectors, but only on the Exchange Online Protection (EOP) level. Also, you need to use the `Set-OutboundConnector` and `Set-InboundConnector` cmdlets, which are the custom wrappers around Send and Receive connectors found in Exchange on-premises.

The HCW will take care of configuring the mail flow between Exchange on-premises and Exchange Online. What it does not do is reconfiguring your public MX record, which determines if inbound messages will land on-premises or in Exchange Online. However, both inbound mail flow options will work, as both environments are set up to accept the same managed domain name and the connectors are configured to transport mail between the on-premises and the Exchange Online organization.

Inbound Mail Flow

Exchange Online depends on the mail-enabled users in Exchange on-premises in conjunction with the Accepted Domain configuration of **Authoritative** or **Internal Relay**, to determine where to redirect the email to the coexistence domain, as shown in Figure 9-17.

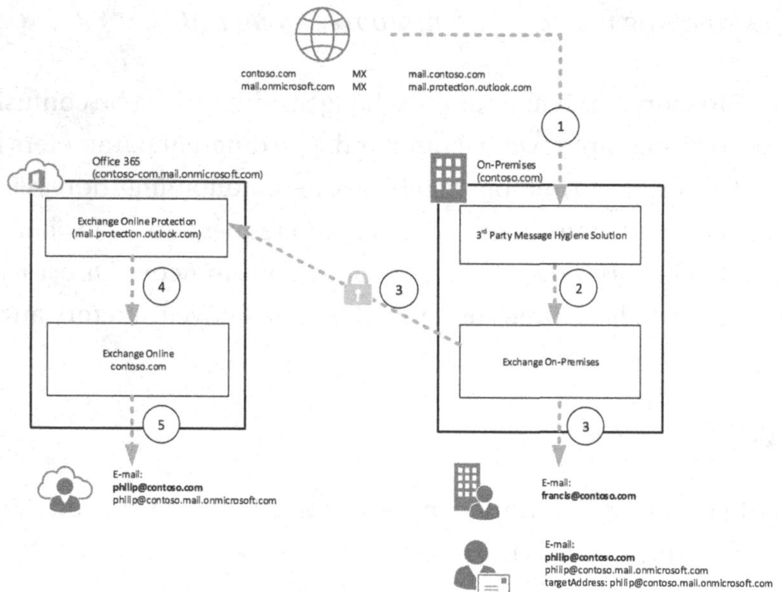

Figure 9-17. *Inbound mail flow routed via on-premises*

A quick walk-through for when Exchange hybrid is configured, and inbound mail flow keeps landing on the on-premises organization. In this example, the sender is contoso.com, and the recipient is either philip@contoso.com, who has his mailbox in Exchange Online, or francis@contoso.com, who has his mailbox on-premises:

1) The mail transfer agent that wants to deliver the mail looks up the **MX** record for contoso.com. This points to mail.contoso.com, so it hands it off to the on-premises third-party gateway.

2) This third-party gateway processes the message and delivers it to Exchange on-premises.

3) Exchange on-premises accepted mail for contoso.com. It also has a matching recipient for francis@contoso.com and delivers the message to the mailbox. For philip@contoso.com, it finds a matching **MEU** (Remote Mailbox). This MEU has a **targetAddress** directing the message to **philip@contoso.mail.onmicrosoft.com**. For this domain, an address space is present on a send connector, **Outbound to Office 365 - <Guid>**, which has been set up by the HCW, and is configured to securely deliver messages. Exchange looks up the MX record for contoso.mail.onmicrosoft.com, which points to **contoso-mail-onmicrosoft-com.mail.protection.outlook.com** (Exchange Online Protection), where it delivers the message.

4) Exchange Online Protection uses an internal connector for the internal address space contoso.mail.onmicrosoft.com domain and hands off the message to Exchange Online.

5) The message is delivered to **philip@contoso.mail.onmicrosoft.com**, which is **philip@contoso.com**.

Caution Third-party gateways between Exchange Online and Exchange on-premises are not supported.

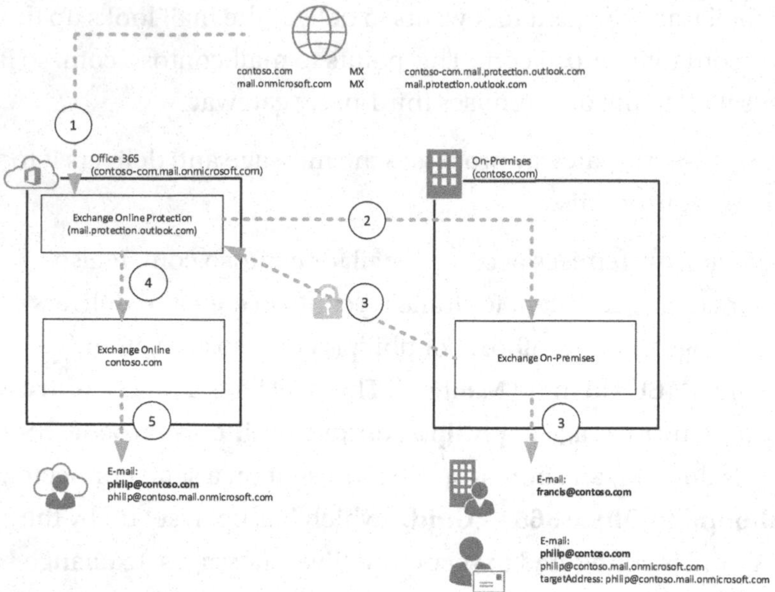

Figure 9-18. *Centralized Mail Transport*

When the MX record is configured to deliver inbound mail to Exchange Online Protection, the following occurs:

1) The mail transfer agent that wants to deliver the mail looks up the MX record for contoso.com. This points to contoso-com.mail.protection.outlook.com (EOP) and so hands it off to EOP.

2) Had Centralized Mail Transport not been configured, the message for philip@contoso.com would have been delivered to his mailbox, and the mail to francis@contoso.com would have been routed to on-premises.

3) If Centralized Mail Transport is configured as shown in Figure 9-18, messages will get routed to Exchange on-premises using the **Outbound to <Guid>** connector which will have the domain set to '*' and **RouteAllMessagesViaOnPremises** set to **$true**.

4) Exchange on-premises knows mailbox francis@contoso.com and delivers the message. For philip@contoso.com, it will again use the configured targetAddress philip@contoso.mail.onmicrosoft.com and deliver the message via the send connector **Outbound to Office 365 - <Guid>**. After the MX lookup, Exchange delivers the message to EOP.

5) Exchange Online Protection delivers the message destined for the internal address space mail.onmicrosoft.com to Exchange Online.

6) The message is delivered to philip@contoso.mail.onmicrosoft.com or philip@contoso.com.

Tip In the HCW, the **Centralized Mail Transport** option is hidden from view. You need to make it visible by selecting **More Options.**

Outbound Mail Flow

Regarding outbound mail flow from Exchange Online, the route again depends on whether your organization has configured Centralized Mail Transport.

A scenario in which the Centralized Mail Transport is beneficial is when you want to secure transport with partners, for example, closed networks where the remote network is only available on-premises or when you have certain third-party agents running on-premises for signatures, for example. By forcing the traffic to flow through your on-premises organization, you create a single point of administration for secure email transport with those partners. However, you also will create a dependency on your on-premises infrastructure and create bandwidth requirements as messages from mailboxes in Exchange Online may pass infrastructure multiple times.

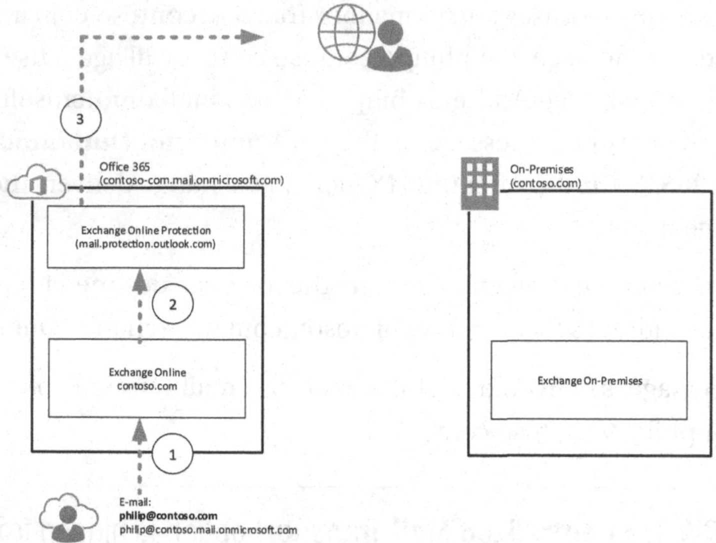

Figure 9-19. *Exchange Online, Outbound Mail Flow*

When your Exchange hybrid is configured to not use the Centralized Mail Transport, the following as shown in Figure 9-19 will happen:

1) The user philip@contoso.com submits a message to joe@fabrikam.com in Exchange Online.

2) Exchange Online sees that it is not authorized for fabrikam.com and routes the message to Exchange Online Protection for delivery.

3) Exchange Online Protection determines that fabrikam.com is external, does an MX lookup, and delivers the message to the configured host.

Caution If the mail transport does not work, verify that there are no appliances sitting in your Exchange infrastructure that may tamper with SMTP traffic, such as removing STARTTLS commands to keep the traffic unencrypted and open to inspection.

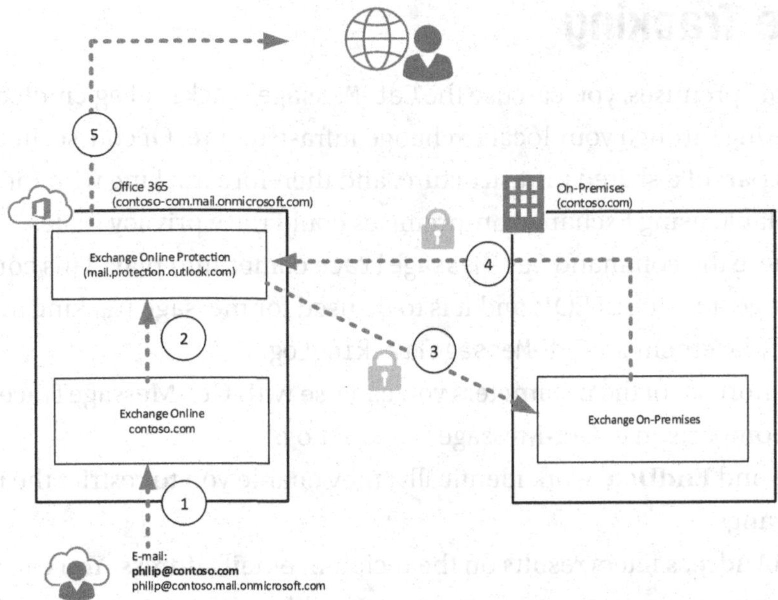

***Figure 9-20.** Exchange Online, Outbound Mail Flow with CMT*

When your Exchange hybrid deployment is configured to use Centralized Mail Transport, the following occurs as shown in Figure 9-20:

1) The user philip@contoso.com submits a message to joe@ fabrikam.com in Exchange Online.

2) Exchange Online sees it is not authorized for fabrikam.com and hands off the message to Exchange Online Protection for delivery.

3) Exchange Online Protection finds a matching connector Outbound to <Guid> which is configured to always route all messages (RouteAllMessagesViaOnPremises) to mail.contoso.com.

4) Assuming you have configured outbound email to be delivered to Exchange Online Protection and there is no connector for fabrikam.com, the message is delivered to Exchange Online Protection.

5) Exchange Online Protection determines fabrikam.com is external, does an MX lookup, and delivers the message.

Message Tracking

In Exchange on-premises, you can use the `Get-MessageTrackingLog` cmdlet to track messages passing through your local Exchange infrastructure. Of course, in Office 365, your tenant is part of a shared infrastructure, and therefore tracking with the details normally available using Exchange on-premises could raise privacy issues.

This is where the command `Get-MessageTrace` comes into play. This command extends message tracking to EOP, and it is to be used for message tracking in Exchange Online, as a replacement for `Get-MessageTrackingLog`.

Here is a short list of the parameters you can use with Get-MessageTrace and how they work in comparison to Get-MessageTrackingLog:

StartDate and **EndDate** work identically; they enable you to restrict the results to a specific date range.

RecipientAddress filters results on the recipient email address. You can specify multiple values using a comma, and you can use wildcards such as *@myexchangelabs.com.

SenderAddress is similar to RecipientAddress, but filters on the sender email address instead. Like RecipientAddress, you can use wildcards.

FromIP allows you to filter on the source IP address for inbound messages, the public IP address of the SMTP server that delivered the message.

MessageTraceID can be used in combination with RecipientAddress to uniquely identify a message trace and obtain more details. A message trace ID is generated for every message processed.

MessageId filters work identical and filters on the Message-ID header field of the message.

Status filters on the delivery status of the message. Options are None, Failed, Pending, Delivered, and Expanded. This is similar to Get-MessageTrackingLog's EventId parameter. It is not identical, as internal routing of messages will be hidden.

ToIP is new. For outbound messages, this filters on the public IP address of the destination server.

Caution You can only trace messages from the last 30 days.

For example, to retrieve all message traces of messages received between July 1, 2021, and July 2, 2021, sent to michel@myexchangelabs.com, you would use something like this:

```
Get-MessageTrace -StartDate 7/1/2021 -EndDate 7/2/2021 -Recipient michel@
myexchangelabs.com | Format-Table -AutoSize Received, SenderAddress,
RecipientAddress, Subject
```

To see all the message traces of email coming from an email domain named "microsoft.com" in the past seven days, showing only the last ten trace events, you would use

```
Get-MessageTrace -StartDate (Get-Date).AddDays(-7) -EndDate (Get-Date)
-SenderAddress '*@microsoft.com' | Select Received, MessageId, Status
| Sort-Object Received -Descending | Select -First 10 | Format-Table
-AutoSize
```

Finally, if the level of detail provided with Get-MessageTrace is not sufficient, you can retrieve more details per message using Get-MessageTraceDetail.

For example, to get the details of the last message delivered, use

```
Get-MessageTrace -Status Delivered | Sort-Object Received -Descending |
Select -First 1 | Get-MessageTraceDetail
```

An example of the output is shown in Figure 9-21. Note that you can send the output to Format-Table for more details available in the Data attribute, such as processing and anti-spam information.

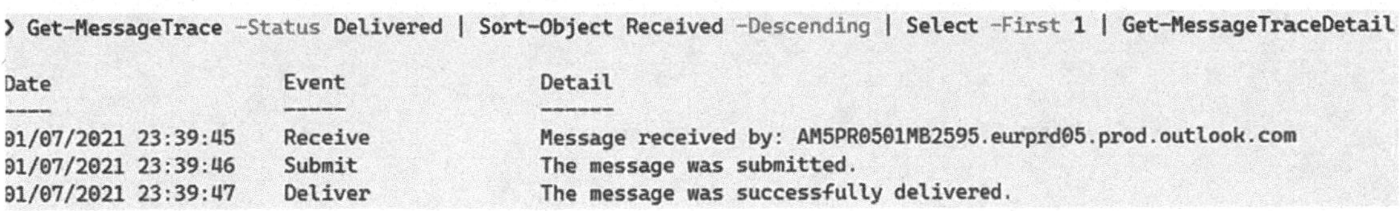

```
> Get-MessageTrace -Status Delivered | Sort-Object Received -Descending | Select -First 1 | Get-MessageTraceDetail

Date                 Event        Detail
----                 -----        ------
01/07/2021 23:39:45  Receive      Message received by: AM5PR0501MB2595.eurprd05.prod.outlook.com
01/07/2021 23:39:46  Submit       The message was submitted.
01/07/2021 23:39:47  Deliver      The message was successfully delivered.
```

Figure 9-21. *Get-MessageTraceDetail*

PART 4

Security and Compliance

CHAPTER 10

Security

Organizations still running Exchange on-premises have it running as part of their business-critical IT infrastructure, either on-premises or in a hybrid configuration. In both cases, there are uptime requirements, and these requirements cannot be met without having the environment properly secured.

For example, depending on your scenario, you may need to arrange protocols and safety measures for communications with parties over the public network—communications that, by default, are in principle open and readable to others. Also, you may wish to lock down the environment by reducing the attack surface, through limiting operations to services and protocols required, or by running Exchange Server on Windows Server core to remove dependencies on libraries which may contain vulnerabilities. Additionally, you may wish to integrate Exchange with solutions such as Windows Defender, to counter zero-day exploits.

Since Exchange 2007, Microsoft has positioned Exchange Server as "secure by default." With the Trustworthy Computing initiative which started in 2002, Microsoft began integrating Security Development Lifecycle (SDL) principles into their development process. These efforts have involved a security review for each feature and component, during which even elementary aspects like default settings have been discussed.

This "secure by default" approach not only meant changes in default settings like the POP3 service; it also instigated architectural changes or introduced features such as the Role-Based Access Control (RBAC), Mailbox servers leveraging self-signed certificates to secure internal communications.

Another thing to note is that starting with Exchange 2019, Exchange has a shorter life span than its predecessors, seven years instead of the usual ten years. This is likely influenced by the rapid development in cloud technology and maintainability of these critical systems, including keeping things secure as possible.

M. de Rooij and J. Wesselius, *Pro Exchange 2019 and 2016 Administration*,
https://doi.org/10.1007/978-1-4842-7331-9_10

In this chapter, we will discuss the following security-related features among other topics:

- Role-Based Access Control
- Split permissions
- Hybrid Modern Authentication
- Multi-factor Authentication
- Message hygiene

With a complex product as Exchange Server, and so intertwined with security matters on other levels, there is always the question of how to cover security. We chose to consider security in context of other topics throughout this book, except where it becomes complicated or is complementary to other functionality. So, if you are looking for publishing Exchange, that can be found in Chapter 3, but topics such as Role-Based Access Control and Hybrid Modern Authentication are contained in this chapter.

Caution Again stating this in the context of this security chapter as well, but one of the most important security measures is to keep your Exchange on-premises servers current, deploying recent Cumulative Updates, as well as keeping things up to date for the operating system and middleware such as the .NET Framework and Visual C++ libraries. At the time of writing, we are few months past the global HAFNIUM crisis, where a substantial number of Internet-facing Exchange servers were compromised with backdoor software. What became visible was that keeping business-critical software up to date is still a problem for many organizations. Shortly after Microsoft released patches for the current Exchange versions, patches were also released for every Cumulative Update since 2017, as the impact of HAFNIUM in relation to organizations still running CUs dating back to 2017 became clear. For more information, see `https://bit.ly/HafniumEx`.

Role-Based Access Control

Before Exchange Server 2010, Exchange had a limited permissions and delegation model. That model grouped around a few security groups (three in Exchange 2003, five in Exchange 2007), and the approach was simplistic and task oriented. For finer-grained permissions, organizations had to resort to measures like using Access Control Lists (ACLs) to restrict permissions in Active Directory. While this worked back then, it could become complex easily and lead to complications when upgrading to newer versions of Exchange which did not support this model. Meanwhile, the predecessor of its role-based access control saw daylight as Authorization Manager, which was made available for Windows Server 2003 and was a role-based security framework for .NET applications.

Role-Based Access Control (RBAC) was introduced in Exchange 2010 and, as the name implies, is a role-based access control permissions model. It allows for fine-grained control over the Exchange environment and underlying Active Directory objects, which cmdlets can be used, and even which parameters are available for a role.

Note Edge Transport servers and its functionality are not part of RBAC security since they typically are not a member server in Active Directory.

The implementation of RBAC revolved around the Universal Security Group (USG) Exchange Trusted Subsystem. That group is effectively managing the Exchange ecosystem, as it not only has full access rights on every Exchange object in the organization but also has permission to manage objects on the Active Directory level by being a member of the local Administrators security group and the Windows Permissions Security Group. All installed Exchange 2019 servers, or more specifically their computer accounts, are members of the Exchange Trusted Subsystem.

Through the RBAC system, you are effectively proxying your actions through Exchange Server, which determines what goes through and what goes not, depending on your role in RBAC. For example, your RBAC role determines ones ability to manage distribution groups or modify its properties, such as the display name. This not only applies to administrators (administrative roles) but to end users as well (user roles). An example of the latter is the ability to manage your distribution groups or change your own display name property.

The RBAC model is based on the concept of assigning who can do what and where, as follows:

- A role is a set of tasks one can perform (what).
- A role group is a collection of roles (who).
- To limit the scope of roles, one can assign scopes (where).

While Exchange 2019 contains predefined roles and role groups that suffice for most organizations, it allows the creation of custom roles and custom role groups. These custom roles can be assigned through Exchange Admin Center or Exchange Management Shell (see Figure 10-1). Creating custom elements for RBAC can only be done through the Exchange Management Shell.

The basic RBAC configuration of administrator or user roles employing predefined objects or changing memberships can be accomplished by using EAC. These options are in EAC ➤ Permissions ➤ Admin Roles. User roles function to manage assignment policies, which are discussed later in this chapter.

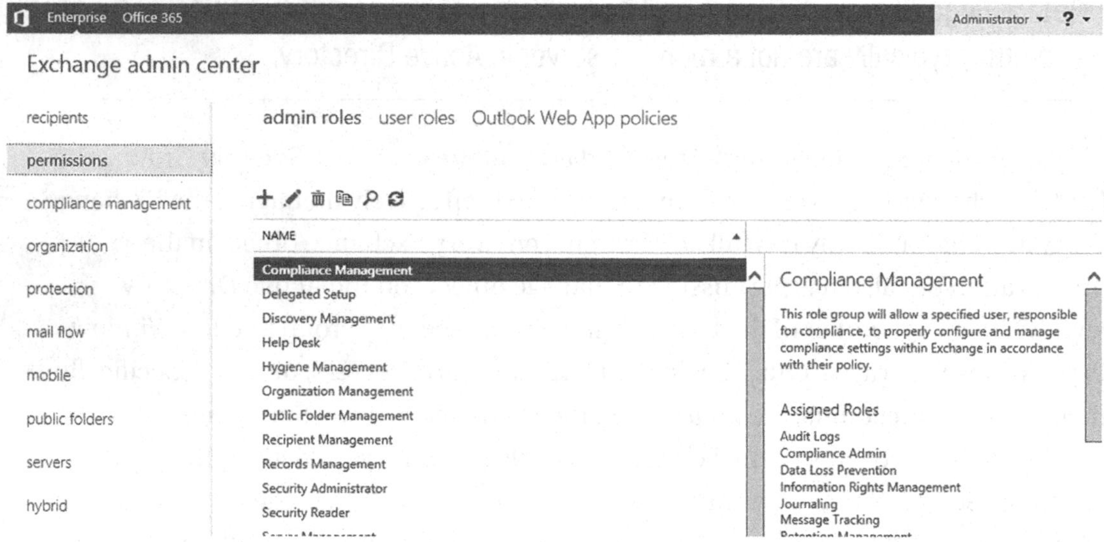

Figure 10-1. *Options for role-based access control in EAC*

Apart from opening the Exchange Management Shell shortcut, to load an Exchange Management Shell in a supported way and which will honor the RBAC configuration, you have two options:

1. Load the functions from the RemoteExchange.ps1 script, which by default is located in the $exbin subfolder, by dot-sourcing it, then call the function to connect to an automatically selected Exchange server:

   ```
   . "C:\Program Files\Microsoft\Exchange Server\v15\bin\
   RemoteExchange.ps1"
   Connect-ExchangeServer -auto
   ```

   You can also connect to a specific Exchange server, specifying the FQDN:

   ```
   Connect-ExchangeServer -ServerFqdn ex1.contoso.com
   ```

2. Connect to Exchange remotely by setting up a remoting session, as follows:

   ```
   $Session= New-PSSession -ConfigurationName
   Microsoft.Exchange -ConnectionUri <FQDN>/PowerShell/
   Import-PSSession $Session
   ```

Caution Loading the Exchange snap-in module directly from PowerShell using Add-PSSnapIn Microsoft.Exchange.* is not supported. This not only bypasses RBAC, but it also may result in non-working Exchange cmdlets as you might be missing permissions in your current security context compared to the permissions through the Exchange Trusted Subsystem using RBAC. However, there is circumstances where this is your only option, such as RBAC misconfiguration.

After connecting to Exchange PowerShell, you will notice your session imports cmdlets into your session. The cmdlets imported are defined by the RBAC role assigned to you. You might notice some cmdlets by default are not available to you, even as an administrator, such as the New-MailboxImportRequest cmdlet.

We will now continue explaining the RBAC model through management roles (what), management scopes (where), and role groups (who). After this, you should be able to connect these pieces of the puzzle and define or troubleshoot your own roles or management role assignments.

Caution RBAC objects are stored in Active Directory, more precisely in the Microsoft Exchange Security Groups OU. Directly manipulating these objects in Active Directory is not supported. Also, if your environment consists of multiple Active Directory sites, take replication latencies into account when making changes to RBAC configuration.

RBAC Components

The components used in the RBAC model and their relationships are shown in Figure 10-2. This section discusses the underlying components, their relationship, and how to put these together. Knowing the concepts, components, and possibilities allows you to troubleshoot or customize RBAC to tailor to specific requirements of your organization.

When planning for RBAC customization, keep the following in mind:

- Determine the organizational structure. In most cases, job responsibilities follow the hierarchy of the organization. Distinguish between role levels, for example, senior vs. junior.
- Define the roles in the organization by detailing their responsibilities and tasks. Categorize the roles, for example, support and sales.
- Attempt to map the roles to corresponding management roles. Identify the gaps as potential new management roles.
- Document the permissions requirements for each position.

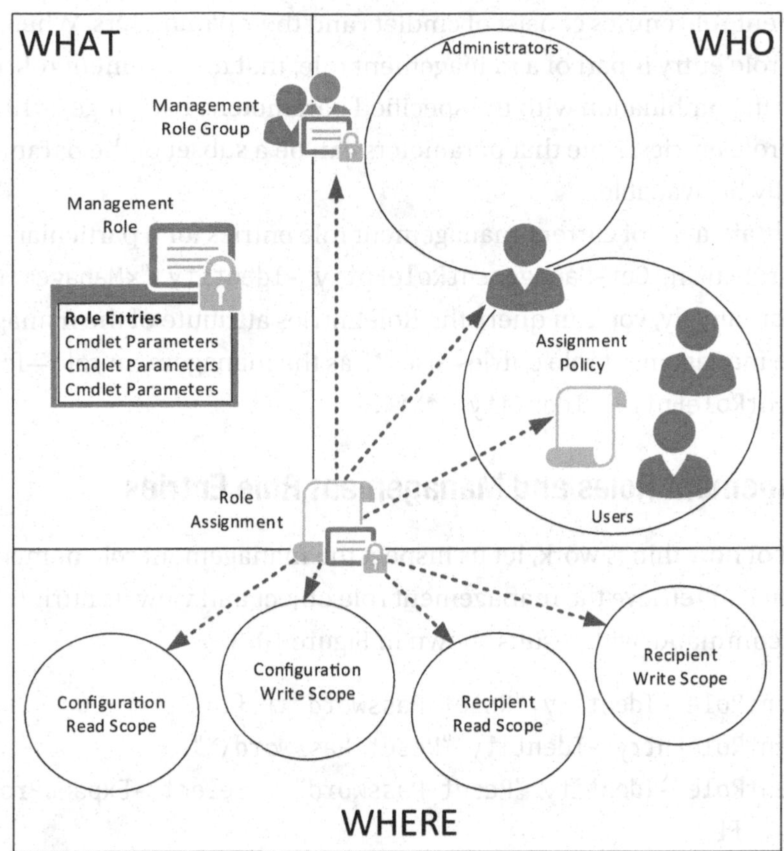

Figure 10-2. *Role-Based Access Control components*

Note To manage RBAC, with the exception of unscoped management roles, you need to be assigned the Organization Management role group. Be careful, though, as the Organization Management role group is managed by the Organization Management role group, and you could create a situation locking yourself out by removing yourself.

The What

The "what" component is set by the management roles and management role entries. A management role defines the job, with its set of cmdlets and parameters that can be used. Exchange 2019 has 94 predefined management roles. You can obtain a list of these by using `Get-ManagementRole`.

Management role entries consist of cmdlets and their parameters. When the management role entry is part of a management role, that management role can use those cmdlets in combination with the specified parameters. Exchange 2019 has 2822 management role entries. Note that parameters can be a subset of the parameters that would normally be available.

You can obtain a list of current management role entries for a particular management role using `Get-ManagementRoleEntry -Identity "<Management Role>\*"`. Alternatively, you can query the RoleEntries attribute of the management role. To view all the management role entries, use "*" as the management role—for example, `Get-ManagementRoleEntry -Identity "*\*"`.

Using Management Roles and Management Role Entries

To get an idea of how things work, let us inspect the management role named "Reset Password." You can retrieve the management role object and view its attributes by using the following command, with results shown in Figure 10-3:

```
Get-ManagementRole -Identity "Reset Password" | fl
Get-ManagementRoleEntry -Identity "Reset Password\*"
Get-ManagementRole -Identity "Reset Password" | Select -ExpandProperty
RoleEntries | fl
```

```
[PS] C:\>Get-ManagementRoleEntry -Identity "Reset Password\*"

Name                          Role                       Parameters
----                          ----                       ----------
Set-Mailbox                   Reset Password             {Password, ResetPasswordOnNextLogon, RoomMailboxPassword}


[PS] C:\>Get-ManagementRole -Identity "Reset Password" | Select -ExpandProperty RoleEntries | fl


PSSnapinName : Microsoft.Exchange.Management.PowerShell.E2010
Name         : Set-Mailbox
Parameters   : {Password, ResetPasswordOnNextLogon, RoomMailboxPassword}
```

Figure 10-3. *Reset Password's management role entries*

The latter two cmdlets show that the Reset Password management role permits the use of the cmdlet *Set-Mailbox,* in conjunction with the parameters *Password, ResetPasswordOnNextLogon,* and *RoomMailboxPassword.* Simply said, users with the Reset Password role can use Set-Mailbox to configure the password for user mailboxes or rooms and configure the requirement for users to reset the password after the next logon.

Custom Management Roles

You can create custom management roles by using the New-ManagementRole cmdlet. In Exchange, there are two types of management roles: normal and unscoped. The normal management role requires you to specify an existing role, which will become known as the parent. This can be a predefined management role or another custom management role. The parent is used as a template but also functions as a limiter; you can remove any superfluous cmdlets or parameters at any level, but you cannot add cmdlets or parameters that are not part of the parent management role.

Caution When you assign a Set-* cmdlet to a management role, you also need to assign the corresponding Get-* cmdlet. In other words, you need to be able to read things you also need to configure.

In this example, you will create a simple custom role for mail recipients. This predefined role is used for managing mail-enabled objects in the organization. You use this command:

```
New-ManagementRole -Name 'Custom Mail Recipients' -Parent 'Mail Recipients'
```

You can verify the capabilities of this new custom role, which will be identical to the capabilities of the Mail Recipients role, by using

```
Get-ManagementRoleEntry -Identity 'Custom Mail Recipients\*'
```

Now, suppose you want to remove the capability of using one of the role entries. To do that, you use the Remove-ManagementRoleEntry cmdlet, specifying <Management Role>\<Management Role Entry>, like this:

```
Remove-ManagementRoleEntry -Identity 'Custom Mail Recipients\Set-UserPhoto'
```

Caution When stripping role entries from a custom management role that will be using EAC, be careful not to remove the Set-ADServerSettings cmdlet. This cmdlet is used during initialization of the session to enable the View Entire Forest option needed to discover the permissions of the currently logged-on user.

Adding or Removing Parameters

To modify the parameters which you can use, use the Set ManagementRoleEntry cmdlet together with AddParameter or RemoveParameter depending on the required operation, as well as Parameter specifying the parameters. For example, if you want to remove the ability to use the preview parameter with Set-UserPhoto, you use this command:

```
Set-ManagementRoleEntry -Identity 'Custom Mail Recipients\Set-UserPhoto'
-Parameter Preview -RemoveParameter
```

To reinstate this preview parameter, you use

```
Set-ManagementRoleEntry -Identity 'Custom Mail Recipients\Set-UserPhoto'
-Parameter Preview -AddParameter
```

As mentioned earlier, re-adding Preview works here because it is also available in the parent Mail Recipients role.

To quickly retrieve roles that use certain cmdlets, parameters, scripts, or script parameters, you can use the Get-ManagementRole cmdlet with the parameter Cmdlet, CmdletParameters, Script, or ScriptParameters.

You can also use GetChildren to retrieve roles that are "children" of the parent role or use Recurse to return a role and all of its offspring. For example, this returns all roles that allow Set-Mailbox:

```
Get-ManagementRole -Cmdlet Set-Mailbox
```

This cmdlet will return all roles allowing the use of a parameter called EmailAddresses with any cmdlets:

```
Get-ManagementRole -CmdletParameters EmailAddresses
```

Unscoped Top-Level Management Roles

A special management role is the unscoped top-level management role. This is a management role which purpose is to provide administrators or specific user accounts permissions to execute scripts or non-Exchange cmdlets. As the name implies, unscoped roles have no scope, as they have no related parent role, contrary to normal management roles.

To create an unscoped management role, you need to be assigned to the Unscoped Role Management Group. To quickly assign the administrator account to this group, you use

```
New-ManagementRoleAssignment -Name 'Unscoped Role Management-Administrator'
-User 'Administrator' -Role 'Unscoped Role Management'
```

If you want to grant permission to a group, use the SecurityGroup parameter instead of User:

```
New-ManagementRoleAssignment -Name 'Unscoped Role Management-Organization
Management' -SecurityGroup 'Organization Management' -Role 'Unscoped Role
Management'
```

Note You need to restart the EAC or the EMS session to see the effects of assigning new permissions to your currently logged-on account.

It is best practice to name the management role assignment by combining the name of the management role group and the user or group you have assigned the role group to. When not specified, this combination will be used as the management role assignment.

Now, when granted the Unscoped Role Management assignment, you can specify the switch UnscopedTopLevel when using the New-ManagementRole cmdlet:

```
New-ManagementRole -Name 'Maintenance Scripts' -UnscopedTopLevel
```

Since we do not use templates like with normal management roles, the newly created unscoped management role will initially be empty regarding permissions. The account creating the unscoped management role will initially get assigned to it, which is necessary to perform delegation of the role to other accounts. It is also something you may notice when, for example, you want to remove the group or assignment. More on that later.

Unscoped management roles are special, in that they allow you to assign scripts or non-Exchange cmdlet permissions to run. The scripts you want to use must reside in the **$exinstall\RemoteScripts** folder, though. When the default Exchange installation folder is used, this location will resolve to **C:\Program Files\Microsoft\Exchange Server\v15\RemoteScripts**.

Note The scripts you want to use with unscoped management roles need to reside in the $exinstall\RemoteScripts folder and need to be present on every relevant Exchange server, that is, on all servers or only on those within a specific region or site depending on your role or permissions.

To allow the execution of scripts via management role entries for an unscoped management role, specify its name as well as any parameters you would allow:

```
Add-ManagementRoleEntry -Identity '<role name>\<script name>' -Parameters
<param1, param2,..> -Type Script -UnscopedTopLevel
```

Note You need to specify every individual parameter required; there is no wildcard option to add all possible parameters at once.

For example, to allow the unscoped management role Maintenance Scripts to execute the script ClearLogs.ps1 using the parameter Days, after distributing this script to every RemoteScripts folder, use the following cmdlet to allow it through a role entry:

```
Add-ManagementRoleEntry -Identity 'Maintenance Scripts\ClearLogs.ps1'
-Parameters 'Days' -Type Script -UnscopedTopLevel
```

Caution When adding scripts to role entries, know that the cmdlet only performs basic validation for the parameters specified. It is not dynamic, so any changes to the script or removal of the script will not be detected, and you need to adjust the related role entries manually.

Earlier, we created an unscoped management role group Maintenance Scripts, which we have given permission to run the script ClearLogs.ps1. All we need to do now is create a role group for the role we created, and add accounts which need to run this script to this group:

```
New-RoleGroup -Name 'RunMaintenanceScripts' -Roles 'Maintenance Scripts'
Add-RoleGroupMember -Identity 'RunMaintenanceScripts' -Member svcExchange
```

The output of these cmdlets as well as the result is shown in Figure 10-4.

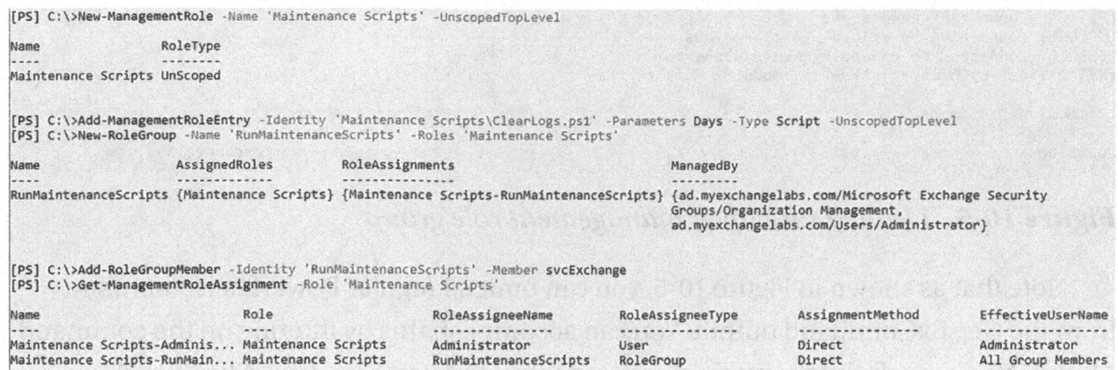

[PS] C:\>New-ManagementRole -Name 'Maintenance Scripts' -UnscopedTopLevel
Name RoleType
---- --------
Maintenance Scripts UnScoped
[PS] C:\>Add-ManagementRoleEntry -Identity 'Maintenance Scripts\ClearLogs.ps1' -Parameters Days -Type Script -UnscopedTopLevel
[PS] C:\>New-RoleGroup -Name 'RunMaintenanceScripts' -Roles 'Maintenance Scripts'
Name AssignedRoles RoleAssignments ManagedBy
---- ------------- --------------- ---------
RunMaintenanceScripts {Maintenance Scripts} {Maintenance Scripts-RunMaintenanceScripts} {ad.myexchangelabs.com/Microsoft Exchange Security Groups/Organization Management, ad.myexchangelabs.com/Users/Administrator}
[PS] C:\>Add-RoleGroupMember -Identity 'RunMaintenanceScripts' -Member svcExchange
[PS] C:\>Get-ManagementRoleAssignment -Role 'Maintenance Scripts'
Name Role RoleAssigneeName RoleAssigneeType AssignmentMethod EffectiveUserName
---- ---- ---------------- ---------------- ---------------- -----------------
Maintenance Scripts-Adminis... Maintenance Scripts Administrator User Direct Administrator
Maintenance Scripts-RunMain... Maintenance Scripts RunMaintenanceScripts RoleGroup Direct All Group Members

***Figure 10-4.** Creating an unscoped management role group*

Notice that there are two assignments created, each with a different role assignment delegation type (property not shown):

- The account creating the role gets a DelegationOrgWide type assignment. This assignment is automatic after role creation, allowing the creator to delegate permissions for the role.
- The assignment created using New-RoleGroup is a normal type assignment. This allows the role assignee to execute the role entries associated with that role group.

Tip If the user executing the Add-RoleGroupMember cmdlet is not part of the ManagedBy property of the role group (i.e., accounts that can manage their membership), you need to specify the BypassSecurityGroupManagerCheck switch to bypass built-in group management checks.

Now, when svcExchange opens a remote EMS session, it will have only the ClearLogs.ps1 script at its disposal, as shown in Figure 10-5. You can quickly test this using the Connect-ExchangeServer cmdlet, with the User and Prompt parameters to provide the account name, and let it prompt for the password. The Auto switch is added to make it connect to any available server:

```
Connect-ExchangeServer -Auto -User 'svcExchange' -Prompt
```

```
[PS] C:\>Connect-ExchangeServer -Auto -Prompt -UserName ad\svcExchange
VERBOSE: Connecting to ex1.ad.myexchangelabs.com.
VERBOSE: Connected to ex1.ad.myexchangelabs.com.
[PS] C:\>Get-ExCommand |Where {$_.Module -NotLike 'Microsoft.PowerShell.*' -and $_.Module -notlike 'PSReadline'}

CommandType     Name                                               Version    Source
-----------     ----                                               -------    ------
Function        ClearLogs.ps1                                      1.0        ex1.ad.myexchangelabs.com
```

Figure 10-5. *Limited unscoped management role group*

Note that as shown in Figure 10-5, you can omit all regular PowerShell commands from the Get-ExCommand output. You can accomplish this by filtering on the command ModuleName, excluding commands offered through Microsoft PowerShell.* and PSReadLine modules, as follows:

```
Get-ExCommand | Where { $_.Module -notlike 'Microsoft.PowerShell.*' -and
$_.Module -notlike 'PSReadLine' }
```

Note also that you allowed only the role to execute the script. There is no single Exchange cmdlet available. If you want to be able to execute Exchange cmdlets through this script or directly, you need to allow them as well, by adding them as role entries using New-ManagementRoleEntry.

This may take a while to set up, as you need to go through scripts to collect information on cmdlet and parameter usage, but it grants you very fine-grained control over permissions, which should make your security officer happy and may prevent disasters from occurring.

Caution When allowing execution of scripts through roles, you need to allow cmdlets and parameters referenced in the script as well. When you overlook this requirement, these will not be available in the security context of the role, and your script will not function.

You can also use unscoped management roles to grant permissions to execute cmdlets provided through other modules as well. In those cases, use the following syntax:

```
Add-ManagementRoleEntry -Identity <role name>\<cmdlet name> -PSSnapinName
<snap-in name> -Parameters <param1, param2, ..> -Type
Cmdlet -UnscopedTopLevel
```

For example, assume you want to grant permission to use a cmdlet named Get-QADUser with the parameter Identity. The cmdlet is part of the PowerShell snap-in named Quest.ActiveRoles.ADManagement. You can create a management role entry as follows:

```
Add-ManagementRoleEntry -Identity 'Maintenance Scripts\Get-QADUser' -Parameters
'Identity' -PSSnapinName Quest.ActiveRoles.ADManagement -UnscopedTopLevel
```

Note that this module needs to be installed and registered on all relevant Exchange servers which could be running the cmdlet.

Cleaning Up

The cmdlet to remove script or non-Exchange cmdlet assignments for unscoped management roles is similar to removing normal management role entries:

```
Remove-ManagementRoleEntry -Identity 'Maintenance Scripts\ClearLogs.ps1'
```

Only user-defined management roles can be removed. Before you can remove a management role, you first need to remove any dependencies on that management role or use the Recurse parameter to perform a cascaded delete:

```
Remove-ManagementRole -Identity 'Custom Mail Recipients' -Recurse
```

If you want to remove an unscoped top-level management role, don't forget to specify the parameter UnScopedToplevel as well, for example:

```
Remove-ManagementRole -Identity 'Maintenance Scripts' -UnScopedTop
Level -Recurse
```

The Where

The "where" component determines where the cmdlets are allowed to read or change objects. From an Active Directory perspective, this scope can be an organizational unit, an Active Directory site, or the entire Exchange organization. The latter is the default scope. It can also be more tailored to specific subsets of recipients, Exchange servers, or databases, targeting objects with specific properties.

RBAC defines two types of management scopes:

- **Regular or non-exclusive scopes** define which objects in Active Directory can be accessed—for example, on the Organizational Unit (OU) or the server level.
- **Exclusive scopes** are like regular scopes, except that they include access to Active Directory objects. Only members of groups with exclusive access can access those Active Directory objects; others will be denied access.

When defining scopes, be aware of the following rules and terminology:

- When you create a custom management role, it will inherit the non-exclusive scope configuration of the parent management role. These inheritable scopes are called implicit, as they are set by the parent.
- Custom scopes are called explicit scopes, as they are not inherited and explicitly defined.

More on implicit and explicit scopes later in the section.

Note Unscoped top-level management roles have no scope definition. The scope properties of these roles will state "Not Applicable."

Regular Scopes

There are two types of regular scopes: recipient and configuration scopes. A recipient scope refers to recipient objects, such as mailboxes, distribution groups, or mail-enabled users. A configuration scope refers to Exchange configuration objects, such as an Exchange server or mailbox databases. For each of these types, you can configure a read or a write scope. Together, this enabled you to assign the following types of scopes to every management role:

- **Recipient read scope** determines which recipient objects the assignee is allowed to read from Active Directory.
- **Recipient write scope** determines which recipient objects the assignee is allowed to create or modify from Active Directory.

- **Configuration read scope** determines which configuration objects the assignee is allowed to read from Active Directory.
- **Configuration write scope** determines which configuration objects, such as Exchange servers or databases, the assignee is allowed to create or modify from Active Directory.

Note An assigned write scope cannot exceed the boundaries of the related read scope. In other words, you cannot configure what you cannot view.

Implicit Scopes

Implicit scopes are predefined for the management roles and are configured through the ImplicitRecipientReadScope, ImplicitRecipientWriteScope, ImplicitConfigReadScope, and ImplicitConfigWriteScope properties of the management role. Child management roles inherit the management scopes of the parent. When a management role is used in a management role assignment, the implicit scopes of the management role apply to the assignment, unless the assignment has explicit scopes defined (which will be explained a bit later). A configured explicit scope will override the implicit scopes, making it an uninheritable explicit scope. The only exception to this override rule is implicit read scopes, which always prevail over explicit scopes. Table 10-1 lists all the available implicit scope definitions.

Table 10-1. *Implicit Scope Definitions*

Name	Recipient Configuration	Description
Organization	Read/write	Recipient objects in the Exchange organization
MyGAL	Read	Read the properties of any recipient within the current user's GAL
Self	Read/write	The current user's properties
MyDistributionGroups	Read/write	Distribution groups managed by the current user
OrganizationConfig	Read/write	Exchange server or database objects in the Exchange organization
None		Blocks a scope

Explicit Scopes

Explicit scopes are user-configurable scopes that override implicit write scopes. Explicit scopes are defined through management role assignments, allowing implicit roles to be used consistently and persisting through inheritance, while allowing for exceptions through configured explicit scopes.

Management role assignments have specific properties for predefined relative scopes. Those scopes are a subset of the implicit scopes that are relative to the role assignee. Options for predefined relative scopes are a subset of the implicit scopes, as follows:

- **Organization** allows assignees to modify recipients in the entire Exchange organization. For example, if a role allows configuration of the display name and user photo, this scope will allow configuring those properties for all recipients in the Exchange organization.
- **Self** allows assignees to modify their own properties. For example, if a role allows configuration of the display name and user photo, assigning this scope will allow that action only for the assignee.
- **MyDistributionGroups** allows assignees to create and manage distribution groups where they are configured as an owner through the ManagedBy property.

Predefined relative scopes are assigned to management role assignments using the RecipientRelativeWriteScope property.

Custom Scopes

When implicit scopes, optionally in combination with predefined relative scopes, meet your requirements, you can use a custom scope. This allows you to define specific targets, such as particular organizational units, recipients, or databases. As with predefined relative scopes, custom scopes override the implicit scopes, except for the read scope. To create custom scopes which can be reused for more than one management role, you can define and assign management scope objects. This also makes them more manageable. More on management scopes later in this section.

When you want to define custom scopes, you can choose from the following types of custom scopes:

- **OU scope** targets recipients within the configured OU. It is configured through the RecipientOrganizationalUnitScope property of management role assignments.
- **Recipient filter** scope uses a management scope object to filter recipients based on properties such as recipient type, department, manager, or location by using an OPATH filter. The filter is configured through the RecipientRestrictionFilter property of the management scope. In addition, you can combine the recipient filter with RecipientRoot to define the filter starting point. The management scope is configured through the CustomRecipientWriteScope property.

Tip When you specify an alternative root location for the recipient filter scope using RecipientRoot, you need to specify RecipientRoot in canonical form (contoso.com/nl/users), not the distinguished name.

- **Configuration scope** uses a management scope object to target specific servers based on server lists or filterable properties, such as the Active Directory site of the server role, or to target specific databases based on database lists or filterable database properties.
- **Server** scope is configured using the ServerRestrictionFilter parameter using an OPATH filter, or the ServerList parameter. Note that configuration objects related to the server, like receive connectors or virtual directories, can also be managed for servers that are in scope.
- **Database scope** is configured using the DatabaseRestrictionFilter parameter using an OPATH filter, or the DatabaseList parameter. Database configuration settings like quota settings, maintenance schedule, or database mounting can be managed for databases that are in scope. In addition, the assignee can also create mailboxes in databases that are in scope.

> **Caution** Defined scopes related to Active Directory locations are not dynamic. For example, when you move or rename organizational units, make sure you adjust any related scopes as well.

Management Scopes

Now we touched on all the possible elements that may come into play when constructing and configuring management scopes, let us talk about the management scopes themselves. We will also provide a few examples to improve understanding of the subject and provide insights on possibilities.

Management scopes are created using the New-ManagementScope cmdlet. Depending on whether you want to provide a recipient scope or server scope, you provide the corresponding parameters and the filter value itself.

For example, to create a scope for the following objects:

- All recipients who are members of a certain group named Staff. This can be achieved by specifying the distinguishedName of the group, for example, cn=Staff,ou=Users,dc=contoso,dc=com.
- They must reside below a top-level OU named NL in contoso.com, which canonical definition would be contoso.com/NL.

you would use

```
New-ManagementScope -Name 'Scope-NL-Staff' -RecipientRoot 'contoso.com/NL'
-RecipientRestrictionFilter {membergroup -eq 'cn=Staff,ou=Users,dc=contoso,
dc=com'}
```

Along the same lines, to create a scope for the Active Directory site London, you could use

```
New-ManagementScope -Name 'Scope-Site London' -ServerRestrictionFilter
{ServerSite -eq 'CN=London,CN=Sites,CN=Configuration,DC=contoso,DC=com'}
```

To create a scope for a fixed set of servers, which can be accomplished using the ServerList parameter, you use

```
New-ManagementScope -Name 'Servers Amsterdam' -ServerList AMS-EXCH01,AMS-EXCH02
```

To create a scope for a database starting with "NL-", you use

```
New-ManagementScope -Name 'Databases NL' -DatabaseRestrictionFilter
{Name -like 'NL-*'}
```

Note that recipient or server filters use OPATH definitions for recipient or configuration restrictions. More information on scope filtering can be found at `http://bit.ly/RBACScopeFilters`.

Exclusive Scopes

The last type of scope to discuss is the exclusive scopes. Exclusive scopes target a specific set of recipients or configuration objects in Active Directory. These objects then become inaccessible for other management role assignments when accessing the same type of object—hence the word exclusive. Even if other assignments have those objects in scope, if they are targeted with an exclusive scope, they can only be managed through the management roles with the exclusive scope assignment.

For example, if you define an exclusive recipient assignment for a top-level OU named NL, other assignments will be blocked from accessing the NL container structure, including assignments with an organization-wide scope. Common usage for roles with these scopes are high-profile recipients, for which exclusive manage recipient roles are assigned, thus blocking the management of these recipients by other management roles.

To create an exclusive scope, use the Exclusive switch when creating or reconfiguring a management role assignment. For example, to create an exclusive scope using a recipient filter for all recipients located in the VIP OU tree, you can use this command:

```
New-ManagementScope -Name 'Scope-Exec Recipients' -RecipientRoot 'contoso.
com/VIP' RecipientRestrictionFilter {Name -like '*'} -Exclusive
```

Now suppose you want to assign a group called Exec Admins the role of Mail Recipients, using the scope you've just created. You would use the **ExclusiveRecipientWriteScope** instead of the **CustomRecipientWriteScope** for the exclusive scope:

```
New-ManagementRoleAssignment -SecurityGroup 'Exec Admins'
-Role 'Mail Recipients' -ExclusiveRecipientWriteScope 'Exec Recipients'
```

The reason for using ExclusiveRecipientWriteScope is to confirm that you are specifying an exclusive scope. If you use CustomRecipientWriteScope, Exchange will notify you that the scope you have specified is exclusive. This way, Exchange not only takes care of configuring the CustomRecipientWriteScope with the scope you provided, but it also sets the RecipientWriteScope to the ExclusiveRecipientScope type to indicate that the scope is exclusive.

You can check the previously set assignment using Get-ManagementRoleAssignment, knowing that Exchange will use the <Role>-<Role Assignee Name> as the assignment name. If that name already exists, it will append sequence numbers. To check, use the following command; Figure 10-6 shows a similar example of the output:

```
Get-ManagementRoleAssignment -Identity 'Mail Recipients-Exec Admins'| fl
*role*,*scope*,*assign*
```

```
[PS] C:\Tools>Get-ManagementRoleAssignment -Identity 'Mail Recipients-Exec Admins' | fl *role*,*scope*,*assign*

RoleAssigneeType              : SecurityGroup
RoleAssignee                  : ad.myexchangelabs.com/NL/Exec Admins
Role                          : Mail Recipients
RoleAssignmentDelegationType  : Regular
RoleAssigneeName              : Exec Admins
CustomRecipientWriteScope     : Scope-Exec Recipients
CustomConfigWriteScope        :
RecipientReadScope            : Organization
ConfigReadScope               : OrganizationConfig
RecipientWriteScope           : ExclusiveRecipientScope
ConfigWriteScope              : OrganizationConfig
AssignmentMethod              : Direct
AssignmentChain               :
RoleAssigneeType              : SecurityGroup
RoleAssignee                  : ad.myexchangelabs.com/NL/Exec Admins
RoleAssignmentDelegationType  : Regular
RoleAssigneeName              : Exec Admins
```

Figure 10-6. *View of the management role assignment*

As shown, the members of the Exec Recipients group are now the only users allowed to manage recipients in the VIP OU (and below). Organization-level managers of Mail Recipients, including administrators with organization management permissions, cannot.

Note Exclusive scopes can overlap. Objects that are part of multiple exclusive scopes can be managed by every assignee of those scopes.

The interaction of regular scopes and exclusive scopes and the possibility to overlap are shown in Figure 10-7.

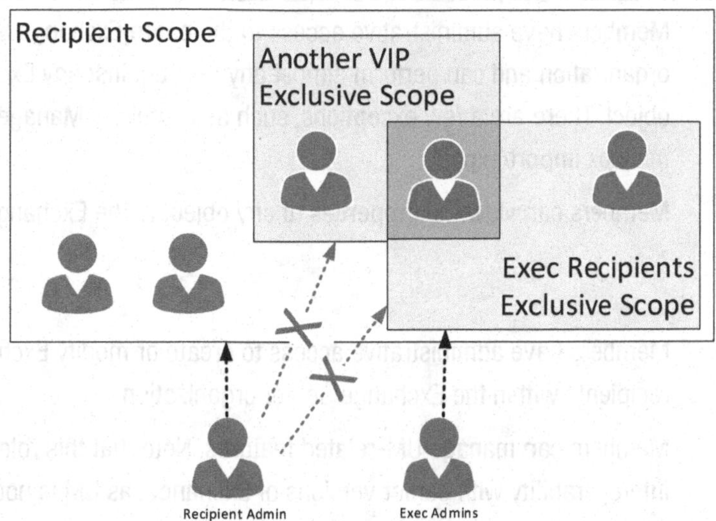

***Figure 10-7.** Regular and exclusive scopes*

The Who

The "who" component in Role-Based Access Control defines who will be assigned the permissions. This information is stored in the management role groups, or role groups which are Universal Security Group (USG) with special flags to indicate they are role groups. By assigning role groups to one or more management roles, you are effectively granting those role groups the permissions that are part of the management role's list of management role entries.

Table 10-2 lists all built-in role group definitions, as well as short descriptions of their predefined capabilities.

Note A management role group is a Universal Security Group with msExchRecipientTypeDetails set to 1073741824.

Table 10-2. *Built-in Role Groups*

Role Group	Description
Organization Management	Members have administrative access to the entire Exchange Server organization and can perform almost any task against any Exchange Server object. There are a few exceptions, such as Discovery Management and mailbox import/export.
View-Only Organization Management	Members can view the properties of any object in the Exchange organization.
Recipient Management	Members have administrative access to create or modify Exchange Server recipients within the Exchange Server organization.
UM Management	Members can manage UM-related features. Note that this role group is for interoperability with earlier versions of Exchange, as UM is not available on Exchange 2019.
Help Desk	Members can view and modify the OWA options of any user in the organization, such as modifying the display name or phone number.
Hygiene Management	Members can configure the anti-virus and anti-spam features of Exchange Server. Third-party programs that integrate with Exchange Server can add service accounts to this role group to grant those programs access to the cmdlets required to retrieve and configure the Exchange configuration.
Records Management	Members can configure compliance features, such as retention policy tags, message classifications, and transport rules.
Discovery Management	Members can perform searches of mailboxes in the Exchange organization for data that meets specific criteria. In addition, they can also configure legal holds on mailboxes.
Public Folder Management	Members can manage public folders on Exchange Server.
Server Management	Members can configure server-specific configuration of transport, client access, and mailbox features such as database copies, certificates, transport queues and Send connectors, virtual directories, and client access protocols. This role group also allows to manage UM settings on previous versions of Exchange Server.

(*continued*)

Table 10-2. (*continued*)

Role Group	Description
Delegated Setup	Members can deploy servers running Exchange Server that have been previously provisioned by a member of the Organization Management role group.
Compliance Management	Members can configure and manage Exchange compliance settings in accordance with organization policy.

Custom Role Group

In addition to the built-in role groups, you can create your own role group. To create a role group, you must be a member of the Organization Management role group. To manage a role group, you must be the manager of the role group, which is determined by the ManagedBy property, or use the BypassSecurityGroupManagerCheck to bypass checks if you are the manager, like regular distribution group management.

To create a role group, you use the New-RoleGroup cmdlet. Give the role group a name and assign to it one or more existing management roles using the Roles parameter, as follows:

```
New-RoleGroup -Name 'Staff Mailbox Manager' -Roles 'Staff Mailboxes'
```

Users or groups can be directly added to the role group using the Members parameter, or manage the members using Add RoleGroupMember or Remove-RoleGroupMember. For example, to add a user Frank to Staff Mailbox Manager:

```
Add-RoleGroupMember -Identity 'Staff Mailbox Manager' -Member 'Frank'
```

The New-RoleGroup cmdlet allows you to specify management roles using the Roles parameter, scopes using the various Scope parameters, and desired role group members using the Members parameter. This way, you can accomplish role assignments using one cmdlet, assuming the required building blocks are built-in or created. It will also allow you to change the manager of the role group. For example, you could use the following cmdlet:

```
New-RoleGroup -Name 'Exec Recipient Management' -Roles 'Mail
Recipients','Staff Mailboxes'
 -CustomRecipientWriteSope 'Exec Recipients' -ManagedBy 'Frank' -Members
'Peter','Judith'
```

This will accomplish the following:

1. A new role group named Exec Recipient Management is created.
2. Users Peter and Judith are added as members of this role group.
3. User Frank is configured as the manager of the role group.
4. The following management role assignments are created, where each assignment will be configured with Exec Recipients as CustomRecipientWriteScope:
   - Mail recipients-Exec Recipient management
   - Staff mailboxes-Exec Recipient management

Linked Role Groups

Some organizations consist of multiple Active Directory forests, which are linked to each other using trusts. A basic example of this is a resource forest containing all Exchange-related resources, which trusts an account forest where all the users and group accounts reside. In this scenario, you need to use linked role groups, creating role groups in the trusting Exchange forest that will be linked to Universal Security Group (USG) in the trusted account forest. Two-way trusts are not required.

Assuming the trust has been set up correctly, you can create a linked role group with the following command:

```
New-RoleGroup -Name '<Role Group Name>-Linked' -LinkedForeignGroup <Name of
foreign USG> -LinkedDomainController <foreign DC fqdn> -LinkedCredential
(Get-Credential) -Roles <Roles>
```

You can then use the Roles property of the role groups to get a list of roles to assign to the linked role. For example, to create a linked role group for the Server Management role group, you use the following:

```
New-RoleGroup -Name 'Server Management-Linked' -LinkedForeignGroup 'Server
Management Admins' -LinkedDomainController dc1.contoso.com -LinkedCredential
(Get-Credential) -Roles (Get-RoleGroup -Identity 'Server Management').Roles
```

> **Tip** To convert existing built-in role groups to linked role groups, use the procedure described at `http://bit.ly/ConvertToLinkedRoleGroups`.

The Glue: Management Role Assignments

After defining the management roles (what), the management scopes (where), and the role groups (who), it is now time to connect the pieces of the puzzle. This is accomplished by so-called management role assignments.

Earlier examples showed how to use `New-ManagementRoleAssignment` to assign a user or Universal Security Group to a management role. Besides these direct role assignments, end users can be granted permission through role assignment policies. But before moving on to management role assignments, let us briefly look at the relevant options when creating an assignment.

- The `Name` parameter can be used to specify the name of the management role assignment. If a name is not provided, Exchange will use the <Role>-<Role Assignee Name> by default. If that name already exists, sequence numbers will be appended to create a unique name.
- The `Computer` parameter specifies the computer account to assign the management role to.
- The `SecurityGroup` parameter specifies the management role group or Universal Security Group to assign the management role to.
- The `User` parameter specifies the name or alias of the user to assign the management role to.
- The `Policy` parameter specifies the name of the management role assignment policy to assign the management role to. The `IsEndUserRole` property of the specified role needs to be `$true`, indicating it is a user role.
- The `Role` parameter specifies the management role to assign.

- The `CustomConfigWriteScope` parameter specifies the regular management scope for configuration objects. If `CustomConfigWriteScope` is specified, you cannot use `ExclusiveConfigWriteScope`.
- The `CustomRecipientWriteScope` parameter specifies the regular management scope for recipient objects. If `CustomRecipientWriteScope` is specified, you cannot use `ExclusiveRecipientWriteScope` or `RecipientOrganizationalUnitScope`.
- The `Delegating` switch specifies if the user or USG is allowed to grant the assigned management role to other accounts.
- The `ExclusiveConfigWriteScope` parameter specifies the exclusive management scope for configuration objects. If `ExclusiveConfigWriteScope` is specified, you cannot use `CustomConfigWriteScope`.
- The `ExclusiveRecipientWriteScope` parameter specifies the exclusive management scope for the recipient objects. If `ExclusiveRecipientWriteScope` is specified, you cannot use `CustomRecipientWriteScope` or `RecipientOrganizationalUnitScope`.
- The `RecipientOrganizationalUnitScope` parameter specifies the OU to scope the role assignment. Use the canonical form when specifying the OU, for example, domain.com/OU/subOU.
- The `RecipientRelativeWriteScope` parameter specifies the type of restriction to apply to the recipient scope. Valid options are `Organization`, `MyGAL`, `Self`, `MyDistributionGroups`, and `None`.
- The `UnScopedTopLevel` switch needs to be specified if the role provided is an unscoped top-level management role.

Tip When assigning management roles, the parameters Computer, SecurityGroup, User, and Policy are mutually exclusive; you can only use one of these parameters per assignment.

Now let us look at some examples to see how to create these assignments using management roles, management scopes, and role groups. The examples assume you have administrators who have the task of managing recipients in the top-level OU called NL. These administrators are named in the USG "NL Admins". Since you only want to filter on an OU, specifying the `RecipientOrganizationUnitScope` parameter will suffice for accomplishing this, as shown in Figure 10-8:

```
New-ManagementRoleAssignment -SecurityGroup 'NL Admins' -Role 'Mail
Recipients' -RecipientOrganizationalUnitScope 'ad.myexchangelabs.com/NL'
```

```
[PS] C:\Tools>New-ManagementRoleAssignment -SecurityGroup 'NL Admins' -Role 'Mail Recipients' -RecipientOrganizationalUnitScope 'ad.myexchangelabs.com/NL
Creating a new session for implicit remoting of "New-ManagementRoleAssignment" command...

Name                        Role             RoleAssigneeName   RoleAssigneeType   AssignmentMethod   EffectiveUserName
----                        ----             ----------------   ----------------   ----------------   -----------------
Mail Recipients-NL Admins   Mail Recipients  NL Admins          SecurityGroup      Direct
```

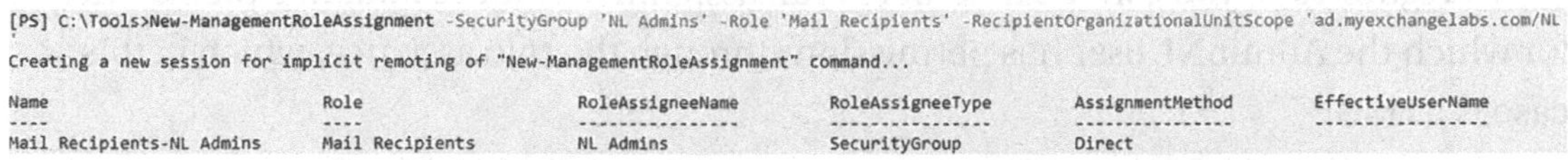

Figure 10-8. *Creating a role assignment with a recipient OU scope*

What we have accomplished:

- Created a management role assignment. Since we omitted the name, it received the default name Mail Recipients-NL Admins.
- Assignment is effective on the Organizational Unit named NL in ad. myexchangelabs.com and below.
- The role assigned is Mail Recipients.
- The role is assigned to members of the security group NL Admins.

Now, assume you want those NL administrators to only manage recipients below the Organizational Unit NL who are in the Amsterdam office. Before you can assign a scope to a role assignment, we first need to create a scope definition for it:

```
New-ManagementScope -Name 'Scope-NL-Amsterdam' -RecipientRoot 'ad.
myexchangelabs.com/NL'
-RecipientRestrictionFilter { City -eq 'Amsterdam' }
```

You can now adjust the previously created assignment and have it use the configured management scope as `CustomRecipientWriteScope`:

```
Set-ManagementRoleAssignment -Identity 'Mail Recipients-NL Admins'
-CustomRecipientWriteScope 'Scope-NL-Amsterdam'
```

To retrieve information regarding effective permissions, you can use the Get-ManagementRoleAssignment cmdlet with the EffectiveUsers switch. This will return what users are granted the permissions given by a management role through the role groups, assignment policies, and USGs that are assigned to them. For example, to return all assignments where the account AdminNL has effective permissions, you would use

```
Get-ManagementRoleAssignment -GetEffectiveUsers | Where {
$_.EffectiveUserName -eq 'AdminNL' } | Select EffectiveUserName, Role,
RoleAssignee, Identity
```

In Figure 10-9, you can see that there is an assignment for the Mail Recipients role, for which the AdminNL user has permissions through the role assignee, which in this case is a USG.

```
[PS] C:\>Get-ManagementRoleAssignment -GetEffectiveUsers | Where { $_.EffectiveUserName -eq 'AdminNL' } | Select
EffectiveUserName, Role, RoleAssignee, Identity

EffectiveUserName Role            RoleAssignee                      Identity
----------------- ----            ------------                      --------
AdminNL           Mail Recipients ad.myexchangelabs.com/NL/NL Admins Mail Recipients-NL Admins\AdminNL
```

Figure 10-9. *Viewing effective assignments using Get-ManagementRoleAssignment*

Tip Use Get-ManagementRoleAssignment with the EffectiveUsers switch to return effective user permissions for the role assignments.

Role Assignment Policy

End users can automatically be assigned permissions by way of role assignment policies. One policy is present by default, the **Default Role Assignment Policy**. This policy contains relative scopes that, when enabled, allow users to manage certain attributes of their own user object or other items, such as distribution groups managed by the end user. The default policy gets assigned when new mailboxes are created. When required, you can modify this default policy or create your own explicit role assignment policy and assign these to specific users.

When using the Exchange Admin Center, these role assignment policies can be found via Permissions ➤ User Roles and opening up the Default Role Assignment Policy. Part of the default settings are shown in Figure 10-10. Notice the several end-user roles that control what tasks a user is or is not allowed to perform.

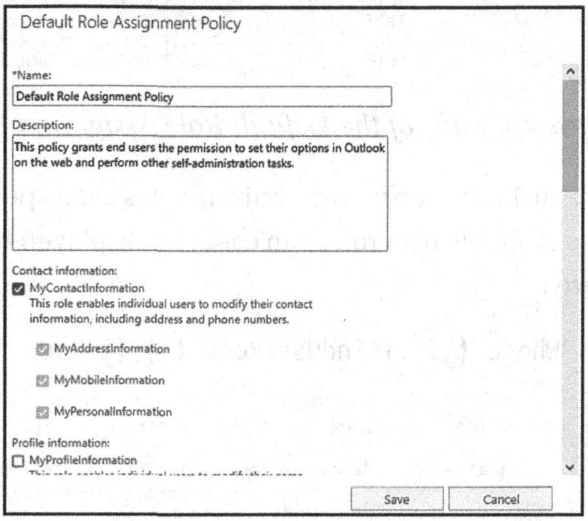

***Figure 10-10.** Default Role Assignment Policy*

To retrieve the current default assignment policy from the Exchange Management Shell, use `Get-RoleAssignmentPolicy`:

```
Get-RoleAssignmentPolicy | Where { $_.IsDefault }
```

The property `Roles` contains the roles assigned, and `RoleAssignments` contains the role assignments that have been created by the policy. To inspect which assignments are made, as well as the scopes that were used in making the assignments, retrieve the Default Role Assignment Policy, and send each element of the `RoleAssignments` property to perform a `Get-ManagementRoleAssignment`; the latter can provide the required scope information:

```
$RAP=Get-RoleAssignmentPolicy | Where { $_.IsDefault }
$RAP.RoleAssignments | Get-ManagementRoleAssignment | ft Role,Recipient*Sco
pe,Config*Scope
```

```
[PS] C:\>(Get-RoleAssignmentPolicy | Where { $_.IsDefault }).RoleAssignments | Get-ManagementRoleAssignment |
ft Role,Recipient*Scope,Config*Scope

Role                              RecipientReadScope RecipientWriteScope    ConfigReadScope   ConfigWriteScope
----                              ------------------ -------------------    ---------------   ----------------
MyTeamMailboxes                         Organization        Organization OrganizationConfig OrganizationConfig
MyDistributionGroupMembership                  MyGAL               MyGAL               None               None
My Custom Apps                                  Self                Self OrganizationConfig OrganizationConfig
My Marketplace Apps                             Self                Self OrganizationConfig OrganizationConfig
My ReadWriteMailbox Apps                        Self                Self OrganizationConfig OrganizationConfig
MyBaseOptions                                   Self                Self OrganizationConfig OrganizationConfig
MyContactInformation                            Self                Self OrganizationConfig OrganizationConfig
MyTextMessaging                                 Self                Self OrganizationConfig OrganizationConfig
MyVoiceMail                                     Self                Self OrganizationConfig OrganizationConfig
```

***Figure 10-11.** Role assignments of the Default Role Assignment Policy*

As shown in Figure 10-11, there are some built-in roles used specifically for the assignment policy. The available user roles can easily be displayed by filtering on the `IsEndUserRole` property:

```
Get-MangementRole | Where { $_.IsEndUserRole } | ft Name,*Scope
```

```
[PS] C:\>Get-ManagementRole | Where { $_.IsEndUserRole } | ft Name,*Scope

Name                              ImplicitRecipientReadScope ImplicitRecipientWriteScope ImplicitConfigReadScope
----                              -------------------------- --------------------------- -----------------------
My Custom Apps                                          Self                        Self      OrganizationConfig
My Marketplace Apps                                     Self                        Self      OrganizationConfig
My ReadWriteMailbox Apps                                Self                        Self      OrganizationConfig
MyBaseOptions                                           Self                        Self      OrganizationConfig
MyContactInformation                                    Self                        Self      OrganizationConfig
MyProfileInformation                                    Self                        Self      OrganizationConfig
MyRetentionPolicies                                     Self                        Self      OrganizationConfig
MyTextMessaging                                         Self                        Self      OrganizationConfig
MyVoiceMail                                             Self                        Self      OrganizationConfig
MyDiagnostics                                           Self                        Self      OrganizationConfig
MyDistributionGroupMembership                          MyGAL                       MyGAL                    None
MyDistributionGroups                                   MyGAL        MyDistributionGroups      OrganizationConfig
MyMailboxDelegation                                    MyGAL         MailboxICanDelegate      OrganizationConfig
MyTeamMailboxes                                 Organization                Organization      OrganizationConfig
MyAddressInformation                                    Self                        Self      OrganizationConfig
MyDisplayName                                           Self                        Self      OrganizationConfig
MyMobileInformation                                     Self                        Self      OrganizationConfig
MyName                                                  Self                        Self      OrganizationConfig
MyPersonalInformation                                   Self                        Self      OrganizationConfig
```

***Figure 10-12.** User Roles available for Role Assignment Policies*

The built-in user roles contain the role entry information that determines which cmdlets the assignee is allowed to run. Table 10-3 contains an overview of each built-in role and its purpose.

Table 10-3. *Built-in User Roles*

Name	Permissions Granted
My Custom Apps	Allows users to view and modify their custom apps.
My Marketplace Apps	Allows users to view and modify their marketplace apps.
My ReadWriteMailbox Apps	This role will allow users to install apps with ReadWriteMailbox permissions.
MyBaseOptions	Enables individual users to view and modify the basic configuration of their own mailboxes and associated settings.
MyContactInformation	Enables individual users to modify their contact information, including address and phone numbers.
MyProfileInformation	Enables individual users to modify their name.
MyRetentionPolicies	Enables individual users to view their retention tags and view and modify their retention tag settings and defaults.
MyTextMessaging	Enables individual users to create, view, and modify their text messaging settings.
MyVoiceMail	Enables individual users to view and modify their voice mail settings.
MyDiagnostics	Enables end users to perform basic diagnostics on their mailboxes, such as retrieving calendar diagnostic information.
MyDistributionGroup Membership	Enables individual users to view and modify their membership in distribution groups in the organization, provided those distribution groups allow manipulation of group membership.
MyDistributionGroups	Enables individual users to create, modify, and view distribution groups, as well as modify, view, remove, and add members to distribution groups they own.
MyMailboxDelegation	This role enables administrators to delegate mailbox permissions.
MyTeamMailboxes	Enables individual users to create site mailboxes and connect them to SharePoint sites.
MyAddressInformation	Enables individual users to view and modify their street addresses and work telephone and fax numbers.
MyDisplayName	Enables individual users to view and modify their display names.

(continued)

Table 10-3. (*continued*)

Name	Permissions Granted
MyMobileInformation	Enables individual users to view and modify their mobile telephone and pager numbers.
MyName	Enables individual users to view and modify their full names and their notes field.
MyPersonalInformation	Enables individual users to view and modify their websites, addresses, and home telephone numbers.

To create a new default assignment policy, use `New-RoleAssignmentPolicy`:

```
New-RoleAssignmentPolicy -Name 'Limited Configuration'
-Roles MyBaseOptions,MyAddressInformation,MyDisplayName
```

The previous cmdlet created an explicit policy. We forgot to make this new policy the default policy by omitting the IsDefault switch. To make this new assignment policy the default policy, reconfigure this policy using `Set-RoleAssignmentPolicy`, and specify its name and the `IsDefault` switch:

```
Set-RoleAssignmentPolicy -Identity 'Limited Configuration' -IsDefault
```

When you want to reconfigure an existing assignment policy as the new default policy, you use `Set-RoleAssignmentPolicy` and specify the `IsDefault` switch, for example:

```
Set-RoleAssignmentPolicy -Identity 'Limited Configuration' -IsDefault
```

To add roles to and remove roles from an assignment policy, you use `New-ManagementRoleAssignment` and `Remove-ManagementRoleAssignment`, respectively.

To configure an assignment policy for a mailbox, use `Set-Mailbox` with the `RoleAssignmentPolicy`:

```
Set-Mailbox -Identity 'Philip' -RoleAssignmentPolicy 'Limited Configuration'
```

To retrieve all mailboxes that have a specific assignment policy configured, filter on the RoleAssignmentPolicy property. There are more ways to accomplish this task. Often, the command used would be something like

```
Get-Mailbox -ResultSize Unlimited | Where { $_.RoleAssignmentPolicy -eq
'Limited Configuration'}
```

However, while simple this is not very efficient. It will retrieve all mailboxes, before applying the filter. Better is to use the "Get-Mailbox" Filter parameter, which allows server-side filtering on RoleAssignmentPolicy:

```
Get-Mailbox -ResultSize Unlimited -Filter "RoleAssignmentPolicy -eq
'Limited Configuration'"
```

Tip When available, using server-side filtering is not only more efficient, it also returns results faster. To see which attributes can be used using server-side OPATH filtering, see **https://docs.microsoft.com/en-us/powershell/exchange/filter-properties**.

Finally, to remove an assignment policy, use Remove-AssignmentPolicy:

```
Remove-RoleAssignmentPolicy -Identity 'Limited Configuration'
```

Auditing

When audit logging is enabled, you can report on changes in elements such as role groups and role assignments.

To verify the status of administrator audit logging:

```
Get-AdminAuditLogConfig | Select AdminAuditLogEnabled
```

The **AdminAuditLogEnabled** property indicates if administrator audit logging is enabled. If it is not enabled, use the following command:

```
Set-AdminAuditLogConfig -AdminAuditLogEnabled $true
```

Tip Exchange's audit logging will only record actions which have been performed through the Exchange ecosystem. To identify changes made directly in Active Directory, you will need to use Active Directory's auditing options or third-party solutions.

To perform audit log inspection via EAC, navigate to **Compliance Management ➤ Auditing**. There, it has pre-made reports to choose from, including the admin audit logs. You can use additional filtering options to narrow down the search.

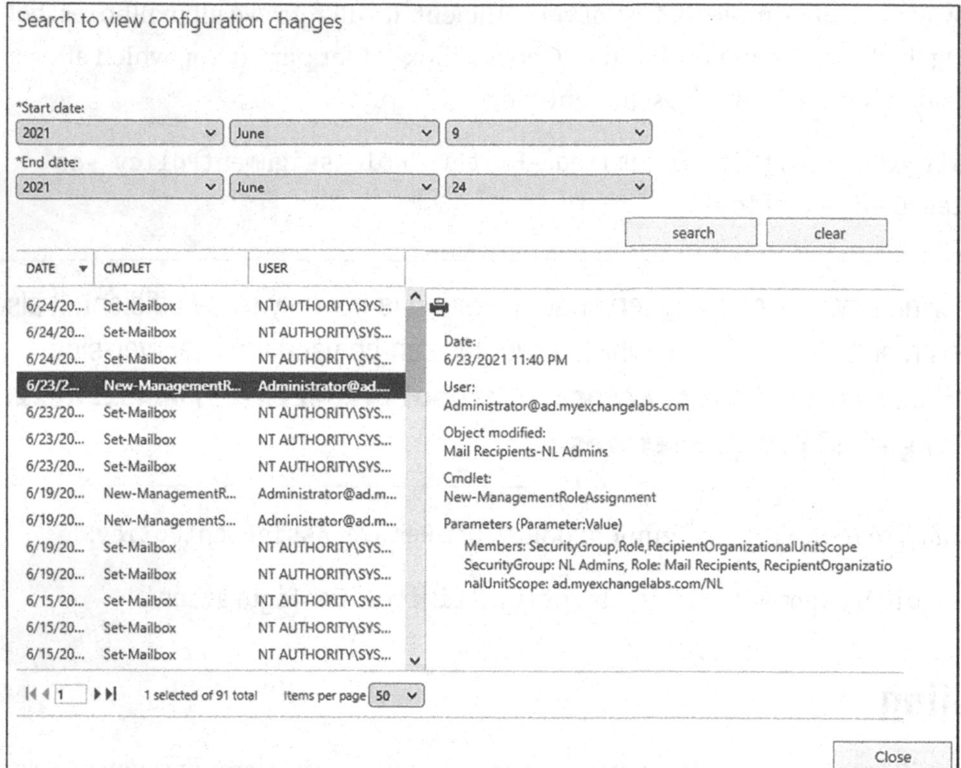

Figure 10-13. *Admin Audit Log reporting from EAC*

Using EMS, you can search the administrator audit logs for all sorts of entries related to RBAC cmdlets using `Search-AdminAuditLog`. For example, to search changes related to management role assignments in the last 24 hours by the administrator, use something like

```
Search-AdminAuditLog -Cmdlets New-ManagementRoleAssignment,Set-
ManagementRoleAssignment
-StartDate (Get-Date).AddDays(-7)
```

The possible output of this command is shown in Figure 10-14.

```
[PS] C:\>Search-AdminAuditLog -Cmdlets New-ManagementRoleAssignment,Set-ManagementRoleAssignment -StartDate (Get-Da
te).AddHours(-24) -UserIds Administrator

RunspaceId           : d75de2f2-60fb-4be6-97b4-a3087bace842
ObjectModified       : Mail Recipients-NL Admins
CmdletName           : New-ManagementRoleAssignment
CmdletParameters     : {SecurityGroup, Role, RecipientOrganizationalUnitScope}
ModifiedProperties   : {}
Caller               : Administrator@ad.myexchangelabs.com
ExternalAccess       : False
Succeeded            : True
Error                :
RunDate              : 6/23/2021 11:40:22 PM
OriginatingServer    : EX1 (15.02.0858.012)
Identity             : AAMkADdiMjI3ZjQ1LTc1OGEtNDcyMy1hOTEyLWEzMmNhNTY4OTIxNABGAAAAAAA1uKPEwHWxSqv1g5ERyAMyBwCBGrUZB
                       1rNQqfjlpT8MvAZAAAAAAEbAACBGrUZB1rNQqfjlpT8MvAZAAARgC7XAAA=
IsValid              : True
ObjectState          : New
```

Figure 10-14. *Auditing log reporting using Search-AdminAuditLog*

There is more on administrator audit logging in Chapter 11.

Split Permissions

In most deployments, Exchange Server is installed using the shared permissions model that is the default installation mode. Sometimes, organizations are not even aware they are using the shared permissions model. In shared permissions, you can create and manage security principals in Active Directory through Exchange cmdlets. This is because the Exchange Trusted Subsystem is a member of the Exchange Windows Permissions Security Group, which has permissions in Active Directory for doing such things as creating user objects or modifying group objects.

More specifically, in shared mode, the following management roles are used to create security principals in Active Directory:

- **Mail Recipient Creation** role, assigned by default to the Organization Management and Recipient Management role groups
- **Security Group Creation and Membership** role, assigned by default to the Organization Management role group

However, depending on your organization's security requirements, or the way your infrastructure is managed, you may need stricter management of security principals in Active Directory. It can also be Exchange is managed by a different team than Active Directory, and the team responsible for Active Directory strictly governs management of security principals.

In a shared model, creating a new mailbox automatically also creates a new user object in Active Directory. While convenient, it might be something your organization does not desire. In those cases, you might have a look at implementing the split permissions model.

When considering implementing a split permissions model, you have two options:

- **RBAC split permissions**—This model is recommended over Active Directory split permissions. The model is flexible, and security principal management remains under RBAC control. The Exchange Trusted Subsystem is still a member of Exchange Windows Permission USG. Exchange servers, services, and specific groups can manage security principals such as distribution groups or role groups. The Exchange tools keep working. Configuring RBAC split permissions is a manual process.
- **Active Directory split permissions**—This model isolates the management of Exchange configuration and Active Directory security principals. The Exchange Trusted Subsystem will not be a member of Exchange Windows Permission USG. This may result in your having to use separate tools for managing Exchange and Active Directory security principals, including managing distribution groups. Finally, third-party Exchange-related products might not work, as they do not have (implicit) permissions on Active Directory (and many third-party software expects it can). Configuring AD split permissions is an automated process.

Tip When using split permissions, the task of installing an Exchange Server can be delegated using the Delegated Setup role group. Administrators can provision placeholder information in Active Directory by using setup.exe /NewProvisionedServer:<server name>. After that, members of the Delegated Setup role group can deploy that server. If those delegates need to perform configuration as well, they need to be added to the Server Management role group. Alternatively, create an assignment using a scope as management boundary.

RBAC Split Permissions

Implementing split permissions on the RBAC level is relatively simple and makes good use of RBAC features. In the shared permissions model, the **Mail Recipient Creation** and **Security Group Creation and Membership** roles are used to create security principals in Active Directory.

Enabling RBAC split permissions is a manual process and will effectively transfer the permission for creating security principals to a user-defined role group, rather than using the built-in **Organization Management** and **Recipient Management** role groups. Assuming you have not enabled Active Directory split permissions yet, you proceed as follows to configure RBAC split permissions:

1. Create a role group that will contain AD administrators that have permission to create security principals.
2. Make regular and delegating role assignments between the **Mail Recipient Creation** role and the new role group. Do the same for the **Security Group Creation and Membership** role group.
3. Remove the regular and delegating role assignments between **Mail Recipient Creation** and the **Organization Management** and **Recipient Management** role groups. Do the same for the **Security Group Creation and Membership** role group.
4. Optionally, reconfigure the `ManagedBy` property of the role group, as this by default will be the creator of the role group.

For example, assuming we are creating a role group ADAdmins, which will become the designated role group for AD administrators as mentioned in step 1. To grant them sole permissions to create and manage security principals in Active Directory, perform the following set of commands which will enable RBAC split permissions using this role group:

```
New-RoleGroup -Name 'ADAdmins' -Roles 'Mail Recipient Creation',
'Security Group Creation and Membership'
```

```
New-ManagementRoleAssignment -Role 'Mail Recipient Creation'
-SecurityGroup 'ADAdmins' -Delegating
```

```
New-ManagementRoleAssignment -Role 'Security Group Creation and Membership'
```

```
-SecurityGroup 'ADAdmins' -Delegating

Get-ManagementRoleAssignment -RoleAssignee 'Organization Management'
-Role 'Mail Recipient Creation' | Remove-ManagementRoleAssignment

Get-ManagementRoleAssignment -RoleAssignee 'Recipient Management'
-Role 'Mail Recipient Creation' | Remove-ManagementRoleAssignment

Get-ManagementRoleAssignment -RoleAssignee 'Organization Management'
-Role ' Security Group Creation and Membership' | Remove-
ManagementRoleAssignment

Set-RoleGroup -Identity 'ADAdmins' -ManagedBy 'ADAdmins'
```

Note the following:

1. Only members of the ADAdmins role group will now be able to create security principals, such as mailboxes.
2. The following cmdlets become unavailable for Exchange administrators: `New-Mailbox`, `New-MailContact`, `New-MailUser`, `New-RemoteMailbox`, `Remove-Mailbox`, `Remove-MailContact`, `Remove-MailUser`, and `Remove-RemoteMailbox`.
3. Certain features in EAC or OWA/ECP might become unavailable for Exchange administrators, because cmdlets mentioned earlier became available.

Tip If you want the ADAdmins role group to also manage Exchange attributes on new objects, assign the Mail Recipients role.

Active Directory Split Permissions

At some point, anyone who will install Exchange in a greenfield scenario using setup interactively is probably familiar with the dialog that is shown in Figure 10-15. It is also available through the `/ActiveDirectorySplitPermissions:true` parameter when running setup in conjunction with preparing Active Directory using `/PrepareAD`.

Exchange Organization

Specify the name for this Exchange organization:

First Organization

Apply Active Directory split permissions security model to the Exchange organization

The Active Directory split permissions security model is typically used by large organizations that completely separate the responsibility for the management of Exchange and Active Directory among different groups of people. Applying this security model removes the ability for Exchange servers and administrators to create Active Directory objects such as users, groups, and contacts. The ability to manage non-Exchange attributes on those objects is also removed.

You shouldn't apply this security model if the same person or group manages both Exchange and Active Directory. Click '?' for more information.

***Figure 10-15.** Active Directory split permissions question during setup*

With Active Directory split permissions, the Recipient Management and Organization Management roles will not be able to create security principals in Active Directory. Active Directory administrators will be responsible for creating security principals in Active Directory. Exchange administrators, being Recipient or Organization Management group members, will be responsible for configuring and managing the Exchange attributes on those security principals, like mailbox-enabling an existing user.

The AD split permissions model is configured through the setup wizard by checking the Apply Active Directory split permissions model or when running `setup.exe /PrepareAD /ActiveDirectorySplitPermissions:true` from the command line.

Depending on whether you are enabling Active Directory split permissions during the initial setup of Exchange 2019 or are switching from the shared permissions or RBAC split permissions model, enabling Active Directory split permissions results in the following changes:

1. An OU named **Microsoft Exchange Protected Groups** is created.
2. The **Exchange Windows Permissions** USG is created in the **Microsoft Exchange Protected Groups** OU. When the **Exchange Windows Permissions** USG already exists, it is moved to **Microsoft Exchange Protected Groups**.
3. When the **Exchange Trusted Subsystem** USG is a member of the **Exchange Windows Permissions Group**, it is removed from that group.
4. When they exist, any non-delegating role assignment to role groups **Mail Recipient Creation** and **Security Group Creation and Membership** is removed.

5. Any existing access control entry (ACE) assigned to the **Exchange Windows Permissions** USG is removed from the domain object, for example, CN=contoso,CN=com. This will be repeated for all domains in the forest, depending on the usage of the `/PrepareAllDomains` switch during setup.

After enabling the Active Directory split permissions model, the following cmdlets will become unavailable: `New-Mailbox`, `New-MailContact`, `New-MailUser`, `New-RemoteMailbox`, `Remove-Mailbox`, `Remove-MailContact`, `Remove-MailUser`, and `Remove-RemoteMailbox`. The following cmdlets will be accessible, but cannot be used to create or manage distribution groups: `Add-DistributionGroupMember`, `New-DistributionGroup`, `Remove-DistributionGroup`, `Remove-DistributionGroupMember`, and `Update-DistributionGroupMember`.

Certain features in EAC or OWA/ECP might become unavailable as related cmdlets or permissions become unavailable.

Tip You can switch back from Active Directory split permissions to shared permissions models using `setup.exe /PrepareAD /ActiveDirectorySplitPermissions:false`. Changes mentioned will be made in the opposite direction, such as the addition of required ACEs to domain objects for **Exchange Windows Permissions** and adding the **Exchange Trusted Subsystem** to **Exchange Windows Permissions**. When switching, role assignments for **Mail Recipient Creation** and **Security Group Creation and Membership** are not automatically recreated.

Hybrid Modern Authentication

In Chapter 9, we showed how to set up an Exchange hybrid deployment and talked about the benefits of having Modern Authentication (OAuth) between two organizations, with Azure Active Directory being trusted for authentication and authorization. With the option to hand off authentication and authorization to Azure Active Directory also come Azure Active Directory security features that build on Modern Authentication, such as Multi-factor Authentication (MFA), or Conditional Access policies to provide access based on sign-in conditions or control over data. Perhaps more importantly, you can also start using identity-related analytics provided in Office 365, such as risky sign-ins. However, for that to work, your Exchange on-premises infrastructure needs to use Modern Authentication exclusively. This is where Hybrid Modern Authentication comes into play.

Note More about Multi-factor Authentication later in this chapter. You can read up on Conditional Access policies, which can also be used to manage MFA requirements when using Azure AD P1 or P2 licenses, at **https://bit.ly/AADCAP**.

Hybrid Modern Authentication (MHA) was introduced in previous editions of Exchange 2016 (CU8) and Exchange 2013 (CU19) in 2017. It allows you to appoint Azure Active Directory as the sole centralized authentication and authorization infrastructure for Exchange on-premises. Instead of supporting Modern Authentication and additionally legacy authentication such as NTLM or Basic Authentication, Exchange ultimately gets configured to exclusively support Modern Authentication. From a technical perspective, it means Exchange will be configured to consume authentication tokens from Azure Active Directory only.

Caution OWA/ECP cannot be used with HMA only, except when you have AD FS or use Azure App Proxy to publish OWA/ECP. More about publishing internal applications via Azure App Proxy at `https://bit.ly/PubAppProxy`.

To be able to deploy HMA, the following prerequisites should be met:

- Exchange Hybrid should be deployed using Full Classic topology; Hybrid Modern or Classic Minimum topologies are not supported.
- OAuth should be set up between Exchange on-premises and Exchange Online. The HCW should have taken care of this.
- Accounts should be synchronized to Azure Active Directory, either managed using the same sign-on with Password Hash Synchronization (PHS) and Pass-Through Authentication (PTA) or federated using AD FS or an alternative Security Token Service (STS) that is supported by Office 365.

- HMA cannot be used together with SSL offloading, as Exchange will be required to perform the encryption. SSL bridging is supported.
- MAPI/HTTP has to be enabled; RPC/HTTP will not work with HMA.
- Clients and services will need to support Modern Authentication (OAuth). This means Outlook 2013 or later, Outlook 2016 for Mac, Outlook Mobile. Third-party apps such as the native Mail app on iOS, Gmail app on Android, or third-party applications such as Thunderbird that support OAuth could be made to work as well.
- HMA cannot be used when Exchange 2010 servers are still present in your organization, which do not support OAuth. This could be the case when you have deployed Exchange 2016 as Hybrid servers.
- With HMA enabled, legacy authentication will keep functioning provided those authentication mechanisms are still enabled. However, with legacy authentication, organizations will not have the security features that are part of Modern Authentication and HMA in particular.
- Outlook for Mobile clients will leverage the caching mechanism in Exchange Online when HMA is enabled. This means that you need to allow this for HMA to work. Details later in this section.

Note Outlook 2013 requires the following registry keys to enable the ADAL libraries and support OAuth:

`HKCU:\SOFTWARE\Microsoft\Office\15.0\Common\Identity\EnableADAL=1`

`HKCU:\SOFTWARE\Microsoft\Office\15.0\Common\Identity\Version=1`

It is recommended to also enable OAuth for Autodiscover: `HKCU:\Software\Microsoft\Exchange\AlwaysUseMSOAuthForAutoDiscover=1`

Deploying Exchange Hybrid in classic mode, with OAuth configured by HCW, using Azure AD Connect to provision identities and Password Hash Synchronization, has been described in Chapter 9.

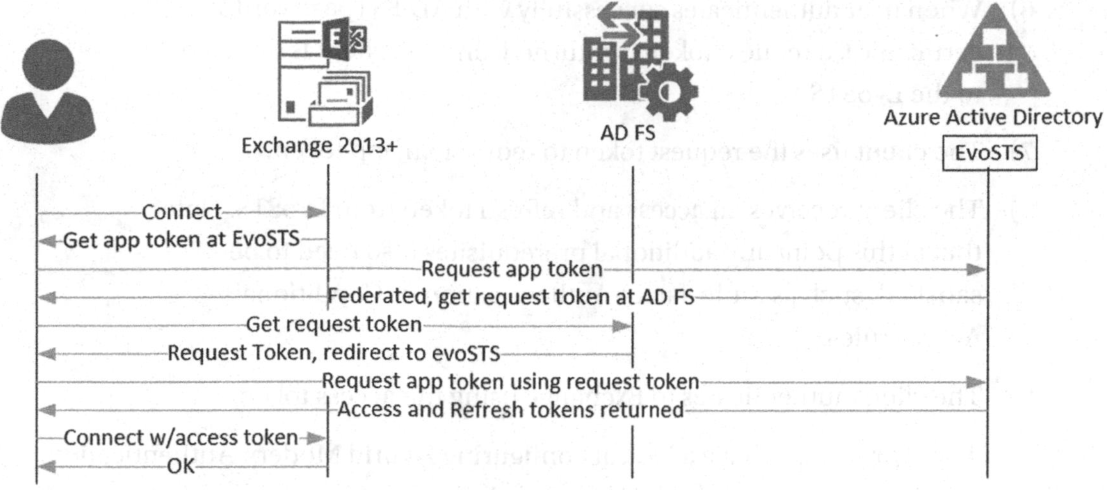

***Figure 10-16.** Hybrid Modern Authentication*

Before we dive into configuring Hybrid Modern Authentication, it helps to get an understanding of how authentication workflow with HMA is set up. Figure 10-16 displays this, and we will briefly walk you through its steps. Note that there are no cached tokens, and integrated authentication has been disabled:

1) The user uses a client that supports Modern Authentication and attempts to connect to Exchange on-premises. In the connect, the client reports it supports Modern Authentication, by means of an "**Authorization: Bearer**" header. The UPN is supplied as the **X-User-Identity** header.

2) Exchange receives the request, sees the header, and returns the URL of the endpoint which the client needs to use to retrieve an application token.

3) The client follows the URL and uses it to request an application token, providing the user UPN, for example, jaap@contoso.com. Now, when that domain is not federated, the user gets to authenticate with Azure Active Directory and proceeds with step 8.

4) When EvoSTS determines that the domain is federated, it sends the client a redirect to the AD FS infrastructure.

5) The client navigates to the provided AD FS endpoint asking for a request token and needs to authenticate.

6) When user authenticates successfully with AD FS (password, certificate), a request token is returned, and the client is directed to the EvoSTS.

7) The client uses the request token to request an app token.

8) The client receives an access and refresh token from EvoSTS. Note that at this point any additional prerequisites also need to be satisfied, such as Multi-factor Authentication or Conditional Access rules.

9) The client authenticates to Exchange using the access token.

We will now proceed to have a look at configuring Hybrid Modern Authentication. Configuration consists basically of the following three steps:

First, we need to add the Service Principal Names (SPN) used by Exchange on-premises to Azure Active Directory. This is because Azure AD will become the default authentication method for authentication requests, external and internal. To collect all URLs involved, use the following commands:

```
$U=  (Get-MapiVirtualDirectory).internalURL
$U+= (Get-MapiVirtualDirectory).externalURL
$U+= (Get-WebServicesVirtualDirectory).internalURL
$U+= (Get-WebServicesVirtualDirectory).externalURL
$U+= (Get-OABVirtualDirectory).internalURL
$U+= Get-OABVirtualDirectory).externalURL
$U+= (Get-AutodiscoverVirtualDirectory).internalURL
$U+= (Get-AutodiscoverVirtualDirectory).externalURL
$U+= (Get-ClientAccessService).AutodiscoverServiceInternalUri
$U | Where-Object {$_.Scheme -eq 'https'} |Select-Object -Unique Authority
```

This will collect all configured external and internal URLs on relevant endpoints, picks only those using HTTPS, and then only returns the unique entries. When you have only mail.contoso.com and autodiscover.contoso.com in use at your organization, this will return only mail.contoso.com and autodiscover. contoso.com. Another trick is to have a look at the certificate, and collect all Subject Alternate Names, as that might do the trick as well.

We then need to verify these SPNs are configured in Azure AD. This is one of those cases where you might need the Microsoft Online module. Use Connect-MSOLService to connect to Office 365, and run the following command:

```
(Get-MsolServicePrincipal -AppPrincipalId 00000002-0000-0ff1-
ce00-000000000000).ServicePrincipalNames
```

If the names collected are not present yet, you need to add them to this list. Unfortunately, Set-MSolServicePrincipal does not offer add/remove using hashtables, so we need to resort to the following code snippet:

```
$spn= (Get-MsolServicePrincipal -AppPrincipalId 00000002-0000-0ff1-
ce00-000000000000).ServicePrincipalNames
$spn.Add( 'https://mail.contoso.com/')
Set-MSOLServicePrincipal -AppPrincipalId 00000002-0000-0ff1-
ce00-000000000000 -ServicePrincipalNames $spn
```

Repeat this step for every name collected at the first step, replacing "mail.contoso.com" with every entry.

Caution When you have configured your Exchange on-premises in Exchange Hybrid with multiple tenants, you need to populate Azure AD for each of these tenants with these SPNs.

Second, you need to verify OAuth is configured on relevant virtual directories in your Exchange on-premises environment:

```
Get-MapiVirtualDirectory | FL server,*url*,*auth*
Get-WebServicesVirtualDirectory | FL server,*url*,*oauth*
Get-OABVirtualDirectory | FL server,*url*,*oauth*
Get-AutoDiscoverVirtualDirectory | FL server,*oauth*
```

If any of the reported authentication methods does not indicate it is configured for OAuth, configure it using Set-MapiVirtualDirectory or other related cmdlets, depending on the type of virtual directory. The HCW should normally have taken care of this, but it cannot hurt to verify virtual directory configuration before enabling HMA.

Tip If your organization is still using RPC/HTTP for Outlook for Desktop, you can gradually move them to MAPI/HTTP by enabling them for MAPI/HTTP at the user level and optionally disable RPC/HTTP for them as well.

To enable MAPI/HTTP, use

```
Set-CASMailbox -Identity <User ID> -MapiHttpEnabled $True
```

To disable RPC/HTTP, use

```
Set-CASMailbox -Identity <User ID> -MAPIBlockOutlookRpcHttp
$True
```

Of course, these commands can be used to target larger groups or mailboxes. Preferably, keep the user mailboxes aligned with user mailboxes to prevent RPC/HTTP and MAPI/HTTP mix-ups.

Finally, when everything is found to be in order and configured correctly, we can activate HMA. Enabling HMA consists of two steps:

1) Configure the default authorization endpoint for Exchange server. This can be accomplished by

    ```
    Set-AuthServer -Identity 'EvoSTS - <Guid>'
    -IsDefaultAuthorizationEndpoint $true
    ```

    where <Guid> is the GUID of your tenant organization. You can also derive this from the Get-IntraOrganizationConnector identity or have a look at the AuthServer's DomainName attribute to pick the right one.

Note The default AuthServer 'EvoSTS - <Guid>' is created by the HCW since September 2020, to accommodate for future multi-tenant support. If you have an older Exchange hybrid deployment, your AuthServer configuration might be called EvoSTS only.

2) Configure Exchange to start supporting clients using OAuth. This can be accomplished by

```
Set-OrganizationConfig -OAuth2ClientProfileEnabled $true
```

After turning HMA on, it might take a short while for Exchange and clients to pick up new settings, and Outlook will need a restart for the new authentication flow to become effective.

To validate HMA deployment from the back end, you can use a script called Test-EASHMA.ps1. It is available from the GitHub repository from Exchange Support and can be downloaded directly from **https://bit.ly/TestEASHMA**. After downloading the script, run

```
.\Test-EASHMA.ps1 <User ID>
```

where User ID is the primary email address of an on-premises mailbox. Without additional parameters, the script will follow basic Autodiscover and bearer tests. You can perform an Exchange ActiveSync test specifying -TestEAS, for example:

```
.\Test-EASHMA.ps1 <User ID> -TestEAS
```

Caution If you have been restricting applications that can access Office 365 data on behalf of a user, applications or scripts such as Test-EASHMA.ps1 that use OAuth may fail authentication because of these restrictions. Also, keep in mind admin and user consent configuration. More on this at `https://bit.ly/ConsentConfig`.

Outlook for Desktop clients can check if they are using Modern Authentication by Shift-right-clicking the Outlook icon in the system tray and selecting **Connection Status**. Something similar to Figure 10-17 should show up.

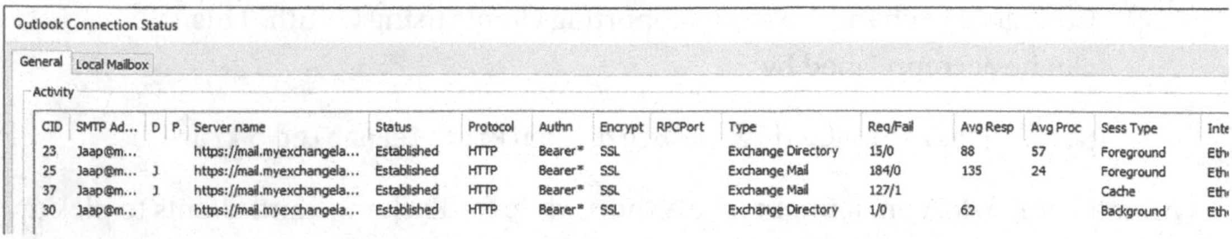

Outlook Connection Status

General | Local Mailbox

Activity

CID	SMTP Ad...	D	P	Server name	Status	Protocol	Authn	Encrypt	RPCPort	Type	Req/Fail	Avg Resp	Avg Proc	Sess Type	Inte
23	Jaap@m...			https://mail.myexchangela...	Established	HTTP	Bearer*	SSL		Exchange Directory	15/0	88	57	Foreground	Eth
25	Jaap@m...	J		https://mail.myexchangela...	Established	HTTP	Bearer*	SSL		Exchange Mail	184/0	135	24	Foreground	Eth
37	Jaap@m...	J		https://mail.myexchangela...	Established	HTTP	Bearer*	SSL		Exchange Mail	127/1			Cache	Eth
30	Jaap@m...			https://mail.myexchangela...	Established	HTTP	Bearer*	SSL		Exchange Directory	1/0	62		Background	Eth

Figure 10-17. *Outlook Connection Status when using Modern Authentication*

The column "Auth" reading Bearer* is evidence that Modern Authentication is used. Note that in the example cached mode was enabled, which creates multiple connections per configured mailbox.

Outlook for Mobile users will need to create a new profile when switching from Basic Authentication to Modern Authentication/OAuth.

Caution Before enabling HMA, be aware that if you have configured any Conditional Access policies, those immediately start to apply to users using clients supporting Modern Authentication with mailboxes hosted in Exchange on-premises as well. Adjust existing policies or create a new one for those users as deemed appropriate.

Should circumstances arise that you need to disable HMA, you can do so by undoing the AuthServer configuration step, for example:

```
Set-AuthServer -Identity 'EvoSTS - <Guid>' -IsDefaultAuthorizationEndpoint
$false
```

Optionally, you can also disable OAuth for clients that support it, but that is usually not required:

```
Set-OrganizationConfig -OAuth2ClientProfileEnabled $false
```

The other changes were usually already in-place or complementary to existing configuration. You only need to undo them if you consider dismantling OAuth functionality completely, but since OAuth is the way forward, that is not an unlikely scenario.

Tip When you experience connectivity issues with HMA, additionally to running the Test-EASHMA.ps1 script, the Exchange Remote Connectivity Analyzer's Office 365 section also contains an Outlook Mobile Hybrid Modern Authentication module for configuration and connectivity tests. The RCA can be accessed at `https://exrca.com`.

Now with OAuth being enabled and Azure Active Directory being default authentication, be advised that legacy authentication is still configured for the virtual directories. You might leave those configured, but you also might wish to start disabling Basic Authentication, especially for mobile clients.

For Outlook Mobile, you can leverage Device Access Rules. With Basic Authentication enabled, Outlook Mobile devices will report as device model **Outlook for iOS and Android**. When HMA is enabled, and the Outlook for Mobile profile has been recreated, all inbound traffic for Outlook Mobile will use caching engine in Office 365 and therefore will report as device type **OutlookService** in Exchange on-premises device logging. Of course, the opposite is also true.

To set up a Device Access Rule to block "Outlook for iOS and Android" devices:

```
New-ActiveSyncDeviceAccessRule -Characteristic DeviceModel
-QueryString 'Outlook for iOS and Android' -AccessLevel Block
```

To set up a Device Access Rule to allow "OutlookService" devices:

```
New-ActiveSyncDeviceAccessRule -Characteristic DeviceType
-QueryString 'OutlookService' -AccessLevel Allow
```

Note Due to the architecture of Outlook for Mobile, if those clients use HMA, their traffic will be channeled through the caching service in Office 365. Evidence of this is traffic coming in from 52.125.128.0/20 and 52.127.96.0/23, and the user agent for this traffic will be OutlookService.

Eventually, you may wish to lock out Basic Authentication altogether on-premises on Exchange 2019 by means of an Authentication Policy. The default policy will allow Basic Authentication, but we can create a new one which will block Basic Authentication for all protocols. Then, when the switchover to Modern Authentication-only is to be made, configure this new policy as default. This will also allow you to easily switch back, in case you missed a legacy application that still requires Basic Authentication, for example.

To create a new Authentication Policy that blocks Basic Authentication for all protocols, use (PowerShell splatting used for readability)

```
$Param= @{
    BlockLegacyAuthActiveSync= $True
    BlockLegacyAuthAutodiscover= $True
    BlockLegacyAuthImap= $True
    BlockLegacyAuthMapi= $True
    BlockLegacyAuthOfflineAddressBook= $True
    BlockLegacyAuthPop= $True
    BlockLegacyAuthRpc= $True
    BlockLegacyAuthWebServices= $True
}
New-AuthenticationPolicy -Name "Block Basic Auth" @Param
```

After creating this new Authentication Policy, you then configure it per user, which is ideal for testing purposes, or set it as the organization-wide default policy:

```
Set-User -Identity <ID> -AuthenticationPolicy 'Block Basic Auth'
Set-OrganizationConfig -DefaultAuthenticationPolicy 'Block Basic Auth'
```

Should you wish to revert to the previous Authentication Policy, named OrgWideDefault, use

```
Set-OrganizationConfig -DefaultAuthenticationPolicy 'OrgWideDefault'
```

Note Similar functionality is available in Exchange Online. Be advised that the settings there are not only reversed, for example, AllowBasicAuthPop instead of BlockLegacyAuthPop, but blocking legacy authentication on-premises blocks all legacy authentication methods, including NTLM. Be aware of this when you still need to migrate mailboxes, as MRS does not support OAuth.

Apart from that, you can block Basic Authentication in Exchange Online and other Office 365 workloads by enabling Security Defaults in your tenant. Note that Microsoft will proactively disable Basic Authentication in your tenant if you do not use it for the last 30 days, as announced in June 2021. This approach is part of an overall campaign to increase security; when organizations require Basic Authentication, they use the self-help in the Office portal, entering Diag: Enable Basic Auth in EXO.

Multi-factor Authentication

In general, authentication is based on something you know (e.g., your password), something you have (e.g., security token or smart card), or who you are (biometrics). By having two factors instead of one, the identities are more secure than they would be otherwise. Multi-factor Authentication (MFA) is the form of authentication whereby the user identifies themselves by using more than one factor. Multi-factor Authentication should be seriously considered for accessing services, and not for administrator-type accounts only. Consider the targeted phishing and social hacking attempts to compromise C-level accounts alone. Studies have indicated that accounts are 99.9% more likely to be compromised when not using MFA.

With MFA enabled, users need to authorize their sign-in by confirming their identity through what is called a contact method. The following contact methods are available in Office 365:

- Mobile phone or office phone numbers for receiving authorization codes through calls
- Mobile phone numbers for receiving authorization codes through text messages
- Mobile App on smartphone

The Mobile App Microsoft provides is available for iOS and Android. It should be considered the most secure option, apart from perhaps being the most convenient for an end user as well, as phone numbers in principle can be spoofed and sending SMS verification messages is not that secure.

Tip Always have at least two Global Administrators when MFA is enabled, or use one break glass account that is exempt from MFA rules or may sign in without MFA, for example, when that sign-in is performed from a trusted location using Conditional Access. That way, when needed, you can still perform administrative tasks when MFA is not possible due to a lost phone etc.

The MFA feature is part of the Office 365 offering. Licensing requirements and features depend on your current subscription plan and what features your organization requires. Currently available MFA-related features for Azure AD Free (plans that do not include Azure AD P1 or P2) as well as Azure AD P1/P2 are

Azure AD Free

- Protect all tenant users using Security Defaults
- Users
    - Use Mobile App as a contact method
- Global Administrators
    - Use Mobile App, phone call, or SMS as a contact method
    - Remember MFA on trusted devices
- Admin controls over Global Administrators' contact methods

Azure AD P1 or P2

- Same features as Azure AD Free, plus
- User extra options
    - Phone call or SMS as a contact method
    - Remember MFA on trusted devices
- Fraud alerting option
- MFA reports, for example, usage and contact methods
- Additional configuration for a phone call contact method
    - Custom call greeting
    - Custom caller ID (US only)

- Trusted IPs or named locations
- Support MFA for on-premises applications

While the feature set for Azure AD Free is rudimentary, it does provide organizations a basic level of protection for everyone, or just those with the Global Administrator tenant role. Do note that in addition to this all-or-nothing (Azure AD Free) or "per-user" configuration, organizations using Azure P1/P2 licenses will have additional options to require MFA, using Conditional Access policies. This brings the full features of CA policies to MFA management, such as triggering MFA based on sign-in location, applying to groups, exclusions, etc. More on configuring Conditional Access policies at **https://bit.ly/AADCAP**.

Caution Security Defaults is an all-or-nothing option. Its underlying policy is fixed and cannot be tailored to different needs. When this is desired, Azure AD P1 or P2 licensing is required.

To enable Security Defaults, navigate to the Azure portal, then open the blade at **Active Directory ➤ Azure Active Directory ➤ Properties**, and click the **Manage security defaults** link at the bottom. Be advised that enabling Security Defaults not only configures MFA for users and administrators but will also block legacy authentication methods, such as Basic Authentication.

Note When enabling Security Defaults, the account used for AD Connect will be excluded from configuring MFA.

To enable individual users for MFA, open the Azure AD portal at portal.azure.com, and navigate to **Azure Active Directory ➤ Users**. There, after selecting one or more users, you will find the option **Per-user MFA**. This will open a new tab or window, shown in Figure 10-18.

Select one or more users from the list. When the users are not MFA enabled, you have the option to enable them for MFA, which will trigger the enrollment process for them. You can also manage their user-related settings, which can trigger predefined actions:

- Require selected users to provide contact methods again. When users are MFA enrolled, they provide contact methods such as the phone number to call to verify their sign-in. This forces them to update those settings.
- Delete all existing app passwords generated by the selected users. This forces users to recreate app passwords for applications which do not support Modern Authentication. Since app passwords are strongly discouraged, you should never have to use this option.
- Restore Multi-factor Authentication on all remembered devices. This will force users to use MFA again on devices on which they selected the "Remember Me" option. This option is controlled by the MFA Service Settings, configurable via **Azure Active Directory ➤ Users ➤ Per-User MFA** and selecting **service settings**.

Note that when users are MFA enabled, apart from disabling them for MFA, you can also enforce them to use MFA. This can be achieved by selecting MFA-enabled users and selecting Enforce. Note that users can then only use applications which support Modern Authentication.

When you have enabled a user for Multi-factor Authentication, that user needs to complete the setup process. The process is initiated when the user accesses Office 365 resources. Alternatively, you can direct the user to **`http://aka.ms/MFASetup`**, where the user can complete the initial setup process. Administrators can configure custom MFA settings, such as fraud alert or custom greetings, from the Azure AD portal, via the blade at **Azure Active Directory ➤ Security ➤ MFA**.

multi-factor authentication
users service settings
Before you begin, take a look at the multi-factor auth deployment guide.
View: Sign-in allowed users Multi-Factor Auth status: Any bulk update

DISPLAY NAME	USER NAME	MULTI-FACTOR AUTH STATUS
Administrator	administrator@myexchangelabs.com	Disabled
AdminNL	adminnl@myexchangelabs.com	Disabled
Francis Blake	francis@myexchangelabs.com	Disabled

Select a user

***Figure 10-18.** Configuring MFA in Office 365*

Administrators can also manage MFA using PowerShell and the Microsoft Online module. Managing MFA this way not only allows organizations to easily configure MFA for existing users or in bulk but also to enhance the current provisioning process with MFA options. For example, by pre-populating contact methods and phone numbers, administrators can prevent users from having to enter their mobile phone or office number for verification.

To configure MFA using the Microsoft Online module for PowerShell, open up a PowerShell session and connect to your Office 365 tenant:

Caution At the moment of writing, the Microsoft Online module does not work with PowerShell 7. The latter is still in preview, so that might change.

```
Connect-MSOLService
```

Next, you define a strong authentication object, as follows:

```
$st= New-Object Microsoft.Online.Administration.
StrongAuthenticationRequirement
$st.RelyingParty= '*'
```

Now you can enable users for MFA by using Set-MSOLUser with the StrongAuthentication Requirements parameter, passing it the strong authentication object created earlier. For example, to enable MFA for user jaap@myexchangelabs.com, you would use

```
Set-MsolUser -UserPrincipalName jaap@contoso.com -
StrongAuthenticationRequirements $st
```

To disable MFA, you clear the StrongAuthenticationRequirements attribute:

```
Set-MsolUser -UserPrincipalName jaap@contoso.com -
StrongAuthenticationRequirements $null
```

Administrators can also predefine the contact methods for users by configuring the StrongAuthenticationRequirement attribute state and providing at least one contact method through the StrongAuthenticationMethods parameter:

```
$st= New-Object Microsoft.Online.Administration.
StrongAuthenticationRequirement
$st.RelyingParty= '*'
$st.State= 'Enforced'
$m1 = New-Object -TypeName Microsoft.Online.Administration.
StrongAuthenticationMethod
$m1.IsDefault = $true
$m1.MethodType = 'OneWaySMS'
```

So, the variable $st now contains a state of preconfigured authentication, and $m1 has one contact method, in this case OneWaySMS. Alternatives for setting the contact method using MethodType are

- `OneWaySMS` texts code to my mobile phone.
- `TwoWayVoiceMobile` calls my mobile phone.
- `TwoWayVoiceOffice` calls my office phone.
- `TwoWayVoiceAlternateMobile` calls an alternate mobile phone number.
- `PhoneAppOTP` shows one-time code in the app—that is, a six-digit number. OTP stands for "one-time password."
- `PhoneAppNotification` notifies me through an app using in-app verification.

When you specify a OneWaySMS, TwoWayVoiceMobile, or TwoWayVoiceOffice contact method, the currently configured mobile phone or office phone number attributes on the user object will be used. Now, to apply the strong authentication method with a specific contact method to user jaap@contoso.com, you use

```
Set-MsolUser -UserPrincipalName jaap@contoso.com
 -StrongAuthenticationRequirements $st -StrongAuthenticationMethods @($m1)
```

Note When users have configured PhoneAppNotification, by default they will also have the PhoneAppOTP contact method configured, which serves as a fallback for situations when there is no data coverage.

If you want to add another authentication contact method, for example, to have the user receive a call on their mobile phone, add it as an element to the StrongAuthenticationMethods attribute:

```
$m2 = New-Object -TypeName Microsoft.Online.Administration.
StrongAuthenticationMethod
$m2.IsDefault = $false
$m2.MethodType = 'TwoWayVoiceMobile'
$methods= [array](Get-MsolUser -UserPrincipalName jaap@contoso.com).
StrongAuthenticationMethods
$methods+= $m2
Set-MsolUser -UserPrincipalName jaap@contoso.com
 -StrongAuthenticationRequirements $st -StrongAuthenticationMethods
$methods
```

At some point, administrators may want to receive a report on which users are enabled for MFA and what contact methods they have configured. The StrongAuthenticationMethods attribute contains the configured method. Using this knowledge, you can construct a command to get a list of MFA-enabled users and their configured methods:

```
Get-MsOlUser | Where-Object {$_.StrongAuthenticationRequirements}
| Select-Object UserPrincipalName, @{name="MFA"; expression={$_.
StrongAuthenticationRequirements.State}}, @{name="Methods";
expression={($_.StrongAuthenticationMethods).MethodType}} | ft -AutoSize
```

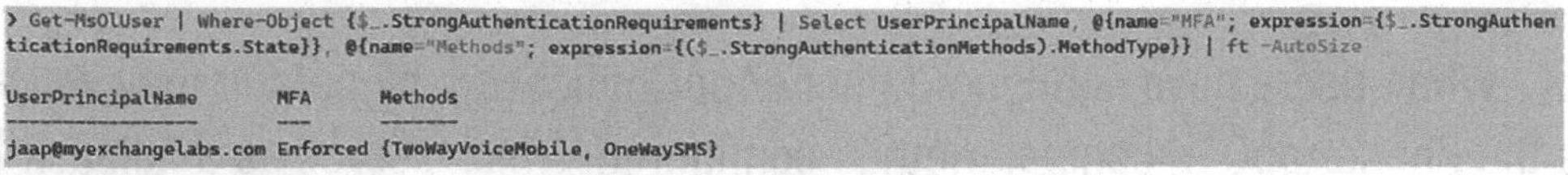

```
> Get-MsOlUser | Where-Object {$_.StrongAuthenticationRequirements} | Select UserPrincipalName, @{name="MFA"; expression={$_.StrongAuthen
ticationRequirements.State}}, @{name="Methods"; expression={($_.StrongAuthenticationMethods).MethodType}} | ft -AutoSize

UserPrincipalName       MFA      Methods
-----------------       ---      -------
jaap@myexchangelabs.com Enforced {TwoWayVoiceMobile, OneWaySMS}
```

Figure 10-19. *Reporting on MFA usage*

App Passwords

App passwords were introduced to ease the transition to OAuth, when only a limited number of applications supported OAuth. App passwords are 16-character passwords generated by Azure AD, which can be used like any regular password for apps that do not support OAuth. You can manage those app passwords from the portal, for example, to invalidate them or refresh.

With nowadays availability of applications supporting OAuth, there is no reason to have app passwords. That said, app passwords do not protect organizations against what they are using MFA for in the first place. Also, while 16-character passwords still take a long time to brute-force crack with nowadays processing power, the secure usage of passwords is a time bomb.

For this reason, we recommend disabling app passwords at the organizational level. In the Azure AD portal, navigate to **Azure Active Directory ➤ Users ➤ Per-User MFA**, select **service settings**, and there disable app passwords by selecting **Do not allow users to create app passwords to sign in to non-browser apps**.

CHAPTER 11

Exchange 2019 Compliance

In today's world of complex electronic communications, many organizations utilize email for communicating both internally and with other organizations. Because everybody has become used to sending and receiving email on all sorts of devices, and because some of the underlying complexities and potential adverse consequences are unknown to end users, many companies want their communications to conform to certain rules—whether those rules are company policies for sending email containing sensitive information to external organizations or are operations to comply with external laws and regulations, such as the Sarbanes-Oxley Act in the United States or the European Union's Data Protection Directive.

Exchange Server 2010 brought features that address some of those concerns. Exchange Server 2013 introduced new ones while extending existing features, albeit using different names for some of them, and the features in Exchange 2013 are carried forward in Exchange 2019.

In this chapter, we discuss the following compliance-related features:

- In-Place archiving
- Online eDiscovery
- Online hold
- Messaging records management (MRM)
- Data loss prevention (DLP)
- Transport rules
- Auditing
- Information rights management (IRM)

M. de Rooij and J. Wesselius, *Pro Exchange 2019 and 2016 Administration*,
https://doi.org/10.1007/978-1-4842-7331-9_11

In-Place Archiving

The In-Place archive mailbox is an extension of a regular mailbox, and it is hosted on an Exchange server or in Exchange Online. This feature was introduced with Exchange Server 2010 as a personal archive or archive mailbox; as of Exchange Server 2013, this feature is known as In-Place Archiving, and the in-place archive is known as the In-Place Archive Mailbox.

An In-Place archive mailbox can be used to offload contents from the primary mailbox, keeping the primary mailbox relatively small and tidy; it also helps organizations manage the space occupied by a large offline cache, or .OST files. However, OST size management has become less of an issue with Outlook 2013 and higher, which contains an option in the form of a slider. This slider limits the information that can be stored in the offline cache to a certain age, and then Outlook can retrieve the non-cached mailbox information from the online mailbox as required. The default setting for the slider is to cache one year of mail data; the maximum time span is "unlimited," and the minimum time span is three days.

It is also possible to control the slider via a Group Policy Object (GPO). For this to work, you need to download the Office 2016 Administrative Template files (ADMX/ADML) and Office Customization Tool from the Microsoft download center. More information about managing Outlook and the slider can be found at `https://bit.ly/OutlookSlider`.

The slider in Outlook 2019 is shown in Figure 11-1.

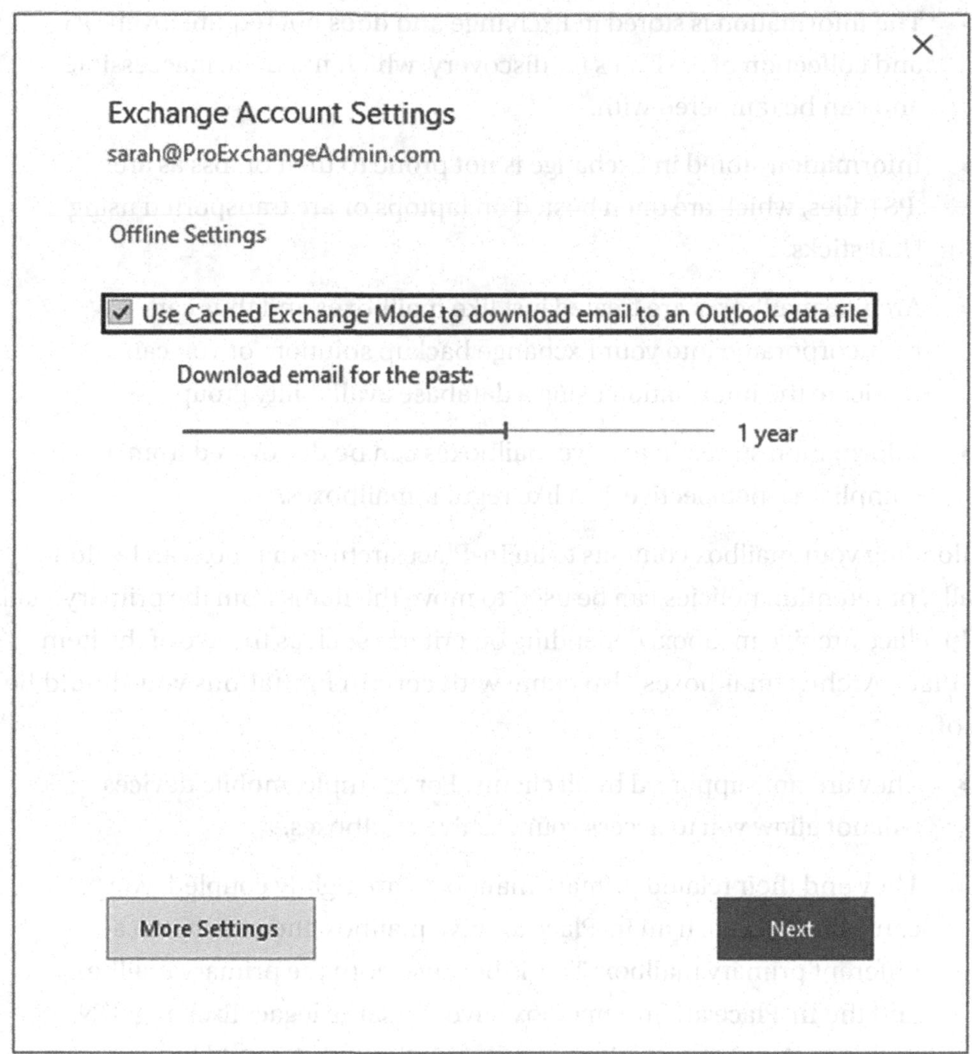

Figure 11-1. *Outlook cached mode slider*

Note Archive mailboxes are always accessed in online mode. Keep this in mind when considering the use of In-Place Archive mailboxes.

Second, and perhaps more important, is that the archive mailbox serves as a much better alternative for the infamous personal folders, or .PST files. This is because archive mailboxes are stored in Exchange (or the cloud when using Exchange Online In-Place Archive mailboxes), and this has several advantages over .PST files:

- The information is stored in Exchange and does not require inventory and collection of .PST files for discovery, which might be inaccessible and can be tampered with.
- Information stored in Exchange is not prone to theft or loss as are .PST files, which are often hosted on laptops or are transported using USB sticks.
- Archive mailboxes are treated just like mailboxes and thus can be incorporated into your Exchange backup solution, or you can replicate the information using a database availability group.
- Information stored in archive mailboxes can be discovered from a compliance perspective, just like regular mailboxes.

Offloading your mailbox contents to an In-Place archive mailbox can be done manually, or retention policies can be used to move the items from the primary mailbox to the In-Place archive mailbox, depending on criteria such as the age of the item.

In-Place Archive mailboxes also come with certain limitations you should be aware of:

- They are not supported by all clients. For example, mobile devices will not allow you to access your archive mailboxes.
- They and their related primary mailboxes are tightly coupled; you can't simply detach an In-Place archive mailbox and attach it to a different primary mailbox. This is because both the primary mailbox and the In-Place archive mailbox have the same legacyExchangeDN property. A possible workaround for this limitation would be to export the contents of the archive mailbox and import them elsewhere. Be advised, though, that if the primary mailbox is deleted, the archive mailbox will be deleted also.

Note In-Place archiving is a premium feature and requires an Enterprise CAL when used on-premises. More information about licenses can be found at `https://bit.ly/OLLicense`. As such, it has specific Outlook licensing requirements. To quickly check how many mailboxes are configured with archive mailboxes, use the (Get-Mailbox –Archive).Count command.

Enabling Archive Mailboxes

When you consider using In-Place archive mailboxes, check if the clients used in your organization support archive mailboxes.

To create an In-Place archive mailbox for Sarah's mailbox, execute the following command in EMS:

```
[PS] C:\> Enable-Mailbox -Identity Sarah -Archive

Name                  Alias           ServerName       ProhibitSendQuota
----                  -----           ----------       -----------------
Colonel Olrik         Sarah           exch01           Unlimited
```

The target database for the archive mailbox will automatically be picked by the mailbox resources management agent. You can also create an archive mailbox on a specific mailbox database by specifying the archive database in the `Enable-Mailbox` command:

```
[PS] C:\> Enable-Mailbox -Identity David -Archive -ArchiveDatabase MDB02

Name                  Alias           ServerName       ProhibitSendQuota
----                  -----           ----------       -----------------
David Honeychurch     David           exch02           Unlimited
```

After an In-Place archive mailbox is enabled, additional mailbox properties will get populated. For example, when you are retrieving the mailbox properties using the Get-Mailbox command, you will see additional archive-related attributes:

```
[PS] C:\> Get-Mailbox -Identity David | Select *Archive*

ArchiveDatabase             : MDB02
ArchiveGuid                 : 992a0666-9f30-4e90-af3c-acaff4691b1a
ArchiveName                 : {In-Place Archive -David Honeychurch}
JournalArchiveAddress       :
ArchiveQuota                : 100 GB (107,374,182,400 bytes)
ArchiveWarningQuota         : 90 GB (96,636,764,160 bytes)
ArchiveDomain               :
ArchiveStatus               : None
ArchiveState                : Local
```

```
AutoExpandingArchiveEnabled : False
DisabledArchiveDatabase     :
DisabledArchiveGuid         : 00000000-0000-0000-0000-000000000000
ArchiveRelease              :
```

The property ArchiveDatabase contains the name of the database where the archive is stored. ArchiveGuid identifies the archive mailbox. The quota settings are inherited from the default values of the hosting database, and they limit the amount of information stored in the archive as well as when a warning is generated. ArchiveDomain contains the SMTP domain of the tenant hosting the archive, and it is set when using an Exchange Archive mailbox, for example, for on-premises, this property remains blank.

ArchiveStatus indicates the status of the archive and can be set to None or Active; the latter is used to indicate when the Exchange Archive mailbox is ready. The property ArchiveState indicates the state of the archive and can be Hosted Pending, Hosted Provisioned, Local, None, or On Premise. When an archive is disabled, the DisabledArchiveGuid will contain the value of the disabled archive. For on-premises archives, ArchiveDatabase will contain the name of the mailbox database hosting the disabled archive.

Caution If you enable a primary mailbox for an In-Place archive mailbox on-premises, it will create a new archive. If you want to reuse a formerly disabled archive, see the section on reconnecting archive mailboxes.

When you have added an archive mailbox to a mailbox, the Autodiscover response will contain an additional alternative mailbox section that provides information to the client, such as that there is an archive mailbox configured for this mailbox. The client can leverage Autodiscover to connect to the archive mailbox. Because the information is contained in the initial Autodiscover response, no additional configuration is required on the client, and the archive will automatically be configured and added onto the supported clients, as shown with Outlook 2019 in Figure 11-2.

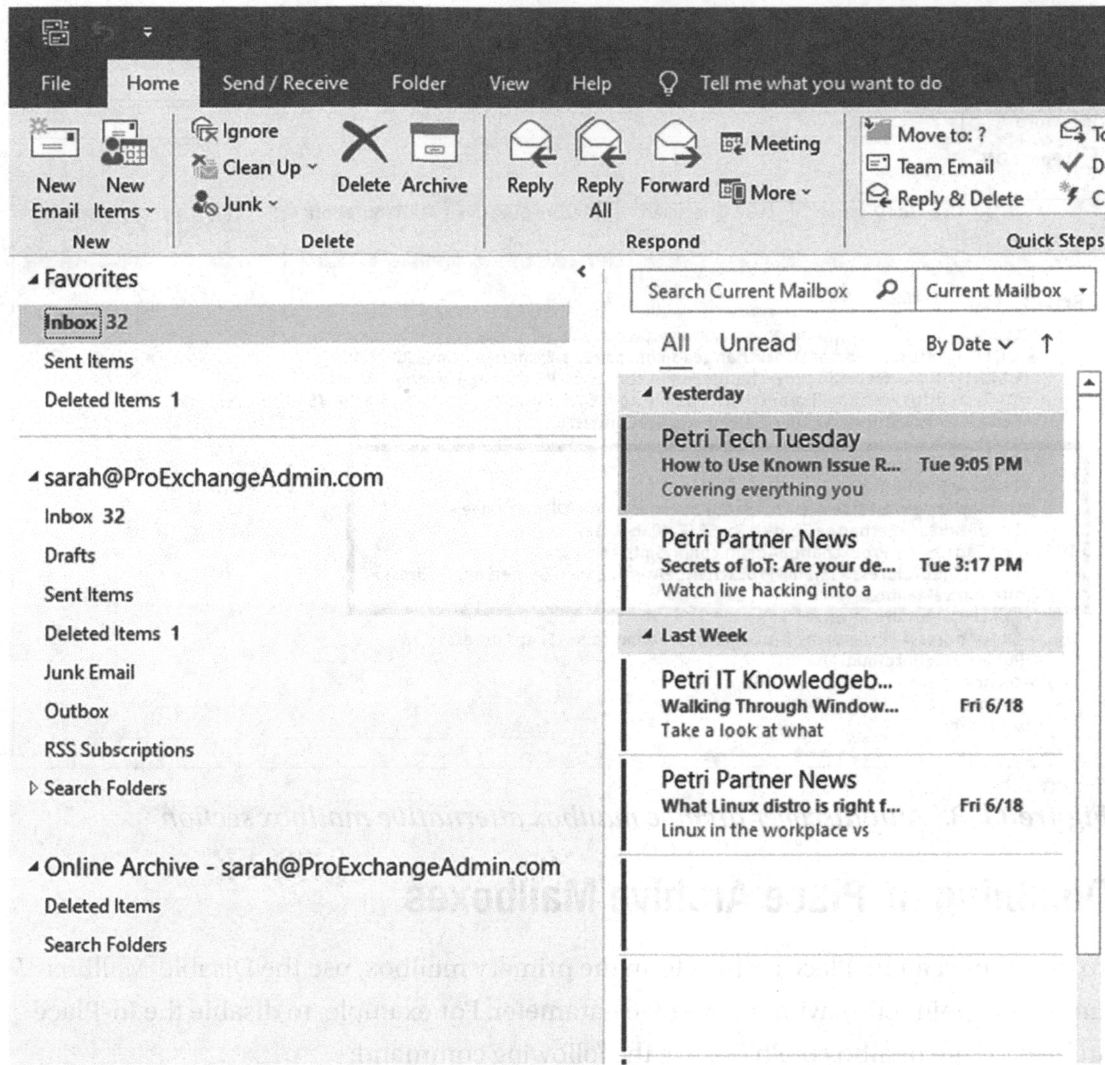

***Figure 11-2.** Outlook 2019 client with the archive mailbox configured*

For example, in the excerpt of the Autodiscover response shown in Figure 11-3, you can see that there is an additional mailbox of type Archive configured, which has the identity shown at the LegacyDN attribute and is accessible through the provided Server attribute.

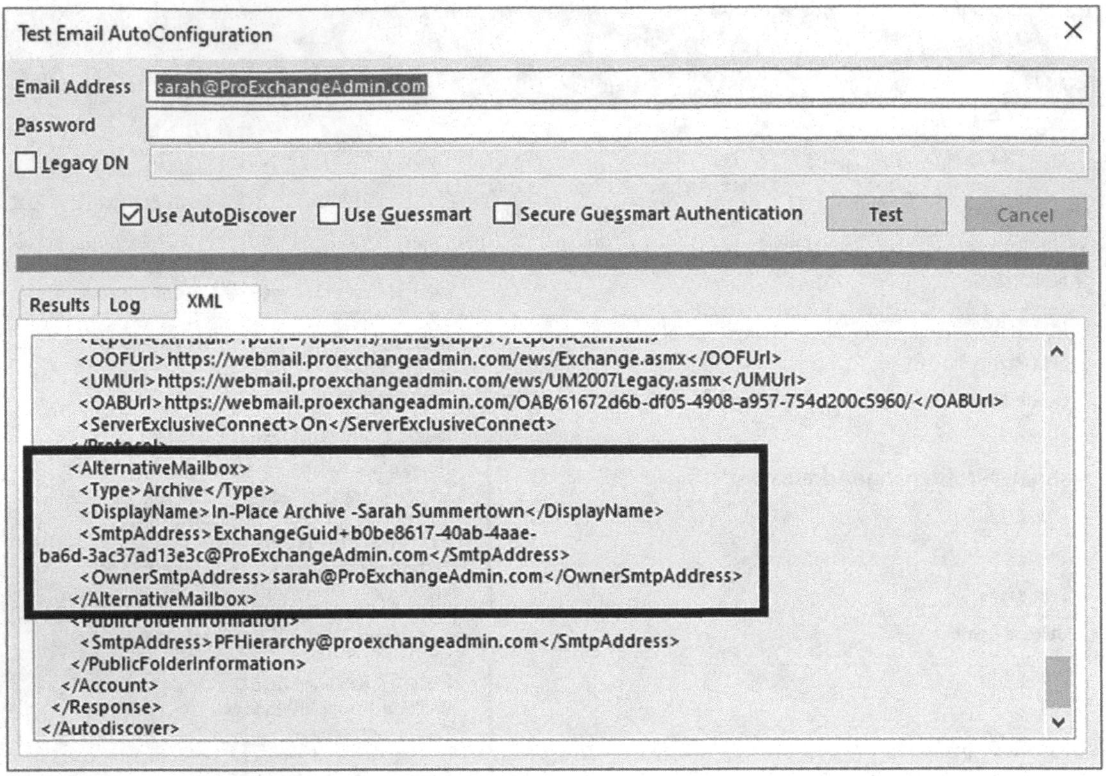

Figure 11-3. *Autodiscover archive mailbox alternative mailbox section*

Disabling In-Place Archive Mailboxes

To disconnect an In-Place archive from the primary mailbox, use the Disable-Mailbox cmdlet in conjunction with the Archive parameter. For example, to disable the In-Place archive for the mailbox of Philip, use the following command:

```
[PS] C:\> Disable-Mailbox -Identity Philip -Archive
```

Note Disconnected In-Place archive mailboxes follow the same deleted mailbox retention settings as their primary mailboxes. By default, this means that they will be removed from the mailbox database after 30 days.

Reconnecting Archive Mailboxes

Just as when you disable a mailbox, the mailbox doesn't get deleted, but it does get disconnected. This means the user object is stripped of its In-Place archive mailbox-related properties, and the In-Place archive mailbox is retained in the mailbox database until the mailbox retention expires; after that, it is physically removed from the database.

Note If you want to reconnect a disabled In-Place Archive mailbox, just enable the In-Place Archive mailbox for the primary mailbox.

As with mailboxes, you can reconnect a disabled on-premises In-Place archive mailbox to a mailbox-enabled user, and this will be the original primary mailbox. To get a list of all disconnected In-Place archive mailboxes, use the following command:

```
[PS] C:\> Get-MailboxDatabase | Get-Mailboxestatistics | Where
{$_.DisconnectDate -and $_.IsArchiveMailbox}
```

To connect an on-premises archive to its original primary mailbox, use the Connect-Mailbox cmdlet in conjunction with the Archive parameter, for example:

```
[PS] C:\> Connect-Mailbox -Identity d972ef60-8eca-4b0b-a36d-cb9d0903883c -
Archive -User Philip -Database MDB2
```

Checking and Modifying Archive Mailbox Quotas

Primary mailboxes and their related In-Place archive mailboxes can have different quota settings. You can query the archive mailbox quota settings for all mailboxes by using the following command:

```
[PS] C:\> Get-Mailbox -Archive | Select Name, Archive*Quota | FT -A

Name              ArchiveQuota                     ArchiveWarningQuota
----              ------------                     -------------------
Sarah Summertown  100 GB (107,374,182,400 bytes) 90 GB (96,636,764,160 bytes)
Glenn Kendall     100 GB (107,374,182,400 bytes) 90 GB (96,636,764,160 bytes)
David Honeychurch 100 GB (107,374,182,400 bytes) 90 GB (96,636,764,160 bytes)
Colonel Olrik     100 GB (107,374,182,400 bytes) 90 GB (96,636,764,160 bytes)
```

You can modify the archive mailbox quota settings using the Set-Mailbox command, for example:

```
[PS] C:\> Set-Mailbox -Identity Philip -ArchiveQuota 200GB -
ArchiveWarningQuota 190GB
```

Relocating the Archive Mailboxes

The primary mailbox and the archive do not need to be hosted in the same mailbox database. This means you can have dedicated mailbox servers for hosting primary mailboxes and for hosting archives.

When you want to relocate only the archive mailboxes to a different database, you can utilize the New-MoveRequest cmdlet in conjunction with the -ArchiveOnly parameter. In addition, you can use the -ArchiveTargetDatabase parameter to specify the target database for the archive mailboxes. For example, to relocate all the archive mailboxes to a database called MDB2, you use the following command:

```
[PS] C:\> Get-Mailbox -Archive | New-MoveRequest -ArchiveOnly -
ArchiveTargetDatabase MDB2
```

Do not forget to clean up your move requests when the archives have been moved successfully; you do this by using this command:

```
[PS] C:\> Get-MoveRequest | Where {$_.Status -eq 'Completed'} |
Remove-MoveRequest -Confirm:$False
```

Exporting and Importing Archive Mailboxes

Should you need to physically move the contents of an In-Place archive mailbox to a different mailbox, you can opt to export and import the information. To export or import mailbox contents, you first need to have the mailbox import/export management role. You can use the Exchange Admin Center to assign this role, or you can use the following command:

```
[PS] C:\> New-ManagementRoleAssignment -Role 'Mailbox Import Export' -User
Administrator
```

Next, you create a network share for hosting the .PST files. Exporting and importing require a network share because it is undetermined which Exchange server will ultimately handle the import or export request in a multi-Exchange server environment. Make sure the Exchange Trusted Subsystem has read/write permissions.

Then, to export the contents in an archive mailbox, you use `New-MailboxExportRequest` in conjunction with the -IsArchive parameter, and use -FilePath to specify the full UNC file name of the .PST file, for example:

```
[PS] C:\> New-MailboxExportRequest -Mailbox Philip -FilePath '\\FS01\PST\
Philip_Archive.pst' -IsArchive
```

To import the contents in a subfolder, you use TargetRootFolder, for example:

```
[PS] C:\> New-MailboxImportRequest -Mailbox Philip -FilePath '\\FS01\PST\
Philip_Archive.pst' -IsArchive -TargetRootFolder 'Imported Archive'
```

When you're finished, you can remove the import and export requests using `Remove-MailboxExportRequest` and `Remove-MailboxImportRequest`.

In-Place eDiscovery

Electronic discovery, or eDiscovery, refers to the discovery or the ability to discover exchange of information. Exchange Server 2010 introduced multi-mailbox search and legal hold, which were features to discover organization-wide contents of mailboxes or to freeze mailbox contents and record changes for legal purposes. Both features are renamed in Exchange Server 2013: multi-mailbox search has become in-place eDiscovery, and legal hold is now known as In-Place hold (there is more on In-Place hold later in this chapter).

Early versions of Exchange did not contain such features and had no options to retain deleted information, let alone retain changed information. If Exchange administrators were requested to provide mailbox information for a certain period, that would most certainly result in having to restore mailbox backups and to extract the requested information.

> **Caution** When you are in a coexistence scenario of Exchange Server 2016 with Exchange Server 2010, you need to move the system mailbox to Exchange Server 2016. If you do not, you will not be able to perform eDiscovery searches, as eDiscovery also stores configuration information in the system mailbox.

Management of In-Place eDiscovery

In-place eDiscovery of information stored in Exchange and management of in-place hold on mailboxes are secure processes dealing with potentially confidential information, and thus they are subject to privacy legislation. To be able to create eDiscovery searches, the user needs to be a member of the RBAC role group Discovery Management. This group is empty by default.

To add users to the Discovery Management group, so as to perform eDiscovery searches or put mailboxes on in-place hold, you use the following command (where Philip is the identity of the user you want to be able to create eDiscovery searches):

```
[PS] C:\> Add-RoleGroupMember -Identity 'Discovery Management' -Member
Philip
```

To list the current members of the Discovery Management role group, you use

```
[PS] C:\> Get-RoleGroupMember -Identity 'Discovery Management'
```

When the investigation is over, do not forget to remove the user from the role group using the following command:

```
[PS] C:\> Remove-RoleGroupMember -Identity 'Discovery Management' -Member
Philip
```

Although this book is primarily targeted toward PowerShell, sometimes a GUI can be very useful, especially for non-repetitive tasks. To use the EAC to perform these tasks, open EAC and navigate to Permissions ➤ Admin Roles and open the Discovery Management group. In the Members section, add the user Philip to this group. The Discovery Management group is shown in Figure 11-4.

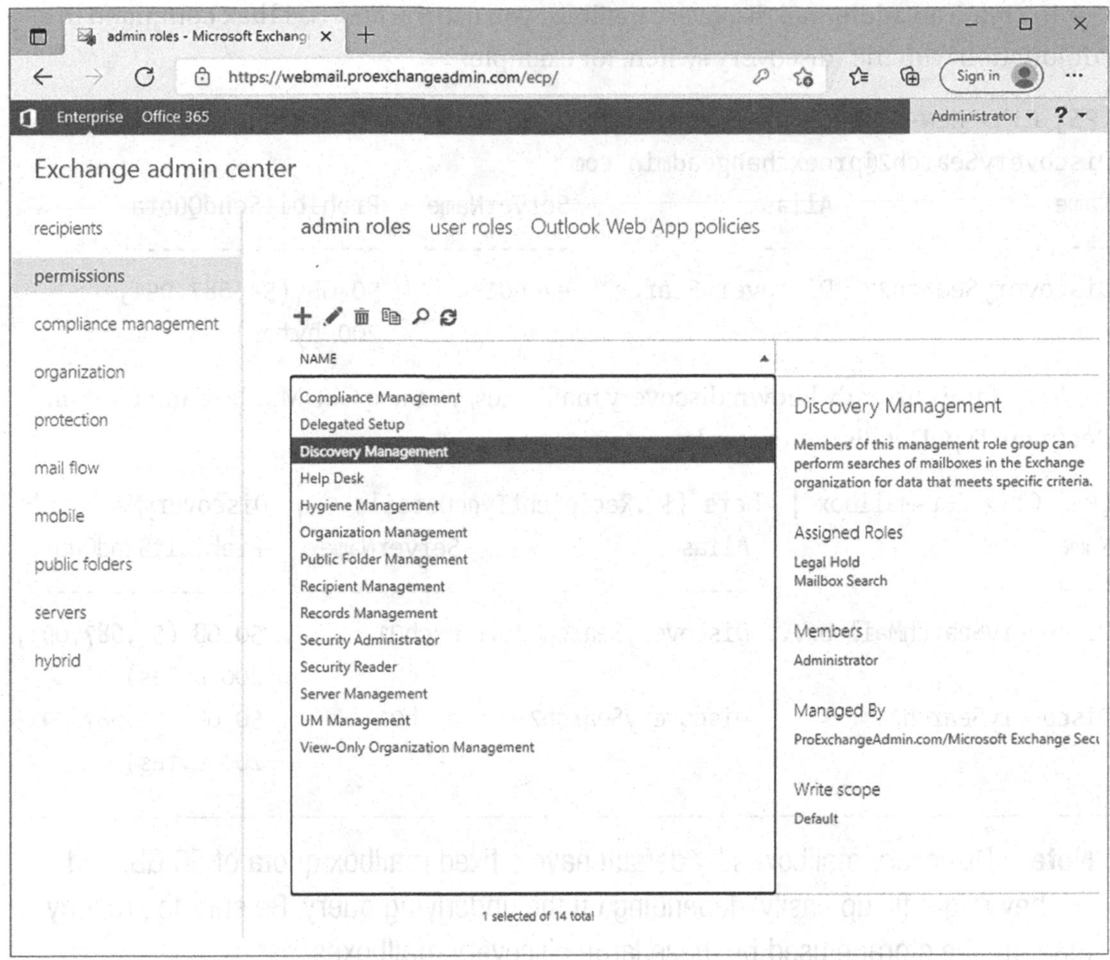

***Figure 11-4.** Managing the Discovery Management role group in EAC*

Discovery Mailbox

A discovery mailbox is a mailbox that can be used for storing contents retrieved as part of an in-place eDiscovery search. During setup, Exchange Servers 2013, 2016, and 2019 create a default discovery mailbox whose name starts with DiscoverySearchMailbox followed by a GUID. You can create additional discovery mailboxes when you need them, for example, to support multiple searches. Because they are like ordinary mailboxes, you can remove a discovery mailbox when it is no longer needed.

To create an additional discovery mailbox, you use the `New-Mailbox` command in conjunction with the -discovery switch, for example:

```
[PS] C:\> New-Mailbox DiscoverySearch2 -Discovery -UserPrincipalName
DiscoverySearch2@proexchangeadmin.com
Name               Alias              ServerName   ProhibitSendQuota
----               -----              ----------   -----------------
DiscoverySearch2   DiscoverySearch2   exch01       50 GB (53,687,091,
                                                   200 bytes)
```

To list the currently known discovery mailboxes, you use Get-Mailbox and filter on RecipientTypeDetails, for example:

```
[PS] C:\> Get-Mailbox | Where {$_.RecipientTypeDetails -eq 'DiscoveryMailbox'}
Name                      Alias                  ServerName   ProhibitSendQuota
----                      -----                  ----------   -----------------
DiscoverySearchMailbox... DiscoverySearchMa...   exch01       50 GB (53,687,091,
                                                              200 bytes)
DiscoverySearch2          DiscoverySearch2       exch01       50 GB (53,687,091,
                                                              200 bytes)
```

Note Discovery mailboxes by default have a fixed mailbox quota of 50 GB, and so they might fill up easily, depending on the underlying query. Be sure to properly manage the storage used by these large discovery mailboxes.

Searching Mailboxes

The easiest way to perform a discovery search is using the EAC. Remember that as an admin we are used to PowerShell, but users that perform these searches are most likely not. To perform a discovery search, follow these steps:

1. Open the Exchange Admin Center and navigate to Compliance Management ➤ In-Place eDiscovery & Hold. Click the + icon to start a new search.
2. Enter a name for the search and optionally add a description. Click Next to continue.
3. Specify a specific mailbox to search, or select the “search all mailboxes” radio button to perform a search on all mailboxes. Be aware, this can take a serious amount of time. Click Next to continue.
4. Choose whether you want to search all content or enter search criteria, such as keywords or a specific date range. When you are finished entering the criteria, click Next to continue. This is shown in Figure 11-5.
5. Select Finish to store the eDiscovery search.

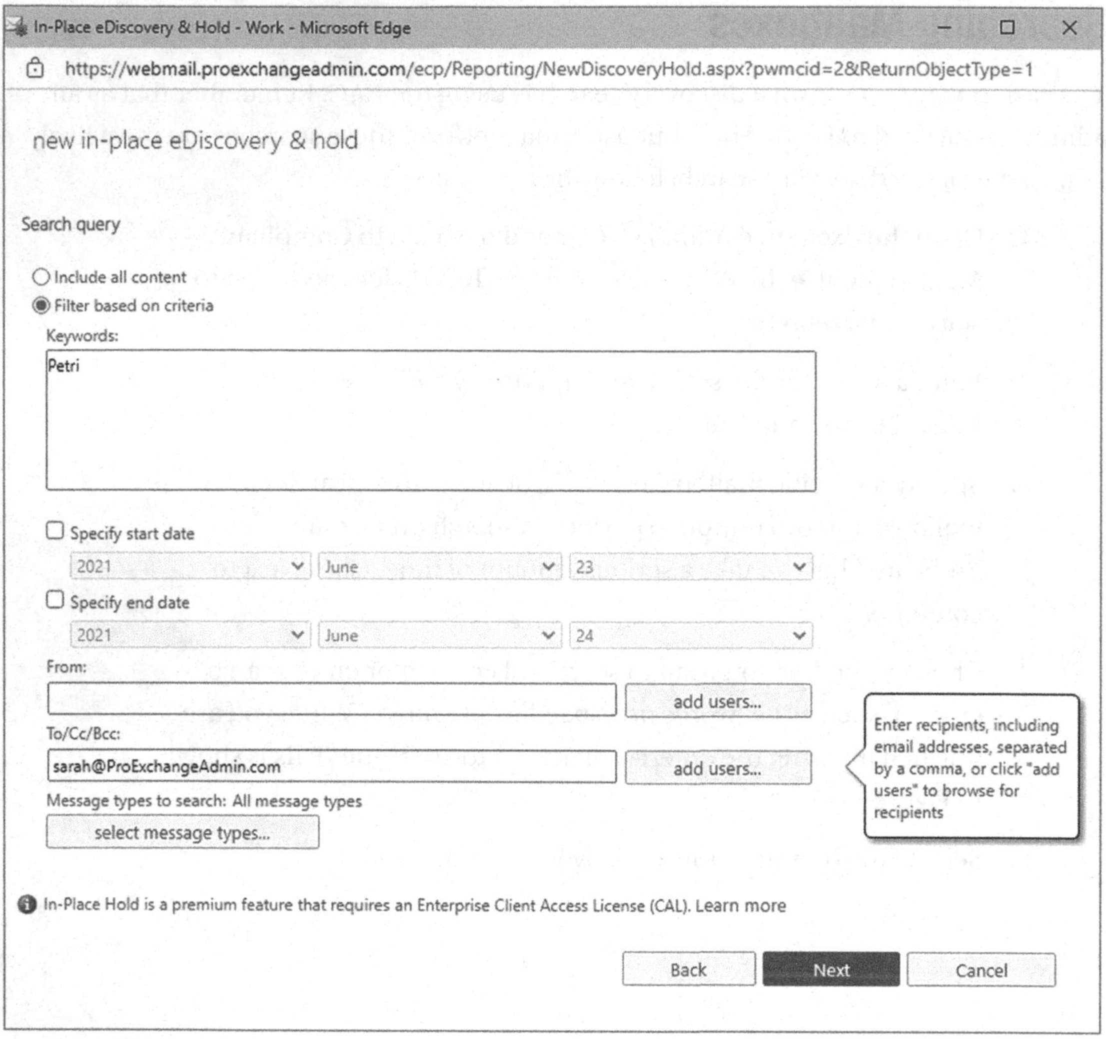

In-Place eDiscovery & Hold - Work - Microsoft Edge
https://webmail.proexchangeadmin.com/ecp/Reporting/NewDiscoveryHold.aspx?pwmcid=2&ReturnObjectType=1

new in-place eDiscovery & hold

Search query

- ○ Include all content
- ◉ Filter based on criteria

Keywords:

Petri

- ☐ Specify start date

2021 | June | 23

- ☐ Specify end date

2021 | June | 24

From:

add users...

To/Cc/Bcc:

sarah@ProExchangeAdmin.com

add users...

Enter recipients, including email addresses, separated by a comma, or click "add users" to browse for recipients

Message types to search: All message types

select message types...

In-Place Hold is a premium feature that requires an Enterprise Client Access License (CAL). Learn more

Back | Next | Cancel

***Figure 11-5.** Search query for a new In-Place eDiscovery and In-Place Hold*

Tip When specifying search query keywords, you can use "and" or "or" Boolean operators to construct queries using multiple keywords. For example, to search for "Fabrikam" and "Options," enter FABRIKAM AND OPTIONS. To influence the evaluation order, you can use parentheses, that is, X AND Y OR Z is not the same as X AND (Y OR Z). To include spaces in a search string, put the string in quotes—for example, "WINGTIP TOYS." To look for words in each other's vicinity, you can use the NEAR(N), where N is the number of words before or after to take into account—for example, FABRIKAM NEAR(5) OPTIONS. Finally, you can use an asterisk (*) for wildcard matching—for example, CON* matches words starting with CON (e.g., consultant, connection, construction).

After defining the discovery search criteria, the results will be shown in the in-place discovery and hold section. Exchange will then start to estimate the amount of data and number of unsearchable items. Note that the query will only be activated when you view or export the results, meaning the query will also return items added after the discovery search was created.

Note Unsearchable items are items that cannot be or are not indexed because of unrecognized, nonindexed file types or encryption. IRM-protected messages can be indexed.

After defining the discovery search, you have the following options:

- Update the search result figures, such as the amount of data and the number of items.
- Preview the search results on-screen.
- Copy the search results to a discovery mailbox. Besides the option to exclude unsearchable items, you can cancel duplicate items so as to have items only returned once, even if they match multiple criteria. Also, you can have Exchange send you an email with a summary of the results.
- Export the discovered items to a .PST file. This option can be useful if you need to ship the information to third parties.

You can also utilize the Exchange Management Shell to perform discovery searches using the `New-MailboxSearch` cmdlet. When using `New-MailboxSearch` to perform discovery searches, you have the following parameter options:

- **Name**—To set the name of the search.
- **EndDate**—To set the end of the search time span.

- **StartDate**—To set the start of the search time span.
- **EstimateOnly**—To indicate you only want an estimate of the number of items.
- **ExcludeDuplicateMessages**—To remove duplicate items from the results.
- **IncludeUnsearchableItems**—To include items not indexed by Exchange Search.
- **LogLevel**—To set the level of logging; options are Supress, Basic, and Full.
- **MessageTypes**—To limit the search to a specific message type. Valid options are Email, Meetings, Tasks, Notes, Docs, Journals, Contacts, and IM. When omitted, all items are searched.
- **Recipients**—To limit the search to certain recipients (examines TO, CC, and BCC fields).
- **SearchQuery**—To specify terms to search for.
- **Senders**—To limit the search to certain senders (FROM).
- **SourceMailboxes**—To specify the mailboxes to be searched.
- **StatusMailRecipients**—To specify users who should receive status reports.
- **TargetMailbox**—To set the mailbox that should receive a copy of the search results.

Note When a start date or end date is specified, it is matched against the receive date or creation date (depending on the item type) of discovered items.

To create a discovery search titled SarahSearch2 for Sarah's mailbox on items received or created between March 1, 2021, and June 30, 2021, of type Email, with the keyword "IT Knowledgebase" and the destination set to DiscoverySearch2, you use the following command:

```
[PS] C:\> New-MailboxSearch SarahSearch2 -SourceMailboxes Sarah -StartDate
3/1/2021 -EndDate 06/30/2021 -TargetMailbox 'DiscoverySearch2' -SearchQuery
'IT Knowledgebase' -MessageTypes Email

Name         CreatedBy                  InPlaceHoldEnabled Status
----         ---------                  ------------------ ------
SarahSearch2 PROEXCHANGE\Administrator False              NotStarted
```

To get a list of your current discovery search entries, you use the `Get-MailboxSearch` cmdlet. To run a discovery search, use `Start-MailboxSearch`. When you have selected to copy the discovered data to a discovery mailbox, you start the mailbox search, which clears any existing results for that specific mailbox search from that discovery mailbox, as follows:

```
[PS] C:\> Start-MailboxSearch -Identity SarahSearch2
```

Note You cannot change the properties of a running discovery search. To do that, you need to restart the search by using Stop/Resume in EAC or by using the cmdlets Stop-MailboxSearch and Start-MailboxSearch.

To modify a discovery search, you use `Set-MailboxSearch`, for example:

```
[PS] C:\> Set-MailboxSearch -Identity SarahSearch2 -StatusMailRecipients
philip@proexchangeadmin.com
```

When the search is finished, the configured StatusMailRecipients will receive a status report, which will look like what is shown in Figure 11-6.

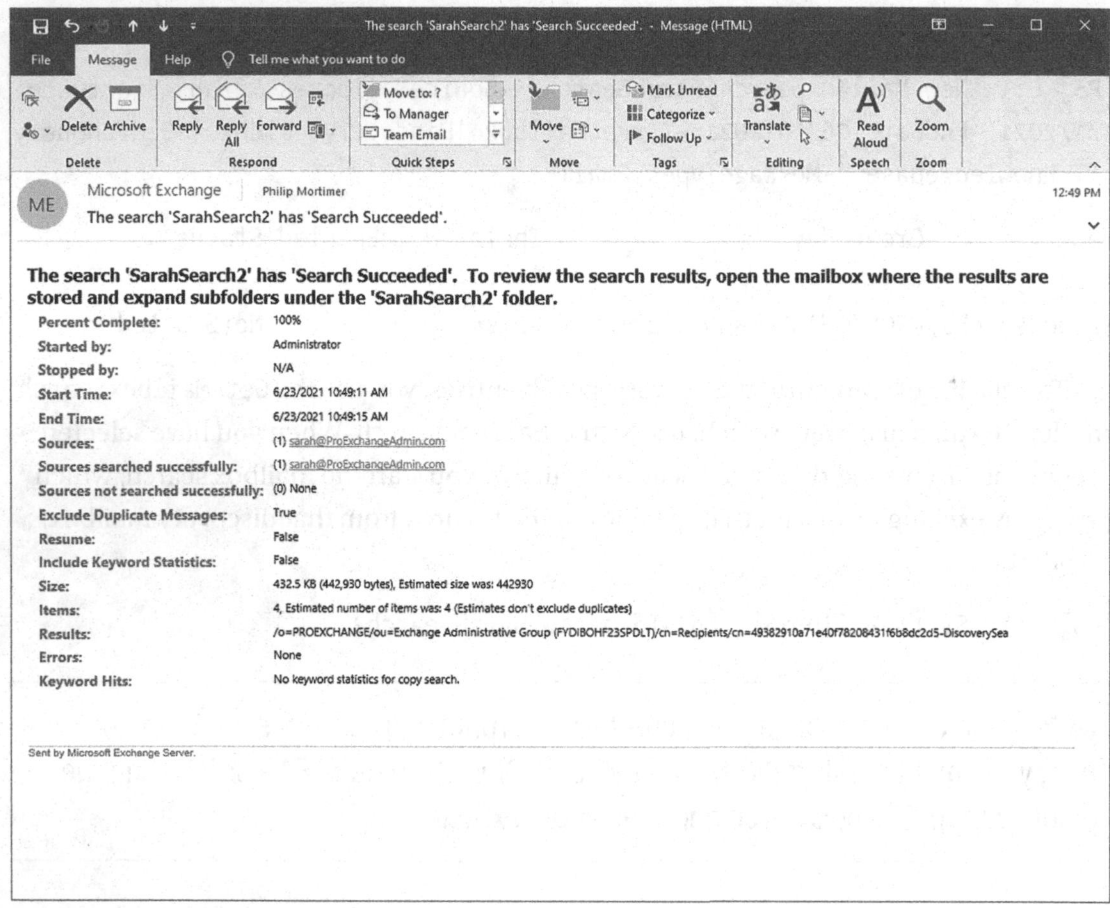

***Figure 11-6.** In-Place eDiscovery search report*

When you explore a discovery mailbox, you will notice the discovered data is stored in a folder named after the discovery search as shown in Figure 11-7.

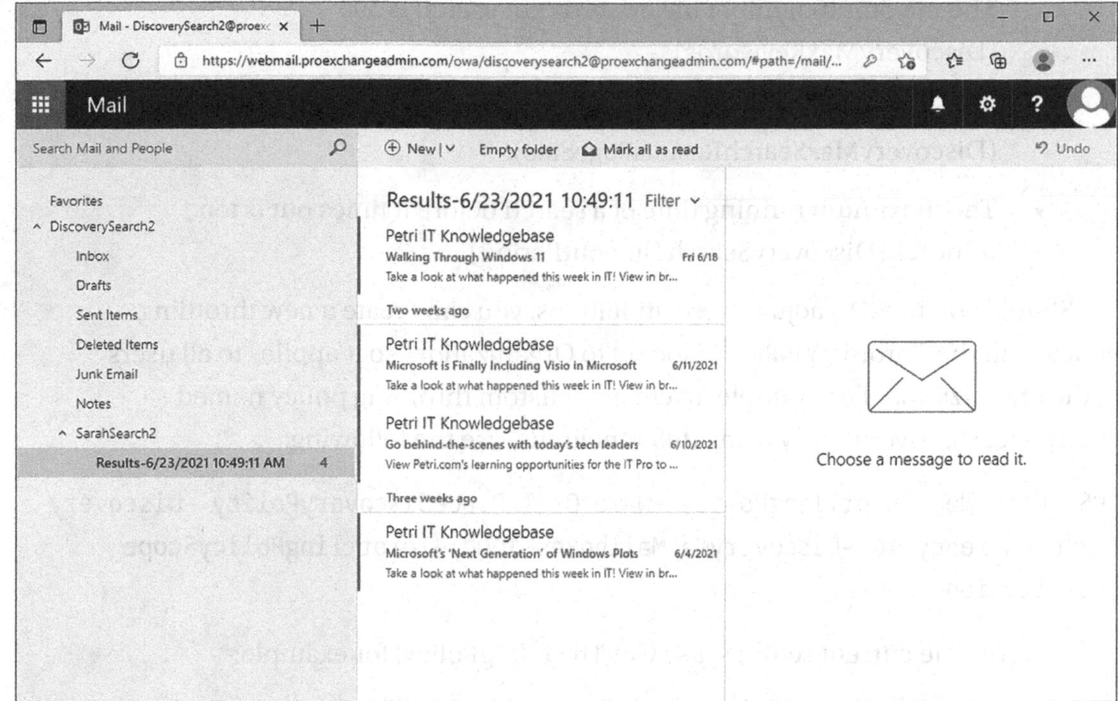

***Figure 11-7.** Contents of an In-Place eDiscovery folder*

While the search is running, you will notice a folder named <SEARCH NAME>. Working. This folder is used to temporarily store the search results and will be renamed after the search is finished.

Finally, you have the option to delete the contents from mailboxes using discovery search. For this purpose, you can use `Search-Mailbox` with the -DeleteContent parameter in combination with a search query, for example:

```
[PS] C:\> Search-Mailbox -Identity Sarah -DeleteContent -SearchQuery
"Bitcoin"
```

To preview the information that would potentially be deleted, you can first use Search-Mailbox with the LogOnly parameter. Be advised that the in-place eDiscovery search process is throttled and by default is subject to the following limitations:

- The maximum number of concurrent searches per user is two (DiscoveryMaxConcurrency).
- The maximum number of mailbox searches per discovery is 5000 (DiscoveryMaxMailboxes).

- The maximum number of keywords per search is 500 (DiscoveryMaxKeywords).
- The maximum number of items displayed per page in preview is 200 (DiscoveryMaxSearchResultsPageSize).
- The maximum running time of a search before it times out is ten minutes (DiscoverySearchTimeoutPeriod).

Should you need to adjust these limitations, you can create a new throttling policy with the ThrottlingPolicyScope set to Organization, so it applies to all users in the organization. For example, to create a custom throttling policy named OrgInPlaceDiscoveryPolicy using different limits, use the following:

```
[PS] C:\> New-ThrottlingPolicy -Name OrgInPlaceDiscoveryPolicy -Discovery
MaxConcurrency 10 -DiscoveryMaxMailboxes 1000 -ThrottlingPolicyScope
organization
```

To verify the current settings, use Get-ThrottlingPolicy, for example:

```
[PS] C:\> Get-ThrottlingPolicy OrgInPlaceDiscoveryPolicy | fl Discovery*
```

In-Place Hold

There could be circumstances when an organization needs to preserve its email records, such as for a legal investigation. It may also be necessary to freeze the contents of a mailbox, preventing them from being processed by the managed folder assistant (MFA) as part of the messaging records management (MRM) process. A possible task of the managed folder assistant is, for example, the automatic removal of items after a certain period.

To support requests to preserve mailbox information, Exchange contains a feature called in-place hold. This feature was introduced with Exchange Server 2010 as litigation hold, but litigation hold is still available in Exchange 2019. In-place hold allows organizations to freeze mailbox contents, prevent manual or automatic updating, and/or not remove expired items that have passed the retention period.

In-place hold integrates with in-place eDiscovery, allowing you to limit the hold items by using criteria such as keywords or senders. It is also possible to specify a time span or to search for specific item types, such as email or calendar items.

Note When the managed folder assistant processes a mailbox, and it finds five or more query-based holds applying to the same mailbox, it will put the whole mailbox on in-place hold. If the number of matching queries drops below five, the MFA will revert to query-based in-place hold again.

Normally, when a mailbox is not on in-place hold, deleted messages are moved to the deleted items folder. When items get deleted from the deleted items folder or when the user shift-deletes the messages, those messages get moved to the recoverable items\deletions folder. This is the folder in which contents are displayed when, for example, you use the Recover Deleted Items option in Outlook. When the managed folder assistant processes the mailbox, the deleted items that had passed the retention period are purged.

When a mailbox is put on in-place hold, though, items that would normally be purged from the recoverable items\deletions folder are instead moved to the recoverable items\discoveryholds folder. These items remain there until the in-place hold is lifted.

Note To use query-based in-place hold, such as queries based on sender or start time, the user requires both the Mailbox Search and the Litigation Hold management roles. Without the Mailbox Search management role, the user cannot specify the criteria and can only put whole mailboxes on in-place hold. The Discovery Management role group is assigned both these management roles.

When a mailbox is put on in-place hold, copy-on-write is used when updating or removing messages from the mailbox. This is to preserve original copies of modified messages and to prevent tampering. Copies of original messages are stored in the recoverable items\versions folder. This is shown in Figure 11-8.

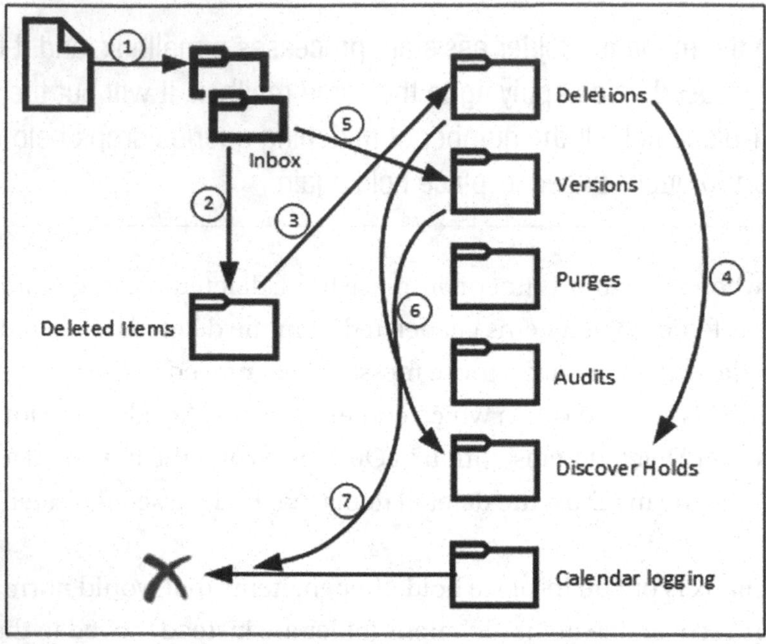

Figure 11-8. *How in-place hold and copy-on-write work*

Here is how in-place hold and copy-on-write work in detail:

1. A message is delivered to the mailbox. The message can be stored in the inbox or any of the other folders.
2. When the user deletes a message, it is moved to the deleted items folder.
3. When the deleted items folder is emptied, the messages are removed from the deleted items folder, or the user hard-deletes a message (shift-delete), and those messages are moved to the recoverable items\deletions folder. The contents of this folder are displayed when the user selects Recover Deleted Items from Outlook or the Outlook Web App.
4. Messages from the recoverable items\deletions folder are purged when the user removes those messages from the recoverable items folder in Outlook or Outlook Web Access. When the mailbox is on in-place hold, messages are moved to the recoverable items\discoveryholds folder instead of getting purged.

5. When the user edits a message, a copy of the original message is stored in the versions folder using copy-on-write.

6. When the mailbox is on in-place hold, expired messages from the recoverable items\deletions folder and recoverable items\versions folder are moved to the recoverable items\discoveryholds folder if they are touched by any current in-place hold query. The managed folder assistant is responsible for keeping track of messages in relation to any in-place hold queries.

7. Expired messages will be purged from the recoverable items\deletions and recoverable items\versions folders when the mailbox is no longer on in-place hold. Messages not touched by any current in-place hold query are also purged from the recoverable items\discoveryholds folder when they expire.

Not listed earlier is that when a user shift-deletes an item, it will go straight to the recoverable items\deletions folder.

To get a sense of how this looks under the hood, you can use tools like MFCMAPI, available from `https://github.com/stephenegriffin/mfcmapi`. Note that to be able to view the recoverable items in MFCMAPI, you need to go to Tools ➤ Options and check the following options:

- Use the MDB_ONLINE flag when calling OpenMsgStore.
- Use the MAPI_NO_CACHE flag when calling OpenEntry.

Warning Low-level utilities like MFCMAPI can be powerful tools providing lots of insight, but they can also operate on the low-level structures and contents of your Exchange data and create inconsistencies or corruption. Tools like these offer great power to administrators, and consequently using them comes with great responsibility.

From MFCMAPI, you can open the mailbox via Session Logon (selecting an Outlook profile), double-click the Mailbox store entry, and expand the root container. This is shown in Figure 11-9.

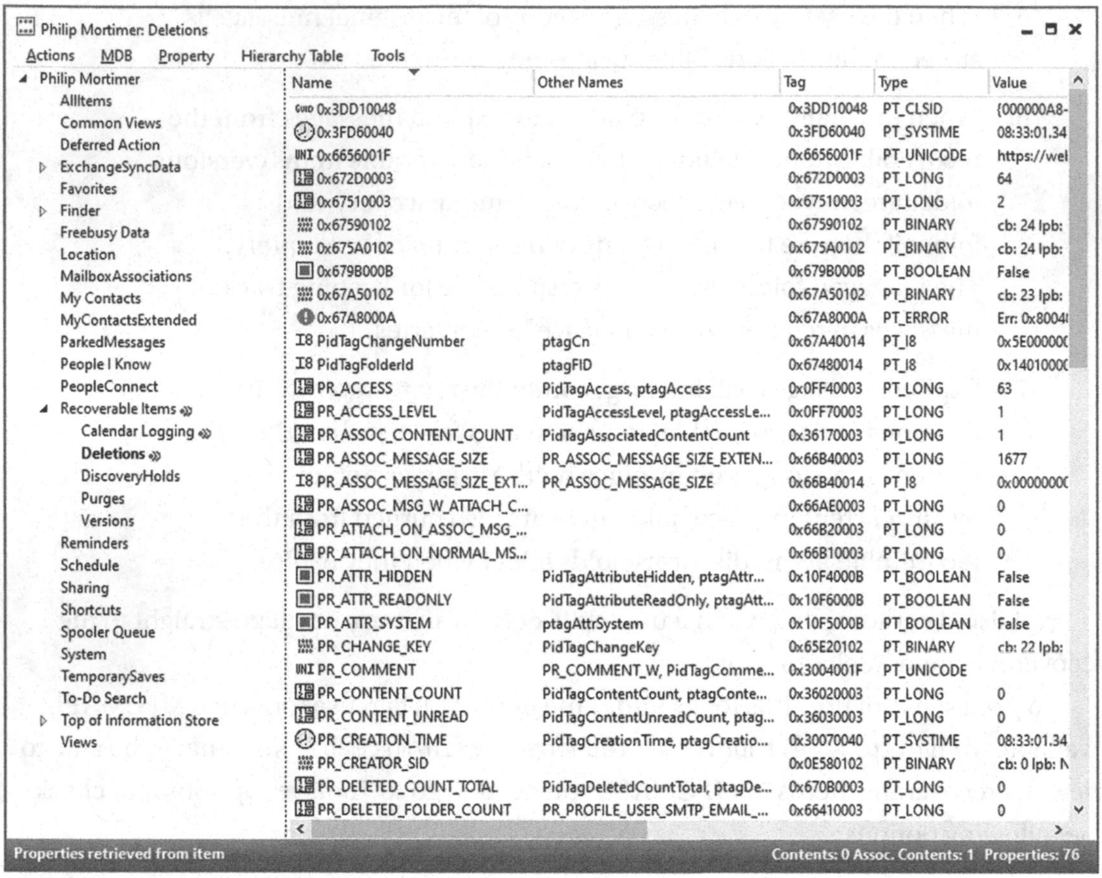

Figure 11-9. Recoverable items folder in the mailbox on in-place hold

Within the recoverable items folder, you will find the deletions, versions, and discoveryholds folders, among others, and you can inspect their contents.

Note You cannot change messages in the versions folder; when you try to save an edited item, the save attempt will fail. You can remove messages from the versions or discoveryholds folders, but these will end up in the purges folder. Messages cannot be removed from the purges folder, thereby preventing (malicious) removal or alteration of original messages.

Enabling In-Place Hold

To put a mailbox on in-place hold using the Exchange Management Shell, you use the same cmdlet as you would use for in-place discovery, `New-MailboxSearch`, additionally specifying the parameter -Inplaceholdenabled while setting it to $True. Since In-Place hold leverages In-Place eDiscovery, you have all the query options of New-Mailboxsearch at your disposal.

The simplest form of in-place hold is a mailbox hold, for which you need only specify the mailboxes to be put on hold. For example, to put the mailbox of a user named Philip on hold, use the following:

```
[PS] C:\> New-MailboxSearch -Name PhilipHoldQuery1 -SourceMailboxes
Philip -InPlaceHoldEnabled $true
```

Note The use of switches and Boolean parameters is not always consequent, despite serving the same purpose. For example, when you want to enable the creation of an in-place archive, you specify New-Mailbox –Archive; but when you want to put a mailbox on hold, you need to set InPlaceHoldEnabled to $true.

The fact that a mailbox is put on hold does not manifest itself in any way for the end user. If it is required and deemed acceptable, you could send the user a notification or utilize the RetentionComment and RetentionURL mailbox settings to put a notice on the account settings section in Outlook, for example:

```
[PS] C:\> Set-Mailbox -Identity Philip -RetentionComment 'Your mailbox is
put on In-Place Hold' -RetentionUrl 'http://intranet.proexchangeadmin.com/
faq/mailboxhold'
```

This message and its clickable URL will be displayed on the Outlook account page, as shown in Figure 11-10.

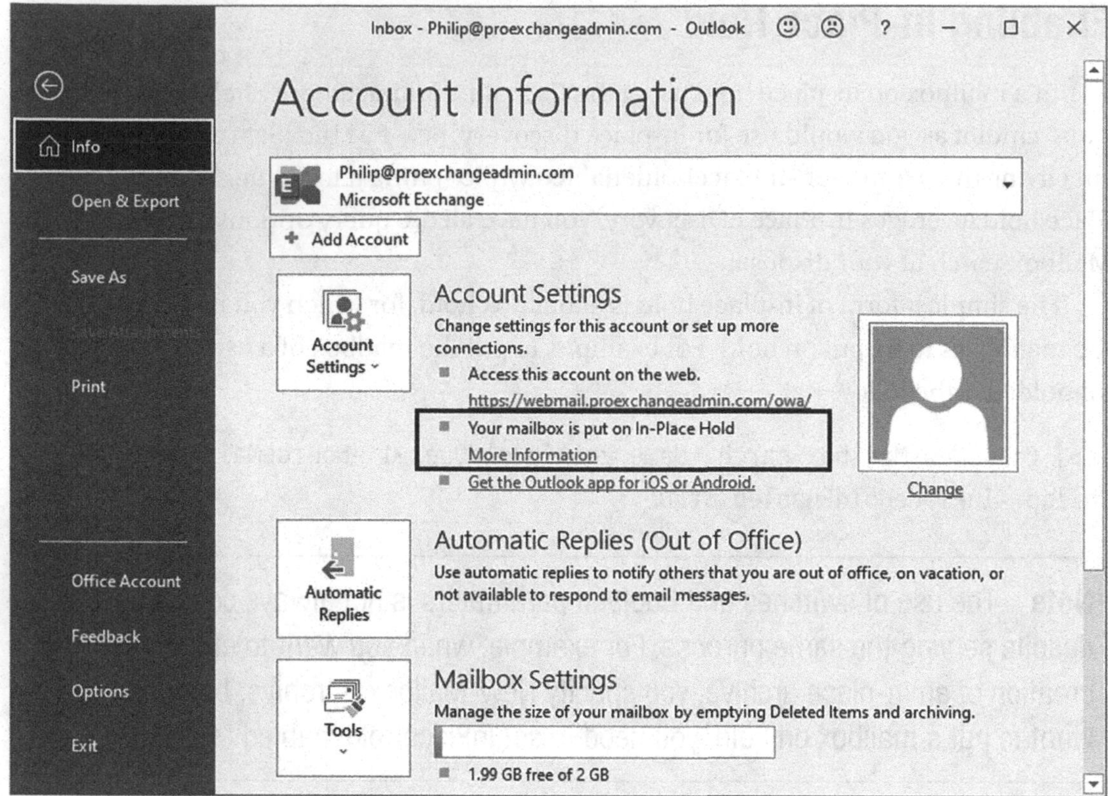

***Figure 11-10.** Outlook notification of in-place hold*

You can clear the message by setting these properties to $null:

```
[PS] C:\> Set-Mailbox -Identity Philip -RetentionComment $null
-RetentionUrl $null
```

To define an in-place hold from the Exchange Admin Center, you perform the following steps:

1. Open the Exchange Admin Center and navigate to Compliance Management ➤ In-Place eDiscovery & Hold.
2. Select New, enter a name and optionally a description, and select Next.
3. Select Specify to indicate which mailboxes to search. Use the + sign to add mailboxes to put on hold. When done, select Next.

4. Choose whether you want to search all content or enter some search criteria, like keywords or a specific date range. When finished entering the criteria, select Next.
5. Check Place for putting on hold the content matching the search query into the selected mailboxes. You can specify if you want to keep the records indefinitely or only for a certain number of days following message receipt or creation. Select Finish to save the query definition and activate the in-place hold.

Note If an in-place archive is configured for the primary mailbox and the mailbox is put on in-place hold, the in-place hold will be applied to the in-place archive as well.

Disabling In-Place Hold

To disable in-place hold, you set the InPlaceHoldEnabled attribute of the related in-place discovery search to $false, as follows:

```
[PS] C:\> Set-MailboxSearch -Name PhilipHoldQuery1 -InPlaceHoldEnabled
$false
```

When an in-place hold is lifted, the mailbox and its messages will again fall under the applicable retention policy regime. Any messages stored in the recoverable items\versions folders as part of the in-place hold will get removed by the managed folder assistant.

Caution When an in-place hold is removed, it may release messages from being placed on hold, thus possibly expiring and removing those messages if they no longer match any other current in-place hold query. After an in-place hold is lifted, the managed folder assistant purges all messages from the discoveryholds, versions, and purges folders.

Note that this does not remove the underlying search; to remove the discovery search definition, use `Remove-MailboxSearch`, for example:

```
[PS] C:\> Remove-MailboxSearch -Name PhilipHoldQuery1
```

Messaging Records Management

In the world of ever-growing mailbox sizes, organizations require controls to manage the volume of email stored within their corporate environments. When these mailboxes are left unmanaged and unrestricted, there could be a disruption of email services and higher storage costs. Additionally, organizations may have a legal obligation to store certain electronic communications for a given period. This makes email management crucial in many organizations.

Messaging records management (MRM) is the feature of Exchange that deals with the organization and management of email by using an established set of rules. Messaging records management was introduced with Exchange Server 2010, based on its managed folders, and is known as MRM 1.0. The MRM version introduced in Exchange Server 2010 SP1 and later, and still in Exchange 2019, is MRM 2.0. In MRM 2.0, mailboxes are managed by definition of the retention policies that have been assigned to those mailboxes. Those retention policies consist of retention policy tags that identify the rules that could be applied to the mailbox or elements of the mailbox. A retention policy tag can be part of one or more retention policies. The retention policies are enforced by the managed folder assistant. Let's discuss these elements next.

Retention Policy Tags

A retention policy tag defines what retention setting is to be used for a message or folder to which that tag is assigned. There are three types of retention tags:

- **Default policy tag (DPT)**—This is assigned to items that do not otherwise have a tag assigned. A retention policy can have only one DPT.
- **Retention policy tag (RPT)**—This tag is assigned to default well-known folders, such as inbox, deleted items, calendar, and so on.

- **Personal tag**—This tag can be assigned by users using Outlook or Outlook Web Access to apply retention settings to specific items or folders.

Note Personal tags are a premium feature and require an Enterprise CAL or Exchange Online Archiving License.

In this section, we will create new policy tags first with the EAC to make it more visible. Later in this section, we will continue with PowerShell.

To create a retention policy tag using the EAC, you do the following:

1. Open the Exchange Admin Center and navigate to Compliance Management ➤ Retention Tags.
2. Click the + sign and select one of the following options:
    - Applied automatically to entire mailbox (default) to create a default policy tag
    - Applied automatically to a default folder to create a retention policy tag
    - Applied by users to items and folders (personal) to create a personal tag
3. Depending on the type of tag you choose, you are now asked to complete the creation of the retention policy tag by providing details such as name, retention period, and action to take. An example is shown in Figure 11-11.

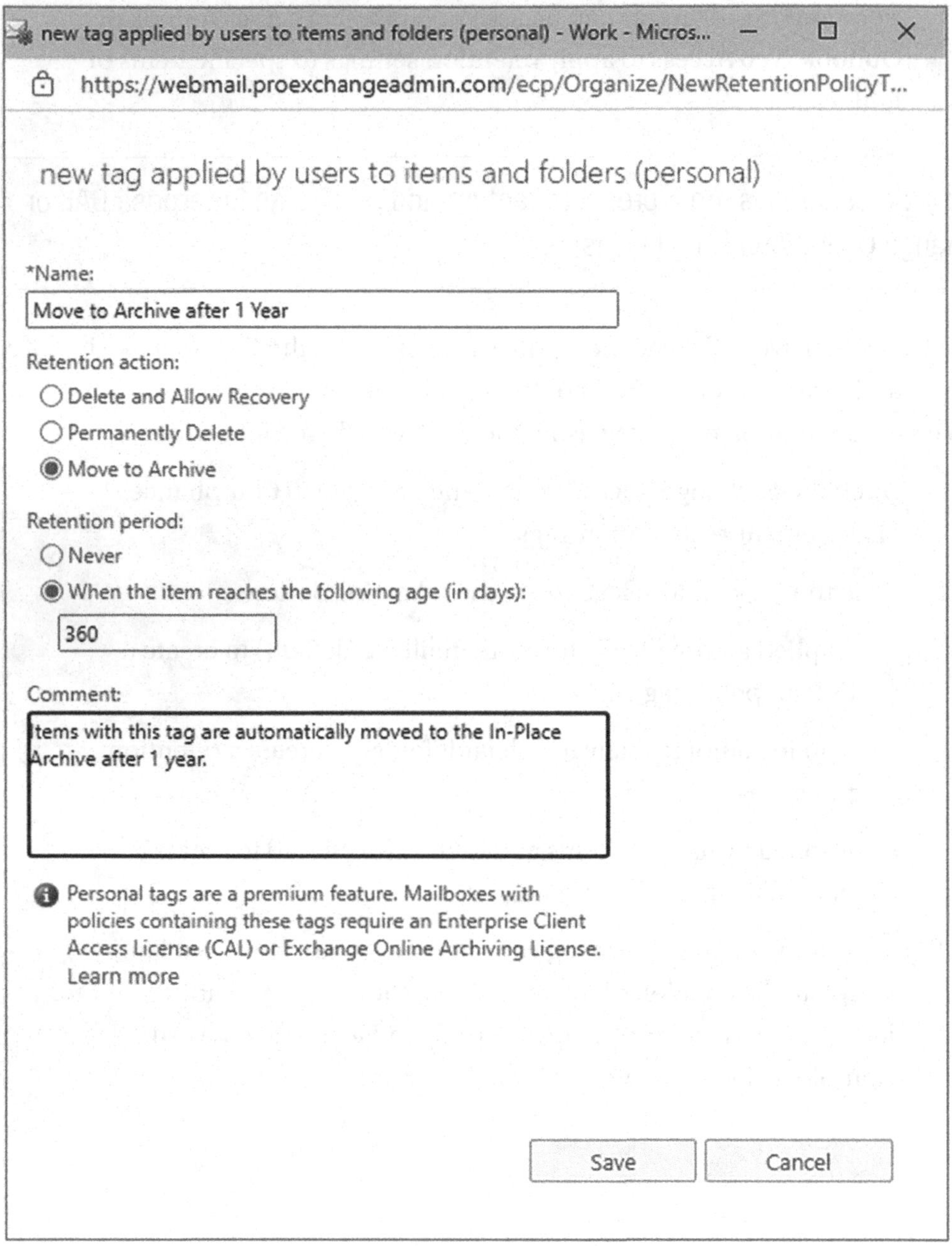

Figure 11-11. *Creating a new retention policy tag in the EAC*

To apply a retention policy to a folder or an item, you select the object in Outlook or Outlook Web Access and right-click to select one of the Assign Policy options in the pop-up menu. This is shown in Figure 11-12.

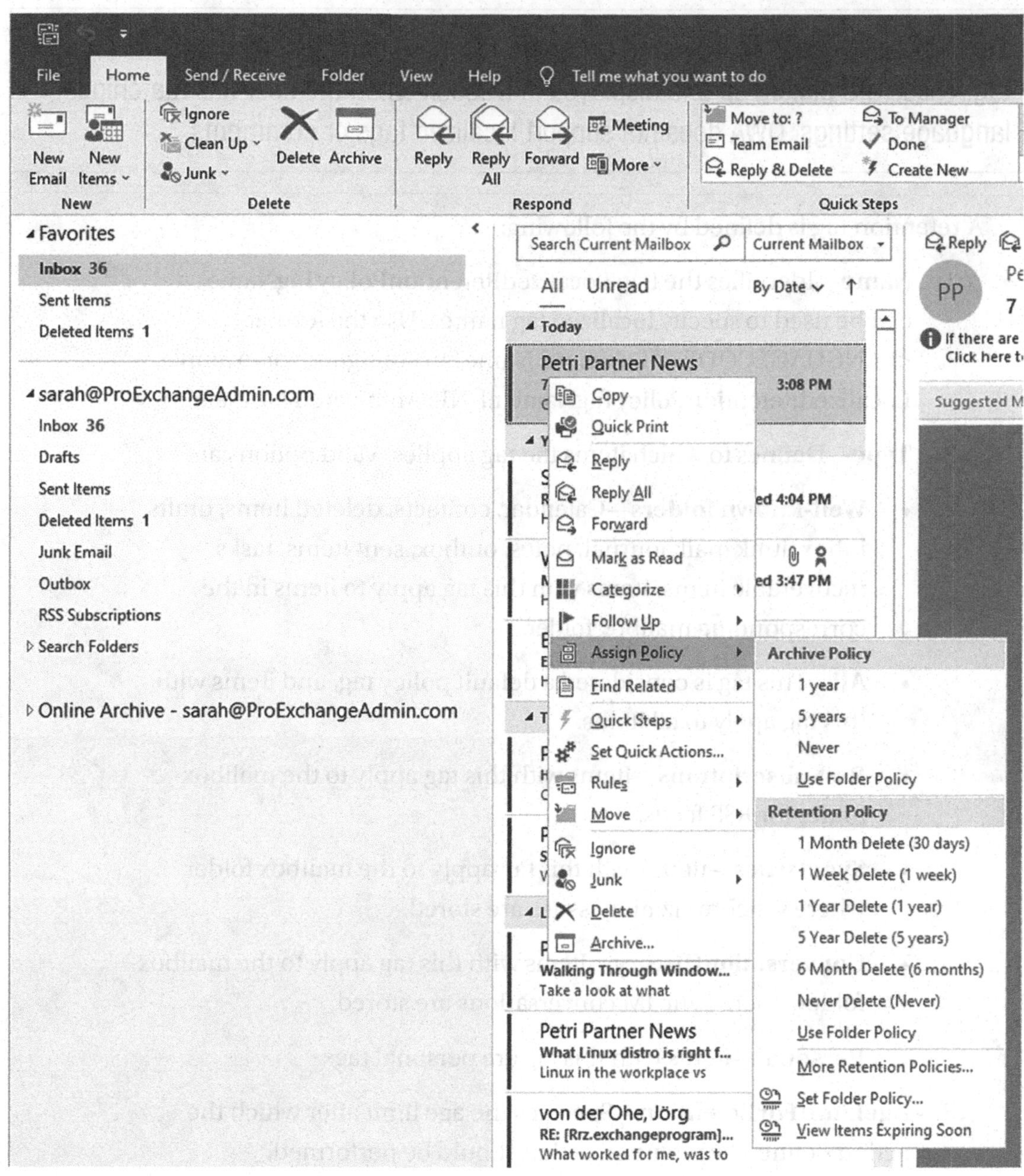

***Figure 11-12.** Applying a retention policy tag in Outlook*

Tip You also have the option to configure localized names and comments on a tag. These are picked up and displayed in Outlook when the user has matching language settings. OWA does not support localized tags or comments.

A retention tag is defined by the following:

1. **Name**—Identifies the tag; LocalizedRetentionPolicyTagName can be used to specify localized tag names. Use the format <LANGUAGECODE>:"Localized Name" to configure, for example, LocalizedRetentionPolicyTagName nl-NL:'Archiveren na 1 jaar'.
2. **Type**—Defines to which items the tag applies. Valid options are
    - **Well-known folders**—Calendar, contacts, deleted items, drafts, inbox, junk mail, journal, notes, outbox, sent items, tasks, recoverable items. Items with this tag apply to items in the corresponding mailbox folder.
    - **All**—This tag is considered a default policy tag, and items with this tag apply to all items.
    - **RssSubscriptions**—Items with this tag apply to the mailbox folder for RSS feeds.
    - **SyncIssues**—Items with this tag apply to the mailbox folder where synchronization issues are stored.
    - **ConversationHistory**—Items with this tag apply to the mailbox folder where Lync IM conversations are stored.
    - **Personal**—Items with this tag are personal tags.
3. **AgeLimitForRetention**—Specifies the age limit after which the action defined by retention action should be performed.
4. **RetentionEnabled**—Set to $true if the tag is enabled.

5. **RetentionAction**—Defines the action to take when the retention limit has been reached. Possible actions are

   - **MarkAsPastRetentionLimit**—Items with this tag are marked as passed the retention limit. This will only result in a visual clue in Outlook—that is, a notice that the item has expired will be shown, and it will appear in strikethrough font.
   - **DeleteAndAllowRecovery**—Items with this tag will be soft-deleted and moved to the deleted items folder.
   - **PermanentlyDelete**—Items with this tag will be hard-deleted and cannot be recovered. When the mailbox is on hold, those items can be found using in-place discovery.
   - **MoveToArchive**—Items with this tag will be moved to the archive (when configured). You can use this tag only for all, personal, and recoverable item types.

6. **Comment**—Used to specify a comment for the tag; LocalizedComment can be used to specify localized comments. Use the same format as with LocalizedRetentionPolicyTagName to create localized information.

7. **MessageClass**—Used to limit the tag to certain items. Currently, only one message class is supported: UM voice mail messages. To select these, specify MessageClass IPM.Note.Microsoft.Voicemail* as the message class. The default message class value is *, which means the tag applies to all items.

A default policy tag is created by establishing a policy tag with the All type. For example, to create a default policy tag that moves items to the archive after a year, you use the following command:

```
[PS] C:\> New-RetentionPolicyTag -Name 'Default 1 year move to archive' -Type
All -AgeLimitForRetention 365 -RetentionAction MoveToArchive
```

To create a retention policy tag for a well-known folder, you specify the type. For example, to create a policy to soft-delete calendar items after two years, you use the following command:

```
[PS] C:\> New-RetentionPolicyTag -Name 'Delete Calendar Items after
2 year' -Type Calendar -AgeLimitForRetention 730 -RetentionAction
DeleteAndAllowRecovery
```

To create a personal tag, you use the Personal type. For example, to create a personal tag that can be used to tag items that should never be processed for retention, you use the following command:

```
[PS] C:\> New-RetentionPolicyTag -Name 'Never Move to Archive' -Type
Personal -RetentionEnabled $false -RetentionAction MoveToArchive
```

To configure a localized string for an existing policy tag, you can use the following command:

```
[PS] C:\> Set-RetentionPolicyTag -Name '1 Week Delete' -LocalizedRetention
PolicyTagName nl-NL:'Na 1 Week verwijderen'
```

Assigning Personal Tags

Personal tags can be assigned by end users using Outlook 2010 or later, Outlook Web Access, or programmatically (Exchange Web Services). To assign a personal tag, you follow these steps:

1. Open Outlook or Outlook Web Access.
2. Right-click the folder or item you want to assign a personal tag to and select Assign Policy.
3. Pick a personal tag from the list. You may also see the following options:
    - **Use Folder Policy**—To revert to the folder retention policy
    - **Set Folder Policy**—To set the parent folder retention policy
    - **View Items Expiring Soon**—To show items that will expire within the next 30 days

You can automatically apply personal tags to items using inbox rules. For example, you can create a rule to automatically apply the "1 Year Delete" tag to electronic newsletters to have them automatically removed from your mailbox by the managed folder assistant after a year. An example with a "1 Year Delete" is shown in Figure 11-13.

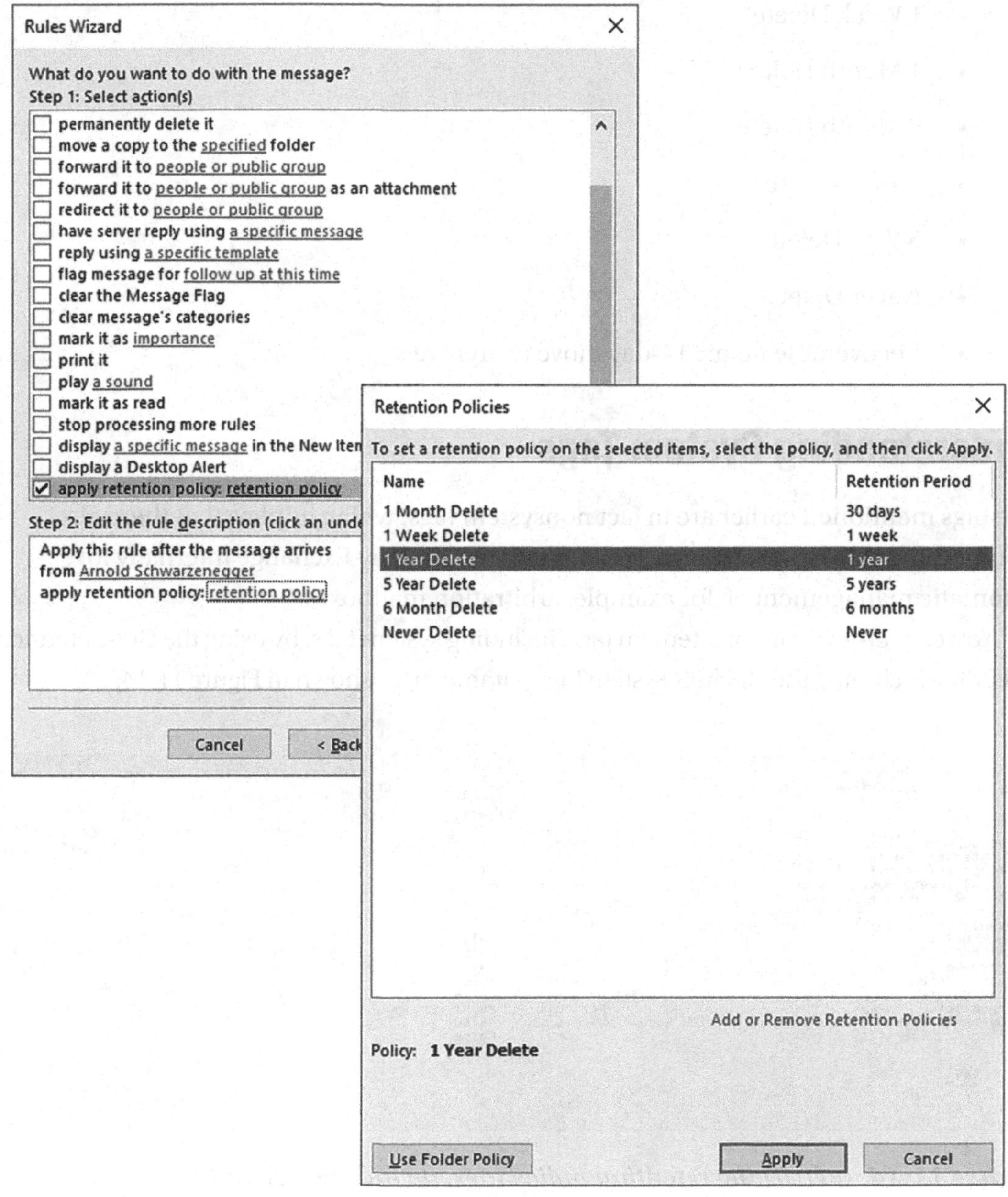

***Figure 11-13.** Applying retention policy tags using inbox rules*

In Exchange, the following retention tags are available by default:

- Default: Two-year move to archive
- Personal: One-year move to archive, five-year move to archive, or never move to archive
- 1 Week Delete
- 1 Month Delete
- 6 Month Delete
- 1 Year Delete
- 5 Year Delete
- Never Delete
- Recoverable Items: 14-day move to archive

Understanding System Tags

The tags mentioned earlier are in fact nonsystem tags, which implies that there also is something called "system tags." System tags are used by Exchange internally for automatic management of, for example, arbitration mailboxes.

You can retrieve a list of retention tags, including system tags, by using the Get-RetentionPolicyTag including the –IncludeSystemTags parameter, as shown in Figure 11-14.

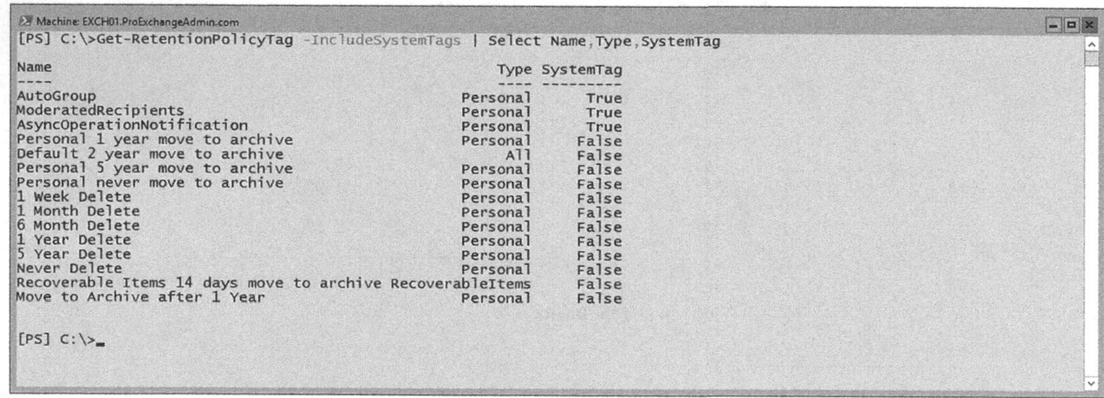

Figure 11-14. *Retrieving retention policy tags, including system tags*

System tags can be queried just like regular retention tags, as shown in Figure 11-15. It is generally recommended you leave these retention tags as is.

```
Machine: EXCH01.ProExchangeAdmin.com
[PS] C:\>Get-RetentionPolicyTag -Identity AutoGroup | Select Name,Age*,*Action

Name      AgeLimitForRetention       RetentionAction
----      --------------------       ---------------
AutoGroup 30.00:00:00          DeleteAndAllowRecovery

[PS] C:\>_
```

Figure 11-15. *Retrieving system tag properties*

Retention Policies

A retention policy is a collection of retention tags assigned to a mailbox. A default policy tag is applied to the assigned mailbox overall, and a retention policy can only contain one default policy tag. Retention policies can also contain retention policy tags that are applied to the related folder in the assigned mailbox. Finally, the user of the mailbox can select those personal tags made available by assigning a retention policy containing those personal tags to that mailbox, thus explicitly overriding any existing retention settings.

In an Exchange Server deployment, by default there are two retention policies available:

- **Default MRM policy**—This is the default retention policy assigned to mailboxes. Note that it contains the default two-year move to archive retention policy tag, which configures the mailbox to automatically move its contents to the in-place archive when such an archive is configured for the mailbox.
- **ArbitrationMailbox**—This policy is by default assigned to system mailboxes and contains, for example, the retention policy tag autogroup, which deletes items after 30 days.

To see which retention policy tags are part of a retention policy, inspect the RetentionPolicyTagLinks attribute:

```
[PS] C:\> Get-RetentionPolicy -Name 'Default MRM Policy' | Select
RetentionPolicyTagLinks
```

To create a retention policy using EAC, you do the following steps:

1. Open the Exchange Admin Center and navigate to Compliance Management ➤ Retention Policies.
2. Select the + sign.
3. In the new retention policy dialog, enter the name of the policy to create. In the retention tags section, use the + and – signs to add or remove retention tags.

This is shown in Figure 11-16.

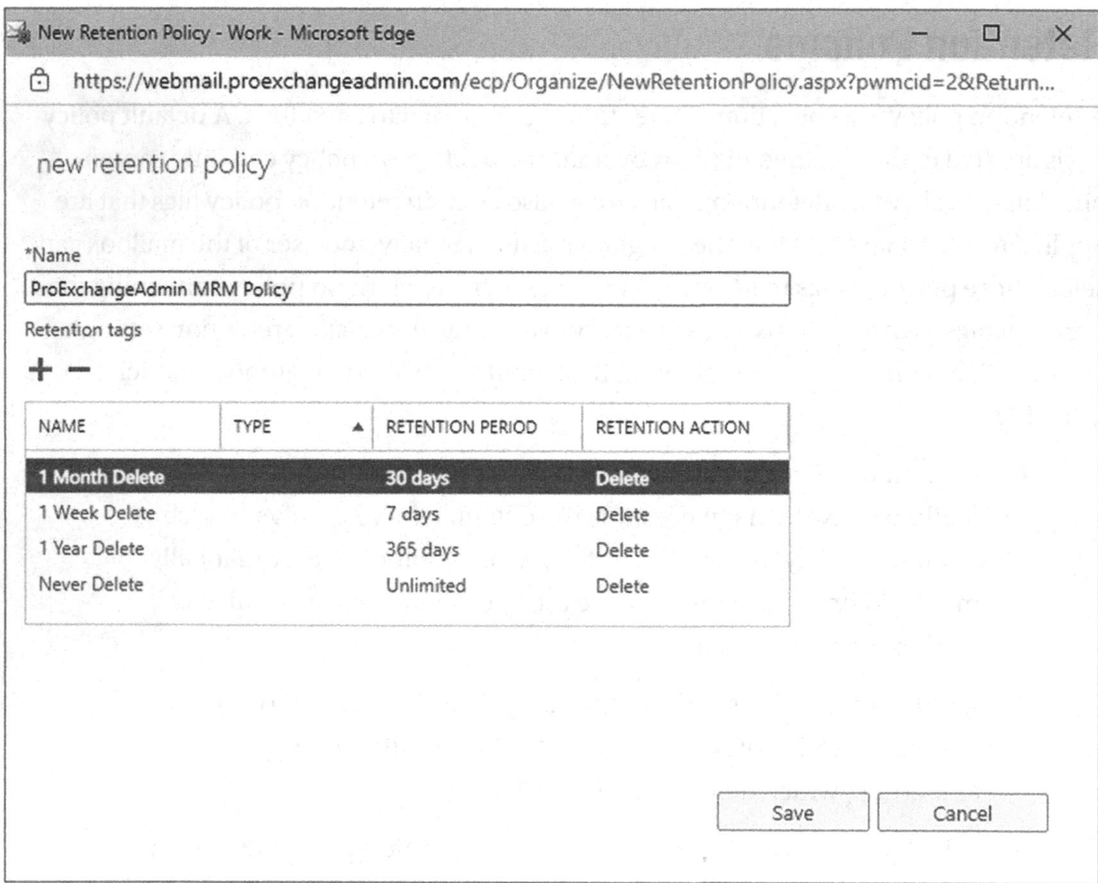

Figure 11-16. *Creating a new Exchange MRM policy*

To create a new retention policy using the Exchange Management Shell, use New-RetentionPolicy and provide retention policy tags as a parameter, separating tags using a comma (thus providing the tags as an array), as follows:

```
[PS] C:\> New-RetentionPolicy -Name 'ProExchangeAdmin MRM Policy' -
RetentionPolicyTagLinks 'Default 1 year move to archive','Never Delete'
```

To add a retention policy tag to a retention policy, you need to add it as an element:

```
[PS] C:\> Set-RetentionPolicy -Name 'ProExchangeAdmin MRM Policy' -
RetentionPolicyTagLinks @{Add='1 Week Delete'}
```

Should you need to remove a retention policy tag from a retention policy, you can remove the element:

```
[PS] C:\> Set-RetentionPolicy -Name 'ProExchangeAdmin MRM Policy' -
RetentionPolicyTagLinks @{Remove='1 Week Delete'}
```

Warning Do not use Set-RetentionPolicy "ProExchangeAdmin MRM Policy"–RetentionPolicyTagLinks "1 Week Delete," as this would overwrite any current retention policy tag entries with the value specified.

Assigning a Retention Policy

For a retention policy and its tags to become effective or available in the case of personal tags, it needs to be assigned to a mailbox. To assign a retention policy to a mailbox using EAC, you do the following steps:

1. Open the Exchange Admin Center and navigate to Recipients ➤ Mailboxes.
2. Select the mailbox you want to assign a retention policy to and click the Edit icon.
3. Select the Mailbox Features section.

4. Select the desired retention policy in the Retention Policy drop-down box.
5. Click Save to save the new setting.

Tip If you select multiple mailboxes, you can use the Bulk Edit option. Select More Options... and click Update below the Retention Policy heading. You will then see a dialog where you can pick a retention policy that you want to apply to the mailboxes you have selected.

When using the Exchange Management Shell, the Set-Mailbox cmdlet is used to configure a retention policy. For example, to apply the Contoso MRM Policy retention policy to Philip's mailbox, you enter

```
[PS] C:\> Set-Mailbox -Identity Philip -RetentionPolicy 'ProExchangeAdmin
MRM Policy'
```

If you want to assign the retention policy to a certain group of people, you can utilize PowerShell's ability to pipe objects to Set-Mailbox. For example, if you want to clear the retention policy on mailboxes starting with P, you assign each one the retention policy value $null, as follows:

```
[PS] C:\> Get-Mailbox -Identity P* | Set-Mailbox -RetentionPolicy $null
```

Managed Folder Assistant

The managed folder assistant (MFA) is responsible for enforcing retention policies on items in mailboxes. It is a background process that checks items in each mailbox against the policy that has been configured on the mailbox (DPT), folder (RPT), and personal tag level. The process is throttled to limit the number of resources and cycles consumed.

You can monitor MFA activity by looking in the application event log for Event ID 9018, generated by the MSExchange mailbox assistants. It will mention what database was processed by the MFA, how many mailboxes were processed, and how long it took. If the MFA could not complete a work cycle, it will also mention how many mailboxes could not be processed.

It is possible that the events do not show up in the Application event log. The EventLevel for the MFA is set to "Lowest," so not all events are logged. It is possible to increase this setting using the `Set-EventLogLevel` command in EMS.

Possible values are

- Lowest
- Low
- Medium
- High
- Expert

To raise the level to "Expert" for troubleshooting purposes, execute the following command:

```
[PS] C:\> Set-EventLogLevel -Identity "MSExchangeMailboxAssistants\
Service" -Level Expert
```

In Exchange 2013, it was possible to configure the MFA Assistant Schedule using the -ManagedFolderAssistantSchedule parameter in the Set-Mailbox command. Although this parameter is still available in Exchange 2016 and Exchange 2019, it is no longer used. The parameter is only available for coexistence scenarios with Exchange 2013.

To change the settings in Exchange 2016 and Exchange 2019, a SettingOverride must be used. To configure the work cycle for MFA and process mailboxes every two days, use the following command:

```
[PS] C:\> New-SettingOverride -Name "MFA WorkCycle Override"
-Component TimeBasedAssistants -Section ELCAssistant -Parameters @
("WorkCycle=2.00:00:00") -Reason "Process mailboxes every 2 days"
```

The WorkCycle format is d.hh.mm.ss, and the default setting is one day. It can be changed, but be careful with system resource planning.

To apply the new work cycle, execute the following command:

```
[PS] C:\> Get-ExchangeDiagnosticInfo -Process Microsoft.Exchange.Directory.
TopologyService -Component VariantConfiguration -Argument Refresh
```

This is shown in Figure 11-17.

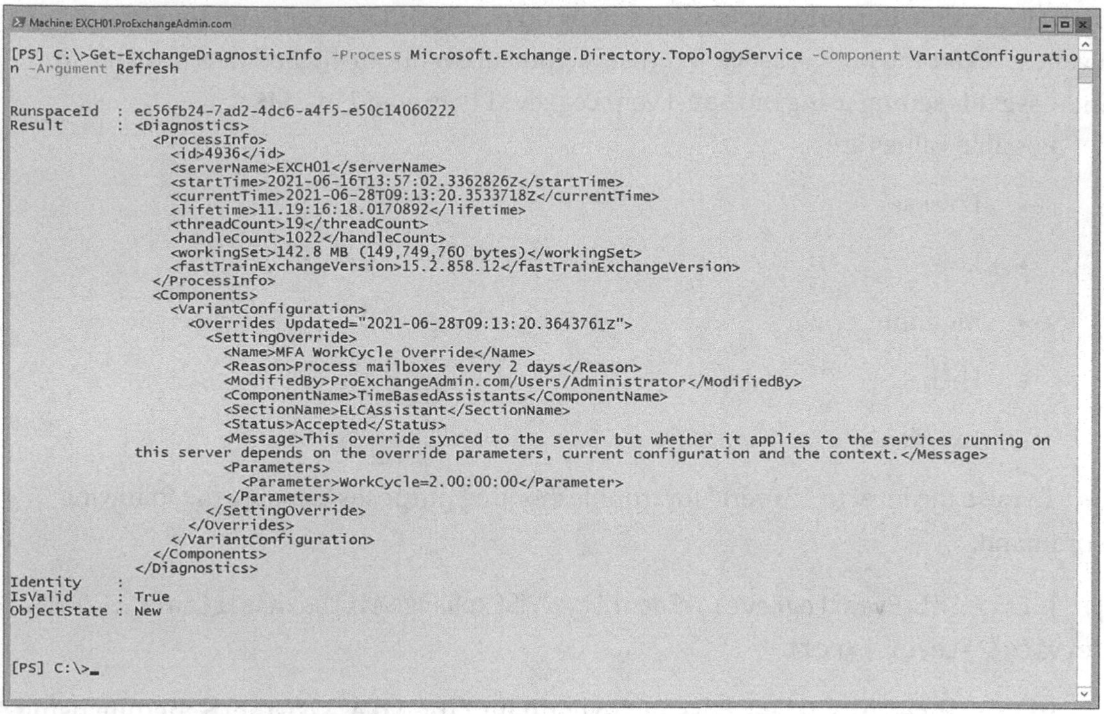

```
Machine: EXCH01.ProExchangeAdmin.com
[PS] C:\>Get-ExchangeDiagnosticInfo -Process Microsoft.Exchange.Directory.TopologyService -Component VariantConfiguratio
n -Argument Refresh


RunspaceId  : ec56fb24-7ad2-4dc6-a4f5-e50c14060222
Result      : <Diagnostics>
                <ProcessInfo>
                  <id>4936</id>
                  <serverName>EXCH01</serverName>
                  <startTime>2021-06-16T13:57:02.3362826Z</startTime>
                  <currentTime>2021-06-28T09:13:20.3533718Z</currentTime>
                  <lifetime>11.19:16:18.0170892</lifetime>
                  <threadCount>19</threadCount>
                  <handleCount>1022</handleCount>
                  <workingSet>142.8 MB (149,749,760 bytes)</workingSet>
                  <fastTrainExchangeVersion>15.2.858.12</fastTrainExchangeVersion>
                </ProcessInfo>
                <Components>
                  <VariantConfiguration>
                    <Overrides Updated="2021-06-28T09:13:20.3643761Z">
                      <SettingOverride>
                        <Name>MFA WorkCycle Override</Name>
                        <Reason>Process mailboxes every 2 days</Reason>
                        <ModifiedBy>ProExchangeAdmin.com/Users/Administrator</ModifiedBy>
                        <ComponentName>TimeBasedAssistants</ComponentName>
                        <SectionName>ELCAssistant</SectionName>
                        <Status>Accepted</Status>
                        <Message>This override synced to the server but whether it applies to the services running on
              this server depends on the override parameters, current configuration and the context.</Message>
                        <Parameters>
                          <Parameter>WorkCycle=2.00:00:00</Parameter>
                        </Parameters>
                      </SettingOverride>
                    </Overrides>
                  </VariantConfiguration>
                </Components>
              </Diagnostics>
Identity    :
IsValid     : True
ObjectState : New


[PS] C:\>_
```

Figure 11-17. *Applying the new work cycle for MFA*

To check the new settings, execute the following commands:

```
[PS] C:\> [xml]$diag=Get-ExchangeDiagnosticInfo -Process
MSExchangeMailboxAssistants -Component VariantConfiguration -Argument "Conf
ig,Component=TimeBasedAssistants"
[PS] C:\> $diag.Diagnostics.Components.VariantConfiguration.Configuration.
TimeBasedAssistants.ElcAssistant
```

This is shown in Figure 11-18.

```
Machine: EXCH01.ProExchangeAdmin.com

[PS] C:\>$diag.Diagnostics.Components.VariantConfiguration.Configuration.TimeBasedAssistants.ElcAssistant
[PS] C:\>[xml]$diag=Get-ExchangeDiagnosticInfo -Process MSExchangeMailboxAssistants -Component VariantConfiguration -Argument "Config,Component=TimeBasedAssistants"
[PS] C:\>$diag.Diagnostics.Components.VariantConfiguration.Configuration.TimeBasedAssistants.ElcAssistant

Classification                           : InternalMaintenance
MaxConcurrency                           : 1024
Enabled                                  : True
EnabledDuringBlackout                    : False
MailboxNotInterestingLogInterval         : 1.00:00:00
SpreadLoad                               : True
SlaMonitoringEnabled                     : True
CompletionMonitoringEnabled              : True
ActiveDatabaseProcessingMonitoringEnabled : True
SlaUrgentThreshold                       : 0.1
SlaNonUrgentThreshold                    : 0.5
WorkCycle                                : 2.00:00:00
GroupMailboxADGroupProcessingEnabled     : True
SpreadLoadPaddingPercent                 : 10

[PS] C:\>_
```

***Figure 11-18.** Checking the new MFA work cycle settings*

Adjusting the work cycle will impact the frequency of which retention policies are checked and enforced on mailboxes hosted on the mailbox server with the adjusted ManagedFolderWorkCycle setting.

You can also manually start the MFA to perform a work cycle. To manually trigger the MFA, use the Start-ManagedFolderAssistant and specify the mailbox you want the MFA to run against. For example, to run the MFA for Philip's mailbox, you would use the following command:

```
[PS] C:\> Start-ManagedFolderAssistant -Identity Philip
```

Note The managed folder assistant will resume processing where it left off, so there is no problem if the MFA cannot complete a work cycle at a particular time. However, the retention policy application and executing retention policy actions might be delayed for unprocessed mailboxes.

Transport Rules

One of the critical components in an Exchange infrastructure is the transport service, which is responsible for processing messages traveling within or entering or leaving an Exchange organization.

Part of an organization's compliance and security requirements could be that messages transported within the organization or messages entering or leaving the Exchange infrastructure must comply with certain rules. Here is where the Exchange Transport rules can come into play. An example of such a restriction is an ethical wall, also known as a Chinese wall, whose purpose is to prevent conflict of interest and disclosure of valuable information.

Note Transport rules can be used to accomplish lots of other goals as well, such as adding disclaimers. They are building blocks for features like data loss prevention and information rights management. If you are interested in these areas, consider employing the transport rules to achieve your ends.

Basically, transport rules are rules that define operations for messages that satisfy certain conditions. Examples of such rules are dropping or redirecting messages and applying information rights management templates. To manage transport rules, you need to be assigned an Organization Management or Records Management role. Transport rules are organization-wide unless their specific conditions narrow the scope, and they are processed by the transport rule agent.

Create a Transport Rule

Let us assume you're working for a law firm where lawyers representing client A (distribution list RepCaseAClientA) may not exchange messages with lawyers representing client B (distribution list RepCaseAClientB). So, you want to create an ethical wall between the users in those groups via a transport rule. To create a transport rule using EAC, you do the following:

1. Open the Exchange Admin Center and navigate to Mail Flow ➤ Rules.
2. Select the + sign and select Create a New Rule from the pop-up menu to create a transport rule from scratch.
3. Enter a name—for example, EW_CaseAClientAClientB.

4. Configure the predicate "Apply this rule if..." as "The sender and the recipient ... the message is between members of these groups," selecting RepCaseAClientA and RepCaseAClientB.

5. Configure the predicate "Apply this rule if" as "The sender is a member of RepCaseAClientA" and "The recipient is a member of RepCaseAClientB."

6. Configure "Do the following" as "Block the message..." as "Reject the message and include an explanation." When configuring, add an explanation like "You are not allowed to send a message to this recipient for legal purposes."

   Note that the message will be returned in a delivery service notification (DSN) message using a default return code of 5.7.1, a common code for access denied types of DSN messages.

7. Optionally, configure "Audit this rule with severity level" if you want to generate audit log entries when the rule is triggered.

8. Click Save to save and activate the rule.

To create a transport rule using the Exchange Management Shell, use the New-TransportRule cmdlet. For example, to institute the same transport rule, use the following command:

```
[PS] C:\> New-TransportRule -Name 'EW_ EW_CaseAClientAClientB'
-BetweenMemberOf1 RepCaseAClientA -BetweenMemberOf2 RepCaseAClientB -
RejectMessageReasonText You are not allowed to send a message to this
recipient for legal purposed ' -Mode Enforce
```

By using the RejectMessageEnhancedStatusCode parameter, you can override the default DSN status code of 5.7.1 for rejected messages.

Caution Transport rules are stored in Active Directory. Therefore, you may experience delays when implementing changes, and you should consider replication latency before those changes will be propagated to Mailbox servers throughout the organization.

When a user in one group tries to send a message to a member in the other group, they will receive a 5.7.1 delivery service notification message indicating failure. The explanation will be shown, and the diagnostic information will indicate that a transport rule has governed rejection of the message, as shown in Figure 11-19.

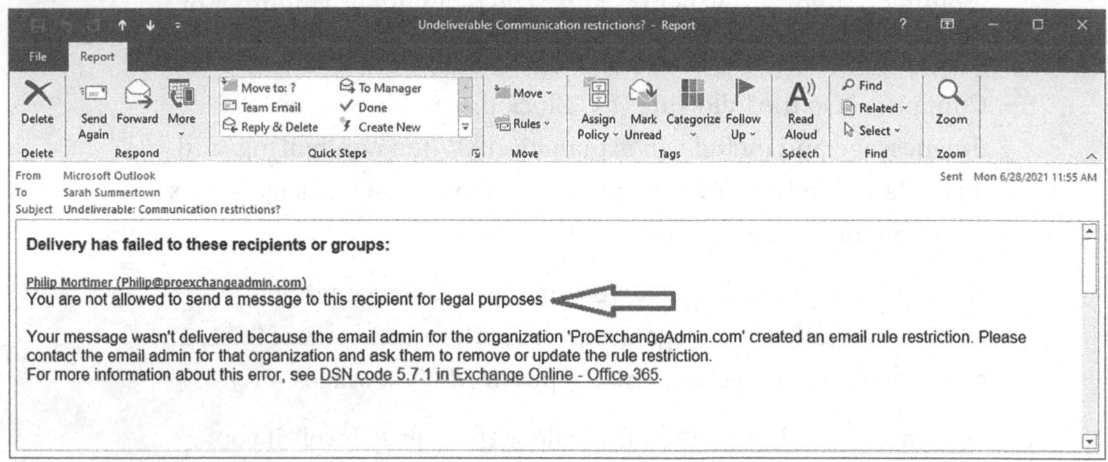

Figure 11-19. *Notification message of the ethical wall delivery service*

Another example of using transport rules for compliance is about a corporate disclaimer. For such disclaimers, you can select to have the disclaimer applied only to messages sent outside of the organization. To accomplish this, you use the scope NotInOrganization (displayed in EAC as Outside the organization. Possible scope options for the sender (FromUserScope) or receiver (SendToScope) are

- **InTheOrganization**—The sender or receiver is located in Active Directory, or the domain name is an accepted, non-external relay domain name using an authenticated connection.
- **NotInTheOrganization**—The domain name of the sender or receiver isn't an accepted domain or is an external relay accepted domain.
- **ExternalPartner (ToUserScope only)**—The domain name of the receiver is configured to use a domain secure security setting.
- **ExternalNonPartner (ToUserScope only)**—The domain name of the receiver is not using a domain secure security setting.

A complication with disclaimers is that inserting text in the body of a message may invalidate any signed or encrypted messages. Because only a signed or encrypted message can be excluded (not both), you can leverage the Exchange message classification to tag the message, using transport rules to tag that encrypted or signed message. In the disclaimer transport rule, you can then select to not apply the rule to tagged messages.

Note If your company policy is to disallow sending signed or encrypted messages externally, you can replace the action of adding the disclaimer by an action that will drop the message, quarantine it, or forward it for moderation.

Message classifications can only be created from the Exchange Management Shell, using the New-MessageClassification. In this example, you would use the label SignedOrEncrypted, as follows:

```
[PS] C:\> New-MessageClassification 'SignedOrEncrypted' -DisplayName
'Signed or Encrypted Message' -SenderDescription 'Signed or Encrypted
Message' -PermissionMenuVisible:$false
```

Note PermissionMenuVisible determines if the message classification can be assigned to messages in Outlook or Outlook Web App. Setting this parameter to $false disables this option.

You create the transport rules that will tag messages using this message classification. First, you create a transport rule that applies the message classification SignedOrEncrypted (ApplyClassification) to encrypted messages (MessageTypeMatches "Encrypted"), as follows:

```
[PS] C:\> New-TransportRule -Name 'Tag Encrypted Messages' -Enabled $true -
MessageTypeMatches 'Encrypted' -ApplyClassification 'SignedOrEncrypted'
```

Next, you create a transport rule that applies the message classification SignedOrEncrypted to signed messages (MessageTypeMatches "Signed"), as follows:

```
[PS] C:\> New-TransportRule -Name 'Tag Signed Messages' -Enabled $true -
MessageTypeMatches 'Signed' -ApplyClassification 'SignedOrEncrypted'
```

Finally, you create the transport rule that applies the disclaimer to outgoing messages:

```
[PS] C:\> New-TransportRule -Name 'Disclaimer' -Enabled $true -SentToScope
'NotInOrganization' -ExceptIfHasClassification 'SignedOrEncrypted'
-ApplyHtmlDisclaimerLocation 'Append' -ApplyHtmlDisclaimerFallbackAction
'Wrap' -ApplyHtmlDisclaimerText '<P>This email and any files transmitted
with it are confidential and intended solely for the use of the individual
or entity to whom they are addressed.</P>'
```

The ApplyHtmlDisclaimerFallbackAction parameter specifies where to put the disclaimer text. In the example, it is appended to the message. By setting ApplyHtmlDisclaimerFallbackAction to Wrap, the message will be wrapped in a new message containing the disclaimer. The parameter ApplyHtmlDisclaimerText specifies the text to use for the disclaimer. Note that the disclaimer text can be HTML, allowing you to use HTML IMG tags, which reference externally hosted images for embedding, or to use a link to point to an online disclaimer.

If you want to use disclaimers for internal communications as well, you will face an additional challenge. As the message passes each Transport service, a disclaimer is added, thereby potentially resulting in multiple disclaimers. Of course, you can add an additional exception that will check the body of the message for disclaimer text fragments. A different and perhaps more elegant approach, though, is to insert a sentinel in the message header after a disclaimer has been appended, and add the condition to exclude messages containing the sentinel.

To implement such a condition and transform the disclaimer created earlier in a global disclaimer, you use the following command, where you set the SentToScope to $null to make it apply to all messages:

```
[PS] C:\> Set-TransportRule -Identity 'Disclaimer' -SetHeaderName
'X-Disclaimer' -SetHeaderValue '1' -ExceptIfHeaderContainsMessageHeader
'X-Disclaimer' -ExceptIfHeaderContainsWords '1'
```

Now, when you receive a message, a disclaimer is added to the message as shown in Figure 11-20.

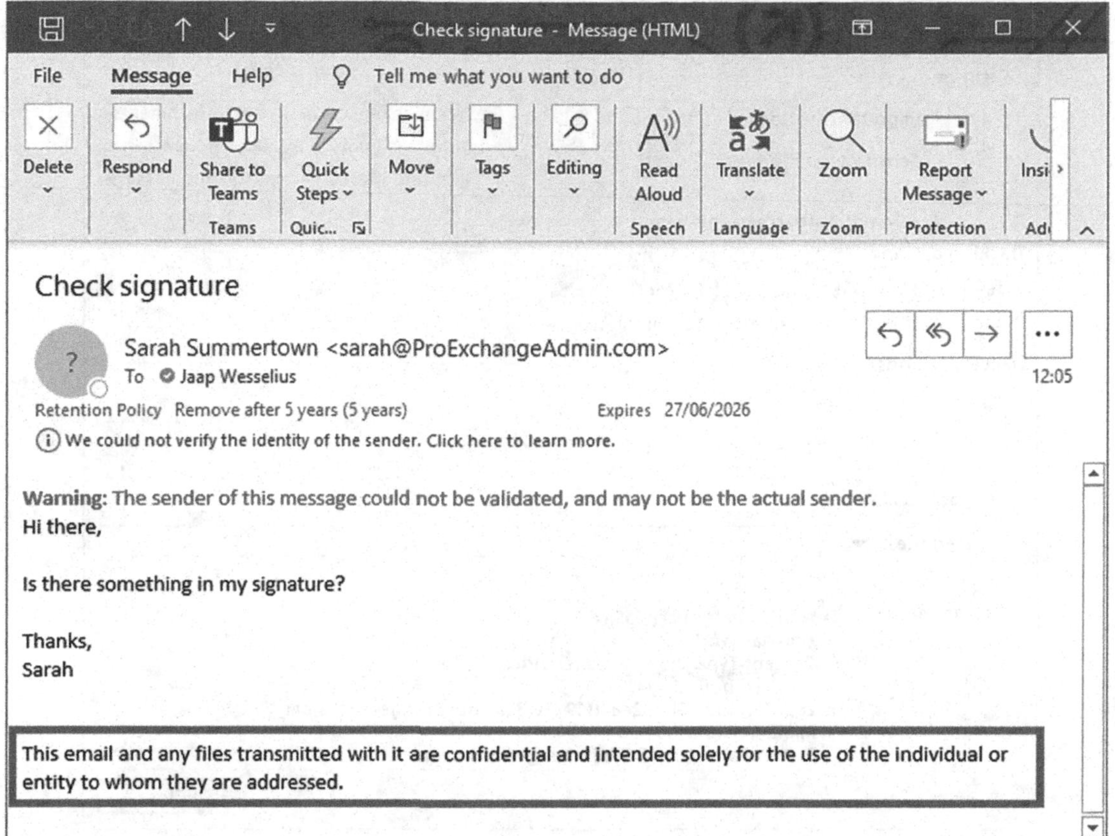

***Figure 11-20.** Disclaimer added to a message using transport rules*

Now, when you receive a message with a disclaimer, you can see “proof” in the header, which will contain an entry X-Disclaimer: 1, as shown in Figure 11-21. That is, the header will contain an additional header entry, X-Disclaimer, which will be set to 1 for messages subject to the rule you just created.

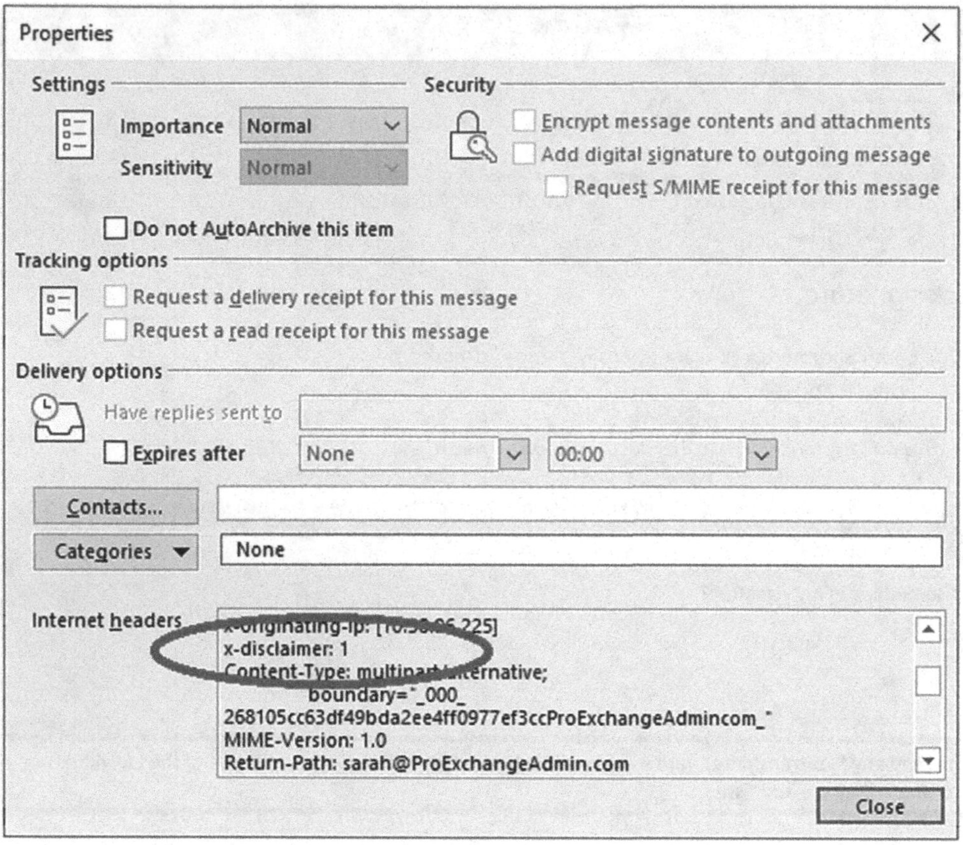

Figure 11-21. *The additional X-Disclaimer header in the previous message*

Priority Ranking for Transport Rules

When you have multiple transport rules configured, the way they are ordered becomes important. For instance, if you have configured one transport rule to tag messages and another transport rule to process the tagged messages, the tagging needs to take place first.

To query the current list of transport rules and their assigned priority, use the Get-TransportRule cmdlet, with results as shown in Figure 11-22.

```
Machine: EXCH01.ProExchangeAdmin.com
[PS] C:\>Get-TransportRule

Name                    State   Mode    Priority Comments
----                    -----   ----    -------- --------
EW_CaseAClientAClientB  Enabled Enforce 0        ...
Tag Encrypted Messages  Enabled Enforce 1
Tag Signed Messages     Enabled Enforce 2
Disclaimer              Enabled Enforce 3

[PS] C:\>_
```

***Figure 11-22.** Retrieve a list of Transport Rules*

The priority property determines the order in which the rules are applied, starting with 0. As you can see in Figure 11-22, the rules to tag messages are first and second, and the rule taking actions based on those tags comes next.

Tip When you have lots of rules, you can speed up the overall processing by the transport rule agent of the message by setting the StopRuleProcessing property of a transport rule to $true. When conditions are met and with this property set to $true, additional transport rules with lower priority will not be evaluated.

When you want to reassign the priority for a transport rule, you can use the Set-TransportRule cmdlet with the -Priority parameter. For example, if you created the disclaimer rule from the example first, it would have a higher execution priority than the tagging rules, as rules are assigned priorities based on their order of creation. To reset the priority of a transport rule with the identity of the disclaimer to 2, you use the following command:

```
[PS] C:\> Set-TransportRule -Identity Disclaimer -Priority 2
```

If you assign a priority that is already in use, it will insert the rule on that position, and the priorities of the other rules will shift one position down.

Journaling

Some organizations may be required to record all inbound and outbound email messages from a compliance perspective. Exchange can help fill that requirement by leveraging the transport rules discussed earlier. When considering the transport rule options, you may have spotted that one possible action a transport rule can perform is copying to a certain recipient. That, in combination with rules that define the conditions under which to journal messages, makes up the journaling option in Exchange.

In Exchange Server, all email is handled by the Transport service. The journaling agent is a transport agent that processes messages on Mailbox servers, either when they are submitted or when they are routed. Exchange provides the following journaling options:

- **Standard journaling**—Configured on the mailbox database and can be used to journal all messages that are either received by or sent through mailboxes hosted on that mailbox database
- **Premium journaling**—Can utilize rules, allowing you to journal based on criteria such as the recipient, distribution group, or internal vs. external messages

---

Note Premium journaling requires an Enterprise CAL license.

So far, a journal rule, or even journaling in general, may sound like just an implementation of a transport rule, but there is a difference. While transport rules can be used to forward messages, journaling generates integral copies of the original messages in the form of journal reports, including the original messages as an attachment with the original header information. This makes journal reports suitable as evidence, as contrasted with forwarded messages retrieved by means of a transport rule. See Figure 11-23 for a sample journal report.

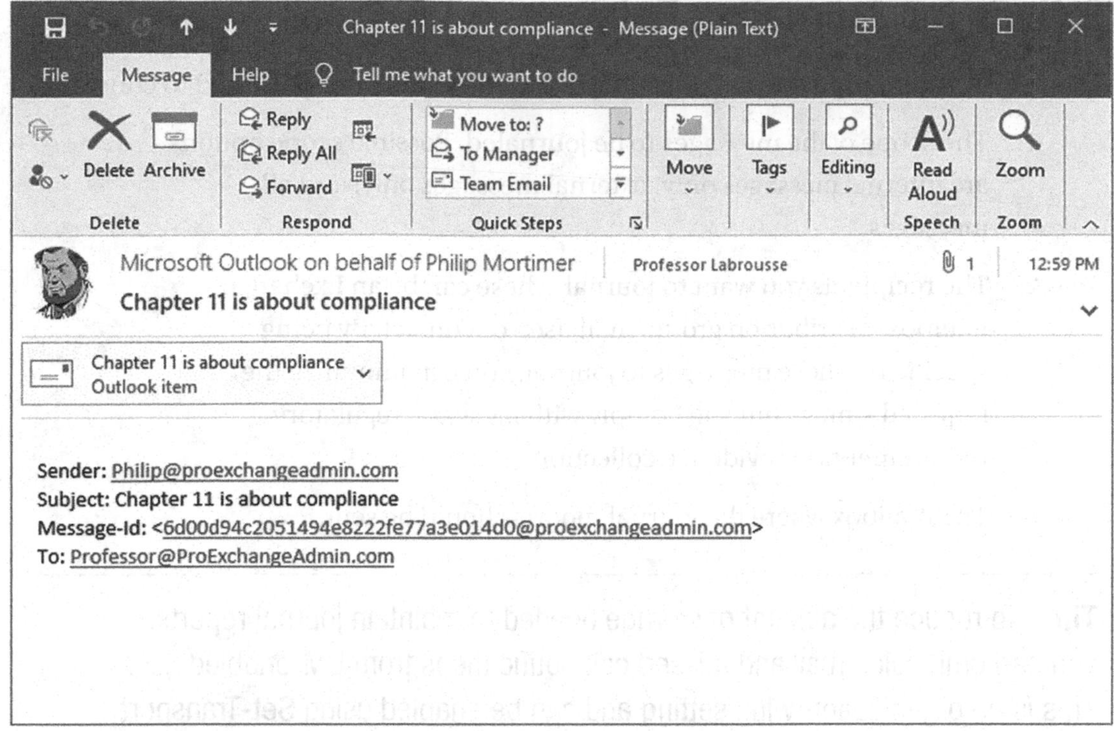

***Figure 11-23.** A journal report shown in Outlook*

A journal report for an externally sent message may differ from that for an internal message. This is because internal messages contain more information in the header regarding the source and destination. The information provided in journal reports contains

- **Sender**—This is the SMTP address of the sender of the message.
- **Subject**—This is the subject of the journaled message.
- **Message-ID**—This is the internal message ID generated by Exchange when the message is submitted in the organization by the Transport service.
- **To**—These are the SMTP addresses of the message recipients. This list includes recipients indicated as TO, CC, or BCC addresses. If groups are expanded, it will also be mentioned at this line.

Options for Journaling Rules

When you are defining a journal rule, there are three parameters you need to consider:

1. The scope of the messages to be journaled. Possible scope options are internal messages only, external messages only, and all messages.
2. The recipients you want to journal. These can be an Exchange mailbox, distribution group, mail user, or contact. By being specific in whose messages to journal, you can minimize the required storage but still comply with legal and regulatory requirements for evidence collection.
3. The mailbox where the journal reports should be sent.

Tip To reduce the amount of storage needed to maintain journal reports, you can omit voice mail and missed call notifications from UM-enabled users. This is an organization-wide setting and can be enabled using Set-TransportConfig –VoicemailJournalingEnabled $false. Or, you can enable journaling of voice mail and missed call notification messages using Set-TransportConfig –VoicemailJournalingEnabled $true. To retrieve the current setting, use Get-TransportConfig | Select VoiceMailJournalingEnabled.

The journaling mailbox is a configured mailbox where the journal reports are collected. The configuration of this journaling mailbox itself depends on the policies that have been set by the organization or by regulatory or legal requirements. For example, you can define a retention policy on the mailbox so there will be some form of automatic housekeeping on the mailbox itself. Also, you can make sure the quota setting doesn't prevent the journal mailbox from receiving journal reports, as the size of that journal mailbox can grow quite big depending on the number of journal reports generated. So, make sure your journal mailboxes are properly managed.

Note You can utilize multiple journal mailboxes for different journal rules. On a side note, you cannot utilize a mailbox hosted in Office 365 for journaling.

In addition, the journal mailbox needs to be treated as a special, secured mailbox, as it may contain sensitive information. It is recommended that you configure your journal mailboxes as follows, where "Journal" is the name of the journal mailbox in this example:

```
[PS] C:\> $ExRcpt= (Get-OrganizationConfig).
MicrosoftExchangeRecipientEmailAddresses | select -ExpandProperty
SmtpAddress
[PS] C:\> Set-Mailbox -Identity 'Journal' -
RequireSenderAuthenticationEnabled $true -HiddenFromAddressListsEnabled
$true -AcceptMessagesOnlyFromSendersOrMembers $ExRcpt
```

Doing this will lock the mailbox and not allow external senders to send messages to it, will hide it from the address books so users will not see it, and will only allow Exchange to send messages to that mailbox.

Note (Get-OrganizationConfig).MicrosoftExchangeRecipientEmailAddresses will return the SMTP addresses of the named Microsoft Exchange recipients. It will contain an entry in the format MicrosoftExchange329e71ec88ae4615bbc36 ab6ce41109e@domain for each configured accepted domain. Note that the primary address is used as the sender for internal DSN messages.

Warning If you ever decide to change the primary SMTP address of a Microsoft Exchange recipient by configuring it directly or indirectly through email address policies, make sure you adjust the AcceptMessagesOnlyFromSendersOrMembers setting accordingly.

Besides establishing the journaling mailbox, you can also define an alternative journal recipient, often used in cases when Exchange encounters problems delivering the journal report to the configured journal recipient. The alternative journal recipient will receive NDRs with the journal report attached, allowing you to resend the original message if the journaling mailbox becomes available again. If there is no alternative journaling recipient configured, Exchange will just requeue the journal report.

Journal reports do not generate NDRs unless an alternate recipient is configured. If an alternative journal recipient is configured, it will receive an NDR with the original journal report. If no alternative journal recipient is configured, Exchange will requeue the journal report indefinitely, and those messages will never expire.

The alternative journal recipient is an organization-wide setting, collecting journal reports for all unavailable journal recipients. Because it collects journal reports for all failing journal recipients, it might grow very fast when an outage hits multiple original journal recipients. Also, because it possibly collects NDRs of journal reports for all journal recipients, be sure to check with your legal department to see if sending all those journal reports to an alternative journal recipient is allowed under existing regulations and applicable laws.

Note Multiple journaling reports could be generated if the number of recipients exceeds the ExpansionSizeLimit setting in %ExchangeInstallPath%\EdgeTransport.exe.config, which could happen after group expansion. The default value is set to 1000 recipients. Multiple journal reports are also generated when a message is bifurcated—that is, the message is split as it gets routed to different destinations.

Create a Standard Journal Rule

To create a standard journal rule using EAC, you do the following:

1. Open the Exchange Admin Center and navigate to Servers ➤ Databases.
2. Select the database you want to enable journaling on and click the Edit icon.
3. Select Maintenance.
4. For selecting the journal recipient, click Browse and select the journal mailbox you want to use for collecting journal reports generated for mailboxes hosted on this database.
5. Click Save to confirm.

This is shown in Figure 11-24.

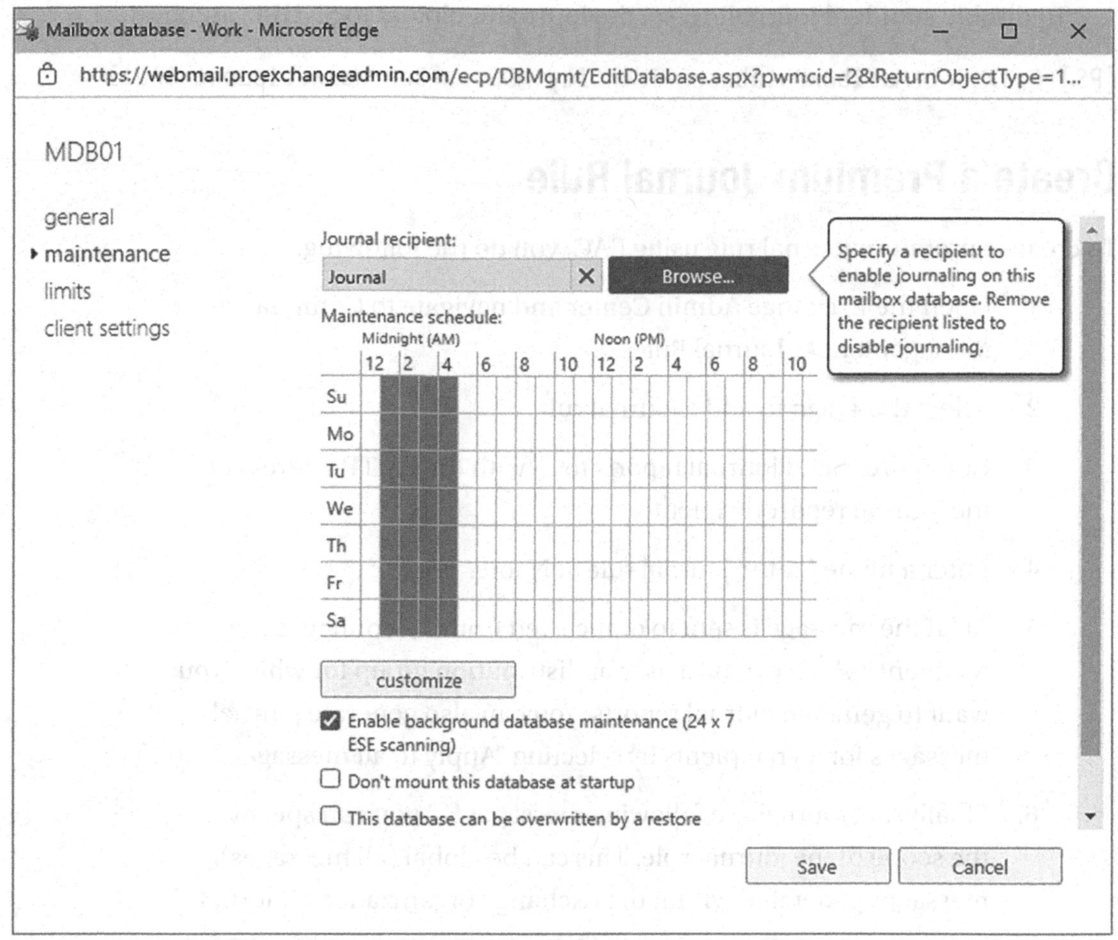

***Figure 11-24.** Configuring standard journaling*

To accomplish this using the Exchange Management Shell, use the Set-MailboxDatabase cmdlet. For example, to enable standard journaling to database MDB1 using journaling mailbox Journal Box 1, use the following command:

```
[PS] C:\> Set-MailboxDatabase -Identity MDB01 -JournalRecipient Journal
```

To check which mailbox database has been configured for standard journaling, use the following command:

```
[PS] C:\> Get-MailboxDatabase | Where {$_.JournalRecipient} | Select
Identity,JournalRecipient
```

To disable standard journaling, set the JournalRecipient to $NULL, as follows:

```
[PS] C:\> Set-MailboxDatabase -Identity MDB01 -JournalRecipient $null
```

Create a Premium Journal Rule

To create a premium journal rule using EAC, you do the following:

1. Open the Exchange Admin Center and navigate to Compliance Management ➤ Journal Rules.
2. Select the + sign to add a journal rule.
3. Configure "Send journal reports to..." with the SMTP address of the journal report recipient.
4. Enter a name for the journal rule at Name.
5. At "If the message is sent to or received from...," configure the recipient, which can be a user or distribution group for which you want to generate journal reports. You can also generate journal messages for all recipients by selecting "Apply to all messages."
6. Finally, at "Journal the following messages...," you can specify the scope of the journal rule. This can be global (all messages), messages generated within the Exchange organization (internal messages only), or messages with an external recipient or sender SMTP address (external messages only).
7. Click Save to save the rule.

This is shown in Figure 11-25.

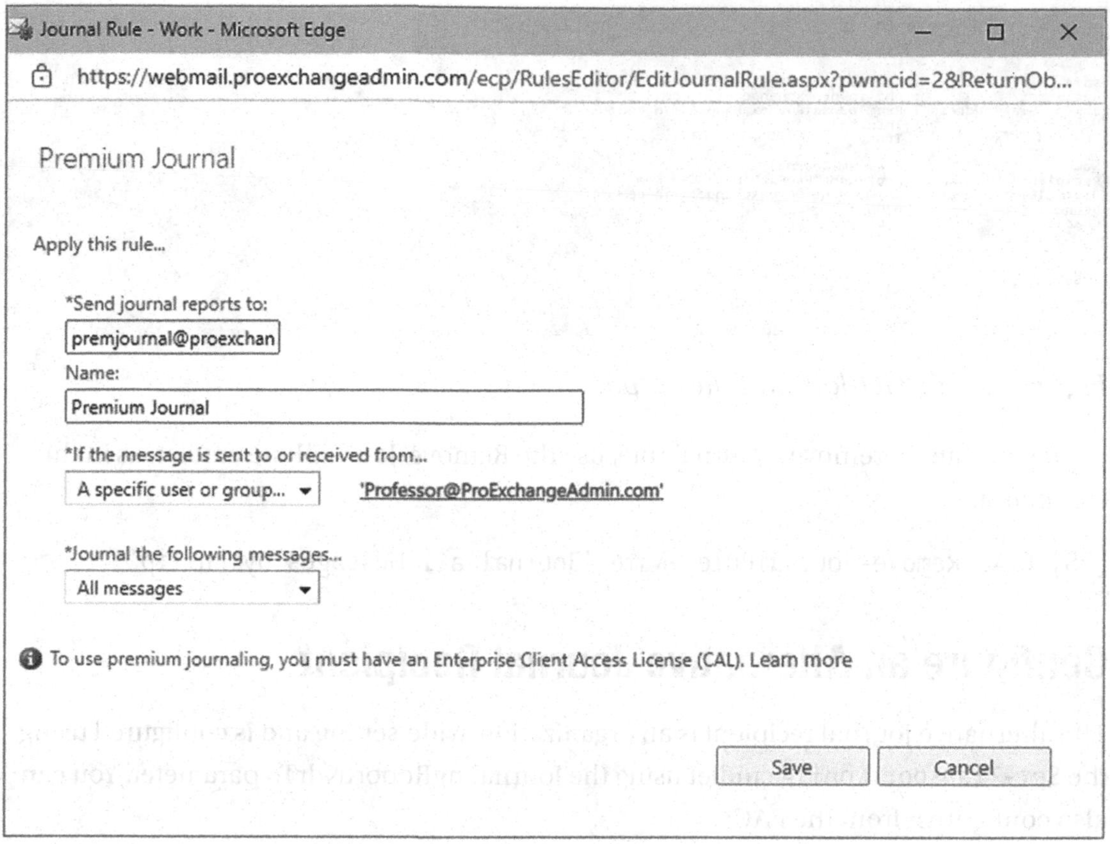

Figure 11-25. *Journal rule creation*

The cmdlet to create a journal rule is New-JournalRule. To create the journal rule in the preceding example, you would use the following command:

```
[PS] C:\> New-JournalRule -Name 'Journal all messages to/from Philip' -
JournalEmailAddress PremJournal@proexchangeadmin.com -Recipient philip@
proexchangeadmin.com -Scope Internal -Enabled $true
```

Possible options for the scope are global, internal, and external.

If you want to see which journal rules are configured, use `Get-JournalRule`, as shown in Figure 11-26.

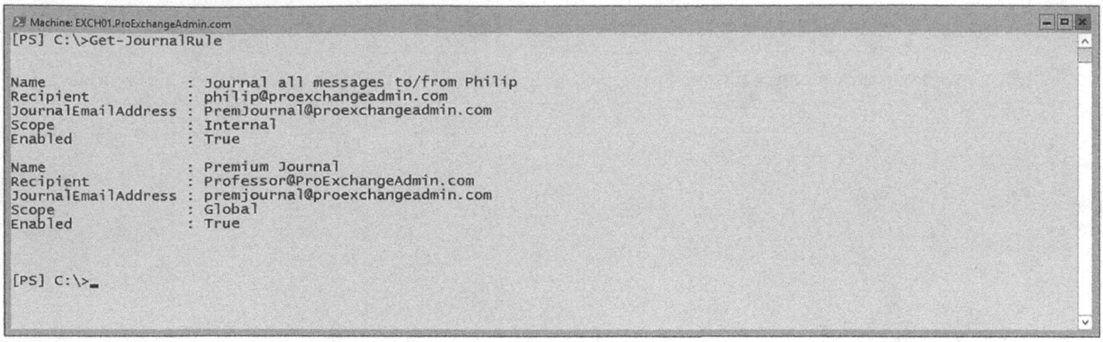

```
Machine: EXCH01.ProExchangeAdmin.com
[PS] C:\>Get-JournalRule

Name                : Journal all messages to/from Philip
Recipient           : philip@proexchangeadmin.com
JournalEmailAddress : PremJournal@proexchangeadmin.com
Scope               : Internal
Enabled             : True

Name                : Premium Journal
Recipient           : Professor@ProExchangeAdmin.com
JournalEmailAddress : premjournal@proexchangeadmin.com
Scope               : Global
Enabled             : True


[PS] C:\>_
```

Figure 11-26. *Get-JournalRule output*

If you want to remove a journal rule, use the Remove-JournalRule cmdlet, as in this command:

```
[PS] C:\> Remove-JournalRule -Name 'Journal all messages by Philip'
```

Configure an Alternative Journal Recipient

The alternative journal recipient is an organization-wide setting and is configured using the `Set-TransportConfig` cmdlet using the JournalingReportNdrTo parameter. You can also configure it from the EAC:

1. Open the EAC and navigate to Compliance Management ➤ Journal Rules.
2. In the top section, just above the + icon you can see the "Send undeliverable journal reports to" section.
3. Click Select Address, select an alternative journal mailbox, and click Save to continue.

To configure the alternative journaling recipient to AlternativeJournal@proexchangeadmin.com, execute the following command:

```
[PS] C:\> Set-TransportConfig -JournalingReportNdrTo AlternativeJournal@
proexchangeadmin.com
```

To remove the alternative journaling recipient, set it to $null.

Warning When an alternative journaling recipient is configured, you must make sure either the original journal recipient or the alternative journal recipient is available. If the alternative journal recipient is configured, messages that cannot be delivered to the original journal recipient are not requeued, and the related NDR, which Exchange will try to deliver to the alternative journal recipient, will be lost.

Data Loss Prevention (DLP)

Part of compliance is not only having the instruments to verify that an organization or its employees are operating within applicable regulations and laws but also providing the controls to manage sensitive data and prevent data leakage, such as credit card information. With email being used to send business reports as well as those invitations for dinner to family, users could be unaware of the sensitivity of the information they are sending or ignorant of the potential business impact of sending certain information over the public network which is the Internet.

An Exchange feature that focuses on managing or preventing the exposure of sensitive information is data loss prevention (DLP). For this purpose, DLP policies can be seen as a package of transport rules that prevent users from sending sensitive information by filtering those messages. Alternatively, you can use policy tips to notify users that they might be sending sensitive information. Policy tips are like mail tips, and they are shown as a notification in Outlook.

Caution Policy tips require Office 2013/2016/2019 Professional Plus. Policy tips do not work when you install Outlook separately.

Exchange has a feature named document fingerprinting, which can be used to identify sensitive material in your organization. By uploading sensitive text-based forms used by your organization, you can create DLP policies to match those forms. For example, you can add HR documents and create a DLP policy to prevent messages containing those HR documents from leaving the Exchange organization.

> **Note** Data loss prevention is a premium feature that requires an Enterprise CAL when used with on-premises Exchange Server 2013.

Creating DLP Policies

There are two ways to create a DLP policy in Exchange Server. The first method is to use a template. This template can be an Exchange-supplied one or one provided by a third party or yourself. After creating a DLP policy using a template, you can then customize the transport rules.

> **Note** To be able to create DLP policies, the user needs to be a member of the Compliance Management group.

You can see which templates are available by using the Get-DlpTemplate cmdlet, as shown in Figure 11-27.

```
Machine: EXCH01.ProExchangeAdmin.com
[PS] C:\>Get-DlpPolicyTemplate

Name                                               Publisher Version
----                                               --------- -------
U.S. Personally Identifiable Information (PII) Data Microsoft 15.0.3.0
U.S. Gramm-Leach-Bliley Act (GLBA)                 Microsoft 15.0.3.0
PCI Data Security Standard (PCI DSS)               Microsoft 15.0.3.0
Japan Financial Data                               Microsoft 15.0.3.0
U.K. Financial Data                                Microsoft 15.0.3.0
France Financial Data                              Microsoft 15.0.3.0
U.S. Financial Data                                Microsoft 15.0.3.0
Japan Personally Identifiable Information (PII) ... Microsoft 15.0.3.0
U.K. Personally Identifiable Information (PII) Data Microsoft 15.0.3.0
France Personally Identifiable Information (PII)... Microsoft 15.0.3.0
Germany Personally Identifiable Information (PII... Microsoft 15.0.3.0
Germany Financial Data                             Microsoft 15.0.3.0
Canada Health Information Act (HIA)                Microsoft 15.0.3.0
Canada Personal Information Protection Act (PIPA)  Microsoft 15.0.3.0
Canada Personal Information Protection Act (PIPEDA) Microsoft 15.0.3.0
Canada Personal Health Act (PHIPA) - Ontario       Microsoft 15.0.3.0
Canada Personal Health Information Act (PHIA) - ... Microsoft 15.0.3.0
U.K. Personal Information Online Code of Practic... Microsoft 15.0.3.0
U.K. Data Protection Act                           Microsoft 15.0.3.0
U.K. Privacy and Electronic Communications Regul... Microsoft 15.0.3.0
U.K. Access to Medical Reports Act                 Microsoft 15.0.3.0
Japan Protection of Personal Information           Microsoft 15.0.3.0
U.S. Health Insurance Act (HIPAA)                  Microsoft 15.0.3.0
France Data Protection Act                         Microsoft 15.0.3.0
Australia Health Records Act (HRIP Act)            Microsoft 15.0.3.0
Australia Privacy Act                              Microsoft 15.0.3.0
Australia Personally Identifiable Information (P... Microsoft 15.0.3.0
Australia Financial Data                           Microsoft 15.0.3.0
Saudi Arabia Financial Data                        Microsoft 15.0.3.0
Saudi Arabia - Anti-Cyber Crime Law                Microsoft 15.0.3.0
Israel Financial Data                              Microsoft 15.0.3.0
Israel Protection of Privacy                       Microsoft 15.0.3.0
U.S. Patriot Act                                   Microsoft 15.0.3.0
U.S. Federal Trade Commission (FTC) Consumer Rules Microsoft 15.0.3.0
U.S. State Social Security Number Confidentialit... Microsoft 15.0.3.0
U.S. State Breach Notification Laws                Microsoft 15.0.3.0
Israel Personally Identifiable Information (PII)... Microsoft 15.0.3.0
Saudi Arabia Personally Identifiable Information... Microsoft 15.0.3.0
Canada Personally Identifiable Information (PII)... Microsoft 15.0.3.0
Canada Financial Data                              Microsoft 15.0.3.0


[PS] C:\>_
```

Figure 11-27. *Retrieving available DLP policy templates*

To create a template-based DLP policy using EAC, you do the following:

1. Open the Exchange Admin Center and navigate to Compliance Management ➤ Data Loss Prevention.
2. Select the + sign and select New DLP policy from the template.
3. Enter a name for the DLP policy, optionally a description. Then, in "Choose a template," you pick the template to use as a basis for your DLP policy.
4. When expanding "More options," you can choose to test the DLP policy first by selecting "Test DLP policy with Policy Tips" or "Test DLP policy without Policy Tips." This is especially helpful when customizing DLP policies, as an improperly configured DLP policy could result in unwanted behavior, like blocking the mail flow of valid messages. You can also initially disable the DLP policy, which is recommended if you need to customize it, as the DLP policy becomes effective after saving it, potentially affecting mail flow.
5. Click Save to create the policy.

This is shown in Figure 11-28.

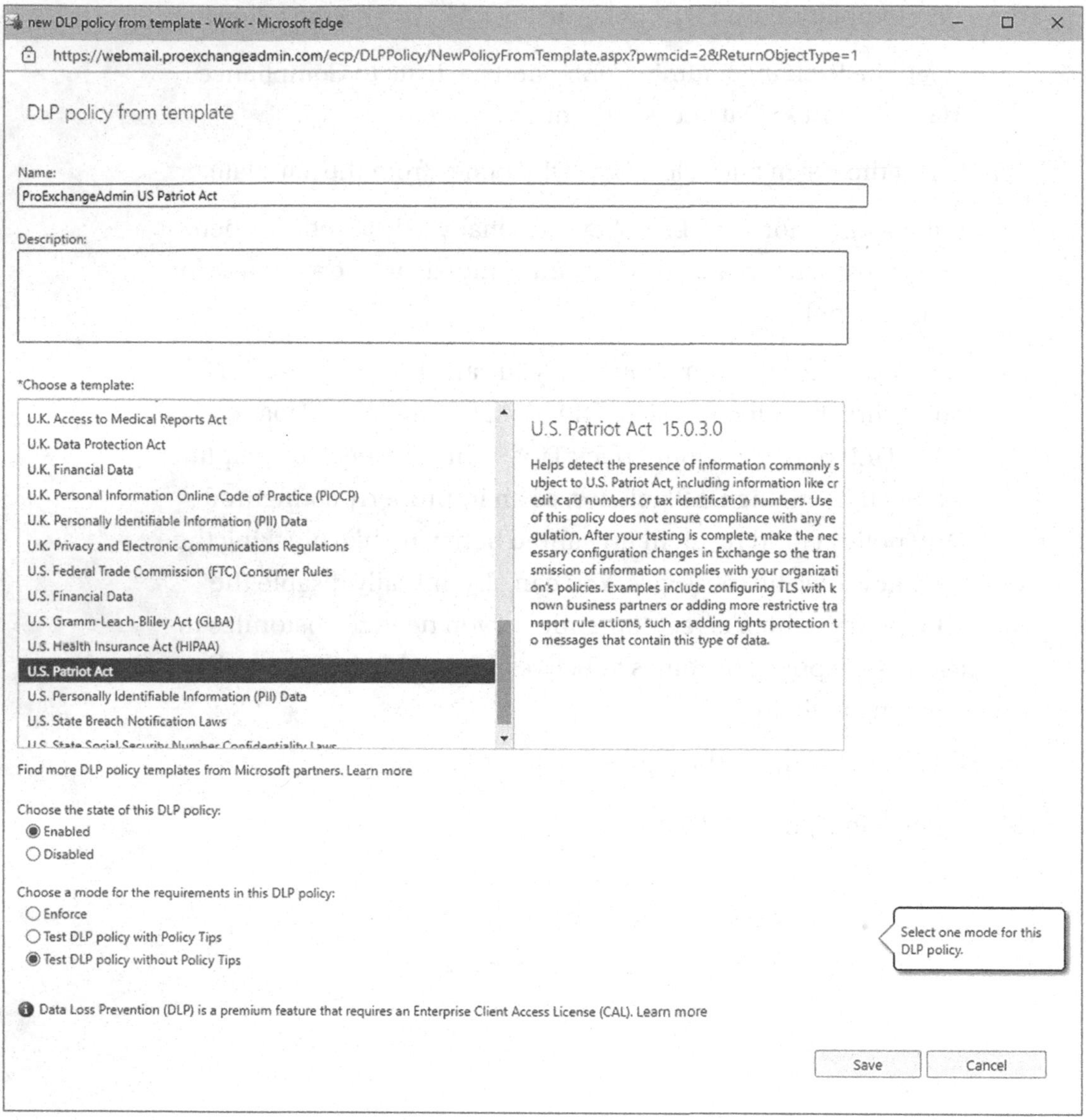

Figure 11-28. *Creating a DLP policy using a template*

If you are happy with the template, you can leave the DLP policy as is. When you want to inspect or customize the DLP policy, in EAC you do the following:

1. In Compliance Management ➤ Data Loss Prevention, select the DLP policy.
2. Click the Edit button.

3. Select Rules.

4. You will now be presented a list of rules contained in the DLP policy. You can turn them on or off individually or edit them to customize each rule.

This is shown in Figure 11-29.

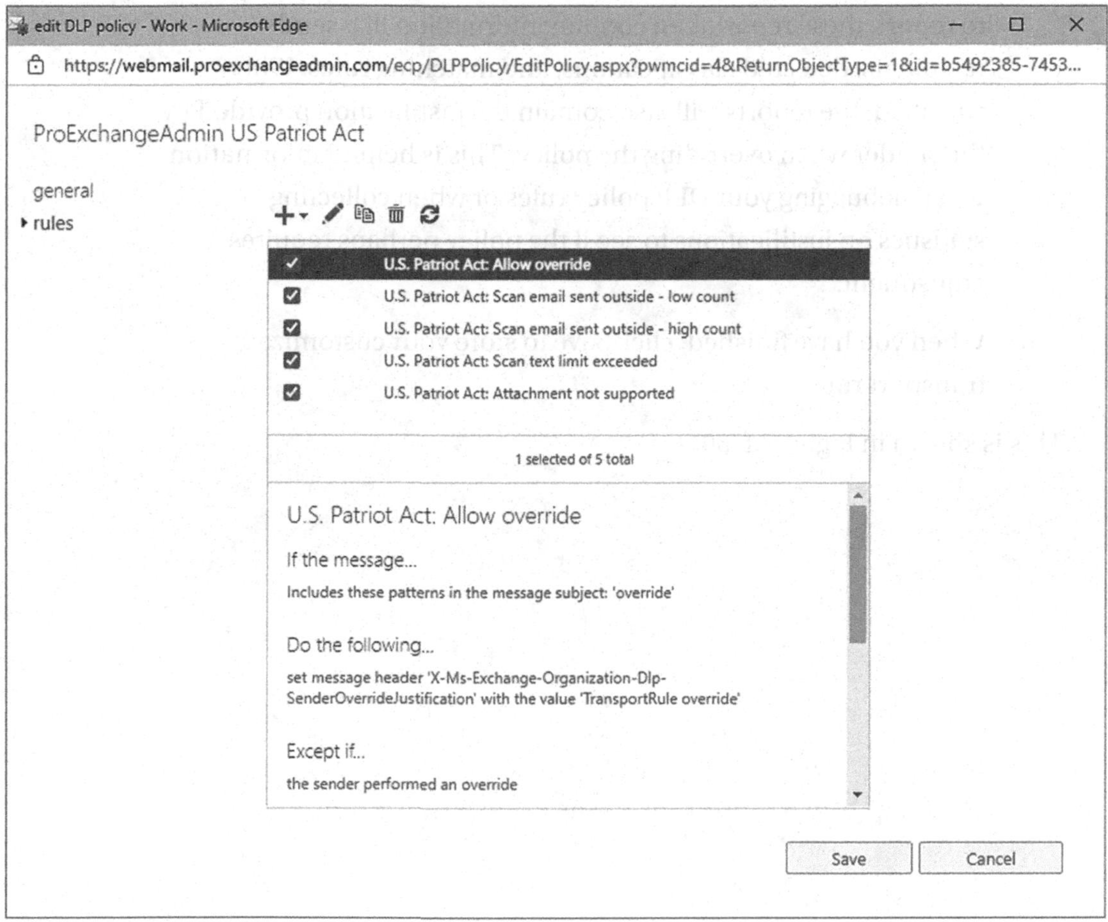

***Figure 11-29.** Editing a DLP policy*

5. When you select Edit (i.e., the Pencil icon), you will have the option to inspect or customize the underlying transport rule that is part of the DLP policy. When testing DLP policy rules, you can temporarily add an action "Generate incident report" (new in Exchange Server 2013 SP1), which you can use to generate reports for matching messages and have those reports sent to the recipients specified. Depending on the selected information to report, these reports can contain information like sender, recipients, detected classifications, and matching rules. When specified, the reports will also contain the justification provided by the sender when overriding the policy. This is helpful information when debugging your DLP policy rules or when collecting statistics on justifications to see if the policy perhaps requires adjustment.

6. When you have finished, click Save to store your customized transport rule.

This is shown in Figure 11-30.

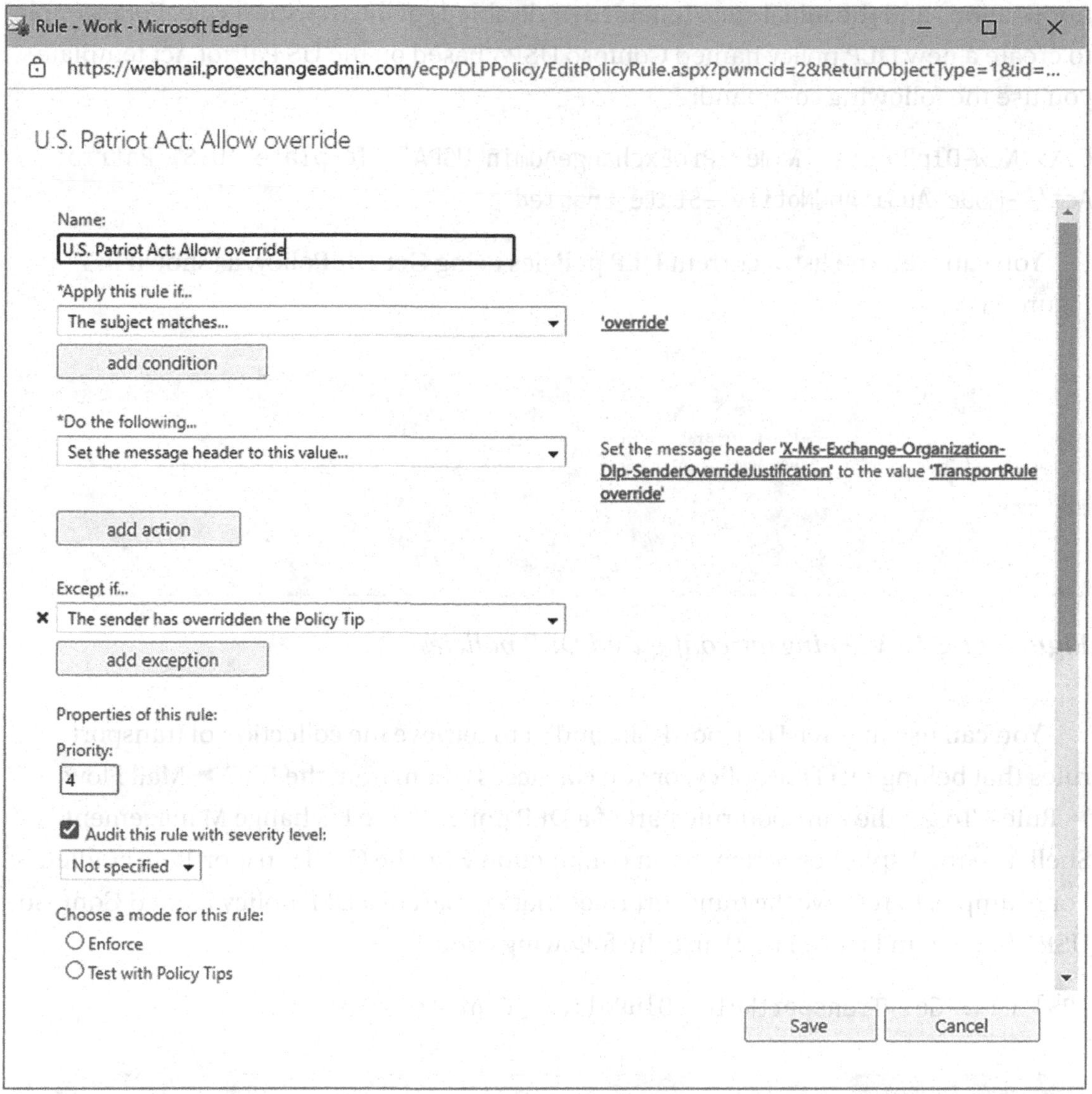

***Figure 11-30.** Editing a DLP policy rule*

If you want to create a DLP policy using the Exchange Management Shell, use the New-DlpPolicy cmdlet, specifying a name and the template to use as a basis for your DLP policy. You can also specify mode (audit, audit and notify, or enforce—the latter will block sending messages with detected possible sensitive information without notification) and the initial state (enabled or disabled) of the transport rule. For example, to create a new DLP policy named Contoso USPA based on the US Patriot Act template, you use the following command:

```
C:\> New-DlpPolicy -Name 'ProExchangeAdmin USPA' -Template 'U.S. Patriot
Act' -Mode AuditAndNotify -State Enabled
```

You can view the list of current DLP policies using Get-DlpPolicy, as shown in Figure 11-31.

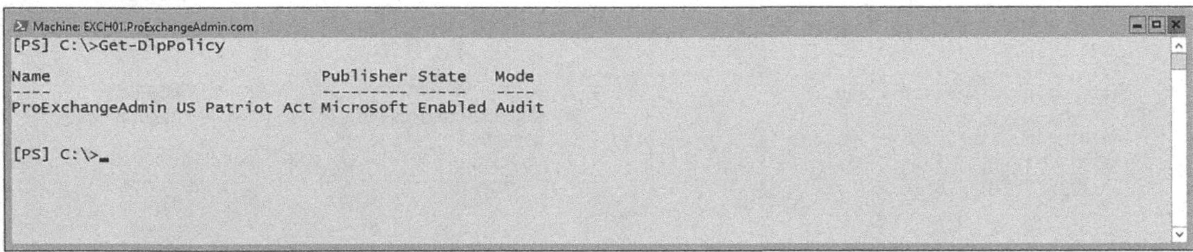

Figure 11-31. *Viewing the configured DLP policies*

You can use the Get-TransportRule cmdlet to retrieve the collection of transport rules that belong to a DLP policy, or you can access them from the EAC ➤ Mail Flow ➤ Rules. To get the transport rule part of a DLP policy in the Exchange Management Shell, use the DlpPolicy parameter in conjunction with the Get-TransportRule cmdlet. For example, to retrieve the transport rules that are part of a DLP policy named Contoso USPA (shown in Figure 11-32), use the following command:

```
[PS] C:\> Get-TransportRule -DlpPolicy 'Contoso USPA'
```

```
Machine: EXCH01.ProExchangeAdmin.com

[PS] C:\>Get-TransportRule -DlpPolicy "ProExchangeAdmin US Patriot Act"

Name                                                State   Mode  Priority Comments
----                                                -----   ----  -------- --------
U.S. Patriot Act: Allow override                    Enabled Audit 4
U.S. Patriot Act: Scan email sent outside - low count Enabled Audit 5
U.S. Patriot Act: Scan email sent outside - high count Enabled Audit 6
U.S. Patriot Act: Scan text limit exceeded          Enabled Audit 7
U.S. Patriot Act: Attachment not supported          Enabled Audit 8

[PS] C:\>_
```

Figure 11-32. *Retrieving DLP policy transport rules*

Note Regular transport rules can be distinguished from transport rules that are part of a DLP policy, in that their DLP policy attribute is not set and their DLP ID is configured as 00000000-0000-0000-0000-000000000000. For DLP policy rules, the DIP ID matches the Immutable ID attribute of the DLP policy.

You can customize policy tips with localized messages or a URL, which you can use to direct users to a page explaining the communications compliance standards. To add these custom elements, go to EAC ➤ Compliance Management ➤ Data Loss Prevention, and select "Customize policy tips" (the cogwheel).

To create custom policy tips using the Exchange Management Shell, use the New-PolicyTip cmdlet. The Name parameter defines what policy tip you want to override, where locale is a supported language locale, as follows:

- **<Locale>\NotifyOnly**—To customize the message used for notifications in <Locale>.
- **<Locale>\RejectOverride**—To customize the message used for notifications in <Locale> when the user is still allowed to send the message.
- **<Locale>\Reject**—To customize the message used when used for notifications in <Locale> and when the sending of the message is prevented.
- **Url**—To add a link to a URL for policy tips. There can be only one URL policy tip. The URL will be accessed when the sender clicks the link in "Learn more about your organization's rule," which will be shown in the policy tip.

For example, to customize the Dutch locale notification when users are notified of possibly sending a message with sensitive information, you could use

```
[PS] C:\> New-PolicyTipConfig -Name 'nl\RejectOverride' -Value 'Uw bericht
bevat mogelijk gevoelige informatie'.
```

> **Note** If the transport rule is configured to only notify users and you configure a custom policy tip for "en\RejectOverride," your custom notification message will not be displayed. You will need to configure a notification message for all three possible modes.

To configure a compliance URL to show with the policy tip (shown in Figure 11-33), you use

```
[PS] C:\> New-PolicyTipConfig -Name 'Url' -Value 'http://compliance.
proexchangeadmin.com'
```

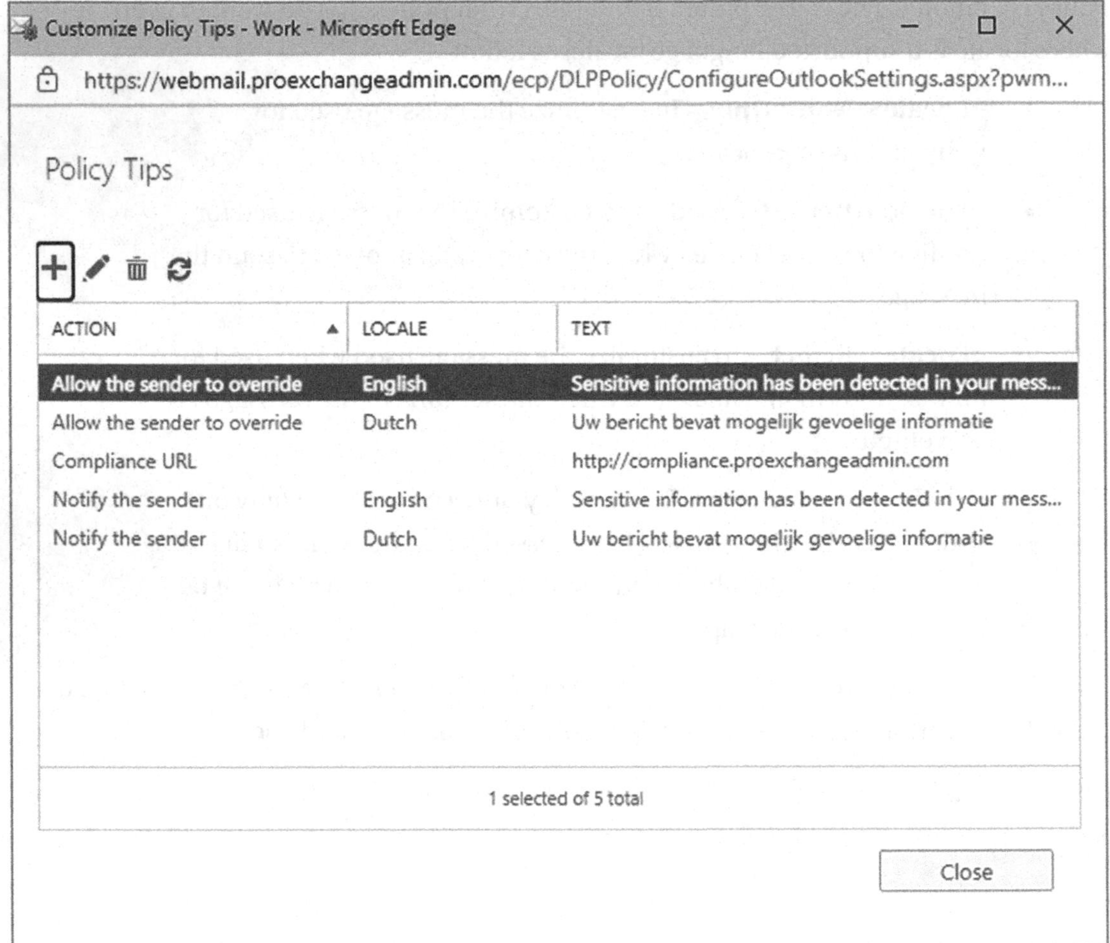

Figure 11-33. *Customizing the policy tips*

To retrieve the current set of customized policy tips, use `Get-PolicyTipConfig`.

Optionally, you can use the locale parameter to only return the custom policy tips for a given locale; for example, `Get-PolicyTipConfigLocale -Locale NL`. Both are shown in Figure 11-34.

```
Machine: EXCH01.ProExchangeAdmin.com
[PS] C:\>Get-PolicyTipConfig

Identity           Value
--------           -----
en\NotifyOnly      Sensitive information has been detected in your message.
en\RejectOverride  Sensitive information has been detected in your message.
nl\NotifyOnly      Uw bericht bevat mogelijk gevoelige informatie
nl\RejectOverride  Uw bericht bevat mogelijk gevoelige informatie
Url                http://compliance.proexchangeadmin.com

[PS] C:\>Get-PolicyTipConfig -Locale NL

Identity           Value
--------           -----
nl\NotifyOnly      Uw bericht bevat mogelijk gevoelige informatie
nl\RejectOverride  Uw bericht bevat mogelijk gevoelige informatie

[PS] C:\>_
```

***Figure 11-34.** Using Get-PolicyTipConfig to list customized policy tips*

The way DLP policy tips manifest themselves to users is like how mail tips operate. A small notification bar is shown when sensitive information is detected, and the DLP policy and related DLP policy rules are configured to generate a notification, as shown in Figure 11-35.

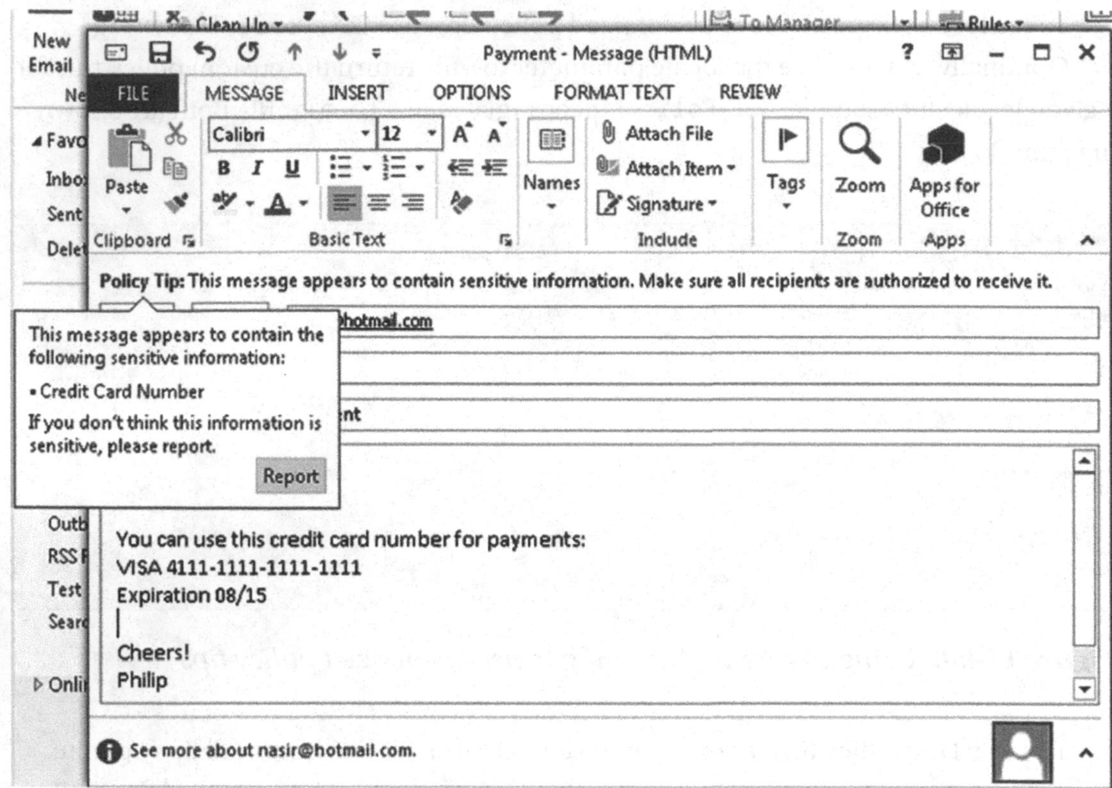

Figure 11-35. *DLP policy tip shown in Outlook*

When such a message is sent (when allowed by the DLP policy) and you have configured to generate incident reports for DLP policy rules, the configured recipients will receive a report as well as a copy of the message attached. The information in the report depends on the selected fields and may include such items as matching rules and data classifications that were detected, including the number of occurrences.

If you want to adjust a DLP policy, use the Set-DlpPolicy cmdlet, for example:

```
[PS] C:\> Set-DlpPolicy -Identity 'Contoso USPA' -Mode Enforce -State
Enabled
```

When you want to remove a DLP policy, you use Remove-DlpPolicy, for example:

```
[PS] C:\> Remove-DlpPolicy -Identity 'Contoso USPA'
```

Note Unfortunately, Exchange Server 2013 does not contain built-in reports for DLP-related incidents. Office 365 does, though, and you can find them at Exchange Admin Center ➤ Compliance Management ➤ Data Loss Prevention ➤ Reports. You can generate information on DLP policy matches for sent mail, received mail, and DLP rule matches for sent or received mail.

Importing and Exporting DLP Policies and Templates

As mentioned earlier, you can import DLP policy templates, or you can import or export a DLP policy collection from XML files. Either way, you can quickly implement a customized DLP policy in an Exchange environment. You can duplicate the DLP policies from a test environment to your production environment. The DLP policy settings are stored in an XML file.

Warning When you import a DLP policy collection, that collection of policies will overwrite any existing DLP policies defined in your Exchange organization.

To import a DLP policy template file, you use the Import-DlpPolicyTemplate cmdlet. For example, to import a DLP policy from a file named C:\ProExchangeTemplate.xml, you would use the following command:

```
[PS]C:\> Import-DlpPolicyTemplate -FileData ([Byte[]]$(Get-Content -Path
'C:\ProExchangeTemplate.xml' -Encoding Byte -ReadCount 0))
```

To import a DLP policy template in the EAC, follow these steps:

1. Open EAC and navigate to Compliance Management ➤ Data Loss Prevention.

2. Click the + icon and select the Import Policy Option.

Alternatively, you can create a new DLP policy directly from a file-based template using New-DlpPolicy with the TemplateData parameter, for example:

```
[PS]C:\> New-DlpPolicy -Name 'DLPPolicy' -TemplateData ([Byte[]]$(Get-
Content -Path 'C:\ProExchangeTemplate.xml' -Encoding Byte -ReadCount 0))
```

Tip Besides importing DLP policy template files from third parties, you can develop your own template file. For more information on developing your own DLP policy template files, see `http://bit.ly/ExchangeDevDLPTemplate`.

You can also import or export the complete collection of DLP policies. To export the current DLP policy collection, use Export-DlpCollection. For example, to export the DLP policy collection to a file named C:\ProExchangeDLP.xml, you would use the following command:

```
[PS] C:\> Set-Content -Path 'C:\Temp\ProExchangeDLP.xml' -Value
(Export-DlpPolicyCollection).FileData -Encoding Byte
```

The XML file will contain all DLP policies, all DLP policy settings, and the related transport rules. This XML file is shown in Figure 11-36.

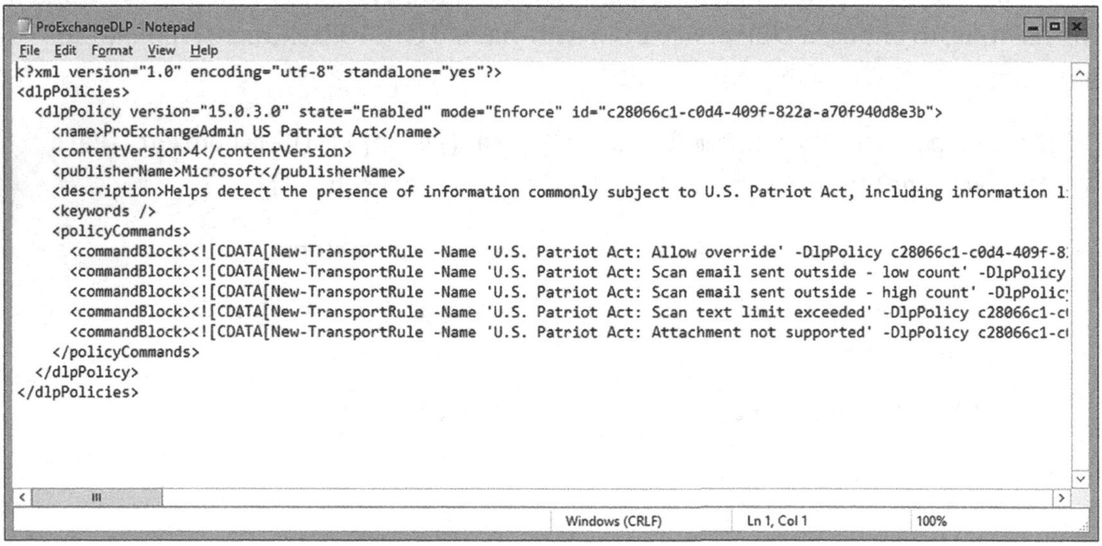

ProExchangeDLP - Notepad

File Edit Format View Help


```
<?xml version="1.0" encoding="utf-8" standalone="yes"?>
<dlpPolicies>
  <dlpPolicy version="15.0.3.0" state="Enabled" mode="Enforce" id="c28066c1-c0d4-409f-822a-a70f940d8e3b">
    <name>ProExchangeAdmin US Patriot Act</name>
    <contentVersion>4</contentVersion>
    <publisherName>Microsoft</publisherName>
    <description>Helps detect the presence of information commonly subject to U.S. Patriot Act, including information l
    <keywords />
    <policyCommands>
      <commandBlock><![CDATA[New-TransportRule -Name 'U.S. Patriot Act: Allow override' -DlpPolicy c28066c1-c0d4-409f-8
      <commandBlock><![CDATA[New-TransportRule -Name 'U.S. Patriot Act: Scan email sent outside - low count' -DlpPolicy
      <commandBlock><![CDATA[New-TransportRule -Name 'U.S. Patriot Act: Scan email sent outside - high count' -DlpPolic
      <commandBlock><![CDATA[New-TransportRule -Name 'U.S. Patriot Act: Scan text limit exceeded' -DlpPolicy c28066c1-c
      <commandBlock><![CDATA[New-TransportRule -Name 'U.S. Patriot Act: Attachment not supported' -DlpPolicy c28066c1-c
    </policyCommands>
  </dlpPolicy>
</dlpPolicies>
```


Windows (CRLF) Ln 1, Col 1 100%

Figure 11-36. *DLP policy collection XML file*

To import a file containing a DLP policy, you use the Import-DlpPolicyCollection cmdlet. For example, to import the DLP policy collection settings stored in C:\ContosoDLP.xml, you would use the following command:

```
[PS] C:\> Import-DlpPolicyCollection -FileData ([Byte[]]$(Get-Content -Path
'C:\ContosoDLP.xml' -Encoding Byte -ReadCount 0))
```

Caution Export-DlpPolicyCollection seems to contain a bug, as it exports the New-TransportRule cmdlets to create the related DLP policy rules, but it forgets to state some mandatory values. For example, it does not save the AttachmentProcessingLimitExceeded value in the XML file, after which Import-DlpPolicyCollection will complain because no value is specified for the AttachmentProcessingLimitExceeded parameter. Try correcting the cmdlets in the XML file and then retry the importing when you encounter this obstacle.

Customizing Your DLP Policy

An alternative to using a template to create a DLP policy is to create a custom DLP policy when you have specific requirements. That DLP policy will be empty after creation, so you need to add your own transport rules to it.

To create a custom DLP policy using EAC, you do the following:

1. Open the Exchange Admin Center and navigate to Compliance Management ➤ Data Loss Prevention.
2. Click the arrow next to the + sign and select New for setting a custom policy.
3. Enter a name, optional description, and initial state for the policy.
4. Click Save to save the empty DLP policy definition.

You can now start adding rules to it by clicking the Edit icon and selecting the rules section, where you can add your custom rules.

If you want to add a custom rule using the Exchange Management Shell, you use New-DlpPolicy, for example:

```
[PS] C:\> New-DlpPolicy -Name 'CustomDLP' -State Enabled -Mode AuditAndNotify
```

After you have established that, you can start adding custom transport rules to the DLP policy using the New-TransportRule cmdlet with the DlpPolicy parameter to attach the transport rules to the DLP policy.

In addition, you can use the mode to determine how the rule operates. Choices for mode are Audit (rule is evaluated but actions are skipped), AuditAndNotify (audit with policy tips), and Enforce (audit and notify plus actions are performed). For example, to create a transport rule to generate policy tips for all messages in which a credit card number is detected and further attach it to a DLP policy named "CustomDLP," you would use the following command:

```
[PS] C:\> New-TransportRule -Name 'Custom DLP: All messages with Credit
Card Number' -DlpPolicy 'CustomDlp' -Mode AuditAndNotify -MessageContains
DataClassifications @{Name = 'Credit Card Number'} -SetAuditSeverity
Medium -NotifySender NotifyOnly
```

Both commands are shown in Figure 11-37.

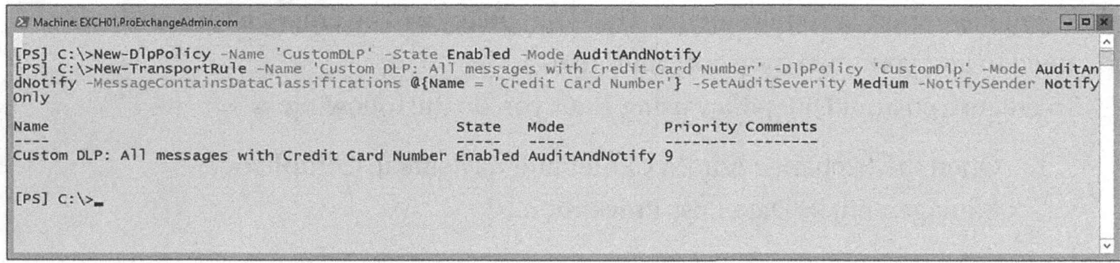

Figure 11-37. *Creating a custom DLP policy rule using New-TransportRule*

Here is a short explanation of the DLP-specific parameter used in this example:

- **DlpPolicy** is used to specify the DLP policy to attach the rule to.
- **NotifySender** is a DLP-specific parameter that determines how a user is notified when entering DLP policy–violating information. It needs to be specified together with the MessageContainsDataClassifications parameter. The options for NotifySender are

- **NotifyOnly**—Notifies the sender that the message is sent.
- **RejectMessage**—Notifies the sender that the message is rejected.
- **RejectUnlessFalsePositiveOverride**—Notifies the sender; the sender can send a message marking it as a false positive.
- **RejectUnlessSilentOverride**—A message is rejected unless the sender overrides policy restriction.
- **RejectUnlessExplicitOverride**—A message is rejected unless the sender overrides, allowing the sender to specify justification.
- If any of the reject options are selected for NotifySender, you can specify a rejection status code and reason using the RejectMessageEnhancedStatusCode and RejectMessageReasonText parameters.
- The parameter MessageContainsDataClassifications is a new predicate in Exchange Server 2013 SP1 and can be used to specify rules for searching for sensitive information. In the example, it was used to filter messages for the classification "Credit Card Number."

  You can also define thresholds for the minimum and maximum numbers of occurrences, as well as for the confidence level, which is a percentage indicating how sure the DLP engine is that the information is a match. For example, something that looks like a credit card number near something else that looks like an expiration date is more likely to be credit card information than something that looks like a series of numbers. Note that when the parameter is omitted, as in the example, a default minimum of 1 occurrence and 100% maximum confidence level are set.
- Not shown in the example but other DLP-specific predicates are ExceptIfHasClassification (to exclude one specific data classification) and ExceptIfHasNoClassification (to apply the rule to messages without a classification). Predicates HasSenderOverride and ExceptIfHasSenderOverride can be used to control rule evaluation whether or not the sender has selected to override DLP policy for the message.

You can verify the creation of the DLP policy rule using `Get-TransportRule` with the DlpPolicy parameter.

Note For more information on creating your own sensitive information, or even your own template containing these definitions, see `http://bit.ly/ExchangeSensitiveInformation`. To get a list of currently defined types of sensitive information, use Get-DataClassification|Sort Name.

DLP Document Fingerprinting

Another interesting feature in Exchange Server is DLP document fingerprinting. This fingerprinting allows you to enhance DLP by customizing your sensitive information types by uploading documents. These documents should represent the information you are trying to protect, for example, HR documents or tax forms. You can then create DLP policy rules to detect these types of documents and take appropriate action.

Note Documents uploaded for document fingerprinting are not stored in the Exchange Information Store. Instead, a hash is generated using the contents of the document used by the DLP engine for detecting matching information. The hashes are stored with the data classification object in Active Directory. There could be one or more document fingerprints per data classification.

To create document fingerprints using EAC, you do the following:

1. Open the Exchange Admin Center.
2. Navigate to Compliance Management ➤ Data Loss Prevention.
3. Select Manage Document Fingerprints.
4. In the document fingerprints window, select the + sign to create a new document fingerprint.
5. In the new document fingerprint window, enter a name for the kind of document fingerprint you are creating and a mandatory description. This is shown in Figure 11-38.

6. In the document list section, select the + sign to add a new document for which you want to create a fingerprint. The document fingerprinting supports the same file types as transport rules. For a list of supported file types, see `http://bit.ly/ExchangeTransportRulesFileTypes`.

7. When you are done uploading the documents to fingerprint, click Save and click close.

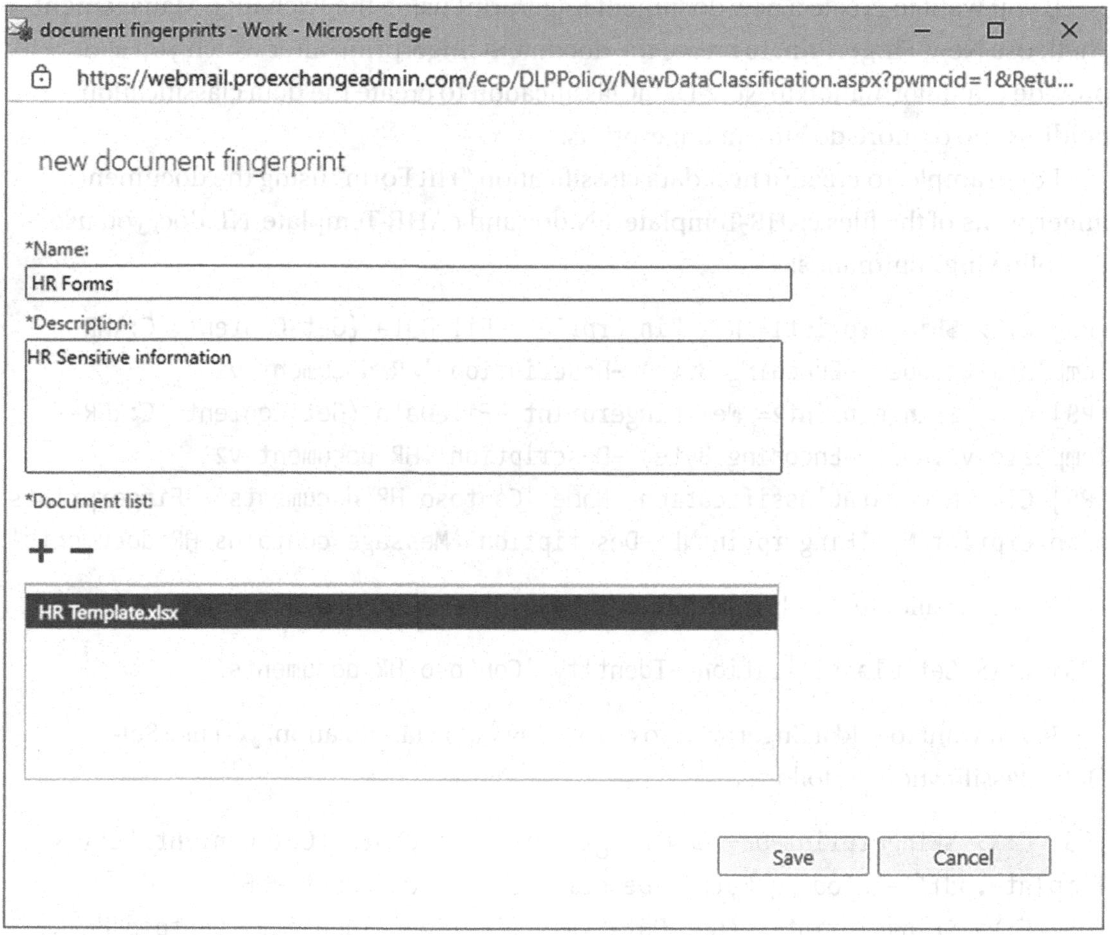

Figure 11-38. *Creating a document fingerprint*

Tip You can add multiple documents to a single document fingerprint. This allows you to create a single fingerprint for the same type of information in various formats—for example, .docx and .pdf—or different versions of the document. You can also configure a localized name to display in supported clients for the fingerprint via Edit document fingerprints ➤ Language settings—for example, EN/'HR Documents' and DE/'HR Documents'.

If you want to create a new document fingerprint using the Exchange Management Shell, use New-FingerPrint to create the document fingerprint, after which you can provide that information to New-DataClassification to create the data classification holding one or more document fingerprints.

For example, to create a new data classification "HR Form" using the document fingerprints of the files c:\HR-Template-EN.doc and c:\HR-Template-NL.doc, you use the following commands:

```
[PS] C:\> $Fingerprint1= New-Fingerprint -FileData (Get-Content 'C:\HR-
Template-v1.doc' -Encoding Byte) -Description 'HR document v1'
[PS] C:\> $Fingerprint2= New-Fingerprint -FileData (Get-Content 'C:\HR-
Template-v2.doc' -Encoding Byte) -Description 'HR document v2'
[PS] C:\> New-DataClassification -Name 'Contoso HR documents' -Fingerprints
$FingerprintEN, $FingerprintNL -Description 'Message contains HR documents'
```

You can validate the classification using Get-Classification, for example:

```
[PS] C:\> Get-Classification -Identity 'Contoso HR documents'
```

If you want to add a fingerprint to an existing data classification, you use Set-DataClassification, as follows:

```
[PS] C:\> $FingerprintPDF= New-Fingerprint -FileData (Get-Content 'C:\HR-
Template.pdf' -Encoding Byte) -Description 'HR document PDF'
[PS] C:\> $Fingerprints= (Get-DataClassification -Identity 'Contoso HR
documents').Fingerprints + $FingerprintPDF
[PS] C:\> Set-DataClassification -Identity 'Contoso HR documents' -
Fingerprints $Fingerprints
```

Changes made to a DLP policy may not take effect immediately. Outlook 2013 caches DLP policies in two local XML files that are refreshed every 24 hours. The files are in the folder %UserProfile%\AppData\Local\Microsoft\Outlook, and their file names start with PolicyNudgeClassificationDefinitions (cached data classifications) and PolicyNudgeRules (cached rule information). Keep this in mind when implementing policy changes in production or when you are testing DLP policies. Luckily, there is a workaround.

Note Outlook will use the locally cached DLP policy information to evaluate the message and attachments against document fingerprints or other DLP policy rules, using the same DLP engine as Exchange. This means attachments are not sent over the network for evaluation.

To force Outlook 2019 to download the latest DLP policies, close Outlook 2013 and remove the following entry from the registry:

```
HKEY_CURRENT_USER\SOFTWARE\Microsoft\Office\16.0\Outlook\
PolicyNudges\LastDownloadTimesPerAccount
```

After removal, start Outlook 2019. When you create a message, the updated DLP policies will be downloaded.

Caution Document fingerprinting does not work for password-protected files or files containing solely images. Also, documents will not be detected if they do not contain all the text used in the document employed to create the document fingerprint. Use documents or forms with blank fields, for example, to create the fingerprints.

Now, you need to create a DLP policy rule in which you specify this data classification to match your sensitive information contents. To do this, follow these steps:

1. Open EAC and navigate to Compliance Management ➤ Data Loss Prevention.

2. Open the DLP Policy and select Rules.

3. Click the + icon to select a new rule. In the “Apply this rule if” drop-down box, select “The message contains any of these sensitive information types” and select the document fingerprint that was created in the previous step.

4. In the “Do the following” drop-down box, select “Reject the message with an explanation” and enter the text “This message contains sensitive HR information.”

5. Click Save and Close to continue.

This is shown in Figure 11-39.

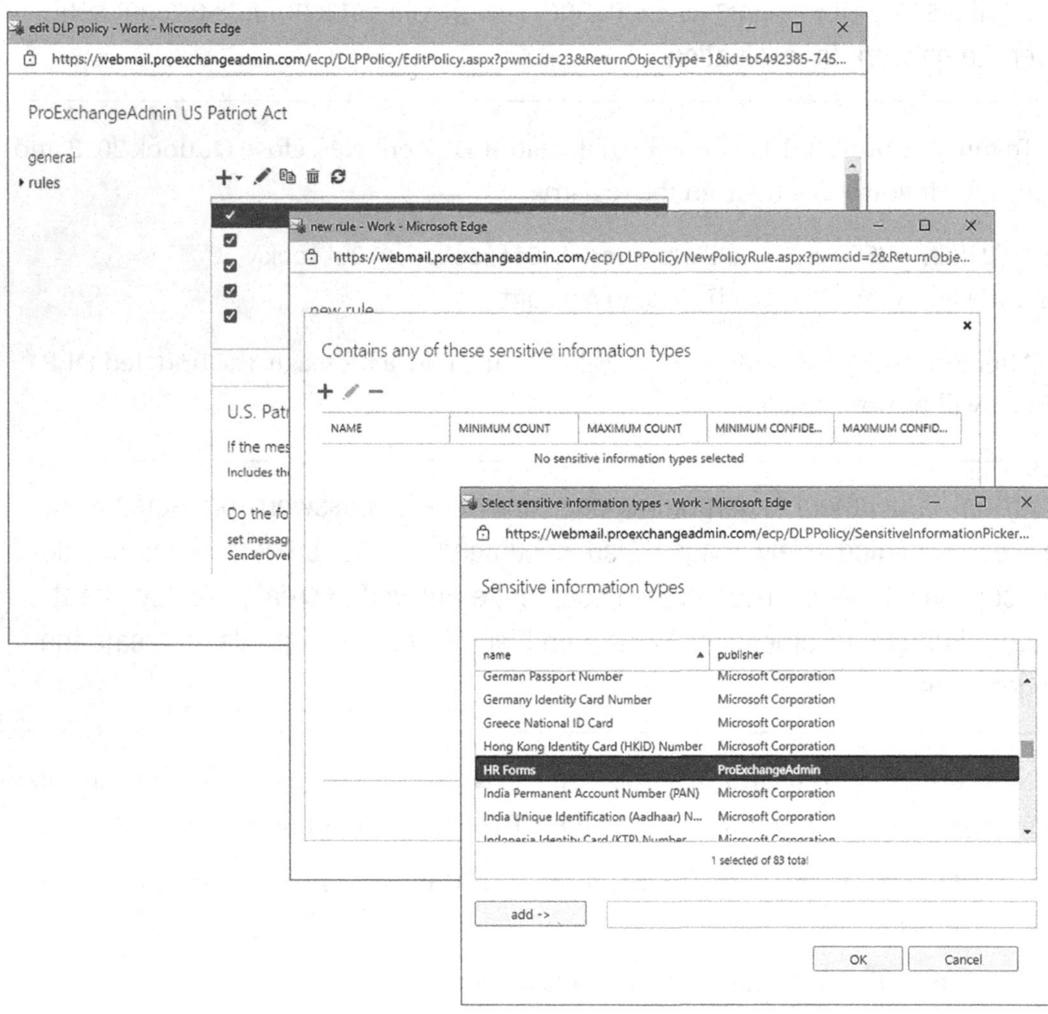

***Figure 11-39.** Creating a DLP policy rule using document fingerprints*

To create such a DLP policy in the Exchange Management Shell, use the New-TransportRule you would also use to create a custom DLP policy rule, for example:

```
[PS] C:\> New-TransportRule -Name 'CustomDLP: HR docs' -MessageContains
DataClassifications @{'Name'='ProExchangeAdmin HR documents'} -NotifySender
'RejectUnlessExplicitOverride' -RejectMessageReasonText 'Delivery not
authorized, message refused' -SetAuditSeverity 'Medium' -Mode
'AuditAndNotify' -DlpPolicy 'CustomDLP'
```

Now, when a user tries to send a message using a document with an attachment that matches the document fingerprint, the sender will get a nondelivery report as shown in Figure 11-40.

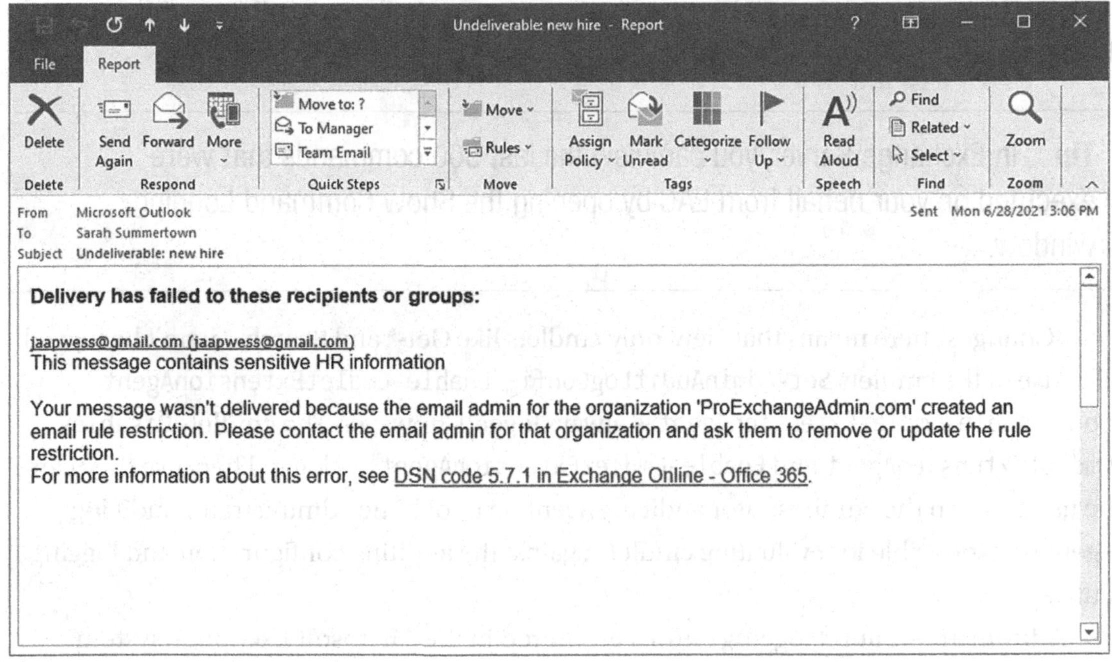

***Figure 11-40.** DLP fingerprint NDR in Outlook*

Auditing

Administrators in an Exchange organization have power, and with power comes responsibility. From a compliance perspective, organizations may require tracking of administrative changes, such as monitoring who made changes to a certain receive connector, or auditing the access to high-profile mailboxes.

The following auditing options are available in Exchange Server:

- **Administrator audit logging**—This allows organizations to audit administrative changes in their Exchange organization.
- **Mailbox audit logging**—This allows organizations to audit mailbox access and changes.

Administrator Audit Logging

The administrator audit logging feature allows auditing of who did what and where in the Exchange organization. Exchange Server can audit all changes performed by administrators in the Exchange Management Shell. Actions performed in the Exchange Admin Center are also logged because EAC constructs and runs cmdlets in the background.

Tip In Exchange Server, you can view the last 500 commands that were executed on your behalf from EAC by opening the Show Command Logging window.

"Changes" here means that view-only cmdlets like Get-* and Search-* won't be logged. The use of the cmdlets `Set-AdminAuditLogConfig`, `Enable-CmdletExtensionAgent`, and `Disable-CmdletExtensionAgent` is always logged, however. The cmdlets `Disable-CmdletExtensionAgent` and `Enable-CmdletExtensionAgent` are logged because they can be used to turn the administrator audit log agent on or off. The administrator audit log agent is responsible for evaluating cmdlets against the auditing configuration and logging entries.

Administrator audit logging entries are stored in the Microsoft Exchange system mailbox, SystemMailbox{e0dc1c29-89c3-4034-b678-e6c29d823ed9}. You can access this mailbox—for example, if you want to move it to a different database—by using Get-Mailbox with the Arbitration parameter, for example:

```
[PS] C:\> Get-Mailbox -Arbitration -Identity 'systemMailbox{e0dc1c29-89c3-
4034-b678-e6c29d823ed9}'
```

If you want to move the system mailbox to a database named "MDB02," for instance, you will use the following command:

```
[PS] C:\> Get-Mailbox -Arbitration -Identity 'systemMailbox{e0dc1c29-89c3-
4034-b678-e6c29d823ed9}' | New-Moverequest -TargetDatabase 'MDB02'
```

If you are concerned about the amount of logged data in the system mailbox after enabling administrator audit logging, you can check the size of the system mailbox, as follows:

```
[PS] C:\> Get-Mailbox -Arbitration -Identity 'systemMailbox{e0dc1c29-
89c3-4034-b678-e6c29d823ed9}' | Get-MailboxStatistics | Format-Table
TotalItemSize
```

Caution When you are in a coexistence scenario of Exchange Server 2016 with Exchange Server 2010, you need to move the system mailbox to Exchange Server 2016. If you do not, Exchange Server 2016 tasks will not be logged in the audit log, and audit log searching will not work.

Administrative audit logging is a global setting enabled by default in Exchange Server. It can be disabled using the following:

```
[PS] C:\> Set-AdminAuditLogConfig -AdminAuditLogEnable $False
```

To enable administrator audit logging, you use

```
[PS] C:\> Set-AdminAuditLogConfig -AdminAuditLogEnable $True
```

If you want to view the current administrator audit logging settings, you use Get-AdminAuditLogConfig, as shown in Figure 11-41.

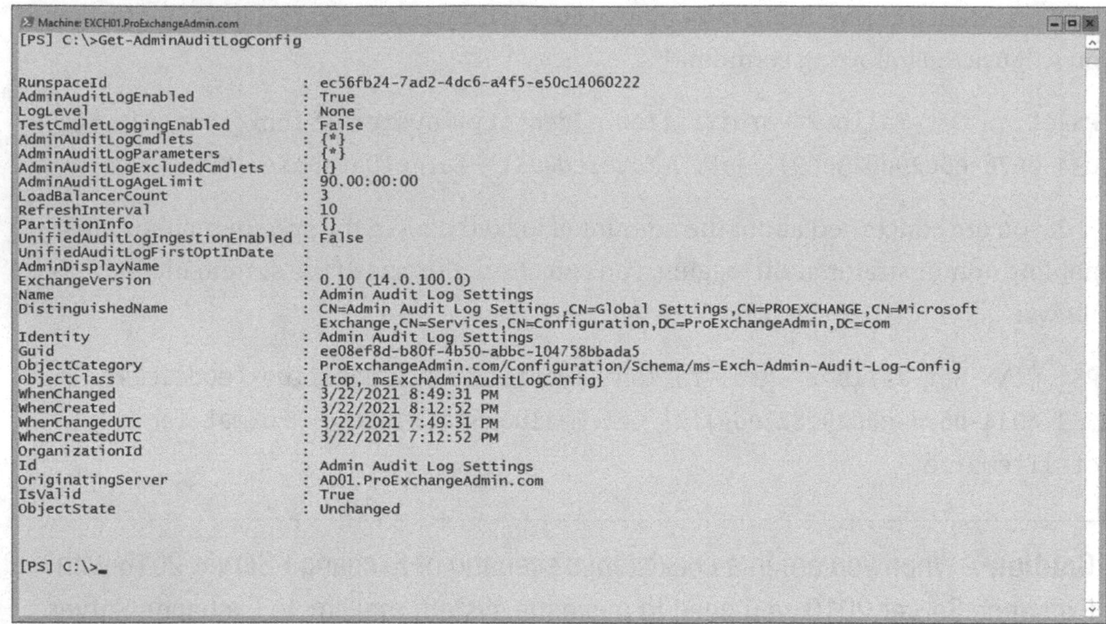

Machine: EXCH01.ProExchangeAdmin.com
[PS] C:\>Get-AdminAuditLogConfig
RunspaceId : ec56fb24-7ad2-4dc6-a4f5-e50c14060222
AdminAuditLogEnabled : True
LogLevel : None
TestCmdletLoggingEnabled : False
AdminAuditLogCmdlets : {*}
AdminAuditLogParameters : {*}
AdminAuditLogExcludedCmdlets : {}
AdminAuditLogAgeLimit : 90.00:00:00
LoadBalancerCount : 3
RefreshInterval : 10
PartitionInfo : {}
UnifiedAuditLogIngestionEnabled : False
UnifiedAuditLogFirstOptInDate :
AdminDisplayName :
ExchangeVersion : 0.10 (14.0.100.0)
Name : Admin Audit Log Settings
DistinguishedName : CN=Admin Audit Log Settings,CN=Global Settings,CN=PROEXCHANGE,CN=Microsoft Exchange,CN=Services,CN=Configuration,DC=ProExchangeAdmin,DC=com
Identity : Admin Audit Log Settings
Guid : ee08ef8d-b80f-4b50-abbc-104758bbada5
ObjectCategory : ProExchangeAdmin.com/Configuration/Schema/ms-Exch-Admin-Audit-Log-Config
ObjectClass : {top, msExchAdminAuditLogConfig}
WhenChanged : 3/22/2021 8:49:31 PM
WhenCreated : 3/22/2021 8:12:52 PM
WhenChangedUTC : 3/22/2021 7:49:31 PM
WhenCreatedUTC : 3/22/2021 7:12:52 PM
OrganizationId :
Id : Admin Audit Log Settings
OriginatingServer : AD01.ProExchangeAdmin.com
IsValid : True
ObjectState : Unchanged
[PS] C:\>_

Figure 11-41. *Administrator audit logging settings*

As you can see from Figure 11-41, there are additional options for administrator audit logging. There are options to restrict logging to certain cmdlets or parameters. These administrator audit logging options are explained next.

Caution The administrator audit logging setting is stored in Active Directory, and depending on replication, it may not immediately be applied. Also, for any current Exchange Management Shell session, it may take up to one hour for the new setting to become effective.

Administrator Audit Logging Options

To restrict logging to only specific cmdlets or only if specific parameters are used, you use `Set-AdminAuditLogConfig` in combination with the AdminAuditLogConfig commands and AdminAuditLogConfigParameters parameters. For example, to log only the cmdlets New-Mailbox and Remove-Mailbox, you would use

```
[PS] C:\> Set-AdminAuditLogConfig -AdminAuditLogCmdlets 'New-Mailbox','Remove-Mailbox'
```

You can also choose to exclude certain cmdlets from being logged using the AdminAuditLogExcludeCmdlets parameters, for example:

```
[PS] C:\> Set-AdminAuditLogConfig -AdminAuditLogExcludeCmdlets 'set-
Mailbox'
```

You can restrict logging when certain parameters are used. For example, to log only the name, identity, Windows email address, and email addresses parameters, you would use

```
[PS] C:\> Set-AdminAuditLogConfig -AdminAuditLogParameters 'Name',
'Identity', 'WindowsEmailAddress', 'EmailAddresses'
```

To cover a set of related cmdlets or parameters, you can use wildcards. For example, to log only cmdlets related to the mailbox and only those parameters containing "address," you would use

```
[PS] C:\> Set-AdminAuditLogConfig -AdminAuditLogCmdlets '*-Mailbox'
-AdminAuditLogParameters '*Address*'
```

The default values for AdminAuditLogCmdlets and AdminAuditLogParameters are *, which causes any cmdlet in combination with any parameter to be logged. If you want to reset these values to their default, you use

```
[PS] C:\> Set-AdminAuditLogConfig -AdminAuditLogCmdlets '*' -
AdminAuditLogParameters '*' -AdminAuditLogExcludeCmdlets $null
```

By default, administrator audit logging is restricted to a 90-day period. After 90 days, the log entries are deleted. You can increase or decrease this limit by using the AdminAuditLogAgeLimit parameter, specifying the number of days, hours, minutes, and seconds that entries should be kept. The format to specify this parameter is dd.hh:mm:ss. For example, to set the limit to 180 days, you use

```
[PS] C:\> Set-AdminAuditLogConfig -AdminAuditLogAgeLimit 180.00:00:00
```

Administrative audit logging only logs information like the cmdlet ran, when it ran, the context, and any specified parameters and values. By configuring the log level to Verbose, it will also log the previous values of any changed attributes: `Set-AdminAuditLogConfig -LogLevel Verbose`. To return to the default logging, you set the log level to None.

By default, test cmdlets are not logged. To log the test cmdlets, set TestCmdletLoggingEnabled to $true, for example:

```
[PS] C:\> Set-AdminAuditLogConfig -TestCmdletLoggingEnabled $true
```

To disable it again, set TestCmdletLoggingEnabled to $false.

Custom Logging Entries

In addition to the administrator audit logging cmdlets, you can create custom entries in the administrator audit log. This can be useful when you want to create markers for when to run scripts or for maintenance stop and starting events, for example.

To create a custom administrator audit log entry, use the `Write-AdminAuditLog` cmdlet, with the Comment parameter to pass the message to log. For example, to log the start of a scheduled maintenance cycle, you could use

```
[PS] C:\> Write-AdminAuditLog -Comment 'start of scheduled maintenance'
```

Caution The maximum size of the comment text is 500 characters.

Auditing Log Searches

Logging information for auditing purposes would be useless if there were no ways to search through or retrieve the logged information. To search the administrator audit log using EAC, navigate to Compliance Management ➤ Auditing, and select to view the administrator audit log or to export the administrator audit log when you want to perform a search and then send the results to a mailbox. An example is shown in Figure 11-42.

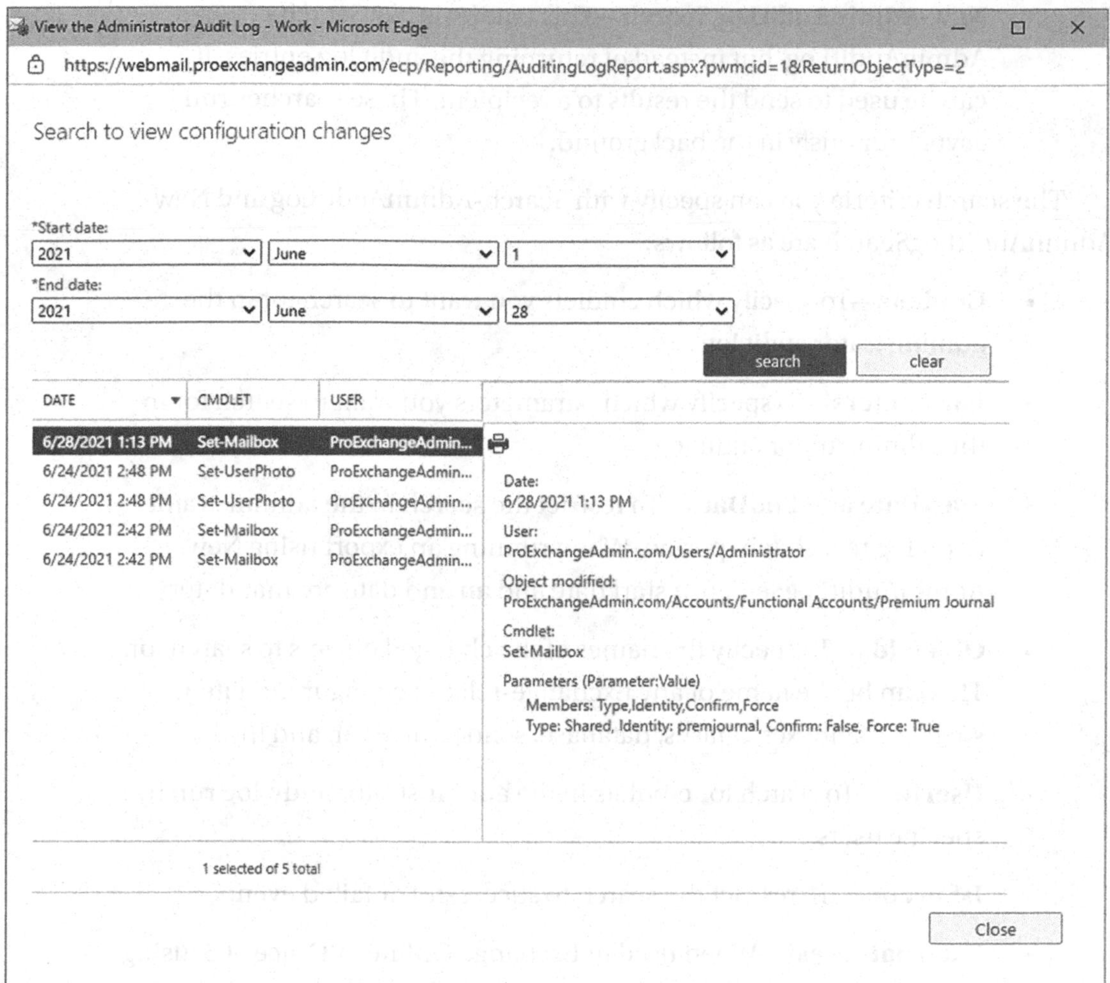

Figure 11-42. *Inspecting the administrator audit log*

EAC is a bit limited when it comes to searching the audit log, as you can only further specify the start and end dates for reports on the administrator audit log. When you want to check the administrator audit log using the EMS using additional search criteria, Exchange provides two cmdlets:

- **Search-AdminAuditLog**—Use this cmdlet to search through the administrator audit log entries based on search criteria. These searches are synchronous.

- **New-AdminAuditLogSearch**—This cmdlet is like Search-AdminAuditLog, but instead of returning the audit log entries, it can be used to send the results to a recipient. These searches run asynchronously in the background.

The search criteria you can specify with Search-AdminAuditLog and New-AdminAuditLogSearch are as follows:

- **Cmdlets**—To specify which cmdlets you want to search for in the administrator audit log.
- **Parameters**—To specify which parameters you want to search for in the administrator audit log.
- **StartDate** and **EndDate**—To restrict the search in the administrator audit log to a certain period. When running an export using New-AdminAuditLogSearch, a start date and an end date are mandatory.
- **ObjectIds**—To specify the names of the changed objects to search for. This can be the name of any Exchange-related configuration items, such as mailboxes, aliases, database, send connector, and the like.
- **UserIds**—To search for cmdlets in the administrator audit log run by specific users.
- **IsSuccess**—To restrict the search to successful or failed events.
- **ExternalAccess**—When used in Exchange Online or Office 365, using $true will return audit log entries generated by Microsoft service administrators; using $false will return audit log entries generated by the tenant administrators.
- **StatusMailRecipients**—Specifies the SMTP addresses of the recipients who should receive the audit log report. This parameter is only valid when using New-AdminAuditLogSearch.
- **Name**—Specifies the subject of the email. This parameter is only valid when using New-AdminAuditLogSearch.

Note It can take up to 15 minutes for Exchange to generate and deliver the report. The raw information in XML format attached to the report generated by New-AdminAuditLogSearch can have a maximum size of 10 MB.

For example, to search the audit log for entries where the Add-TransportRule cmdlet was used on an object (in this case, transport rule) named "HR Documents" since June 21, 2021, 3:15, you would use the following:

```
[PS] C:\> Search-AdminAuditLog -Cmdlets Remove-TransportRule -ObjectIds 'HR Documents' -StartDate '6/21/2021 3:15'
```

Tip As with many cmdlets, only the first 1000 entries are returned. When necessary, use -ResultSize Unlimited to return all matching audit log entries.

To return all cmdlets run by an administrator against objects named Philip, you would use

```
[PS] C:\> Search-AdminAuditLog -UserIds Administrator -ObjectIds Philip
```

To return all audit log entries where the `New-ManagementRoleAssignment` or `Remove-ManagementRoleAssignment` cmdlets were run, you would use

```
[PS] C:\> Search-AdminAuditLog -Cmdlets New-ManagementRoleAssignment,
Remove-ManagementRoleAssignment
```

To run the same query against the past 24 hours and send the results to a recipient named philip@proexchangeadmin.com, you would use

```
[PS] C:\> New-AdminAuditLogSearch -Name 'ManagementRoleAssignment Changes'
 -Cmdlets New-ManagementRoleAssignment, Remove-ManagementRoleAssignment
 -StatusMailRecipients philip@proexchangeadmin.com -StartDate (Get-Date).
AddDays(-1) -EndDate (Get-Date)
```

You can also search for specific parameter usage and/or use ExpandProperty to get an overview of all changed values using parameters. For example, if you want to show changes in the circular logging settings of mailbox databases in the last seven days, you will use

```
[PS] C:\> Search-AdminAuditLog -Cmdlet Set-MailboxDatabase -StartDate
(Get-Date).AddDays(-7) -EndDate (Get-Date) | Select RunDate,
CmdletName -ExpandProperty CmdletParameters
```

You can retrieve a list of current searches using `Get-AuditLogSearch`. This will return both administrator audit log searches and mailbox audit logging searches. You can optionally specify "created after" and "created before" to limit the time span of the items returned. The returned information contains the name, the name of the job or email subject, and the recipients of the report. The time span used for the report is returned as a UTC time stamp in StartDateUtc and EndDateUtc. The attribute "Type" can be used to differentiate between administrator audit log searches ("Admin") and mailbox audit log searches ("Mailbox"):

```
[PS] C:\> Get-AuditLogSearch | Format-Table Name, Type, CreationTime,
StartDateUtc, EndDateUtc, StatusMailRecipients -AutoSize
```

This cmdlet will return a list of current audit log searches, and the audit log entries are returned as a set of objects. The structure of the returned administrator audit log entries is as follows:

- **ObjectModified**—Contains the object modified.
- **CmdletName**—Contains the cmdlet run.
- **CmdletParameters**—Contains the parameters specified with the cmdlet.
- **ModifiedProperties**—Is only populated when the log level is set to Verbose. When set, this field will contain the modified properties of "ObjectModified."
- **Caller**—Contains the user account that ran the cmdlet.
- **Succeeded**—Reports if the cmdlet ran successfully.
- **Error**—Contains the error message if the cmdlet did not run successfully.

- **RunDate**—Contains the time stamp when the cmdlet ran.
- **OriginatingServer**—Indicates which server ran the cmdlet.

As you can see, the CmdletParameters, as well as the ModifiedProperties when applicable, will by default only display the parameter name or the name of the attribute changed. To see the related value, expand the CmdletParameters or ObjectModified attribute.

For example, to find the last logged `New-TransportRule` cmdlet and view what parameters and configuration values were used, you can use the following commands:

```
[PS] C:\> $LogEntry= Search-AdminAuditLog -Cmdlets New-TransportRule | Sort
StartDate -Desc | Select -First 1
[PS] C:\> $LogEntry
[PS] C:\> $LogEntry.CmdletParameters
```

Mailbox Audit Logging

Along with the auditing administrative changes, an organization might require tracking the access or changes made to individual mailboxes, especially mailboxes potentially containing sensitive information from a business or privacy perspective. This also applies to nonpersonal mailboxes, which are mailboxes attached to a disabled user account and which are used by multiple mailbox users commonly referred to as "delegates."

Mailbox audit logging can audit access and changes performed by the mailbox owners, delegates, and administrators. After enabling the mailbox audit logging, you can additionally limit the audit log to record only log certain operations—for example, creation, movement, or deletion of messages. You can also specify the logon type to audit—for instance, owner, delegate, or administrator.

You cannot enable mailbox audit logging using EAC. To enable mailbox audit logging from the EMS, use the Set-Mailbox cmdlet, setting AuditEnabled to $true, for example:

```
[PS] C:\> Set-Mailbox -Identity 'Philip' -AuditEnabled $true
```

To verify that the auditing is enabled and see what has been the logged, check the audit attributes of the mailbox as shown in Figure 11-43 using the following command:

```
[PS] C:\> Get-Mailbox -Identity 'Info' | Select Name, Audit*
```

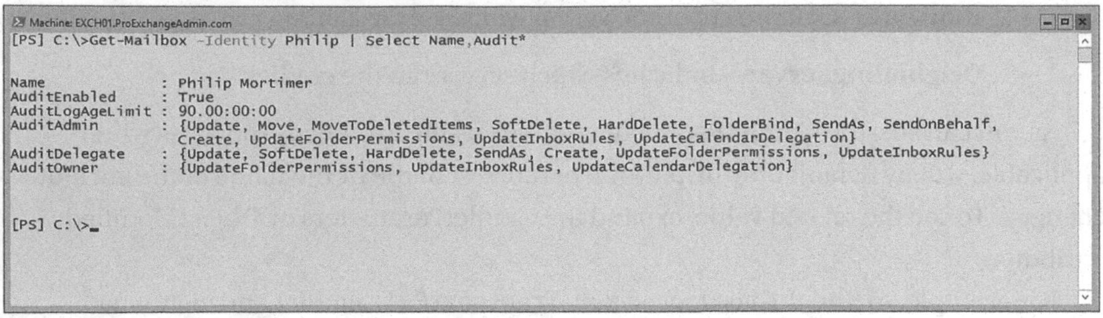

```
Machine: EXCH01.ProExchangeAdmin.com
[PS] C:\>Get-Mailbox -Identity Philip | Select Name,Audit*

Name               : Philip Mortimer
AuditEnabled       : True
AuditLogAgeLimit   : 90.00:00:00
AuditAdmin         : {Update, Move, MoveToDeletedItems, SoftDelete, HardDelete, FolderBind, SendAs, SendOnBehalf,
                     Create, UpdateFolderPermissions, UpdateInboxRules, UpdateCalendarDelegation}
AuditDelegate      : {Update, SoftDelete, HardDelete, SendAs, Create, UpdateFolderPermissions, UpdateInboxRules}
AuditOwner         : {UpdateFolderPermissions, UpdateInboxRules, UpdateCalendarDelegation}


[PS] C:\>_
```

Figure 11-43. *Verifying the mailbox audit logging settings*

To disable mailbox audit logging, you use

```
[PS] C:\> Set-Mailbox -Identity 'Info' -AuditEnabled $false
```

Mailbox Audit Logging Options

As seen earlier when verifying the mailbox audit logging settings, there are several options that can be used to determine what is logged per type of logon—that is, owner, delegate, or administrator. Not all actions can be logged for all logon types. Table 11-1 lists the mailbox audit logging options.

Table 11-1. *Mailbox Audit Logging Options*

Action	Description	Owner	Delegate	Administrators
Copy	Item is copied to another folder	No	No	Yes*
Create	Creation of an item (e.g., item received). Folder creation is not audited	Yes	Yes*	Yes
FolderBind	Folder access	No	Yes	Yes*
HardDelete	Permanent deletion of an item	Yes	Yes*	Yes
MessageBind	Item access	No	No	Yes
Move	Item is moved to another folder	Yes	Yes	Yes*
MoveToDeletedItems	An item is deleted (moved to Deleted Items)	Yes	Yes	Yes*

(*continued*)

Table 11-1. *(continued)*

Action	Description	Owner	Delegate	Administrators
SendAs	A message is sent using SendAs permissions	-	Yes*	Yes*
SendOnBehalf	A message is sent using SendOnBehalf permissions	-	Yes	Yes
SoftDelete	An item is moved from Deleted Items to Recoverable Items	Yes	Yes*	Yes
Update	Updating of item properties	Yes	Yes*	Yes*

**Default option*

To log a specific action for a certain logon type, use the parameter AuditOwner for logging owner actions (this includes delegates with full access mailbox permissions), AuditDelegate for logging actions performed by delegates, and AuditAdmin for logging actions performed by administrators.

Note FolderBind operations are consolidated. Only the first occurrence of FolderBind per folder in a three-hour time span generates a mailbox audit log entry.

For example, to enable mailbox audit logging on a shared mailbox called "Olrik" and only log Send As actions for delegates as shown in Figure 11-44, use the following command:

```
[PS] C:\> Set-Mailbox -Identity 'Olrik' -AuditEnabled $true -AuditDelegate
SendAs -AuditAdmin None -AuditOwner None
```

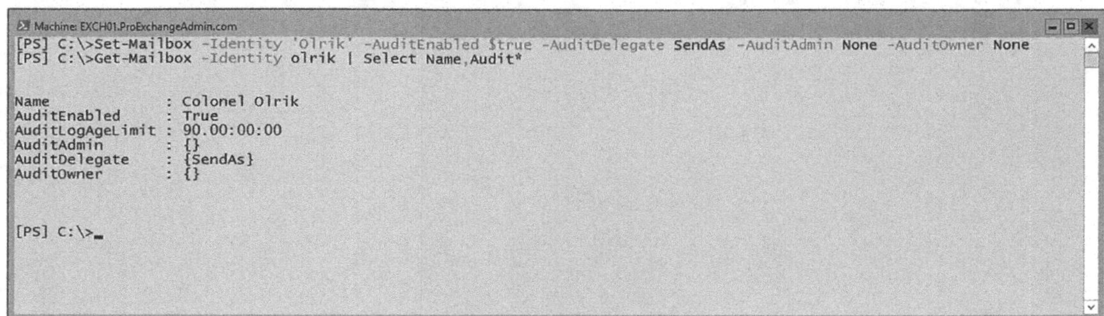

Figure 11-44. *Configuring mailbox audit logging*

When mailbox audit logging is enabled, the audit log entries are stored in the mailbox itself, in the audits folder located in the recoverable items folder. When a mailbox is moved, the recoverable items are also moved, including any existing audit log entries.

The default retention period of mailbox audit log entries is 90 days. You can adjust that retention period by using Set-Mailbox with the AuditLogAgeLimit parameter. For example, to set the retention period of the mailbox audit log for Philip's mailbox to 180 days, you would use

```
[PS] C:\> Set-Mailbox -Identity Philip -AuditLogAgeLimit 180
```

Note If the mailbox is on in-place hold, the mailbox audit log entries will not be removed after the retention period.

If you are concerned about the amount of logged audit data in the mailbox after you have enabled the mailbox audit logging, you can use the following commands to check the size of the folder mailbox:

```
[PS] C:\> Get-Mailbox -Identity Olrik | Get-MailboxFolderStatistics -
FolderScope RecoverableItems |  Where { $_.Name -eq 'Audits' } | Select
FolderSize
```

In this command, Get-MailboxFolderStatistics retrieves statistical information on the folders. By using FolderScope, you can configure it to look into a specific well-known folder. As mentioned earlier, the mailbox audit log entries are stored in the recoverable items folder in a subfolder named "audits." So, you set the scope to Recoverable Items to only return that folder. Next, you use Where to filter the folder name "audits," of which you display its FolderSize property.

Searches of the Mailbox Audit Logging

To search a mailbox audit log using EAC, you navigate to Compliance Management ➤ Auditing. Exchange EAC provides seven options for generating mailbox audit log reports:

- **Run a non-owner mailbox access report**—This option allows you to generate a report on non-owner access to mailboxes. You can select the search period, the auditing-enabled mailboxes to investigate, and the type of access.
- **Run an administrator role group report**—This option allows you to search for changes made to role groups. This can identify security breaches.
- **Run an in-place eDiscovery and Hold report**—This option lets you search for changes made to In-Place eDiscovery and In-Place holds.
- **Run a per-mailbox Litigation Hold report**—This option lets you search for mailboxes that have Litigation Hold enabled or disabled.
- **Export mailbox audit logs**—This option allows you to export the mailbox audit logs and send them as an attachment to selected recipients. As with administrator audit logging, the searching and reporting options are limited when managed through EAC. In the EMS, mailbox audit logging provides the following cmdlets for searching and reporting:
    - **Search-MailboxAuditLog**—Use this cmdlet to search the mailbox audit logs based on search criteria. These searches are synchronous.
    - **New-MailboxAuditLogSearch**—This cmdlet is similar to Search-MailboxAuditLog, but instead of returning the audit log entries, it can be used to send the results to a recipient. These searches run asynchronously in the background.
- **Run the admin audit log report**—This option will show you the admin audit log, similar to the Search-AdminAuditLog in EMS. An example is shown in Figure 11-45.
- **Export the admin audit log**—This option is an addition to the previous option and lets you export the results to an XML file and have it sent to specified recipients.

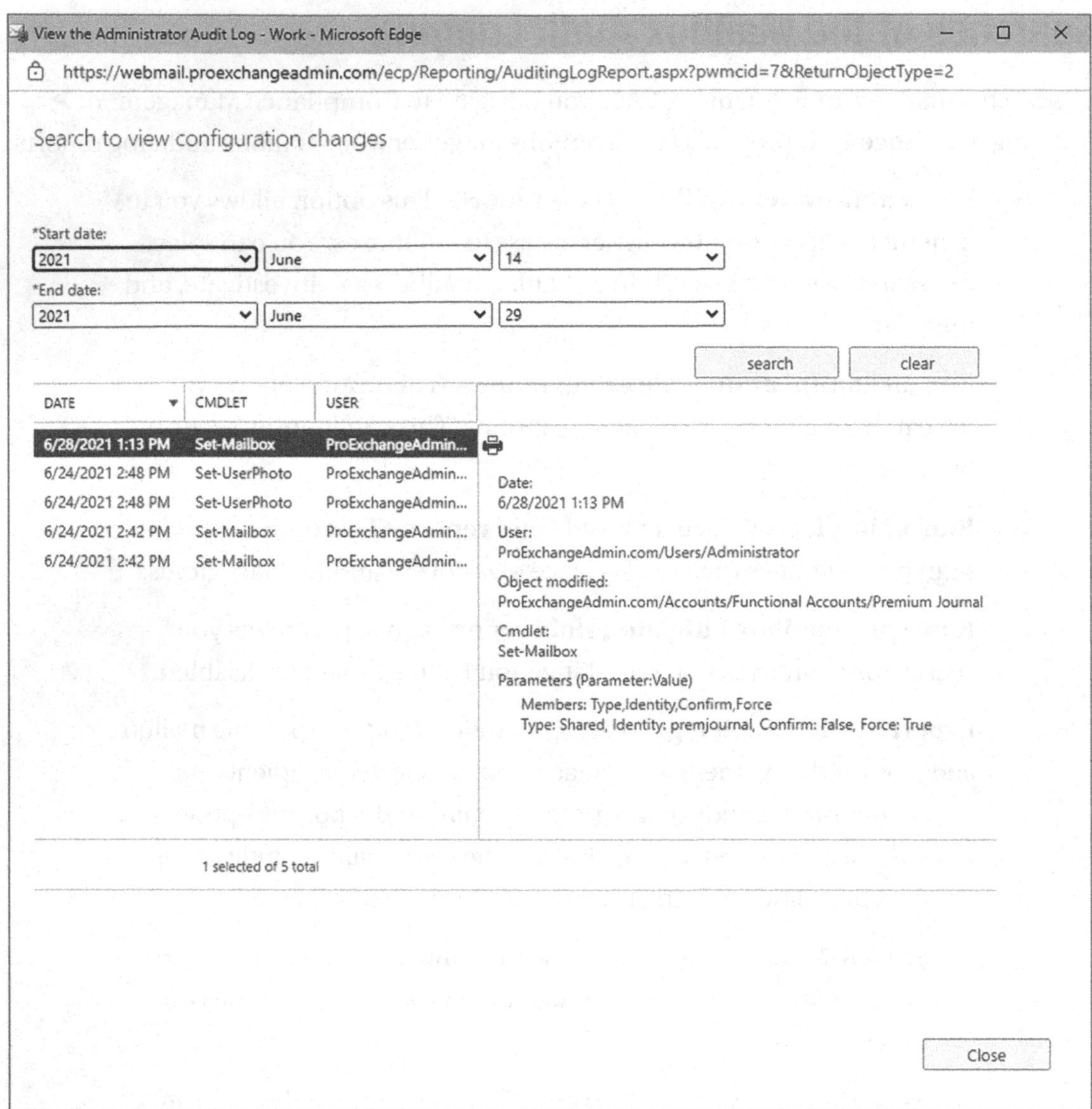

Figure 11-45. *Report of configuration changes in the Exchange organization*

Note These cmdlets are similar in usage and purpose to the administrator audit logging searching cmdlets, Search-AdminAuditLog and New-AdminAuditLogSearch.

The search criteria you can specify with SearchMailboxAuditLog and New-MailboxAuditLogSearch are the following:

1. **Identity**—To specify the mailboxes to search for audit log entries. This parameter is only available when using Search-MailboxAuditLog.
2. **Mailboxes**—To specify the mailboxes to search for audit log entries. When neither identity nor mailboxes is specified, all mailbox auditing-enabled mailboxes will be searched.
3. **LogonTypes**—To specify the logon types to search. Valid logon types are
   - Admin for administrator logon types
   - Delegate for delegate logon types, including users with Full Access
   - External for Microsoft service administrators in Exchange Online or Office 365
   - Owner for primary owner
4. **ShowDetails**—To retrieve details of each audit log entry. This parameter is mandatory when LogonTypes is set to Owner and can't be used together with the mailboxes parameter. This parameter is only available when using Search-MailboxAuditLog.
5. **StartDate** and **EndDate**—To restrict the search in the administrator audit log to a certain period. When running an export using New-AdminAuditLogSearch, the start date and end date are mandatory.
6. **ExternalAccess**—To search for audit log entries generated by users outside of your organization such as Microsoft service administrators in Exchange Online or Office 365.

7. **StatusMailRecipients**—Specifies the SMTP addresses of the recipients that should receive the audit log report. This parameter is only available when using New-MailboxAuditLogSearch.
8. **Name**—Specifies the subject of the email. This parameter is only available when using New-MailboxAuditLogSearch.

When used without specifying parameters, `Search-MailboxAuditLog` will return all auditing-enabled mailboxes, as follows:

```
[PS] C:\> Search-MailboxAuditLog
```

To see what auditing information is returned by mailbox audit logging, let us pick a single audit log entry while specifying ShowDetails to include detailed information, as follows:

```
[PS] C:\> Search-MailboxAuditLog -ShowDetails -ResultSize 1
```

A lot of information is available per audit log entry. You may notice a few unpopulated fields, which are due to the operation. Folder names are not logged for SendAs operations. Here is a short list of some of the important fields:

- **LastAccessed**—Contains the time stamp when the operation was performed.
- **Operation**—Is one of the actions Copy, Create, FolderBind, HardDelete, MessageBind, Move, MoveToDeletedItems, SendAs, SendOnBehalf, SoftDelete, and Update.
- **OperationResult**—Shows if the operation succeeded, failed, or partially succeeded.
- **LogonType**—Shows who performed the operation, whether the owner, a delegate, or an administrator.
- **FolderPathName**—Contains the folder name that contains the item.
- **ClientInfoString**—Contains information about the client or Exchange component that performed the operation.
- **ClientIPAddress**—Contains the IPv4 address of the client computer used.

- **InternalLogonType**—Contains the type of logon performed by the non-owner.
- **MailboxOwnerUPN**—Contains the UPN of the mailbox owner.
- **DestMailboxOwnerUPN**—Contains the UPN of the destination mailbox owner for cross-mailbox operations; CrossMailboxOperation contains information about whether the operation is across mailboxes.
- **LogonUserDisplayName**—Contains the display name of the logged-on user who performed the operation.
- **ItemSubject**—Contains the subject line of the item affected.
- **MailboxResolvedOwnerName**—Contains the display name of the mailbox.

For example, to search all auditing-enabled mailboxes for log entries generated for non-owner access by delegate or administrator logon types, you could use

```
[PS] C:\> Search-MailboxAuditLog -LogonTypes Delegate,Admin -ShowDetails |
Format-Table LastAccessed, MailboxResolvedOwnerName, Operation, LogonType,
LogonUserDisplayName, ClientIPAddress, ItemSubject -AutoSize
```

Note Use ResultSize to limit the number of entries when using Search-MailboxAuditLog.

In this example, you query the mailbox "Info," which is mailbox auditing enabled, for non-owners' access to a specific folder. Because you cannot specify the operations to search for directly as a Search-MailboxAuditLog parameter, you can pipe the output through Where-Object. Using this technique, you can filter entries so that only certain operations are shown, for example FolderBind (i.e. folder access) and Folder Path name. Of the objects returned, you then select certain fields for displaying:

```
[PS] C:\> Search-MailboxAuditLog -Identity 'Info' -LogonTypes
Delegate, Admin -ShowDetails | Where { $_.Operation -eq 'FolderBind'
-and $_.FolderPathName -eq '\Inbox' } | Format-Table LastAccessed,
InternalLogonType, LogonType, LogonUserDisplayName, FolderPathname
```

When required, you can narrow your search to a certain period by specifying the start date and end date as well.

In addition to Search-MailboxAuditLog, you can use New-MailboxAuditLogSearch to gather mailbox audit log information in the background and have it sent as an email attachment to specific recipients. The parameters you can use are similar to those you can use with Search-MailboxAuditLog, only you can't use identity for reporting on a specific mailbox; you need to specify the message subject (name) and recipients (status mail recipients).

That said, to create a background mailbox audit log query on delegate access to a mailbox called "Info" from January 1, 2014, to February 1, 2014, you could use

```
[PS] C:\> New-MailboxAuditLogSearch -StartDate '1/1/2014' -EndDate
'4/1/2014' -Mailboxes 'Info' -ShowDetails -LogonTypes Delegate -Name
'Mailbox Info - delegate access audit report' -StatusMailRecipients philip@
proexchangeadmin.com
```

You can use Get-AuditLogSearch to list current audit log searches. The generated export of audit information in XML format is sent as an attachment to Philip.

The XML contains the same elements as the Search-MailboxAuditLog output, allowing organizations to perform additional processing or reporting using the information contained in the XML file. For example, when you store the attached XML file locally, you can import it using PowerShell by using

```
[PS] C:\> [xml](Get-Contents .\SearchResults.xml)
```

Note Do not try to import an XML file using Import-CliXml. The purpose of Import-CliXml is to import serialized PowerShell objects, usually generated using the Export-CliXml cmdlet.

A simple query to retrieve the information contained in SearchResults.xml and select certain information from audit log events is as follows:

```
[PS] C:\> [xml](Get-Contents .\SearchResults.xml) | Select -ExpandProperty
SearchResults | Select -ExpandProperty Event | Format-Table LastAccessed,
LogonType, Operation, LogonUserDisplayName, FolderPathName -AutoSize
```

Bypass of Mailbox Audit Logging

Applications may implicitly use administrator permissions when processing mailboxes, generating excessive amounts of audit log information for mailboxes that have mailbox auditing enabled for MessageBind or FolderBind operations. Examples of such applications are backup and archiving solutions. Audit log information generated by these applications are likely not of interest to the organization with regard to compliance and are viewed only as creating "noise" in the mailbox audit logs while also claiming valuable system resources in the process.

To create exceptions for these types of applications, Exchange Server 2013 can be configured to bypass mailbox auditing using mailbox auditing bypass associations. These bypass associations can be assigned to user or computer accounts. The cmdlet to configure bypass associations is Set-MailboxAuditBypassAssociation. To configure bypass for an account named "BesAdmin," for example, you would use

```
[PS] C:\> Set-MailboxAuditBypassAssociation -Identity 'BesAdmin' -
AuditBypassEnabled $true
```

To remove the bypass association for "BesAdmin," you set AuditBypassEnabled to $false:

```
[PS] C:\> Set-MailboxAuditBypassAssociation -Identity 'BesAdmin' -
AuditBypassEnabled $false
```

To retrieve the accounts currently associated with mailbox auditing bypass, you use

```
[PS] C:\> Get-MailboxAuditBypassAssociation | Where { $_.AuditBypassEnabled
} | Select Name
```

Caution When configuring mailbox auditing bypass associations, bear in mind that some organizations need to closely monitor these bypass associations, as these accounts will not generate mailbox audit log information. Alternatively, organizations can leverage role-based access control to restrict those configuring bypass associations using the Exchange Management Shell. You can also monitor the msExchBypassAudit attribute of user objects in Active Directory.

Summary

This chapter surveyed the compliance features in Exchange servers 2013, 2016, and 2019 and showed how these features can help organizations meet their business requirements stipulated by laws or regulations. In-place archiving, in combination with managed records management, can be helpful in monitoring the contents of the primary mailbox by using retention policies to automatically offload contents into the in-place archives or to remove them after a certain period.

In-place discovery can be used to search for information, allowing organizations to create exportable sets of content using discovery mailboxes for external investigations. When required, organizations can make their mailboxes immutable by using in-place hold for legal investigations or other purposes. To investigate activities related to mailboxes, organizations can leverage their mailbox auditing to log mailbox access or specific operations on mailboxes or even on specific folders.

Transport rules automatically process messages or control mail flow. Data loss prevention including document fingerprinting helps organizations control leakage of sensitive information.

Finally, regarding the Exchange environment itself, organizations can use administrator auditing to log or report changes in the Exchange environment.

Index

A

M. de Rooij and J. Wesselius, *Pro Exchange 2019 and 2016 Administration*,
https://doi.org/10.1007/978-1-4842-7331-9

B

C

E

N

O

P, Q

R

W, X, Y, Z